THEORIES OF COUNSELING AND PSYCHOTHERAPY

A Case Approach

Second Edition

NANCY L. MURDOCK

University of Missouri–Kansas City

Merrill
is an imprint of

PEARSON

Upper Saddle River, New Jersey
Columbus, Ohio

Library of Congress Cataloging-in-Publication Data

Murdock, Nancy L.
   Theories of counseling and psychotherapy : a case approach / Nancy L. Murdock. —2nd ed.
      p. cm.
   Includes bibliographical references and index.
   ISBN 978-0-13-228652-7
   1. Counseling. 2. Psychotherapy. 3. Counseling—Case studies. 4. Psychotherapy—Case studies. I. Title.
   BF637.C6M846 2009
   158′.3—dc22

                                                                                    2007046223

Vice President and Executive Publisher: Jeffery W. Johnston
Publisher: Kevin M. Davis
Acquisitions Editor: Meredith D. Fossel
Editorial Assistant: Maren Vigilante
Senior Project Manager: Linda Hillis Bayma
Production Coordination: Kelli Jauron, S4Carlisle Editorial Services
Design Coordinator: Diane C. Lorenzo
Photo Coordinator: Shea Davis
Cover Designer: Jason Moore
Cover image: SuperStock
Operations Specialist: Susan Hannahs
Director of Marketing: Quinn Perkson
Marketing Coordinator: Brian Mounts

This book was set in Garamond by S4Carlisle Publishing Services. It was printed and bound by Courier Westford, Inc. The cover was printed by Phoenix Color Corp.

Photo Credits: Aaron T. Beck, MD, p. 314; AP Wide World Photos, pp. 64, 273; Brief Family Therapy Center, p. 460; Corbis/Bettmann, pp. 29, 105; Craig Ferre Photography/The William Glasser Institute, p. 352; Dulwich Centre, p. 490; © Images.com/CORBIS, p. 376; Gestalt Journal Press, p. 198; Heidi Hancock, p. 1; Omikron/Photo Researchers, Inc., p. 232; PH College, p. 514; © Roger Ressmeyer/CORBIS. All Rights Reserved, p. 147; Joseph Siroker, p. 179; and Virginia Satir Global Network, p. 405.

Pearson® is a registered trademark of Pearson plc
Merrill® is a registered trademark of Pearson Education, Inc.

Pearson Education Ltd.
Pearson Education Singapore Pte. Ltd.
Pearson Education Canada, Ltd.
Pearson Education—Japan

Pearson Education Australia Pty. Limited
Pearson Education North Asia Ltd.
Pearson Educación de Mexico, S.A. de C.V.
Pearson Education Malaysia, Pte. Ltd.

Merrill
is an imprint of

10 9 8 7 6 5 4 3 2 1
ISBN-13: 978-0-13-228652-7
ISBN-10:   0-13-228652-1

To my parents,
Mary Elizabeth Frojd Murdock
and
Sandlan John Murdock
Who taught me to love life and learning.

PREFACE

There is nothing so practical as a good theory.
—Kurt Lewin

WHY I WROTE THIS BOOK

The quote from Kurt Lewin aptly captures my philosophy on the role and use of theory. I have been teaching about counseling theory for longer than I care to say, and I consider myself something of a theory freak. I admit that I think theory is fun. However, over the years I have learned that theory is not very useful if you don't know how to apply it; application is what makes theory practical and good. I have struggled to teach the application of theory to my students, trying different methods and models along the way. Knowing that it is sometimes difficult for me, how can I expect the application process to be easy for students just learning the basics of counseling theory? That's why I wrote this book; it is an effort to demonstrate the value of theory through its application. Theory comes alive when it is used to understand a client presentation. The pitfalls and strengths of an approach are never more evident than when it is put to use in this way.

The task of understanding a client presentation in a theoretical structure creates a situation in which you need to know the thory in a way that is different from simply knowing its constructs and techniques. At times it is tempting to give up the attempt to apply a theory to a given client presentation, because the theory under consideration just doesn't seem to fit as well as some other one. My experience has been that when this situation occurs, the potential for learning is great. Clients don't offer their problems in theory-laden terms. They tend to speak in their own language, and it is your job to do the best you can to understand that language in ways that are helpful. In essence, you need to interpret the client's presentation in theoretical terms. Another situation in which I have found theory most useful is when my clients have me confused. Instead of operating on automatic pilot, I am forced to ask, "Now what on earth just happened here?" My theory helps me calm down and sort out what initially seems chaotic.

In each chapter of this book, I have tried to present the various theories in a straight-forward, understandable way. What distinguishes this book from others is that I immedi-ately illustrate the application of a construct or process by showing how it relates to a client case described at the beginning of the chapter. I chose to use different client cases for each chapter for at least two reasons. First, I wanted to show that theory could apply to clients who range across the broad spectrum of individual and cultural diversity and present with many kinds of distress. Second, I did not want my readers to lose interest from reading about the same case chapter after chapter. In essence, I have tried to make this book as engaging as I possibly could without compromising the intellectual quality of the presen-tations. However, it is an engaging and useful exercise to apply different theories to the same case, so I would urge the users of this book to undertake this task as a way of com-paring the approaches in a meaningful way.

THE THEORIES I CHOSE

A question always arises about which theories to include in a text like this one. Some choices are obvious; others less so. I included classical psychoanalysis—even though true analysis may not be common these days—because it is the foundation of the profession and the springboard for many other systems. If you ever write something that generates as much love and hate as Freud's work did, you have really created something important. I chose other theoretical approaches based on several criteria: (a) currency—whether the theory is used by professionals in the real world; (b) potential to contribute to understand-ing of the counseling process even if the reader does not adopt the theory wholesale; and (c) comprehensiveness—the extent to which the theory provides a conceptual structure as well as guidelines for counseling and associated techniques.

MY PHILOSOPHY

I am a Counseling Psychologist and a scientist-practitioner, and these aspects of my pro-fessional identity influence the structure and content of the presentations in this book. Counseling psychologists attend to individuals' strengths and are oriented toward health as much as (or more than) they are toward dysfunction. I prefer to look at people through a positive lens, seeing personal strength and the potential to change in every life moment. To focus primarily on deficits seems to me to be a disservice to the human spirit. This em-phasis leads to the use of terms such as *client* instead of *patient* and *dysfunction* rather than *disorder*. I also include sections in each theory chapter that describe the theory's version of the healthy personality.

An important element of the identity of a Counseling Psychologist is a commitment to the scientist-practitioner model. The scientist in me wants some confirmation that a theoretical structure is valid. This is not to say that I endorse the idea of one true reality; rather, I consider myself an intellectual pragmatist. I simply want some evidence that the version of reality presented by a given theoretical structure actually helps me to understand the counseling process and to help my clients. The sections on research support in each theory chapter grew out of this empirical bent. If I were to be totally honest, I'd have to say that, philosophically, I lean toward the contextual perspective, rooted in Frank and Frank's (1991) work and further supported and elaborated by Bruce Wampold. You'll find this model described in Chapter 16. It would be nice if we could find the one true theory, but for now I think that that possibility is fairly remote, and the data seem to support this position.

Another defining feature of Counseling Psychology is attention to individual and cultural diversity. We are all aware that our world is changing and that, historically, counseling and psychotherapy have been mired in a Caucasian, Western European, male model. The failure to recognize the biases inherent in this model (e.g., emphasis on individualism, a lack of attention to social and cultural forces in people's lives) is, to be blunt, unethical. I have attempted to address these issues systematically in each chapter. I have also selected clients and counselors of diverse backgrounds for the case presentations.

My concern about the effects of sex bias in language has led me to the solution of alternating the singular pronouns used in this text. In the theory chapters the pronouns used match those of the client and counselor in the case study. If the client is female, references to client issues and processes in the discussion of theory employ feminine pronouns. If the therapist is male, reference to therapist activities or processes employ masculine pronouns. The diverse cases include men and women in both client and counselor roles. In Chapters 1 and 16, pronouns are alternated randomly.

PREFACE TO THE SECOND EDITION

I am very excited to introduce the second edition of this book. Having never experienced the process of revision, I was quite overwhelmed by the task initially. In addition to generally updating the content throughout the book, I had two other goals for this revision: adjusting chapter selection based on input from instructors and students and updating the research evidence relevant to each theory. We've also added several new features to this edition, which I will briefly describe here.

NEW CHAPTERS

You will find three new chapters in this edition: Neoanalytic Approaches, Existential Therapy, and Narrative Therapy. The chapter on Interpersonal Theory, which described the MRI approach and the interpersonal circle, has been dropped. Some of the content in that chapter has been moved to Chapter 13, Family Systems Theory (for example, the section on Ordeal Therapy). The choice of the chapters to add was based on several factors. The staff at Merrill listened carefully to feedback from reviewers, instructors, and students about what was missing in the text and these three topics were mentioned most frequently. Of the three chapters, Neoanalytic Approaches is the most difficult to read and use, but neoanalytic theory is increasingly recognized as useful to know. Most psychoanalytically oriented therapists are aware of and draw on these perspectives. Existential Therapy was added for similar reasons. Many individuals opined that any therapist needed an awareness of these issues. Chapter 15, Narrative Therapy, discusses a relatively recent development that is in tune with the constructivist orientation that will be evident if you make even a quick review of major journals in our profession. Narrative therapy happens to be the best-formulated version of constructivist therapy around, in my opinion (not counting Solution-Focused Therapy, which of course is already in the book).

ORIGINAL SOURCE READINGS

Texts such as this one, in which the same author or authors write about many approaches, have the advantage of consistency in the level and structure of the presentations, but the disadvantage of depriving the reader of the opportunity to truly experience the voice of the original proponent(s) of the theory. Believing that this experience is valuable to students of counseling, we added a new feature to each chapter: an excerpt from a major theorist associated with that approach.

GENERAL UPDATING, WITH AN EMPHASIS ON NEW RESEARCH

In what was a daunting task, I updated the research evidence sections in all of the chapters. In many cases much more research was available than could be summarized, so my review is selective. Where new sources were available on advances in basic constructs and principles of theory, I added these as well. As you might expect, in some cases (such as cognitive theory and solution-focused therapy) lots of material was available. In others (most notably, classic psychoanalysis) new research directly relevant to the approach was scant.

A VIDEO SERIES: THEORIES IN ACTION

Perhaps the most exciting addition to this edition is the video series, *Theories in Action*. Then-editor Kevin Davis and I discussed this idea when I was writing the first edition but he wisely decided to hold off at that time, knowing that I would be exhausted after completing 14 chapters. However, we revived the idea for the second edition, and I hope you will share my excitement and enthusiasm for this project. The DVD that accompanies each copy of the text contains six 20-minute sessions with the client, Helen, from different theoretical perspectives: Classic Psychoanalysis, Gestalt Therapy, Feminist Therapy, Cognitive Therapy, Narrative Therapy, and Family Systems Therapy. Following each session is a brief review in which the counselors answer two questions: (a) what they did in the session that was most characteristic of their approach and (b) what they would do in the next session with Helen. Adopting instructors will also be able to access the full 50-minute sessions from which the sessions on the DVD were derived by searching www.pearsonhighered .com under ISBN 0-13-502517-6.

COMPANION WEBSITE: A VIRTUAL LEARNING ENVIRONMENT

Readers can access chapter summaries, self-assessment items, weblinks, and critical thinking questions based on the *Theories in Action* video series at www.prenhall.com/murdock.

INSTRUCTOR'S MATERIALS

The *Online Instructor's Manual with Test Bank* is free to adopters of this text. This electronic material includes chapter outlines and a test bank with multiple choice and short answer questions. The *Online PowerPoint Slides* provide lecture outlines. Adopting professors can access these supplements on the Instructor's Resource Center with an access code by searching www.pearsonhighered.com under the ISBN 0-13-228652-1.

ACKNOWLEDGMENTS

All of my teachers—both students and professors—deserve mention; however, the list of names would be so lengthy I must simply acknowledge my graduate program at Virginia Commonwealth University and all of the students over my postgraduate career as significant educators in my journey to becoming a teacher of theory. Numerous students have read and commented on chapters of this book, and I truly appreciate their helpful feedback. I am also deeply indebted to all of the clients with whom I have been fortunate to work over my career.

My fortune cookie really let me down on the sunny fall day almost 10 years ago when Merrill Executive Editor Kevin Davis showed up unexpectedly in my office. I tend to eat at least once a week at a local Chinese restaurant, and I am sure that my fidelity results in special fortunes coming my way. Usually, my cookies tell me something meaningful, or at least something that I try to turn into self-fulfilling prophecy (e.g., the ones that say "you will be rich and famous"). Occasionally, the cookies tell me something I don't want to hear (e.g., "troubles loom ahead"), but I pay attention nonetheless. On this day, my cookie gave me no warning that my life was about to change.

No doubt I was looking out my office window wishing I could be outside when Kevin knocked on my door. In retrospect, I am glad that I had not succumbed to my impulses because if I had, you might not be reading this book. Although I had vaguely contemplated writing a book, it was Kevin who helped me see that I had an idea that might turn into one. I am very grateful for the support, encouragement, and wisdom that Kevin contributed throughout the writing process.

Numerous reviewers are responsible for significant improvements in the first edition of this book, and I am thankful for their willingness to read and comment on the chapter drafts: James Archer, Jr., University of Florida; Jerry Chandler, University of Central Oklahoma; Kevin A. Fall, Loyola University–New Orleans; Marijane Fall, University of Southern Maine; Mary A. Herman, Mississippi State University; James W. Lichtenberg, University of Kansas; Christopher J. McCarthy, University of Texas at Austin; Woodrow Parker, University of Florida; Herman C. Salzberg, University of South Carolina; and Thomas Scofield, University of Nebraska at Kearney. Roberta Nutt, of Texas Women's University provided extra input on Chapter 13, Feminist Therapy. Second edition reviewers include: Dulin Clark, Penn State University; James Kreider, Kansas University; Marcy Marinelli, University of Maryland; David Powers, Loyola College; Charles L. Ridley, Indiana University; Edward H. Robinson, III, University of Central Florida; Jim Sells, Northern Illinois University; and Heather C. Trepal, University of Texas at San Antonio.

It was important to me to have client cases for study that, while interesting in content, were fairly representative of the clients we see and covered a diverse spectrum. In all cases, identifying information was changed to protect the identity of the individuals. Some of these cases were loosely based on my own clients, who have taught me much about being a counselor. Others were contributed by students, and so special thanks go to Shawn Roberson, Natalie Wilcox, Laura Shaughnessey, and Meredith Porter. Thanks also to Aaron Rochlen, who allowed me to use the case of Theo for Chapter 3 and to Kate Forristall and David Donovan, who created the case of Helen, used in Chapter 6.

In the preface to the first edition of this text I thanked many individuals for their help and support. I am fortunate that I can again express my appreciation to these folks, and add a few more. The support group that attempted to keep me sane and put up with me moaning about being frustrated and behind schedule includes (in no particular order): Julie and Mike Horton (and Riley and Conner), Tamera Murdock, Amy Winn, Holly Garcia, Laura Logan, Phil and Genie Reid, and Bob Lewis (who is still the only person other than editors who actually had the patience and perseverance to read all of the chapters). Heidi Hancock, as good a friend as she is a photographer, provided the photo for Chapter 1. Special thanks to Jeffrey J. Bentley and Jezebel vom Drache Feld for their love and encouragement.

The patience and support of the faculty, staff, and students of the Division of Counseling and Educational Psychology at UMKC and Dean Linda Edwards were also instrumental in the revision process. April Connery, doctoral student in Counseling Psychology, was heroic in her role as research assistant, tracking down an amazing range of resources and finding the typo in the spelling of Scarlett's name in Chapter 1. She and three other members of my research group contributed interesting content for boxes you will find in Chapters 3, 6, and 9.

Once again, the staff at Merrill has been fabulous. Kevin Davis, although he has graduated to a higher plane, worked with me to develop the new ideas and features in this edition, and was extremely patient with my struggles to finish this revision. Meredith Fossel, who assumed editorship in August of 2006, has been equal in her support, creativity, and patience.

The video project represents the combined efforts of a group of hard-working, talented individuals, to whom I extend my most sincere gratitude. Peter Morello, associate professor of Communication Studies at UMKC served as producer, working closely with Kevin Mullin, instructor and studio engineer in Communication Studies, our ace camera and editing expert. Kate Forristall, the actress who portrayed Helen the client, was magnificent—many who viewed the rough cuts of the video had no idea that she was not a "real" client. Huge thanks go to David Donovan, who you will see as the psychoanalyst, for his help in finding Kate and many of the other therapists you will see in the series. It is also his office that provides the lovely backdrop for the counseling sessions. It is difficult to find the right words to express my appreciation (and awe) for the hard work and enthusiasm of Kate, David, and the other therapists—Paul Anderson, Jennifer Lundgren, Jim Kreider, Linda Moore, and Shelley Stelmach—without them, my dreams for this project would have remained unrealized.

Finally, I pay tribute to my parents, Mary Elizabeth Frojd Murdock and Sandlan John Murdock, and to my sisters, Kathy Winn and Cecelia Niemann, for helping me to become the person who could write this book. One of my fondest memories involves asking my mother why cats purr. She sent me off to complete my first literature search in the hope of answering this question. Among other things, my sisters taught me to swim, dance, and write in cursive, important skills at which I have had varying rates of success. Most important, my family taught me the value of relationships and attention to others that is so necessary to becoming a professional helper.

Nancy L. Murdock

DISCOVER THE COMPANION WEBSITE ACCOMPANYING THIS BOOK

THE MERRILL COMPANION WEBSITE: A VIRTUAL LEARNING ENVIRONMENT

Technology is a constantly growing and changing aspect of our field that is creating a need for content and resources. To address this emerging need, Merrill has developed an online learning environment for students and professors alike—Companion Websites—to support our textbooks.

In creating a Companion Website, our goal is to build on and enhance what the textbook already offers. For this reason, the content for each user-friendly website is organized by chapter and provides the professor and student with a variety of meaningful resources. Common features of a Companion Website include:

- **Chapter Objectives**—outline key concepts from the text.
- **Interactive Self-quizzes**—complete with hints and automatic grading that provide immediate feedback for students. After students submit their answers for the interactive self-quizzes, the Companion Website **Results Reporter** computes a percentage grade, provides a graphic representation of how many questions were answered correctly and incorrectly, and gives a question-by-question analysis of the quiz. Students are given the option to send their quiz to up to four e-mail addresses (professor, teaching assistant, study partner, etc.).
- **Essay Questions**—these questions allow students to respond to themes and objectives of each chapter by applying what they have learned to real classroom situations.
- **Web Destinations**—links to www sites that relate to chapter content.

To take advantage of the many available resources, please visit the *Theories of Counseling and Psychotherapy: A Case Approach* Companion Website at

www.prenhall.com/murdock

Brief Contents

Contents

Note: Every effort has been made to provide accurate and current Internet information in this book. However, the Internet and information posted on it are constantly changing, so it is inevitable that some of the Internet addresses listed in this textbook will change.

CHAPTER 1

Theory Is a Good Thing

Scarlett comes to counseling because she is troubled about an important relationship. It seems that her husband, Rhett, whom she realizes that she loves deeply, does not seem to return her love and has, in fact, vanished. Scarlett is also mourning the death of her 6-year-old daughter, Bonnie, 6 months ago. Sad and angry at the same time, Scarlett feels helpless to do anything about her situation. She blames Rhett for the problems in their relationship. Scarlett reports that she is not eating or sleeping well, and she has panic attacks and fainting spells almost on a daily basis.

Scarlett is the eldest daughter of a farmer; she has two younger sisters. Her father died 8 years ago in a fall from a horse. There is some evidence that Scarlett's father was drinking at the time; he was bereft because his farm had been plundered by an invading army and his wife had died of scarlet fever. This invasion cost the formerly wealthy family much, creating a situation in which Scarlett and her sisters had to scratch out a living for a number of years. Eventually, Scarlett started a successful business on her own. She has been married three times; Rhett is her third husband.

Scarlett has known Rhett for a long time. For years, Rhett had professed to be in love with Scarlett; she did not respond to him because she was in love with another man. After Scarlett lost her second husband, she agreed to marry Rhett. Scarlett describes her relationship with Rhett as distant, but reports that both she and Rhett doted on their daughter, Bonnie. During the years of the marriage, Scarlet did not feel that she loved Rhett; she simply tolerated him because he could support her and their daughter.

Six months ago, Bonnie died in a fall from her pony. Rhett and Scarlett were devastated and uncharacteristically took comfort in each other. In the grip of this grief, Scarlett finally realized that she loved Rhett. However, Rhett became angry at Scarlett and disappeared into a dark foggy night. Although Scarlet at the time vowed "tomorrow is another day," she is struggling with hurt and anger along with her grief about Bonnie.

You are Scarlett's counselor. She looks at you, imploring you to help her get Rhett back. How are you going to help her? She is crying, fainting, and having panic attacks. Should you address these symptoms first or help her make a plan to find Rhett and bowl him over with her love (which is what she wants most)? How do you help Scarlett with her grief over the loss of her daughter? What is the contribution of Scarlett's family background and more recent history to the current situation?

A consistent, coherent approach to helping Scarlett is found in the careful application of counseling theory. I do not mean just any theory that I make up off the top of my head. Although I am pretty smart, I don't think that writing down my ideas about people and the nature of change is going to produce a system that will reliably guide your work as a beginning therapist. Rather, I direct your attention to a set of theories that have received much work and scrutiny, for the most part, over many years. These theories are known to be helpful in our work as counselors. Before addressing them, however, I will offer some basic definitions.

WHAT IS THEORY?

On the surface, defining theory seems easy. Most definitions specify that a theory is composed of a set of concepts and their defined relationships, all intended to explain some phenomenon of interest. Why do we theorize? According to Maddi (1996), theories are meant "to foster understanding of something hitherto not understood" (p. 485). Put another way, theories, in a perfect world, should explain and predict behavior. In the counseling profession, we also hope that they tell us how to help our clients.

The theories you are most interested in are theories of counseling or psychotherapy. All of these theories attempt to explain the process of helping clients change; they all offer some sort of prescription for what one person, the therapist, can do to help the other person, the client, who has sought assistance. To complicate matters, however, some theories of counseling address how people are made (psychologically), developmental issues, and descriptions of healthy and unhealthy psychological functioning. Other theories bypass these issues as simply not relevant to helping the client change.

WHAT IS PSYCHOTHERAPY?

Although I am guessing that almost everyone who reads the previous question has an answer to it, it is probably useful to offer a definition of counseling or psychotherapy as a starting point for further discussion of the link between theory and therapy. Here are a few.

Division 17, the Society of Counseling Psychology of the American Psychological Association, described counseling as "helping to overcome obstacles to their personal growth, wherever these may be encountered, and toward achieving optimum development of their personal resources" (Committee on Definition, Division of Counseling Psychology, 1956, p. 283).

Wampold (2001) took a slightly different view: "Psychotherapy is a primarily interpersonal treatment that is based on psychological principles and involves a trained therapist and a client who has a mental disorder, problem, or complaint; it is intended by the therapist to be remedial for the client's disorder, problem, or complaint; and it is adapted or individualized for the particular client and his or her disorder, problem, or complaint" (p. 3).

Which definition do you think is better? As you can see, what we assume everyone knows is not necessarily so. What are the implications of using language such as "overcome obstacles to their personal growth" versus "remedial for the client's disorder, problem, or complaint"? These kinds of philosophical differences supply the underpinnings for the various theories of psychotherapy that will be presented in this book.

One nagging question always surfaces at this point: Is there a difference between counseling and psychotherapy? Traditionally, psychotherapy was considered the realm of "personality change" and "*depth* work," whereas counseling was seen as shorter in duration, problem-focused, and much less intense. Currently, most people do not differentiate between counseling and psychotherapy, acknowledging that the difference between the two activities is more in the ideology of the speaker than in the actuality of the event. I will therefore use *counseling* or *therapy* (and *counselor, psychotherapist,* or *therapist*) interchangeably in this book.

WHY BOTHER WITH THEORY?

Once you've tentatively decided what counseling is, the next step is to consider how to do it. A long-standing tradition, dating from Sigmund Freud, is that the practice of psychotherapy is guided by the use of a theory. For Freud, of course, there was *one* theory. In the 2000s, we can count over 400 different approaches to counseling (Corsini & Wedding, 2005). The situation may seem bewildering, and you may be wondering, Do I have to have a theory?

We've all heard the phrases "that's just theoretical" or "Theoretically . . . " The general message seems to be that theory is one thing, reality is another. Theory is something that is the concern of ivory-towered fuzzy-headed intellectuals, and it is well known they live their lives far from reality.

I respectfully differ. I believe that theory is practical and important. Theory is fun. Theory works. Theory is essential to human life. Counselors who don't have theory are likely to get lost in their very genuine efforts to help their clients.

These claims may seem pretty extravagant. In this chapter, and indeed in the rest of this book, I intend to convince you that these observations make some sense—that theory plays a critical role in your work with clients. I will explain a little more.

THEORY IS FUN

You probably think I am exaggerating a little in this statement, but really, for me, theory is fun. Looking at all of the different ways to understand human activity is entertaining to those of us who are people watchers, or even worse, nosy busybodies who are always asking, Now *why* did he or she do that?

THEORY WORKS

As you will see before this chapter is over, we are pretty certain that the major counseling theories are effective. Each of the theories I present explains why people behave as they do, how to help them grow, and how to change aspects of their lives if they wish to do so. Careful, critical application of these principles seems to result in decreases in psychological symptoms and other signs of psychological health. I'd also risk saying that good psychotherapy results in increased self-understanding and, ultimately, can produce changes in lives that increase happiness.

THEORY IS ESSENTIAL TO HUMAN LIFE

I suppose I will admit to a little exaggeration in my choice of the above heading. I am talking about theory in a very general way here. What I mean is that humans can't exist unless they have ways of organizing the bath of information in which we constantly splash. Stop reading for a moment and just attend to everything *around* and *in* you. Note your physical environment—are you reading this book outside on a grassy lawn? Is it warm? Cold? What about your body? Is your stomach growling? What thoughts are going through your head?

I think you might be getting my point—how do we know which stimuli to attend to and which to put in the background? How do we tell the difference between a dog and a horse? The answer to these questions, of course, is theory, or put another way, some structure into which we fit information to create meaning. We sometimes call these structures schemas, which are defined as cognitive structures that help us organize information. The interesting thing about schemas is that they can be both helpful and harmful. First, a schema helps us organize information into a coherent whole (think about "elephant" and list the qualities of elephant). We do this instantaneously because our schema is already present in our minds. Schemas make us more efficient processors of information. Schemas also help us to communicate. We can talk to other people because they have similar schemas (never mind whether these things are real or simply agreed-upon interpretations of the world). The downside of schematic processing is that we tend to quickly identify information that is consistent with our schema and may ignore or forget information that is *not* consistent.

You can see the implications of schema theory for counselors. Theory, our professional schema, help us organize information about human experience, life, the universe, and our clients. It can make us more efficient and directed in our work. However, theory can also bias our perceptions, seducing us into tunnel vision of the worst sort. The problem is that despite these dangers, it is probably impossible to avoid using schemas in information processing, and I'd argue that it is equally impossible to avoid using some kind of theory-like structures and assumptions in working with clients. Using a formal theory simply makes the assumptions and predictions explicit and open to examination.

COUNSELORS WHO DON'T USE THEORY MAY GET LOST

What about those who don't think about theory or, even worse, reject it outright? Consider a metaphor.

If I wanted to travel from Lake Lotawana, Missouri, to Key West, Florida, how would I proceed? I consider flying on a plane, and then reject that notion in favor of my trusty old Miata, which I have always wanted to drive down the 7-mile bridge. So driving is the thing, but do I just pack my bags and sail out the door? Well, some folks might—but we will leave this approach for another paragraph. What I would do is find a map of the United States.

As I scrutinize my map, I discover several things. First, many major roads (interstate highways) would seem very efficient, well-trodden paths. There are also the back roads, scenic, but perhaps less efficient. In essence, it appears that there are many ways to get from Lake Lotawana to Key West. Depending on the criteria you use (speed, beauty, traffic), each has strengths and weaknesses.

In my view, counseling theory provides the counselor with a map. On this map, counselor and client can locate where they are right now and see the path to where they want to go. The theory specifies the "good" way to go. In the blooming wild of the world, the theory tells the therapist which of the zillion bits of information presented in human experience are important, and how to organize them.

To refuse to adopt some form of theory is to be driving around without a map. Consider what would have happened if I had packed my bags, hopped in the car, and just started driving. Would I have gotten to Key West? Who knows? I could have ended up in California or Boston.

However, you might accurately point out that I probably had some idea that Key West is south and east of Lake Lotawana. That is a good point, and by analogy, beginning therapists often have some ideas about what directions to take with their clients. There are some potential problems, though, with this loose sense of understanding. Proceeding with a vague idea will probably lead to a lot of wrong turns; at best, it will probably take much longer to get there. You might even get lost.

If you are a risk-taking, adventurous, free-spirited type, you might be tempted to argue that maps are stultifying; it is much more exciting to set out unfettered. Sticking to the map keeps you from seeing out-of-the-way places that are interesting and potentially enriching. I have three responses to that argument. First, using a map does not mean that you *have* to take the interstate. You still have the option of taking the less-frequented roads. Second, you can always take side trips. Third, and most important, there is an ethical issue: You are not traveling alone. Your client is in the car with you and expects that you know how to drive and where you're going. Although free-spirited wandering might be helpful to some clients, it could be very dangerous for others.

YOUR TASK: FIND YOUR MAP

As a beginning therapist, I remember being pretty nervous as I thought about greeting my first client. I recall that I had lots of theories in my head, but I did not feel very secure with any particular one. I was wandering around with too many maps and no idea which one to use.

The best advice I can give you is to find a map that you can live with in the form of one of the established theories of psychotherapy. As a beginner, you will find it much easier to learn from the masters than to invent your own theory. Taking this approach does *not* mean that you become a thick-headed, single-minded devotee of dogma. In fact, it is unethical to do so because the unique needs and characteristics of the client require you to be somewhat flexible. Theory should be applied in a critical way, with the recognition that other approaches exist (and are apparently valid, too) and that theories contain biases that can be dangerous to clients. Also, starting with one good theory does not mean you will stay with that theory forever. In fact you will probably change orientations several times over your career as a therapist. What I am suggesting is that you deliberately choose where you start and what map you will follow. By doing so, you will learn how to apply a theory while at the same time having some comfort in adhering to an approach that has survived some years of scrutiny by those who have more experience than you have.

Am I advocating that you pick one theory and relentlessly pound your clients with it, regardless of the feedback you get? Aren't there times when other approaches or techniques not stipulated by your theory would be more helpful? Of course there are. In fact, I support a kind of technical eclecticism—relying on one theoretical structure (or as you gain experience, an integration of two or more similar approaches) but using techniques from others, *with a clear idea about why these techniques help you toward your theoretically defined goals.*

What I don't advocate is theory-hopping, treating theories like clothes that are easily discarded depending on the occasion. First, I am not sure that psychologically or intellectually we are able to change theories easily because an important part of choosing a theory is to find one that fits with your assumptions about life. Theories differ along these lines. Second, I think that theory-hopping can lead to a very superficial understanding of theoretical perspectives. Sometimes you just have to hang in there to really get to know a theory.

One other consideration about flexibility in theoretical approach is extremely important. Theories have biases, and sometimes these interfere with the understanding of your client, particularly in terms of ethnicity, culture, sexual orientation, gender, physical ableness, and so forth. You must be very sensitive to potential problems in this realm. Any time you pick up that the client is not comfortable with your approach, check it out! Consult with the client, your supervisor, your peers (being careful to maintain client confidentiality). Never persist in using a theory that seems problematic to your client.

Now that you have accepted the challenge of finding your map, the next hurdle looms ahead: what theory should you pick? There are a number of ways to look at this question. I will review several in this chapter, and then revisit this complicated issue in my final chapter.

CHARACTERISTICS OF GOOD THEORY

You may be thinking that the way to choose a theory is simply to pick the best one. Of course! Unfortunately, there are several yardsticks proposed to measure theory. One way of starting our examination of theory is to begin with the notion that good theory corresponds to reality (however you define that); that is, its ideas are accurate and so are its predictions. Testing theory against the qualities of the world is the business of science, and the practice of counseling and psychotherapy has its roots in the scientific tradition.

For a very long time the ideals and products of science have been an important part of the enterprise of counseling and psychotherapy. Sigmund Freud, arguably the first theoretical psychotherapist, considered himself a scientist, and this tradition is alive today in the scientist–practitioner model, the dominant training model of professional psychologists (i.e., counseling, clinical, and school psychologists; Raimey, 1950). The same kind of respect for the scientific roots of intervention is evident in other counseling professions as well (e.g., professional counseling). What does the scientist–practitioner model mean? Does it mean that you have to be a scientist and a therapist? Do you have to conduct research and do counseling to qualify?

Questions about whether individuals can truly integrate the elements of the scientist–practitioner model have raged for years (Nathan, 2000). At one extreme, the model is interpreted to mean that professionals should routinely engage in both science and practice in their everyday activities. Proponents of this view have been disappointed to find that very few practitioners engage in scientific research. Interestingly, some research indicates that individuals who are mainly scientists—college and university professors who teach counseling and psychotherapy—do practice what they preach (Murdock & Brooks, 1993). Over 60% of a sample of university faculty reported that they regularly worked with clients in some form (mostly individual counseling). Thus, it is at least possible to realize both components of the scientist–practitioner model, although it appears that, for practical reasons, very few professionals do.

A more moderate position on the model is that those who are mostly counselors or therapists (the largest group of scientist–practitioners) should approach their work with a scientific attitude. This perspective is the one I advocate, given the lack of incentives for most practitioners to do research. What does being a "scientific practitioner" mean? I propose that individuals in this mode understand the relationships among theory, research, and practice and are able and willing to read and evaluate research relevant to their practice. They approach their work with a critical, evaluative attitude and with the best interests of their clients firmly in mind.

Now that you understand the basic orientation, we can proceed to examine some of the qualities that have been identified as important in determining what a good theory is: precision and testability, empirical validity, parsimony, stimulation, and practicality.

PRECISION AND TESTABILITY

A theory should have clearly defined constructs and should clearly specify the relationships among them (Maddi, 1996; Monte & Sollod, 2003). This kind of arrangement makes the theory easier to use. Because scientist–practitioners like to test theory to see if it approximates our current view of reality, the constructs should be easy to measure, or to use the professional word, they should have operational definitions or be easily operationalized. An operational definition is a statement that describes how the construct is to be measured "in terms that differ from the data it is meant to explain" (Maddi, 1996, p. 486).

Take the notion of defense mechanisms. How would you measure the presence or absence of a defense mechanism? For example, if you were thinking that a defense mechanism causes some behavior (say, aggression), you'd want to measure the level of the defense mechanism and then measure aggressive behavior. To rely on aggression as the measure of the defense mechanism is problematic because other constructs could possibly explain the occurrence of aggressive behavior (habit, situational cues, an angry personality type).

Let's consider the Rational Emotive Behavior Therapy construct of rational belief. Skip quickly to Chapter 9 and read the section on beliefs. Is the idea of rational belief clearly defined? How would you identify the presence of a rational or irrational belief? Could you easily measure whether an individual had rational or irrational beliefs?

Good theory generates predictions about behavior that are testable. For example, if defense mechanisms are operative, aggressive behavior results. If distorted thoughts are active, then psychological distress results.

Another quality related to testability is refutability (Monte & Sollod, 2003). In essence, you should be able to deduce what kind of information would lead to disconfirmation of the theory. However, because a theory is refutable does not mean it will be abandoned if

TABLE 1.1
DISCREDITED PSYCHOLOGICAL TREATMENTS

Treatment	Mean Rating(SD)	Percent Not Familiar
Angel therapy for treatment of mental/behavioral disorders	4.98 (.14)	46.4
Use of pyramids for restoration of energy	4.98 (.13)	28.0
Orgone therapy for treatment of mental/behavioral disorders	4.97 (.17)	16.9
Crystal healing for treatment of mental/behavioral disorders	4.95 (.21)	21.0
Past lives therapy for treatment of mental/behavioral disorders	4.92 (.27)	7.2
Future lives therapy for treatment of mental/behavioral disorders	4.88 (.33)	30.5
Treatments for PTSD caused by alien abduction	4.85 (.40)	20.5
Rebirthing therapies for treatment of mental/behavioral disorders	4.75 (.46)	4.8
Color therapy for treatment of mental/behavioral disorders	4.68 (.62)	50.6
Primal scream therapy for treatment of mental/behavioral disorders	4.61 (.72)	4.8

Note: SD=standard deviation; percent not familiar indicates the proportion of participants in the poll who were unfamiliar with the particular treatment.

Source: Adapted from Norcross, J. C., Koocher, G. P., & Garofalo, A. (2006). Discredited Psychological Treatments and Tests: A Delphi Poll. *Professional Psychology: Research and Practice 37,* 515–522 (p. 518). Adapted with permission.

disconfirming evidence emerges. The history of science shows us that it is indeed difficult to discard a theory because what constitutes good evidence is often a topic of debate (Kuhn, 1970). An interesting illustration of this phonemenon can be seen in Norcross, Koocher, and Garofalo's (2006) report on discredited psychological treatments. In this study, Norcross et al., using a technique called Delphi polling, asked a sample of experts to rate a set of psychological treatments on the degree to which they were discredited. Ratings were made on a scale of 1 (not at all discredited) to 5 (certainly discredited). Table 1.1 shows their top 10 results. With this evidence in mind, the issue of empirical validity will be taken up more extensively in the next section.

EMPIRICAL VALIDITY

A good theory should have some empirical support (Maddi, 1996). From a scientist–practitioner perspective, this is a given. The question is, What constitutes empirical support?

> One theorist's placebo (e.g., nondirective discussion) is another's favorite treatment. (Haaga & Davison, 1989, p. 502)

Sigmund Freud's idea of empirical support was his own case descriptions, which he wrote mostly after the fact. These days, uncontrolled methods such as these are not considered good empirical support because they reflect one person's views and are therefore subject to much bias (Heppner, Kivlighan, & Wampold, 2007). More appropriate are controlled case studies, in which specific, standardized measurements are made over the course of counseling, and the interventions performed are well defined and verified (i.e., the extent to which the therapist faithfully performed the treatment is ascertained).

Over the years, great debate has raged about what evidence is considered acceptable in terms of validating the psychotherapy enterprise. In 1952 Hans Eysenck raised eyebrows and tempers in the then-young profession of psychotherapy. Eysenck, a behaviorist, set out to study the effects of psychotherapy, which at that time was roughly categorized as either psychoanalytic or eclectic (note that behavioral methods were not considered in the "therapy" grouping). Eysenck (1952) compared the rates of improvement of clients in the two types of counseling to two groups of "untreated" individuals, state hospital patients and individuals who had made disability claims with their insurance companies on the basis of psychoneurosis. Over 2 years, the improvement rate for the untreated individuals was 72%. In contrast, Eysenck found that only 44% of clients in psychoanalytic therapy and 64% of clients in eclectic therapy improved. He concluded that these data "fail to prove that psychotherapy, Freudian or otherwise, facilitates the recovery of neurotic patients. They show that roughly two-thirds of a group of neurotic patients will recover or improve to a marked extent within about two years of the onset of their illness, whether they are treated by means of psychotherapy or not" (Eysenck, 1952, p. 322).

Of course, this kind of conclusion greatly disturbed professionals who believed in the benefits of therapy. Numerous rebuttals to Eysenck were published that included various recalculations of his data and criticisms of his "control" groups. Without summarizing these sometimes tedious arguments, it is probably safe to say that the most useful thing about Eysenck's original study was that it caused professionals to realize that something more was needed to back up their statements regarding the effectiveness of psychotherapy.

Over the years since Eysenck's article, huge numbers of studies have been conducted to test the effects of psychotherapy, and there is now agreement within the profession that psychotherapy is indeed effective (Lambert & Ogles, 2004; Wampold, 2001). In what is generally cited as the authoritative reference on psychotherapy outcome, Lambert and Ogles (2004) conclude that "providers as well as patients can be assured that a broad range of therapies, when offered by skillful, wise, and stable therapists, are likely to result in appreciable gains for the client (p. 180). The sheer amount of data gathered since the original 1952 challenge is overwhelming, but can generally be classified into three sets: meta-analytic studies, what I call "exemplar" outcome studies, and perhaps most controversial, consumer survey data (Seligman, 1995).

Meta-analysis is a statistical technique that combines the results of a selected set of studies into an overall index of effectiveness, called effect size. Effect size tells us whether, across all studies, the treatment being observed is associated with significant differences between treated and untreated groups, or differences between two theoretical or treatment approaches. For example, the earliest meta-analyses compared counseling to no treatment and found effect sizes in the 0.75 to 0.80 range (Smith & Glass, 1977, Smith, Glass, & Miller, 1980). These results indicate that across the research studies compiled, the average client in psychotherapy improved more than about 80% of clients who were not treated (Lambert & Ogles, 2004). Meta-analysis has also demonstrated that psychotherapy is at least equal to, and perhaps more powerful than, antidepressant medication (Gloaguen, Cottraux, Cuchherat, & Blackburn, 1998; Robinson, Berman, & Neimeyer, 1990; Steinbrueck, Maxwell, & Howard, 1983). In what is a disappointing finding for some, the various theoretical orientations have been repeatedly shown to be equally effective with a wide variety of client presentations (Lambert & Ogles, 2004; Wampold, 2001).

What I call "exemplar" studies are those that are generally recognized as stringent comparisons of psychotherapy groups to no treatment groups following the best scientific procedures. They are also called efficacy studies and are based on the clinical trials approach adopted from pharmacy research. Efficacy studies involve random assignment of participants (clients) to treatments, rigorous controls, carefully specified treatments, fixed numbers of sessions offered to clients, narrowly defined entrance criteria (e.g., clients having only one identified disorder), and independent raters to assess client dysfunction and improvement. An important feature of these kinds of studies is that they use treatment manuals that detail the expectations for what the therapist will do. Of the exemplar studies I describe here, the National Institute of Mental Health Treatment of Depression Collaborative Research Program (TDCRP) and the Project MATCH studies are true clinical trials (efficacy) studies; the Temple study was not because it admitted clients presenting a wide range of concerns.

The Temple study (Sloane, Staples, Cristol, Yorkston, & Whipple, 1975) compared short-term Psychoanalytically Oriented Therapy and Behavior Therapy with a minimal contact control group. Experienced therapists provided the treatments to 90 clients over a 4-month period who were randomly assigned to one of the three groups. Therapist adherence to their approaches was assessed, and independent observers rated client outcomes, as did the participating counselors and clients. A 1-year follow-up assessment was included, along with pre- and posttherapy tests of symptoms. Across all measures of outcomes, the treated groups improved significantly more than the control group. Differences between the two therapeutic approaches were negligible.

Critics of meta-analysis and the early exemplar research suggest that the problem in finding differential effectiveness of counseling approaches can be attributed to ignoring significant client factors in these studies. Such client factors are usually operationalized as diagnosis as exemplified in the *Diagnostic and Statistical Manual of Mental Disorders, Fourth Edition,* (DSM-IV-TR, American Psychiatric Association, 2000). Perhaps specific approaches will work best for specific diagnoses. A second exemplar study adopted this philosophy, attempting to assess psychotherapy for depression. The National Institute of Mental Health (NIMH) Treatment of Depression Collaborative Research Program (TDCRP) focused solely on depression and compared psychotherapeutic treatment to antidepressant and placebo groups. The antidepressant and placebo groups also received clinical management, which apparently amounted to "minimally supportive therapy" (Elkin, 1994, p. 135). The two treatment types were interpersonal psychotherapy, a variant of psychoanalytically oriented therapy (see Box 1.1 for an overview), and cognitive behavioral therapy (most similar to Beck's Cognitive therapy; Chapter 10). Thus, clients were randomly assigned to one of four treatment groups: interpersonal psychotherapy, cognitive-behavioral therapy, antidepressant plus clinical management, or placebo plus clinical management. Ten experienced therapists, carefully trained, administered the counseling at three research sites across the United States. A total of 239 clients participated, exhibiting a range of nonbipolar, nonpsychotic depression.

Using multiple outcome measures, the study found virtually no differences among the four treatment groups. All groups showed improvement following treatment, even the placebo group. What remains unclear is whether the unexpected improvement in the placebo-clinical management group was a result of the placebo pill or the clinical management. Thus, this study clearly supports the effectiveness of psychotherapeutic

Box 1.1

Klerman and Weissman's Interpersonal Psychotherapy

THEORY

The interpersonal psychotherapy (IPT) approach is a present-oriented, short-term therapy that was developed for clients who present with depression. Based in attachment and communications theories and with recognition of the importance of social factors in everyday functioning, IPT includes a medical model of depression used to educate clients, but then focuses on current interpersonal issues as the targets of intervention.

Four Relationship Problems

IPT theory identifies four basic interpersonal problems: grief, interpersonal role disputes, role transitions, and interpersonal deficits (Klerman, Weissman, Rounsaville, & Chevron, 1984; Markovits & Swartz, 1997; Stuart, 2006). **Grief** is defined as the persistence of depressive symptoms beyond a normal period of mourning following the death of a person significant to the client. **Role disputes** are when two or more individuals disagree on the nature of their relationship. Current overt or covert conflict with another is present. Three general phases of role dispute are distinguished: renegotiation, impasse, and dissolution. Clients who are in the midst of a major life change are generally struggling with **role transition**, which includes events such as divorce, retirement, job change, or being diagnosed with a major physical illness. The **interpersonal deficits** category of problems is the last-resort category. It signifies a long-term pattern of interpersonal deficits or lack of relationships. Prognosis is considered to be poor for these clients (Markowitz & Swartz, 1997).

IPT does not present a causal theory of depression; depression is probably the result of many factors. Interpersonal problems can either cause or exacerbate depressed mood. What is important in IPT is that the client accept a conceptualization that her depression is linked to a specific area of interpersonal functioning, one of the four problem areas (Weismann & Markowitz, 1994).

THERAPY

Two kinds of assessment are important in IPT. First, the counselor confers a formal (DSM-IVTR) diagnosis. A complete medical evaluation of the client is recommended (Klerman et al., 1984). Second, the counselor conducts an interpersonal inventory with the client (Stuart, 2006). All of the important interpersonal relationships in the client's life are reviewed with the goal of establishing a link between changes in one or more of these relationships and the onset of the depression.

Counseling focuses on current problems, not historical events. In this approach, the therapist is an active problem solver and advocate for the client. Although the therapeutic relationship is used as a vehicle for change, no transference interpretations are used. Clients are expected to become experts on depression and to use this expertise to work actively to solve their problems (Markowitz & Swartz, 1997).

Conceptualized as a time-limited (12–16 weeks) weekly therapy (Weissman & Mardowitz, 1994), IPT has two basic interlocking goals (Klerman et al., 1984): to reduce the client's depressive symptoms and to remedy the interpersonal difficulties associated with the depression. The client and counselor must agree on the conceptualization of the problem; this agreement promotes the therapeutic relationship and also signals the strategies and goals of the therapy (Markowitz & Swartz, 1997).

IPT has three stages (Klerman & Weissman, 1993). In stage 1 (the first three sessions or so), assessment, diagnosis, and conceptualization are the focus.

The medical model conceptualization of depression is presented to clients, and they are given the "sick role." Clients are told that depression results from the interaction of biological and environmental factors (i.e., life events). Advocates of this approach argue that making psychological dysfunction partly biological in nature relieves clients of the overwhelming responsibility for their problems and allows separation of the problems from clients' sense of self (Markowitz & Swartz, 1997). Adopting the sick role is significant because it relieves clients from significant social responsibilities and stressors, but also creates in clients a commitment to working in therapy (Weissman & Markowitz, 1998).

Stage 1 also involves giving clients the conceptualization of their depression in one of the four areas: role dispute, role transition, grief, and interpersonal deficits. Only one of these areas should be identified for each client.

In stage 2, attention is focused on the problem area that was identified in stage 1 (Markowitz & Swartz, 1997). Counselors with grieving clients help them mourn and then support them in establishing new activities and relationships. Clients experiencing role disputes examine the nature of the dispute and devise ways to resolve it. Counselors attempt to help clients in role transition negotiate the life changes smoothly and to the best outcomes. The interpersonal deficits category is the most difficult to treat, according to Markowitz and Swartz (1997), because it is basically a default category. These clients tend to have lots of interpersonal problems and very few supportive relationships. Clients are encouraged to understand the connection between depression and social difficulties and to learn new social skills.

Stage 3 of IPT is termination and comprises the last few sessions of therapy. Client and counselor discuss the client's progress and acknowledge the ending of the therapeutic relationship. The potential for relapse and triggers that might be associated with it are discussed (Markowitz & Swartz, 1997).

TECHNIQUES

IPT is basically an eclectic approach. The following seven categories of intervention are presented; example of specific techniques within the categories are excerpted from Klerman, and colleagues (1984, pp. 142–153), which is generally considered the treatment manual for IPT.

Exploration: Nondirective exploration of the problem; supportive acknowledgement

Encouragement of affect: acceptance of painful emotion; facilitating suppressed affect

Clarification: rephrasing; attending to contradictions

Communication analysis: identifying problems in communication such as assuming that one is understood; communicating ambiguously on nonverbal channels

Use of the therapeutic relationship: encouraging client to reveal thoughts and feelings about the therapist and the therapeutic relationship; used to help client learn about other relationships

Behavior-change techniques: advice and suggestions; education; modeling

Adjunctive techniques: forming a therapeutic contract

interventions, but also calls into question the specificity of these effects because the therapies did not outperform the reference conditions (the drug and placebo groups).

Project MATCH represented yet another step in outcome research. This elaborate research project was specifically designed to see if client characteristics moderated treatment effects for a specific problem, in this case alcohol dependence and abuse (Project MATCH Research Group, 1997). In this very large and powerful study, over 1,500 clients received either cognitive behavioral treatment (12 sessions), motivational enhancement (4 sessions), or a treatment designed to help clients begin to work on the Alcoholics Anonymous 12 steps (12 sessions and clients were encouraged to attend AA meetings). Ten client characteristics thought to predict client response to the type of treatment were carefully assessed (e.g., alcohol involvement, gender, motivation).

The results of Project MATCH were consistent with previous studies. There were no differences in the effectiveness of the three treatments, and virtually no effects of client factors were found. Of the client characteristics, only one significant difference was apparent— clients who were relatively low in psychological distress did better with the 12-step approach than the others did. These differences were not evident in more distressed clients.

Several other carefully conducted studies have shown similar outcomes. One of these was Crits-Cristoph et al.'s (1999) study of treatments for cocaine dependence, in which clients received individual drug counseling plus group drug counseling (GDC), cognitive therapy plus GDC, supportive-expressive therapy plus GCD, or GDC alone. The drug counseling conditions used nonprofessional counselors. Surprisingly, GDC plus individual drug counseling produced the best results. Shapiro et al. (1994) compared psychodynamic interpersonal and cognitive-behavior therapy for depression and found the approaches equivalent. Generally, then, the results of exemplar studies tend to confirm meta-analytic findings that there are no differences in the effectiveness of theoretically-based treatments.

A final, and controversial, approach to studying counseling outcome involves what has been called the *effectiveness* approach to emphasize the difference between this and the efficacy or clinical trials method (Seligman, 1995). The *Consumer Reports* (CR) study is the most famous effectiveness study, and in fact, the distinction between efficacy and effectiveness was proposed by Seligman, who consulted with CR on the research and presented it to the psychological community in the *American Psychologist*. The intent of the CR study was to assess the outcomes of counseling *as it is actually practiced in the real world* (Seligman, 1995). Fixed numbers of sessions, strict adherence to manuals, and random assignment are serious distortions of what actually happens when real people go to therapy.

Further, clients usually have more than one specific problem (which they don't present as DSM-IV diagnoses), and the client and the counselor are concerned with overall client functioning, not just improvement in specific symptoms. This approach is quite controversial, for it does away with control groups, random assignments, and all of that other hard-core scientific stuff. Instead, effectiveness studies simply ask clients about their experiences using a large-scale survey method.

Imagine having folks rate therapy the way they do washing machines. Actually, that's what the *Consumer Reports* study did. CR sent out 180,000 surveys instructing individuals to complete the section on mental health if in the past 3 years they had sought help for stress or emotional difficulties. A total of 4,100 respondents reported having obtained professional help of some kind (e.g., attended support groups, visited physicians or mental health professionals); of these, 2,900 reported having received the services of a mental health professional. Twenty-six specific questions explored the participants' experiences with counseling. Without getting too detailed, the results of this study suggested that the efficacy studies were perhaps right—the vast majority of the respondents reported improving as a result of counseling. The amount of improvement was correlated with the length of counseling. Most relevant for our study of theory was that, once again, no theoretical approach was found to be superior to any other.

Even long before the era of meta-analyses, clinical trials, and effectiveness studies, Rosenzweig (1936/2002) captured the state of psychotherapy outcome research by quoting the Dodo bird from Carroll's *Alice in Wonderland:* "*Everybody* has won and *all* must have prizes" (p. 5). However, this verdict is not fully accepted by all scholars involved in psychotherapy research (Ollendick & King, 2006). In fact, a large group of psychologists support a movement to develop a list of treatments that work—known as empirically supported treatments, or ESTs. The idea behind the EST movement is that identifying specific treatments that are efficacious for specific problems is the solution to the Dodo bird dilemma.

The EST movement began in Division 12 of the American Psychological Association (APA), the Society of Clinical Psychology. Later, a special issue of the *Journal of Consulting and Clinical Psychology* was published presenting a review of literature in focused areas with the intent of identifying ESTs. In the special issue, ESTs were defined as "clearly specified psychological treatments shown to be efficacious in controlled research with a delineated population" (Chambless & Hollon, 1998, p. 8). This provision meant that the treatments considered had to be assessed within an efficacy design, specifically a randomized clinical trial study. If two independent research teams demonstrated that the treatment was better than no treatment, the treatment was labeled *efficacious.* A treatment was considered *efficacious and specific* for a given population or problem if it produced better outcomes when compared to "conditions that control for nonspecific processes" (e.g., client expectation or effects of attention of an interested other, p. 8) or other recognized treatment approaches.

It is not possible to summarize the results of the entire special issue here. Some examples of the approaches labeled efficacious include Cognitive Therapy for panic disorder and depression, Exposure Therapy for agoraphobia and obsessive-compulsive disorder (this with response prevention), and Cognitive-Behavior Therapy for generalized anxiety disorder (Crits-Cristoph, 1997; DeRubeis & Crits-Christoph, 1998). Very few approaches were labeled efficacious *and specific*—that is, better than comparison approaches for a given disorder. Efficacious and specific approaches include Cognitive Therapy for generalized anxiety disorder and panic disorder, exposure plus response prevention for obsessive-compulsive disorder, and Exposure Therapy for agoraphobia. However, DeRubeis and Crits-Christoph point out that the conclusion that Cognitive Therapy is specific for depression relative to other psychological treatments is probably premature, particularly in light of results found in such careful and powerful studies as the NIMH TDCRP study.

The EST movement set off a major controversy within professional psychology. Opponents of the movement criticize it on the grounds that it is biased toward cognitive and behavioral approaches (i.e., those approaches that are easily manualized) and that the requirement for clinical trials methodology was too strict. Others reiterated the criticisms elaborated by Seligman (1995) (i.e., clinical trials don't represent reality). Various political, philosophical, and methodological issues are still debated heatedly (Norcross, Beutler, & Levant, 2006). One of the bottom line issues is that if we conclude that there are no specific effects of psychotherapy, what are we to tell managed care organizations about what kind of therapy is acceptable? The lack of such a stance leaves those who pay for the treatment (and presumably have less knowledge about its intricacies than we do) free to determine the treatment clients receive based on other factors (e.g., length, cost; Beutler, 1998).

A different way of looking at empirically supported interventions was proposed by Division 17, the Society of Counseling Psychology (SCP) of the American Psychological Association (Wampold, Lichtenberg, & Waehler, 2002). In an issue of *The Counseling Psychologist,* the division's Special Task Group presented seven principles by which research concerned with empirical support for interventions could be reviewed; these are shown in Figure 1.1. In the first principle, the task group proposed four levels of specificity in counseling outcome research and suggested that the credential "empirically supported" could apply at each level. Level 1 is the most general level, the level of types of actions such as prevention, psychotherapy, and classroom intervention. Level 2 of this system includes major approaches to level 1 activities, such as group therapy, career exploration, or cognitive-behavior therapy. Level 3 is the level of the Division 12 empirically supported treatment, the application of major approaches (as in level 2) to specific problems or populations. Level 4 interventions are specific approaches (from within the major modalities or approaches) to specific populations or problems. An example of this level would be

---

1. Level of specificity should be considered when evaluating outcomes.
2. Level of specificity should not be restricted to diagnosis.
3. Scientific evidence needs to be examined in its entirety and aggregated appropriately.
4. Evidence for absolute and relative efficacy needs to be presented.
5. Causal attributions for specific ingredients should be made only if the evidence is persuasive.
6. Outcomes should be assessed appropriately and broadly.
7. Outcomes should be assessed locally and freedom of choice should be recognized.

FIGURE 1.1 Society of Counseling Psychology's Principles of Empiricall Supported Interventions.
Source: Wampold, B. E. Lichtenberg, J. W., & Waehler, C. A. (2002). Principles of empirically support: Intervention in counselling psychology. *The Counseling Psychologist, 30,* 197–217.

"well-specified Prevention Program A for persons with Risk Factor B and Cultural Characteristic C" (Wampold et al., p. 205).

The SCP task force argued that level of specificity should not be defined solely by DSM-IV diagnosis because many other dimensions are meaningful in understanding the client or treatment effects. For example, differences attributable to individual and cultural diversity are not considered in the original EST approach, nor are client values or other client characteristics. A final important point the task force made was that outcomes should be assessed globally rather than simply in terms of symptom remission, the usual practice in clinical trials studies. Clients and counselors, as I noted earlier, care about quality of life, too. Many people come to counseling for that basic reason, not because they have specific, identifiable symptoms.

What does this new perspective mean in terms of understanding the empirical support for what we do? Basically, it means that there are different ways of cutting the pie, so to speak. These principles were demonstrated in three articles in the same issue of *The Counseling Psychologist* that reviewed empirical support for career counseling, family interventions, and anger management (Deffenbacher, Oetting, & DiGiuseppe, 2002; Sexton & Alexander, 2002; Whiston, 2002). Each article reviewed the evidence for the intervention on all four levels of specificity, if appropriate. Each article also considered available research evidence in light of the other six principles. These reviews produced a broad and informative stack of information and also highlighted the strengths and weaknesses of the existing research.

A second perspective on the Dodo bird verdict is called the *common factors* approach. Observing the similarities among outcomes has led to the proposal that there are commonalties among therapies that are the *real* curative factors (Lambert & Ogles, 2004). Lambert and Ogles (2004) proposed the taxonomy of common factors shown in Table 1.2, and opined that "interpersonal, social, and affective factors common across therapies still loom large as stimulators of patient improvement" (p. 163). One of the most often cited common factors is the therapeutic relationship or alliance. Estimates of the effect of the therapeutic relationship range up to 30% of the variance in client outcomes (Asay & Lambert, 1999). Wampold (2001) maintained that the therapeutic relationship "accounts for dramatically more of the variability in outcomes" (p. 158) than do any specific factors offered based on theoretical approaches. For example, in the TDCRP study, alliance accounted for up to 21% of the variance in outcomes, whereas differences in treatments (e.g., interpersonal psychotherapy, cognitive-behavior therapy, placebo, drug) accounted for only 2%.

Other common factors that have been proposed are (a) client and counselor sharing similar views of the world, (b) positive client expectations, and (c) rituals or interventions that are acceptable to client and counselor (Fischer, Jome, & Atkinson, 1998). Fischer and colleagues (1998) suggested that our understanding of counseling relationships between diverse individuals (i.e., when client and counselor differ on significant dimensions such as sex, race, ethnicity) could be understood using a common factors perspective. For example, the counselor's possession of knowledge about the client's culture aids in building shared worldview, which may in turn contribute to the therapeutic alliance and allow the counselor and client to formulate culturally appropriate rituals or interventions. Understanding the culture of the client may also boost client expectations (hope and faith) by giving the counselor credibility in the eyes of the client.

In summary, the research on counseling and counseling theory suggests that many approaches can be taken to helping clients grow or alleviate troubles that bring them to

TABLE 1.2

LAMBERT AND OGLE'S COMMON FACTORS

Support Factors	Learning Factors	Action Factors
Catharsis	Advice	Behavioral regulation
Identification with therapist	Affective experiencing	Cognitive mastery
Mitigation of isolation	Assimilating problematic experiences	Encouragement of facing fears
Positive relationship	Cognitive learning	Taking risks
Reassurance	Corrective emotional experience	Mastery efforts
Release of tension	Feedback	Modeling
Structure	Insight	Practice
Therapeutic alliance	Rationale	Reality testing
Therapist/client active participation	Exploration of internal frame of reference	Success experience
Therapist expertness	Changing expectation of personal effectiveness	Working through
Therapist warmth, respect, empathy acceptance, genuineness Trust		

Source: Lambert, M. J., & Ogles, B. M. (2004). The efficacy and effectiveness of psychotherapy. In M. J. Lambert (Ed.) *Bergin and Garfield's Handbook of Psychotherapy and Behavior Change,* 5th Ed. (pp. 139–193). NY: John Wiley and Sons. Used by permission.

therapy. As I describe each theoretical viewpoint in this book, I will also provide a summary of research relevant to the approach. We will return to the issue of empirical validity in Chapter 16.

PARSIMONY

The principle of parsimony or simplicity (Maddi, 1996) says just that: The simplest explanation that can handle the data is the best. If comparing two theories, one elaborate and one very simple, that are both effective, then choose the simple one. Sounds good, right? Well, there are a few problems with taking such an approach. First, who makes the rules that say what's simple and what's not? Second, what is simple today may be simplistic tomorrow or next week. A more complex theory may be just right.

STIMULATION

Good theories get people excited (Maddi, 1996). The best theories prompt thought, writing, and research. Good theory can also provoke attempts to disconfirm it, although whether theories can actually be disconfirmed is a subject of debate. One wonders, though, about approaches that become "fadlike" and the devotees who, like worshipers, may not be the best critics of their faiths.

PRACTICALITY

Practicality implies applicability. For our purposes, all of the approaches in this book are practical; I chose them because they provide solid conceptual frameworks that are well-known for their applicability. Some roadmaps are easier to use than others, and I will note that the approaches presented in this book vary to some degree on this criterion. Also, the degree to which an approach lends itself to particular problems and other modes of counseling varies considerably.

SO HOW DO I CHOOSE A THEORY?

Well, to start, you have to know some theories. That's why we have books about theory. Once you have the basics of the major theories, perhaps you will be a step farther down the path.

Will you choose based on the "good theory" criteria? As scientist–practitioners, we have an obligation, I think, to consider the empirical merits of a theory, which we will do for each of the theories presented in this book. The controversy over empirically supported treatments is not yet settled, so prudent professionals should be conversant with these issues.

The question always arises, Why do I *have* to pick a theory? Can't I borrow from several (or more) of the major ones? In fact, many therapists do this; it is a theoretical stance called *eclecticism*. Consider Table 1.3, which shows the theoretical orientations found in six studies conducted between 1982 and 2001. Based on these data, it appears that the most popular orientation is eclectic, with about 30–40% of the respondents choosing this option. The exception is Jensen et al., who cited 70%. However, their sample size was much smaller than

TABLE 1.3
THEORETICAL ORIENTATIONS OVER THE YEARS

	1982[1]	1983[2]	1986[3]	1990[4]	2001[5]	2001[6]	2003[7]
Eclectic	41	30	40	70	39	36	29
Cognitive	10	8	11	5	21	16	28
Psychodynamic	11	18	10	9	10	21	15
Other	9	8	5	2	7	5	7
Systems	N/A	3	5	3	5	3	3
Interpersonal/Sullivan	N/A	1	2	1	5	3	4
Behavioral	7	6	6	8	4	3	10
Existential	2	4	3	0	3	1	N/A
Person Centered	9	2	8	1	2	2	1
Humanistic	N/A	4	4	1	2	2	1
Gestalt	2	3	2	0	2	2	N/A
Psychoanalytic	N/A	9	2	N/A	1	8	N/A
Adlerian	3	2	2	0	1	N/A	N/A

N/A means not assessed.
[1] Smith, 1982; $N = 422$, 1/2 Division 12 (Clinical Psychology), 1/2 Division 17 (Counseling Psychology)
[2] Prochaska & Norcross, 1983; $N = 410$, Division 29 (Psychotherapy)
[3] Watkins et al., 1986, $N = 716$; Division 17
[4] Jensen, Bergin, & Greaves, 1990; $N = 122$, Division 12 members
[5] Murdock, 2001; $N = 691$, Division 17 members
[6] Norcross, Hedges, & Castle, 2001; $N = 538$, Division 29
[7] Norcross, Karpiak, & Santoro (2005)

those in the other studies, so the higher percentage may be an anomaly related to the sample. This kind of research is usually cited as evidence that therapists are mostly eclectics. Let me draw your attention to two issues. First, even if we consider the high end of the range, 40% is less than half of a sample. Over 60% of these therapists endorsed a single orientation.

Second, studies of those who endorse an eclectic orientation suggest that eclectics do identify with particular orientations from among the major theoretical approaches. In Jensen and colleagues' sample of clinical psychologists, 63% and 62% of the eclectics said they were cognitive or psychodynamic, respectively (they were allowed to choose more than one approach). Fifty-six percent indicated a behavioral orientation. In my own research (Murdock et al., 2001), we asked individuals to identify their first and second choices of orientations. Of the participants who specified eclectic as their primary theoretical orientation, 15% did not specify a second theoretical influence. Of the 85% who did indicate a second theory, the most frequent response was cognitive (39%). Other respondents indicated psychodynamic, systems, and humanistic, ranging from 9% to 12% of the sample of eclectics. The largest proportion of these eclectics (more than 83%) characterized themselves as synthetic eclectics, indicating that they integrated two or more theoretical approaches. An interesting sidelight to this study was our exploration of who the therapist chooses for a therapist (see Box 1.2 for the results).

Box 1.2

Do Counselors Seek Counseling?
With Whom? Some Revelant Data

Beginning with Freud, personal therapy has been thought to be important in the development of counselors. Whether for growth or remediation, mental health professions have long encouraged counselors and therapists to undertake personal therapy (American Psychological Association, 1992; Geller, Norcross, & Orlinsky, 2005; Norcross, Strausser-Kirtland, & Missar, 1988). Various studies have looked at the kinds of personal problems experienced by psychologists, but few have examined their perceptions of their psychotherapy (Good, Thoreson, & Shaughnessy, 1995; Mahoney, 1997; Pope & Tabachnick, 1994). An exception was a study by Watkins, Lopez, Campbell, and Himmel (1986), who found that 66% of their sample had engaged in personal counseling; their counselors' orientations most often fell into the category labeled "other," which the researchers defined as a mixture of approaches that was not identified as "eclectic" by respondents. Norcross and Guy (2005) surveyed the surveys on therapists' therapies, which on average found that 72% of therapists in the United States report having been in personal therapy. They also found that insight-oriented psychotherapists were more likely to have had personal counseling than were therapists of other orientations.

In a 2001 study, my colleagues and I surveyed Counseling Psychologists, asking, among other things, about their experiences with personal counseling (Goodyear et al., in press; Murdock 2001). We sent questionnaires to 1,500 APA members who identified themselves as Counseling Psychologists; 691 returned surveys. These Counseling

Psychologists were employed in a wide variety of settings (e.g., independent practice, university counseling centers, academic faculty positions).

In our sample, a large percentage of respondents, 84.5%, reported having been in personal therapy. This percentage is comparable to or higher than those reported in previous surveys.

We found that participants who self-identified as "clinical practitioners" were more likely to have engaged in personal counseling than those who identified in other ways (e.g., researcher, administrator, academician, supervisor). We looked at participants' theoretical orientations and their perceptions of the importance of personal counseling to the work of a psychotherapist. Our respondents were very similar to those of Norcross and colleagues in that those who endorsed psychodynamic theoretical orientations were the most likely to have sought personal counseling (97%), followed by humanistic/existential types (93%). Behaviorally oriented psychologists were least likely to have undergone therapy (71%). Psychodynamic respondents also thought that personal counseling was more important than did respondents of other theoretical orientations (cognitive therapists had the lowest importance ratings). Table A shows the theoretical orientations of the therapists' therapists, demonstrating that the most popular orientation was psychodynamic or eclectic. When we compared the theoretical orientations of respondents to those of their counselors, we found that 32% of our respondents had counselors of the same or similar theoretical orientations. However, we found no relationships between a match of theoretical orientations and reported satisfaction with counseling.

TABLE A
THEORETICAL ORIENTATIONS OF COUNSELORS' COUNSELORS

Orientation	Percent of Respondents
Psychodynamic	24.5
Eclectic	20.1
Humanistic	9.9
Cognitive	8.3
Systems	7.1

So why hasn't eclecticism taken over the profession? Certainly the idea of doing what will work best for the client is an attractive one. Several factors probably account for the fact that we have not overwhelmingly jumped on the eclecticism bandwagon. For one thing, it is hard to say exactly what eclecticism is . . . which theories do you borrow from? From our data, my hunch is that eclectics borrow from several approaches within the same general theoretical domain—for example, Beck's cognitive therapy and rational emotive behavior therapy. A second question is, do you borrow ideas about how human beings function, or do you steal techniques? If so, how do you know which technique to use when? These are some tough questions, particularly for a beginning therapist. I'd also note that it is difficult to scientifically test eclecticism because by definition the counselor does different things with different clients at different times. I don't know about you, but that would make me a little nervous.

So, whether you turn out to be an eclectic or a single-theory proponent, knowing the major approaches to counseling and psychotherapy is essential. Even eclectics need to know the approaches from which they borrow.

WHAT ABOUT ME?

With all of this argument about science, empirically supported treatments and so on, you are probably wondering how you fit into the picture. What is the relationship between who you are and which theoretical approach you choose? When quite a few approaches seem effective, you probably don't just want to choose one at random.

You need to find an approach that is consistent with your assumptions about people, your values, and your preferred way of relating to others. Studies of therapists' choices of theories are rare; those that are available document that personality style is associated with theoretical orientation (Murdock, Banta, Stromseth, Viene, & Brown; 1998; Tremblay, Herron, & Schultz, 1986). For example, Walton (1978) found that psychodynamic types "perceive themselves as complex and serious. RET therapists (now Rational Emotive Behavior Therapy) maintain a diametrically opposed position, namely, simple and humorous" (p. 392). Because different studies look at different characteristics, it is difficult to fully integrate the results, and it is probably risky to apply them directly. In Box 1.3, I describe a study of philosophical assumptions and personality characteristics that some of my students and I did to give you an example. However, what is clear is that you need to fit your theory (and it needs to fit you).

Philosophical assumptions about people are also involved with theory choice, as you can see from the study described in Box 1.3. Although you might not want to use the dimensions identified by Coan (1979), you will still want to consider the assumptions made by different theories about the nature of human beings. To help you with this assessment, I have incorporated a section on basic philosophy for each of the theories I describe in this book.

The way we relate to others is core in how we conduct ourselves as counselors. As our study suggested, the way we choose to relate to others is probably connected to our choice of theory. Activity level is also an important consideration; as I tell my students, I could *never* be a psychoanalyst because that would require me to sit still too long (literally and metaphorically). I prefer an active approach to helping. For this reason, I am a family systems theorist and therapist.

You may also want to consider the type of practice that you plan to engage in as another factor. Although I present classic psychoanalysis in this book, not many therapists make a living doing classic analysis exclusively. Psychoanalysis requires a very special kind of client to engage in therapy for long periods of time. These clients are few and far between. If you don't have a trust fund, you might want to consider a different orientation.

HOW TO USE THEORY

The problem with theory is that if you don't know how to apply it, it seems sort of worthless. That's probably where the ivory tower thing came from—it is sometimes difficult to see the connection between the theory and what you see as the "real" world, the client who actually comes in the door asking for help. It is my mission in this book to help you learn

Box 1.3

Joining a Theoretical Club

Some years ago (after gaining some experience in teaching theories of counseling), I began to wonder about what really determined therapists' choices of theoretical orientation. Several students agreed that this might be an interesting research question, so we developed a study to try to find out. We surveyed more than 100 therapists and counselors, some students in graduate programs, and some professionals working in the field. We asked these therapists to identify their theoretical orientations and then to rate (a) the degree to which they endorsed a set of philosophical assumptions (derived from Coan's 1979 model) and (b) their perceptions of their interpersonal behavior on the dimensions of interpersonal control (dominant–submissive) and affiliation (friendly–hostile).

The theoretical orientations of our respondents fell into five broad groups: psychoanalytic, cognitive/cognitive-behavior, systems/interpersonal, person-centered, and existential/Gestalt. Here's how our five groups fell out, with the location of their names indicating their relative placement on the dimensions:

PHILOSOPHICAL ASSUMPTIONS

Emphasis on Behavioral Content	*Emphasis on Experiential Content*
Cognitive/Cognitive behavioral	Psychoanalytic
Systems/Interpersonal	Person-centered
	Existential/Gestalt

Elemental Emphasis	*Holistic Emphasis*
Psychoanalytic	Person-centered
Systems/Interpersonal	Existential/Gestalt
Cognitive/Cognitive behavioral	

Emphasis on Physical Causation	*Emphasis on Psychological Causation*
Systems/Interpersonal	Existential/Gestalt
Cognitive/Cognitive-behavioral	Psychoanalytic
	Person-centered

Interpersonal Behavior: Interpersonal Dominance	
High	Low
Psychoanalytic	Existential/Gestalt
	Person-centered
	Systems/Interpersonal
	Cognitive/Cognitive behavioral

to actually use theory through applying it to individuals. I limit my presentation to individual counseling and psychotherapy (with the exception of the family systems chapter) and will illustrate the application of each theory to a client. This method gives you an example of the application process. Before you go on to the theories, I think I can give you a start on the application process by providing a general model of case conceptualization, or the application of theory to the individual client.

A STEP-BY-STEP GUIDE

In the interest of helping you learn how to apply theory, I now present one model that describes how to do this. My model presents a series of questions to answer within three broad steps to conceptualization. If you answer these questions, the application process will be easier and more accurate.

STEP 1: KNOW YOUR THEORY

To fully understand your theoretical perspective, answer the following questions:

1. What does the theory say is the primary or core motivation of human existence? Theories vary on how explicitly they address this issue as well as on what the motivations actually are. Psychoanalysis, for example, rests on a model of humans as driven by conflicting instinctual forces. Behavior therapists are less vocal on this issue; they see humans as motivated to survive and adapt to the environment.
2. What are the major constructs of the theory?
3. What is the process of development from the theory's perspective (if it specifies one)? Some theories are very detailed in their descriptions of psychological development, such as Psychoanalysis. Others don't have much to say about how people grow psychologically (Solution-Focused Therapy) or offer somewhat vague, general statements about it (Person-Centered or Cognitive Therapy). A useful question here is, What stages are key in development, if any?
4. What is psychological health? What is psychological dysfunction? If you can tell what the theory sees as healthy, you can probably deduce what it sees as unhealthy.

An important point to note at this juncture is that you must *always* take into account the client's cultural background in the theoretical conceptualization process. When I say culture, I mean the term in its broadest sense—differences among people that are a function of age, race or ethnicity, sex, sexual orientation, religion, and so on. Theories, for the most part, are pretty blind to these differences. They generally assume that everyone is just like everyone else. Worse, theories are inherently biased because they are the products of the cultural experience of the theorist who created them and the times in which they were created. Definitions of psychological health vary from culture to culture. What was considered psychologically healthy 25 years ago may not be so today.

5. Who are the important individuals in a client's life? Parents? Siblings? In the case of Bowen family systems theory, the perspective is multigenerational. At least three generations are thought to be important in any client's presentation.
6. Relatively speaking, how important are behavior, cognition, and affect in the client's situation? For the rational emotive behavior therapist, thoughts are the most important aspect

of the person. For Gestalt therapists, emotion is primary. The behavior therapist is most interested in actions.

When considering the behavior, affect, and cognition triad, it would be a mistake to neglect any of the three components because they are all important to understanding a theory. What I am trying to emphasize here is that the relationships of these components can help to define a given theoretical approach.

STEP 2: KNOW YOUR CLIENT

Two sorts of information are critical here. The first is general information that is essential to understanding the person, such as demographics (age, sex, race or ethnicity, sexual orientation, ableness, religion, or other cultural information). You probably want to know things such as family composition, current living situation, and physical health.

The second kind of information you want is theoretically oriented. If you are a Cognitive therapist, you ask about the client's thoughts. If you are a Reality therapist, you look at the individual's current relationships and the relative satisfaction of the other important needs specified by that theory.

Some theoretical approaches seem to deny this kind of information seeking. For instance, the Gestalt therapist doesn't want to know "stuff"; she or he wants to have an experience with the client. I propose that even though therapists may not seem to actively search for information in the form of questioning, they are gathering it nonetheless. The Gestalt therapist is looking for "holes" in the personality, areas where experience is blocked. Person-centered therapists are looking for areas of clients' experience that do not fit with their views of themselves. In my opinion, it is wise to acknowledge and make explicit this search.

STEP 3: PUT IT TOGETHER

Now you have to fit the knowledge you have together, carefully. This step is a process of translating the client's presentation into the terms of the theory. Here is another helpful question:

7. Does the client's presenting problem fit with the views of the theory about psychological functioning? Sometimes the fit seems perfect. The client comes to the interpersonal therapist with stormy relationships. The individual psychology counselor gets the client who is very insecure.

When the pieces don't seem to fit well, you really struggle. Clients don't usually come to counseling speaking in theoretical terms. Client Janey comes to the rational emotive behavior therapist talking about problems with relationships. Oh no. She's supposed to have irrational beliefs! However, if you take a step back, and really know your theory, you will realize that your job is to figure out how these relationship problems are driven by irrational thinking. The psychoanalyst's client wants to be more assertive. The analyst does not immediately morph into a behavior therapist. Instead, she thinks about what lack of assertion means in a psychoanalytic framework (something about discomfort in relationships that probably stems from early trauma).

In rare cases, the conflict between the client's presentation and the theoretical orientation of the therapist is not resolvable. Often, this situation arises because the client is from a different culture (and again, I mean this term in its broadest sense) than that from which the theory sprung. Consider this simple example: A Chinese client comes to a Bowen family systems therapist. The therapist may see the client's problem as stemming from a lack of differentiation from his[1] in family of origin. If the therapist works to get the client to differentiate, problems arise because these efforts may be in conflict with Chinese norms about how individuals relate to parents and other family members. If you run into a case of serious mismatch, I'd suggest, as I did earlier, that you consult with your supervisor as a first step.

HOW THEORY IS PRESENTED IN THIS BOOK

Now that you know the issues involved in being a theoretical scientist practitioner, it is time to proceed to the theories themselves. I will close this chapter by explaining my structure for presenting the major approaches to counseling that I have chosen. (If you want to know why I chose these, see the Preface.)

A Case Study

Each chapter begins with a case study. Most are actual clients, either based on my former clients or modified from case studies offered by students and helpful professionals. Information that could potentially identify the clients has been changed.

I begin with an actual client case because my interest is in teaching how to *apply* theory, not just read it. In my mind, theory is meant to be used on the ground, even if it was developed in an ivory tower. In each chapter I apply the theory immediately after a major section or heading so that you can see how the theory works for the individual client. I have chosen to use different clients in each chapter, partly to keep you from getting bored, but more to emphasize the diversity and complexity that you will face in your profession.

Background

For each theory, I present relevant background information, historical aspects of the theory, and a few places you can go to get current information on the approach (mostly websites). One of the more interesting parts of reading background sections, I think, is to look at the life of the person who developed the theory in relation to the theory. In many cases I provide relevant information about the major proponent of an approach.

Basic Philosophy

I have attempted to capture the view of human nature underlying the approach in this section. I believe that examining how a theorist or theory views human existence is an important basis from which to start your exploration of the theory.

---

[1] Concern about sex bias in language leads me to the following solution about singular pronouns: in the theory chapters, pronouns match the sex of client and counselor; in Chapters 1 and 16 masculine and feminine pronouns are alternated randomly.

HUMAN MOTIVATION

A very basic quality of a theory is found in its assumptions about the primary motives of human behavior. Sometimes these are explicit in the theory; at other times I had to infer them.

CENTRAL CONSTRUCTS

To understand any theoretical approach, you need to understand the central constructs it presents. These constructs are essential to the theory's predictions about health and dysfunction and tie into the developmental progression (if any) proposed in the theory.

THEORY OF THE PERSON AND DEVELOPMENT OF THE INDIVIDUAL

Many theories propose a developmental sequence that is critical to understanding the behavior of the individual. In this section I outline developmental concepts if the theorist proposes them—and some don't.

HEALTH AND DYSFUNCTION

To help your clients, you must understand the theory's ideas about healthy individuals as well as how dysfunction is conceptualized. Because I am a counseling psychologist, I am prone to looking first at an individual's strengths; emphasizing the nature and characteristics of the healthy person from a theoretical perspective is one way of honoring the strengths of a client. No matter how distressed your clients, you will find some aspects of health and strength in them.

You've noticed by now that I choose the term *dysfunction* rather than *mental disorder* or *pathology* or a number of other terms. I do this for two reasons. The first relates to my dislike of seeing folks as "sick" rather than emphasizing strengths. Second, the theories I present disagree wildly about the nature of dysfunction. Some are more on the "disorder" end of the continuum; others simply refuse to use a medical model that conceptualizes human problems as disease. These latter approaches tend to see dysfunction as faulty learning, complaints, or even normal reactions to oppressive environmental conditions.

NATURE OF THERAPY

This section in each chapter has subsections in which I attempt to describe how therapy goes in the approach. I describe assessment, the general atmosphere, and assumptions of the therapy, including the expectations for the length of counseling and the activity level of the counselor. Next, I outline the expectations of the participants in the therapeutic relationship (roles) and then, finally, the goals of the counseling enterprise based in the theoretical approach.

Assessment. In this section I attempt to describe two approaches to assessment, formal and informal. Some theories use both kinds; others, only one. When I say formal, I mean ritualized kinds of procedures, such as giving tests (e.g., the Rorschach) or administering structured techniques (e.g., Adlerian early recollections). Informal assessment means things such as talking with the client or simply observing the client's behavior during the counseling session.

Overview of the Therapeutic Atmosphere. Here I describe the general tenor of the counseling sessions. Issues such as structure of sessions, general approach to the client, and the expected length of therapy are included.

Roles of the Client and Counselor. In many cases, the theory specifies distinct roles for the therapist and client. Some are more "medical" in nature, such as in psychoanalysis, in which the doctor–patient model is evident. Other theories specify egalitarian relationships between client and counselor.

Goals. The map of your theory helps you to determine your destination in terms of its definition of the healthy person.

PROCESS OF THERAPY

In this section I attempt to describe any critical events, processes, or stages associated with an approach. Sometimes this section includes information on the theory's conceptualization of resistance, transference, and countertransference (don't worry if you don't know what these are right now—you'll get to them in the next chapter). Theorists sometimes propose stages of counseling. Generally, what you see in this section will vary somewhat from theory to theory.

THERAPEUTIC TECHNIQUES

After a general introduction, various techniques associated with the theory are presented.

EVALUATION OF THE THEORY

I chose a number of dimensions upon which to evaluate the theories I present. First, I provide a general summary of critiques of the approach that are found in the literature.

Qualities of the Theory. Following this general summary, I proceed to evaluate the approach on two of the qualities of good theory described earlier, operationalization (or testability) and empirical support. I decided not to discuss parsimony because it doesn't seem like a useful criterion. Practicality and stimulation were neglected because I chose approaches that have high values on these dimensions.

Research Support. In this section I review the research that is relevant to the theory. I chose to divide the research into two categories. First, I review the outcome research on the approach. Does it work? What kind of outcome research is available? Next I focus on studies that potentially test the theory's explanatory power. Just because an approach produces client improvement does not mean that its explanations of *how* that happens are verifiable. I believe that one way of furthering our knowledge about psychotherapy is to test the process. Understanding how approaches produce change is as important as knowing that they do.

ISSUES OF INDIVIDUAL AND CULTURAL DIVERSITY

Theories are often, and quite rightly, criticized for bias. This bias can take many forms, and to be ethical counselors, we must examine approaches we use to understand how we could go wrong. Clearly, Caucasian individuals, mostly male heterosexuals, developed most counseling theories. The level of awareness of the theorists about individuals from other backgrounds varies from theory to theory.

THE CASE STUDY

In this section, which is probably the least consistent in terms of what is included, I attempt to assess the fit between theory and client case presented in the broadest sense. If some things were difficult to conceptualize from the theoretical perspective, I describe them. If the process was easy, I say that too. One thing for sure is that doing case conceptualization is not an easy task. There are almost always going to be bits and pieces that you struggle to understand from the theory's viewpoint.

Summary

To close each chapter, I attempt to summarize the important aspects of the theory, the relevant research, and the criticisms of the approach.

ANOTHER RESOURCE ON LEARNING TO USE THEORY

As I have probably made clear by now, learning to use theory is important, but the process of doing so can be difficult and trying. To further assist you in this process, I've developed another resource that should help, the video series that accompanies this book, called *Theories in Action*. On your DVD, you'll find six counseling sessions with the same client, Helen. The therapists are experts in six different theoretical orientations presented in the book: Psychoanalytic, Cognitive, Family Systems Theory, Feminist, Narrative, and Gestalt. After each session, the therapists and I discuss what they did in their sessions that was particularly characteristic of their approaches, and what they would do with Helen in the next counseling session. It is my hope that watching these experts work with Helen will further help you to learn how to apply theory.

CLOSING REMARKS

As I close this chapter, I am remembering my own struggles to find a theoretical home. I think that you will find something to offer in each of the approaches I present, as I did when I was a neophyte counselor. It took quite a while for me to settle where I am, and even longer to believe that I was really using my theoretical approach. As you begin your counseling adventure, I hope you appreciate the value of counseling theory in the helping process. If I have done a really good job, you should be feeling some excitement about what the rest of this book offers.

Visit Chapter 1 on the Companion Website at **www.prenhall.com/murdock** for chapter-specific resources and self-assessments.

CHAPTER 2

Psychoanalysis

Sigmund Freud

Barb is a 47-year-old Caucasian female. She has been divorced twice, the second time 6 years ago. Barb has a high school education and works as a cashier in a grocery store. She speaks rapidly and in great detail. Barb has difficulty sitting for prolonged periods of time, sometimes appearing to be in physical pain during counseling sessions. She has difficulty making eye contact with her counselor.

Barb comes to counseling because she is depressed, experiences mood swings, and has bouts of crying and panic attacks. She has many physical maladies and complaints. These conditions include arthritis in the hands, repeated sinus infections, headaches, numbness in the face, dizziness without known neurological causes, fallen bladder, and injured knees.

Barb is also troubled by her perception that she is too dependent on her current boyfriend and has mixed feelings about the relationship. Barb says that she would like to become a "stronger person." She feels unloved, unwanted, and unneeded. Barb reports that she is "tired of catering to men," but wants to be able to trust men and find someone to "sweep her off her feet."

Barb reports that she has experienced physical and sexual abuse. She remembers being fondled by a male family friend around the age of 5. Barb's mother left the home when Barb was 10; Barb and her younger siblings (two sisters and a brother) remained with their father. From the age of 10 until about age 16, Barb's father sexually abused her.

At age 17, Barb married her high school sweetheart and had two children in the next 3 years. Shortly after they were married, her husband showed her letters to prove that he had been involved with another woman before their marriage, and he continued to be unfaithful to Barb throughout their 10-year marriage. Barb describes him as "perverted" because he would force her to participate in sexual acts that she perceived as "dirty" and was only concerned with his own sexual satisfaction. She characterized her husband as physically and emotionally abusive. During these 10 years, Barb attempted suicide three times. In the first

29

attempt, she overdosed on prescription pain medication. Several months later, she jumped off a two-story building. In another incident, Barb reports that she jumped out of a moving car.

Barb characterizes her second husband as affectionate, protective, and warm, but uncommunicative. She married him 5 years after her divorce from her first husband. Barb reports that she had great difficulty learning to trust this man, and then after 8 years of marriage he left her.

Currently, Barb is dating a 50-year-old man. Although she describes him as safe, his lack of commitment, alternately withdrawing and clinging behavior, and critical comments are making Barb feel insecure. She is also involved with a married man, even though she thinks that this relationship is not in her best interests.

Barb has not seen her mother since she left the family when Barb was 10. She has some contact with her siblings, but describes her relationships with them as distant. Barb maintains that they do not like her. Her father remarried about 8 years ago and moved to another state. Barb does not visit her father, stating that she does not like his new wife.

BACKGROUND

Psychoanalysis was founded by Sigmund Freud (1856–1939). Freud was a prolific writer; the dates of his work span over 45 years (from 1893 to 1938), and during his professional lifetime he revised his theory many times. However controversial this theory is, his influence on the profession of counseling and psychotherapy has been enormous. Consider that before Freud, although some philosophers had debated the idea of the unconscious (Gay, 1988), no one had systematically applied the idea to psychological functioning. Also, Freud and his colleague and mentor, Joseph Breuer, were the first to explore the "talk" therapy approach as a treatment for psychological dysfunction (Breuer & Freud, 1895/1937).

Sigmund Freud was an interesting character and has been the subject of many biographies, including his own in 1925 when he was 69 years old (Freud, 1925/1989). Depending on whom you read, Freud is characterized as a meticulous scientist or an arrogant controller who could not tolerate dissent in his ranks. Perhaps the safest view is to see him as a combination of both. At times he presented himself as the humble scientist, at times the wounded victim of a rejecting scientific community, and at times in a dogmatic, stubborn tone. Freud was also known to be a workaholic (18- to 20-hour workdays were common) who seemed to have neurotic symptoms from time to time. During the late 1890s Freud undertook his self-analysis, the content of which is partially revealed in several of his works, including *The Interpretation of Dreams* (1900/1953).

Much has been made of Freud's complex family constellation. Freud was the first child of his mother, Amalia, who was Jacob Freud's (Freud's father) second or third wife (there is some controversy surrounding even this simple fact). Jacob's two sons from his first marriage were about the same age as Freud's mother (who was 20 years younger than Jacob), and one of these men had a son, Freud's nephew, who was older than Freud. Thus, Freud's early environment gave him interesting puzzles to investigate, and some speculate that his theories are a reflection of this somewhat unusual family constellation (Gay, 1988).

Sigmund Freud lived most of his life in Vienna, Austria. He was an exemplary student who entered the University of Vienna at age 17. After finally deciding on a career in medicine (with dominant interests in the scientific aspects), Freud obtained his medical degree in 1881. Although he wanted to continue his already recognized work in the medical laboratory, he reluctantly took up the clinical practice of medicine as a way to support his eagerly anticipated marriage to Martha Bernays.

Before his marriage in September 1886, Freud journeyed to Paris to study with the famous neurologist Jean-Martin Charcot, investigator of hysteria and champion of hypnosis in medical practice. At the time, Charcot was investigating hysteria, the appearance of physical symptoms that apparently had no physiological bases. Although the malady was thought to be an exclusively female problem (the name comes from "wandering uterus"), Charcot discovered that hysteria also affected males (Gay, 1988). Peter Gay, an eminent biographer of Freud, maintains that "Freud was amazed and impressed to see Charcot inducing and curing hysterical paralyses by means of direct hypnotic suggestion" (1988, p. 49), a novel approach to this puzzling syndrome. Freud was quite excited by Charcot's work and used it as a basis for his subsequent theoretical efforts.

Freud returned from Paris and began to work in the everyday practice environment, while still pursuing his scientific interests. Freud's first published book on hysteria was coauthored with Joseph Breuer in 1895 (*Studies in Hysteria*, Breuer & Freud, 1895/1937). According to Gay (1989) Freud first used the word *psychoanalysis* in 1896 (p. xxxvi). One of Freud's most widely acclaimed books, *The Interpretation of Dreams*, was published in 1899; it is an interesting bit of trivia that this book actually had a copyright date of 1900 (Gay, 1988).

Freud's theories about the sexual origins of the neuroses and sexuality in children were quite controversial. If you wish, you can begin your excursion into psychoanalysis by reading a selection from *An Outline of Psycho-analysis* (1940/1949) written by Freud, in Box 2.1.

Box 2.1

An Excerpt from an Outline of Psycho-Analysis

A dream, then, is a psychosis, with all the absurdities, delusions and illusions of a psychosis. A psychosis of short duration, no doubt, harmless, even entrusted with a useful function, introduced with the subject's consent and terminated by an act of his will. None the less it is a psychosis, and we learn from it that even so deep-going an alteration of mental life as this can be undone and can give place to the normal function. Is it too bold, then, to hope that it must also be possible to submit the dreaded spontaneous illnesses of mental life to our influence and bring about their cure?

We already know a number of things preliminary to such an undertaking. According to our hypothesis it is the ego's task to meet the demands raised by its three dependent relations—to reality, to the id and to the super-ego—and nevertheless at the same time to preserve its own organization and maintain its own autonomy. The necessary precondition of the pathological states under discussion can only be a relative or absolute weakening of the ego which makes the fulfilment of its tasks impossible. The severest demand on the ego is probably the keeping down of the instinctual claims of the id, to accomplish which it is obliged to maintain large expenditures of energy on anticathexes. But the demands made by the super-ego too may become so powerful and so relentless that the ego may be paralysed, as it were, in the face of its other tasks. We may suspect that, in the economic conflicts which arise at this point, the id and the super-ego often make common cause against the hard-pressed ego which tries to cling to reality in order to retain its normal state. If the other two become too strong, they succeed in loosening and altering the ego's organization, so that its proper relation to reality is disturbed or even brought to an end. We have seen it happen in dreaming: when the ego is detached from the reality of the external world, it slips down, under the influence of the internal world, into psychosis.

Our plan of cure is based on these discoveries. The ego is weakened by the internal conflict and we must go to its help. The position is like that in a civil war which has to be decided by the assistance of an ally from outside. The analytic physician and the patient's weakened ego, basing themselves on the real external world, have to band themselves together into a party against the enemies, the instinctual demands of the id and the conscientious demands of the super-ego. We form a pact with each other. The sick ego promises us the most complete candour—promises, that is, to put at our disposal all the material which its self-perception yields it; we assure the patient of the strictest discretion and place at his service our experience in interpreting material that has been influenced by the unconscious. Our knowledge is to make up for his ignorance and to give his ego back its mastery over lost provinces of his mental life. This pact constitutes the analytic situation.

No sooner have we taken this step than a first disappointment awaits us, a first warning against over-confidence. If the patient's ego is to be a useful ally in our common work, it must, however hard it may be pressed by the hostile powers, have retained a certain amount of coherence and some fragment of understanding for the demands of reality. But this is not to be expected of the ego of a psychotic; it cannot observe a pact of this kind, indeed it can scarcely enter into one. It will very soon have tossed us away and the help we offer it and sent us to join the portions of the external world which no longer mean anything to it. Thus we discover that we must renounce the idea of trying our plan of cure upon psychotics—renounce it perhaps for ever or perhaps only for the time being, till we have found some other plan better adapted for them.

There is, however, another class of psychical patients who clearly resemble the psychotics very closely—the vast number of people suffering severely from neuroses. The determinants of their illness as well as its pathogenic mechanisms must be the same or at least very similar. But their ego has proved more resistant and has become less disorganized. Many of them, in spite of their maladies and the inadequacies resulting from them, have been able to maintain themselves in real life. These neurotics may show themselves ready to accept our help. We will confine our interest to *them* and see how far and by what methods we are able to 'cure' them.

With the neurotics, then, we make our pact: complete candour on one side and strict discretion on the other. This looks as though we were only aiming at the post of a secular father confessor. But there is a great difference, for what we want to hear from our patient is not only what he knows and conceals from other people; he is to tell us too what he does *not* know. With this end in view we give him a more detailed definition of what we mean by candour. We pledge him to obey the *fundamental rule* of analysis, which is henceforward to govern his behaviour towards us. He is to tell us not only what he can say intentionally and willingly, what will give him relief like a confession, but everything else as well that his self-observation yields him, everything that comes into his head, even if it is *disagreeable* for him to say it, even if it seems to him *unimportant* or actually *nonsensical.* If he can succeed after this injunction in putting his self-criticism out of action, he will present us with a mass of material—thoughts, ideas, recollections—which are already subject to the influence of the unconscious, which are often its direct derivatives, and which thus put us in a position to conjecture his repressed unconscious material and to extend, by the information we give him, his ego's knowledge of his unconscious.

Despite the rejection of, or indifference to, his work, Freud persevered and gradually gathered a group of adherents. He established the Wednesday Psychological Society in 1902 for the purpose of discussing psychoanalytic ideas (Gay, 1988). Over the years, the membership of this group included Carl Jung and Alfred Adler, among others. Interesting stories are to be found in the "politics of psychoanalysis" (Freud's own term) that space prohibits telling here (see any of the Freud biographies for these).

Freud remained in Vienna until the Nazis invaded in 1938, then immigrated to London. He was close to death due to cancer of the jaw (probably a result of his favorite vice, cigars). Choosing his own end on September 23, 1939, Freud obtained from his physician a lethal dose of morphine (Gay, 1989). He was survived by his daughter, Anna Freud, whose story is also an interesting one (Monte, 1999). Anna was Freud's youngest child and was very close to her father. In her 20s, Anna received training analysis from her father. Without the benefits of any formal training in medicine or psychology, she became an analyst and Freud's intellectual heir. Anna was a staunch advocate of her father's ideas, yet made significant contributions of her own in her psychoanalytic approach to working with children (You will read more about Anna's ideas in Chapter 3). It is indeed significant that Freud was willing to analyze Anna, a serious deviation from the standards of abstinent conduct that he developed for analysts. Some authors suggest that this violation of analytic rules was a reflection of the importance he placed on "having a trustworthy and competent intellectual heir after so many previous failures and betrayals" (Monte, 1999, p. 181).

Freud's ideas laid the foundation for the profession of psychology and the practice of psychotherapy as we know it today. Most of the prominent theories of counseling and psychotherapy either incorporate Freud's ideas or were formulated in reaction to them. Despite some arguments that psychoanalysis is a dated and discarded theory of human behavior, both ideologically "pure" as well as variations of psychoanalysis thrive currently. You can watch a classic psychoanalytic session with the client Helen on the *Theories in Action* DVD, conducted by Dr. David Donovan.

The American Psychoanalytic Association has a webpage at http://apsa.org, and the International Psychoanalytical Association can be found at www.ipa.org.uk. Both of these sites offer links to other current information about psychoanalysis. The Psychoanalysis division of the American Psychological Association (Division 39) is one of the larger divisions of the APA and sponsors a journal, the *Journal of Psychoanalysis.*

BASIC PHILOSOPHY

Freud was a pessimist, and thus psychoanalysis presents a rather gloomy view of human nature. Arguing against those who characterized human nature as inherently positive, Freud maintained that "unfortunately what history tells us and what we ourselves have experienced does not speak in this sense but rather justifies a judgement that belief in the 'goodness' of human nature is one of those evil illusions by which mankind expect their lives to be beautified and made easier while in reality they only cause damage" (Freud, 1933/1964, p. 104).

For Freud, human behavior is produced by conflicts between genetically built-in drives, the instincts of self-preservation, sex, and destruction. Although Freud acknowledged the influence of environmental events and genetic predispositions, in his view the most dominant force in human behavior is the sexual instinct, which he thought was innate.

In psychoanalytic theory, a great deal about a person is determined before the age of 6. Children are viewed as enacting a genetically determined developmental sequence, which under normal circumstances progresses until about the sixth year, whereupon the psychological developmental process goes dormant. At puberty, development resumes.

Freud's views of children were much more complex than the views current when he was writing. He believed that kids are sexual beings and have murderous fantasies in the search for gratification of primal wishes (i.e., satisfaction of the sexual instinct; Freud, 1940/1964). According to Freud, all psychopathology has its roots in early development and arises out of conflicts among various psychic entities.

Our psychoanalytic therapist, Glenda, begins her work with Barb with the assumption that her current behavior is jointly the result of her genetic inheritance and the experiences of her childhood. First, she is female, which for Freud is an essential determinant of personality structure. Second, she recalls some sexual experience before age 6 and sexual abuse as a teenager. The trauma of both sequences of sexual abuse would be enough to cause problems on its own, but the nature of her symptoms depends heavily on Barb's early development.

Freud thought that as humans we are not very good at knowing the reasons for our actions. We blissfully endorse the comforting myth that our conscious thought directs our behavior. He said, "The truth is that you have an illusion of a psychic freedom within you which you do not want to give up" (Freud, 1920/1952, p. 52). Freud maintained that forces of which we are unaware (the unconscious) are the most powerful sources of behavior. Evidence for the existence of the unconscious is, according to Freud, found in such everyday occurrences as forgetting, mistakes, "slips of the tongue," and dreams. In these events, which we typically dismiss as meaningless, Freud saw the relaxation of the censor that typically keeps unconscious material from surfacing. A good example of such a slip is when a man about to be married is queried by his future in-laws about his religious affiliation. He replies "prostitute" instead of "Protestant." Freud would see this mistake as evidence of the unconscious sexual urges that are close to the surface because of the excitement and stress of impending marriage (and accompanying sexual gratification, of course).

Glenda expects Barb to have little awareness of the real sources of her symptoms. Barb will likely attribute her crying, anxiety attacks, and so on, to environmental factors, but the analyst's position is that these are likely the result of the inhibitions in development resulting from the early sexual experience and later sexual abuse.

Glenda sees evidence of Barb's unconscious functioning in several ways. For instance, Barb might "accidentally" use her father's name in place of the family friend who sexually abused her. Such a substitution would be very significant indeed to Glenda. Barb also relates dreams in her analysis, and Glenda looks in these accounts to understand the workings of Barb's unconscious. In one dream, Barb describes a scenario in which she is captured and tormented by a sea monster. She is rescued by an old man in white robes who is riding a mule, but feels confused and tearful when this happens. Glenda realizes that in this dream Barb is reliving her experiences of sexual abuse. The monster is the abuser, and water is thought to be related to sexual feelings and actions (think about waves). Glenda understands Barb's confusion and tears in response to her rescue as representing conflicting feelings of relief, the loss of possible sexual gratification (which is unconscious), and the resurgence of anxiety and fear connected to her abuser, who was an older man. An interesting facet of the dream is that the scary man is riding a mule (an infertile animal).

HUMAN MOTIVATION

Freud was convinced that human behavior is driven by intrapsychic conflict (Freud, 1940/1964). Specifically, the instinctual urges in the unconscious are considered unacceptable by the conscious mind and society, so the psychic apparatus exerts energy to keep these urges at bay. Behavior is thus a compromise between the warring mental forces.

Glenda knows that Barb's current behavior is a compromise between unacceptable urges and reality. Her mixed feelings about her relationship with her current boyfriend are probably the result of (a) pleasure due to satisfaction of sexual urges and (b) guilt about expressing sexuality. She is also involved in a socially less-acceptable sexual relationship (with a married man), which would also result from conflicting sexual and moralistic impulses.

CENTRAL CONSTRUCTS

INSTINCT THEORY

Freud hypothesized that humans have instinctual urges that are innate, resulting from their evolutionary heritage. These instincts must be expressed or the individual will become dysfunctional (Freud actually used the word *ill;* 1940/1964, p. 150). In his early writings he identified the most basic instinct as Eros, or life. Later on he described the destructive instinct (more commonly called Thanatos, or the death instinct; Freud, 1949/1969). Aside from direct expression through satisfaction of the need, instincts can also be expressed in four other ways (Rickman, 1957, p. 77): (a) turning into the opposite, (b) turning back on the person, (c) repression (or banishment to the unconscious), and (d) sublimation (expression in socially approved activity).

The life instincts are thought to be composed of those directed toward self-preservation (for example, hunger and reproduction continue the individual and the species). Although it is tempting to see the life and death instincts as opposing one another, Freud indicated that they sometimes can fuse. For example, Eros prompts the person to eat, which allows the destructive instinct to be expressed as destroying the food (Freud, 1940/1964). When a child is learning to control her[1] bowel and bladder functioning, the death and love instincts can fuse into sadism because the child becomes angry at the loved caretaker who forces the child to control elimination.

In Barb's case, Glenda sees the destructive or death instinct as responsible for her suicide attempts. Her depression, crying, and destructive attempts can be seen as the result of a need for punishment for her unacceptable sexual urges. Problems around Eros seem to give rise to her disruptive relationships with men; she simultaneously seeks forbidden sexual gratification and reacts angrily to the rejection she has experienced from men.

Freud had much more to say about Eros than he did about Thanatos because the latter was a late addition to the theory (Freud, 1923/1961). The instincts are unconscious and possess a store of energy, which in the case of Eros is called libido. The term *libido* has become synonymous with sexual drive even though Freud protested that it was a much more general drive. Libido is considered a very basic drive, because it is responsible for the perpetuation of the human species.

Instinctual energy always seeks objects in which to invest (normally, people); such attachment discharges the energy of the instinct and creates pleasure. At birth, libido is directed only to the self, a state known as primary narcissism. Next, and rather quickly, the mothering one becomes the primary object of the libido. As the child develops, she continues to invest life energy in other people or objects until, as an adult, she finds mature love in the investment of libido in a person of the opposite sex. Further journeys of the libido will be described under the discussion of sexual development.

It is important to note that problems in development lead to fixation of the libido at that stage of development. Fixation is rarely total in the neuroses, so the individual continues on a modified developmental path. However, later trauma can lead to regression to the point of fixation, the primary means whereby old, unresolved conflicts become symptoms.

Glenda hypothesizes that Barb's libido is fixed somewhere in her early development, probably around the age of 5 or 6. She is arrested in her development, which explains why she has difficulty with intimate relationships in her adult years. Glenda thinks that Barb, to some extent, reproduces in her current relationships aspects of those she experienced early in life. These immature ways of relating to others tend to get her in trouble.

TOPOGRAPHIC MODEL: THE ICEBERG APPROACH

In his early work Freud differentiated among three types of mental content. Beginning with the most obvious, he recognized the conscious awareness of the individual. To the consternation of

---

[1] Pronouns in the theory chapters of this book will match the sex of the client and counselor. Male and female pronouns in Chapters 1 and 16 are alternated randomly.

many, however, he denied it as the source of most behavior. Instead, he saw most behavior as stemming from the unconscious, so that what we typically think of as driving our behavior (our conscious thought) is only the tip of the iceberg. The real motivations lie beneath the surface of the stormy ocean, the instincts in the unconscious. Some mental content moves easily from conscious to unconscious, and this material Freud termed the preconscious. Even though he later revised his model (see the structural model that follows), Freud continued to use the terminology of the levels of consciousness to describe mental events.

STRUCTURAL MODEL: THE BIG THREE

Later Freud asserted that there were three basic divisions or entities in the mind, which he termed the It, I, and over-me (Freud, 1933/1964). The more familiar Latin terms of **id, ego,** and **superego** were evidently substituted in translation to English and have since become the terms of choice (Karon & Widener, 1996).

If you want to see an id, look at a newborn baby. The id is the most primitive of psychic entities, the residence of the instinctual urges. It seeks immediate gratification of its instinctual needs. Consider what happens when a baby gets hungry—the message is, Feed me right now!

Freud emphasized that the id has no real contact with reality, writing, "No such purpose as that of keeping itself alive or of protecting itself from dangers by means of anxiety can be attributed to the id" (Freud, 1940/1964, p. 148). Totally unconscious, the id operates on the **pleasure principle;** it seeks pleasure and avoids pain. Another term for this type of mental processing is **primary process** because it is the most basic, primitive form of psychic activity. The id's version of pleasure is the satisfaction of instinctual impulses through the discharge of energy associated with them. In this process of discharge, the instinctual energy is attached to objects, including people.

The psychic entity with which we are most familiar is the ego. The ego develops out of the id in response to pressure from the child's environment to restrain instinctual drives. Operating according to **secondary process,** or the **reality principle,** the ego strives for satisfaction of the id impulses while at the same time preserving the person. Because of the nature of the instinctual impulses, outright gratification of them could result in damage to the organism, or even death, and the ego's job is to prevent these outcomes.

The superego is the last psychic entity to develop; it is the internalized version of parental or other authority figures. We know the superego as our conscience, and it is also the vehicle for the ego-ideal, or our vision of the perfect ego. Freud maintained that the superego "observes the ego, gives it orders, judges it and threatens it with punishments, exactly like the parents whose place it has taken" (1940/1964, p. 205).

Figure 2.1 was proposed by Nye (1986) as an illustration of the relationships between the structural and functional models of psychoanalytic theory. The drawing emphasizes that all three psychic entities have unconscious elements, with the id entirely and safely in the unconscious. Note that portions of the ego are unconscious, primarily the defenses and processes most intimately related to dealing with the id.

Barb's ego seems to be struggling with unconscious forces that result in her current dysfunctional behavior. Her basic id impulses are at war with the demanding and rigid superego. She

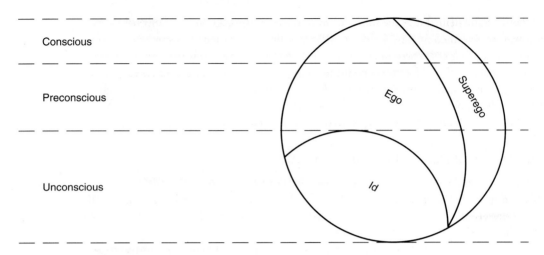

Conscious

Preconscious

Unconscious

FIGURE 2.1. An Integration of the Structural and Topographical Models of the Personality.
From *Three psychologies: Perspectives from Freud, Skinner, and Rogers* 5th edition by Nye. © 1996. Reprinted with permission
of Wadsworth, a division of Thomson Learning: www.thomsonrights.com. Fax 800-730-2215.

> *has sexual urges that seek fulfillment, yet the internal voice of her superego tells her that sex
> and intimacy are forbidden and dangerous. The superego exerts its control in the form of Barb's
> depression and crying. Glenda guesses that this punishment has resulted in a poor self-concept
> and an exceedingly strict ego-ideal. The impulses of Barb's id are fighting for gratification but
> are so unacceptable that they are not directly expressed in behavior. Her ego, although taxed,
> is still intact, and therefore Barb is able to participate in the counseling relationship.*

REPRESSION

One of the most important processes in psychoanalytic theory is **repression**, the act of
containing or pushing unacceptable psychic material to the unconscious. The process of
repression is unconscious and is always involved in symptom formation, although not all
repression results in symptoms. Repression uses psychic energy and can result in the person
being developmentally "stuck" at the psychological stage of a traumatic event, a mechanism
called **fixation.** Although some would characterize repression as one of the most important
defense mechanisms (discussed later), Freud also wrote of it as a more general psychic process.

> *From a psychoanalytic perspective, it is interesting that Barb retains the memories of her
> childhood sexual abuse. The symptoms that she is experiencing likely result from the
> repressed emotion related to the abuse. Early sexual experience, in Glenda's view, would
> overgratify the sexual instinct; this overgratification would explain Barb's pronounced
> desires to fulfill sexual needs with a safe male. These desires are seen in her many attempts
> to establish relationships, but their dysfunctional nature is evident in that she does not pick
> safe men. Barb seems doomed to repeat her early experiences, a sign of fixation.*
>
> *Barb's psychic processes are repressed, and the memories that trigger them are accessible
> only through lengthy analysis. Glenda proceeds carefully in conceptualizing these memories,*

*because one psychoanalytic understanding would be that these memories are wish fulfill-
ments; they represent childhood fantasies of gratification of the sexual drive. That is, the
abuse may have happened only in Barb's fantasies. A second type of interpretation would
be that the abuse was real. Either explanation would lead Glenda to expect fairly significant dysfunction in Barb's relations with men.*

Symptoms as Symbols

For Freud, symptoms were symbols of psychic conflict. In his earlier writings he always
described them as expressions of unacceptable sexual impulses: "Every time we should be
led by analysis to the sexual experiences and desires of the patient, and every time we
should have to affirm that the symptom served the same purpose. This purpose shows
itself to be the gratification of the sexual wishes; the symptoms serve the purpose of sexual
gratification for the patient; they are a substitute for satisfactions which he does not obtain
in reality" (1920/1952, p. 308). The most obvious examples of such symbolization are
things such as uncontrollable vomiting, which was thought to symbolize morning sickness
accompanying a wish for impregnation (Nye, 1986). In one of his most controversial cases,
that of Emma E., Freud interpreted repeated bleeding from the nose as a wish to be taken
care of (Masson, 1984). Freud also said that symptoms could serve as a defense against
unacceptable wishes. In either case they are attempts to keep the unacceptable thoughts or
desires from surfacing in the conscious. Glove anesthesia, in which only a portion of the
arm becomes paralyzed, was thought to be a defense against masturbation. In addition,
Freud's later theorizing included the destructive drives as the source of symptoms; for
instance, a suicide attempt would represent the activity of the death instinct.

*Barb's symptoms are, in Glenda's view, symbolic of her conflicts around sexual impulses and
fixation at an early developmental stage. Her depression is the result of her superego punishing her for her unacceptable sexual wishes. Her panic attacks probably result when these
wishes come close to the conscious and would be dangerous or socially unacceptable to express. Barb's physiological symptoms, particularly the neurological ones, are probably representative of mental drives that are not being expressed. Quite likely, they symbolize
unconscious sexual desires. Her face may be numb because she wishes for forbidden kisses.
Barb's fainting spells may be reflective of a wish to "swoon" over the man who will "sweep
her off her feet," most likely her father.*

Defense Mechanisms

In addition to repression, the ego also has other ways to prevent unacceptable wishes from
emerging into awareness. These tactics are called defense mechanisms (Hall, 1954). As
noted earlier, repression is often listed as one of the defenses. Defense mechanisms are triggered when anxiety signals that unconscious material is threatening to break into the conscious mind. The defense mechanism distorts reality so that the actual wish does not enter
consciousness and interfere with the ego's functioning or the safety of the individual.

The operation of defenses is recognized through their extreme manifestations; the individual's perceptions or reactions seem extraordinarily strong. Freud cautioned that defense
mechanisms, even the relatively healthy ones, are only able to discharge a fraction of the

energy attached to the instinctual impulses. For example, transforming aggression into the socially approved racquetball game would not fully satisfy the instinctual drive.

Depending on which source one consults, the list of defenses varies, and Freud himself apparently never enumerated them in one place. *Repression*, described earlier, is the cornerstone of the psychic defenses. A brief description of others follows.

Identification is operating when the qualities of another person are taken into the individual's personality (Hall, 1954). For males, this process is the key to resolving the Oedipal complex (discussed later), but it is also seen in other situations in which individuals are threatened by another person. For this reason, this defense is sometimes termed "identification with the aggressor," although identification through positive emotions is also possible.

Displacement occurs when an unwelcome impulse is deflected onto another person, presumably someone who is less dangerous than the original target. The classic example of displacement is the man who gets angry with his boss, but instead of aggressing against the boss, he comes home and yells at his wife, his kids, the dog, and the goldfish.

Projection is the externalization of an unacceptable wish. People who are paranoid, for example, externalize their instinctual rage by perceiving others as out to get them. This strategy reduces the anxiety associated with the aggressive drives by placing the aggression in the external world. In some cases, the projection of one's aggression allows the angry individual to act on these urges and thereby achieve some degree of instinctual gratification.

Reaction formation is when an unacceptable urge is transformed into its opposite. Rage is transformed to love, and sexual desire to hate. For example, a man's rage against his younger sister that stemmed from sibling rivalry could be transformed into an overly solicitous love.

Sublimation, thought to be one of the healthiest of the defense mechanisms, is the funneling of the unacceptable impulse into a socially acceptable activity. For instance, Freud thought artists sublimated their libidos into creative products. Football players are likely sublimating aggressive drives. According to Maddi (1996), the expression of love toward a socially approved other is a form of sublimation because it represents the disguised expression of incestuous wishes (p. 39).

Regression is seen when a threatened individual retreats to an earlier stage of development, typically to one in which she is fixated. When the demands of a current situation are overwhelming and the person's current defenses and ego operations are unable to handle the stress, she reverts to earlier ways of dealing with life. A school-aged child chastised for lying to a parent may resort to thumb-sucking or curling up in a fetal position to deal with the attack on the ego.

Barb is likely employing several defense mechanisms that revolve around the issues of sexuality in her life. She has repressed her sexual desire for her father and her subsequent feelings of anger and hatred toward men who reject her advances. She may be using reaction formation to deal with some of these feelings that do threaten to emerge into awareness, because she continues to value and seek intimate relationships. However, she is doomed by her fixation, which causes her to repeat the patterns of the past—seeking men who will ultimately abuse and then reject her. When involved in interpersonal conflict with men, Barb probably regresses to earlier coping mechanisms of being passive and distant. Her belief that her siblings don't like her is probably a projection of her own hostile feelings for them as usurpers of parental attention.

THEORY OF THE PERSON AND DEVELOPMENT
OF THE INDIVIDUAL

Freud formulated a complex theory of early human development that focused primarily on sexual development. Shocking his Victorian professional community, Freud proposed that humans are inherently sexual creatures and that even infants and young children have sexual urges. He further proposed that humans are inherently bisexual, with gender identification resulting from an inherent tendency toward maleness or femaleness, along with the way in which a key developmental crisis is resolved (see the later discussion of the Oedipal complex).

According to psychoanalysis, humans progress through a series of stages of sexual development beginning at birth and ending with mature sexual identity in puberty. The psychosexual stages are identified by the satisfaction of sexual drive via different zones of the body, termed erotogenic zones (Freud, 1933/1964). Too much or too little satisfaction can lead to too much investment of the libido at a given stage (fixation), resulting in the individual having difficulty negotiating subsequent stages. Fixations vary in intensity. We all have minor ones, but when a large amount of energy is attached at one of the developmental stages, problems can result later in life.

The first erotogenic zone is the mouth, and therefore, the first stage of sexual development is termed the **oral** stage. The infant (or little id) first obtains nourishment from sucking at the mother's breast (thereby satisfying the self-preservation instinct). This satisfaction quickly becomes independent from nourishment, which for Freud was evidence that sucking was satisfying sexual needs as well. Think of all the kids you have seen sucking on pacifiers, their thumbs, and other assorted objects. The oral stage lasts roughly from birth through the first year.

Minor fixations at the oral stage are seen in such oral activities as nail biting, smoking, and overeating. More intense fixation can result in the oral character types (Maddi, 1996). Maddi described these characters as focused on the activities of taking (oral aggressive) and receiving (oral incorporative).

The second stage of development is the **anal** stage, in which satisfaction is gained through the functions of elimination. Freud characterized this stage as sadistic, suggesting that the libidinal and destructive urges fused at this stage to create sadism. Initially, the infant values her excretions, particularly the feces, producing them as "presents" for those whom she especially values (Freud, 1920/1952). As an example of this early attitude, a certain niece of mine placed hers in a jar in the refrigerator for her parents to find.

Later in this stage, the infant comes into conflict with the environment for the first time in her young life when the lessons begin about when and where she can gain gratification of pleasurable urges. Toilet training, in which the child is forced to produce urine and feces only at certain times, can have a great impact on later personality characteristics, according to psychoanalysis. Harsh toilet training can result in individuals who are stingy, orderly, and precise (anal retentive characters), whereas excessive praise leads to people who are overgenerous, messy, and vague (anal expulsive characters; Maddi, 1996).

The most important stage of human psychosexual development for psychoanalytic theory occurs between ages 4 and 6 and is known as the **phallic** stage. The focus of sexual gratification becomes the genitals, and little boys and girls begin to notice differences in their bodies. Children are sexually curious prior to this age, particularly about the origin of babies, which they have concluded come from the anus. However, as their knowledge increases, they begin to suspect that something else is going on, and both sexes, according to Freud, turn their attentions to the penis. Up to this point, kids have assumed that both sexes possess a penis. However, with the awakening of satisfaction in the genital areas, it becomes evident that boys have one and girls don't. This realization is often the result of accidental viewing of a girl's or woman's genitals, but can also be set off by the trauma of observing adult or parental sexual intercourse. In any case, the discovery that male and female genitals differ is critical; at this point the course of development for boys and girls takes sharply different courses.

As a boy begins to masturbate, he has fantasies about doing something of the sort with his primary love object (an attachment established in the oral phase, you recall), his mother. At this point, he has entered the **Oedipal** stage, named for the mythical Greek character who unknowingly killed his father and married his mother. However, the little boy becomes aware that girls do not have penises and worries that this might happen to him. Also, the little boy remembers earlier warnings of adults when they caught him masturbating—they threatened to cut off the offending member. **Castration anxiety,** a powerful force in male development, ensues. The little boy fears that his father, the rival for his mother's attention, might find out about his incestuous desires for his mother and exact the ultimate revenge, castration. After all, there are a lot of people in the world who don't have penises. The terrified boy therefore represses the desires for his mother, and Freud maintained that in most cases, the complex is "destroyed" (Freud, 1933/1964, p. 92). As a result of this process, the superego makes its first appearance, developed out of the identification with the parents, particularly the father (identification with the aggressor). Identification compensates for the necessary loss of attachment to the mother while defending against the threatening father.

The development of women was much more puzzling to Freud; he devoted a lecture to this topic, although acknowledging therein that "psychology too is unable to solve the riddle of femininity" (1933/1964, p. 116). Like little boys, girls' initial attachment is to the mother, yet to become fully female, they turn from her to attach to the father, but then must seemingly renounce this second important attachment. Freud maintained that early development in girls was masculine in nature, culminating in discovering the clitoris as a source of pleasure analogous to the penis. However, the little girl soon afterward discovers that she does not truly have a penis, the realization that starts the castration complex for women. The primary form of the castration complex among girls is **penis envy**, which Freud thought often was never resolved. In fact, Freud thought that unresolved penis envy was responsible for homosexuality in women as well as the pursuit of "masculine" professions (Freud, 1933/1964). Both courses of development are considered abnormal and represent a continued quest for a penis.

The resolution of the female castration complex resulting in normal femininity begins when the girl renounces clitoral masturbation and seeks to sexually attach to her father as a way to gain the wished-for penis. She becomes hostile to her mother, blaming the mother for her (the girl's) lack of a penis. However, this wish for the penis of her father is frustrated, and so is the next transformation of the wish, that for a "penis-baby" from her father. Unfortunately, the press to resolve the Oedipal complex among girls, castration anxiety, is not present, so girls are much slower to resolve the complex, if at all. They are thereby limited in their superego development and are prone throughout life to envy and jealousy. They feel inferior because their clitoris can't compare to a real penis. Women continue to search for a penis of their own and really only find one in bearing a male baby. Freud said, "A mother is only brought unlimited satisfaction by her relation to a son; this is altogether the most perfect, the most free from ambivalence of all human relationships" (1933/1964, p. 133). The girl's relationship with her mother remains ambivalent or hostile unless she reidentifies with the mother on the birth of her own children.

After the Oedipal stage, the individual enters **latency**, which is a usually a period of sexual quiescence. The sexual urges are usually repressed; however, Freud cautioned that occasionally some manifestations of sexuality may break through or that some individuals may remain sexually active throughout the latency period. In essence, repression is not always total during latency, and behavior during this period is variable (Freud, 1924/1989).

Mature sexuality, according to Freud, develops during the **genital** stage, which we enter during adolescence. During this phase, the sexual instinct becomes integrated with the reproductive function. The process toward mature sexuality can become derailed during the genital phase if excessive pleasure has been derived from one of the other erotogenic zones during early development. The individual then becomes too invested in foreplay to the detriment of intercourse, thereby leaving unfulfilled the reproductive function of sex (Freud, 1924/1989).

Glenda is certain that Barb has unresolved Oedipal issues. First, the question of the early sexual abuse is important; it is uncertain whether she was actually abused, or whether these memories are wish fulfillments of an Oedipal nature. In Freud's view, the course of development would be very similar in either case. If the abuse was actual, the symbolic gratification of the Oedipal complex would strongly fixate Barb in the Oedipal period. This would cause her to search continually for her father as a love object and results in her duplication of faithless father in her choice of a faithless first husband and a view of men as untrustworthy. The symbolic attainment of her father would also likely intensify her hatred for her mother, resulting perhaps in stormy relationships with other women.

If the abuse was an Oedipal wish fulfillment, the abuser is transformed into "a family friend" because the actual representation of her father in this context is unacceptable. That Barb recalls this memory indicates that her repressive processes were not at full strength, a sign that her psychic system was overtaxed. In either case, she emerges from this stage with an unresolved Oedipal complex.

Barb demonstrates her ambivalent, Oedipal relations with men in the relationship with her current boyfriend. She is worried about being too dependent on him, yet wants a man to sweep her off her feet. Glenda sees these conflictual urges as evidence of Barb's unresolved conflict and the incomplete identification with the female role.

HEALTH AND DYSFUNCTION

Healthy people are able to love and work. They have a minimal level of repression because they have mostly resolved their Oedipal complexes in ways resulting in less fixation at that stage and therefore less leftover unconscious material. Thus, the goal of psychoanalysis is to bring unconscious material into the conscious; that is, to reduce repression. Individuals who successfully complete psychoanalysis are those who are able to work through unconscious conflicts by allowing them to surface into the conscious and to recognize them as the sources of current behavior and symptoms. It is probably important to note that one can never get rid of the id or superego, so the story of life is the ego's attempts to manage these pressures along with the demands of the external environment (reality). In fact, one interpretation of the Freudian psychoanalytic theory is that a healthy person is the one who uses the healthiest defenses (Maddi, 1996).

Dysfunctional people are individuals who have unresolved unconscious conflicts, particularly those of an Oedipal nature. Freud maintained that all dysfunction originates by age 6 and is due to unsuccessful resolution of the stages of psychosexual development. "Among the occurrences which recur again and again in the youthful history of neurotics which are scarcely ever absent . . . observation of parental intercourse, seduction by an adult, and threat of castration" (Freud, 1917/1963, pp. 368–369). In adults, dysfunctional behavior is the result of fixation due to unresolved conflicts plus some kind of activating, traumatic experience. The adult trauma reactivates the childhood fixation, resulting in symptoms (Freud, 1920/1952).

Before discussing the psychoanalytic understanding of various psychological dysfunctions, it is critical to note that most of Freud's work was with a very narrow sample of clients. Most of his clients were neurotics, and in the parlance of the day, either suffering from hysteria or obsessive-compulsive neurosis. Today these dysfunctions would be called conversion disorders and obsessive compulsive disorder or personality. Freud's discussions of other types of dysfunction were far less detailed.

Anxiety forms the basis of dysfunction, and Freud identified three kinds: neurotic, moral, and realistic (Freud, 1933/1964). Realistic anxiety is the appropriate affective reaction to real danger to the organism. Birth anxiety is the original realistic anxiety.

Neurotic anxiety is the fear of libido. It is based in realistic anxiety because if the libidinal drives are expressed, danger to the organism could result. Moral anxiety is the fear of the punitive superego. The nature of the response is identical in all three types of anxiety, but moral and neurotic anxiety are responses to an internal rather than environmental threat.

By far the most important in Freud's work was neurotic anxiety, which results when an emerging instinctual urge is close to consciousness. The ego, perceiving the state of danger that would arise if the demand were satisfied, allows the anxiety to surface as an aversive experience. In most cases, repression then does away with the unpleasant state, and the unsatisfied urge is relegated back to the unconscious. If the energy of the psychic apparatus is overtaxed, the drive can be converted into a symptom that is symbolic of the conflict that generated the anxiety.

The most common client for Freud, and perhaps the most interesting, presented with what was then termed hysterical neurosis, which was originally thought to occur only in females (the result of dysfunction of the uterus). Charcot and Freud were the earliest advocates of the psychic determinants of hysteria and its existence in individuals of both sexes. Charcot thought that any kind of trauma created hysteria, whereas as early as the 1890s, Freud was beginning to assert the sexual origins of hysteria. His insistence on this principle disrupted his relationship with mentor Joseph Breuer, with whom he had coauthored his first book (*Studies in Hysteria;* Breuer & Freud, 1895/1937).

Early on in his explorations of neurosis, Freud noticed that his clients almost always related memories of early sexual experience, mostly perpetrated by male relatives. He initially assumed that the stories that his clients were telling were true and located in these traumas the origins of neurotic symptoms. This assumption is called the seduction hypothesis. However, later Freud abandoned this notion, seeing these "scenes" as the fantastic creations of his analysands based on Oedipal longings. The renunciation of the seduction hypothesis is first seen in an 1897 letter to his confidant, Fliess, and his first public acknowledgement was in 1905 (in *Three Essays on Sexuality*, Masson, 1984). The decision to treat these client recollections as fantasy is considered critical among the adherents of psychoanalysis because it opened the way to the understanding and exploration of the Oedipal complex. Box 2.2 presents an interesting but controversial examination of why Freud abandoned the seduction hypothesis.

Box 2.2

A Failure of Courage? Another View of Freud's Abandonment of the Seduction Hypothesis

Freud's early work with hysterical clients initially led him to believe that these afflictions were caused by sexual trauma (mainly sexual abuse by a male relative) early in life. This position came to be known, somewhat misleadingly, as the seduction hypothesis or theory. In 1905 Freud changed his mind about the reality of his clients' memories of childhood seduction, declaring that he "overrated the importance of seduction in comparison with the factors of sexual constitution and development" (Masson, 1984, p. 129). He also wrote, "At that time, my material was still scanty, and it happened by chance to include a disproportionately large number of cases in which sexual seduction by an adult or by older children played the chief part in the history of the patient's childhood. I thus overestimated the frequency of such events (though in other respects they were not open to doubt)" (cited in Masson, 1984, p. 129). Freud gave several reasons for his altered opinion, including (a) the fact that he was not able to cure his clients based on this hypothesis, (b) the fact that the incidence of hysteria would indicate an unbelievably high rate of sexual offenses by fathers, (c) his conviction that the unconscious has no sense of reality, and (d) the fact that in most severe psychoses, unconscious content does not surface (Masson, 1984). Most analytic writers agree that if Freud had not changed his opinions, he would not have gone on to discover other significant aspects of psychological functioning, such as the Oedipal complex and the role of fantasy in human psychology.

Paul Masson, however, painted another picture of the situation. Masson (1984) maintained that Freud relinquished the seduction theory for reasons other than those stated in his writings. First, Freud was ostracized by the medical community for his assertions that neuroses resulted from childhood sexual experiences. At the time, the Victorian attitudes toward sex precluded discussion of the topic, and some number of medical authorities dismissed the accounts of sexual abuse among both children and adults as "hysterical lies."

Even more interesting is Masson's argument that Freud changed his opinion partly to cover up for a surgical mistake made by his good friend, Wilhelm Fliess. One of Freud's early analytic clients, Emma Eckstein, had come to Freud with stomach complaints and menstrual difficulties. Both Freud and his colleague Fliess considered menstrual problems to be the result of masturbation. Fliess, however, believed that sexual problems (such as masturbation) originated in the nose, and thus could only be cured by a surgical intervention, removal of the turbinate bone. In early 1885 Freud and Fliess apparently decided that this operation was the solution to Emma's problems.

After the surgery, great complications arose, including hemorrhaging that threatened Emma's life. Various remedies were tried, to no avail. Finally, a surgeon called to consult examined Emma and found that in performing the operation, Fliess "had 'mistakenly' left half a meter of surgical gauze in Emma's nose" (Masson, 1984, p. 66). Masson argued that the hemorrhaging was a normal result of a botched surgical procedure, but that Freud was motivated to save his friend's reputation. Instead of publicly acknowledging the error, Freud conceptualized Emma's hemorrhaging as the result of hysterical "sexual longing" (Masson, 1984, p. 67).

Masson suggested that Freud's rejection of the seduction hypothesis was the result of the reaction of the medical community to his theory and the need to protect his friend and colleague. Further, Masson contended that his own investigation into this issue caused the orthodox psychoanalytic community to shun him, rescinding his access to the Freud archives. Masson argued that his motivation was to force psychoanalysts to believe their clients, rather than dismissing their stories as fantasy.

Prominent scholars of the history of psychoanalysis have found fault with Masson's work (Monte & Sollod, 2003; Roazen, 2002). However, perhaps the most important lesson learned from this debate is that sexual abuse has been and still is underreported. Counselors would be wise to think carefully before they attribute their clients' reports to need-driven fantasies.

Hysteria, which is now called conversion disorder, is a condition in which an individual displays physiological symptoms that seem to have no valid physical basis. For example, a woman might display "glove anesthesia," numbness from the elbow downward to the hand, a condition that is neurologically impossible. As noted earlier, glove anesthesia is thought to result from guilt about masturbation and the accompanying fantasies (probably Oedipal in nature). The term *conversion* conveys the basic assumption about such conditions: that they are anxiety converted to symptoms. In Freud's view, hysteria results from the anxiety produced by the unacceptable sexual impulses threatening to break into consciousness. In the case of adult neurotics, unresolved childhood conflicts have been triggered in adult life, and the hysterical symptoms, according to psychoanalysis, always symbolize the childhood event.

Phobias are a special class of hysteria in which sexual impulses are first repressed, then converted to anxiety, and finally attached to some external object (Freud, 1920/1952). The phobic then creates structure that keeps the dreaded object at a distance, which represents the feared libido. For example, agoraphobia (literally, "the fear of the marketplace") is the fear of sexual impulses surfacing when the individual finds herself in a social setting. Freud gives the example of an individual who feels sexual urges toward those she passes when walking down the street. The individual displaces the danger (anxiety) into the environment and avoids it, thereby protecting herself (Freud, 1920/1952).

Obsessive-compulsive neurosis is conceptualized as having its roots in fixation in the anal stage of development. The sadistic urges developed at this time are a significant feature of obsessional neurosis and are the result of harsh toilet training. Reaction formation is a common defense of these individuals. Freud wrote, "The obsessive thought 'I should like to murder you' means nothing else but 'I should like to enjoy love of you' " (1920/1952, p. 353).

In the case of depression, it is difficult to reconcile Freud's terminology with today's nomenclature. Freud identified two kinds of depressive syndromes: melancholia and mourning. The contemporary counterparts of these classifications are not clear. Melancholia sounds like what we might term major depressive disorder. Mild to moderate depressions (other than mourning) seem to be the result of a hypercritical superego, as in melancholia.

Mourning and melancholia both begin with the loss of an object, often a loved person (or something that is representative of a loved object). Mourning is the gradual withdrawal of libido from attachment to the object, a process that simply takes time. Melancholia is the result of an extremely critical superego (Rickman, 1957). However, in the case of this more severe disorder, the ambivalent feelings toward the lost loved one (object) become part of the ego through identification. Thus, the superego turns the rage felt toward the lost object onto the ego. Freud maintained that the complaints that the melancholic turns against herself (being worthless, for example) are actually really directed at the loved person.

The terminology of Freud's time also creates confusion around the subject of the psychoses. The surrounding medical community referred to these conditions as dementia praecox, or with the newer term *schizophrenia;* Freud called them paraphrenia (Rickman, 1957, p. 105). Conceptually, however, Freud discussed these conditions as forms of narcissism (Freud, 1920/1952). He thought that psychosis results when the libido abandons all object attachments and instead attaches to the ego. The individual becomes egotistical and sometimes hypochondriacal (when some of the libido attaches to a body organ). In all psychological dysfunction, but particularly the psychoses, "there is a splitting of the ego" (Freud, 1940/1964, p. 202), in which two separate ideations or impulses coexist—those of the ego and id. If the instinctual element becomes strongest, the stage is set for psychosis.

Glenda sees some of Barb's symptoms as hysterical in nature, such as the dizziness and numbness. Her ego is not strong because of the amount of energy fixated in her early development. Barb does not have a successful work or love life, which supports the position that her symptoms are hysterical and reflects libidinal energy at work and the repression of memories of sexual abuse or fantasies of sexual relations with her father. Barb's panic attacks and headaches likely happen when some event activates her fixation in the phallic stage during which the Oedipal complex was unsuccessfully resolved. Her anxiety signals the possible emergence of a forbidden sexual urge, and her depression and mood swings result from her superego's punishment for the unacceptable urges. Glenda also understands Barb's troubles with men as a result of her unresolved Oedipal complex and the trauma of the sexual abuse she experienced in adolescence, which probably reinforced her fixation.

NATURE OF THERAPY

ASSESSMENT

Freud considered assessment very important in his approach to his clients, but only had what we would call informal approaches to this task. After determining that his client's symptoms were psychological rather than physiological, Freud recommended a 2-week trial period to ascertain that the client was suitable for analysis (Freud, 1912/1958). Primarily, Freud sought to make a differential diagnosis between hysterical or obsessive neurosis and schizophrenia (paraphrenia) because he thought the latter untreatable by psychoanalysis. A continuing assessment in psychoanalysis is seen in the search for clues to the unconscious in the clients' free associations, dreams, and errors.

In more contemporary forms of psychoanalytic therapy, formal assessment is often used to gain some information about the nature of the client's defenses and unconscious conflicts. The classic (and some would say the only) way to access unconscious material is by using ambiguous stimuli, such as the Rorschach inkblot test (Rorschach, 1942). In these methods, clients are asked to associate to the stimuli, and the therapist records and analyzes these productions. The ambiguity of the stimuli creates a situation in which unconscious processes are thought to be projected onto the cards, and can then be deduced from the nature of the client's responses.

Other psychoanalytic writers endorse the idea of doing a mental status exam (a structured, formal assessment of psychological functioning including orientation to person, place, time, reality testing, and so forth) and an assessment of ego strength (Yalof, 2005). This evaluation leads, according to Yalof, to both a formal DSM-IV-TR diagnosis as well as a "diagnosis" from a psychoanalytic perspective.

OVERVIEW OF THE THERAPEUTIC ATMOSPHERE

Freud spent many years searching for the most efficient ways to access the unconscious. His early attempts relied heavily on hypnosis because he had observed the famous Charcot recreating the symptoms of hysteria through this method. Because he found that some individuals were not very hypnotizable, Freud abandoned the practice in favor of placing his hands on clients' foreheads to evoke memories. Interestingly, in his early attempts to grasp the unconscious, he would exhort his clients to remember and was quite interpretive and forceful in his approach. Later on he deplored such behavior, terming it "wild analysis" (Freud, 1910/1957). At one point, Breuer and Freud were treating a client together and came to believe that the source of a cure for hysteria was catharsis, or emotional expression (the client called it "chimney sweeping"; Breuer & Freud, 1895/1937).

Gradually, Freud came upon the position with which we familiarly associate analysis— that the therapist is to remain "abstinent," or a neutral stimulus, in the therapeutic relationship. He described the attitude of the therapist as one of "evenly suspended attention" (Freud, 1912/1958, p. 111). Freud banished the personality of the therapist from the interaction, leaving the client free to project her unconscious material into the analytic situation.

One of the most conspicuous features of classical psychoanalysis is the analytic couch. Freud's couch was a gift from one of his clients (Gay, 1988). These and other incidents (such as inviting clients to meals and analyzing his own daughter) suggest that although Freud preached abstinence and strong client–counselor boundaries, he liberally broke the rules too.

Freud had at least two reasons for the use of the couch and the tradition of the analyst sitting behind it, out of the client's view. First, preventing the client from seeing the analyst helped to maintain the abstentious atmosphere. The therapist, who is admonished to let the client's unconscious work, might reveal something or otherwise influence the client through her facial expression. Freud also admitted that he simply did not like to be stared at for 8 hours a day (Freud, 1913/1958, p. 134).

Psychoanalysis is a long-term process. Freud believed in seeing his clients daily (i.e., six days a week), some of them for years. Mild cases required 3 days of analysis a week. Some analysts even took their clients along on vacations!

Glenda, who typically performs classical analysis, would like Barb to come to therapy 5 days a week. However, arrangements might be made for less frequent sessions if financial concerns interfere. After a few exploratory sessions (in which assessment of suitability for analysis was the focus), Glenda asks Barb to lie on the couch and obey the "fundamental rule" (discussed next).

Freud finally settled on **free association** as his primary analytic technique. He insisted that his clients obey the **"fundamental rule"** of psychoanalysis: The client is to reveal "everything that comes into his head, even if it is disagreeable for him to say it, even if it seems to him *unimportant* or actually *nonsensical*" (italics in original, Freud, 1940/1964, p. 52). Freud explained to his clients that what happens in analysis is different from everyday conversation. They were not to try to make any sense; they were only to be totally honest with him.

Glenda describes the fundamental rule to Barb, even using Freud's own words. When Barb agrees to this contract, Glenda feels she can proceed with the analysis.

ROLES OF CLIENT AND COUNSELOR

Both the nature of the theory and its historical roots in medicine combine to create the roles of the client and counselor in psychoanalysis. Freud was a physician first, and his belief that we are unable, for the most part, to access our unconscious led to the doctor role for the therapist and the patient role for the client. The client must comply with the fundamental rule, and in turn, the therapist will correctly interpret the client's productions. In addition, it is the therapist who decides what is real and not real (see the sections on resistance, transference, and countertransference that follow). Freud urged his students to take the surgeon as a model "who puts aside all his feelings, even his human sympathy, and concentrates his mental forces on the single aim of performing the operation as skillfully as possible" (Freud, 1912/1958, p. 115).

Freud believed that to achieve the proper attitude as a psychoanalyst, candidates should undergo analyses themselves. "It may be insisted, rather, that he should have undergone a psychoanalytic purification and have become aware of those complexes of his own which would be apt to interfere with his grasp of what the patient tells him" (Freud, 1912/1958,

p. 116). This analysis is termed the training, control, or personal analysis. Interestingly, Roazen (2002) presents evidence that Carl Jung (see Chapter 3), Freud's student and later nemesis, originated the idea of the training analysis, not Freud.

Glenda takes the orientation that she is the expert, able to listen to and understand Barb's associations in terms of Barb's unconscious process. Glenda remains relatively passive and opaque in her sessions with Barb, becoming active only when she has something to interpret to Barb. She expects Barb to cooperate with the analytic goals by freely expressing everything that comes to mind.

GOALS

The goal of psychoanalysis is to help the client uncover and resolve unconscious conflicts and to strengthen the ego by redirecting energy to conscious processes. The psychoanalyst is not really interested in symptoms; these will go away if the analysis succeeds. In fact, simple removal of a symptom is useless because the conflict will inevitably be expressed through some other symptom, a phenomenon known as symptom substitution (Yates, 1960).

Glenda attempts to help Barb understand how her current behaviors and symptoms are related to unconscious conflicts in her past. As Barb free associates, her repressed memories and emotions slowly begin to surface. Barb examines her early memories, particularly those of her relationship with her parents and siblings. With Glenda's help, Barb will begin to gain awareness of psychic material and events that have long been unavailable to her conscious mind.

PROCESS OF THERAPY

Arlow (2005) identified four phases of psychoanalytic treatment. However, before describing these phases, you should understand some important psychoanalytic constructs relevant to intervention.

INSIGHT

The goal of psychoanalysis is insight. The client will understand the sources of her current behavior and symptoms as stemming from unresolved unconscious conflicts originating in childhood. In essence, the counselor is teaching the client to think in psychoanalytic terms.

RESISTANCE

In any analysis, one will see the workings of the unconscious ego and superego in the form of resistances. Because it is dangerous for unconscious material to surface, the psychic apparatus fights to keep it out of awareness, using any means possible. Early forms of resistance to treatment can be seen in such tactics as having nothing to say, being late to or missing sessions, being unable to pay the analyst, and so forth. All of these are "grist for the mill" for the psychoanalyst, and they are eventually interpreted to the client. The most powerful, and in the end the most healing, resistance is the transference neurosis (discussed next).

TRANSFERENCE

Over the years of his work, Freud came gradually to the conviction that transference is the key to successful psychoanalysis. Every client inevitably recreates a pivotal former relationship with the analyst, and the secret is to analyze and resolve this transference neurosis. Freud called the transference "ambivalent" (1940/1964, p. 175) because it is composed of both positive and negative emotions toward the therapist. Most often, the therapist is placed in the role of the client's mother or father. Thus, the client can fall in love with the analyst (the erotic component), but then become angry when the analyst does not return this love or show her special favor. Much of the transference reaction is rooted in the Oedipal complex.

After a number of sessions, Barb will begin to develop a therapeutic bond with Glenda. At first, this bond is likely to be positive, but as the relationship develops, ambivalence and resistance will start to emerge. Barb may be initially quite loving of her therapist, perhaps wanting to recapture the ruptured relationship with her mother. An alternate possibility is that she will be trying (unconsciously) to recreate her special relationship with her father. She will want to know all about Glenda, ask for special favors (such as changing the time of her appointments or not having to lie on the couch). As the analysis progresses and Glenda refuses to gratify such wishes, Barb may become angry with Glenda, refusing to free associate or discounting Glenda's interpretations. She may also develop new and troubling symptoms. The ambivalent feelings Barb has toward her therapist stem from her Oedipal impulses of seeing her mother as a competitor and responsible for her lack of a penis. If Barb transfers her feelings for her father to Glenda, then Barb's anger will duplicate Barb's rage at her father's rejection of her.

COUNTERTRANSFERENCE

Countertransference is what happens when the therapist has not had a proper training analysis. Conflicts from the counselor's past are projected into the analytic situation, and the therapist loses her objectivity. The client becomes "special" to the counselor (a positive countertransference), or the therapist begins to want to argue or gets angry with the client. The counselor may find herself looking forward to or dreading seeing a particular client. The only way to resolve countertransference is for the analyst to seek the aid of her training analyst or a professional consultant.

At the conclusion of her academic training, Glenda underwent her training analysis as a requirement for her certification as a full-fledged analyst. As a result, Glenda is now able to listen neutrally to Barb's associations and avoid responding on the basis of her own conflicts. In the event that Glenda feels that she is reacting emotionally to Barb's associations and behaviors, Glenda will seek analysis to work through her own difficulties.

PHASES OF THERAPY

The four stages of psychoanalytic treatment are (a) the opening phase, (b) development of transference, (c) working through, and (d) resolution of the transference (Arlow, 2005, p. 35).

Opening Phase. The first few sessions with the client are typically conducted face-to-face and are an attempt to see if analysis is appropriate (Arlow, 2005). The client must have a certain level of psychological sophistication to engage in the analytic process, and the problem presented should be suitable from the perspective of psychoanalytic theory. The counselor observes the client's presentation and listens to her story. If the analyst decides that the client is a good candidate for analysis, the fundamental rule is explained and the client is asked to take her place on the analytic couch. The analysis then begins, with the client relating whatever comes to mind and the therapist observing these productions to get an idea of the client's conflicts and characteristic defenses. This stage lasts 3 to 6 months (Arlow, 2005).

Development of Transference. As the client continues to free associate, she eventually gets closer to relating her current difficulties to unconscious material. At about this time, the therapist begins to become a very important figure in the client's life as the client starts to transfer to the analyst feelings associated with past significant others (Arlow, 2005). According to Arlow, "the professional relationship becomes distorted as the patient tries to introduce personal instead of professional considerations into every interaction" (2005, p. 36). The therapist analyzes these interactions and interprets them to the client, starting with relatively benign, surface observations and progressing to interpretations involving deep unconscious material. This process is called analysis of the transference.

Working Through. As therapy progresses, the transference appears in many forms and is analyzed. Once an incident is analyzed and the client accepts the therapist's interpretation, new memories from the client's past are likely to surface, providing new material for analysis (Arlow, 2005). Repeated and more elaborate analysis of the transference constitutes the working through phase, which results in the client becoming more confident about the relationships between her current thoughts, feelings, and behavior and her past.

Resolution of Transference. When the analyst and client decide that the client has insight into her conflicts and the transference process, a date is set for termination of the therapy. Commonly, this event is marked by a resurgence of the client's symptoms because the client does not want to give up the therapist. This infantile urge is then analyzed by the client and therapist. New memories and fantasies can surface during this stage of treatment, which are then interpreted, until the client finally deals with her fantasies about what life will be like with no therapist (Arlow, 2005). At this point, therapy can end.

THERAPEUTIC TECHNIQUES

Very few techniques are available to the therapist in psychoanalysis, but they are considered quite powerful. Generally, the counselor is to be passive, rather than active, so the lack of overt technique is consistent with this attitude.

FREE ASSOCIATION

As I indicated earlier, the most important weapon in the therapist's arsenal is free association. Only in the special environment created by the fundamental rule will the unconscious start to show itself.

INTERPRETATION

The second powerful technique available to the psychoanalyst is interpretation of the client's material as it relates to conflicts from the past. Because Freud had found that premature interpretions evoked resistance in his clients, he insisted that none be made until the client was almost ready to discover the connections herself. Further, one must have developed a sufficient level of relationship with the client (the transference) prior to interpretation. In general, interpretation in the early part of therapy is oriented toward more "surface" material, and deep unconscious material is addressed later in the therapy.

Interpretation plays a part in the two other techniques described here, analysis of the resistance and dream analysis. Correct interpretations of the transference are critical so that the client can finally see that her behavior is not based in the actual relationship between therapist and client, but in relationships in the past.

Glenda is interested in the associations Barb produces as she engages in the analytic process. Barb's initial productions will be not very close to her unconscious urges, so Glenda is very general and cautious in interpreting the material. For instance, Barb may talk about her feelings about men, but instead of bringing up Oedipal issues, Glenda will likely talk to Barb about feeling unloved and rejected while at the same time longing for a savior. Later, Glenda could tentatively relate Barb's feelings about men to those about her father, her abuser, and finally to Glenda (who by then represents a powerful, important person in Barb's life).

ANALYSIS OF THE RESISTANCE

The psychoanalyst must always be alert for signs of client resistance. Minor, common resistances (such as forgetting appointments or having nothing to say) must be interpreted for the client, lest they get in the way of treatment. Symptoms may begin to disappear, and the client may begin to think that she is getting well. However, the wise analyst knows that this is yet another form of resistance, called flight into health. As analysis continues, resistances connected with more threatening material, such as the transference neurosis, are interpreted and analyzed much more cautiously. In fact, the transference neurosis will have to be reinterpreted many times (called "working through") before the client can resolve it.

At some point in the analysis, Barb will show signs of serious resistance. She may openly refute Glenda's interpretations, grow silent, or miss sessions. Glenda will remain calm in the face of such resistances, gathering information to make her case convincing. Barb may at some point begin to feel better and want to discontinue analysis. Glenda will interpret this "flight into health" as Barb's aversion to dealing with difficult material. Glenda will then offer repeated interpretation of the feelings of being unloved and worthless until Barb begins to accept these. New information will surface and be interpreted, perhaps at deeper levels. When the time is right, Glenda will begin to offer more intense interpretations involving Oedipal material.

DREAM ANALYSIS

The special place of dreams in psychoanalytic theory is considered to be one of Freud's most original and important contributions. His 1900 book, *The Interpretation of Dreams*, was probably the work of which Freud was most proud, and is considered by many his finest. Freud considered dreams to be symbolic wish fulfillments. He wrote, "A dream is itself a neurotic symptom and, moreover, one which possesses for us the incalculable advantage of occurring in all healthy people" (Freud, 1920/1952 p. 87). The content that the dreamer reports is known as the **manifest content.** However, the most important part of a dream is the **latent content,** that which has been disguised by **dreamwork** for the usual reasons (i.e., the content is unacceptable to the conscious). Elements in the dream are only substitutes for the latent material that is of the most interest to psychoanalysis. When a client reports a dream, the analyst then asks her to free associate to the content. The alert analyst then listens and interprets the latent content from the manifest content.

As you might have divined, an "overwhelming majority of symbols in dreams are sexual symbols" (Freud, 1920/1952, p. 161). Box 2.3 shows a list of dream elements and their hypothesized underlying contents. However, when examining such lists, remember that symbols may have multiple determinants, and that dream elements may even represent the opposite of what they appear to be. For example, in one of Freud's most famous cases, the client (the wolf man) had dreamed that he woke up and saw a pack of wolves sitting motionless outside of his window. Freud interpreted this dream as symbolic of the wolf man's early observation of vigorous parental sexual intercourse, but the stillness of the wolves represented the opposite (Freud, 1918/1955).

Box 2.3

The Meaning of Dream Symbols

In *A General Introduction to Psychoanalysis* (1920/1952), Freud wrote that "the number of things which are represented symbolically in dreams is not great. The human body as a whole, parents, children, brothers and sisters, birth, death, nakedness—and one thing more" (here Freud meant sex; p. 160). By far, the majority of symbols in dreams, according to Freud, have to do with sex. Following is a list of symbols presented by Freud in this work, along with their possible interpretations.

Symbol	*Interpretation*
House	With smooth walls, a man
	With ledges and balconies, a woman
Exalted personages (queens, emperors, kings, etc.)	Parents
Little animals or vermin	Children, brothers, sisters
Water (falling into, climbing out of)	Birth
Traveling by train	Dying
Clothes, uniforms	Nakedness
The number three	Male genitals
Long and upstanding objects (sticks, umbrellas, trees, etc.)	Penis

Symbol	Interpretation
Objects that can penetrate (knives, fire-arms)	Penis
Objects from which water flows (springs, taps)	Penis
Objects capable of elongation (pencils that slide in and out of sheaths)	Penis
Balloons, aeroplanes, zeppelins	Penis (the property of erection)
Flying	Erection
Reptiles and fishes	Penis
Serpent	Penis
Objects that enclose a space (pits, jars, bottles, boxes, chests, pockets)	Female genitalia
Cupboards, stoves	Uterus
Rooms	Uterus
Doors and gates	Opening of the vagina
Church, chapel	Woman
Snails and mussels	Woman
Fruit	Breast
Woods and thickets	Pubic hair (both sexes)
Landscape	Female genitalia
Machinery	Male genitalia
Jewel case	Female genitalia
Blossoms or flowers	Female genitalia
Play	Masturbation
Sliding or gliding	Masturbation
Teeth falling out or extracted	Punishment (castration) for masturbation
Dancing	Sexual intercourse
Riding or climbing	Sexual intercourse
Experiencing some violence	Sexual intercourse
Mounting ladders, steep places, stairs	Sexual intercourse
Windows or doors	Body openings
Key	Penis
Oven	Uterus
Plow	Penis

Barb reports to Glenda that she had the following dream: She is at work (in the grocery store) and is carrying two bags of groceries when she trips and falls, scattering the contents of the bag and breaking glass items. What caused Barb to fall was a broom that was carelessly left in the grocery aisle area by Carlos, one of the other workers in the store.

Most likely, Glenda would see Barb's dream as Oedipal in nature. The bag represents her womb, full of goodies. Barb trips over a phallic object (the broom), and everything is broken. Clearly, Barb is expressing her desire for sex or perhaps her fear of it. Glenda has to discover which interpretation is correct based on Barb's associations to the dream. Because Barb reports being afraid and anxious in the dream (manifestly attributed to fear of punishment by her boss), Glenda concludes that Barb's dream represents her fear of forbidden sex; that is, sex with her father. Carlos is merely a safe substitute for Barb's father, inserted into the dream by the dream censor. Barb's superego takes the form of the boss.

ANALYSIS OF THE TRANSFERENCE

The ultimate key to a successful analysis is the analysis of the transference neurosis. The client will unconsciously transfer onto the counselor qualities of significant individuals in her past, particularly parental figures. Feelings associated with these early interactions are evident in the client–counselor relationship, which, in the analyst's view, are unreal because the analyst has been properly abstinent in the therapeutic environment.

Cautiously, the counselor interprets the client's behavior and feelings, starting with the least threatening aspects. Early on, the transference is often affectionate and positive, resulting in clients idealizing the therapists as they would their "good" parents. The analyst can enlist this energy, encouraging the client to work hard to understand her unconscious material. Over the course of the therapy, the deeper issues emerge into the transference, and this transference is usually erotic in nature or hostile, resulting in powerful resistance (Freud, 1915/1958). For example, a female client might perceive a male therapist as unloving and uncaring, echoing the earlier rejection by her own father in the Oedipal phase. Male clients may transfer to a female analyst feelings about their mothers, becoming angry when the therapist refuses to gratify their wishes to be special. You will note that these examples involve cross-sex pairings. However, in many cases, transference feelings are not dependent on the sex of the analyst. For example, feelings of anger directed at an authority or power figure could be transferred to a therapist of either sex.

The job of the analyst, then, is to interpret the transference, showing the client that the feelings that she is having are not real, but instead rooted in the past. This process is long and sometimes tedious because transference tends to pop up again and again in the relationship. Analysts call this process "working through."

As her work progresses, Barb will begin to feel that Glenda does not care about her, a transference of her feelings of being unwanted, mistreated, and unloved that result from her unresolved Oedipal complex. Barb is also likely to become angry at Glenda, attributing her anger to Glenda's uncaring treatment of her. Glenda interprets these feelings as transference of feelings resulting from the longing associated with her father's abuse and abandonment. Some of Barb's feelings might also stem from her rage at her mother for stealing her father away. Barb's transference is likely to be quite ambivalent, however, vacillating between desperately seeking Glenda's love (reflecting Barb's longing for her father) and anger at his abandonment early on (the result of the Oedipal fantasies or abuse she suffered at that early age) and his abuse of her as a teen. Feelings of distrust of Glenda could also appear as a result of Barb's feelings about her father or her ambivalent feelings about her mother. Glenda will patiently interpret these feelings for Barb, slowly demonstrating that Barb's reactions are based in her psychological conflicts rather than in reality.

Eventually, Barb will come to recognize that the feelings and impulses she has toward Glenda are not real. Together, Glenda and Barb work through multiple examples of this transference until Barb understands fully the nature of her psychological processes. Barb will probably always have some of the same tendencies to be angry at men and mistrusting of others, but she will have insight into them and will be more able to operate based on ego rather than id or superego processes. After a lengthy analysis, Barb is finally ready to begin termination, but shortly after she and Glenda begin to discuss ending the analysis, Barb's symptoms, which have almost disappeared, reemerge. Glenda helps Barb see that this resurgence is the result of Barb's not wanting to give up the safe analytic relationship. When Barb can fully acknowledge this interpretation, she is truly ready to end the analysis.

EVALUATION OF THE THEORY

There is no doubt that psychoanalytic theory has had a major impact on many professional and scholarly disciplines, including literature, psychology, and the practice of counseling and psychotherapy. Reactions to psychoanalytic theory are rarely neutral; it seems to be both the most idolized and criticized theory in existence. Numerous prominent theorists of counseling admit that their approaches were developed partly in reaction to psychoanalytic theory (e.g., individual psychology, Rational Emotive Behavior Therapy, Reality Therapy, Cognitive Therapy, Person-Centered Therapy). Because of the sheer volume of literature that critiques the psychoanalytic approach, it is simply impossible to summarize succinctly in this section. Thus, I will attempt to hit only the high points of these evaluations, leaving the interested scholar a lot of fascinating reading.

Psychoanalysis has also spawned a second generation of analytically oriented theories, generally subsumed under the headings psychoanalytic (small *p*), neoanalytic, or psychodynamic. They are also called self psychology, ego psychology, or object relations theory (St. Clair, 2004). Theorists associated with these approaches are Fairbairn, Kohut, Kernberg, Klein, Jacobson, Mahler, and Winnicott. Their theories share an interest in mental representations of self and others (i.e., objects) and how these influence relationships. You will read more about these theorists in Chapter 3, Neoanalytic Approaches.

QUALITIES OF THE THEORY

Precision and Testability. One of the most common critiques of Freud's theory is that it is not very testable. Entities such as the id, ego, and superego are not easily observed directly; researchers must be satisfied with only indirect evidence of their existence. A second problem with psychoanalytic theory relates to falsifiability. It is very difficult to disconfirm psychoanalytic theory. Consider, for example, the idea of resistance. If an analyst makes an interpretation that the client rejects, the client can be said to be resisting because the client is too threatened to acknowledge it. If the client accepts the interpretation, it is right, end of story. Monte (1999) gives the following example:

> Imagine telling the mythical "man on the street" that sometime between ages three and six years, he lusted after his mother, hated his father, and was terrified that his father would remove his penis. If our man on the street protests that this is nonsense or berates us for being offensive, we must point out to him that he is incredulous or offended precisely because he is repressing these experiences! And, indeed, the more he protests, the more we are prone to assume that he is threatened by these ideas because he, like all males, has *repressed* his Oedipal strivings. What possible evidence could the man produce

that would *disconfirm* our theoretical assertion that he was Oedipal as a child? (Monte, 1999, p. 97, italics in original)

It is difficult to derive precise predictions from psychoanalytic theory that might be easily tested. In psychoanalytic interpretation, things are often their opposite (as with the wolf man or defense mechanisms). Further, reading Freud in the original reveals his heavy reliance on metaphor in his descriptions of psychic functioning. Maddi cautions that such language impairs the precision and clarity of the theory (1996, p. 492). Finally, because of the various revisions of psychoanalytic theory, different interpretations can be made of the same or similar phenomena.

Other views of the testability of psychoanalytic theory are less negative. Borenstein (2005) and Westen (1998) have argued persuasively that significant support exists for some of the basic assumptions of psychoanalytic theory. Borenstein contends that other branches of psychology have co-opted psychoanalytic constructs and amassed data in support of them. Evidence for this argument can be found in Westen's (1998) review, summarized in the theory-testing section. Seeing this state of affairs as partially a public relations problem, Borenstein suggests that psychoanalysts need to reclaim the scientific heritage that was so important to Freud.

Empirical Validity. A good theory should have some empirical support. As you will see in the research support section, the evidence bearing on psychoanalytic theory is mixed. Research reviewed in Chapter 3 is also relevant to psychoanalytic theory.

RESEARCH SUPPORT

Outcome Research. As with the other major theoretical approaches, outcome research has generally supported the efficacy of psychoanalytic psychotherapy (Lambert & Ogles, 2004). However, we should note that most outcome research is not assessing traditional (5 days a week on the couch) psychoanalysis. For instance, the Temple study (Sloane et al., 1975) found that psychoanalytic psychotherapy (weekly sessions for 3 months) was as effective as Behavioral Therapy, and that both were more effective than no treatment. Meta-analytic studies (Crits-Christoph, 1992; Svartberg & Stiles, 1991) support the efficacy of short-term psychodynamic therapy treatment compared to no therapy, but the findings are mixed when short-term dynamic therapy is compared to alternative treatments. Short-term dynamic therapy is psychoanalytically based, but tests of this mode are probably not good tests of traditional psychoanalysis.

The Menninger Foundation conducted an intensive study of psychoanalysis, called the Psychotherapy Research Project, or more commonly, the Menninger Project (Wallerstein, 1986, 1989). Funded by several private and public sources, the project investigated various forms of psychoanalytic psychotherapy, including traditional psychoanalysis. The clients of the Menninger Foundation tended to be "seriously emotionally ill" (Wallerstein, 1989, p. 195) and were often sent to the foundation as a last resort. This project attempted to discriminate among classic psychoanalysis, expressive psychotherapy, and supportive psychoanalytic treatment, but generally found that the distinctions between the three approaches were not as clear as expected. A major aim of the study was to use naturalistic methods that did not disturb the psychotherapy process. For this reason, outcome data are not amenable to summary.

Leuzinger-Bohleber and Target (2002) reported on the "German studies" of psychoanalytic therapies, which focused on the outcomes of long-term intervention. This study, conducted in the late 1990s, relied heavily on retrospective reports of therapists and clients, although they did administer the Symptom Check List-90R (SCL-90R; Derogatis, 1994). Like other large studies of therapy, they found that most clients in analytic therapy of some form reported improvement, as did the therapists. SCL-90R scores revealed that the former clients were mostly below the mean score defined as "clinical" based on German norms.

Masling, Bornstein, Fishman, and Davila (2002) presented an interesting study of gender differences in psychoanalytic research. They wanted to see if there is any evidence, given the often-touted bias against women in analysis, that research on psychoanalytic constructs was equally biased. Specifically, they looked to see if research used male participants more often than female and also, whether psychoanalytic constructs could better predict the behavior of men than women. A meta-analysis of 98 studies revealed that effect sizes were stronger for predictions of males' behavior when both females and males were included in studies. However, when studies that only looked at one sex were examined (separately), effect sizes were roughly the same. These findings are hard to explain, for they suggest that psychoanalytic theory predicts the behavior of males better than females when both sexes are the subject of study but predicts equally well when participants in research are of one sex only. Masling et al. suggest that investigators in these two types of studies may be considering different questions, but don't offer any evidence to support this hypothesis.

Theory-Testing Research. Theory testing research does exist in the psychoanalytic realm, although many of the empirical studies of pure psychoanalytic theory are dated and can be questioned on methodological grounds. For example, Levin (1966) examined penis envy and found that "career women" showed more penis envy than did married women who did not work outside of the home. However, the measure of penis envy was based on the Rorschach test, another projective device with debatable psychometric properties, at least when considering the measurement of penis envy. In yet another test of the penis envy construct, Johnson (1966) expected that more females than males would fail to return special pencils after completing a test in a psychology class, indicating that penis envy was operative among the women. Results of the study confirmed Johnson's prediction. A more recent replication of the study failed to support the hypothesis that women would steal more pencils/penis symbols (Skinner, 1977). Is coveting pencils a good measure of penis envy? You can see the difficulty in operationalizing this psychoanalytic construct.

Eysenck and Wilson (1973) presented an interesting and informative book in which studies testing psychoanalytic theory are presented, each followed by Eysenck and Wilson's methodological evaluation. On the basis of their review, Eysenck and Wilson concluded that "the studies looked at in this volume give little if any support to Freudian concepts and theories. . . . several of the studies dealing in particular with treatment and with 'single case' investigations give results powerfully challenging Freudian hypotheses" (1973, p. 392). However, Eysenck has long been known as a critic of the psychoanalytic approach. Other reviews paint a more positive picture (e.g., Kline, 1972; Sears, 1943), although these authors could be accused of the opposite kind of bias.

More recently, Westen (1998) summarized the research on five postulates of psychoanalytic theory:

1. The existence and centrality of unconscious processes
2. Conflicting feelings and motivation that result in ambivalence and compromise
3. The role of childhood experiences and their impact on adult relationships
4. The importance of mental representations of the self, others, and relationships in social interaction
5. The idea that development involves learning to regulate sexual and aggressive tendencies and that it progresses from immaturity and dependence to maturity and independence.

Adapted from Westen, 1998, pp. 334–335.

Reviewing an impressive amount of literature from cognitive, developmental, and social psychology, Westen concluded that there is ample support for the five propositions. For example, Westen reported that the idea that unconscious processes influence overt behavior is "no longer controversial" (p. 336). Studies of subliminal exposure (exposure to stimuli in very brief intervals that are not registered in conscious awareness) confirm the idea that these stimuli can affect emotion, preferences, and attitudes. Westen presented similar evidence in support of the other psychoanalytic assumptions. Scientists who want to dismiss Freud's theoretical work had better read this article.

Other recent research centers on constructs that are involved in psychoanalytic therapy such as interpretation and the working alliance (Henry, Strupp, Schacht, & Gaston, 1994). In a major review of these research areas, Henry and colleagues (1994) concluded that transference interpretations were not related to good therapy outcomes. However, they noted that client emotional expression following such interpretations is linked to positive outcome, but only slightly more so than nontransference interpretations that induce client affect. The research on Core Conflictual Relationship Themes summarized in Chapter 3 is also relevant to classic psychoanalytic theory.

Of interest to psychoanalytic theorists and researchers is the construct of working alliance, or the relationship between client and therapist that allows the work of therapy to proceed. The research assessing the relationship between the working alliance and counseling outcome has cut across many theoretical orientations and generally finds that the relationship is modestly related to outcome in the expected direction (i.e., more positive alliance is related to better outcome; Lambert & Ogles, 2004). Of note is that clients' and independent observers' ratings of the alliance are more predictive of outcome than therapists', raising a question about therapists' objectivity when assessing their relationships with clients (Henry et al., 1994). None of these findings are supportive of the theoretical structure of psychoanalysis specifically.

A major area of research that bears on psychoanalytic constructs is centered on what is termed the repressed memory controversy (Enns, McNeilly, Corkery, & Gilbert, 1995; Kluft & Loftus, 2007; Loftus, 1993; Loftus & Ketcham, 1994). This debate centers on whether individuals traumatized at an early age, particularly in the case of sexual abuse, can repress and then later accurately recall memories of the incidents. These questions can be seen as relevant to the validity of Freud's construct of repression. Enns and colleagues (1995), in their review of the historical, political, and scientific issues involved in this debate, discussed Freud's repudiation of the seduction hypothesis as perhaps the first incident of denying the memories of abused women.

The issues discussed in the area of repressed memory have been characterized as political rather than scientific (Brown, 1995). The recent interchange of opinions has been connected to the establishment of the False Memory Syndrome Foundation, an organization that was founded to investigate what they termed "false memory syndrome," seen primarily in cases in which a survivor of sexual abuse recovers previously repressed memories of the abuse. The proponents of false memory syndrome contend that psychotherapists induce such memories via suggestive psychotherapeutic techniques.

At the heart of the repressed memory controversy is the question of whether we do in fact repress memories of events in our lives, a question that would certainly be relevant to psychoanalytic theory. Research using retrospective self-report has shown that a certain percentage of victims of sexual abuse report that at some time in their lives they were unable to remember the abuse (Briere, 1995; McNally, Perlman, Ristuccia, & Clancy, 2006). On the other side, research suggests that it is relatively simple to implant created memories (Loftus & Ketcham, 1994). Briere (1995) pointed out that short of observing someone's abuse and then following their later reports, establishing the validity of the self-reports used in the recent memory studies is almost impossible. The implications of this controversy for psychoanalytic theory are mixed: it appears that there is some empirical evidence supporting the existence of repression, but support for the ability to accurately regain and report repressed memories is still a topic of controversy (Kluft & Loftus, 2007).

ISSUES OF INDIVIDUAL AND CULTURAL DIVERSITY

Psychoanalysis shares with many other theories of counseling the position that the individual rather than the surrounding environment needs to change. This assumption is countered by feminist and cultural critiques of the theory that insist that many aspects of society are detrimental to individuals, that oppression of women and minorities is debilitating, and that asking individuals to adapt to an oppressive social system is wrong.

Feminists have been critical of Freud since the early days of the feminist movement (Enns et al., 1995; Kaplan & Yasinski, 1980). To begin with the obvious, the idea that the strongest motivator of female behavior is the envy of the penis is seen as outrageous and demeaning. What women envy is the traditionally conferred power of men in society, not their anatomy! Feminists also criticize Freud's views of women as passive, inferior, and immoral, traveling through life in an endless search for a penis to remedy their inherent inferiority (Kaplan & Yasinski, 1980). Karen Horney, a psychoanalytic theorist in her own right, had a great deal to say about Freud's theories, pointing out that he neglected "womb envy" as a source of men's fear of things feminine (1932, 1930/1967). In an early response to these criticisms, Freud characterized them as "denials of the feminists, who are anxious to force us to regard the two sexes as completely equal in position and worth" (Freud, 1925, p. 258). In a larger sense, some of the problems identified by feminists are an unavoidable complication in every theory: a theorist is a product of his or her environment and culture, and the theory is directly or indirectly infused with the normative expectations of the culture. Clearly, Freud was a participant in, and influenced by, a culture that was sexist—the role of women was restricted and less valued than that of men.

More recently, some feminists have concluded that psychoanalytic theory, particularly the more recently developed offshoots, can be saved (Zanardi, 1990). Chodorow (1989) identified two general approaches to feminist psychoanalysis: the interpersonal approach and the French postmodern approach. The interpersonal approach attempts to revalue femininity through the use of object relations, self psychology, and Jungian approaches. A more indirect variant of psychoanalysis, the postmodern approach to psychoanalysis, is more often used in literary criticism than in psychotherapy.

From a cultural perspective, it is clear that psychoanalysis is rooted in European values. Intellectualism, individuation, and individual achievement are goals in this theory that might not necessarily translate across cultures. The value of insight is by no means treasured in other than European-influenced cultures (Sue & Sue, 2003). Psychoanalysis, in its pure form, is probably only accessible to individuals who have the economic means to pay for intensive treatment. Thus, a class bias exists: how many individuals from lower socioeconomic levels have the time and financial resources to devote years to exploring their inner experiences?

From a gay, lesbian, or bisexual (GLB) perspective, Freud called homosexuality a perversion, meaning that it was a deviation from what the theory considered normal sexual development. He did not overtly disparage GLB orientations, saying, "The most important of these perversions, homosexuality, scarcely deserves the name" (Freud, 1925/1989, p. 423). However, the use of the term *perversion* and the assumption of heterosexuality as normal sexual development suggests, according to some authors, a negative moral judgment (Murphy, 1984). Contemporary authors have noted that given Freud's notion that humans are inherently bisexual, it is possible to reconceptualize GLB sexuality as a healthy developmental path (Cornett & Hudson, 1986; Murphy, 1984).

THE CASE STUDY

The client conceptualized in this chapter, Barb, presented some of the features often associated with typical "good candidates" for psychoanalysis. She appeared to be motivated and interested in investigating her psychological processes. Furthermore, her issues seemed to relate to sexual trauma, neatly fitting in with psychoanalytic thought about the origins of dysfunction in sexual development. Some of Barb's symptoms appeared to fit quite well with a psychoanalytic understanding, such as the fainting and numbness in the face.

The most difficult aspect of Barb's history from a conceptual standpoint involves the validity of her early sexual experiences. As noted earlier, the final version of Freud's theory would predict that most likely the memories of the early abuse by the family friend were fantasy born out of Oedipal longings. To be fair to Freud, it is important to note that he did not deny that sexual abuse of children occurred. However, he clearly stated that his clients' reports of this abuse were mostly untrue. Current data on sexual abuse indicate that it is very prevalent, which would lead us to conclude that Barb's memories are probably accurate. However, the aftereffects of both real abuse and fantasy abuse would presumably be fixation in the Oedipal stage. The resolution of the validity dilemma is therefore a moot point from a practical perspective.

Summary

Psychoanalytic theory is based on the idea that humans are motivated by conflicts between unconscious and conscious forces. The expression of instinctual drives (libido and Thanatos) is not acceptable to society, so the psychic apparatus evolved to suppress them. Freud proposed that the psyche was composed of three entities: the id, ego, and superego. Dysfunction arises when the instinctual urges (most notably libido or sexual drives) threaten to break into consciousness and are symbolized as symptoms.

Freud proposed an elaborate model of human development, the psychosexual stages. The most important of these stages is the phallic stage, in which children become aware of the anatomy of the other sex. The process of resolution of the Oedipal complex arising in this stage is different for girls and boys. For boys, who have developed a desire to possess their mothers, the complex is resolved through castration anxiety. The boy fears that his father will find out about his incestuous desires and cut off his penis. He resolves this conflict through identification with the father. Girls notice that they have no penis and develop penis envy. They turn away from their mothers, but because sex with father is forbidden, they repress this urge. They continue their lives in search of a penis, most notably through the birth of a male baby.

Psychoanalysis is a long-term process conducted in a doctor–patient model. The client free associates in a process that eventually yields unconscious material. The therapist remains abstinent so that the client can project unconscious conflicts onto the therapist. This projection, which typically involves Oedipal wishes, is called transference, and is at the heart of the psychoanalysis. The psychoanalytic therapist interprets the client's unconscious material with the goal of helping the client achieve insight into her conflicts.

Psychoanalysis has long had many critics. It is considered by some to be untestable, and direct empirical support for the outcome of traditional psychoanalysis is sparse. The theory also is based in a male, western European model, so it draws criticism from feminists and other scholars of diversity.

Visit Chapter 2 on the Companion Website at **www.prenhall.com/murdock** for chapter-specific resources and self-assessments.

Anna Freud

CHAPTER 3

Neoanalytic Approaches

Theo came to counseling after being told by his girlfriend, Tamia, that if he did not seek help, she would end their three-year relationship. He is a 22-year-old, tall, African American male currently in his final year of college at a large university with a major in Math and Computer Science. He plans to enter the military after graduation.

Although he presents calmly, Theo says that he feels as if he "is going to explode." He believes that he needs counseling to better understand his problems controlling his anger and how it relates to his behaviors. Most recently, Theo became angry with Tamia after she failed to return his phone call and stayed out "partying" all night. He indicated that Tamia claimed she had told him about her plans and that his anger felt controlling and threatening. Theo also expressed concern about his inability to control his anger when dealing with his family and professional relationships.

Theo is the middle child of three boys. When Theo was 10 years old, his parents divorced and Theo's mother relocated with the boys. Two years later, his parents reconciled and remarried. Theo reported that he did not want his parents to remarry and still believes they should not be together because of their regular arguments about financial issues and his father's constant business travel. He noted that his older brother took care of him and his younger brother and tried to maintain peace in the household.

Both of Theo's parents completed college at historically Black colleges. Although supportive of Theo going to college, they wanted him to attend a historically Black college, especially because most of Theo's primary and secondary school education took place in primarily White schools. Theo said that even though he chose not to follow his parents' wishes, he still identifies strongly with his African-American heritage. He chose to attend a predominantly White college because he did not want to follow in his parents' footsteps. He reports that going to college was a way of getting away from them and, particularly, "a lot of fighting and yelling."

BACKGROUND

The psychoanalytic crowd is an interesting subset of the psychotherapeutic community. Within the group of therapists who would characterize themselves as psychoanalysts, there are a number of different theoretical camps, ranging from pure classicists (i.e., orthodox Freudians) to a relatively recently developed constructivist approach, *relational psychoanalysis*. In between are several other identifiable theoretical variants that contribute to how psychoanalytic therapists currently practice. These are the *object relations* theorists, the *ego* psychologists, and *self* psychologists, *interpersonal* theorists, and *intersubjectivists*. All of these theorists/therapists consider themselves direct intellectual descendents of Freud, but all extend Freud's theory or deviate slightly or significantly from orthodox psychoanalysis; hence my choice of the label neoanalytic to describe them.

Psychoanalysts like to write about their particular perspectives, and a glance at the major journals shows that they also seem to argue a lot about the validity of the various strains of psychoanalytic theory. The orthodox analysts criticize the relationists for being "impure" and "not analytic," and the relationists see the traditionalists as living in the past and clinging to outdated ideas. Psychoanalysts like fancy terms and seem to favor elaborate writing styles and so in the midst of the arguments, the variety of names and terms becomes absolutely bewildering at times.

The biggest bone of contention seems to be conceptualizations of motivation. Traditional Freudian theory is often referred to as *drive theory* because of Freud's conviction that the genetically wired-in instinctual drives (sex and aggression) motivated behavior (this is sometimes referred to as the genetic or engergic position). Contemporary variants of psychoanalysis can be characterized according to the degree to which they accept or reject drive theory (Wolitzky & Eagle, 1997). In fact, a classic in the modern analytic literature is Greenberg and Mitchell's (1983) *Object Relations in Psychoanalytic Theory*. In this book, Greenberg and Mitchell classify theorists into the degree to which they buy (or say they buy) Freud's notion that behavior is motivated by the drives or seeing motivation as a function of an inherent need to relate to other human beings. Across the four approaches presented in this chapter, ego psychologists tend to be traditionalists, more or less building on Freud's original notions. Relational analysts are the most radical in their rejection of drive theory. There is some argument about the status of self psychology in this regard, because its originator, Heinz Kohut, seemed in his early writings to accept drive theory. Later, Kohut seemed to abandon this perspective for one more relational in nature (Fosshage, 2003). Otto Kernberg, according to Greenberg and Mitchell, liked to maintain that he was a drive theorist, but their analysis of his theory suggests otherwise. Object relations (with the exception of Melanie Klein, who accepted traditional drive theory) and relational theorists adopt the view that humans are motivated by the need to relate to others.

Drives vs. relationships aside, the most important relationship for all of these theorists is that with the primary caretaker. Thus, the mother-child relationship is often the focus of attention (for the most part, they were writing prior to our current enlightened views of child care). The mother is most important because she has the breast, the source of biological sustenance for the infant.

Newer versions of analytic thought go beyond Freud's theory in the area of development. For example, these systems are thought to be helpful in understanding more severe forms of dysfunction, such as psychosis, and borderline (meaning to psychosis) and narcissistic states. These types of problems are thought to originate earlier than the neuroses with which Freud was concerned. Thus, the neoanalytic theorists discuss "pre-Oedipal" development. Some of the neoanalytic strains are relatively traditional in their approaches to intervention, relying on free association, interpretation, and an abstinent analyst (traditional ego psychology and object relations); others emphasize the working alliance (the psychoanalytic term for the therapeutic relationship) as the primary vehicle of change. All recognize the power of the unconscious. According to Greenberg and Mitchell (1983), it is the content of the unconscious that differentiates the drive and relational theorists: for the drive theorists, the unconscious contains the unacceptable impulses of sex and aggression. For the relational theorists, the unconscious "consists of particular images of the self and others which have been similarly rejected" (Greenberg & Mitchell, 1983 p. 382).

The view of human nature among the neoanalytics varies. For instance, Melanie Klein, considered an object relations theorist, wrote a lot about the aggressive instincts, suggesting a rather negative view. Although she did acknowledge libidinal energy (which leads the infant to a state of love), she characterized the early stages of development as scary; the infant is beset by conflicting feelings (particularly aggression) and shifting emotional states (Mitchell & Black, 1995). You can read some of Klein's thoughts in the original in Box 3.1. The other object relations theorists, the self psychologists, and relational psychoanalysts seem to offer at least a neutral view of human nature. The ego psychologists, who turned away from the battleground metaphor of Freud's system, emphasized the ego's adaptive capacities, perhaps offering a more positive view of humans.

Box 3.1

Melanie Klein

In my view—as I have explained in detail on other occasions—the introjection of the breast is the beginning of superego formation which extends over years. We have grounds for assuming that from the first feeding experience onwards the infant introjects the breast in its various aspects. The core of the superego is thus the mother's breast, both good and bad. Owing to the simultaneous operation of introjection and projection, relations to external and internal objects interact. The father, too, who soon plays a role in the child's life, early on becomes part of the infant's internal world. It is characteristic of the infant's emotional life that there are rapid fluctuations between love and hate; between external and internal situations; between perception of reality and the phantasies relating to it; and, accordingly, an interplay between persecutory anxiety and idealization—both referring to internal and external objects; the idealized object being a corollary of the persecutory, extremely bad one.

The ego's growing capacity for integration and synthesis leads more and more, even during these first few months, to states in which love and hatred, and correspondingly the good and bad aspects of objects, are being synthesized; and this gives rise to the second form of anxiety—depressive anxiety—for the infant's aggressive impulses and desires towards the bad breast (mother) are now felt to be a danger to the good breast (mother) as well. In the second quarter of the first year these emotions are reinforced, because at this stage the infant increasingly perceives and introjects the mother as a person. Depressive anxiety is intensified, for the infant feels he has destroyed or is destroying a whole object by his greed and uncontrollable aggression. Moreover, owing to the growing synthesis of his emotions, he now feels that these destructive impulses are directed against a loved person. Similar processes operate in relation to the father and other members of the family. These anxieties and corresponding defences constitute the 'depressive position', which comes to a head about the middle of the first year and whose essence is the anxiety and guilt relating to the destruction and loss of the loved internal and external objects.

It is at this stage, and bound up with the depressive position, that the Oedipus complex sets in. Anxiety and guilt add a powerful impeius towards the beginning of the Oedipus complex. For anxiety and guilt increase the need to externalize (project) bad figures and to internalize (introject) good ones; to attach desires, love, feelings of guilt, and reparative tendencies to some objects, and hate and anxiety to others; to find representatives for internal figures in the external world. It is, however, not only the search for new objects which dominates the infant's needs, but also the drive towards new aims: away from the breast towards the penis, i.e. from oral desires towards genital ones. Many factors contribute to these developments: the forward drive of the libido, the growing integration of the ego, physical and mental skills and progressive adaptation to the external world. These trends are bound up with the process of symbol formation, which enables the infant to transfer not only interest, but also emotions and phantasies, anxiety and guilt, from one object to another.

Source: Klein, M. (1952). The origins of transference. *International Journal of Psychoanalysis, 33,* 433–438.

What might be considered a very basic philosophical difference among the neoanalytic writers is whether they are objective positivist thinkers (as was Freud) versus relativistic, constructivist ones. Freud was very interested in promoting psychoanalysis as a natural science operating on some objectively real material and discovering laws of nature. In this view, the analyst was the scientist charged with accurately interpreting client material and was thus an expert source who knew the right and wrong for the client. There was a clear and consistent truth, rooted in physical reality (for Freud, neuroanatomy, although he could never demonstrate this). Some of the descendents of Freud tend to take this approach, but current analysts, particularly the relational and self theorists, for example, are more constructivist in philosophy. Simply put: they view "reality" as inseparable from the observer—one person's truth may not be the same as another's. "Reality" in the therapeutic relationship is constructed by client and counselor; prompting the notion of the *two-person psychology*, which emphasizes the roles of the client and counselor in therapeutic events. This demise of the totally objective therapist/observer arose from the revolution of thought in the so-called "hard" sciences spurred by Einstein's relativity theory, quantum physics, and Heisenberg's uncertainty principle that eventually trickled into the social sciences, and then into psychoanalytic thought (Curtis & Hirsch, 2003).

Neoanalytic approaches do not add any new techniques beyond what have been already described by Freud. They do discuss new ways of viewing the effects of classical technique, and most emphasize the relationship between the therapist and client as curative in and of itself (beyond the effect of insight gained via transference interpretation). Therefore, the techniques sections in this chapter are brief and focus on how the traditional techniques of free association, dream analysis, and interpretation are used in the service of the approach described.

Most analysts practicing today draw on one or more of the various analytic strains, and perhaps all of them (Karon & Widner, 1995). In this chapter, I will present four major variants of neoanalytic thought: Ego Psychology (EP), Object Relations (OR), Self Psychology (SP) and Relational Psychoanalysis (RP). Although this delineation of these general orientations seems logical to me, you should be aware that there is controversy about how to divide up current psychoanalytic thought into camps. For example, some see Kohut, whom I separate out from the others, as an OR theorist, whereas others would characterize his approach as relational. Only a deeper study than I can provide would allow you to fully understand these arguments. Lest I neglect one other important theoretical offshoot of psychoanalysis, a summary of the views of Carl Jung, one of the earliest of Freud's followers, is presented in Box 3.2.

Box 3.2

Analytical Psychology—Carl Jung's Version of Psychoanalysis

Carl Gustav Jung was born on July 26th, 1875 in Kesswil, a village in northeast Switzerland. Like many other famous psychologists (E. G. Wilhelm Wundt, Edward Thorndike, and Ivan Pavlov) Jung's father was the head of a church. Jung spent most of his life in Switzerland, although he did make one trip to America in 1909. Jung made many contributions to the field of psychology, most notably his work on personality types and his theory of personality.

Originally one of Sigmund Freud's students, Jung eventually broke from Freud over the issue of sexuality as the prime motivator of human behavior. For Jung, sexuality was only one of the things that could influence psychological process; of equal or more importance was the individual's quest for individuality and meaning (Raff, 2007).

Although the most well-known influence on Jung's work was that of Sigmund Freud (Casement, 2002), like many people in Europe during the late 1800s, Jung was fascinated by philosophy, the occult, myths, and symbols (Douglas, 2005). Jung's understanding of the common elements of societal symbols led Jung to the perspective that there are common elements of human experience, which Jung called archetypes. Jung was also heavily influenced by eastern philosophies and perspectives, which can be seen in his focus on the balance of intra-psychic forces, an essential theme throughout Jung's theory.

TYPOLOGY OF THE PERSONALITY

Jung called the psychological makeup of the person the *psyche*. In the center of Jungian personality structure is the *ego*. The ego is the "I," or the "Me," and contains the aspects of the personality of which people are conscious. The *persona*, also in the person's consciousness, is the aspect of the personality that is presented to the external world (Douglas, 2005). The persona essentially acts as a socially appropriate ego by presenting to observers the parts of the personality that the individual judges socially acceptable.

To balance the conscious ego Jung hypothesized the existence of the *personal shadow*. The personal shadow lies in the individual unconscious and includes the aspects of the person that the individual views as negative, harmful, or painful. Jung believed that the personal shadow also could contain positive aspects of a person's personality that were underdeveloped or unrecognized, and further, that the individual unconscious as a whole could be a source of creativity and comfort for the individual (Douglas, 2005).

The *collective unconscious* is a set of knowledge, beliefs, and experiences shared by all humans. The most important elements in the collective unconscious are patterns known as *archetypes*. Jung believed that the specific characterization of these archetypes can change over time, and across cultures, but even if the visual and culturally specific details changed, the essential characteristics of the specific archetype did not. As an example consider the Hero archetype. For some people this archetype may appear as an image of a knight in shining armor. For others, the Hero might manifest as a samurai. Although these images are visually different, they share the essentials of the hero archetype. Presaging our current attention to cultural diversity, Jung therefore believed that accurate identification of a client's archetypal images required an understanding of the client's culture and her or his personal understanding of that culture.

Two other important archetypes are the *animus* and the *anima*. The *animus* represents the masculine aspects of an individual and the *anima* the feminine. These archetypes closely resemble their Chinese counterparts the yang and the yin. Much like the concepts of the yang and the yin, Jung believed that every person had both the animus and the anima and individuals should strive to understand and develop both aspects of the personality. Such understandings of the archetypes leads to better self-understanding and more fulfilling relationships with people of the other gender.

Jung added to the classic Freudian conception of the unconscious the realm of human potential. The unconscious did include negative feelings, but for Jung it was also the seat of human potential, creativity, and existential meaning (Douglas, 2005). This view of the unconcious is one of the key ways in which Jung's theory was different than Freud's psychoanalysis.

JUNGIAN TYPOLOGY

One of the most easily recognizable contributions of Jung has been his theory of personality typology (Douglas, 2005). Jung theorized that there are three basic dimensions of the personality. Each of these dimensions has two opposite concepts that balance each other. A person usually will display qualities of both concepts to some degree, but will typically favor one over the other. As with the rest of his theory Jung emphasized balance between these aspects of type. Introversion needed to be balanced by extroversion, thinking by feeling, sensing by intuition, and judging by perceiving.

Jung theorized that a healthy psyche had a balance between *introversion* and *extroversion*. Although most people today understand introversion and extroversion as an orientation towards people, Jung found a deeper meaning for these concepts. Introversion is the tendency for a person to explore the inner self. Introverted people need time alone for this exploration, which is primarily directed at understanding their affective reactions. Jung hypothesized that the libido, or driving energy, of an introvert was oriented towards a deeper understanding of themselves and a deep understanding of the internal lives of others. Thus, the introvert has a few friends, but those friends are very close. An extroverted person, on the other hand, finds meaning in external objects and relationships. The libido of an extroverted person pushes the person to be near others and find meaning in life through relationship with other people.

The second personality dimension is *thinking* and *feeling*. Thinking individuals favor cognition, logic, and rational thinking. A thinking person likes to understand all of the details of the options available and then make decisions based on logic. A feeling person enjoys experiencing the ebb and flow of emotions and affect. Joy, depression, desire, and satisfaction are the experiential playground of the feeling person.

Sensation and *intuition* make up the third dimension. A person who favors sensing will believe only what they can see, or smell, taste, touch, and so forth. They are skeptical of things that they can not sense. A person that is more oriented towards using intuition, on the other hand, seeks to understand the missing or mysterious forces that one can not actively perceive. An intuitive person is often good at picking up on subconscious cues such as body language, changes in voice tone, and less-than-obvious emotional meaning. An intuitive person may be willing to trust a hunch more than his or her senses.

The most commonly used assessment of types is the *Myers-Briggs Type Indicator* (MBTI; Myers, & McCaulley, 1985), and it includes a fourth dimension, *judging or perceiving*. A person who favors judging will often make a decision based on incomplete information and seek immediate action. A perceiver likes to have as much information as possible before making a decision. A perceiver would be less hasty than a judger in making decisions. Decisions that need to be made quickly might also be a source of a large amount of anxiety for the perceiver. A balanced person might seek as much information as possible, but still be able to make a decision based on incomplete information and adapt later based on new information.

Jungian typology has been used in a wide array of counseling activities and has been found to be useful in counseling centered on helping individuals function in collaboration with others (Douglas, 2005). Helping individuals understand their own and others' typologies is thought to improve a wide range of relationships. Even if people have never heard of Jung, many people have completed the MBTI and are familiar with their own personality type. This widespread knowledge is a testament to the veracity of Jung's theories and work that Jungian analysts since have done to continue his work.

PSYCHOLOGICAL DYSFUNCTION AND THERAPY

Jung believed that a part of human development was the tendency to develop *complexes*. A complex is a particularly sensitive aspect of the personality. A person can develop a complex centering on life events that he or she does not understand or events that are too painful to incorporate into the ego; the complex is formed and relegated to the personal unconscious. Complexes can give rise to symptoms as a person tries to resolve the complicated emotions, sensations, memories, and meaning behind the complex. To alleviate the symptoms a person needs to bring the complex into consciousness and incorporate it into the ego (Casement, 2002).

To take an example, let's say that Peter had an inconsistent relationship with his older sibling, Dan. Much of the time Dan was very nice to Peter, caring for him and having fun with him, but occasionally Dan would get angry and violent and would hit Peter. Peter looked up to Dan, and greatly admired him. Due to Dan's violent outbursts, however, Peter also held strong emotions of fear and anger toward Dan. When Peter was 12, Dan was killed in a car accident. Peter's feelings about Dan's death were too painful to incorporate into his ego, and so the feelings were repressed into the personal unconscious. Now the feelings have become a part of Peter's shadow. As an adult, the emotions now are a complex that may express itself unconsciously in a number of ways throughout Peter's life. For example, Peter may unconsciously sabotage close relationships with mentors. Peter is unconsciously protecting himself from the anticipated loss of the mentor. Peter may also project anxiety and mistrust onto the mentor, making the mentor uncomfortable with the relationship and tempted to end it. Peter's complex is affecting his relationship, but, consciously, it appears to Peter that it is the mentor who is abandoning him. To Peter there is no such thing as a good mentor.

Although Jung's theory of psychotherapy is decidedly psychoanalytic in its focus on the unconscious, early childhood, and transference, it is in many ways similar to humanistic approaches. Jung believed that successful therapist understood four critical principles of psychological functioning (Douglas, 2005).

The first principle was that the psyche is a self-regulating system. The client knows what is needed to heal and to resolve his or her complexes. The second is that the unconscious serves a protective function within the personality, shielding the ego from painful feelings and thoughts. The unconscious is also a source for creativity and inspiration and a resource for understanding the self. The third essential principle is that the counseling relationship plays a major role in successful therapy. Jung's final assertion is that personal growth can occur across the lifespan. Complexes can be created and resolved throughout a person's life.

Jung divided therapy into four stages. Similar to parts in a musical score these stages can be solo, or they can occur together in harmony. The first part of therapy is called *confession*, in which the counselor explores the client's history, ego, and unconscious. The confession stage emphasizes what Carl Rogers would later come to call unconditional positive regard. The counselor explores the client's personality and past in a nonjudgmental way. This acceptance relieves the person of shame and guilt normally associated with hidden aspects of self. Jung indicated that during the confession stage transference will be strong and essential. The client will project onto the counselor many aspects of the self that are currently being explored (Douglas, 2005).

Elucidation, or exploration of the transference is the second stage of therapy, in which the counselor begins to point out to the client the transference and to explore its source. In classical Jungian therapy the counselor explores events in very early childhood, a period ranging from birth to about 4 years old. *Education* is the third stage of therapy, in which the client and counselor begin to implement insight achieved in elucidation through action. Most clients do not reach the fourth stage of therapy, *transformation*. In the transformation stage, the client nears self-actualization. According to Jung, self-actualized people value both conscious and unconscious experiences. People who achieve self-actualization have achieved a balance between their consciousness and unconscious, as well as between the external environment and their internal psyche. Jung believed that self-actualized persons were rare, but he did think it was possible.

Each of these four stages of therapy is woven in, out, and around the melody of the relationship between the counselor and client. Some clients may only engage one of these stages of therapy; other clients may encounter two or three stages of therapy. Reaching the fourth stage of therapy is unusual, and most often occurs with clients that are in their later years of life.

CONCLUSION

Jung's theory focuses on the internal conflicts of an individual as well as the existential meaning of the individual's life. His theories and life are influential partially because of his intense focus on balancing internal struggles with the importance of maintaining a meaningful existence. Jung died in 1961. He had survived two world wars and had seen the growth and development of psychoanalysis, as well as several other schools of psychology. Although some of Jung's ideas have been seriously questioned, Jungian analysts have continued to develop and prosper amongst psychologists today. Through gaining an understanding of Jung's theory of therapy and personality we can catch a glimpse of one of the great contributors to today's psychological world.

Contributed by J. Rico Drake.

EGO PSYCHOLOGY:
ID LOSES THE LIMELIGHT, TEMPORARILY

OVERVIEW

The post-Sigmund history of psychoanalysis begins with Anna Freud. Analyzed by her father in the years 1918–1922, Anna was truly her father's intellectual heir. (More information about Anna Freud can be found at the website of the Anna Freud Center, http://www.annafreudcentre.org/) She is known as one of the founders of child psychoanalysis (along with Melanie Klein) and for her development of theory about defenses. Anna Freud and her intellectual descendents evolved into what is known as the Ego Psychology (EP) school, which dominated American psychoanalysis for many years (Wallerstein, 2002). It was considered very close to traditional psychoanalysis, but added attention to the adaptive functions of the ego, in addition to the defensive ones described by Anna in her landmark book, *The Ego and the Mechanisms of Defense*, 1936.

Another important ego psychologist was Heinz Hartmann. Hartman, who was analyzed by Freud and studied for a while with sociologist Max Weber, contributed several important ideas to EP. His best known book was *Ego Psychology and the Problem of Adaptation* (1939), in which he freed the ego from subservience to superego, and more importantly, from the id. Still, his loyalty to classical drive theory prompted Greenberg and Mitchell (1983) to characterize him as a "transitional figure" and "caught between two models" (pp. 236, 268). Although some might categorize her as an OR theorist, I also include in this section Margaret Mahler's view of psychological development, because it is a well-known model of ego growth. Other important EP writers are Joseph Sandler, Hans Loewald, and Otto Kernberg. However, I discuss Kernberg's work in the OR section, because for the most part, he relies upon these constructs more than he does drive/structural theory.

Wallerstein (2002) writes eloquently of the history of EP in America, the oldest chronologically of the neoanalytic approaches. It ruled American psychoanalysis in the 1950s and 1960s and its proponents deemed themselves qualified to determine who was "analytic" and who was "unanalytic" (the latter being a clear excommunication from the community). Its stranglehold on American psychoanalysis was nudged by Sullivan's interpersonal psychiatry, and really shaken by Kohut's self psychology. As a result, many EP theorists have integrated OR or RP notions into their work (Kernberg, 2005). Wallerstein also describes several modifications of EP traditional EP theory (those proposed by Brenner, Loewald, Kernberg, and Sandler) but it is difficult to decide what is truly the state of EP in American psychology today. Therefore, most of what is presented in this section is traditional EP theory, leaving you to pursue this issue further if you wish.

CENTRAL CONSTRUCTS

Structural Model. EP theorists retain Freud's original structural model, composed of id, ego, and superego, along with the sex and aggressive drives (see Chapter 2). However, whereas in traditional Freudian theory the emphasis was on instincts (drive) and therefore id functioning, in EP theory, the emphasis is on ego functioning. Both Anna Freud and Hartmann were interested in the development of the ego, seeing it as more than a mere product of the need to control id impulses (Quintar, Lane, & Goeltz, 1998). For Hartman, at least, ego develops independently from the id, unlike in Freud's version in which it develops out of the id. The ego is much more alive and energetic in this approach, prompting the use of the term *ego autonomy* in these writings.

Hartman contended that the ego had its own store of energy (separate from id) gained through transforming instinctual into ego energy through a process he called *neutralization* (Fine, 1979). The EPs examined ego functions such as cognition, reality testing, and judgment as well as the defenses described by Anna Freud (Wolitzky, 2005). A special focus in the EP perspective is on how the ego adapts to the environment, which includes id and superego demands as well as those from the external world.

Jezebel, Theo's EP therapist, thinks that Theo is struggling with conflicts between id, ego, and superego. The anger he feels is a transformed version of id impulses, which ego and superego are fighting. Based on his ability to function in college, it appears that Theo's ego function is intact, and to a large extent, adaptive.

Jezebel thinks that she sees evidence of Theo's conflicts in his relationships with Tamia and his parents. His id, with all of its sexual and aggressive energy, is pushing Theo toward the potential gratification offered by Tamia. When she stays out all night partying, Theo worries that she could be with other men, and aggressive id impulses become prominent in his relationship with her. He lashes out in anger. His anger with his parents likely has roots in repressed aggressive impulses as well, particularly toward his father. He rebels against them by refusing to go to an historically Black institution for college.

On the other hand, Theo's superego and ego keep him from acting out the id's impulses. His apparent concern over his difficulty with anger is a sign that his superego is operating. That he comes to counseling is probably the result of these superego commands and the rational decision of the ego to attempt to better function in his current situation.

Defenses. As noted in this chapter, some of Anna Freud's most significant work was in the area of ego defenses. The major forms of defense are listed in this chapter. Anna Freud elaborated on the reasons for defenses in identifying three kinds of danger to the ego: the wrath of the superego, the threat of the drives, and the dangers of the outside world (Monte, 1999). In Box 3.3, you can read about Anna's additional defenses.

Theo seems to be dealing with his aggressive impulses through repression, identification with the aggressor, and displacement. He is well past the Oedipal stage, but his behavior suggests an incomplete resolution of this conflict, and he is still experiencing unresolved aggression toward his father as a result. Rather than expressing this aggression, which would be dangerous, he represses it, but also damps down the drive by identifying with his father, the aggressor, and displacing the aggression onto safer targets, such as Tamia. Jezebel considers

---

Box 3.3

Anna Freud's Defenses

In addition to the defenses formulated by her father, Anna Freud added the following to the list of the ways we escape threatening psychological material:

Denial—rejection of external events that are associated with psychically threatening material

Identification with the Aggressor—becoming like a feared other (as in the Oedipal resolution for boys)

Asceticism—seen mostly in adolescents. Adolescents are so threatened by their emerging sexual desires that they renounce all desires or pleasures

Altruistic Surrender—gratifying one's own desires through the fulfillment of another's; sort of a mix of projection and identification

Turning-against-self—redirecting threatening impulses against the self rather than into the environment

Reversal—changing into the opposite

Isolation—removing emotion or meaning from events

Undoing—associated with obsessive-compulsive types; use of rituals to cancel threatening thoughts or behaviors

Adapted from Monte, 1999, pp. 204–207.

that Theo sees himself as an angry person because he identifies with his father, the Oedipal aggressor. However, he displaces his anger onto Tamia and other safer targets, such as peers and faculty members who frustrate him even in the smallest ways.

Conflict-Free Sphere. Contributed by Hartmann (1939), this construct concerns the EP assumption that not all of psychological life is driven by conflict between the environment, id, ego, and superego. According to this view, there are areas of ego function that are independent of the id and superego, such as thinking, perception, memory, and learning (Fine, 1979; Greenberg & Mitchell, 1983).

Jezebel observes that Theo is able to function in a wide range of circumstances, indicating the function of his ego in the conflict-free zone. His anger has not created enough problems to jeopardize his standing in school. It has, however, put his relationship with Tamia in peril, so the adaptive aspects of his ego have prompted him to enter counseling.

Average Expectable Environment. Hartmann also added the concept of the *average expectable environment* to EP theory (Fine, 1979). If the average expectable environment exists, the infant, who is born with the capacity to adapt to and use this kind of environment, will grow in healthy ways. If the infant is born into a situation that does not meet this level of support, problems ensue. For example, if a mother is depressed, she will fail to attend to and nurture her infant; this neglect will lead to psychological (and possibly physical) deficits in later life.

Although it is not totally clear from Theo's presentation, Jezebel thinks that there may have been some deficits in his early environment, which led to the inadequate resolution of the Oedipal conflict. However, she expects that his very early environment was sufficient for him to grow and develop to a large extent. Departures from the average expectable environment could include lapses in attention from his mother, perhaps because of the disruptive, conflicted relationship with his father.

THEORY OF THE PERSON

The early EPs essentially adopted Freud's developmental and personality theory in toto. So, they follow the psychosexual model of development, with all its implications, such as the assumption that personality is formed by the ways in which the child's instincts are gratified (or not; see Chapter 2) and the phallic stage as a critical developmental phase. Later EPs started paying more attention to earlier stages of development (such as in Mahler's writing, described next).

Although Anna Freud theorized about child development with her work on developmental lines, Mahler's work has remained more prominent historically. Mahler described the "psychological birth of the infant," contending that "the biological birth of the human infant and the psychological birth of the individual are not coincident in time. The former is a dramatic and readily observable, and well-circumscribed event; the latter a slowly unfolding intrapsychic process" (Mahler, 1972, p. 333). Beginning at about the 4th month of life and completed around age 3, development in this model is the progression from symbiosis to separation and individuation.

In the first month after birth, the infant is in the state of *normal autism*, in which he can't differentiate between self and mother. In classical terms, the infant is in a state of absolute primary narcissism (St. Clair, 2000). Around the second month, what Mahler called *normal symbiosis* begins, in which the infant becomes increasingly aware of the mother but as a part of him, not a separate identity. The infant is fused with the mother. If the mothering is good enough, the four subphases of separation and individuation begin around 4–5 months. First, the child enters the *Differentiation and Body Image* period, in which he gradually tolerates physical distance from the mother, but can be seen to check back to mother to orient himself.

The next subphase is *Practicing*, which begins as the child learns to walk. The peak of this phase is when the child can walk by himself upright and thus gains a totally new perspective on the world. The child is, at this point, egotistical and narcissistic, as can be seen in the typical "no" period that is often observed in children of this age. NO! screams the infant in response to the parent's directive, the ultimate sign of independence.

If parenting is adequate, at about 17 months, the child returns to earth and recognizes that he can't really be alone without the parent. He experiences separation anxiety. This event heralds the onset of the *Rapprochement* subphase, during which the relationship with the mother is ambivalent. The child's newly found autonomy conflicts with his separation anxiety. In crisis, the child vacillates between closeness and autonomy. This crisis peaks between 18 and 24 months.

The final phase of development is called *Emotional Object Constancy and Individuality*. In this subphase, the child internalizes a positive mother image so that he can truly be separate from her. This subphase has no defined endpoint, and involves ego and superego elaboration.

Jezebel thinks that Theo has negotiated the phases of separation and individuation fairly successfully. He appears to have an elaborated ego and superego, and to be struggling with conflicts more from the Oedipal situation than with earlier ones. However, another way of seeing Theo's presentation might be that he is indeed experiencing difficulties resulting from early development that led to the inadequate resolution of the Oedipal conflict. The angry, ambivalent relationship with Tamia is in essence the recreation of the relationship he has with his mother. He gets angry at her when she "disappears" on him, suggesting that he is stuck in the rapprochement subphase; he has some strong but mixed feelings about his mother and father. Perhaps both explanations are useful, thinks Jezebel, in helping Theo.

HEALTH AND DYSFUNCTION

EP theorists, for the most part, accept the version of psychological health proposed by Freud: healthy repression of instinctual drives, the ability to love and work, and so on (see Chapter 2). They would add that health is observed in the quality of the ego's adaptation to the environment (Wolitzky, 2005). Also like Freud, the EPs consider the Oedipal complex as the source of much dysfunction. However, the views of many EP theorists seem to foreshadow the OR theorists in that they emphasize the quality of the very early stages of life and the adequacy of the environment around the infant. Problems in the early environment can cause dysfunction later in life. For example, Mahler contended that if the mother does not provide a secure enough base for the developing child, the child will show problems in establishing independence, or in EP terms, developing an autonomous ego. For Hartmann, if the average expectable environment is not present, the child's development will be compromised.

Brenner (1982) proposed that behavior is a function of *compromise formations*. Conflict is found in the interplay of four psychic motivations: the pressure of the drives, the push of the superego, the ego's motivation to adapt to reality (i.e., the external world) and the ego's need to avoid or minimize anxiety and depression. To integrate the OR perspective, Brenner indicates that all object relations are a product of the negotiation of these forces; in essence, relationships and their internalized representations are compromise formations (Wallerstein, 2002).

Jezebel judges that Theo shows adequate ego and superego development, although he is displaying some oedipal issues that result in compromise formations through the use of less than optimal defenses such as displacement, displacement of aggression, and identification with the aggressor. To some extent, the defensive functions allow gratification of sexual and aggressive instincts in modified forms directed at less-than-threatening entities (e.g., colleagues and Tamia). However, that Theo is feeling badly enough to seek counseling suggests that the sheer amount of energy (perhaps evoked by the stresses of the college environment) is threatening to overwhelm Theo and damage the delicate balance of the compromise. If this happens, Theo's superego threatens, he would be annihilated.

NATURE OF THERAPY

Assessment. Very little formal assessment is used in an EP approach (Wolitzky, 2005). Instead, the clinical interview serves as the primary mode of assessment, with the intent of observing current and past functioning and to gain information regarding defensive operations and core unconscious conflicts contributing to the client's current presentation. However, as in traditional analysis, the counselor is simultaneously determining the suitability of the client for psychoanalytic therapy. Formal diagnosis (i.e., DSM-IV-TR) may be used, but the psychoanalytic therapist is really more interested in underlying dynamics than client symptoms (Wolitzky, 2005).

Jezebel concludes that Theo is a good candidate for psychoanalytic therapy. She is not concerned about formulating a DSM diagnosis for Theo. She is more interested in observing how he interacts with her, and his descriptions of his everyday life. She is looking for clues to his psychological dynamics, observing that although he is docile in the early interviews, his descriptions of anger in other aspects of his life suggest conflicted dynamics.

Overview of the Therapeutic Atmosphere and Roles of Client and Counselor. It seems difficult to summarize the EP orientation to therapy. In some sources, EPs appear to adopt the neutral, objective stance of the classic analysts in their work. This stance would be taken by a traditional EP counselor, and implies a doctor-patient model, in which the expert therapist interprets the material provided by the client (Wolitzky, 2005). However, other interpretations see the EPs moving away from the authoritarian model. For example, Mitchell and Black (1995) indicate that the EP understanding of the resilience of the ego leads these therapists to be interested in enlisting the client as an ally in therapy, who contributes significantly to the work of understanding unconscious material. The latter orientation might suggest a more egalitarian approach to client-counselor roles.

Buckley (2003) maintained that although Hartman's influence led to an austere, abstinent therapist as in the classic analytic model, later theorists in the EP group proposed a more interactive model of therapy. For example, Buckley interprets Loewald (1989) as promoting the idea that psychoanalysis produces ego development through internalization of the relationship between therapist and client, implying a more constructivist view of the process.

A contemporary EP therapist, Jezebel approaches Theo with a warm and friendly manner. She recognizes the importance of his collaboration in the therapeutic endeavor. Theo responds in kind, discussing his anger somewhat uncomfortably.

Goals. EP therapists still accept Freud's original goal of psychoanalysis: to make the unconscious (most importantly, the repressed) conscious (Greenberg and Mitchell, 1983). However, they would add that a second important goal of EP therapy is to improve the client's adaptation to her world (Wolitzky, 2005).

Jezebel hopes that when he is finished with therapy that Theo can understand the unconscious roots of his behaviors and the defenses he uses to cope with the unconscious conflicts. He will gain insight into the anger he feels toward both of his parents, and how he repressed the real roots of this anger in the attempt to protect his fledgling psychological structure. She also intends to try to help him to adapt better to his environment and hopes that his insight into his dynamics will carry into future situations.

PROCESS OF THERAPY

Therapy in a EP model changes depending upon which variant of EP one is reading. Anna Freud seemed to be most interested in classical technique: analyzing defense and transference (Freud, 1936). Other EPs see the transference as recreating early relationships and emphasized the emotional support or empathy provided therein (Mitchell & Black, 1995).

In classical EP tradition, the client free associates and the analyst interprets. *Transference* is considered very important. *Countertransference* is considered a very bad thing (see Chapter 2).

Jezebel attends to the interpersonal process that she and Theo create, but is also aware that she needs to observe and interpret drive-related processes. She is aware, as a result of her own training analysis, of her tendencies to countertransference and guards against these.

THERAPEUTIC TECHNIQUES

Techniques in a traditional EP approach are the same as in classic psychoanalysis. Free association, interpretation (particularly of the transference), and dream analysis are the mainstays. However, it is interesting that that free association came to be recognized as a goal of analysis, not a technique, for the EPs emphasized the pervasiveness of ego defense processes, both outside and within the therapeutic relationship (Mitchell & Black, 1995). In this respect, Anna Freud commented:

> Even today many beginners in analysis have an idea that it is essential to succeed in inducing their patients really and invariably to give all other associations without modification or inhibition, i.e., to obey implicitly the fundamental rule of analysis . . . such docility in the patient is in practice impossible. The fundamental rule can never be followed beyond a certain point. The ego keeps silence for a time and the id derivatives make use of this pause to force their way into consciousness. The analyst hastens to catch their utterances. Then the ego bestirs itself again, repudiates the attitude of passive tolerance which it has been compelled to assume, and by means of one or other of its customary defense mechanisms intervenes in the flow of associations. (1966, pp. 13–14)

Jezebel asks Theo to talk about whatever occurs to him. As he does, she looks for evidence of defenses operating and then, for indications of the accompanying underlying conflicts. As she becomes fairly confident about her hypotheses, she offers them to Theo in the form of interpretations, first of the defenses and later of the underlying conflictual themes. Theo initially talks quite a bit about his anger with Tamia, and then shifts gradually to speaking about his parents and early experience with them. It takes a while for this shift to happen, because Theo's defenses are operating. As he begins to address his early experiences, his emotions become more vivid and eventually, Theo's anger becomes directed at Jezebel. She carefully begins to interpret these processes so that Theo can gain insight into them.

OBJECT RELATIONS: THE LEGO APPROACH

OVERVIEW

Within the object relations group there are several important theorists. Most spectacular was Melanie Klein, who was considered a heretic by the psychoanalytic establishment as represented by Anna Freud and her followers. She accepted drive theory, but still emphasized the importance psychic representations of relationships and primitive fantasy, particularly aggressive urges. Her ideas were considered so deviant that in the late 1920s, the European psychoanalytic world split into the London school (Klein and her followers) and the Viennese school (Anna Freud et al.). Still, Klein is seen as having a major impact on psychoanalysis, even as it is practiced today (Mitchell & Black, 1995). You can read more about the controversy surrounding Klein and Anna Freud in Box 3.4.

Other important OR names are R. D. Fairbairn, and Donald Winnicott. In terms of allegiance to drive theory, Fairbairn was probably the most radical of the OR group, for he theorized that drives were directed at objects, not simply at the pleasure of expressing the drive or some combination of object-seeking and drive release. Fairbarn, Klein, and associates were considered to be of the British school of object relations, but Klein and her followers are generally considered distinct enough to be referred to as Kleinians. Eventually, an American school developed, and the most prominent of writers in this realm was Otto Kernberg.

At first, the term *object* may seem a little odd in a theory that deals with people, but it stems directly from Freud's use of it to describe the targets of the instincts. In traditional theory, the most important objects are people, who can satisfy libidinal or aggressive urges. The object relations theorists generally reject classic drive theory and instead argue that we

Box 3.4

Melanie Klein and Anna Freud: Feuding Leaders
of the Development of Child Analysis

In 1927, Sigmund Freud wrote a stern letter to his colleague and eventual biographer, Ernest Jones. In this letter, Freud accused Jones, then president of the British Psycho-Analysis Society, of masterminding a campaign against his daughter, Anna Freud (Paskauskas, 1988). Freud reprimanded Jones for publishing the proceedings of the Symposium on Child-Analysis in the *International Journal of Psycho-Analysis* (of which Jones was the editor). Freud maintained that the publication of the proceedings demonstrated that Jones and the British Psycho-Analysis Society favored Melanie Klein's version of psychoanalysis over Anna Freud's (Klein et al., 1927) and he labeled Jones' criticisms of Anna's child analysis as "impermissible" (Paskauskas, 1988, p. 624).

Jones' criticism of Anna Freud's child analysis techniques and praise for Klein's led Freud to wonder whether Ernest Jones' condemnation of Anna Freud was really directed at him (Paskauskas, 1988). However, Ernest Jones was not the only psychoanalyst siding with Klein. A decade before the Symposium was published, those who championed child analysis began gradually dividing into two separate camps, one commanded by Melanie Klein and the other by Anna Freud. Whereas British Psychoanalysts in London accepted Klein's theories of child analysis, Viennese analysts supported Anna Freud's techniques (Donaldson, 1996).

Freud's scolding led Ernest Jones to defend his decision to publish the Symposium. Jones stated that he was simply attempting to ensure a fair hearing of both Melanie Klein's and Anna Freud's sides of the argument (Paskauskas, 1988). He contended that the imbalance resulted from the refusal of the other major psychoanalytic journal, *International Zeitschrift fur Psychoanalyse*, to publish Klein's work. By publishing the Symposium in his *International Journal of Psycho-Analysis*, Ernest Jones was trying to allow Melanie Klein the chance to more broadly defend her theories against the assault of Anna Freud.

Born in Vienna in 1882, Melanie Klein, along with Anna Freud, is among the most influential women psychoanalysts in the history of the discipline. Her contributions were primarily to developmental theory and specifically regarding the analysis of children. In response to Ernest Jones' urging, Melanie Klein began to work on her developing theories in London (Grosskurth, 1986), when in early 1927, Anna Freud published the *Introduction to the Technique of Child Analysis* (Freud, 1974). In her book, Anna attacked Klein's methods of child analysis, giving them the dreaded label of "un-Freudian" (Donaldson, 1996, p. 160). As a result, the Symposium of Child-Analysis was organized for Melanie Klein to respond to Anna Freud's criticisms.

In creating their theories of child analysis, Melanie Klein and Anna Freud drew from different components of Sigmund Freud's work: developmental theory versus therapeutic techniques. Anna Freud focused on Freud's theory of child development, concluding that the traditional analytic techniques applied to adults could not be applied to children because adult psychoanalysis is based on the interpretation of the patient's free associations and free association requires a level of linguistic capabilities that children have not yet acquired. Therefore, she developed a new therapeutic technique, a pedagogical form of child analysis that had the goal of developing and strengthening a child's ego in hopes of repressing the impulses of the id (Freud, 1974). Anna's theory presented no challenge to Freud's theory of the psychic development of the child.

In contrast, Melanie Klein chose to incorporate adult analytic techniques into child analysis, focusing on Freud's clinical practices and modifying his theories of development. In fact, part of what was so controversial was that Klein posited that consideration of the death instinct should be incorporated into theorizing about the development of the superego, which she saw as emerging prior to the resolution of the Oedipus complex. Through the analysis of her own children and the children of colleagues, Melanie Klein observed a harsh and punitive superego that emerged very early on, and she theorized that a child's relationship with the mother is the foundation of this entity, not the Oedipal complex as Sigmund Freud had contended (St. Clair, 2004). Klein thought that the aggressive tendencies that the child experienced during the oral and anal stages were evidence of the child's sadistic fantasies (related to the aggressive instincts) that were projected onto the mother and then introjected as hostile objects (Klein, 1926). Through projective identification, these punitive introjects became the superego.

Klein also believed that in an analytic session, a full transference relationship was created between the child and analyst. Specifically, Klein contended that the negative transferences were particularly important because the child's hostile and aggressive impulses were what brought the child to analysis to begin with. Klein believed that in order to make therapeutic progress, the analyst must interpret (sometimes forcefully) the negative transference and bring it to the forefront (Donaldson, 1996). In response, Anna Freud criticized Melanie Klein's ideas, saying that Klein's method of analyzing a child's aggressive fantasies was dangerous because the child's developing ego is not strong enough to deal with bringing aggressive impulses out of the unconsciousness (Freud, 1974).

Melanie Klein gave the opening paper in the fateful Symposium, in which she describe her views of Anna Freudian child analysis, attacking some of the central aspects of Anna's theory (Klein, 1927). Klein maintained that focusing on the child ego and relying on an educative approach was inadvisable because it leads children to repress hostile impulses, negating the goal of therapy. Klein also posited that ignoring the Oedipus complex prevents the analyst from uncovering the child's source of anxiety (Klein, 1927). The paper ended with Melanie Klein claiming that her own approach was superior to Anna Freud's, because her technique achieved a stronger and more lasting analysis of the child compared to Anna Freud's techniques (Klein, 1927). After Klein presented, other speakers gave shorter presentations commending her approach. Ernest Jones' closing speech made it evident which child psychoanalyst he personally supported, giving the British Psycho-Analytic Society's final vote of approval to Kleinian child analysis (Jones, 1927). The publication of the proceedings then cemented the split between Kleinism and Freudianism that endured for years (Donaldson, 1996).

Contributed by Ashley Heintzelman.

seek objects (mostly other people) in and of themselves, not as means to satisfying instinctual drives as Freud thought (Wolitzky & Eagle, 1997). Because the object-seeking process begins very early in life, the object relations writers focus on early developmental stages (pre-Oedipal) and the mother-child relationship.

CENTRAL CONSTRUCTS

Objects. The term object is used in several ways in OR theory, and this is part of the difficulty in reading these theorists. The first use refers to *external* objects, things and people in the environment (Hamilton, 1988). Ultimately, the most important type of object is the *internal* object, a psychological structure, formed through the internalization of interactions with important others, early in life (Scharff & Scharff, 1995). The first object of interest is the breast. Internalized objects become part of the developing child's self and the quality of the child's relationships with them, particularly affecting the attachment to them, determine the functioning of the individual.

Kernberg called internal representations of relationships *bipolar intrapsychic representations* (Cashdan, 1988). These are composed of three elements: an image of the self, an image of the other person, and associated emotions (Cashdan, 1988, p. 17). The emotion associated with the internalized object contributed to the development of the instinctual drives, according to Kernberg.

Paul is Theo's object relations therapist. He speculates on the nature of Theo's internal world, trying to sense the nature of the objects that populate it. He thinks that Theo's parents are certainly represented, as are his siblings. He has a self representation as well. Anger is clearly attached to these representations, evidence of the aggressive drive. Sexual urges are likely associated with Theo's internal representations of his mother and Tamia.

Projection. Projection, along with introjection and splitting are, according to OR theorists, initially ways of relating to the breast and the primitive emotions associated with it (St. Clair, 2000). The aim of these defenses is to protect self-integrity and at the same time, the attachment object (Hamilton, 1989, p. 1553). Initially concerned with the relations with breast and mother, these processes then generalize to other objects (people) important to the infant.

Projection is seen when the feelings associated with the object are fused with the object and projected into the external world so that they are safer. The happy infant who has just had a meal projects these feelings onto the breast and it becomes the good breast. Likewise, the hungry, angry infant associates these feelings with another breast, the bad one. Mothers and other important individuals in the infant's experience become good and bad in the same way.

Paul believes that Theo may project his anger with his mother's unsatisfying breast onto her and his father. He sees them as angry with him for a number of reasons (e.g., his choice of college), but this anger is really Theo's primitive anger with the unsatisfying breast projected onto them so that it is less threatening.

Introjection. A second way to make a scary world safe is to take the bad aspects of it and internalize them so that they can be controlled. Introjection is the term used by Klein to describe this process, and although it makes the external world safer, it is problematic because it creates a scary internal world for the infant. Some theorists would say that good objects are introjected as well.

Paul wonders if Theo has introjected the bad breast. The anger he shows may be the anger at the bad breast but the projection has resulted in these feelings becoming unconscious and thus liable to pop out in his current life. For example, his anger at Tamia could be a result of this process.

Splitting. Splitting is another process by which the infant manages good and bad affect (Cashdan, 1988). It is a normal process by which dangerous feelings, objects, and impulses are separated from pleasant ones and this makes them easier for the infant to manage. The infant's good and bad emotion is at first not associated with any specific object; however, the breast (or bottle) quickly becomes the first object. When the breast satisfies the infant's hunger, it is good; when it doesn't, it is bad. This process broadens so that people can be good or bad, most notably early on, the mother. Moms aren't perfect, and so it is inevitable that they will fail to gratify the infant and become partly bad. To deal with the anxiety associated with experiencing both the good and the frustrating breast/mother, the infant psychologically introjects and then splits the two and so has an inner world populated by good and bad objects. Infants tend to repress the bad mom, making the conscious version of her an idealized one (Cashdan, 1988). Parts of the ego associated with these painful objects are repressed as well. Fairbairn contended that the repressed bad object is further split into the *rejecting* and *exciting* objects (Scharff & Scharff, 1985). Rejecting objects are associated with aggressive urges and exciting with sexual, or libidinal, drives.

Paul thinks that Theo's splitting mechanisms have broken down, possibly as a result of the stress of being in college and his unsuccessful attempts to attach to Tamia. The anger associated with the repressed portions of the objects (of the breast, mother, and father), is surfacing, and is directed toward other objects. That is, some repression is still functioning, keeping the real objects of the angry feelings (i.e, the breast and parents) in the unconscious.

Projective Identification. Another protective function described by the OR theorists is projective identification, and it is surely one that is difficult to grasp. Originally described by Klein, this process begins when the infant projects some scary feelings outward onto another object (such as the breast or the mother). However, these dangerous impulses are now outside and uncontrollable. The only solution is to continue to relate to the scary object by taking them back inside the self, through internalization. The bad object thus becomes a part of the infant. Although most often discussed in terms of scary/dangerous impulses, projective identification can also involve positive feelings, such as when drives are satisfied (St. Clair, 2004). Cashdan (1988) goes on to indicate that this process induces the target of this process to feel and behave in ways consistent with the projective identification.

Through projective identification, Theo has taken the bad breast into his self. The excitement and frustration he feels related to his mother's inconsistent support has resulted in both sexual and angry feelings attached to these objects, but these feelings are too threatening to leave outside of him. Similarly, Theo has identified with his father, who abandoned the family early on. The anger Theo feels related to the abandonment is thus directed back at himself and is also bleeding out into his other relationships.

THEORY OF THE PERSON AND DEVELOPMENT OF THE INDIVIDUAL

The process of development, according to the OR theorists, is from a primitive, pristine self through fragmentation to whole experiencing—the infant, if given the correct environment, gradually develops the capacity to resolve splitting and to integrate the various internal objects into wholes. The self is inherent in the human condition and present at birth (Scharff & Scharff, 1995). It develops thorough interaction with others, building psychic structure through the internalization of objects.

Klein's view of infant development is one beset with turmoil. You can read a bit of her writing on this topic in Box 3.1. The infant first experiences anxiety because the death instinct threatens annihilation of the infant self; this situation is accompanied by feelings of persecution (Klein, 1952). Simultaneously, the feeding and care of the mother result in the internalization and idealization of the good object, the breast. The feelings of persecution and wishes to destroy are projected to the bad breast, which withholds from the infant. To deal with these intense emotions, the infant splits them into two internal objects. The infant vacillates between these states, shifting from love to hate and aggression, the latter feelings producing anxiety and guilt. Simultaneously, these are both external objects, as are mother (to which the breast eventually generalizes), and eventually, the father. This phase occurs in the first 6 months of the infant's life and is referred to as the *paranoid-schizoid* position.

Around 6 months, according to Klein, the infant begins to perceive the mother as a whole person, and as the good and bad objects begin to synthesize, realizes that the aggressive, hateful emotions associated with the bad breast are directed at her. This development brings on the *depressive* position because the child recognizes his terrible hate and aggression toward the mother object and wishes to repair the relationship (Scharff & Scharff, 1997). Associated with the depressive position, in Klein's view, is the beginning of the Oedipus complex, with its associated feelings of love, aggression, guilt, and anxiety (Klein, 1952).

Klein thought that we never really outgrow these two positions—we struggle to resolve these issues throughout life. However, healthy people tend to function more out of the depressive than the paranoid-schizoid position (Scharff & Scharff, 1997).

Paul sees Theo's present functioning as resulting from his early experience with his parents, particularly his mother. He is probably standing in the depressive position, because he seems to function fairly well in his life. However, the uncontrollable anger he reports could be associated with the paranoid-schizoid position; possibly he never fully made the transition out of this stage and cycles back to it periodically. He may be experiencing Oedipal feelings about his father, and his anger at his mother could be the result of his conflicting feelings of anger and love for her, never resolved. Later, when she agreed to reunite with his father, she symbolically deprived Theo of Oedipal satisfaction.

Winnicott, who styled himself as a follower of Klein, had quite a bit to say about child development. He coined the engaging term "good enough mother" to describe a mom that mostly met the infant's needs, one who created (or is) a safe *holding environment* (Mitchell & Black, 1995). The mother's role involves two processes. First, she ensures that the infant's needs are met and in doing so, allows the infant to believe that she has created needed objects, which helps the infant develop an associated degree of omnipotence necessary for ego development. Second, mother allows the infant periods of quiet time. Failure to provide either of these results in fragmentation of the self, for the self develops out of the gradual reconciliation of internal and external realities.

An interesting and unique contribution of Winnecott is the idea of the *transitional object*. A transitional object is something inanimate, like a teddy bear or blanket, and in the words of Greenberg and Mitchell (1983), these entities provide "a developmental way station between hallucinatory omnipotence and the recognition of objective reality" (p. 195). The child in his omnipotence believes that he's created the bear because he desires it. The parent goes along with this notion but at the same time, the object is a real one that exists in the external world. This ambiguity helps the child make the transition from fantasy to interacting with a real world.

Paul considers Theo from Winnicott's perspective and guesses that his mother did not provide an adequate holding environment, for his anger is evidence that he has not consolidated his objects into a sense of self. Because Theo's mother and father were embroiled in their fights (likely resulting from their own faulty object relations), quiet times were few, and the constant fighting distracted his parents so much that they to some extent neglected his needs. It is too threatening to deal with the anger attached to his mother, so the internalized object associated with her is likely split, and the bad part repressed.

Theo still has his battered old panda bear who was his chum as a small child. He still has warm feelings when he glances at Rudy, who is on a shelf in his bedroom.

Fairbairn and other later OR theorists saw development as the process of resolving the twin pulls of individuation and attachment to others (Hamilton, 1989). In Fairbairn's view, infants' strong emotions are threatening (they might overwhelm the nascent sense of self), so they externalize these emotions onto the parents. If the parent can accept the emotion (in Fairbairn's terms, to contain it) and still maintain a bond with the infant (creating a *holding environment*), the infant will eventually learn how to do this himself (Hamilton, 1989).

Paul thinks from Fairbairn's perspective: Theo has likely externalized his anger at his mother's compromised ability to form a bond with him onto both of his parents. That's why he is so angry with their fighting.

HEALTH AND DYSFUNCTION

Broadly speaking, OR theorists see psychological dysfunction as the result of faulty early development, with an emphasis on the object relations that result from less-than-optimal parenting (i.e., bad mothering). For instance, Fairbairn thought that infants repressed threatening objects, but these have effects on the individual nonetheless. The individual is essentially doing away with aspects of the self, yet this repression leaves feelings of frustration and negative feelings about the self. The person then becomes terrified of abandonment, and when threatened with it reacts with rage or extreme neediness (Cashdan, 1988).

From Winnicott's perspective, failures of the mother to provide a holding environment cause the child to experience *impingement*. The mother either fails the child in the area of omnipotence or in providing quiet time to consolidate. Development stops, and the child doesn't develop a healthy core sense of self. Instead, the child develops a false self in order to deal with the external world and also to protect what little self has developed (Greenberg & Mitchell, 1983).

Kernberg saw dysfunction as stemming from a lack of integration of object representations, or in his rather ungainly term, *unmetabolized bipolar intrapsychic representations* (Cashdan, 1988). Difficulty in the integration process is typically due to excessive, defensive splitting. For example, Kernberg writes a lot about individuals who display borderline personality organization, or borderline personality disorder, in DSM-IV-TR terminology. He sees these individuals as harboring a lot of negative affect, mostly aggression, which is intolerable and has to be split off (Levy et al., 2006).

One controversial aspect of Kernberg's theory is that this aggression can be the result of either constitutional (i.e., inherited) or environmental forces (e.g., experiences of abuse). Whatever their origin, these feelings result in a negative emotional tenor that dominates interpersonal relationships, and thus, negative objects (actually part-objects) are internalized. The object representations can't be integrated into the self, resulting in *identity diffusion*, Kernberg's diagnostic label. In Kernberg's words "identity diffusion is represented by a poorly integrated concept of the self and of significant others. It is reflected in the subjective experience of chronic emptiness, contradictory self-perceptions, contradictory behavior that cannot be integrated in an emotionally meaningful way, and shallow, flat, impoverished perceptions of others" (1984; p. 12). The self is fragile and constantly shifting between good and bad states. These shifts also appear in how these individuals deal with other people in their lives; they alternate between seeing people as very bad and very good and behave in ways that convey these perceptions.

Paul sees Theo as having internalized the bad objects created by his parents' treatment of him and the environment that their conflicted relationship created. These feelings have mostly been repressed, but the stress that Theo experiences in having to grow up and negotiate the complex interpersonal environment of college is taking its toll. He hasn't developed a healthy self, or set of integrated internal objects. He has used the defenses of projection, introjection, and splitting to manage the inadequacies of his early environment, but these defenses are breaking down and his anger is beginning to surface. The surfacing of the anger is scary for Theo—it is powerful, and unconsciously Theo fears that if it comes out, it will destroy important objects, most significantly, his parents.

NATURE OF THERAPY

Assessment. OR therapists are not likely to use any formal assessment. As with most analysts, they are more interested in observing the client's behaviors and verbal content as clues to underlying dynamic processes.

Paul simply listens to Theo and tries to get a sense of his internal world. He closely observes Theo's reactions to him and listens carefully to his stories of his stormy relationship with Tamia and others. Paul is looking for clues to Theo's object relations.

Overview of the Therapeutic Atmosphere and Roles of Client and Counselor. Like the ER theorists, OR therapists look very much like orthodox psychoanalysts when they do therapy. However, they are more likely to attend to the environment of therapy than do classic analysts—they see the therapy relationship as replicating the early relationship with the caregiver.

Again, however, Klein stands out. According to Walker (1957), Klein's approach to therapy was influenced by her work with children, and differed from classic analysis in the following ways. First, she emphasized the early phases of experience, because she was convinced that neuroses were seated much earlier than did Freud, and probably in the oral phases of development. As noted earlier, Klein was much more interested in the aggressive impulses of the client. She advocated the early use of very deep interpretation (Walker, 1957); instead of proceeding from surface to depth, she would offer interpretations based on early developmental dynamics much sooner than would a traditional analyst. Mitchell and Black (1995) characterize the relationship between analyst and client in Kleinian therapy as

> much more fundamentally enmeshed than in Freud's view. It is not as if the patient is simply revealing the contents of her own mind to a generally neutral (except when distracted by countertransference) observer; the patient experiences the analytic situation in terms of her primitive object relations. At times, the analyst is a good breast, magically transformative; interpretations are good milk, protective, nurturing, restorative. At times, the analyst is a bad breast, deadly and destructive; interpretations are poisonous, destroying from within if ingested. (p. 107)

Winnicott saw the analytic situation as providing the holding environment that the client did not experience as an infant (or they otherwise wouldn't be a client). The therapist should avoid impinging on the client so that the true self can then safely emerge and replace the false self (Kernberg, 1984; Mitchell & Black, 1995). Likewise, Fairbairn thought that analytic change emerged from the new relationship established with the analyst (Mitchell & Black, 1995).

Of recent interest among contemporary analysts is the notion of the therapist's authority in the analytic situation and associated discussions of therapeutic neutrality. Kernberg (1996) addresses this issue, and contends that therapists must retain their authority based on education, training, and skills, but they must also recognize their own input into the therapeutic relationship. He writes "technical neutrality, in short, does not imply anonymity, and natural behavior does not imply that the analyst is not in a consistent, stable, professional role relationship with the patient. Nor does technical neutrality imply that the psychoanalyst's personality will not influence the patient, in the same way as the patient necessarily will influence the analyst through countertransference reactions" (p. 146).

Paul takes a moderate approach to Theo, trying to establish a stable, safe therapeutic environment with him. He realizes that who he is will affect Theo, but also is alert for evidence that suggests that Theo's object relations are surfacing in the therapeutic relationship.

Goals. For OR theorists, good therapy will restore healthy object relations and thus a solid sense of self. Winnicott saw the goal of therapy as development of the self. Fairbairn's goal was for the client to develop new ways of relating to others, ways that were not tied to the faulty patterns the client brought to therapy. Kernberg would see the goal of therapy as the integration of the part-objects within the self, and the resulting abilities to maintain a continuous sense of self and others, empathize with them, and reflect on one's own experience (Levy et al., 2006).

Paul hopes that Theo will be able to withstand the necessary surfacing of his internal object world so that he can build a more integrated sense of self through the therapeutic work they will do. He anticipates that it will take a while for Theo to be able to deal directly with the emotions associated with his parents because they are so scary, so he begins with Theo's current relationships, which are the topics of his early free association.

Process of Therapy

OR therapists are very interested in *insight*. However, with clients who display severe dysfunction, the kind of insight expected is a little different than that expected with typical neurotic clients. As noted in text that follows, transference interpretations with the former clients are restricted initially to here-and-now events, implying that insight is first about the dynamics of the therapy relationship; later, the focus becomes historical events.

OR theorists are also very interested in *transference* phenomena. They accept that clients will bring to therapy their old ways of relating, and will unconsciously recreate early relationships in the relationship with the analyst. For instance, Fairbairn thought that as hard as the client tried to do otherwise, he eventually comes to experience the therapist as "the old, bad object" (Mitchell & Black, 1995 p. 122) from earlier relationships.

In classical analysis, the therapist deals with the transference objectively, interpreting the transference to the client from an unemotional, neutral standpoint (unless the therapist is a bad analyst, caught up in countertransference). Some of the OR theorists, such as Klein, accepted this idea of the therapist's role. For example, Kernberg characterized analysis as having three key components: (a) the analyst's technical neutrality; (b) the use of interpretation; (c) a goal of developing of a full-fledged transference neurosis, which is resolved through interpretation. Even in maintaining technical neutrality, however, Kernberg (1984) advocates warmth and empathy, and further, that the therapist must be able to empathize with what the client can't deal with in himself.

Kernberg acknowledged working with relatively disturbed individuals made technical neutrality difficult to maintain, due to the strong negative transference displayed by these clients. As a result, he recommended that early in therapy, transference interpretations be confined to only immediate therapeutic situation; genetic interpretations (those based on the client's developmental history) are saved for the later stages of therapy. Acting out of the transference, both within and outside of therapy, is to be blocked, sometimes requiring the therapist to sacrifice neutrality to make directive interventions. Positive transference is not to be interpreted; instead it is used to build the working alliance (Kernberg, 1984).

For OR theorists, what happens in transference with the more severely disturbed clients is best explained by the nature of the primitive defenses they need to employ to protect their fragile selves. Noting that these primarily negative transferences seem to develop really quickly, Kernberg thought that projective identification was behind them (St. Clair, 2004). The client, because of his unintegrated internalized objects, brings in to therapy the aggressive, scary object representations of the parents left over from early experiences, and projects these onto the therapist. As a result, the client does not trust the therapist, and fears him. The client may then attempt to protect the self in one of two ways: either by being hostile and sadistic, or reacting like a frightened child.

Countertransference is seen as an aid to understanding the client (Scharff & Scharff, 1995). Because the client projects his disordered object relationships into the analytic situation, the therapist's reaction to the client becomes diagnostic information about the client's internal dynamics and ways of operating. However, in relation to the more severely disturbed clients, the shifting and mostly negative aspects of the transference can elicit corresponding aggressive and hostile responses on the part of the therapist (Kernberg, 1996; St. Clair, 2004). Kernberg (1996) recommends ongoing peer consultation as a way for the therapist to examine his input into the transference.

Paul hopes that he can help Theo understand the relation between his early experiences and his current relationship problems. He will be alert for Theo's responses to the therapeutic relationship, as well as possible historical roots of his current behaviors and feelings. Paul thinks that Theo will eventually become angry with him in the way that he expresses anger toward others in his life. Paul will accept this anger, first discussing it as it applies in the relationship between the two of them, then in Theo's current relationships, and then eventually as it relates to Theo's earliest experiences with his bad objects, his parents, particularly his mother. If Theo's anger threatens to get out of control, Paul will set boundaries on the expression of such and will work with Theo to structure his life outside of therapy to minimize its effects. In this process, Paul remains attentive to his feelings when he is with Theo, and his possible input into their relationship dynamics. He will seek consultation if he believes that his responses are interfering with his work with Theo.

THERAPEUTIC TECHNIQUES

As in traditional psychoanalysis, the most potent of technique in OR is *interpretation*, particularly of transference. Kernberg speaks of the "three-person" model of therapy, in which "the analyst is immersed, on the one hand, in a transference-countertransference relationship, and on the other, as maintaining an objective distance, from which observations and interpretations of the patient's enactments of internal object relationships can be carried out" (2001, p. 536).

Some OR theorists believe that the relationship in therapy is the curative factor, not the actual content. For example, Winnicott believed that the holding environment created in therapy provides the proper relationship that was missing in the client's early life. In this environment, the client, who is developmentally stuck at the stage where parenting failed, can get unstuck and move forward (Greenberg & Mitchell, 1983).

A recent approach, based on Kernberg's work, is known as Transference Focused Psychotherapy (TFP; Levy et al., 2006). In TFP, a structured approach begins with the development of a treatment contract specifying the expectations of therapist and client.

The major techniques of TFP are clarification, confrontation, and transference analysis of the here-and-now events of the therapeutic relationship. Clarification refers to the attempts of the therapist to understand the client's experience, helping the client to improve his ability to self-reflect (difficulties in self-reflection are thought to result from the poorly integrated self). The TFP therapist also confronts discrepancies in the client's communications, which then can be linked to psychic splits hypothesized to underlie the problems in self-integration. Transference interpretations link the therapist-client interaction to early object relations.

Paul patiently listens to Theo and tries to maintain a relatively neutral, but supportive therapeutic environment. He will interpret expressions of Theo's anger in the relationship and lead him to see how it is connected to his feelings about his parents, particularly his mother. Throughout the therapy relationship, Paul will try to provide the correct, supportive, holding environment that is essential if Theo is to express his anger and fear on the way to gaining insight.

SELF PSYCHOLOGY—IT'S ALL ABOUT ME

OVERVIEW

As the label suggests, SP focuses on the development of the self. Heinz Kohut (1913–1981), the founder of this approach, was born in Vienna but eventually relocated to Chicago in 1939, fleeing the invasion of Austria by the Nazis. He began his professional work as a traditional analyst, but over the years developed his own perspective, which was first readily apparent in his 1971 book, *The Analysis of the Self: A Systematic Analysis of the Treatment of the Narcissistic Personality Disorders.* In his second book, *The Transformation of the Self* (1977) he further developed his ideas. Kohut died in 1981 but was in the process of writing his final book, *How Does Analysis Cure?* which was published in 1984 (Strozier, 2006). More information on Kohut and SP can be found at the website of the International Association for Psychoanalytic Self Psychology, http://www.psychologyoftheself.com/kohut/index.htm.

SP's subtitle might be "it's all about me," for Kohut developed his ideas primarily through his work with clients who were labeled as narcissistic personalities, and this perspective is very focused on one's conception of the self, as you will see. Originally, he seemed to see his work as a complement to traditional theory that applied to the narcissistic syndromes (St. Clair, 2004). However, toward the end of his life, Kohut characterized his work as more broadly applicable and as a contribution separate and parallel to that of Freud (Mitchell & Black, 1995). Nonetheless, Kohut is often seen as trying to have the best of both worlds: he did not reject classical drive theory completely, but reserved it for cases in which the client presented with a relatively intact self system (i.e., what Freud called the neuroses). In doing so, he softened the nature of the drives: for instance, the normal Oedipal stage impulses were joyful and assertive rather than libidinous and aggressive. However, drive theory was not to be used to understand the character or personality disorders, such as narcissism. SP was the better alternative here because it emphasized problems in development that predate the Oedipal conflicts that are the focus of drive theory (St. Clair, 2004). This adaptation prompted Greenberg and Mitchel (1983) to label Kohut's theory a mixed model. However, Kohut's ideas were considered radical enough by the "mainstream" psychoanalytic crowd to deserve the dreaded label "unanalytic," bestowed by Anna Freud herself (Mishne, 1993).

CENTRAL CONSTRUCTS

Selfobject. Kohut coined a special term, *selfobject,* to emphasize his position that infants can't differentiate between the self and other. Although the term tends to be a bit fuzzy and difficult to pin down, selfobjects are referred to as parts of the self and also as individuals in the environment that are relevant to the self. Kohut uses the term self-selfobject relationships to describe the role of the selfobjects, but most other writers simply refer to selfobject relations, as I will in the following sections.

Selfobjects exist to soothe and support the infant as it grows from the primitive selfless state to an individual with a self, but the need for selfobjects never disappears. The most important selfobjects are the parents, who need to be good selfobjects but also to occasionally frustrate the infant to spur growth (Kohut, 1984). If these relationships are satisfactory, the infant's self will develop in healthy ways (Quintar, Lane, & Goeltz, 1998).

Sharlene is Theo's self-psychology therapist. In thinking about Theo's presentation, she speculates that he has some problems with his selfobjects—he probably has not established a totally integrated self. Sharlene wonders if Theo's parents provided the optimal levels of gratification and frustration as he was developing—their stormy history suggests that it is possible that their preoccupation with their own issues resulted in higher levels of frustration than would be desired, resulting in Theo developing negative selfobjects.

Disintegration Anxiety. Kohut added the conception of disintegration anxiety to analytic theory, maintaining that it is the most basic form of anxiety experienced by human beings. Although he acknowledges that "the attempt to describe disintegration anxiety is the attempt to describe the indescribable," Kohut characterizes it as the fear of psychological death (Kohut, 1984, p. 16). Mollon (2007) noted that the threat of fragmentation is present even in individuals with relatively healthy (cohesive) selves, and that all psychic defenses operate to ward off this horrendous, primal, anxiety.

Theo is probably suffering the effects of disintegration anxiety, although largely unconsciously. This anxiety, which stems from faulty object relations that do not support a coherent sense of self, is terrifying, and he represses it and instead it is expressed as anger toward important selfobjects who failed to provide him security and protect him from nothingness. It is also transferred to important others in his current situation, most notably, Tamia.

THEORY OF THE PERSON AND DEVELOPMENT OF THE INDIVIDUAL

As you might expect, Kohut's view of development emphasizes the self (St. Clair, 2004). The self develops through relationships with the selfobjects. Two processes are important in the healthy establishment of the self, mirroring and idealizing and two selfobjects must be developed: the *grandiose-exhibitionistic self* and the *idealized parental imago.* Little kids need to say "Look at me! Aren't I great?" This is the operation of the grandiose-exhibitionistic self, and it needs *mirroring* from the parents, which consists of parental approval and admiration. The development of the parental imago requires *idealizing*, or the parent allowing the child to see him or her as perfect, and communicating to the child that he or she is enjoying it.

Idealizing and mirroring comprise what Kohut called the empathic relationship between parent and child (St. Clair, 2000). Generally, healthy parents do this well, but inevitably, there is some disruption in the process, and the child's needs for idealizing or mirroring are not met. These disruptions, if mild, push the child toward the development of a cohesive self because the child's response is to, in small steps, take these functions into the self. These disruptions in empathy are called *optimal frustrations* (Kohut, 1984) and with these, gradually, the self develops through the internalization of the grandiose-exhibitionistic self and the parental image through the process Kohut called *transmuting internalization* (St. Clair, 2000). If all goes well, these representations broaden into good feelings about the self and the idealized superego (Kohut, 1984). Most importantly, the child develops a coherent sense of self.

The self develops with two poles, corresponding to the two types of selfobjects. Personality type, for Kohut, is determined by which of the two poles is dominant (Greenberg & Mitchell, 1983). If the grandiose-exhibitionistic aspects are strongest, the individual will be assertive and ambitious. If the idealized selfobject is dominant, the person will hold strong ideals and values.

Kohut seems ambivalent about traditional drive theory and psychosexual stages. He really thought that the kinds of clients we are dealing with now differed from those that Freud saw. He acknowledges, for example, the Oedipal stage of development, but in his later writings, sees it as a phase of joy and affection for the parents (Kohut, 1984). For Kohut, the intense sexual and aggressive impulses sometimes seen at this stage are a product of faulty development (see the following section on dysfunction).

Theo's mother and father attempted to be good parental objects for him, at times playing with him and admiring the products of his play. For instance, Theo's panda bear, Rudy, learned to talk, and his mother would engage in animated conversations with him. Theo also idealized his parents, particularly his father, who he saw as important and powerful.

HEALTH AND DYSFUNCTION

In an SP model, healthy people have healthy selves, generally defined as *structurally complete* (Kohut, 1984). Kohut rejected the traditional Freudian notion that the pinnacle of health is a heterosexual individual who has successfully negotiated the Oedipal stage of development. He wrote that "there are many other good lives, including some of the greatest and most fulfilling lives recorded in history, that were not lived by individuals whose psychosexual organization was heterosexual-genital or whose major commitment was to unambivalent object love" (1984, p. 7).

Kohut believed that the need for selfobjects is lifelong. It is the way in which one seeks and uses selfobjects that differentiates between healthy and dysfunctional people. He opined "we must be in possession of available nuclear self-esteem and ambitions, on the one hand, and of core ideals and goals, on the other, in order to seek out mirroring selfobjects and be nourished by their response to us and in order to seek out idealizable selfobjects and be enlivened by the enthusiasm we feel for them" (1984, p. 77).

According to SP, the basic problem leading to dysfunction is self-related and can be traced to deficits in early experiences with caregivers. Greenberg and Mitchell (1983) put it thus: "the cause of pathology, as Kohut sees it, is *chronic* failure in empathy, attributable to parental character pathology (p. 355, italics in original). These chronic failures result in a kind of "black hole" where the self should be, typically observable only through the extreme emotional reactions associated with threat (Mollon, 2007).

Kohut (1984) recognized three different types of dysfunction: the psychoses, narcissistic personality disorders, and the structural-conflict neuroses. In the psychoses, a rudimentary self has not been developed. He believed that although one could work with these individuals in therapy, it would be nearly impossible to help them create a true self because doing so would require demolishing the defenses that have been erected to compensate for the missing self. Instead, the analyst can help the client shore up the already existing defenses (Kohut, 1984).

SP theory is perhaps best illustrated by Kohut's analysis of narcissistic personality disturbances (Kohut, 1984). This term is used in a broad sense in SP theory, rather than in the narrow, DSMIV-R Narcissistic Personality Disorder sense. In these clients, a basic sense of self has been formed, but there are significant deficiencies in it. In fact, what is really wrong is that the individual has developed neither the idealizing or grandiose aspects of the self. The chronic failures (as compared to optimal ones) result in an "enfeebled" self susceptible to *narcissistic injury* (Kohut, 1984). Disintegration anxiety is operative because the person's sense of self is fragmented. In extreme cases, the "black hole" effect described earlier, is apparent (Mollon, 2007).

In referring to the structural-conflict neuroses, Kohut meant the types of dysfunction that were the focus of traditional analysis: those emanating from the phallic stage of development. As I noted earlier, in SP theory, the Oedipal stage is not considered pivotal in the development of dysfunction—instead, "the child of healthy parents enters the oedipal phase joyfully" (Kohut, 1984, p. 14). If the parents cherish the child's emerging displays of assertiveness and affection, all will be well. If they do not serve as good selfobjects in this phase, what Kohut termed the Oedipal complex will emerge (he used the term complex to distinguish these processes from normal oedipal phase events). The child will experience two kinds of anxiety: primary and secondary. Primary anxiety, or *disintegration anxiety*, the fear of the loss of the self (i.e., the loss of one or more selfobjects without which the self can not exist), is the most primal horror that humans can experience (Kohut, 1984). Secondary anxiety is what occurs when the healthy Oedipal self is lost and the Oedipal sexual and aggressive urges become prominent, leading to castration anxiety in boys, and the wish for a penis among girls.

In essence, Kohut is arguing that the motor of psychological disturbance is disintegration anxiety, present in all stages of life. It is the result of faulty parenting—parents failed significantly in either their mirroring or idealizing functions—resulting in flawed selfobject relations and an incoherent sense of self.

Sharlene thinks that Theo's issues arise from faulty early parenting. His parents were likely too distracted by their own conflicts to provide enough mirroring and idealization when he was a very young child. As a result, transmuting internalization failed, his selfobjects are not soothing, and he experiences disintegration anxiety. His sense of self is shaky and easily threatened, as when Tamia went out all night with friends. When she stood up for herself, Theo erupted, because in doing so, she challenged his sense of himself. It seems to Sharlene that although Theo's problems are the result of much earlier dynamics, they are somewhat attached to the Oedipal complex. Theo experiences prominent aggressive urges, and Sharlene wonders about his sexual urges as well.

NATURE OF THERAPY

Assessment. The SP therapist would not be a fan of formal assessment. Instead, the counselor relies on her observation of the client, particularly upon the client's behavior in session, to determine the nature of the self-deficits brought to therapy.

Sharlene carefully observes Theo's behavior in sessions, watching for his emotional reactions to her and tries to gauge the level of coherence of his self-structure. He relates fairly easily to her at first, when discussions are fairly mundane.

Overview of the Therapeutic Atmosphere and Roles of Client and Counselor. Kohut (1984) claimed that the relationship in SP therapy differs from that in traditional psychoanalysis in that it is warmer and more informal. The SP therapist is more willing than a traditional analyst to be emotionally available to the client. Kohut explains this difference in orientation to the client as resulting from the expanded concept of empathy in SP theory—the SP therapist (seeing the client's problem as stemming from early deprivation) construes the client's neediness and narcissistic demands as the welcome appearance of needs that have been repressed. However, the SP counselor does not gratify these needs (that would be a huge mistake) but does empathize with them. In contrast, a traditional analyst might conceptualize this neediness as avoidance of aggressive and libidinal urges associated with Oedipal conflicts.

Despite the assertion that SP analysis is informal and relaxed, the client is still a patient in this approach. The therapist must empathize with the client, but must also provide the correct interpretation of the client's transference manifestations.

While attempting to provide an empathic environment for Theo, Sharlene is aware that she must maintain some sense of authority in the therapy relationship. She maintains the most objective stance she can, and does not respond to Theo's bids for admiration or sympathy.

Goals. The goal of SP intervention is to correct deficits in self structure, or as Kohut put it in the title of his 1977 book, it is the restoration of the self (Kohut, 1977).

Sharlene hopes that in providing the correct environment and interpretations for Theo, he can integrate the fragmented aspects of his personality into a coherent self. He will reexperience his rage at his parents (and the associated internal selfobjects), but as Sharlene provides the proper idealizing and mirroring responses, he will eventually reintegrate these objects and establish a more stable sense of who he is. He will initially perceive events as totally related to himself and threatening; later, he will use his more stable, objective cognitive processes to objectively evaluate events in his life.

Process of Therapy

Therapy in a SP model is very similar to traditional psychoanalytic therapy in many ways. The key technique used in this approach is interpretation, particularly of transference phenomena. Dream analysis is also used in SP therapy. However, the end goal of therapy is different than that of other forms of psychoanalytic treatment: it is rebuilding the self rather than insight or expansion of the ego's capacities.

The core of therapy in the SP model is empathy; "the most important rule governing the self psychological approach . . . is that *understanding always precedes explanation*" (Kindler, 2007, p. 65; italics in original). Therapy reactivates the client's early needs for selfobjects that were frustrated. Essentially, the therapist must function as a selfobject to the client, providing mirroring or idealization functions that were absent in the client's early environment (Kohut, 1984). In this process, the therapist will inevitably fail; if these failures are optimal, transmuting internalization will occur and the client will build self-structure. *Resistance* in the SP model is seen as the client's attempts to avoid a repetition of early assaults on the core of the self.

The signature aspect of SP therapy is that the person of therapist is considered essential to the transference process—the client must either establish a mirroring or idealizing transference (Greenberg & Mitchell, 1983). The therapist basically serves as a selfobject for the client; the process of cure thus recapitulates that which went awry in the client's development (Kindler, 2007; Kohut, 1984). The very human therapist fails the client at times, and these failures, if optimally frustrating, lead to transmuting internalization and the accompanying new self-structure. Kindler (2007) discusses the *disruption-repair sequence* in SP therapy. This process happens in three stages: defense analysis, development of the transference, and the creation of an empathic relationship between the self and selfobject that has been split off and repressed (Kohut, 1984).

Sharlene struggles to empathize with Theo, providing mirroring and idealizing as he needs it. When she fails, she is aware that the disruption will prove helpful if she can repair the relationship. Theo transfers his early frustrations into the relationship, getting angry with her when she ends a session on time, but somewhat abruptly. In the next session, Sharlene brings this anger up with Theo, and tries to link it to his early experiences with his parents. The working through of such interpretations becomes the vehicle by which Theo can integrate the selfobjects that he has split off and repressed.

Therapeutic Techniques

According to Kohut (1984), the most important technique in SP analysis is *interpretation*. As noted by Kindler (2007), two elements must be in place for the interpretation to be effective: understanding and explanation. Understanding provides the optimal frustration that leads to new self structure because although the empathic response of the therapist legitimizes the feelings and needs of the client, the therapist still does not gratify the needs. The empathic bond established (or reestablished) in this process substitutes for the direct satisfaction of the client's need and in the context of this relationship, transmuting internalization brings about new self structure.

Sharlene empathizes with Theo, knowing that she will fail in the idealizing and mirroring transferences. She talks about these failures with him, and through this process, Theo's defenses and repression recede and he is able to reintegrate the problematic selfobjects he carries in his self structure. Transmuting internalization follows the disruptions of the alliance and slowly, Theo builds new self structure. He is less apt to feel slighted by others and to react with anger to these events.

RELATIONAL PSYCHOANALYSIS

OVERVIEW

The fourth wave of psychoanalytic thought is loosely called the relational school. The most distant roots of this approach can be found in the work of Sandor Franzecki, contemporary of Freud and for a brief time, his analysand. Also considered key is Harry Stack Sullivan, who in establishing what he called interpersonal psychiatry in the late 1940s argued that the analyst was a participant observer rather than an abstentious blank screen. The term relational psychoanalysis is confusing because it is sometimes used by some to describe a point of view within contemporary psychoanalysis rather than a specific theory (Ghent, 2001). At other times, it seems the term is used to identify a specific theoretical approach, attributed mostly to Stephen Mitchell, who founded the International Association for Relational Psychoanalysis and Psychotherapy shortly before his death in 2000. The website of this organization can be found at http://www.iarpp.org/html/index.cfm. In the inaugural issue of the organization's newsletter, Ghent (2001) writes that "the term relational was first applied to psychoanalysis by Greenberg and Mitchell back in 1983 when they abstracted the term from Sullivan's theory of interpersonal relations and Fairbairn's object relations theory. Common to these models of psychic development was the notion that psychic structure—at the very least, those aspects of psychic structure that are accessible to psychotherapeutic intervention—derive from the individual's relations with other people" (p. 7). Oddly enough, the "bible" of the relational approach is titled *Object Relations in Psychoanalytic Theory* (1983), written by Jay Greenberg and Stephen Mitchell. This rendition of relational analysis focuses most closely on Mitchell's model, which he calls the *relational-conflict* model (Mitchell, 1988).

CENTRAL CONSTRUCTS

Self. RP theorists discuss the self as the repetitive pattern of experiences and behaviors across time, along with the meanings associated with them (Mitchell, 1992). Mitchell, in writing about the self, maintains that because of its temporal nature, we each have many different selves, some that we experience as more authentic than others. However, the need for security (see the following section on anxiety) causes us to modulate our expression of self because we fear that authentic expression might cause anxiety, anger, or withdrawal in significant others upon whom we are dependent (Mitchell, 1992). These later expressions are called the inauthentic or false self.

Min-Wei, the relational analyst, considers Theo's presentation. He guesses that Theo brings to therapy a set of meanings and behaviors based on his lifelong relationship experiences. Min-Wei assumes that Theo experienced anxiety early in his life, perhaps as a result of observing his parents' stormy relationship. Theo would have also learned a great deal about relation-ships in observing his parents, and others, in his early years. He likely learned that relation-ships are fragile and conflicted, with partners often threatening to abandon the other. These meanings and patterns are Theo's current version of self, which is to some degree inauthentic.

Relational Matrix. The focus of the RP therapist is on relationship; the client's presenta-tion is interpreted through the construct of relational matrix (St. Clair, 2004). The rela-tional matrix is a hypothetical construct, consisting of the self, the object to which the self is relating, and the patterns of interaction between the two (Mitchell, 1988).

Several relational matrices are relevant to Theo's current presentation. Most prominent is the one with Tamia, which is intermittently stormy and angry. Min-Wei thinks that this pat-tern is one that is lifelong; probably it was learned in the relational matrix with his parents.

Drive Theory. RP theory rejects the notion of instinctual drives. However, it does not aban-don the notion that conflict, aggression, and sexuality are important in human relation-ships. Sexuality is seen as the most intense form of relatedness (in terms of intimacy) and a vital sphere in which relational events emerge (Curtis & Hirsch, 2003). Aggression is viewed as the result of frustration or identification with an aggressor. Conflict is routinely found in relationships (compare this perspective to the traditional analytic view that con-flict is intrapsychic—between id, ego, and superego).

Min-Wei assumes that Theo's anger is rooted in relationship conflicts, and perhaps is even one of the interaction patterns that he learned through observing his parents. These early lessons are evident in his current relationships. Min-Wei guesses that feelings of desire and anger are scary to Theo, because in his parents' relationship they seemed to result in strife and abandonment. Also, Theo learned that his parents' anger disrupted his relationships with them as individuals—sometimes the anger was turned on him, and at other times, anger resulted in one of his parents leaving.

Anxiety. Sullivan saw anxiety as key in the early life of the infant; indeed it drives the need to attach (Mitchell, 1988). Infants innately seek secure environments, and anxiety on the part of the infant or caretaker creates a *not* secure situation.

Beneath Theo's cool exterior also lies anxiety, Min-Wei thinks. This anxiety stems from his discomfort with relationship and his inauthentic self, which in turn are related to his lifelong relationship experiences. He fears intimacy because it brings conflict.

THEORY OF THE PERSON AND DEVELOPMENT OF THE INDIVIDUAL

RP theorists tend to rely on developmental theory that emphasizes the significance of early events that are thought to lead to the development of the self. RP models accept the no-tion of learned ways of relating to others as critical in human motivation (Greenberg, 1999). Mitchell (1988) contends: "There is a powerful need to preserve an abiding sense of oneself as associated with, positioned in terms of, related to, a matrix of other people, in terms of actual transactions as well as internal presences" and further, "there is not 'self,' in a psychologically meaningful sense, in isolation, outside a matrix of relations with others" (p. 33). There is, in the RP system, some recognition of the genetic or biological influences such as temperaments, but the most important part of personality in this view is learned relationship patterns (Curtis & Hirsch, 2003).

Min-Wei assumes that Theo's current ways of being in relationships (his self, or personality) are related to his experiences growing up. He has learned how to respond to others through observing relationships around him, and also from the consequences of his attempts to relate to others. He has been unsuccessful in his relationships because he fears intimacy, angers easily, and therefore, guards himself carefully, afraid to reveal his real self and emotions in relationships, particularly with Tamia.

Health and Dysfunction

In RP theory, dysfunction is seen as resulting from developmental problems that have prevented the individual from forming a coherent, consistent experience of self and others (Greenberg & Mitchell, 1983). Healthy individuals live rich lives in which the experience and expression of the authentic self are more common than expressions of inauthentic selves (Mitchell, 1992).

Problems develop when the individual, having experienced dysfunctional relationships throughout his development, forms a "narrowed relational matrix" (Mitchell, 1988). As a result, the person seeks relatedness to others, but does so using old patterns of relationships that are narrow and restricted.

Theo's current struggles are probably linked to his narrow relationship matrix. His limited ways of relating to others are linked to the environment in which he developed and the consequences of these relationships. Theo learned very early on that intimate relationships were dangerous. Intimacy leads to anger, which destroys relationships. Still, he has difficulty controlling his anger because his sense of self is shaky and he unconsciously fears injuries to it. The way to defend against hurt and abandonment is, paradoxically, to get angry.

Nature of Therapy

Assessment. As in the other neoanalytic approaches, the RP therapist is not interested in formal assessment or diagnosis. He simply wants to understand the client as best he can and the characteristic way that he relates.

Min-Wei begins his work with Theo simply by asking what brings him in to counseling. Theo responds openly, and Min-Wei observes Theo's presentation carefully. He notes how Theo interacts with him, feeling simultaneously seduced and pushed away.

Roles of Client and Counselor. According to Curtis and Hirsch (2003) RP practitioners prefer to see clients more than once a week to encourage development of the transference relationship. Modern analysts who adopt a relational perspective tend to see the therapeutic relationship differently than more traditional theorists. In traditional analytic theory, the therapist is objective and neutral, striving to stay out of the client's process in treatment. RP theorists have abandoned this notion, preferring instead the notion of the *two person field*. These therapists recognize therapy as an interpersonal encounter that engages both the client and counselor. Greenberg and Mitchell (1983) comment: "events within the analysis are not understood as preset and unfolding from the dynamic structures of the patient's neurosis. Rather, they are created in the interaction between the patient and the analyst" (p. 389). Transference and countertransference, rather than being a product of the client's conflicts, are seen as mutually influenced by both therapist and client. These recognitions seem to imply a less authoritative model of therapy than in traditional analysis.

Min-Wei is aware of his input in the relationship with Theo. He wonders what effect his person will have on the interaction with Theo, and how transference might develop. Approaching Theo with a warm, congenial manner, Min-Wei attends closely to his own reactions to Theo as well.

Goals. The goal of the RP approach is to help clients change relationship patterns that have proven problematic enough to get them to therapy. The client must give up the old, constricted relationship patterns developed earlier in life. Ultimately, these changes should bring about more authentic and fulfilling experiencing of the self.

Min-Wei hopes that Theo can, through the therapy process, develop new and freer ways of relating to others. If he can do so, Theo will find that his life is more meaningful and relationships more fulfilling. Min-Wei will focus on helping Theo understand the role of intimacy and anger in relationships, connecting these to what he observed and experienced in relation to his parents. It will also be important to see how these dynamics play out in relation to Min-Wei and Tamia.

PROCESS OF THERAPY

One of the most distinct features of RP is that an important goal of the therapy is to offer the client new ways of interacting with others. As Greenberg and Mitchell (1983) put it: "the patient is viewed as having lived in a closed world of archaic object relationships which lead to neurotic self-fulfilling prophecies. Through his new interaction with the patient, the therapist is able to enter that previously closed world and to open the patient to new relational possibilities" (p. 391). The analyst attempts to create a safe environment in which the client can experience the therapist as a new object of relationship first, so that when transference issues do emerge, the client and therapist can readily identifiable interactions based on these (Greenberg, 1999).

Although the term *transference* is used by RP theorists, it is always emphasized that "the analyst can never function entirely 'outside' the transference" (Greenberg & Mitchell (1983, p. 389, quotes in original). It is acknowledged that the client brings his relationship history/patterns to therapy, but the therapist influences how these play out by how he responds (or doesn't) to them. For instance, in Greenberg's (1999) reformulation of analytic neutrality, he points out that for some clients, the aloof, abstentious analytic stance may too closely replicate how the clients parents treated them. Taking this stance will cause the client to immediately make the therapist the old object, which disrupts the therapeutic process. The analyst in this situation might consider disclosing some of himself to the client to prevent this premature transference, and thereby better understand the client's relational patterns (Greenberg & Mitchell, 1983).

Ultimately, Mitchell (1992) maintains that the process of RP involves both the therapist and client in a unique encounter, such that "doing analysis, either as a patient or as an analyst, involves a struggle to reach a fully authentic experience of a particular kind that, when fully engaged, makes possible a kind of freedom and authenticity that is both rare and precious" (p. 19).

Min-Wei asks Theo to talk about whatever he wants, alert for signs of relationship patterns from the past. Well aware that he is in a relational matrix with Theo, Min-Wei tries to be as authentic as he can in the relationship, and readily admits to his own feelings and thoughts when appropriate. Theo tends, at first, to be superficial in his conversations with Min-Wei, avoiding emotional expression. Min-Wei feels distant from Theo, and comments on this. Theo erupts, contending that Min-Wei does not understand him. As calmly as possible, Min-Wei tries to get Theo to talk about these feelings.

THERAPEUTIC TECHNIQUES

Techniques in the RP model are essentially the same as in all of the other neoanalytic models. The therapist and client engage in a discussion (whether it is called free association or not) and the therapist interprets the client's productions. Dream analysis is used if dream content emerges. Discussion of the relationship between therapist and client is common and the ultimate goal is to relate these interchanges to the client's early interactions with significant others.

Theo and Min-Wei work together to sort out what in their interaction is unique to their relationship and what might be coming in from Theo's previous relationships. Min-Wei works to help Theo see the parallels between his relationship with him and those with Tamia and his parents. In this process, Min-Wei tries to help Theo develop new ways of relating to others that will help him feel less like he is about to explode. Hopefully, Theo can learn how to relate to others without the anger that has bothered him before he came to counseling.

EVALUATION OF NEOANALYTIC APPROACHES

My first and most vehement comment about these approaches is that they are very difficult to read! Writers in this area seem to like very convoluted, complicated styles of writing and create nifty-sounding terms that are hard to understand (self-selfobject relations, for example). Even when the terms and concepts are relatively simple, writers often work at very abstract levels or discuss very specific client presentations or problems (e.g., narcissism, envy). Further, the newer writings seem to be spread about in different sources (chapters, journal articles), making the area seem disjointed. Terminology varies from writer to writer, creating a perception that there are many variants of neoanalytic thought, when in fact, many of the ideas and concepts are quite similar to one another. Mitchell (1998) wrote "there are cultist features of traditional psychoanalytic institutions and literature. Analysts have often claimed for themselves an esoteric knowledge of mysterious realms expressed in a thick jargon that is inaccessible to the uninitiated. Because they felt they had singular, proprietary rights over access to the unconscious, some traditional psychoanalytic authors claimed a unique knowledge of the underpinnings of all human experience" (pp. 5–6). Although he was referring specifically to traditional analyses, many of these qualities are seen in neoanalytic writing as well.

The neoanalytic approaches seem less comprehensive than many of the other theories presented in this book. Several of them focus on particular client presentations (such as Kohut's focus on narcissism), and at times, are less easily applied to other client problems. Unless they specifically adopt the bulk of classical analysis, which some do, these theorists seem to be presenting valuable theory that is somewhat limited in scope.

However, there is some significant level of agreement that these approaches are very useful in dealing with clients who present with fairly severe disruption in their lives. Until fairly recently, the neoanalytics were about the only theorists to write extensively about the personality disorders. This tendency makes sense, because the notion of formal (traditional DSM) diagnosis springs from a medical model, and many of the neoanalytic writers are physicians (i.e., psychiatrists).

Qualities of Theory

The four groups of theories presented in this chapter are essentially equivalent to classic analytic theory in terms of *precision* and *testability*. Although it was a major goal of the post-Freudians to clarify and build upon Freud's work, the constructs they developed and invoked tend to be difficult or impossible to directly observe. Proponents of these theories still seem to rely on single-case analysis, and uncontrolled clinical cases at that. It would be difficult to disconfirm these theories as well.

Although variants of neoanalytic theory have been tested in outcome research (see below) and found to be effective in helping clients, it would be erroneous to say that the four approaches presented in this chapter are *empirically valid*. Most of the outcome research conducted tests further variants of psychoanalytic theory, such as brief dynamic therapy or Time Limited Dynamic Psychotherapy (see next section). These approaches do not directly test the postulates of the approaches in this chapter.

Research Support

Outcome Research. In addressing the effectiveness of the various neoanalytic approaches, most writers tend to rely on the various large studies of psychoanalysis, which, by now, are relatively dated (see Galatzer-Levy, Bachrach, Skolnikoff, & Waldron, 2000, for an extensive description of these studies). For example, Galatzer-Levy et al. describe the Columbia Psychoanalytic Center and the New York Psychoanalytic Institute studies, which found that clients generally improved as a result of psychoanalysis.

It is interesting that the Menninger project, discussed in Chapter 2, was based in the EP model (Wallerstein, 1986). This project followed clients in what were conceptualized as two distinct approaches to treatment: supportive vs. expressive. Supportive therapy, thought to be less powerful than expressive, emphasized support for the client's defenses and the avoidance of deep interpretation. Expressive therapy, on the other hand, more resembled traditional analysis, with focus on interpretation and insight. The Menninger project essentially found no differences in the effects of these two approaches.

A more recent report details the efforts of Fonagy and Target (1996) to study children seen at the Anna Freud Center. Ratings on a scale of general adjustment showed that significant improvement in 62% of children treated with intensive psychoanalysis and 44% who received less-intensive psychotherapy. Improvement was related to severity of diagnosis (with less severely disturbed children improving more), longer treatment, and interestingly, children whose mothers received analysis improved more than those who did not.

In a smaller study, Maina, Forner, and Bogetto (2005) presented a comparison of brief dynamic therapy (BDT), supportive psychodynamic therapy (SPT), and a wait-list control group in a sample of 30 clients presenting with depressive symptoms. BDT is considered more active and directive than SPT, and it emphasizes insight into individuals' lifelong patterns of interpersonal and intrapersonal conflict. Participants were randomly assigned to one of the three groups, and engaged in a range of 15 to 30 sessions. Outcome measures indicated that both treatment groups showed more improvement than the controls as posttest. Some evidence indicated that at a 6-month follow-up, BDT produced better outcome than SPT.

Another variant of psychoanalytic treatment is Supportive-Expressive Psychodynamic Therapy (SE therapy in short; Crits-Christoph & Connolly, 1998). This time-limited approach places more emphasis on the working alliance and relationships in general than traditional psychoanalytic therapy. In this model, the focus is on the client's maladaptive relationship patterns, much like interpersonal or relational approaches to analysis. Crits-Christoph and Connolly (1998) present outcome data for SE a manualized approach, finding evidence of effectiveness with diverse presenting concerns such as anxiety, opiate dependence, and depression. However, most of these studies did not use comparison treatments.

Theory-Testing Research. One aspect of the SE therapy research program that is of interest to testing analytic theory is the researchers' work on Core Conflictual Relationship Themes (CCRT). Much effort has been devoted to the measurement of this construct, using actual client material. Crits-Christoph and Connolly (1998) report that the results of these studies suggest that clients tend to show some similarity in their relationship patterns across the various relationships they navigate. Although very tentative in nature, this conclusion provides some support for psychoanalytic theory. However, it is useful to observe that the hypothesis of consistent relationship patterns would be acceptable to many theoretical approaches to counseling. This group has also assessed the relationship between therapists' interpretations and found a positive relationship between accuracy (with respect to the client's CCRT) and outcome and working alliance (Crits-Christoph & Connolly, 1998).

A fairly recent model of psychoanalytic therapy that rests on a program of research is Strupp's Time Limited Dynamic Therapy TLDP (Binder, Strupp, & Henry, 1995). Using Sullivan's ideas about individuals' tendencies to develop stable ways of relating to others, TLDP focuses on cyclical maladaptive patterns, which are "central or salient pattern of interpersonal roles in which patients unconsciously cast themselves; the complementary roles in which they cast others; and the maladaptive interaction sequences, self-defeating expectations, negative self-appraisals, and unpleasant affects that result" (pp. 55–56).

Research on attachment theory would probably be cited by many as supportive of neoanalytic models. Loosely rooted in psychoanalytic models (Mahler is sometimes cited here), this theory emphasizes the importance of the early child-caretaker relationship and argues that these influences can be seen well into adulthood. Attachment theory is very much in vogue at present, and the resulting data seem to support these notions (Cassidy & Shaver, 1999).

Issues of Individual and Cultural Diversity

Although psychoanalysis proper has been heavily criticized for gender and cultural bias, analysis as it is practiced today (other than orthodox analysis) can be seen as much more flexible in its views of clients from diverse backgrounds and of other-than-heterosexual orientations. One clear example of this is found in attitudes toward homosexuality. Although Freud seemed somewhat ambivalent about homosexuality, traditional psychoanalytic thought has historically labeled this orientation as deviant. In contrast, Chodorow (2002) points out that as early as the late 1970s, Mitchell (1978) had provided a substantial critique of the pathological view of homosexuality. Most analysts today would tend to take this position. Kassoff (2004) finds relational psychotherapy, in particular, useful with GLBT clients because the constructivist emphasis within the theory welcomes multiple views of reality and is consistent with recognizing diverse sexual orientations.

Certainly, the early theorists' emphasis on the relationship with the mother can be seen as biased. Taken to the extreme, the mother can be seen as the font from which all dysfunction flows.

With the exception of perhaps the relational and interpersonal perspectives, the neoanalytics could be charged with the overemphasis on individualism that plagues many theories of psychotherapy. This shortcoming may make these theories less than optimal for use with clients from cultural backgrounds that emphasize collectivism, respect for family over individual needs, and so forth. Even from the relational perspective, the notion of authentic self may be culturally encapsulated, for the submission of the authentic self to less authentic versions, say, in response to familial requirements, would be seen as less than optimal for some clients.

The Case Study

The case of Theo seemed to lend itself well to each of the approaches presented in this chapter. His primary problem was relationship, which is a focus of the current neoanalytic approaches. Anger is also easy to understand through these lenses. However, Theo is African-American and so caution must be taken in applying these relatively individualistic approaches with him.

Summary

Neoanalytic approaches to counseling and psychotherapy originated in Freud's models but to some varying extent, extend or modify it. Ego analysts seem the closest to tradition, whereas the relational models deviate most noticeably from it. Almost all of the neoanalytic approaches emphasize earlier forms of experience than did Freud. The neoanalytic approaches presented here also use essentially the same techniques: free association, interpretation (particularly of transference), dream analysis, and so forth. The goals of these theoretical systems differ significantly: ego psychology's resemble traditional psychoanalytic goals (insight, love, and work), object relations and relational perspectives emphasize changing relationships (and in the case of OR theory, change in internal objects as well), and self psychology the integration of a fragmented self.

Most analysts today are probably influenced by more than one of these orientations. The theories in the neoanalytic area seem less comprehensive than traditional analytic theory; hence using different parts of each at times would seem relatively natural. Research support for these theories is about as good as what is found for classic analytic theory. Issues of cultural and individual diversity seem less problematic in the more current approaches, although individualism and gender bias may rear their unpleasant head in some applications.

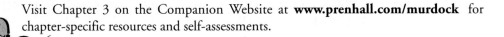 Visit Chapter 3 on the Companion Website at **www.prenhall.com/murdock** for chapter-specific resources and self-assessments.

CHAPTER 4

Individual Psychology

Alfred Adler

James is a 17-year-old African American male who is small and slender and wears glasses. Division of Family Services referred James for counseling to address problems that may affect his adjustment to a new adoptive home. His presenting problems include defiance of authority, lying, stealing, and a history of inappropriate sexual behavior. Various individuals around him (foster parents, caseworkers) have commented unfavorably on his "attitude." He is currently in high school, but comes to counseling during summer vacation.

James is the second child of his birth mother, Denise, who was 18 years old when he was born. Denise also had three other children, James' older sister, Karen, and two younger brothers, Carl and Jeff. James' birth mother and father were not married, and James' father was not the father of any of the other children. Little is known about him except that he is deceased.

When James was 8, he and his siblings, ages 9, 6, and 3, were placed in foster care as a result of severe neglect. His mother had problems with alcohol and had a "nervous breakdown." His stepfather left the home that same month. Conditions at the home prior to the time of placement were very poor. Fourteen people were living in a two-bedroom house strewn with dirty clothes and dishes. No meals were prepared, and no one assumed responsibility for the children. The police had frequently been called to the house in response to loud fights often involving dangerous weapons. Reportedly, Denise's method of handling behavior problems was to lock the children in their rooms for extended periods of time. James was physically abused by his stepfather on at least one occasion.

Following their initial placement in foster care, James and his siblings had a long history of placements. Between foster homes, James lived in residential treatment centers. His mother and stepfather were sporadically involved with the children, but eventually, parental rights were terminated. James was often in trouble at school for stealing or fighting. His grades were poor.

When he was 15, James was removed from the most recent foster home for violent behavior and placed in emergency foster care. He was told that this was the end of the line for him. He seemed to make more of an effort to settle down and was then again placed in a foster home. James apparently got along well with his new family. Conditions seemed ideal. Then, the family started taking in other foster children in addition to their own two children. Now there are five children in the home in addition to the foster parents' children and James. The foster parents are talking about getting a divorce, and there is much turmoil in this household.

James is looking forward to getting back to school, mostly for his social life and also to get out of his "crazy" house. He has many friends and seems to be popular with girls. James recently got a job and was very proud of himself. However, he was fired when he got drunk and his employer saw his friends carrying him out of the building. In counseling, James is struggling to verbalize his feelings, take responsibility for his own actions, and not blame others for his problems. He seems motivated to work, but admits it would be a lot easier if everyone else would change. His goals are to finish school, get a job, and live on his own. James also wants to continue to work on his temper and getting along with others.

BACKGROUND

Alfred Adler (1870–1937), the founder of Individual Psychology (IP), was born in Vienna, Austria, the second son of a grain merchant. There were six children in his middle-class Jewish family. As a child, Alfred was characterized as frail and fearful, suffering from rickets and problems with his vocal chords that resulted in stuttering (Manaster, 1977). At age 5 Adler contracted pneumonia and almost died, an experience to which he attributed his choice to become a physician—he was motivated to overcome death (Ansbacher & Ansbacher, 1956; Monte & Sollod, 2003). Once again, we can see the connections between a theorist's life and his creation: Adler's triumph over his early inferiorities seems to have set the stage for both his medical career and his theoretical ideas.

At age 25 Adler received his medical degree and began work as a practicing physician. Two years later he married Raissa Timofejewna. It is interesting that Raissa is characterized as an "irreligious political revolutionary" and "an ardent feminist who disliked domesticity" (Hoffman, 1994, p. 48), given Adler's progressive ideas about the critical need for equality of men and women. Adler and Raissa had four children, two of whom, Kurt and Alexandra, later became psychiatrists and furthered Adler's work. Valentine, the Adlers' oldest daughter, seemed to realize Alfred and Raissa's socialist political ideology when she emigrated to Russia and lived in dangerous opposition to the Stalin regime. Sadly, "Vali" disappeared in 1937, causing her parents, and particularly her father, great worry and anguish. Vali had evidently been imprisoned for espionage and died after 2 years in prison, at age 44. Alfred Adler died not knowing what had become of his daughter.

In 1895, three years after his graduation from medical school, Adler published his first work, which discussed the damage caused by the horrendous working conditions among tailors at the time. In this study he first demonstrated his special interest in bettering social conditions. Indeed, one of his prominent followers, Heinz Ansbacher, contended that "his most outstanding personal characteristic was his interest in and sympathy with the 'common man' " (Ansbacher & Ansbacher, 1956, p. 201; quotes in original). Adler was a member of the Social-Democratic movement, a social reformist group, and these values are clearly evident in his theory (K. Adler, 1994). When Adler first began his medical practice, it was in a lower-middle-class neighborhood of Vienna (Ansbacher & Ansbacher, 1956).

In 1902 Adler became a member of Freud's Vienna Circle. The nature of the relationship between these two giants of psychological theory has been the subject of much argument (Ansbacher, 1962; Fiebert, 1997; Gay, 1988). Although Adler is typically viewed as Freud's student, Adler and his followers protested that categorization, pointing out that Adler had published a preliminary version of his theory prior to his contact with Freud (Sweeney, 1989). There was apparently no contact between Freud and Adler prior to Freud's invitation to Adler to join his Wednesday night discussion group (Hoffman, 1994). Abraham Maslow, the well-known humanistic psychologist, reported that Adler vehemently denied being a follower of Freud, having established from the beginning of their relationship that his views differed from Freud's (Maslow, 1962). According to Maslow, Adler maintained that Freud spread the story that Adler was a disciple who had gone astray, and he was very angry with Freud for doing so, calling Freud a "swindler" and "sly" (Maslow, 1962, p. 125).

Despite the controversy, it is clear that Adler was an active member of Freud's group from 1902 until 1911, and Freud designated Adler as his successor as president of the Vienna Psychoanalytical Society. By this time, significant theoretical differences had begun to develop between the two men that eventually resulted in Adler's resignation from the society in 1911. The central issue under debate was the primary motivation for human behavior: Freud, of course, saw this as pleasure or sex; Adler wanted to make it interpersonal/social (Monte & Sollod, 2003). Apparently, this divorce was not amicable (Gay, 1988). Adler then established the Society for Free Psychoanalytic Research (Ansbacher, 1929/1969), later renamed the Society for Individual Psychology, and in 1914 established the first journal devoted to individual psychology, *Zeitschrift fur Individualpsychologie* (Mozdzierz & Mozdzierz, 1997). *The Neurotic Constitution*, Adler's first major book, was published in 1912.

After World War I, Adler's commitment to furthering social change led him to help establish child guidance clinics in Vienna schools. In these clinics he taught teachers and other laypersons how to use his ideas to understand the behavior of the children with whom they worked.

With the rise of the Nazis, Adler emigrated to America in 1929 and encouraged his associates to do the same (Hoffman, 1994). Raissa, his wife, remained in Vienna, and according to Adler biographer Hoffman, continued to work as a central figure of the Communist Party in Austria. By the time Adler moved to the United States, many American psychologists had become interested in individual psychology, including G. Stanley Hall, the founder of the American Psychological Association (Ansbacher, 1970). Adler accepted a professorship at Columbia University and continued an active teaching schedule. He was on a lecture tour in Aberdeen, Scotland, when he collapsed and died of a heart attack in 1937 at age 67.

Although a bibliography of his work is lengthy, most of what bears his name was not truly written by Adler himself. Instead, much of the material was gathered from his public lectures and edited and presented by others (Ansbacher, 1929/1969). You can read a bit of this work in Box 4.1. Adler's ideas have been developed and promulgated by a number of talented followers. As noted earlier, Kurt and Alexandra Adler followed in their father's

Box 4.1

An Excerpt from Adler's *The Science of Living*

In the author's own case the interest in psychology developped out of the practice of medicine. The practice of medicine provided the teleological or purposive viewpoint which is necessary for the understanding of psychological facts. In medicine we see all organs striving to develop toward definite goals. They have definite forms which they achieve upon maturity. Moreover, in cases where there are organic defects we always find nature making special efforts to overcome the deficiency, or else to compensate for it by developing another organ to take over the functions of the defective one. Life always seeks to continue, and the life force never yields to external obstacles without a struggle.

Now the movement of the psyche is analogous to the movement of organic life. In each mind there is the conception of a goal or ideal to get beyond the present state, and to overcome the present deficiencies and difficulties by postulating a concrete aim for the future. By means of this concrete aim or goal the individual can think and feel himself superior to the difficulties of the present because he has in mind his success of the future. Without the sense of a goal individual activity would cease to have any meaning.

All evidence points to the fact that the fixing of this goal—giving it a concrete form—must take place early in life, during the formative period of childhood. A kind of proto-type or model of a matured personality begins to develop at this time. We can imagine how the process takes place. A child, being weak, feels inferior and finds itself in a situation which it cannot bear. Hence it strives to develop, and it strives to develop along a line of direction fixed by the goal which it chooses for itself. The material used for development at this stage is less important than the goal which decides the line of direction. How this goal is fixed it is difficult to say, but it is obvious that such a goal exists and that it dominates the child's every movement. Little is indeed understood about powers, impulses, reasons, abilities or disabilities at this early period. As yet there is really no key, for the direction is definitely established only after the child has fixed its goal. Only when we see the direction in which a life is tending can we guess what steps will be taken in the future.

It is true that when the word "goal" is mentioned, the reader is likely to have a hazy impression. The idea needs to be concretized. Now in the last analysis to have a goal is to aspire to be like God. But to be like God is of course the ultimate goal—the goal of goals, if we may use the term. Educators should be cautious in attempting to educate themselves and their children to be like God. As a matter of fact we find that the child in his development substitutes a more concrete and immediate goal. Children look for the strongest person in their environment and make him their model or their goal. It may be the father, or perhaps the mother, for we find that even a boy may be influenced to imitate his mother if she seems the strongest person. Later on they want to be coach-men because they believe the coachman is the strongest person.

When children first conceive such a goal they behave, feel and dress like the coachman and take on all the characteristics consistent with the goal. But let the policeman lift a finger, and the coachman becomes nothing. . . . Later on the ideal may become the doctor or the teacher. For the teacher can punish the child and thus he arouses his respect as a strong person.

The child has a choice of concrete symbols in selecting his goal, and we find that the goal he chooses is really an index of his social interest. A boy, asked what he wanted to be in later life, said, "I want to be a hangman." This displays a lack of social interest. The boy wished to be the master of life and death—a role which belongs to God. He wished to be more powerful than society, and he was thus headed for the useless life. The goal of being a doctor is also fashioned around the god-like desire of being master of life and death, but here the goal is realized through social service.

Adler, A. (1929). *The Science of Living*, H. L. Ansbacher, Ed. and Trans. (Original work published 1929). NY: Doubleday. Reprinted with permission.

footsteps (Hoffman, 1994). Rudolph Dreikurs, the founder of the Alfred Adler Institute of Chicago, was Adler's student and instrumental in popularizing and extending Adler's ideas about working with children. Other prolific writers in IP theory are Harold Mosak, Donald Dinkmeyer, Hans Ansbacher, and Rowena Ansbacher. The influence of Adler's theory can be seen in many theoretical approaches devised since his—for example, in Rational Emotive Behavior Therapy, Family Systems Theory, and Reality Therapy. In fact, Sweeney (1989) reported that Albert Ellis, the founder of Rational Emotive Behavior Therapy, was a member of the American Society of Adlerian Psychology.

Currently, Adlerians are a relatively small but very active group. The *Journal of Individual Psychology* is filled with articles on research and practice. Several new books have recently appeared, among which are those authored by Jon Carlson, Richard Watts, and Michael Maniacci (2006), and Warren Rule and Malachy Bishop (2006), prominent contemporary Adlerians. Mosak and DiPietro presented *Early Recollections* (2006), an intensive examination of this important individual psychology construct and technique. The Adler School of Professional Psychology can be found at the Web address www.adler.edu, with branches in Chicago, Fort Wayne, and Vancouver, B.C. There are Adler institutes in New York, Toronto, and San Francisco and national and international associations, the North American Society of Adlerian Psychology and the International Association of Individual Psychology.

BASIC PHILOSOPHY

Adler can be considered a growth theorist with an optimistic view of the human condition (Eckstein, Milliren, Rasmussen, & Willhite, 2006). He believed humans had an innate tendency to strive for perfection and that this striving was the most important motivator of behavior (Adler, 1929/1969). Equally as important in psychological functioning is the interest in society, for without the support of others, humans would not survive (Dreikurs, 1953). This "social interest" is inherent in the human constitution, but also is the tendency to feel inferior. The ways these two influences are balanced determine the psychological world of the individual.

One watchword of IP theory is *holistic*. Adler said, "Very early in my work, I found man to be a (self-consistent) unity. The foremost task of Individual Psychology is to prove this unity in each individual—in his thinking, feeling, acting, in his so-called conscious and unconscious, in every expression of his personality" (as cited in Ansbacher & Ansbacher, 1956, p. 175). Thinking, feeling, and behaving, and perhaps even physiological functioning, are an integrated system directed toward pursuit of the individual's goals.

Adler is described as a soft determinist (Ansbacher & Ansbacher, 1956), which means that although he did think that human behavior can be understood given general principles and laws, these understandings are only probabilistic. For Adler, the individual creates his life path, but that very creativity enables him to change that path and his ultimate goal at any given time. A very popular quote from Adler is: "The important thing is not what one is born with, but what use one makes of that equipment" (Adler, as cited in Ansbacher & Ansbacher, 1956, p. 176). Here Adler is saying that it is what one does that matters, not one's genetic or biological inheritance. Adler believed that individuals could very well triumph over physical challenge and that these struggles often led to significant contributions to society.

One of the earliest social constructivists, Adler believed that individuals' perceptions, rather than some objective external criterion, determined their views of reality. Of the influences of heredity and environment, he said,

> It is neither heredity nor environment which determines his relationship to the outside. Heredity only endows him with certain abilities. Environment only gives him certain impressions. These abilities and impressions and the manner in which he "experiences" them—that is, the interpretation he makes of these experiences—are the bricks which he uses in his own "creative" way in building up his attitude toward life. It is his individual way of using these bricks, or in other words his attitude toward life, which determines this relationship to the outside world. (Adler, as cited in Ansbacher & Ansbacher, 1956, p. 206)

Known as a social activist, Adler believed that societal change was needed to improve the health of humankind. For example, he characterized the development of striving for power and superiority as the "most prominent evil of our civilization" (Adler, 1927/1998, p. 62). He also had a lot to say about the cultural phenomena of overvaluing masculinity and the belief in the "alleged inferiority of women" (Adler, 1927/1998, p. 106).

Sandy is the IP counselor assigned to work with James. She begins her work by reflecting on the basically positive nature of humans, and knows that even though James appears very troubled, within him is the strength and potential to work toward a better existence. Although James inherited some things and experienced many others, Sandy sees that he has created his view of the world around him, and also that this picture can be changed.

HUMAN MOTIVATION

Humans are motivated to strive for superiority. "We all strive to reach a goal by the attainment of which we shall feel strong, superior, and complete" (Adler, as cited in Ansbacher & Ansbacher, 1956, p. 104). IP uses a variety of terms interchangeably for this motive, such as will to power, striving for significance, or wish to overcome. What is most critical to recognize in the IP view of humans is that people are seen as being "pulled" by their goals (of superiority) rather than driven by their instincts (as in the psychoanalytic view; Ansbacher, 1970).

Paradoxically, humans are also beset by feelings of inferiority. We are born in a relatively undeveloped, defenseless form, are smaller and less powerful than those around us, and depend on our caretakers for existence. Naturally, a child feels weak and inferior and strives to overcome this feeling. Another innate, but initially less developed human inheritance is the need to belong. Adler thought that the need to belong ensured survival because when we are infants, the people around us give us food and water, keep us safe, and so forth.

Ultimately, the motivation for human behavior is how the individual reconciles the search for significance and feelings for others. For Adler, this resolution is an individual, creative process. A person can only be known through his or her personal plan to achieve superiority, which carries the scheme for dealing with feelings of inferiority and a certain level of belongingness.

Sandy thinks that James hides his feelings of inferiority well. He undoubtedly has these feelings, but he comes off as powerful and arrogant (the "attitude"). He doesn't seem to have a sense of belonging to society as a whole, but may have a feeling that he is connected to the friends he hangs with.

CENTRAL CONSTRUCTS

LIFESTYLE

According to Adler, everyone develops a plan for his life by the age of 5 or 6. This plan, which Adler called the *lifestyle*,[1] guides individuals' entire lives, including their perceptions of, and actions in, the world (Carlson et al., 2006). Ansbacher and Ansbacher (1956) list several of Adler's definitions for this complex construct, including "self or ego, a man's own personality, the unity of the personality, individuality, individual form of creative opinion about oneself and the problems of life, the whole attitude to life" (p. 174).

The lifestyle is the child's way of adapting to the circumstances around him (Dreikurs, 1953). Every lifestyle has a goal, and the goal has two important qualities: (a) the individual is largely unaware of it, and (b) it is a fiction, by which Adler meant that it is not based in external reality, but created by the individual (Ansbacher & Ansbacher, 1956). Thus, sometimes the goal is referred to as the fictional goal (Ansbacher & Ansbacher, 1956; Dinkmeyer & Sperry, 2000). A person's goal arises out of the interaction of two influences, the need for significance and feelings of community, or social interest. According to Adler, the only way to truly understand another human being is to understand the goal of the lifestyle. *All behavior is purposeful, oriented toward achieving the lifestyle goal.*

The creative power of the individual explains how the individual interprets and combines his environment, genetic inheritance, and experiences into the lifestyle and associated goal (Ansbacher & Ansbacher, 1956, p. 177). The way a person strives for significance (i.e., his goal) is unique. Take, for example, the case of identical twins. Identical twins raised in the same family could still have different lifestyles and goals because, from the perspective of IP, they have different perceptions of the world and/or use their creative powers differently given the same basic material. Their perceptions of their own

---

[1]This term is in various sources, spelled life style, life-style, and lifestyle with equivalent meaning. The latter will be used in this chapter.

abilities and the surrounding environment may be very different, creating different beliefs and goals. It is entirely possible that even if they look exactly alike, behaviorally they will be quite different. Alternatively, because they have genetically identical constitutions and physically appear the same to those around them, they might be treated identically, which may, in turn, lead them to very similar perception schemes.

Parental and other family influences are very important in the development of lifestyle: "the family is the individual's first society" (Schneider, 2007, p. 43). Parents are models for beliefs and values. However, Adler warns us not to automatically assume that parental influences singularly "cause" the lifestyle because, above all, the development of the style is a personal, creative, interpretive process. Nonetheless, Adler wrote about the results of abuse, neglect, and pampering at a time when little attention was being devoted to raising children. For instance, Adler thought that pampered children grow up with the notion that the world should always provide everything they want, immediately. The neglected or abused child sees the world as a scary or hostile place. Children who are suppressed through overly strict or punitive environments might develop a drive to gain freedom (Adler, 1929/1969).

Sandy observes that James was neglected as a child, and she guesses that this early experience resulted in a view of the world as a confusing, hostile place. His natural feelings of inferiority may have been magnified by his chaotic early environment. In what Sandy knows is the critical period for the development of lifestyle, it is questionable whether James actually had a family. His situation appears to have been one of neglect, at best. James appears to have established a lifestyle and goal oriented more toward personal superiority than social contribution. His goal probably goes something like this: Others are evil and dangerous so I must defeat them before they hurt me. He probably learned these methods through experiences in his life before he was placed in foster care. In other words, James's current behavior is partly a reflection of what he needed to do to survive in a terrible situation.

Sandy doesn't know much about James' inherited strengths and weaknesses, but it does appear that he had virtually no stability in his family, which has resulted in the absence of significant role models to influence his developing lifestyle. If James was indeed physically abused, both the physical abuse and emotional oppression may have resulted in a feeling of being suppressed. Sandy knows that Adler thought that suppressed children may naturally develop a drive to gain release, and she hypothesizes that this dynamic may contribute to James' rebellious life pattern.

SOCIAL INTEREST

A very important contribution of IP is its emphasis on the social embeddedness of the human condition (Carlson et al., 2006). For Adler, the measure of the individual was the degree to which he cares about his society. "We find adaptation to the community is the most important psychological function, both in the individual and in society" (Adler, 1927/1998, p. 25). The individual who chants, "Nobody loves me; everybody hates me; I'm going to go out and eat worms" would definitely be viewed as dysfunctional by the individual psychologist. Adler was so passionate about the importance of social interest that in a chapter entitled "The Absolute Truth," he discussed his conviction that humans can never truly find the absolute truth. Instead, he wrote, "Our sole recourse in this dilemma is to accept the logic of our communal life on earth as though it were an ultimate, absolute truth that can be approached step by step" (Adler, 1927/1998, pp. 21–22). Not to be confused with extroversion, true social interest is seen in the contributions the individual makes to his community (Ansbacher & Ansbacher, 1956, p. 141).

Only the *potential* for social interest is innate; these feelings must be nurtured and supported in children. During development, problems encountered by children usually result in diminished levels of social interest. Adler identified two general classes of problems: those that arise from physical disability and those stemming from environmental influences such as faulty parenting or social factors such as sexism, racism, or classism (Adler, 1927/1998). When a child has physical problems (such as slow development or physical disability), society does not typically react in nurturing ways, and thus his development is stunted. Children who experience negative reactions from others based on sex, race, or class may learn that the way to survive is to look out for number one. Parents can pamper, neglect, or suppress children, resulting in distorted attitudes about social relationships. Healthy children are those who are encouraged to empathize with others and contribute to society as a whole. In sum, "in order to understand what goes on in an individual, it is necessary to consider his attitude toward his fellow man" (Adler, as cited in Ansbacher & Ansbacher, 1956, p. 127).

Sandy thinks that James grew up in an environment that did not support and encourage social interest. In fact, his early environment was at best neutral on this dimension, but the fighting and possible abuse point toward a situation that was antithetical to the development of social feeling. Because James is African American, Sandy wonders if he has experienced some of the racism or oppression still present in our society, particularly with regard to young African American men.

Sandy is encouraged by the glimmers of social feelings evident in James' recent behavior. Judging from his history, James was uncooperative, and at times openly rebellious. He engaged in socially useless behaviors such as stealing, aggression, and lying. However, lately he shows interest in interacting with his peers, which is a very positive sign, given his background. Sandy will attempt to nurture these feelings and to help James channel them into socially useful acts.

INFERIORITY FEELINGS

The familiar term *inferiority complex* was in all likelihood not Adler's (Ansbacher & Ansbacher, 1956). Adler used the word *feelings* rather than *complex*, probably to avoid the Freudian aura conveyed by the latter term (Brachfeld, 1951, as cited in Ansbacher & Ansbacher, 1956). Adler apparently discovered the power of the term *inferiority complex* when he found out (while touring the United States) that he had been called the "father of the inferiority and superiority complex" (Brachfeld, 1951, as cited in Ansbacher & Ansbacher, 1956, p. 256). After Adler finally adopted the inferiority complex, it was typically reserved for abnormal inferiority feelings.

Inferiority feelings are a normal part of life because "to be human means to feel inferior" (Adler, as cited in Ansbacher & Ansbacher, 1956, p. 115). We are always moving up from down, or from minus to plus in our self-estimates (Monte & Sollod, 2003). These feelings "are the cause of all improvements in the position of mankind. Science itself, for example, can arise only when people feel their ignorance and their need to foresee the future; it is the result of the strivings of human beings to improve their whole situation, to know more of the universe, and to be able to control it better. Indeed, it seems that all human culture is based upon feelings of inferiority" (Adler, as cited in Ansbacher & Ansbacher, 1956, p. 117).

Feelings of inferiority begin at a very early age, when the child realizes that he is much smaller and weaker than those around him. How the child is treated by others and how he interprets and reacts to the situation is critical (Ansbacher & Ansbacher, 1956). If others demand too much of the child, he is repeatedly confronted with his inferiority. If he is treated like a piece of precious china, he surely has a different interpretation. How adults relate to children is very important, and some cultural traditions are harmful, such as the idea that children are not to be taken seriously (Adler, 1927/1998). "Ridicule of children is practically criminal," cautioned Adler, because it causes the child to feel insignificant and inferior (1927/1998, p. 61).

But what about people who seem to be entirely lacking in inferiority feelings? The answer lies in the *superiority complex*, in which the individual builds a false sense of significance, devoid of social interest. Although the term is used less often, Adler maintained that people who display this complex are merely signaling that they feel inferior and are using these behaviors to escape their problems (Ansbacher & Ansbacher, 1956, p. 260). In a sense, all those who have inferiority feelings also have superiority complexes in one form or another. The usual manifestation of the superiority complex is the show-off or braggart. Consider, for example, the arrogance of some adolescent males. Of aggressive children, Adler said, "We will always discover . . . an inferiority complex and a desire to overcome it. It is as if they were trying to lift themselves on their toes in order to appear greater and to gain by this easy method success, pride and superiority" (1929/1969, p. 29).

Individuals who present themselves as helpless or weak are also signaling superiority in that everyone else around them must take care of them. Similarly, the display of depression, neglect of one's appearance, and extreme grief can create power for the individual because these behaviors demand that others pay attention.

Sandy thinks that James is surely revealing his feelings of inferiority through his superiority complex. Presenting as cool and unflappable, he uses socially useless ways to gain power such as stealing and aggression, thereby building a feeling of significance that is based on defeating others. A second aspect of his social presentation is his ability to be charming with the ladies. Both of these faces, Sandy knows, are defenses against the very real sense of discouragement James hides. It is a good sign that now and then James reveals these feelings in counseling. In the past James has apparently fought off these feelings by seeking power over others in his environment through angry, violent behavior. He finds superiority in deceiving others through lies and theft and builds a sense of power through sexual behavior deemed "inappropriate." However, James seems to be in the midst of a reconsideration of these means. He shows signs of social feelings and verbalizes the intent to begin to seek significance through friendships and continued education.

BASIC TASKS

"For a long time now I have been convinced that all the questions of life can be subordinated to the three major problems—the problems of communal life, of work, and of love," Adler wrote (as cited in Ansbacher & Ansbacher, 1956, p. 131). These problems can be solved in socially useful or useless ways because, in reality, all three tasks involve social interest. One can't love without a wish to contribute to the betterment of another, and work usually contributes to society to some degree (if it is not criminal activity).

Adler believed that solving the task of communal life, or society, is achieved through cooperation (Ansbacher & Ansbacher, 1956). Society cannot exist without this attitude, and the task of society flows naturally into that of occupation because society can't exist without division of labor among its members.

Most people succeed to some extent at the occupational task (Dreikurs, 1953). People are typically able to find an occupation, although they vary along the dimension of social usefulness. For example, teaching children is an occupation with high social interest, whereas trading on the stock market would seem less so. Adler was one of the earliest vocational guidance counselors, saying, "it is an advantage to ask children early what their occupation is going to be, and I often put this question in schools so that the children are led to consider the point" (Ansbacher & Ansbacher, 1956, p. 431). The choice of one's life work is a good indication of the lifestyle. "In a child's choice of occupation we can observe his whole style of life" (Adler, cited in Ansbacher & Ansbacher, 1956, p. 431). Think, for instance, of the different views of the world expressed when a little girl says that she wants to be (a) an aerospace engineer or (b) a fashion model.

Adler described love as "the most intimate devotion towards a partner of the other sex, expressed in physical attraction, comradeship, and the decision to have children" (as cited in Ansbacher & Ansbacher, 1956, p. 432). Two features of this important task are notable. First, Adler refers to the "other" rather than the "opposite" sex. In using this terminology, Adler sought to downplay the so-called competition between the sexes. Second, for Adler, only heterosexual relationships were worthy; homosexuality was a reflection of fear of accepting the challenge of a male–female relationship. Of the latter, Adler said, "it is a revolt against the demands of social life, and aims at a fictitious, subjectively founded triumph" (as cited in Ansbacher & Ansbacher, 1956, p. 425). He was even more specific about lesbian orientations, saying that they could result from the masculine protest (discussed later) or the wish to gain power by taking on the masculine role (Ansbacher & Ansbacher, 1956). Contemporary Adlerians do not take this perspective, of course, and in addition, add that the task of love includes learning to love ourselves (Carlson et al., 2006).

Mosak and Dreikurs maintained that Adler alluded to two other life tasks: (a) coping with the self and (b) the existential task (Mosak & Dreikurs, 1977a, 1977b). The first task "means nothing more or less than to stop fighting with oneself" (Mosak & Dreikurs, 1977a, p. 101). This fight arises from the deeply embedded notion of dualism, encouraging a belief that within each of us is good and evil, bad and good, moral and immoral, lazy and strong. These dualities are false, leading only to an internal battle that can't be won. Further complicating the problem is that the culture in which we live gives very little information about our individual value, and hence we are constantly uncertain of our own worth. Our task is therefore to find ourselves worthy despite occasional human imperfection.

The existential task is concerned with finding one's place in the cosmos. Coming to terms with religion is part of this task. Mosak and Dreikurs (1977b) discussed negotiating this task through traditional religious paths, but also acknowledged the existence of atheism and agnosticism. The existential task includes developing a general picture of the nature of human beings, coming to terms with the existence or nonexistence of an afterlife, and considering the meaning of life (Mosak & Dreikurs, 1977b).

James is having some difficulty in each of the life tasks. Sandy has already noted that James has had difficulty cooperating with others, but she also observes that he is showing signs of wanting to contribute to society in that he enjoys his friends. James seeks and obtains employment, a good sign, but then finds a way to lose it by failing to cooperate on the job (getting drunk). Reportedly popular with the ladies, James seems to be experimenting with the task of love, but is only in the early stages of work on this problem. Sandy can't see it easily, but she also guesses that James is struggling to come to terms with himself. He has received some consistently negative feedback from the world, and this is bound to affect his self-view. Because of the immediate turmoil in his life, Sandy suspects that he has not had the leisure to consider existential questions.

BASIC MISTAKES

Within the lifestyle, Shulman (1973) identified six classes of basic mistakes, or erroneous beliefs, that can lead to problems in living:

1. distorted attitudes about self (I am a worthless worm)
2. distorted attitudes about the world and people (the world is hostile and people are out to get me)
3. distorted goals (perfectionism, I must rule all)
4. distorted methods of operation (overdoing)
5. distorted ideals (the "real man")
6. distorted conclusions (a) pessimism, (b) _____ conquers all (e.g., love, reason, money), (c) cynicism (you can't trust anyone), (d) fanaticism (Shulman, 1973, pp. 40–42)

Sandy thinks that James is harboring more than one of the basic mistakes. He seems to have the idea that the world should change, not him, although he is beginning to recognize the problem with this attitude. He has in the past pursued the distorted goal of ruling the world, and it is likely that he has difficulty trusting anyone. Although he does not show it, he probably believes that he is not a very worthwhile person. His methods of operation have been faulty (for instance, physical aggression and stealing). These behaviors also suggest that he holds a stereotypical picture of masculinity—the "real man" image of the masculine protest (discussed later). He probably thinks that power conquers all.

THEORY OF THE PERSON AND DEVELOPMENT OF THE INDIVIDUAL

As noted earlier, Adler believed that the pattern of an individual's life was set by about age 5. As a result of heredity, environment, and the individual's own creative work, the lifestyle is developed very early on and is relatively immune to change (Ansbacher, 1929/1969).

The child begins life as a small and relatively helpless creature. This observation prompted Adler to assume that we all begin life with significant inferiority feelings (Ansbacher & Ansbacher, 1956). As the child observes the environment around him, he forms his own impressions (interpretations of life), which are the beginnings of the lifestyle. Looking around at the immediate environment, the child observes the ways of adults and figures out how to gain power within this system. The child's physical condition and family situation contribute to how he meets the problems of life, but Adler emphasized that the creative power of the individual is most important in how he solves these problems. Because children are immature, they often do not use common sense, instead resorting to their own interpretations, which are more idiosyncratic in nature. This reasoning Adler called **private logic** (Adler, 1929/1969) and is contrasted with common sense (Carlson et al., 2006). Such misunderstandings may lead to mistaken goals of superiority (for those with low social interest) such as the need to always be taken care of or to defeat others. The opposite situation also occurs when individuals triumph over horrible life circumstances and become socially contributing people. Adler gave the following example:

> One man with unhappy experiences behind him will not dwell on them except as they show him something which can be remedied for the future. He will feel, "We must work to remove such unfortunate situations and make sure that our children are better placed." Another man will feel, "Life is unfair. Other people always have the best of it. If the world treated me like that, why should I treat the world any better?" . . . A third man will feel, "Everything should be forgiven me because of my unhappy childhood." In the actions of all three men, their interpretations will be evident. (Ansbacher & Ansbacher, 1956, p. 209; quotes in original)

Family influences therefore are very important in the development of children and fall under the general term *family constellation*. Perhaps the most familiar construct from IP theory is **birth order**. Adler believed that the position of a child in the family could have a marked impact on his development. There are at least two ways to look at the phenomenon of family position (Shulman & Mosak, 1977). First, we can consider simple ordinal position—whether the child was born first, second, third, and so forth. A second system is that of birth order—first, middle, last, or only. Adler tended to use the second system (Ansbacher & Ansbacher, 1956), and it is important to note that Adler emphasized the *psychological* position of the child, not the actual ordinal position (Stein & Edwards, 1998). For example, if for some reason the first-born child becomes incapacitated, the second-born may take over that role (Dinkmeyer, Dinkmeyer, & Sperry, 1987). Likewise, children who are born many years after their eldest sibling are thought to constitute a "new" family (Adler, 1931/1998). It is also very important to remember that Adler saw the characteristics typical of the different birth orders only as "tendencies; there is no necessity about them" (Adler, 1929/1969, p. 92). Other variables such as the sex of the child and the size of the family also influence birth order. Therefore, it is with some trepidation that I present a summary of the characteristics thought to be associated with the various birth orders.

First-born children are monarchs, basking in the undivided attention of their parents. Because they receive so much attention, they are generally very good at interacting with adults. They are then "dethroned" by a new child, a very unfortunate occurrence from the first child's perspective (Adler, 1929/1969, p. 12). As a result, the first born may then conclude that power is a very important thing. Also, the first born is often given responsibility within the family, such as taking care of later siblings. These factors create a tendency for first borns to seek positions of authority later in life (Adler, 1927/1998). The first born tends to love rules and may be quite conservative in his approach to life (Ansbacher & Ansbacher, 1956). Paradoxically, Adler thought that first borns were the most likely to be problem children, with the next most likely troublemakers being youngest children. The tendency to rebel comes when the first born is unable to accept his changed situation (Ansbacher & Ansbacher, 1956).

The usurpers, the second borns, spend their lives trying to catch up to the first born. They are likely to live their lives in opposition to the first born (Sweeney, 1989). The outcome of this competition can be that the second born surpasses all others in the family. However, if the first born is too outstanding, the second child may give up and become discouraged (Sweeney, 1989).

Middle-born children often feel "squeezed" between older and younger siblings (Sweeney, 1989). Lacking access to the advantages (e.g., parental attention, caretaking by elder children) offered to the other children, they may feel especially disadvantaged. Sweeney (1989) maintained that middle borns are likely to react to the elder, not the younger, sibling, much like second-born children.

Youngest children are the center of attention, but still the smallest, and Adler pointed out that "no child likes to be the smallest, the one whom one does not trust, the one in whom one has not confidence, all the time" (Adler, 1927/1998, p. 150). Thus, although these kids occupy a privileged position in one sense, they may develop extreme power urges trying to be the very best. A second type of youngest is the one who does not have the self-confidence to strive, or whose older siblings are unsurpassable. This child may give up and become cowardly and evasive (Adler, 1927). Sometimes this child, because he has so many parents, becomes pampered (Stein, 2000). Only children grow up in the world of adults and like being the center of attention. They may not learn how to cooperate with other children (Stein & Edwards, 1998).

Only children have a competitor, but it is not a sibling; it is father (Adler, 1931/1998). Often, they are very sophisticated, using advanced language and interacting well with adults (Stein, 2000). Some of these children may grow up in a very conservative environment, according to Adler, because their parents have experienced life as dangerous (Adler, 1927/1998, p. 155). These children are often overprotected, resulting in their having difficulty achieving independence; they lead self-centered, socially useless lives (Adler, 1927/1998; Stein, 2000).

Other aspects of family constellation include family values and atmosphere, examples set by parents, and the child's role in the family (Peven & Shulman, 1986). Adler asserted that it was the mother's job to teach the child cooperation, yet she must also relate to her husband and the world around her as well, facing all of these tasks "calmly and with common sense" (Adler, 1931/1998, p. 101). She gives the child his first experience with a trustworthy human being.

The father's influence comes into play later in the child's life, and his role is to "prove himself a good companion to his wife, to his children, and in society" (Adler, 1931/1998,

p. 106). He needs to be aware of the overvaluing of the male position and avoid perpetrating the myth that his work is superior to his wife's.

Adler maintained that it was the parents' job to teach children social interest, and to "learn to lessen the family egoism" (Adler, 1927, p. 122). Mistakes made in the family will come back to haunt in later life; failing to learn cooperation and courage will result in the development of problems.

The parental relationship "sets a pattern for all interpersonal relationships in the family" (Dinkmeyer & Dreikurs, 1963). In addition, Adler argued that what children see in their parents' relationship will influence their views of partnership and the nature of the other sex (Adler, 1931/1998). Adler pointed out that children will be quick to exploit differences between parents, so parents must model cooperation with each other.

Gender is another very important influence in how kids develop. Adler's frequent discussions and condemnation of the male bias in society makes him seem like the very first feminist (Nelson, 1991). At first glance, Adler can seem quite sexist because he equated superior and inferior to masculine and feminine. What he was really doing was describing how society perceived the sexes (Mosak & Schneider, 1977). Both sexes struggle with this social pressure in the form of the **masculine protest**. "Our civilization is mainly a masculine civilization, and the child gets the impression that while all adults enjoy superior powers the man's position is superior to the woman's" (Dreikurs, 1953, p. 47). According to Mosak and Schneider (1977), what Adler meant by the confusing use of the term *protest* was that because of the valued male role, both sexes are prompted to declare (protest) their masculinity. The little boy resolves, "I'm going to be a real man," and he protests against anything that seems to imply that he is not and thereby not superior (Dreikurs, 1953, p. 47). Adler pointed out that "almost everywhere the women's part in life is undervalued and treated as secondary" (Adler, 1931/1998, p. 98) and argued that this societal attitude had grave consequences. He said, "one must therefore keep in mind the difficulties under which a girl's development takes place. We cannot expect a complete reconciliation with life, with the facts of culture and the forms of our living together, as long as women are not granted equal rights with men" (Adler, 1982, p. 15).

Confronted with the biases of society, girls may take several paths. The masculine protest can be transformed, so that it is "covered and changed, and [she] seeks to triumph with feminine means. Very often one finds during the analysis the wish to change into a man" (Adler, 1982, p. 36). Other women become resigned to their inferior status. Still others dislike and resist the traditional female role and may become lesbians as a result (Ansbacher & Ansbacher, 1956). According to Dreikurs (1953), women who are unwilling to accept their defined roles are adopting masculine goals.

Dreikurs, however, added that most people have some form of a masculine goal because they desire strength and power. This last position is the one Adler eventually came to; he concluded that the masculine protest was a special case of the more general human tendency to strive for power (Nelson, 1991). Further, not all individuals are beset by the need to protest; some are quite comfortable with their respective genders, presumably those who are relatively low in inferiority feelings and high in social interest (Mosak & Schneider, 1977).

Adlerian theorists recognize four types of personalities that are the function of social interest and the individual's activity level. Because the terms used to label these are fairly descriptive, I will simply list them here, following (Monte & Sollod, 2003, p. 181): (a) The ruling-dominant type (b) the getting-leaning type, (c) the avoidant type, and (d) the socially useful type. I am sure that you recognize that the last one is considered to be the healthiest in IP theory.

James is a second-born male. His situation, in Sandy's view, is a good illustration of the dangers of taking birth order hypotheses as literal truth. James does not exhibit the typical striving of the second born. Instead, he looks more like a first born who is rebelling to achieve power. James and his siblings experienced a chaotic family environment until James was 8, which clearly would have confused roles and responsibilities among children and adults. The series of foster placements following James' seventh year probably exacerbated his confusion and at the same time reinforced his rebellion against the hostile environments he experienced. His acting out gained him power and attention. Sandy guesses that James' first family environment provided role models for masculinity that demonstrated the typical "he man" picture, including the use of physical force to gain power. In fact, his stepfather physically abused him, suggesting that James learned early that physical aggression was a way to gain notice and control over others. Sandy thinks that James is mostly displaying the ruling-dominant type, although at times he seems to do a little getting-leaning.

HEALTH AND DYSFUNCTION

Healthy people, according to individual psychology, have well-developed social interest and therefore contribute to society as they go about solving the tasks of life. They are able to meet problems head on, courageously, and solve them in socially constructive ("useful") ways. Adler wrote, "The nearer to health and normality an individual is, the more he can find new openings for his strivings when they are blocked in one particular direction" (as cited in Ansbacher & Ansbacher, 1956, p. 190). The healthy person succeeds at the tasks of life, contributing to the community and finding a partner of the other sex and socially useful work. The healthy person has the courage to be imperfect because that is the normal state of human life (Dreikurs, 1953).

"All failures—neurotics, psychotics, criminals, drunkards, problem children, suicides, perverts, and prostitutes—are failures because they are lacking in social interest," Adler wrote (Ansbacher & Ansbacher, 1956, p. 156). The individual who is psychologically unhealthy has the goal of personal superiority, and the lifestyle is consequently aimed at protecting self-esteem, a process called *safeguarding* (Rule, 2006). Psychological dysfunction equals discouragement, because the individual has lost the "courage to proceed on the useful side of life" (Adler, as cited in Ansbacher & Ansbacher, 1956, p. 255). These individuals have underdeveloped social interest and strive for power and superiority in ways that are socially useless. "Problems are solved in a self-centered private sense rather than a task-centered common sense fashion" (Ansbacher & Ansbacher, 1956, p. 2; quotes deleted).

Safeguarding, the defense against inferiority feelings and discouragement, can take many forms (Carlson et al., 2006). Psychological symptoms are nonconscious forms of safeguarding. Forms of safeguarding that are more accessible to consciousness are making excuses, aggression, distancing from tasks perceived as threatening, and restricting one's possibilities in life.

Adler discussed a variety of psychological dysfunctions, but he saw all as the result of mistaken lifestyles that were selfish rather than socially oriented and characterized by a drive to protect the person's sense of power or value in the face of challenging life tasks. Most generally, Adler saw neurosis (anxiety, depression) as failure in life (Ansbacher, 1970). Identified by their hesitating attitudes, neurotics display a marked tendency to evade life tasks (Dreikurs, 1953). As Dreikurs (1953) put it, "Neurosis is like a mock battle field outside the war zone—a long way behind the front of life, a side show" (p. 88). Adler called the neurotic the "yes, but" personality—always wanting to achieve, but finding reasons why he can't (as cited in Ansbacher & Ansbacher, 1956). The neurotic uses excuses to evade responsibility for life tasks, at which his inferiority feelings tell him he will fail. The neurotic tolerates suffering from symptoms to avoid the even more traumatic outcome of failure.

Neurotics are striving for superiority, but because their life plans lack social interest, they choose to walk on the "useless" side of life (Ansbacher & Ansbacher, 1956), pursuing goals that are individualistic rather than contributing to the collective good. "The common function of neurotic behavior in all its varied forms is, . . . to provide safeguards for the self-esteem which is bound up with the hidden goal of superiority" (Ansbacher & Ansbacher, 1956, p. 263).

Neurosis has its roots in childhood. In some way, children become overburdened and lose courage. Three general kinds of children have high potential to be neurotic (Ansbacher & Ansbacher, 1956). The first is the child who experiences *organ inferiority* early in his development. The second is the *pampered*, or spoiled, child. The third potential neurotic is the *neglected* child. However, whether these children become troubled depends on an "exogenous factor," which is a task that demands cooperation (Ansbacher & Ansbacher, 1956, p. 296). If the child or adult is overwhelmed by a challenging cooperative task that he believes he can't meet, neurosis will surface.

Children who experience physiological problems, or organ inferiority, become focused on their bodies and have difficulty seeing that life meaning is achieved by contributing to others. The natural process of comparing one's self to others may make the situation worse, and if others pity, ridicule, or avoid the child, the situation becomes even more damaging (Ansbacher & Ansbacher, 1956). It takes exceptional creativity and the presence of strong social training for the child with organ inferiority to grow up psychologically healthy (Ansbacher & Ansbacher, 1956).

The pampered child achieves superiority by having others do everything for him. Experiencing instant gratification, he never learns how to tackle and solve life problems, and thus his feeling of inferiority is intensified. Also, many pampered children develop behaviors that are disliked by adults but compel attention, such as extreme discouragement, oversensitivity, and physical and psychological disturbances that indicate the need for help (Ansbacher & Ansbacher, 1956). Adler cautioned against blaming the parents for the pampered child's style because "it is the creation of the child, and is very frequently found even where there is no evidence whatever of pampering by another person" (Adler, as cited in Ansbacher & Ansbacher, 1956, p. 242). An example of the IP conceptualization of parenting is illustrated in Box 4.2.

The neglected child never had the chance to learn about love and cooperation (Ansbacher & Ansbacher, 1956). He sees the world as hostile and ungiving because he has never found a trustworthy other. As a result, neglected children are likely to resist the

Box 4.2

The Case of Little Hans: Fear of Castration or Pampered Child?

When we examine the facts they tell us only that the name Oedipus is poorly chosen; the complex characterizes a pampered child who does not want to give up his mother.

(Adler, as cited in Ansbacher & Ansbacher, 1956, p. 185)

One of Sigmund Freud's most discussed cases was that of Little Hans, the boy who developed a phobia of horses (Schoenewolf, 1990). Freud, who was seeking information about childhood sexuality, served as a consultant to Hans' father, Max, who attempted a kind of psychoanalytic treatment of his son. The father recorded what Hans said and reported to Freud. Based on advice from Freud, the father would interpret Hans' statements or behaviors to Hans. For Freud, Hans showed all of the normal developmental signs. He became obsessed with his "weewee-maker" at about age 3 and evidenced significant distress upon the birth of his sister around the same time. During the year after his sister's birth (at about age 4), Hans developed a phobia of horses, fearing that the horse would bite him or fall down while pulling his cart and kill him.

Working through the father, Max, Freud proceeded to analyze Hans and eventually published the story of the analysis as "Analysis of a Phobia in a Five-Year-Old Boy" (Freud, 1909). Concluding that the horses represented the father, Freud interpreted Hans' symptoms as stemming from the Oedipus complex. Hans' fears of his father (the horse) stemmed from his sexual desires for his mother. If his father found out about Hans' feelings about mother, he might go so far as to bite him (i.e., castrate him). Hans' particular fear of horses falling down while pulling a cart was given two interpretations: (a) that the kicking and thrashing of the prone horse represented the boy's wish for his father to die and (b) that the overturned cart represented his mother's womb, carrying the competitor (other possible siblings) who would fall out if the cart fell.

Taub (1995) reconceptualized the case of Little Hans from the individual psychology perspective. As you might expect based on the different views of development held by Adler and Freud, Taub's conceptualization emphasized striving for significance rather than Oedipal drives. Hans was a very pampered child who was greatly affected by the birth of his little sister. His lifestyle formed around his efforts to do everything he could to regain his throne, which was lost when his little sister was born. Taub described a hypothetical course of individual therapy for Little Hans, beginning with two sessions with his parents and progressing to play therapy for Hans.

Counseling with the parents revealed that Hans had been told that a natural expression of his curiosity about sex (masturbation) would result in his penis falling off or the doctor removing it. This information scared Hans and at the same time intensified his preoccupation with weewee-makers. His father's interpretation of Hans' fear of horses (relating it to Hans' wish to sleep with his mother and his resultant fear of dad) further confused and scared Hans. At the same time, Hans' fears and curiosity about sex became a "family project" (Taub, 1995, p. 339). His father dutifully wrote down everything Hans said about sex, and he received much parental attention for his behavior. From an individual psychology perspective, Hans' anger and anxiety were understandable because they were associated with the loss of his superior position in the family and his bed being moved out of his parents' room. As a result of his distress, Hans' parents focused on his every behavior and he became a pampered child.

Looking at the family environment in which Hans' behaviors appeared, Taub conjectured that his mother encouraged Hans' increased desires for comfort and cuddling because she wished to avoid her relationship with Hans' father. The father was understandably upset with the disruption Hans caused in their sexual relationship. Hans' mother was upset about the father's criticism of her affection for Hans and generally angry about the father's critical behavior. Taub maintained that if the parents ignored some of Hans' behaviors (i.e., masturbation) and worked out their own relationship, the overall situation would improve. Hans also needed to be given age-appropriate, accurate information about weewee-makers and the origins of babies. Play therapy would allow Hans to experience a safe and nonjudgmental relationship. Hans liked play therapy because in this environment he was special and was allowed to express his fears and jealousy about his sister. However, the therapist took care not to excessively praise or dote on Hans, and to treat him with "respect, confidence, and encouragement" (Taub, 1995, p. 343). Working with Hans and his family allowed the therapist to encourage in Hans both social interest and other modes of seeking significance.

Psychoanalysis and individual psychology thus generate two very different views of Little Hans. We are fortunate to have such exemplar cases to provide us with very real lessons about the effects of theoretical structure on our thoughts about clients. It is indeed exemplary of Freud that he was willing to expose his clinical work to public scrutiny. It is courageous of Taub to present the individual psychology perspective on this famous case.

attempts of others to influence them, and are often openly rebellious. In other instances, they become passively resistant (Dreikurs, 1953).

Unlike many counseling theorists, Adler proposed an understanding of the most difficult cases, the psychotics. "The loftiest goals are to be found in the most pathological cases, that is, in the psychoses" (Adler, as cited in Ansbacher & Ansbacher, 1956, p. 314). Schizophrenics, and particularly paranoiacs (it is not clear whether Adler was including paranoiacs under the general heading of psychoses), have the goal to be godlike in order to fend off their very deep inferiority feelings. The goal is so high that they almost completely lose interest in others and so lose their common sense and contact with reality as seen by most of us. "Insanity is the highest degree of isolation" (Adler, as cited in Ansbacher & Ansbacher, 1956, p. 316). Adler portrayed the psychotics' withdrawing from others as the result of being badly unprepared for life. Psychotics lack interpersonal skills and occupational interests and are afraid that they will fail in everything, including relations with the other sex. Finally they retreat so far that others cannot understand them. In the case of the paranoid person, his distrust of others leads him to oppose socially accepted views of reality by creating his own reality, politics, and religion (Ansbacher & Ansbacher, 1956, p. 318).

James is a neglected child. His early life circumstances were chaotic and impoverished, lacking a stable family structure. Some evidence indicates that he has been abused, both in his first family and in subsequent foster families. Sandy thinks that it is remarkable that James is not more hostile than he is. Perhaps he was able to trust someone in his early environment so that he did not totally lose his faith in others.

Until recently, James has displayed a disinterest in contributing to society, walking on the useless side of life. Sandy knows that this life pattern would classify James as neurotic— he strives for self-esteem at the expense of others. On the surface, little of the hesitating, discouraged attitude of the neurotic is visible in James, but when he relaxes in therapy sessions, he admits to Sandy that he is a little scared to really try hard in school or to become more deeply involved with people around him. Sandy knows that he is harboring the feelings of unworthiness characteristic of neurotics, and that he is afraid to fully engage in the tasks of life because he might fail. Instead, he puts up his macho front so that no one can tell that he truly feels inferior and at the same time is angry at the world for treating him so badly.

NATURE OF THERAPY

ASSESSMENT

Individual psychologists advocate two types of assessment, formal and informal. Each will be discussed separately even though the informal certainly occurs during formal assessment.

Formal Assessment. Formal assessment consists of obtaining information that helps to understand the lifestyle through relatively structured means. Schneider (2007) notes that the lifestyle assessment process is typically a significant contributor to the therapeutic alliance. Several techniques are used.

Adler developed an **interview** structure for assessing lifestyle (Ansbacher & Ansbacher, 1956). Formulating different interview guides for use with children and adults, Adler recommended using a series of questions covering various life areas (e.g., assets, social relationships, interests, discouraged behaviors) only loosely when attempting to understand a client (Ansbacher & Ansbacher, 1956, p. 405). A sample of the questions Adler suggested is shown in Figure 4.1. Eckstein, Milliren, Rasmussen, and Willhite (2006) indicated that nowadays, some IP therapists will use the full formal interview method, but others will use a less structured and briefer method.

"The question" is another important IP assessment technique (Mosak and Maniacci, 1999). The client is asked, "What would be different in your life if (the symptom disappeared)?" (Mosak & Maniacci, 1999, p. 135). Responses to the question can tell the counselor two things. First, if the client says something vague such as, "I'd feel better," the counselor should consider the possibility of a physical basis for the presenting problem. However, many times the client's response will not involve such responses;

For Use with Children

Disorders

1. Since when has there been cause for complaints? In what sort of situation, objective and psychological, was the child when the disorder was first noticed?

The following are significant: change of environment, beginning of school, change of school, change of teacher, birth of sibling, failure in school, new friendships, diseases of the child or of the parents, divorce, remarriage, or death of the parents.

2. Was the child conspicuous in some way already at an earlier age? Was this through mental or physical weakness, cowardliness, carelessness, reserve, clumsiness, jealousy, dependence on others when eating, dressing, washing, or going to bed? Was the child afraid of being alone or of darkness? Does he understand his sexual role, the primary, secondary, or tertiary sexual characteristics? How does he regard the opposite sex? How far has he been enlightened on his sexual role? Is he a stepchild, illegitimate, foster child, or orphan? How did his foster parents treat him? Is there still a contact? Did he learn to walk and talk at the right time? Without difficulty? Was the teething normal? Were there striking difficulties in learning to write, draw, do arithmetic, sing, or swim? Did he attach himself very particularly to a single person? To either his father, his mother, a grandparent, or nurse?

One should notice hostile attitudes toward life, causes for the awakening of inferiority feelings, tendencies to exclude difficulties and persons, and traits of egotism, sensitivity, impatience, heightened affects, activity, greediness, and caution.

3. Did the child give much trouble? What and whom does he fear the most? Did he cry out at night? Did he wet the bed? Is he domineering? Towards weaker children or towards stronger children as well? Did he show a strong desire to lie in the bed of one of the parents? Was he intelligent? Was he much teased and laughed at? Is he vain about his appearance in regard to his hair, clothes, shoes? Does he pick his nose or bite his nails? Is he greedy when eating? Has he stolen? Has he difficulties with bowel movements?

These questions aim to clarify whether the child strives for preeminence with greater or lesser activity, and furthermore, whether defiance has prevented the adaptation of his drives to the culture.

Social Relationships

4. Did he make friends easily? Or was he quarrelsome, and did he torment persons and animals? Does he attach himself to younger or older boys or girls? Does he like to be the leader or is he inclined to isolate himself? Does he collect things? Is he stingy or greedy for money?

These questions concern the child's ability to make contact and the degree of his discouragement.

5. How is he now in all these respects? How does he behave in school? Does he like to go? Does he come in late? Is he excited before school and does he get into a rush? Does he lose his books, or school bag? Is he excited about homework and examinations? Does he forget or does he refuse to do his schoolwork? Does he waste

(continued)

FIGURE 4.1. Lifestyle interview.

time? Is he lazy and indolent? Does he concentrate little or not at all? Does he disturb the class? How does he regard the teacher? Is he critical, arrogant, indifferent? Does he ask others to help him with his lessons, or does he wait until help is offered? Is he ambitious in gymnastics and sports? Does he consider himself entirely or partially talented? Is he a great reader? What sort of literature does he prefer? Does he do poorly in all subjects?

These questions reveal the preparation of the child for school, the result of the going-to-school "experiment," and his attitudes toward difficulties.

6. Correct information about his home conditions, diseases in the family, alcoholism, criminal tendencies, neuroses, debility, lues, epilepsy, the standard of living, deaths in the family, and the age of the child when they occurred. Is he an orphan? Who dominates the family? Is the upbringing strict, nagging or pampering? Are the children made afraid of life? How is the supervision? Are there step-parents?

Through these questions one sees the child in his family position and can appraise what impressions were conveyed to him.

7. What is the child's position in the sibling sequence? Is he the oldest, the youngest, the only child, the only boy, the only girl? Are there rivalry, much crying, malicious laughter, blind depreciation tendencies toward others?

This is significant for the character of the child and his attitude toward people in general.

Interests

8. What thoughts has the child had on the choice of occupation? What occupation have his family members? How is the marriage of his parents? What does he think about marriage?

These questions allow conclusions regarding the courage and confidence of the child in the future.

9. What are his favorite games, stories, characters in history and fiction? Does he like to spoil other children's games? Does he get lost in fantasy? Is he a cool-headed thinker and does he reject fantasy?

These questions give hints regarding the models of superiority the child may have.

Recollection and Dreams

10. What are the child's earliest recollections? What are his impressive or recurring dreams? Falling, flying, powerless, missing the train, racing, being a prisoner, anxiety dreams?

In these experiences one often finds an inclination toward isolation, voices warning toward caution, impulses of ambition, tendency to passivity, preferences for certain persons.

Discouraged Behavior

11. In what respect is the child discouraged? Does he feel neglected? Does he respond to attention and praise? Has he superstitious ideas? Does he avoid difficulties? Does

FIGURE 4.1. Continued.

he try his hand at various things only to give them up again? Is he uncertain about his future? Does he believe in the injurious effect of heredity? Was he systematically discouraged by his environment? Is his outlook on life pessimistic?

These questions yield important viewpoint for the fact that the child has lost his self-confidence and seeks his way in an erring direction.

12. Are there further bad habits? Does the child make faces? Does he act stupid, childish, or funny?

These are not very courageous attempts to attract attention.

Organ Inferiorities

13. Has the child speech disabilities? Is he awkward, ugly, club-footed, knock-kneed, or bow-legged? Did he have rickets? Is he poorly developed? Is he abnormally stout, tall, or small? Has he eye or ear defects? Is he mentally retarded? Is he left-handed? Does he snore at night? Is he remarkably handsome?

These questions refer to life-difficulties which the child usually overrates. Thus he may arrive at a permanent mood of discouragement. One finds a similar faulty development also in very handsome children. They come to believe that they should be given everything without effort and thus they miss the proper preparation for life.

Inferiority [Symptom] Complex

14. Does the child speak openly of his inability, his "lack of talent" for school? For work? Or for life? Does he have thoughts of suicide? Is there any connection in point of time between his defeats and his disorders (waywardness, gang formation)? Does he overrate outward success? Is he submissive, bigoted, rebellious?

These questions refer to forms of expression of extensive discouragement. They often occur after attempts to get ahead have come to grief, not only on account of their inherent inappropriateness, but also on account of insufficient understanding on the part of the environment. The symptoms are substitute satisfactions in a "secondary theater of operations."

Positive Assets

15. Name the things in which the child is successful.

These are important hints, for it is possible that the interests, inclinations and preparations of the child point to a different direction from that which he has taken so far.

For Use with Adults

In case of adult failures I have found the following interview schedule to be valuable. By adhering to it the experienced therapist will gain an extensive insight into the style of the life of the individual already within about half an hour. My own inquiries take the following sequence, although they do not always adhere to it. Those who are not familiar with

(*continued*)

FIGURE 4.1. Continued.

medical questioning will not fail to notice the similarity between this and our sequence. For the Individual Psychologist, thanks to the system by which he works, the answers will yield many a glimpse that would otherwise have remained unnoticed.

1. What are your complaints?
2. What was your situation when you first noticed your symptoms?
3. What is your situation now?
4. What is your occupation?
5. Describe your parents as to their character, and their health. If not alive, what illness caused their death? What was their relation to yourself?
6. How many brothers and sisters have you? What is your position in the birth order? What is their attitude toward you? How do they get along in life? Do they also have any illness?
7. Who was your father's or your mother's favorite? What kind of upbringing did you have?
8. Inquire for signs of pampering in childhood (timidity, shyness, difficulties in forming friendships, disorderliness).
9. What illnesses did you have in childhood and what was your attitude toward them?
10. What are your earliest childhood recollections?
11. What do you fear, or what do you fear the most?
12. What is your attitude toward the opposite sex? What was it in childhood and later years?
13. What occupation would have interested you the most, and if you did not adopt it, why not?
14. Is the patient ambitious, sensitive, inclined to outbursts of temper, pedantic, domineering, shy, or impatient?
15. What sort of persons are around you at present? Are they impatient, bad-tempered, or affectionate?
16. How do you sleep?
17. What dreams do you have? (Of falling, flying, recurrent dreams, prophetic, and examinations, missing a train)
18. What illnesses are there in your family background?

FIGURE 4.1. Concluded.
From *The Individual Psychology of Alfred Adler* by Heinz L. Ansbacher & Rowena R. Ansbacher. Copyright © 1956 by Basic Books, Inc. Copyright renewed 1984 by Heinz L. and Rowena R. Ansbacher. Reprinted by permission of Basic Books, a member of Perseus Books L.L.C.

it will instead be more detailed and give hints to the client's lifestyle goals, or what Adlerians tend to call preferred movement (Schneider, 2007).

IP counselors are very interested in **family constellation,** or the characteristics of clients' families, including birth order, parental influences, and family dynamics (Shulman, 1973). These qualities can be assessed casually or through a structured interview developed by Dreikurs (1952–53). The interviewer asks the client to describe himself, his siblings, and his parents and includes questions about relationships among family members.

Sandy prefers to use the informal mode of assessing lifestyle and family constellation. She gently encourages James to talk about his family life, both before his foster placements and after. She looks for clues about how James learned to strive for significance in his self-centered, aggressive style. These hints are found in his very early environment and the success such behaviors had in James getting what he wanted, particularly the attention of important others. Because James sees his problems as mostly the result of other people and therefore does not present symptoms, Sandy asks James the question this way: "What would be different in your life if folks got off your back?" James' initial response is, "Then I'd be able to do what I want whenever I want without anyone hassling me." Sandy sees this answer as reflecting James' self-centered lifestyle, because he wishes to pursue his own agenda without consideration for, or contribution to, others. However, when James begins to relax and trust Sandy, he indicates that he'd like to finish school, get a job, and maybe find a real girlfriend. These goals seem much more responsible and socially useful.

Adler believed that "there is no such thing as a random or meaningless recollection" (Adler, 1927/1998, p. 41). Thus, the IP counselor is very interested in **early recollections** (ERs; Carlson et al., 2006; Mosak & Di Pietro, 2006). The client's memories of his early childhood are considered reflective of his *current* views on life, or lifestyle (Mosak & Di Pietro, 2006). It does not matter if they are real—they nonetheless provide valuable clues about the individual's life plan and goals (Ansbacher & Ansbacher, 1956). Early recollections also reveal information about the person's level of social interest. For instance, Louise remembers building a sand castle at the beach. If she remembers helping her little brother build the castle, her social interest would be more evident than if she remembers building it alone. If you are interested in using ERs, you would be wise to consult Mosak and Di Pietro (2006) who give a detailed treatment of the assessment and interpretation of these.

One of James' earliest memories is of his mother and stepfather fighting. The stepfather threw a chair across the room and then stormed out of the house. A second memory is of playing in a field with his older sister Karen and falling down after stubbing his toe. Karen kissed the toe and made it better.

Sandy is both disturbed and encouraged by these early recollections. The first memory indicates a negative view of adult relationships and a view that problems are solved through fighting and physical aggression. The second memory, however, suggests that James can recognize and accept caring in others. Maybe he does know something about cooperation with others because it takes some cooperation for two children to play together.

Adler carefully distinguished his theory about **dreams** from that of the psychoanalytic perspective. Rather than dealing with the past, in the IP system, dreams are seen as future oriented. Dreams are thought to represent some problem currently confronting the person and are filled with private logic (Bird, 2005). They often offer solutions to the problem, but these solutions are sometimes simplistic (Ansbacher & Ansbacher, 1956). For instance, if you dream about flying, Adler would contend that you are struggling with whether to take a particular action. The dream gives you a sense of buoyancy, as well as the sense that you can do what others cannot (fly). Thus, this dream conveys an inflated sense of superiority (Ansbacher & Ansbacher, 1956, p. 363). Because of the influence of the individual's private logic on dreams, dream symbols can not be interpreted through a fixed system such as Freud's (Bird, 2005).

James tells Sandy that he had a dream that he was Dennis Rodman. Because James does not play sports at all, much less basketball, Sandy assumes that his dream reflects his exaggerated superiority feelings. That he picked Dennis Rodman, an unconventional player to say the least, would be interesting to Sandy.

Informal assessment. From an individual psychology perspective, assessment begins the instant the counselor meets the client. Adler thought that every action of the client provides information about the client's person, right down to the client's handshake. The counselor watches carefully all of the client's behavior, verbal and nonverbal.

The first time James appears for his appointment, Sandy closely observes the way he presents himself. She notices that he carries himself in a confident, almost cocky way, and that he is dressed in a hip fashion. He does not offer to shake hands with Sandy, and when he sits down, he leans back and crosses his legs. Although he is not actively hostile, he does not seem engaged in the counseling process. Sandy tentatively hypothesizes that James has some stake in appearing "cool" and that his general manner of relating to others is "cooler than you." She wonders if he uses this display to keep people away from him.

Overview of the Therapeutic Atmosphere

Mosak (2005) identified three important factors in IP counseling: faith, hope, and love. The client must develop faith in the counselor. This attitude is encouraged by the therapist's confidence in herself and her willingness to listen nonjudgmentally to the client. Hope is also essential for the discouraged client. The counselor should encourage the client to accept the challenges of life and therapy. Hope may also come from feeling understood by the counselor. Love for the client is in the most general sense, of course. The client must feel that the counselor cares for him. The counselor's empathic listening is important in establishing this condition, but she must avoid the "pitfalls such as infantilizing, oversupporting or becoming a victim of the patient" (Mosak, 2000, p. 70).

A critical goal of the therapist in IP counseling is to understand the client through understanding his lifestyle. To this end, IP counselors use active listening, empathy, and observation in their attempts to build a picture of the client's ways of operating in the world (Mosak & Maniacci, 1999).

Adler thought that the length of therapy depended on the level of cooperation displayed by the client. However, "An Individual Psychology treatment, properly carried out, should show at least a perceptible partial success in three months, often even sooner" (Adler, as cited in Ansbacher & Ansbacher, 1956, p. 344).

Sandy works very hard to understand James' views on life. She asks him to tell his story and uses her basic counseling skills to let James know that she is actively trying to enter his world as best as she can. Telling him that she is sure that his life can get better, Sandy tries to give James a sense of hope for his future. She has faith in his ability to change. Sandy's confidence in him and true expression of acceptance, understanding, and caring create a relationship in which James can begin to trust himself and his counselor.

ROLES OF CLIENT AND COUNSELOR

The relationship in Adlerian counseling is egalitarian (Sweeney, 1989); the therapist must avoid any semblance of superiority (Dreikurs, 1953). Manaster (1990) asserted that IP counseling is a "face-to-face, cooperative learning endeavor with, it might be said, two experts—the patient, the expert on himself or herself; and the therapist; the expert on helping the patient to relate to the theory and its emphasis on social interest" (p. 46).

The IP counselor is an educator (Dreikurs, 1953) and encourager. The educational function requires the counselor to be active and directive (Carlson et al., 2006). To be a good encourager, the counselor should be warm and human (Peven & Shulman, 1986). As part of being human, the counselor admits her own fallibility and models a courageous approach to life by being willing to make mistakes and acknowledge them.

Despite the egalitarian roles espoused by the IP approach, the client is still a learner in the process of counseling (Schnieder, 2007). The client has choices in his life, but first he must recognize his faulty lifestyle. The therapist's job is to point out the client's mistakes.

GOALS

Adler wrote, "In practice we attempt to undo the great errors, to substitute smaller errors, and to reduce these further until they are no longer harmful" (as cited in Ansbacher & Ansbacher, 1956, p. 187). An IP therapist tries to help the client understand and change his faulty lifestyle and selfish goals so that he can achieve success in the tasks of life. Dreikurs (1953) observed that the way to psychological health was correction of "their attitude to their fellow beings" (p. 85) and the modification of life goals. Further, "success in psychological treatment depends on the therapist's ability to make fearless co-operators in life out of timid and discouraged people" (Dreikurs, 1953, p. 85). In summary, the goals of IP counseling are to give the client insight into his lifestyle, allowing the possibility of change in the direction of increased social interest. Four criteria are named by Carlson et al. (2006): decreasing symptoms, increasing functioning, increasing the client's sense of humor, and producing a change in client's perspectives (p. 130).

Sandy approaches James with respect, assuming that he has choices in this relationship as in any other. She treats James as an equal, even though she knows that part of her job is to help him understand his faulty lifestyle. Working in a cooperative and encouraging manner with

James helps him to assume responsibility for his situation and at the same time exposes him to a relationship high in social interest.

PROCESS OF THERAPY

Adlerians see counseling as progressing through four phases: "(1) establishing the client-therapist relationship; (2) collaborating to understand the client's lifestyle and patterns of movement; (3) generating insight into useful and less useful lifestyle patterns; and (4) anchoring a reorientation of lifestyle choices to the client's current life task challenges" (Schneider, 2007, p. 39). In the relationship phase, empathy is critical; Adler maintained that "it is essential for the practitioner to possess, in a considerable degree, the gift of *putting himself in the other person's place*" (Adler, 1929/1969, p. 25; italics in original). The IP counselor uses attending behavior and active listening to develop a trusting relationship with the client that is based on the client feeling understood. Conveying the certainty that the client has the power to change is also critical; encouraging the client begins from the very start of therapy and is an important process throughout the relationship. (Dinkmeyer et al., 1987). Clear goals need to be agreed on because a mismatch between client and counselor goals can lead to resistance (the sources of resistance are discussed later). Dinkmeyer and colleagues (1987) suggested that in this first stage the counselor can also begin to offer some tentative hypotheses about the purpose of the client's behavior as one form of empathy.

James would be most happy if people would just let him do what he pleases. Sandy begins her work with him in an accepting way, trying very hard to understand his perspective and actively communicating her understanding to James. She tries to determine how she and James can agree on goals for their meetings and concludes that she can go along with James' idea to get people "off his back" because that probably involves his taking responsibility for his actions and acting in more socially contributing ways.

The second phase of counseling is lifestyle analysis and assessment (Dinkmeyer et al., 1987). The IP counselor asks questions about the life tasks and tries to understand the client's lifestyle and associated goals. Adlerian counselors recognize that clients' lifestyles come into the therapy session with them (Mosak & Maniacci, 1999). The therapist is ever alert for the client's *movement*—that is, she is always watching the client's efforts to achieve his goals. For instance, a depressed client's behavior will include speaking negatively about himself. The IP therapist might interpret this behavior as movement toward a goal that included being the center of attention, or avoiding responsibility for life tasks. After all, if the client is a worthless unit, he can hardly be expected to attempt to tackle the serious, difficult challenges of life. At the same time, the client is achieving the socially useless goal of superiority by commanding the undivided attention of others.

Dinkmeyer and colleagues (1987) suggested that discovering the person's "number one priority" is helpful in understanding lifestyle (p. 96). According to these authors, there are four types of priorities: ruling, getting, avoiding, and socially useful (p. 97). The client's goals and basic mistakes are connected to the relative importance he places on these priorities.

Sandy works to try to understand James' ways of achieving significance. In his very early environment, he probably was praised for being the "tough guy" or was ignored. He likely felt neglected and scared. James apparently received parental attention when he acted out. As a result, James' past behavior seems to have prioritized ruling and getting over other things. Now he appears to be changing his focus and placing more socially useful goals in the forefront. He wants to finish school, get a job, and learn to relate more productively with others. These goals clearly indicate a shift in priorities.

The third stage of counseling is insight, in which the counselor helps the client understand his lifestyle, and become aware of how he chooses to function and why (Dinkmeyer & Sperry, 2000). Interpretation therefore plays a major role in this phase. To be most facilitative, interpretation is usually offered tentatively, in a questioning manner. "The counselor is modeling the courage to be imperfect, which often teaches as much as an insightful interpretation" (Dinkmeyer & Sperry, 2000, p. 101). Occasionally, the counselor will offer a deliberately exaggerated version of the client's life goals or priorities, hoping to get the client to laugh at himself.

Sandy approaches James gently and tentatively with interpretations about his lifestyle. She empathizes with his tough early environment and indicates that she understands how he became so active and rebellious as a way of offsetting the feelings induced by neglect and abuse. Sandy might say, "Y' know, it seems a little bit like in the past you've felt cornered, so that you had to 'get' folks before they 'got' you—you had to be the most powerful, so they wouldn't mess with you." She might joke with him about his presentation as a really cool dude, showing the world that nothing affects him. She would only very carefully approach the feelings of fear that he experienced early on; in the best case, she would let James express these himself before working with them.

If the insight stage is successful, the counselor and client enter the reorientation phase. The client, accepting the counselor's interpretations and aware of his mistakes and faulty goals, works with the counselor to find ways to behave differently. New, more realistic, and socially appropriate goals are established (Dinkmeyer & Sperry, 2000).

James slowly becomes aware of how his mistaken goals have led to a troubled existence. He concedes that he has bullied people, trying to boost his sense of power and worth. Even though James has difficulty acknowledging this motivation, Sandy senses that he is truly struggling with his life and tells him so.

Resistance in IP counseling is seen as arising from several possible situations. Adler thought resistance represented "lack of courage to return to the useful side of life" (Ansbacher &

Ansbacher, 1956, p. 338). Other individual psychologists have suggested that resistance can also arise when the client and therapist are working toward different goals. For example, the client tends to continue moving toward his faulty goals, and the counselor may wish to discuss the underlying dynamics of the client's behaviors (Peven & Shulman, 1986). A second source of resistance, according to Peven and Shulman, is found in the therapist's challenging interpretations, which can call forth some clients' animosity toward society.

Because Adler was interested in child development, he devoted much thought to how to understand and help the parents of dysfunctional children. He emphasized that parents who consult the counselor should never be blamed for the misbehavior of the child (Ansbacher & Ansbacher, 1956). The parents come to the counselor already feeling insecure and inferior, and Adler advised that the counselor support and encourage them. This support allows the counselor to create an atmosphere in which she can offer suggestions tentatively to the parents.

James may resist Sandy's attempts to help him understand his lifestyle, particularly if she rushes him. He has been neglected and abused and is probably very sensitive to others' attempts to control him. He does not trust easily. James verbalizes that he is working toward taking more responsibility for himself and his actions; Sandy thinks that it might be better to work in this area at first with James to avoid engaging his rebellious tendencies.

THERAPEUTIC TECHNIQUES

Although the list of techniques available to the IP counselor in this section is quite lengthy, it is not totally inclusive. IP therapists are technical eclectics because "Adlerian theory allows, if not demands, that therapists use any and all techniques that hold promise and can be understood as in keeping with the theory" (Manaster, 1990, p. 46). For example, Carlson et al. (2006) suggest using a two-chair dialog to help clients resolve decisional conflict. The client switches back and forth between chairs expressing the pros and cons of the situation. Interestingly, these authors maintain that the client's real choice is indicated by the chair in which she finally stops.

With that said, I present a brief description of some of the major techniques endorsed by IP counselors. Further and more elaborate discussions of IP techniques can be found in Carlson et al. (2006) or Mosak and Maniacci (1998).

INTERPRETATION

Interpretation of the client's behavior is one of the key interventions in the IP counselor's arsenal. The counselor uses all of the information she has collected to form hypotheses about the client's lifestyle and associated goals, and then carefully and tentatively offers these insights (Sweeney, 1989). Adler cautioned that hitting the client over the head with interpretation would not be helpful, saying, "nobody who has understood anything of Individual Psychology would attempt to cure by upbraiding the patient, as if we could do good by taking up a moralistic attitude. A patient has to be brought into such a state of feeling that he likes to listen, and wants to understand. Only then can he be influenced to live what he has understood" (as cited in Ansbacher & Ansbacher, 1956, p. 335). According to Dinkmeyer and Sperry (2000), interpretation is intended to create awareness of "(1) lifestyle, (2) current psychological movement and its direction, (3) goals, purposes, and intentions, and (4) private logic and how it works" (p. 99).

James will not easily accept that his "attitude" is a dysfunctional way to gain significance in the world, devoid of courage and social interest. Sandy must be very careful in helping James to see that he seeks power over others to defy the feelings of inferiority he harbors. Sandy will gently and carefully help him to see that his lifestyle has been one in which he had to gain power by deceiving or hurting others before they hurt him. His logic seems to be that others are evil anyway, so they deserve what they get. However, his current movement seems a little more useful; he is verbalizing more responsibility for his life and more useful goals. Sandy would be sure to point this part out and encourage James to do more.

ENCOURAGEMENT

Equally as important as interpretation is encouragement because it helps the client find his own strengths and recognize his power to affect the world through choice (Dinkmeyer et al., 1987; Eckstein et al., 2006). Encouragement is not the same as praise; ideally, it happens before the client attempts a desired change or action (Thompson & Rudolph, 2000). Encouragement can also be used to combat the sense of discouragement that some clients bring to counseling. For example, an IP therapist can help a client to distinguish between *failing* and *being a failure* (Mosak & Maniacci, 1998).

Sandy would let James know that she has confidence in him as a human being. She thinks that he could achieve the goals he talks about, but is careful not to set him up by placing too much emphasis on them. She is genuinely supportive of him, encouraging him when he takes actions directed toward doing better at school and in relating to others. She searches for instances in his life that were successful so that she can help him build on these. For instance, Sandy might compliment James on getting his job or getting through a day at school without fighting.

NATURAL AND LOGICAL CONSEQUENCES

One way to encourage clients to assume responsibility for their choices is to allow them to experience the consequences of their behaviors. Natural consequences refer to simply letting events take their course; that is, the world imposes these consequences. Too often we try to "save" others by preventing negative consequences. Parents who call the teacher to excuse Suzy's missing homework are doing just this. Often we have to stand a little discomfort to let natural consequences happen. For instance, I once counseled a family in which the parents were very upset with their teenage daughter for leaving her dirty clothes on the bathroom floor. Even though it was not pleasant for the parents to do so, I advised the natural consequence of simply leaving the clothes where the daughter had left them.

Imagine the effect on a 13-year-old of not being able to wear her favorite items of apparel because they were dirty! This young woman quickly learned to pick up her clothes and place them in the laundry hamper, I can assure you.

Logical consequences are those resulting from an intervention by another person (Sweeney, 1989). They teach the social rules of life (Mosak & Maniacci, 1999). In the previous example, the parents who decide to pick up their teen's clothes could also decide where to place them, thereby depriving her of the valuable articles for some period of time. Logical consequences are different from punishment (in which Adlerians do not believe) because they are based on social rules logically related to the undesirable behavior. They are imposed with a friendly attitude and an emphasis on the target's choice (Sweeney, 1989). Adler maintained that "punishment, especially corporal punishment is always harmful to children. Any teaching that cannot be given in a spirit of friendship is wrong teaching" (1931/1998, p. 106).

James experienced the natural consequences of his irresponsible behavior when he lost his job after getting drunk at work. His foster parents, if they caught him stealing something, could take something of his away for a period of time as a way of imposing logical consequences.

ACTING AS IF

Many clients excuse their behavior by saying, "if only . . ." The technique of acting as if is designed for this situation. Whatever the "if only" is, the client is asked to act as if it were true (Watts, Peluso, & Lewis, 2005). Tracy might bemoan the fact that she is not pretty and confident, explaining why she has so few friends and is therefore miserable all of the time. Jerry, the IP counselor, might then ask her how she would act if she were pretty and confident. Then he would direct her to act that way for the next week. This technique helps the IP counselor to change the client's view of herself and also to learn or exhibit previously unexplored behaviors.

Initially, James is not a good candidate for the "acting as if" technique because he presents a tough guy front. He tends to blame others for his behaviors, rather than saying, "if only I was, I could do better." However, over time James becomes more comfortable with Sandy and is able to trust her. At this point he is able to acknowledge that he feels insecure in "normal" social situations, such as at work or school. He says, "If only I was more confident with people, I wouldn't have to dis them so much." Sandy asks James to act as if he is confident for the next week, just to see what happens.

PUSHING THE BUTTON

Mosak (1985) devised the push-button technique for clients who think that they don't have control of their emotions. The client is instructed to visualize a pleasant scene or event and to study the accompanying feeling. Next, the client imagines a scene that evokes negative feeling (e.g., pain, embarrassment, anger) and attends to that feeling. Finally, the client is asked to revert back to the original, pleasant emotion. Thus, the counselor teaches the client that he creates his emotions by choosing what to focus on.

Sandy asks James to conjure up the feelings he has when he's around a girl he likes. Then she instructs him to think about being fired from his job and focus on those emotions. Next, Sandy asks him to refocus on the first set of feelings. Sandy and James then discuss how he was able to change his mood by changing his thoughts.

CATCHING ONESELF

Once the client has accepted the counselor's interpretation, he can practice catching himself in his unique way of achieving power. With a little practice, he can even catch himself before beginning to engage in the undesirable behavior. Tamera tends to avoid playing sports by putting herself down. In this way, she avoids the failure that she fears. If she could catch herself when she begins to disparage herself and reorient herself with "it's OK if I'm not perfect," she might improve her relationships with others, not to mention her physical skills.

James has a tendency to fly into temper tantrums and throw things. Sandy thinks that this is one way he fights off his inferiority feelings—by proving how powerful he is. He also verbally puts others down, with the same motive. Sandy asks James to observe his thoughts and feelings closely, to perhaps learn to recognize when he is feeling inferior or that someone has put him down. Eventually, he might be able to interrupt his patterns and change how he relates to others when feeling insecure.

CREATING IMAGES

Mosak (2005) discussed helping the client use imagery to exemplify his faulty goals. In many cases, these images can even be used humorously, allowing the client to laugh at himself. For example, a client who controls others through constantly failing and needing help could be instructed to think of himself as Charlie Brown who battles the tree-eating kite. Every time Charlie tries to fly his kite, the tree somehow wins. Then he has to visit Lucy, the 5-cent psychiatric professional!

Sandy has James think of himself as Arnold Schwarzenegger any time he feels the impulse to overpower others through intimidation. She winks and calls him Arnold when he starts speaking in these ways, and says "hasta la vista."

PLEASING SOMEONE

Adler advocated confronting the client's faulty lifestyle by advising him to think daily about how to please someone (Ansbacher & Ansbacher, 1956, p. 347). If the client obeys this directive immediately (which is rare, according to Adler), the counselor has succeeded in turning his interest toward others and thereby increasing social interest. If the client refuses, the real motivations (purpose) behind the symptoms emerge. Rather than confronting those motivations, the counselor continues to insist on attending to others. For instance, Adler related an instance in which the client responded to the directive to please others by objecting that others did not please him (Ansbacher & Ansbacher, 1956). Adler simply told the client not to worry about others, but that he (the client) must accomplish the task for his own health (p. 347).

Sandy decides to have James do a pleasing task. Even though it might be difficult and new for James, she asks him to do something nice for his foster mother in the next few days. James struggles with what this task might be, but finally settles on offering to take on a small task around the household, taking out the garbage. He surprises Sandy by saying that he might be willing to take on this duty on a permanent basis.

PARADOXICAL INTENTION

In this counterintuitive technique, sometimes called antisuggestion (Carlson et al., 2006), clients are encouraged to intensify their symptom. For instance, Billy could be asked to practice his temper tantrums to become even better at them. Billy might also be told that his tantrums are very effective in distracting his mother from making him take responsibility for household tasks, and so he should practice even harder. Using this kind of rationale is what Adler called "spitting in the soup" or exposing the function of the symptom (Carlson et al., 2006; Mosak & Maniacci, 1998). The idea behind paradox is to increase the client's awareness of the symptom and its consequences (Dinkmeyer et al., 1987). Also, paradox can help clients give up symptoms because they begin to look absurd.

Sandy can't think of a really good paradoxical directive for James. She could have him practice getting angry, only at a certain time of the day. If James complied, the social function of the anger would be removed. If James did not comply, he'd have a smooth day, which might not be a bad thing for him. Another option is to tell James that he is cool, but not quite cool enough, since others seem not to fully appreciate how cool he is. She asks him to find some ways to be even more cool and observe others' reactions to him. Sandy hopes that James will start to examine what cool means and how putting others down prevents him from truly connecting with them.

EVALUATION OF THE THEORY

IP theory is a "grand" theory that, like psychoanalysis, tries to explain everything. Many of its assumptions are difficult to test. An active community of researchers and writers, however, is busily advancing Adler's work. The level of devotion of these adherents could be considered either a strength or a weakness.

Adler's thoughts had significant influence on many subsequent theorists, including Carl Rogers, Albert Ellis, and Abraham Maslow (Hoffman, 1994). The influence of Adler's description of the basic mistakes can be clearly seen in contemporary cognitive and cognitive-behavior theory.

Perhaps Adler's greatest contribution is that he developed a theory that recognized and even emphasized the effects of social class, racism, and sex on the behavior of individuals. Adler was far ahead of his contemporaries in this sense, and his ideas are even more salient in our increasingly pluralistic society.

Some critics contend that IP theory is too simple and that it is only common sense (Mosak & Maniacci, 1999). All behavior is explained by referring to inferiority feelings, striving for power, and social interest. Of course, Adler would reply that common sense is the highest form of reasoning.

The changing nature of families is a potential problem for classic IP theory. Developed mostly around the conventional two-parent nuclear family, the theory may have more difficulties in validly explaining what happens in a single-parent family that includes grand-parents in the household, for example. Stepfamilies (i.e., multiple family units) might also pose similar problems.

QUALITIES OF THE THEORY

Precision and Testability. IP theory has many of the same weaknesses as psychoanalysis in terms of testability. Many of the constructs in IP theory are difficult to operationalize and measure, at best. Monte and Sollod (2003) observed that the major ideas in IP theory (for instance inferiority feelings or safeguarding strategies) are not very open to disconfirmation. Much like psychoanalysis, IP theory can explain almost any pattern of behavior. If a client acts out, it is because of a superiority complex that is compensating for feelings of inferiority. If a client is passive, it is because she is afraid to risk exposing herself to failure, naturally because she feels inferior. No specific predictions can be derived that would specify which behavior will result. Both stem from the basic inferiority complex.

IP theory is not the most precise theory in the bunch. Adler seems to have relied on commonsense terms that most people think they understand, rather than clearly defining his constructs. For instance, what exactly constitutes pampering? Many of IP theory's constructs are so broad that they are difficult to define or measure. An example would be lifestyle, which, as noted earlier, was defined in many different ways by both Adler and those who followed him. On the other hand, some aspects of the theory are definitionally clear, and predictions can be generated about them. For instance, Adler provided very clear predictions about the behaviors of children in the various birth orders. Unfortunately, we can't seem to agree on the right way to measure these. Social interest has been measured in several different ways, as has lifestyle.

In spite of these problems, researchers have worked hard to define some of the IP constructs, mostly through self-report measures (Watkins & Guarnaccia, 1999). For instance, researchers have developed measures of social interest, early recollections, and lifestyle. General hypotheses can be derived from the theory, but as noted earlier, they are not always as precise as we would like. When more specific predictions can be derived, such as those about the personality correlates of the various birth orders, there is often great disagreement about how to define and measure the constructs. Illustrating this controversy, Jordan, Whiteside, and Manaster (1982) presented seven different schemes for birth order, based on the number of children and the sex of sibling as well as ordinal position.

Empirical Validity. Some research seems to support the major constructs and predictions of IP theory. Most of this research is published, however, in the *Journal of Individual Psychology* rather than more generic psychological journals, leaving questions of potential interpretive bias open. Very little organized outcome research has appeared in the literature, and IP counseling has not been a subject of the major psychotherapy outcome studies. Major constructs such as superiority and inferiority complexes have received little attention, probably because they are so hard to measure.

RESEARCH SUPPORT

Outcome Research. Outcome research testing IP counseling is scarce; the few outcome studies I could locate were very dated. For instance, Shlien, Mosak, and Dreikurs (1962) reported on an outcome test of time-limited therapy (maximum of 20 sessions) in which one of the approaches was IP (the other was person-centered therapy). A Q-sort method was used to measure outcome, in which clients sorted adjectives into two piles, one for their "real" selves and one for their "ideal" selves. Shlien and colleagues (1962) reported that these two sorts matched more closely after counseling compared to before counseling and concluded that IP theory was supported. Although a case could be made that increases in self-ideal are supportive of IP theory, it is more directly predicted by person-centered theory.

Several smaller studies have provided some support for IP theory. Zarski, Sweeney, and Barcikowski (1977) examined the relations between counselor social interest, client satisfaction with counseling, and client outcome as measured by the California Psychological Inventory (CPI). Results showed a positive correlation between counselor social interest and counseling outcome as measured by a client satisfaction inventory and client self-acceptance and sociability as measured by the CPI scales. This study would seem to support IP theory in that good counselors would be those with high social interest. However, it is important to note that (a) client self-acceptance and sociability may not be the best measures of client outcome and (b) this study was not experimental in nature so no causal relationships between counselor social interest and client outcome can be assumed.

Krebs (1986) and Burnett (1988) reviewed the literature on the effectiveness of Adlerian parenting programs and found some support for these interventions, but the majority of the studies reviewed could be criticized on methodological grounds. Overall, then, I tend to agree with Watkins and Guarnaccia's (1999) contention that IP researchers need to do more and more rigorous outcome research.

Theory-Testing Research. Watkins and Guarnaccia (1999) reviewed research on four major constructs of IP theory: birth order, social interest, early recollections, and lifestyle; they concluded that the research evidence supports IP theory. In an earlier review, Watkins (1982) came to a similar conclusion. However, overall, most of the research on IP theorists is conducted by IP advocates and is therefore subject to potential investigator bias. As noted earlier, much of the research has been published in the *Journal of Individual*

Psychology, an obviously IP-oriented journal. Many of the studies of IP constructs seem to suffer from a lack of specificity of predictions based on the theory. That is, an investigator will study a construct (early recollections, for instance), find some findings (that accounting students' recollections include more references to nonfamily members than music students'), and then explain how these fit the theory. More convincing results would be obtained if strong theoretical predictions could be made at the outset. Finally, significant methodological problems can be found in many of the studies that are cited in support of IP theory. The current state of research in the IP arena seems to be similar.

That said, I think it is important to commend the Adlerians for the energy they devote to testing, extending, and applying their theoretical approach. With few exceptions, the investigative activity around other counseling theories pales by comparison to what the IP theorists are doing. To illustrate, I will briefly review some of the research in each of the areas identified by Watkins and Guarnaccia (1999) as well as research in the area of career/vocational behavior, a topic of recent interest to IP advocates.

Career/Vocational Behavior. Watts and Engels (1995) surveyed research relevant to the life task of work or vocation. Examining studies investigating birth order, early recollections, lifestyle, and social interest, they concluded that although the research is sparse, some evidence for IP theory could be gleaned. Elliot, Amerikaner, and Swank (Amerikaner, Elliot, & Swank, 1988; Elliot, Amerikaner, & Swank, 1987) presented two interesting studies. They examined early recollections (ERs) as predictors of vocational choice and found that ERs could be coded for vocational themes. Further, the ER codings predicted career choice as well as other, more traditional predictors of career choice (i.e., the Vocational Preference Inventory). In a more recent study, Kasler and Nevo (2003) reported similar findings, only they used the Self-Directed Search.

Amerikaner and colleagues (1988) reasoned that individuals higher in social interest would, in general, be more satisfied vocationally. They based this prediction on Adler's contention that social interest is vital to success in life in general, and to vocational success and satisfaction with work in particular. Amerikaner and colleagues' results confirmed the predicted relationship between social interest and career satisfaction, lending support to IP theory. Other studies have failed to support IP theory, such as a study of vocational preference and lifestyle by Gentry, Winer, Sigelman, and Phillips (1980). These investigators found no relationship between lifestyle and vocational preferences, which should logically be linked according to IP theory.

Social Interest. Three instruments have been developed to measure social interest: the Social Interest Scale (SIS; Crandall, 1981), the Social Interest Index (SII; Greever, Tseng, & Friedland, 1973), and the Sulliman Scale of Social Interest (SSSI; Sulliman, 1973). Each of the instruments has identifiable weaknesses (Watkins, 1994). Even more troubling is Bass, Curlette, Kern, and McWilliams' (2002) finding that across five measures of social interest, correlations were very small (0.08–0.22) suggesting that the scales were measuring different constructs. When measurement tools are weak, it is difficult to draw conclusions about the theoretical predictions tested using these instruments. On the other hand, one could take the pragmatic position and say that these measures are the best we have right now, and only cautiously rely on the findings. Taking this second perspective, then, we find that overall, social interest as measured by all three major scales has been found to correlate positively with altruism, trustworthiness, religious belief, increasing age, volunteerism, vigor, marital adjustment, and a number of other personality variables (Johnson, Smith, & Nelson, 2003; Leak, 2006; Sweitzer, 2005; Watkins, 1994). Also, social interest has been found to be negatively related to characteristics such as narcissism, depression, and hostility. To give one example of a study testing IP predictions, Crandall (1981) found that the Social Interest Scale (SIS) scores of a group of convicted felons were significantly lower than those of a comparison group of college students and university employees. This finding would seem to directly confirm Adler's contention that individuals who violate the law have low social interest.

Psychometric arguments aside, research continues on social interest. One example is provided by Johnson et al., (2003), who tested the relations between birth order, family characteristics, and social interest, using the SIS. Although birth order was not related to social interest, family characteristics such as levels of conflict and cohesiveness, were. Thus, these results partially support IP theory. Sweitzer (2005) found that the relationship between social interest and self-concept was weaker in conduct disordered adolescents than in a comparison group, again providing some support for the theory.

Birth Order. Birth order is by far the most controversial area of IP theory. Large amounts of research have been conducted on the effects of birth order, and it is generally concluded that birth order is related to personality but that many other factors are involved in the relationship between birth order and other variables (Monte & Sollod, 2003). Because there is so much research in this area, I will proceed to present only a selective review.

Watkins (1992b) reviewed 25 studies of birth order published in the *Journal of Individual Psychology* from 1981 to 1991. He concluded that although many of these studies could be criticized for not accounting for intervening variables (e.g., sibling sex, age spacing, cultural factors, and socioeconomic status), support was found for some birth order predictions. The clearest support is found in studies of first borns—they are, consistent with the theory, generally found to be more dominant and responsible (Watkins, 1992b, p. 365). However, as Ernst and Angst (1983) pointed out, comparisons of first to later borns are risky because these birth positions tend to be confounded with socioeconomic status (higher SES families tend to have fewer children) and many other factors. Thus, differences that are found between first and later borns may be the result of some of these other factors, not birth order.

Adams (1972) reviewed a large collection of birth order studies and concluded that first borns tend to show greater educational achievement, are more affiliative, and are more dependent than their siblings. Further, they tend to be more conforming and responsible than later borns. Some of these conclusions seem directly related to Adler's ideas (conservatism, responsibility, academic achievement in the sense that it represents responsibility and the adoption of "adult" roles and values), whereas others seem either unrelated or contrary to predictions from IP theory (e.g., affiliation, dependence). For example, Laird and Shelton (2006) thought that later borns would be more dependent, and as a result, would engage in more problematic drinking behavior than first borns. This hypothesis was confirmed in Laird and Shelton's study, but it should be noted that they did not assess for dependency, just alcohol use behaviors and birth order. Also less than clear was the theoretical basis for the link between dependency and problem drinking.

One greatly debated aspect of birth order research revolves around the use of actual ordinal position versus psychological position. As noted earlier, Adler argued that the child's conception of his ordinal position mattered, not the actual order of birth. Unfortunately, most studies of birth order do not assess psychological position, relying only on actual birth order. An instrument has been developed to assess psychological birth order, the Psychological Birth Order Inventory (Cambell, White, & Stewart, 1991). It yields scores that measure psychological characteristics thought to be associated with the various ordinal positions (e.g., the "oldest" scale measures feelings of powerfulness and desire to achieve). However, it appears that this instrument has not been used a great deal, and some studies report less-than-desirable psychometric qualities (i.e., low reliability).

Neglecting the sex of siblings and intervals between children is also a problem with the birth order research (Jordan et al., 1982; Watkins, 1992b). Whether your older sibling is female or male would seem to make a difference in how you related, competed, or affiliated with them. One fairly recent study (Lawson & Brossart, 2004) attempted to address this issue, examining sibling structure and relationship with parents. These authors found that younger brothers of brothers were more intimate with their parents, yet experienced more intimidation from them. Older females with brothers were observed to be less intimate and to experience less parental intimidation. As you probably have noted, these results do not seem to directly bear on IP theory except in a very general way.

Other difficulties in birth order research include the issue of the overall frequencies of the different birth orders. Studies that examine the relative proportions of a particular birth order in an expected situation (for example, are first borns more likely to become politicians?) often overlook the fact that, in general, birth orders are not distributed equally in the population (i.e., in a country with an increasing population, there are more first borns than later borns; Adams, 1972).

Early Recollections. Early recollections (ERs) have been the subject of some attention in the research literature, with inconclusive results (Watkins, 1992a). At a very basic level, some argue that attempting to create standardized scoring systems for ERs is contrary to Adler's conception of the individualistic, holistic approach to people (Kal, 1994). Others disagree (e.g., Bishop, 1993), and it is noteworthy that attempts have been made to standardize the measurement of ERs. The most often-used system in this research is the *Manaster-Perryman Manifest Content Early Recollection Scoring Manual,* which includes 42 variables that form seven clusters: characters (family, mother, father), themes, concern with detail, setting, active/passive, internal/external control, and affect (positive/negative) (Manaster & Perryman, 1974). Note that these variables do not seem especially linked to IP theory, except in very general ways.

Watkins (1992a) maintained that the ER research was supportive of IP theory in that the ERs of counseling clients are more negative and anxiety ridden than those of individuals not in counseling, and further, that they tend to change when clients receive treatment, becoming more positive in theme. Watkins cites other findings that are somewhat supportive of IP theory, but also points out a number of weaknesses in the current research, including the lack of theoretical specificity noted earlier. So, support for the ER construct can be said to be weak, at best.

Lifestyle. As noted earlier, several measures of lifestyle have been developed, for the most part, by the same set of researchers. In what seems to be the earliest attempt to measure life style, Kern (1976) developed the Life Style Inventory Questionnaire (LSIQ). A self-report measure, the LSIQ provides information about birth order, sibling relationships, and so forth, that allows judges to classify people into one of eight categories of lifestyle (e.g., intellectualizer, rebel, getter, driver, superior). In a study of Catholic priests, Newton and Mansager (1986) found that judges using this instrument classified the priests reliably into a lifestyle termed "the right, superior, or good life-style" (p. 369).

The Life-Style Personality Inventory (LSPI; Wheeler, Kern, & Curlette, 1991) measures seven lifestyle themes (conforming/active, conforming/passive, controlling/active, controlling/passive, exploiting/active, exploiting/passive, and displaying inadequacy). The LSPI also includes a measure of social interest. Reliability data for the scales were found to be acceptable; validity data are more sketchy. An extension of the LSPI is the Basic Adlerian Scales for Interpersonal Success-Adult form (BASIS-A; Wheeler, Kern, & Curlette, 1993). Both the LSPI and the BASIS-A ask respondents to answer items as they recollect childhood experiences rather than in reference to current functioning. The assumption is that by asking about childhood perceptions, defensiveness is reduced, thereby avoiding social desirability bias in responding (Wheeler, Kern, & Curlette, 1991). Also, Adler maintained that it was the person's interpretation of his or her life that mattered rather than the reality.

Research using the lifestyle inventories seems inconsistent, probably because of the differing structures of the instruments. Lifestyle has been related to coping styles, patterns of substance use, and relationship functioning (Herrington, Matheny, Curlette, McCarthy, & Penick, 2005; Keene & Wheeler, 1994; Kern, Gfroerer, Summers, Curlette, & Matheny, 1996; Lewis & Osborn, 2004; Logan, Kern, Curlette, & Trad, 1993). In general, this research is still in the preliminary stages and provides only modest support for IP theory. For example, Lewis and Osborn (2004) found that the belonging/social interest lifestyle theme (as measured by the BASIS-A) was positively correlated with problematic alcohol use among college students. They saw this result as counter to the theoretical prediction that this relationship would be negative. However, they did note that one possible explanation for the finding was that the belonging/social interest scale was actually measuring extraversion or sociability, instead of the Adlerian construct. In contrast, Herrington et al. (2005) confirmed expected relationships between lifestyle (belonging) and anxiety.

ISSUES OF INDIVIDUAL AND CULTURAL DIVERSITY

Adler was probably one of the first theorists to recognize the effects of class differences, and he was certainly an early advocate of equality between the sexes. He recognized the socially-based constraints that women experienced and clearly acknowledged the devaluation of the female role in the majority culture of his time. From this perspective, then, we could say that his theory might be somewhat less biased than other approaches in terms of gender considerations. However, he did have fairly stereotypical views of women's roles, characterizing them as demonstrating "masculine" goals if they pursued traditionally male occupations. Feminists would see these values as upholding the patriarchy.

IP theory's focus on social involvement and the importance of relationships would be consistent with the values of cultures that hold collectivistic as compared to individualistic worldviews such as Asian or Native American (Thompson & Rudolph, 2000). For example, Johansen (2005) argued that the basic philosophy of IP was consistent with that of individuals who are of Islamic faith. Adler was aware of the negative effects of racism and classism; this quality clearly differentiated him from his contemporaries. The egalitarian therapeutic relationship and emphasis on cooperation among individuals and with society are also strengths of this theory when working with women and clients from diverse backgrounds.

At the same time, the theory emphasizes individual choice, control, and responsibility, constructs that are Western in orientation. Insight (into lifestyle) is also important in IP counseling; this orientation may be inconsistent with the values of cultures that are action oriented (such as the African American community; Sue & Sue, 2003). On the other hand, Perkins-Dock (2005) argues that several principles of IP make it appropriate for work with African American families, such as "(a) concept of collective unity and social interest, (b) importance placed on the family atmosphere, (c) emphasis on collaborative goal setting, (d) influence of a multigenerational legacy, and (e) flexibility of intervention strategies" (p. 235).

One significant criticism of Adler refers to his views on homosexuality. Referring to these lifestyles as perversions (Ansbacher & Ansbacher, 1956), Adler characterized the choice of a GLB lifestyle as evading the task of love. More recently, his intellectual descendents have argued that Adler's conceptualization needs revision (Chernin & Holden, 1995) and have offered strategies for helping lesbian and gay couples (Fischer, 1993). There is also some evidence that Adler was more tolerant in his views than his writings would suggest. McDowell related an anecdote (in Manaster, Painter, Deutsch, & Overholt, 1977) in which a social worker consulted Adler about a client who was gay. According to this account, upon learning that the client was homosexual, Adler inquired if the client was happy. When McDowell responded that he was, Adler replied, "Well . . . why don't we leave him alone? Eh?" (1977, p. 82).

THE CASE STUDY

IP theory fits James' presentation well because of its emphasis on the influence of the early environment and on the client's ways of operating in the world, or lifestyle. Adler's ideas seem to help in understanding James' story. James is African American, and Adler's recognition of racism clearly applies to this case. IP theory would recognize that as a young African American male, James has likely experienced some aversive interactions with people that were largely based on his race. However, this theory's emphasis on the development of life goals before the age of 6 may overlook the effects of experiences James had subsequent to his first foster placement. Adler had little to say about nontraditional family structures, but he would insist that it was James' interpretation of his environment that was most influential in determining his current functioning.

Summary

IP theory teaches that human life is intricately tied to two basic motivations—the striving for power, or superiority, and the need for belonging, or social interest. An individual develops a unique lifestyle, which is the blueprint for how these needs are met. The lifestyle is formed by the age of 6 and is influenced by the early environment of the child (i.e., birth order, sex, family values). However, what the individual makes of his experience is a creative process; the influences of family, physical environment, and heredity are only part of the equation.

Individuals who are healthy fulfill the basic tasks of life: love, work, and community. They are courageous and able to take responsibility for their lives. Dysfunctional individuals are discouraged. They are selfish and often timid, "yes but" personalities. They walk on the useless side of life and avoid challenge and responsibility.

The goal of IP therapy is to help the client understand his faulty lifestyle. The counselor takes an optimistic outlook, and the relationship is egalitarian. Faith, hope, and love are important qualities of the counseling relationship. Numerous techniques are available to the IP counselor.

Adler was the first major theorist of counseling to recognize the power of social conditions. However, IP theory has been criticized for being commonsense and simplistic. Many of the major assumptions of IP theory are difficult to test, and the research evidence for the system is questionable methodologically.

Visit Chapter 4 on the Companion Website at **www.prenhall.com/murdock** for chapter-specific resources and self-assessments.

CHAPTER 5

Person-Centered Therapy

Carl Rogers

Richard is a 48-year-old male Caucasian. He is a high school graduate and has worked as an insurance salesperson for the past 3 years. Prior to this period he worked at the management level for a telecommunication company, but left this job because he found it too stressful.

Richard presents with depressed mood that affects his physical, social, and occupational functioning. He reports experiencing this depression for about the past 2 years. During this period, Richard characterizes himself as often fatigued, socially withdrawn, and ineffective in work. His income has dropped significantly during the last 2 years. Richard feels guilty for having to rely on his wife, Sandy, as the primary income provider. According to Richard, Sandy often expresses disapproval of him nonverbally, such as when she is writing checks for the monthly bills. The couple argues quite frequently about financial matters.

Richard and Sandy have two adult children (Natalie and James) who have completed college within the past 5 years. Richard reports that both children currently earn more than his present income. This situation makes him feel inadequate. As a result, Richard feels emotionally distant from Natalie and James, and sees them as closer to Sandy.

Richard's social activities typically involve his wife and are work-related. He spends his spare time with his computer or reading. He reports having no close friends.

During counseling sessions Richard seems uncomfortable, has difficulty maintaining eye contact, laughs nervously during the shortest periods of silence, and comments on his discomfort with the lack of structure. Although he seems motivated to change, Richard seems to have difficulty discussing his situation.

BACKGROUND

Person-centered therapy is the creation of Carl Ransom Rogers (1902–1987). Developed over a span of over 40 years, the approach has been known by three different names. Rogers first called his model nondirective therapy. As his ideas continued to evolve, he renamed it client-centered therapy. In the 1980s he began using the term person-centered approach in recognition that the theory had been applied far beyond the counseling situation (e.g., teaching, group leadership, international affairs; Rogers, 1980; Zimring & Raskin, 1992).

Rogers was born into what he describes as "a home marked by close family ties, a very strict and uncompromising religious and ethical atmosphere, and what amounted to a worship of the virtue of hard work" (Rogers, 1961, p. 5). His family moved to a farm when Rogers was 12, and as a result, Carl became interested in agriculture, particularly the scientific aspects (Rogers, 1961). He majored in agriculture in his first 2 years of college, but then found his interests changing; he eventually began theological training at Union Theological Seminary in New York. However, after taking courses at Columbia University in psychology, he changed his path again and entered the clinical psychology program there.

Receiving his degree in 1931 (from a program that emphasized traditional experimental psychology and testing), Rogers' first job was as a staff psychologist in the Child Study Department of the Society for Prevention of Cruelty to Children in Rochester, New York. There the beginnings of Person-Centered Therapy were established as Rogers struggled to help the underprivileged clients of this agency. Finding the traditional psychoanalytic methods favored at this clinic increasingly unsatisfactory in his work, Rogers slowly began to form his theory of counseling. He described several incidents that spurred his development, and perhaps the most touching occurred when he had all but given up on a troubled boy and the boy's mother. He had struggled mightily to get them to understand the Oedipal roots of their problems, and had finally become resigned to his inability to help them. At the end of what was to be the final session, he was explaining the situation to the boy's mother. Suddenly, she asked if Rogers would accept adults for counseling and launched into an anguished description of her troubles. As Rogers put it, "Real therapy began then and ultimately it was highly successful—for her and for her son" (1961, p. 11). These early experiences led Rogers to conclude that it was really the client who knew what the problem was and where to go to solve it. This assumption is the foundation of the person-centered approach.

Rogers moved to Ohio State University in 1940 and then to the University of Chicago (1945–1957), where he established the Student Counseling Service, later renamed the Counseling and Psychotherapy Center. An account of the development of the center and of the beginnings of Rogers' research program can be found in Cornelius-White and Cornelius-White (2005). An interesting tidbit: the technology at the time was so primitive that the famous first-ever recording of a therapy session (in which the therapist was anonymous but according to Patterson, 2000, surely Rogers) was accomplished using glass disks, and it took ten of these to record ONE therapy session.

Rogers' last traditional academic appointment was at the University of Wisconsin (1957–1963). He then moved to the Western Behavioral Sciences Institute in La Jolla, California, and later founded the Center for Studies of the Person in La Jolla, where his professional career ended. Along the way he wrote many articles and books, the most prominent of which are probably *Counseling and Psychotherapy* (1942), *Client-Centered Therapy* (1951), *On Becoming a Person* (1961), and *A Way of Being* (1980). You can read an excerpt from *On Becoming a Person* in Box 5.1.

Broadening his approach, Rogers became one of the leaders of the encounter group movement in the late 1960s and '70s (Kirschenbaum, 2004). In the last years of his life, Rogers led large workshops all over the world aimed at resolving conflict, for which he was

Box 5.1

A GENERAL HYPOTHESIS

One brief way of describing the change which has taken place in me is to say that in my early professional years I was asking the question, How can I treat, or cure, or change this person? Now I would phrase the question in this way: How can I provide a relationship which this person may use for his own personal growth?

It is as I have come to put the question in this second way that I realize that whatever I have learned is applicable to all of my human relationships, not just to working with clients with problems. It is for this reason that I feel it is possible that the learnings which have had meaning for me in my experience may have some meaning for you in your experience, since all of us are involved in human relationships.

Perhaps I should start with a negative learning. It has gradually been driven home to me that I cannot be of help to this troubled person by means of any intellectual or training procedure. No approach which relies upon knowledge, upon training, upon the acceptance of something that is *taught*, is of any use. These approaches seem so tempting and direct that I have, in the past, tried a great many of them. It is possible to explain a person to himself, to prescribe steps which should lead him forward, to train him in knowledge about a more satisfying mode of life. But such methods are, in my experience, futile and inconsequential. The most they can accomplish is some temporary change, which soon disappears, leaving the individual more than ever convinced of his inadequacy.

The failure of any such approach through the intellect has forced me to recognize that change appears to come about through experience in a relationship. So I am going to try to state very briefly and informally, some of the essential hypotheses regarding a helping relationship which have seemed to gain increasing confirmation both from experience and research.

I can state the overall hypothesis in one sentence, as follows. If I can provide a certain type of relationship, the other person will discover within himself the capacity to use that relationship for growth, and change and personal development will occur.

THE RELATIONSHIP

But what meaning do these terms have? Let me take separately the three major phrases in this sentence and indicate something of the meaning they have for me. What is this certain type of relationship I would like to provide?

I have found that the more that I can be genuine in the relationship, the more helpful it will be. This means that I need to be aware of my own feelings, in so far as possible, rather than presenting an outward façade of one attitude, while actually holding another attitude at a deeper or unconscious level. Being genuine also involves the willingness to be and to express, in my words and my behavior, the various feelings and attitudes which exist in me. It is only in this way that the relationship can have *reality*, and reality seems deeply important as a first condition. It is only by providing the genuine reality which is in me, that the other person can successfully seek for the reality in him. I have found this to be true even when the attitudes I feel are not attitudes with which

I am pleased, or attitudes which seem conducive to a good relationship. It seems extremely important to be *real*.

As a second condition, I find that the more acceptance and liking I feel toward this individual, the more I will be creating a relationship which he can use. By acceptance I mean a warm regard for him as a person of unconditional self-worth—of value no matter what his condition, his behavior, or his feelings. It means a respect and liking for him as a separate person, a willingness for him to possess his own feelings in his own way. It means an acceptance of and regard for his attitudes of the moment, no matter how negative or positive, no matter how much they may contradict other attitudes he has held in the past. This acceptance of each fluctuating aspect of this other person makes it for him a relationship of warmth and safety, and the safety of being liked and prized as a person seems a highly important element in a helping relationship.

I also find that the relationship is significant to the extent that I feel a continuing desire to understand—a sensitive empathy with each of the client's feelings and communications as they seem to him at that moment. Acceptance does not mean much until it involves understanding. It is only as I *understand* the feelings and thoughts which seem so horrible to you, or so weak, or so sentimental, or so bizarre—it is only as I see them as you see them, and accept them and you, that you feel really free to explore all the hidden nooks and frightening crannies of your inner and often buried experience. This *freedom* is an important condition of the relationship. There is implied here a freedom to explore oneself at both conscious and unconscious levels, as rapidly as one can dare to embark on this dangerous quest. There is also a complete freedom from any type of moral or diagnostic evaluation, since all such evaluations are, I believe, always threatening.

Thus the relationship which I have found helpful is characterized by a sort of transparency on my part, in which my real feelings are evident; by an acceptance of this other person as a separate person with value in his own right; and by a deep empathic understanding which enables me to see his private world through his eyes. When these conditions are achieved, I become a companion to my client, accompanying him in the frightening search for himself, which he now feels free to undertake.

I am by no means always able to achieve this kind of relationship with another, and sometimes, even when I feel I have achieved it in myself, he may be too frightened to perceive what is being offered to him. But I would say that when I hold in myself the kind of attitudes. I have described, and when the other person can to some degree experience these attitudes, then I believe that change and constructive personal development will *invariably* occur—and I include the word "invariably" only after long and careful consideration.

Rogers, C.R. (1961). *On becoming a Person*. (Boston: Houghton Mifflin).

posthumously nominated for a Nobel peace prize (Kirschenbaum, 2004). He died in 1987 of a heart attack during surgery to repair a broken hip (Weinrach, 1990). Rogers was survived by two children; his wife had died in 1979. His daughter, Natalie, became a therapist, eventually writing her own book combining person-centered counseling with other expressive therapeutic techniques (N. Rogers, 1993).

Carl Rogers was a pioneer in many ways. Rogers was the first to use the term *client* to refer to someone seeking psychotherapy. In explaining his use of this term, he said, "The client . . . is one who comes actively and voluntarily to gain help on a problem, but without any notion of surrendering his own responsibility for the situation" (1951, p. 7). Perhaps Rogers' most significant contribution was his willingness to submit the counseling process to the rigors of research. He was the first to record counseling sessions, and he used these recordings as a basis to test his ideas. Many times the transcripts or recordings used in research and publications featured Rogers as the counselor. One of these recordings was the basis for the book *Counseling and Psychotherapy* (1942), which presented the first complete transcription of a counseling case ever printed. Braving the psychotherapeutic unknown, Rogers designed and conducted an extensive study of person-centered therapy with schizophrenics while he was on the faculty of the psychology and psychiatry departments at the University of Wisconsin (see Box 5.2).

Rogers' impact on the profession of psychology was recognized by the American Psychological Association (APA) when in 1956 he was chosen as one of the first three individuals awarded the American Psychological Association award for distinguished scientific contribution. Later

---

Box 5.2

The Wisconsin Schizophrenia Project

In 1957 Carl Rogers was looking for new challenges. He moved to the University of Wisconsin and became a member of the departments of psychology and psychiatry. He wondered if the client-centered therapeutic approach that was so successful with the college students at the University of Chicago would be as helpful with other kinds of clients. In collaboration with the members of the Psychotherapy Research Group at the University of Wisconsin Psychiatric Institute, he set out to test whether client-centered therapy would work with schizophrenic clients (Rogers, 1967).

The study took place over a 5-year period. Eight therapists, all of whom were essentially person centered in their orientations, volunteered to provide counseling. Rogers was one of the therapists. Three groups of participants were identified: acute schizophrenics, chronic schizophrenics, and normal persons (not hospitalized, reporting no dysfunction). A total of 48 participants entered the study and were randomly assigned to therapy or control groups. Multiple measures were used, including a battery of psychological tests (the Rorschach and the Minnesota Multiphasic Personality Inventory, among others) and measures of the therapeutic relationship. Rating scales were developed to measure the important constructs of person-centered theory, including empathy, unconditional positive regard, and therapist congruence. Measures of the therapy process included the level of client experiencing and the ability of the client to engage in relationships. Overall, this study was a tremendous undertaking.

Unfortunately, the study did not flow as well as Rogers had planned. One member of the research team committed an ethical violation. It is not absolutely clear what happened from Rogers' account, but some of the data apparently disappeared, and much of the statistical analysis had to be repeated (Rogers, 1967). Discord was rampant among the research team, and although the study was eventually completed and published,

Rogers characterized the period as "without doubt the most painful and anguished period in my whole professional life" (Rogers, 1967, p. 371).

The results of the study were mixed. Analyses showed some isolated differences between the treatment and control groups (e.g., treated hospitalized clients showed a slightly higher release rate than nontreated hospitalized clients), but overall, the therapy group showed no greater improvement when compared to the control group. All hospitalized individuals showed positive change regardless of whether they received person-centered counseling. Some support for the theory was found in that clients who perceived higher degrees of two of the therapeutic conditions, empathy and congruence, showed better outcomes on two indicators (objective test scores and ratings by clinicians) than did clients who perceived low levels of these conditions. One interesting finding was that clients' and independent observers' ratings were similar in their evaluations of the therapeutic relationship, but therapist ratings were negatively correlated with the ratings of the other two groups. That is, therapists' ratings tended to be high when the clients' (or raters') were low, and vice versa.

Rogers and his colleagues found the results of the study somewhat encouraging. The link between the relationship conditions and outcome seemed promising, and the fact that the researchers were able to develop reliable measures of these indicators was significant. Rogers concluded that the same conditions of good therapy work with schizophrenic clients as well as neurotics. In fact, Rogers suggested that one of the most important insights gained from the study might be that, generally, the schizophrenic clients were more like the typical clients he worked with than they were different (Rogers, Gendlin, Kiesler, & Truax, 1967, p. 93).

(1972) he was recognized with the APA award for distinguished professional contribution, becoming the only person ever to receive both awards. He also served as president of the APA in 1946.

Seeman (1990) argued that a theory is by necessity the theorist's autobiography. The comparability between Rogers' theory and his life was quite evident in his increasing willingness to reveal his person in both his writings and in his work with clients. Over his professional career he became more and more convinced that the genuineness of the therapist was critical to the therapeutic process, and he applied this assertion to his life as well. At least four times (in 1961, 1972, 1980 and 1987; see Kirschenbaum & Henderson, 1989) he wrote accounts of his personal experiences, which are excellent demonstrations of the person-centered philosophy in action. Monte (1999) commented that the nondirectiveness of Rogers' approach likely had its roots in reaction to his strict early environment.

Carl Rogers applied person-centered concepts in areas beyond counseling and psychotherapy, coming to see his theory as more of an approach to interpersonal relations and learning than simply as a theory of client change. For instance, he wrote about marriage (Rogers, 1972) and education (Rogers & Freiberg, 1994), and conducted encounter groups all over the world in the interests of contributing to world peace (Rogers, 1980). Rogers lives on in the *Three Approaches to Psychotherapy* videotapes, in which he demonstrated person-centered therapy with a client named Gloria (Shostrom, 1965; see Box 5.3). The session with Gloria is considered a classic demonstration of the ideal therapeutic relationship, and is still the topic of

Box 5.3

The Meaning of the Missing 249 Words

In 1965 a film series was presented that changed the world of counseling and psychotherapy. In the *Three Approaches to Psychotherapy* (Shostrom, 1965), a courageous woman named Gloria served as a client for three therapists, Carl Rogers, Fritz Perls, and Albert Ellis. Each of the three segments begins with the theorist explaining his views, proceeds to a 20-minute counseling session with Gloria, and then concludes with the theorist's evaluation of his work. At the end of the third interview, Gloria presents her reactions to the three theorists. Gloria's interaction with Rogers has been characterized as exemplifying his incredible ability to form intense, satisfying relationships with people, a demonstration of his almost uncanny therapeutic ability (Weinrach, 1990). Gloria and Carl corresponded for 15 years after the interview, up to her death at age 45, and met once in this period.

One section of the Gloria–Carl interaction has been the subject of controversy. Toward the end of the film, Gloria tells Carl, "I'd like you for my father." Carl responds, "You look to me like a pretty nice daughter." In his taped discussion after the session, Rogers mentions that this interaction might be labeled transference and countertransference, but dismisses that conceptualization as intellectualizing and a disservice to the value of the relationship.

As a result of a rather surprising discovery, the meaning of Gloria and Carl's interchange was the topic of a hot debate in the journal *Psychotherapy* (Bohart, 1991; Weinrach, 1990). Six months after Carl Rogers' death, Weinrach (1990) located a 249-word segment of the interview that was not included in the film. Evidently, the film ran out, but a separate audio recording of the session continued. In the segment, Gloria and Carl had continued their conversation, and Gloria indicated that her search for a loving father figure was a "neurosis." Weinrach suggested that if it had been known that Gloria's longing was, for her, a typical pattern, "or worse yet, a long-standing neurotic need" (1990, p. 283), Rogers would have lost the therapist-guru status that he gained from the film. Instead, Rogers would have been seen as merely a human therapist who missed the boat in failing to interpret Gloria's transference reaction. Even more problematic, in Weinrach's view, was the fact that Rogers appeared to be bound up in counter-transference feelings for Gloria, which was what caused his failure to respond to her transference. Also, Weinrach maintained that if Rogers had acknowledged these dynamics, he would have been supporting a theory against which he had argued for a long time (psychoanalysis), thereby questioning his own. In essence, Weinrach implied that had the missing 249 words been included in the film, Rogers would have been discredited.

Bohart (1991) defended Rogers, contending that Weinrach's views are based in a theoretical perspective (psychoanalytic), not absolute truth. Agreeing with Rogers that reference to transference processes is not productive, Bohart maintained that "what Weinrach is really saying is that he prefers a transferential interpretation of the Rogers–Gloria interaction" (Bohart, 1991, p. 497). Further, he wrote, "to accuse Rogers of making a therapeutic mistake because he did not deal with transference is equivalent to saying that Rogers made a mistake because he did not operate in terms of the theoretical constructs that Weinrach . . . ascribe(s) to" (p. 497). Pointing out that Gloria tends to discount her experience (when she calls her wish for an accepting male figure neurotic), Bohart noted that classifying Gloria's feelings as transferential would validate her mistrust of her person, a damaging event from a person-centered perspective. With regard to Rogers' responses to Gloria, Bohart questioned if it is "'countertransferential' to like and respect one's client, or (heaven forbid) to actually *express* such sentiments" (p. 501, italics in the original).

In responding to Bohart, Weinrach (1991) defended his conceptualization of the transferential nature of the Rogers–Gloria interaction. He acknowledged that Rogers had always elicited in him a wish to have such a grandfather and wondered "what feelings Rogers' persona has evoked in Bohart that influenced him to write such an impassioned defense of Rogers" (1991, p. 505). Further, Weinrach wrote, "Bohart appears to be applying the therapeutic principle of unconditional positive regard to everything Rogers did, including Rogers' demonstration with Gloria" (Weinrach, 1991, pp. 505–506). Weinrach concluded by suggesting that the film be only regarded as an historical artifact at best, and a negative example at worst. Evidently, Bohart chose not to respond to Weinrach's rebuttal.

This entertaining interchange is probably best viewed as a good demonstration of the way theoretical lenses can influence the interpretation of events. Working from a psychoanalytically influenced view, Weinrach saw Gloria and Carl's interaction as transference and countertransference. This perspective, with its attention to client–counselor interaction as a recapitulation of early experience, would evaluate the interchange as a negative therapeutic event because Rogers did not recognize the processes and intervene. In contrast, Bohart endorsed a person-centered approach, seeing the Gloria–Carl interaction as an authentic exchange of intimate feelings, a positive event from this perspective. Until the unlikely time that one of these two theories is elected as the "truth" of psychotherapy, the lesson to be learned is that what we know as "reality" can be viewed from multiple perspectives.

discussion and the stimulus for research projects in contemporary professional counseling (e.g., Bohart, 1991; Weinrach, 1990, 1991). The Center for Studies of the Person continues Rogers' work and has a website at www.centerfortheperson.org. Other Internet sites of interest are the World Association for Person-Centered and Experiential Psychotherapy and Counseling (http://www. pce-world.org). the Association for the Development of the Person Centered Approach (http://www.adpca.org), the British Association for the Person-Centered Approach (http:// users.powernet.co.uk/bapca) and the Person-Centered Expressive Therapy Institute (http:// members.aol.com/exartspc/index.htm), founded by Rogers' daughter, Natalie Rogers. The scholarly journal *Person-Centered Review*, launched in 1986, apparently ended in 1990, but the World Association currently publishes *Person-Centered and Experiential Psychotherapies*. It appears that the prominence of the person-centered approach has decreased in the United States over recent years, but in Europe, PC theory is one of the most dominant theoretical approaches of late (Kirschenbaum & Jourdan, 2005). Lively programs of research and intervention continue in other countries, such as Germany and the United Kingdom (Lietaer, 1990) and there are Person-Centered organizations in many countries around the world (Kirschenbaum & Jourdan, 2005, present a list of 18). Elements of Rogers' approach can also be clearly seen in contemporary programs of training for interpersonal and counseling skills (Egan, 2006; Hill, 2004; Ivey & Ivey, 2007).

BASIC PHILOSOPHY

The hallmark of Person-centered (PC) theory is the basic premise that human beings are inherently good. Carl Rogers was quite clear about this conviction, writing that "the basic nature of the human being, when functioning freely, is constructive and trustworthy. . . . We do not need to ask who will control his aggressive impulses; for as he becomes more open to all of his impulses, his need to be liked by others and his tendency to give affection will be as strong as his impulses to strike out or to seize for himself. He will be aggressive in situations in which aggression is realistically appropriate, but there will be no runaway need for aggression" (Rogers, 1961, p. 194). The major portions of PC theory were developed in the late 1950s and 1960s mostly in reaction to two influences: (a) the psychoanalytic model that dominated the atmosphere at Rogers' job (Rogers, 1961) and (b) the positivistic, behaviorist tradition that was becoming prominent in psychology in the 1960s (Rogers, 1977).

In Rogers' view, human behavior is the result of an innate need to grow and develop common to all living organisms (Rogers, 1980). If left alone, the person will follow the road to full human potential, showing none of the negative tendencies postulated by other theorists (for example, Freud's aggressive instinct). Rogers wrote, "contrary to those therapists who see depravity at men's core, who see men's deepest instincts as destructive, I have found that when man is truly free to become what he most deeply is, free to actualize his nature as an organism capable of awareness, then he clearly appears to move toward wholeness and integration" (1966, p. 193). The PC therapist recognizes that humans sometimes act in destructive or antisocial ways but maintains that these tendencies are a product of experience in the environment, not built in to the human psyche (Merry & Tudor, 2006).

Daryl, Richard's person-centered therapist, begins with the assumption that Richard is inherently a positive, forward-moving individual. Even though Richard is exhibiting some emotion and behavior that might be labeled by others as dysfunctional, Daryl is sure that within Richard is the potential to grow and actualize, establish meaningful and productive relationships with others, and work effectively. He sees glimmers of this in Richard's evident willingness to engage in counseling and small sparks of hope that appear when Daryl responds supportively to him.

Person-centered counselors are committed to the notion that clients are self-directing and able to accept full responsibility for their actions (van der Veen, 1998). Each person has within him the resources and strengths to grow and become a better person. This respect for the individual's autonomy leads to an attitude of equality in the therapeutic interaction, and this mutuality of involvement is critical in any context to which PC theory is applied (van der Veen, 1998). Rogers spoke of freedom as an important element of the counseling relationship. He believed that the client (and the counselor as well) should be free to explore every aspect of the self within the therapeutic environment. "There is also a complete freedom from any type of moral or diagnostic evaluation, since all such evaluations are I believe, always threatening" (Rogers, 1961, p. 34).

Person-centered therapy is characterized as humanistic and phenomenological (Ruthven, 1992). Proponents of humanistic approaches trust the individual, viewing people as oriented toward growth and harmony with others. Rogers' approach is phenomenological in that he argued that the most important factor in understanding a given individual is his (the individual's) perceptions of reality, because for the person, perception is reality.

Daryl approaches Richard as an equal and encourages him to determine the nature and content of the counseling relationship. He relies on Richard to provide the basic material of counseling, asking Richard what he wants to discuss. Although this attitude seems somewhat surprising to Richard and tends to make him a little uncomfortable, Daryl persists in his gentle support of Richard's choices and decisions within the counseling session. In no way does Daryl assess, diagnose, or evaluate Richard; he simply does his best to understand Richard's world.

HUMAN MOTIVATION

Person-centered theorists believe that the only motivation of human behavior is the tendency to grow to full potential in constructive, positive ways. Living beings strive to maximize the organism (a term used by Rogers to mean the whole person or other living entity) and avoid experiences that are detrimental to it. PC theorists see no inherent aggressive or destructive tendencies in people, although aggression or assertion may sometimes be used as a means to grow, such as when an individual asserts himself to obtain something that enhances his existence. For example, killing animals for food would be seen as an aggressive act directed toward the actualization of the organism.

Daryl knows that Richard is motivated to grow and enhance himself and live in harmony with his environment, which includes other people. At the beginning of counseling, Richard's behavior may not seem to consistently stem from this tendency—he seems somewhat stuck at present—but Daryl knows that it is there and only needs to be released from interference. Daryl will constantly look for and respect Richard's growth tendencies throughout the counseling interaction.

CENTRAL CONSTRUCTS

EXPERIENCE

Rogers used the term *experience* in two ways. Experience as a noun refers to everything that is going on in the individual at a given moment (Rogers, 1959). Of particular importance in experience are emotions because we tend to suppress, deny, or distort these in the service of social rules. Although Rogers recognized that unconscious processes might exist, they are not considered in the definition of experience because they cannot be studied objectively (Rogers, 1959); thus, experience is confined to events that are potentially available to consciousness.

The use of the term *experience* as a verb means the process of the person receiving what is going on around and within him, the "sensory or physiological events which are happening at the moment" (Rogers, 1959, p. 197). This term is special to PC theory because in order to grow, humans must experience accurately, discriminating between events that contribute to the organism's well-being and those that are harmful. The degree to which experience is perceived without distortion or disruption determines the level of the individual's functioning.

Daryl is aware that the accurate perception and symbolization of experience is critical to Richard's psychological well-being. Richard is clearly attending to what is going on in the environment around him as well as his psychological experience (he can report feelings of depression). However, Richard's desire to come to counseling and his admission that he is depressed suggest that Richard's experiencing is derailed in some way.

ACTUALIZING TENDENCY

The most basic human process is the actualizing tendency, which is the "inherent tendency of the organism to develop all its capacities in ways which serve to maintain or enhance the organism" (Rogers, 1959, p. 196). This process involves both the person's biological and psychological growth. Growth is always in the direction of autonomy and thus leads to internal regulation of the individual's existence. Growth is also toward greater levels of complexity (Rogers, 1980).

Daryl looks for signs of the actualizing tendency in Richard. Even though Richard's uncomfortable presence and evident depression seems less than growthful, when Richard talks about his struggles, Daryl can sense the presence of a tendency to grow in Richard's desire to live a better, less isolated life.

ORGANISMIC VALUING PROCESS

Rogers thought that humans engaged in an ongoing process of evaluating experience, measuring it event by event to determine if it contributes to one's growth or detracts from it. Humans move toward growth-producing experiences and away from those that do not contribute to or interfere with growth. In the healthy person, the basis for this constant evaluation of experience is the actualizing tendency. To take a simple example, when a child touches a hot stove, she snatches her hand away because it does not promote the growth of her organism to get burned!

Ideally, Daryl would look for signs of the operation of the organismic valuing process in Richard's behavior. Signs of this process are observable at times, but other times Richard's behavior might seem to be motivated by other considerations. For example, Richard seems to fully enjoy his leisure pursuits (reading and working on his computer), but he avoids his family and other social relationships. Because healthy interpersonal relationships are growth enhancing, Daryl hypothesizes that in those situations, Richard is not acting in accordance with his organismic valuing process. Daryl knows that fluctuations of this type are natural, and perhaps even more pronounced in individuals coming to counseling because the need for counseling suggests that some processes are awry.

SELF

As humans grow and experience the world, a portion of this experience becomes labeled as the self. All experiences that the person recognizes as "me" and the values that are attached to them become the *self-concept* (Rogers, 1959). For instance, if I discover that I am good at doing the tango, this experience becomes a part of my self-concept. If I value tango dancing, then this experience contributes to a positive self-concept.

Rogers thought that if experiences were inconsistent with our self-concepts, or negatively valued, we would have difficulty allowing ourselves to perceive them. For example, if it is difficult for me to get up in the morning, then my self-concept could include the construct that I am not a morning person. If there are negative values associated with not being a morning person, this experience will contribute to a negative self-concept to the degree to which I allow myself to acknowledge it. I could, in fact, insist that I always get up at 5:00 a.m., but none of my friends would believe me! A third self-construct important in PC theory is the *ideal self*, the self the person would like to be. My ideal self may contain the characteristics "tango dancer" and "morning person," only one of which is consistent with my actual experience.

Richard probably has a negative self-concept. He is able to recognize and reveal several "negative" aspects of himself—he is socially withdrawn and ineffective at work. Because he unfavorably compares himself with his children, Richard feels inadequate. Very little in Richard's self-description seems positive, and Daryl also guesses that Richard's ideal self is so close to perfection as to be unobtainable by a human being.

SELF-ACTUALIZING TENDENCY

An aspect of the general actualization tendency, the self-actualizing tendency, refers to the propensity of the self to grow and maximize. When the individual is functioning well, the actualizing and self-actualizing tendencies function in concert. What is good for the organism is also perceived as good for the self; what is bad for the organism is therefore bad for the self. Hugging another person is good for me both physically and in terms of self needs.

NEED FOR POSITIVE REGARD AND SELF-REGARD

All human beings have a need for positive regard, and this need extends to the self-system. We value the love of others and also have a need to positively value ourselves. Rogers is not clear whether the need for regard is innate or learned, but he is quite specific in saying that the need for positive regard of the self is learned through experiencing it from others important to the individual (Rogers, 1959).

Richard's need for positive regard is evident in his reactions to his wife Sandy's disapproval. He is falling short in the area of positive self-regard, as seen in his feelings of inadequacy when he compares his achievements to those of his children.

CONDITIONS OF WORTH

The need for positive regard motivates individuals to seek love from important others around them (Rogers, 1959). When the individual perceives that some aspect of himself (whether it is perception, feeling, or behavior) is evaluated positively by someone important to him and other aspects are not, conditions of worth arise. The need for love is so intense that we will deny parts of our experience that are deemed unacceptable (unlovable) by significant others. A classic example of this dynamic is when Suzy becomes frustrated and angry. From a PC perspective, anger is a natural part of human existence. It does not detract from the growth of the organism. If her parents consistently display negative reactions to Suzy's anger, she will tend to deny or distort the experience of anger in the future. She will begin to feel anxious or "bad" when she begins to get angry, and in an attempt to align her perceived and ideal selves, may even start to view herself as someone who never gets angry. In contrast, if Suzy's parents accept her anger nonjudgmentally, she will have no need to distort or disown the experience. She can experience the anger and then go about her business.

Initially, conditions of worth are external; that is, they are the reactions of others (such as parents) who value behaviors differentially, often based on societal norms (e.g., boys don't cry, girls don't shout). What happens quite often, however, is that individuals are reinforced for behaviors that are consistent with conditions of worth, and after a while the conditions are internalized as parts of the self (Rogers, 1959). When this transformation happens, the individual is not evaluating experience through the organismic valuing process; rather, he values experiences based on whether they are consistent with the internalized conditions of worth. He is said to be operating on an *external* locus of evaluation (because his values are not self-generated) rather than an *internal* locus of evaluation (the organismic valuing process). Because conditions of worth are based on societal rules, they are not always consistent with the actualizing tendency. In fact, they are often at odds with the actualizing tendency.

Daryl knows that Richard's self is conditional. His guilt and depression are likely the result of aspects of his experience that are inconsistent with his internalized conditions of worth. For example, Richard apparently holds the value that to be worthwhile, he should earn a certain amount of money; specifically, that he should be the primary provider for his family. He is not fulfilling the condition that men are strong and provide for their families. That his children make more money than he does only confirms his negative perceptions of self. Daryl also guesses that Richard's decision to change occupations was inconsistent with his conditional self, which dictates that men don't buckle under stress and do not show "weak" emotions. He is just not good enough.

THEORY OF THE PERSON AND DEVELOPMENT OF THE INDIVIDUAL

Life is an active process (Rogers, 1980, p. 118). "In short, organisms are always seeking, always initiating, always 'up to something'" (Rogers, 1980, p. 123, quotes in original).

Even in the worst conditions, all organisms strive to grow in positive directions. So begins the journey of the infant.

The infant, motivated by the actualizing tendency, evaluates experience based on the organismic valuing process. "Experiences which are perceived as maintaining or enhancing the organism are valued positively. Those which are perceived as negating such maintenance or enhancement are valued negatively" (Rogers, 1959, p. 222). Babies naturally move toward the positive and away from the negative.

As the child grows, part of the experience becomes defined as the self. The differentiation of self is an offshoot of the actualizing tendency—that is, reaching full human potential involves developing a sense of who one is. Further experience leads to establishing a defined self-concept. With the development of the self, the need for positive regard from others emerges along with the need for positive self-regard.

Gradually, the child becomes aware that certain self-experiences are valued positively or negatively by others around him. Parents, teachers, and other important figures in the child's life have reactions to the child's behaviors that are essentially "good boy" or "bad girl." Because the need for positive regard is so compelling, these evaluations are internalized, and conditions of worth are established. The child begins to seek self-experiences that are consistent with the conditional self and avoid or deny those that are inconsistent. For example, Mary might initially find the experience of playing in squishy mud pleasurable (i.e., consistent with the organismic valuing tendency). However, Mary's mom berates her for messing up her beautiful white dress and shoes. The pleasurable experience of mud-playing then becomes a negative one because Mary experienced negative regard from her mother. Eventually, Mary internalizes this condition of worth and can never again be dirty; in fact, she might develop a compulsive tendency to wash her hands.

In the perfect world, individuals could develop in an atmosphere of unconditional positive regard. Rogers was careful to say that unconditional positive regard does not mean positively valuing all of a child's behaviors. "A parent 'prizes' his child, though he may not value equally all of his behaviors" (1959, p. 208). Given an accepting environment, children could develop unfettered by conditions of worth, and the needs for positive regard and positive self-regard would not be at odds with the organismic valuing process.

Richard is clearly conditional in his self-regard. Daryl does not have much information about Richard's early experiences, but Daryl speculates that people important to Richard early in his life were conditional in their evaluation of him. For example, Richard's current discomfort with his occupational situation (the change in jobs and income) probably results from his early internalization of the value that work is an important definition of who he is as a man. The change of jobs, which could be perceived as taking care of himself, is probably viewed as inconsistent with traditional values of "never give up" and "tough it out." Daryl guesses that Richard might have been raised in an environment in which feelings were off limits, and therefore he is hesitant and uncomfortable disclosing them to those close to him, including Daryl.

HEALTH AND DYSFUNCTION

The "good life," according to Rogers, is a process, not a destination (Rogers, 1961). The healthy person is a *congruent* person; put simply, his perception of self is consistent with what he experiences. He is open to experience and has an internal locus of evaluation (the organismic valuing process). The individual trusts himself to follow the right paths, guided by his organismic valuing process (Rogers, 1961). Because the individual has no internalized conditions of worth, experiences can be accepted freely into awareness and evaluated on the basis of the needs of the organism. The individual has a positive self-concept and unconditional self-regard. All experience is perceived accurately, without distortion; the person naturally orients toward experiences that actualize and away from those that do not contribute to the maximization of potential.

Healthy individuals are creative and take risks in life. "He would not necessarily be 'adjusted' to his culture, and he would almost certainly not be a conformist. But at any time and in any culture he would live constructively, in as much harmony with his culture as a balanced satisfaction of needs demanded" (Rogers, 1961, p. 194; quotes in original). An important part of accepting all of one's experience is the authentic expression of the self, with all of the feelings that accompany being human.

In PC theory, dysfunction is defined as *incongruence* between self and experience. The individual's self is conditional; some experiences are inconsistent with internalized conditions of worth. The actualizing and self-actualizing tendencies are in conflict because the individual is busily trying to evaluate self-relevant experiences according to conditions of worth rather than via the organismic valuing process. The conditional self and the organismic experience are inconsistent, and therefore the actualizing and self-actualizing tendencies are divorced from each other.

When a person encounters experiences that are inconsistent with the conditional self, the experiences are generally "subceived"—that is, only dimly perceived. A clear recognition of the incongruent thought, emotion, or perception could cause a change in the self-concept, and people who are conditional do not welcome such changes. Experiences such as these are threatening to the self because they endanger the person's ability to obtain positive regard from others (and to positively regard the self). The incongruent information results in anxiety. As a result, the individual becomes *defensive* and rigid, either denying or distorting the experience. Defensiveness is the hallmark of the person traditionally described as "neurotic" (Rogers, 1959; my quotes). The incongruent person's behavior is inconsistent; sometimes his behavior is guided by the conditional self and sometimes by the organismic valuing process. The individual is vulnerable because he is constantly defending against experiences deemed unacceptable. He is anxious, rigidly protecting the self-concept. The locus of evaluation is external (paradoxically, because it resides in internalized conditions of worth) rather than internal (i.e., the organismic valuing process; Rogers, 1959).

If the person is very incongruent (i.e., a lot of experiences are unacceptable to the self) and if incongruent experiences are very powerful or sudden, the individual's defenses can become overwhelmed, and the experience is symbolized in awareness (Rogers, 1959). The self-structure is damaged and so the individual becomes *disorganized*. Similar to the neurotic, sometimes his behavior is guided by the conditional self, and at other times the "real" self (i.e., the organismic valuing process) rallies and directs behavior, but these swings are much more severe. The result looks much like what we typically describe as psychosis. Rogers (1959) gives the example of the acute psychotic exhibiting sexual behavior that is typically deemed inappropriate in social situations. Such a person is simply following his actualizing tendency (i.e., sex is good for the organism), but conditions of worth have led him to deny his sexuality. When the self is shattered by too much incongruence, these behaviors are expressed because the need for sexual experience is symbolized in awareness (Rogers, 1959).

Despite his use of terms such as *neurotic* and *psychotic*, Rogers did not have much use for traditional diagnostic procedures and systems. Referring to the previously discussed categorization of individuals into defensive versus disorganized, Rogers said, "this seems to be a more fundamental classification than those usually employed, and perhaps more fruitful in considering treatment. It also avoids any concept of neurosis and psychosis as entities in themselves, which we believe has been an unfortunate and misleading conception" (1959, p. 228).

Translating a bit, then, in PC theory, the roots of all dysfunction are found in incongruence. Depression, for example, would be seen as probably involving negative self-concept that resulted from an excess of conditions of worth. Experiences inconsistent with the conditions would be subceived, and the extent of the depression would depend on the type and nature of the experiences perceived. Anxiety would be seen as resulting from the subception of incongruence and the need to defend the conditional self.

Richard is incongruent. He behaves in his session with Daryl uncomfortably, showing signs of anxiety in his nervous laugh. He seems unwilling to reveal himself, possibly because his internalized conditions of worth disallow the authentic expression of feelings. He dares not talk about his anxiety, or the feelings behind it, because they are contrary to his conditional view of himself, which probably involves being strong. He is fearful of showing Daryl who he really is because he fears conditional reactions from others and as yet has no reason to believe that Daryl is different. He reports being depressed, and Daryl sees this sadness as resulting from Richard's inability to realize his conditional self.

NATURE OF THERAPY

ASSESSMENT

Person-centered counselors do not use any form of assessment. Many are adamantly antidiagnosis. Rogers thought that assessing and diagnosing clients turned them into objects and distanced the counselor from the therapeutic interaction.

After welcoming Richard to counseling, Daryl asks how he can help. Daryl does not conduct an "interview" or direct the flow of Richard's conversation in any way.

OVERVIEW OF THE THERAPEUTIC ATMOSPHERE

Rogers saw therapy as an encounter between two individuals. He vehemently rejected the idea that the counselor was an expert and argued that the therapist's attitude, or philosophy, was critical to the success of the relationship. In his book *On Personal Power* (1977), Rogers presented the following analysis of the counseling process:

Most procedures in psychotherapy may be placed on a scale having to do with power and control. At one end of the scale stand orthodox Freudians and orthodox behaviorists, believing in a politics of authoritarian or elitist control of persons "for their own good," either to produce better adjustment to the status quo or happiness or contentment or productivity or all of these. In the middle are most of the contemporary schools of psychotherapy, confused, ambiguous, or paternalistic in the politics of their relationships (though they may be very clear regarding their therapeutic strategies). At the other end of the scale is the client-centered, experiential, person-centered approach, consistently stressing the capacity and autonomy of the person, her right to choose the directions she will move in her behavior, and her ultimate responsibility for herself in the therapeutic relationship, with the therapist's person playing a real but primarily catalytic part in that relationship. (pp. 20–21. Reprinted by permission of Sterling Lord Literistic, Inc. Copyright by Carl R. Rogers.)

ROLES OF CLIENT AND COUNSELOR

In PC counseling, the counselor and client are equals, with the therapist serving as a companion in the client's search for himself (Rogers, 1986a). Describing his experience, Rogers said, "As a therapist, I do not want to lead the client, since she knows, better than I, the pathway to the sources of her pain. . . . What I wish is to be at her side, occasionally falling a step behind, occasionally a step ahead when I can see more clearly the path we are on, and taking a leap ahead only when guided by my intuition" (Rogers, 1986a, pp. 207–209).

The counselor's job in PC theory is to provide the climate that will release the client's potential. He does not function as an expert or guide in any way. Two tasks of the therapist are critical—that of struggling to understand the experience of the client, while at the same time being open to his own experience in the therapeutic relationship.

The role of the client is to be who he is. He is expected to be in contact with his experience as much as is possible and is the guide in the therapeutic journey. Initially, the degree to which the client is able to experience and express is directly related to the level of incongruence present. Clients who are in extreme incongruence will be less comfortable verbalizing their experiences than those who are more congruent.

Daryl approaches Richard as a partner in an interpersonal encounter. In no way does Daryl take a teaching, evaluating stance or offer any advice to Richard. Instead, Daryl attempts to engage with Richard in a personal, authentic way and to understand Richard's experience as much as possible. Richard is expected to reveal himself to the extent he feels comfortable.

GOALS

The goal of PC therapy is to facilitate the client's journey toward full potential. If the right conditions are achieved, the client experiences the counselor's acceptance and is, in turn, able to accept his experience more fully and thereby become more in touch with his actualizing tendency. A narrower version of the goal of PC counseling is for the client to move from being incongruent to being congruent. Successful PC counseling should result in diminishing or eliminating conditions of worth, and thus, incongruence between self and experience.

Daryl hopes that Richard can become aware of the experiences that are incongruent with his conditional self and accept these experiences as valuable aspects of himself. If counseling is successful, Richard will embrace all aspects of himself, freely living aspects of himself that he subceives and denies or distorts, such has his "failure" to live up to the ideal of the strong, supportive male. Getting in touch with his natural organismic valuing process will allow Richard to evaluate his experiences as negative or positive based on whether they contribute to his actualization. For example, taking care of himself by changing jobs to reduce stress would be something Richard would value, rather than feel bad about. Once Richard is able to experience and express his feelings to others authentically (because he is not rejecting them to achieve positive self-regard in concert with his internalized conditions of worth), he will be able to relate in more unconditional and open ways with others, including his wife and kids.

PROCESS OF THERAPY

Dryden and Mytton (1999) identified three historical stages in the evolution of PC theory. The earliest stage emphasized the nondirective nature of the counseling interaction (in the 1940s and 1950s). In a cathartic model, the client expresses and releases emotion, and the therapist is prohibited from offering any advice or interpretation. Insight was to be achieved by the client on his own. The counselor, through his reflection of the client's feelings, conveys understanding and acceptance of the client.

The attitude of the therapist was the emphasis of the second stage in the development of PC theory (late 1950s and early 1960s). During this stage, Rogers decided that the "techniques" of the nondirective approach (e.g., repeating the client's words, avoiding giving advice) were becoming the approach. Dissatisfied with this interpretation of his approach as mechanical and passive, Rogers began to focus on the attitude of the counselor in relation to the client, particularly the belief that the impetus for change was within the client. The counselor only needed to accurately understand and support the client in his journey inward.

Dryden and Mytton maintained that the spark for the third transformation of PC theory (in the mid- to late 1960s) came out of Rogers' experience as a therapist. They explained that Rogers was working with a very disturbed client that he did not like; he felt "trapped by her dependence upon him" (1999, p. 64). Eventually, Rogers realized that he felt so immersed in the relationship that he could not separate himself from the client. The crisis was so severe that he referred the client and found a temporary geographic cure. After literally fleeing with his wife for a period of time, Rogers then entered therapy with a colleague. This incident led to his recognition that it was critical to be honest in the therapy relationship. He believed that if he had been honest with his client, the relationship might not have become so destructive. Rogers' later versions of PC theory therefore placed great emphasis on the congruence, or genuineness, of the therapist.

For Rogers, all that was needed to release the innate growth tendencies of the client was for the therapist to provide the optimum atmosphere and for the client to perceive it. The counselor creates this environment by holding the right attitudes toward the client and the counseling venture. Simply put, the counselor works to create the facilitative climate for the client's growth by providing what Rogers called the necessary and sufficient conditions for change: congruence, unconditional positive regard, and empathic understanding (also sometimes termed the "core conditions"; Rogers, 1957). Because these concepts are so vital to the theory, they will be discussed separately.

Before discussing the conditions of therapy, however, it is necessary to note that the precursor to counseling is that the client and the counselor must be in psychological contact. When two individuals "make a difference" (Rogers, 1959, p. 207) in the experiential field of each other, they are in contact.

CONGRUENCE

Also called genuineness, transparence, or realness (Rogers, 1980), congruence refers to the counselor's freely flowing awareness of his experience in the therapeutic moment. "The more the therapist is himself or herself in the relationship, putting up no professional front or personal façade, the greater is the likelihood that the client will change and grow in a constructive manner (Rogers, 1980, p. 115). Not only is the therapist aware of his own experience, but this awareness is apparent in both verbal and nonverbal expression; feelings and reactions can be communicated to the client if this seems helpful. As his theory developed, Rogers became convinced that congruence was key to good therapy, writing, "for more than a decade I have been trying to state that genuineness, or congruence, and the expression of such genuineness, is probably the most important part of the therapeutic relationship" (Rogers et al., 1967, p. 511).

Rogers attempted to clarify what he meant by congruence, writing,

> It might be well to state some of the things that it does not imply. It does not mean that the therapist burdens his client with the overt expression of all of his feelings. It does not mean that he blurts out impulsively anything which comes to mind. It does not mean that the therapist discloses his total self to the client. It does mean, however, that he does not *deny* to himself the feelings that he is experiencing, and that he is willing *transparently* to be any persistent feelings which exist in the relationship and to let these be known to the client if appropriate. It means avoiding the temptation to present a façade or hide behind a mask of professionalism to adopt a confessional-professional relationship. (Rogers 1967, p. 101; italics in original)

Although Rogers thought it would be best if the therapist did not experience any persistent negative feelings about the client, if they happen, these too should be expressed because negative feelings would be more harmful if they were hidden (Rogers, 1966, p. 185). To hide negative feelings would be to put up a false front, which would surely be picked up by the client.

Rogers did recognize that it is impossible to be congruent every minute of one's life (Rogers, 1959, 1980). He said, "indeed if this were a necessary condition there would be no therapy" (1959, p. 215) because no one can be completely aware of his experience all of the time. What is critical is that the therapist be present and aware of his experience in the moment of interaction with the client: "thus it is that imperfect human beings can be of therapeutic assistance to other imperfect human beings" (Rogers, 1959, p. 215).

Daryl strives to be fully himself in his sessions with Richard. He attends to what Richard is communicating, both verbally and nonverbally, but is also aware of his own experience in the relationship with Richard. At times Daryl reveals to Richard what he is feeling in the interaction, as, for example, when he tells Richard that he feels distant from him.

UNCONDITIONAL POSITIVE REGARD

The counselor approaches the client with complete acceptance and caring (Rogers, 1980). Rogers spoke often of "prizing" to describe this attitude, and added that it was risky to experience these feelings because we fear being trapped by them. It is scary to invest such feeling in others because they could disappoint us, or they may become demanding. In fact, Rogers thought that these fears were primarily responsible for our adoption of the "professional attitude" toward clients, which creates distance between counselor and client and protects against hurt (Rogers, 1961, p. 52). He said, "It is a real achievement when we can learn, even in certain relationships or at certain times in those relationships, that it is safe to care, that it is safe to relate to the other as a person for whom we have positive feelings" (Rogers, 1961, p. 52). Rogers did note one exception to the rule of unconditional positive regard. In working with the "extremely immature or regressed individual, a conditional regard may be more effective in getting a relationship under way . . . than an unconditional positive regard" (Rogers, 1966, p. 186).

In order to be effective, Daryl must accept Richard without any conditions or evaluations. He finds himself prizing Richard as another human being, and communicates this to Richard in a genuine, caring way.

EMPATHY

Empathy is achieved when one individual perceives the internal experience of another as if he were that person, "without ever losing the 'as if' condition" (Rogers, 1959, p. 210). In his later works Rogers conceived of empathy as a process, rather than a state, saying that it meant "temporarily living in the other's life, moving about in it delicately without making judgements" (Rogers, 1980, p. 142). If the counselor achieves truly accurate empathy, he can even perceive meanings and feelings with which the client is not totally in touch.

The counselor must communicate empathic understanding to the client. However, Rogers warned against trying to make the client aware of totally unconscious feelings because that would be too threatening (Rogers, 1980, p. 142). Instead, the counselor "aims to dip from the pool of implicit meanings just at the edge of the client's awareness" (Rogers, 1966, p. 190).

Unfortunately, according to Rogers (1980), the early concept of accurate empathy grew into a rigid focus on the counselor's responses. "Reflecting the client's feelings" became synonymous with the PC approach. Teaching reflection of feelings as a skill became popular, and Rogers thought that this approach often led to robot responses (Rogers, 1986b). When I was in graduate school, "I hear you saying . . . " was a kind of joke phrase. Rogers said, "I was so shocked by these complete distortions of our approach that for a number of years, I said almost nothing about empathic listening, and when I did it was to stress an empathic attitude, with little comment as to how this might be implemented" (Rogers, 1980, p. 139). Instead, Rogers emphasized that when he appeared to be "reflecting feelings" what he was really doing was trying to check whether his "understanding of the client's inner world [was] correct" (Rogers, 1986b, p. 376). Merry and Tudor (2006) further clarify that the PC counselor would never focus on feelings to the exclusion of other aspects of the client's experience, such as thoughts, physical sensation, or fantasy.

Daryl strives to fully understand what it is like to be Richard. He attempts to "walk in Richard's shoes" as much as possible without losing the boundaries between himself and Richard. At times Daryl finds himself wanting to mention to Richard something he is not quite sure Richard has recognized—feelings that Richard has denied or distorted. For instance, Daryl senses Richard's feelings of inadequacy around his role as husband and provider. Richard becomes anxious if these feelings and their meaning start to surface. In the supportive atmosphere of their relationship, Daryl tries to help Richard to move toward experiencing these feelings. He does not, however, push Richard into experiencing these feelings or in any way insist that Richard acknowledge them if Richard is not ready.

A Fourth Condition?

In his last writings, Rogers began to discuss a fourth characteristic of helping relationships (Rogers, 1986a). Acknowledging that he had no scientific basis for his idea, Rogers maintained that when he was at his best as a therapist, he believed that he entered a "slightly altered state of consciousness . . . full of healing" (1986a, p. 198). This transcendent state leads to behaviors that are impulsive, but they almost magically fit with the client's experience. "At those moments it seems that my inner spirit has reached out and touched the inner spirit of the other" (Rogers, 1986a, p. 199). Despite Rogers' discussion of this transcendent state, subsequent treatments of his theory have paid little attention to this fourth condition.

Stages of the Therapeutic Process

Rogers saw the counseling process as a gradual progression from incongruence to congruence and observed stages through which clients passed on this journey. An interesting side note is that Rogers developed this "process conception" (1958, p. 142) at a time when he was preparing his address to be given when he was awarded the APA award for distinguished scientific contributions. He did not want to discuss his previous work; instead, he wanted to take a new look at personality change, and what emerged was a view of the change process from an observer's perspective (Rogers, 1961). Spending numerous hours reviewing audiotapes of counseling sessions, Rogers said that he was "trying to listen as naively as possible. I have endeavored to soak up all the clues I could capture as to the process, as to what elements are significant in change" (1958, p. 142). Through this study, Rogers identified seven stages of the change process (Rogers, 1958). As I describe these in the following sections, I quote liberally from Rogers' (1958) writing in an attempt to convey the rich and vivid description for which he was known.

Stage 1. The individual in this stage is not likely to show up in the counselor's office voluntarily. Change is not on the agenda because he typically does not see that any problems exist. "Feelings and personal meanings are neither recognized nor owned"

(p. 143), and the person is afraid of intimate relationships. This person tends to talk about externals, not himself, and has a rigid self-structure.

Stage 2. "When a person in the first stage can experience himself as fully received then the second stage follows" (1958, p. 144). Rogers was not certain about how this contact is made, but once it is, the individual moves a little further along the continuum of experiencing. He begins to talk about subjects that are not related to the self, but he displays no sense of responsibility for problems—they are external to him. Although people do come to counseling when they are in this stage, Rogers considered them very tough customers.

Stage 3. Many clients who come to counseling on their own power are in this stage. If the person continues on the path established in stage 2, he takes small steps toward more fluid experiencing and expression. In stage 3, the client discusses self-experiences and feelings but in a largely distant and objectified manner; he does not experience them fully. Feelings are perceived, but as bad things. Although the self is still rigid, it is dimly recognized. The client also recognizes contradictions in experience.

Stage 4. In this stage the individual begins to express more intense feelings, but they are still largely from past experience. The client begins to become aware of incongruence between the self and experience and begins to take some responsibility for his difficulties. Sometimes feelings even sneak into the present, but this experience is scary, and the person has difficulty accepting them.

Stage 5. If the proper climate of acceptance is established, the fourth stage then "sets in motion still further loosenings, and the freedom of organismic flow is increased" (p. 144). Stage 5 clients experience feelings and express them freely as they experience them. This experiencing is not completely without fear, and the feelings that sneak through are sometimes surprising to the client. The person more frequently expresses "ownership of self feelings" (Rogers, 1958, p. 145) and an accompanying urge to be authentic in accepting the feelings. The client begins to sense an internal frame of reference (the organismic valuing process) for experience. Rogers characterized this stage as "several hundred psychological miles from the first stage described" (p. 145).

Stage 6. Rogers described stage 6 as a "very distinctive and often dramatic phase" (p. 146). The client experiences "with immediacy and richness" a feeling that has been previously "stuck" (p. 146). The feeling is fully accepted by the client. In this moment, the self is no longer an object, it "*is*" this feeling. This is a being in the moment, with little self-conscious awareness" (p. 146; italics in original). Incongruence between self and experience is dramatically symbolized in awareness, and is thereby transformed to congruence. In essence, the client *becomes* the aspect of the self that was denied because of conditions of worth. According to Rogers, once the client experiences this process, it is irreversible.

Stage 7. The last stage identified by Rogers is seen both within and outside of the counseling relationship. "There is a growing and continuing sense of acceptant ownership of . . . changing feelings, a basic trust in his own process" (p. 148). The client, having learned to trust himself, consistently uses the organismic valuing process as the basis for living. The self becomes the process of experiencing rather than a perceived object. "There is the experiencing of effective choice of new ways of being" (p. 149). Conditions of worth are replaced by values and constructs loosely held, generated from within. "The client has now incorporated the quality of motion, of flow, of changingness into every aspect of his psychological life" (p. 149). Genuineness and free, consistent, and clear communication characterize relationships.

Not every client will reach the final stage of change (Rogers, 1961). In fact, Rogers was aware that some people do not value fluidity and would disagree with his ideas altogether. If a client started at stage 1, Rogers indicated that it could take years to get to stage 7 and that this progression would be a rare event. More likely, clients come to counseling at stage 2 and end at stage 4 with both parties in the relationship being justifiably satisfied with this outcome.

Rogers (1987) recognized two kinds of client **resistance** to the therapy process. First, there is the natural reluctance to avoid the painful experience of divulging to one's self and to the counselor feelings previously denied. After all, these feelings have been denied for a reason. The second type of resistance, however, is created by the counselor and arises as a result of "offering interpretations, making diagnoses and other judgments" (Rogers, 1987, p. 186). If the counselor creates a safe relationship through providing the core conditions, the client will have no need to protect himself by resisting.

Richard appears to be in stage 3. He experiences depression and feelings of inadequacy, "bad" feelings. Uncomfortable with the lack of structure and apparently avoiding self-relevant topics, Richard seems hesitant to make real contact with Daryl. If Daryl is able to remain accepting, genuine, and empathic, Richard will begin to lose the rigid structure that protects him from experiences not allowed into his conditional self. He will begin to experience feelings in the present (such as pain or anger) and will begin to accept these experiences into himself.

THERAPEUTIC TECHNIQUES

There are no techniques in Person-centered therapy! In fact, techniques as we typically view them (things such as challenging the client, interpretation, and so forth) are seen as guiding and objectifying the client, instead of allowing him to find his own experience, and thus, solutions. As noted earlier, when the professional world began to focus on "reflection of feeling" as the primary technique in PC counseling, Rogers objected, seeing as more important the *attitude* conveyed by the counselor as the truly critical element.

Over the years, lack of specific technique connected to the nondirectiveness of PC theory has been perceived as a significant weakness of this approach. Recent evolutions of person-centered theory involve the use of directive, active interventions by the counselor that are intended to increase clients' levels of experiencing (e.g., Gendlin, 1996; Greenberg, Watson, & Lietaer, 1998). Lietaer (1990) described these innovations, saying, "most characteristic perhaps—at least in European countries—is the fact that client-centered therapists have shaken off their phobia of directing" (p. 33). Josefowitz and Myran (2005) further discuss the role of activity in PC counseling and identify two general "types" of PC therapists. They call the first "experientialists" and include here those interested in Gendlin's (1996) focusing approach and proponents of Process-Experiential Therapy (Elliot, Watson,

Goldman, and Greenberg, 2004). These therapists are likely to allow for greater therapist activity and directiveness, as compared to the "non-directive client-centred group" which, as the name implies, emphasize the need to give the client control of the direction of therapy (Joseofwitz & Myran, 2005, p. 330). Process-Experiential therapy weaves together PC, Gestalt, and existential approaches (see Chapter 7, Box 7.3 for a brief description of this approach) and draws techniques from each of these approaches, including interventions such as empty chair dialogues (Greenberg et al., 1998). Another group of theorists integrates classic PC theory with cognitive psychology, emphasizing the role of information processing in client change (Sachese, 1990; Wexler & Rice, 1974; Zimring, 1990). Gendlin emphasized the experience of the client, developing a technique called focusing (Gendlin, 1990, 1996). Again, all of these techniques are aimed at intensifying client experiencing within counseling sessions with the goal of loosening up "stuck" feelings.

On the other end of the spectrum is Prouty's Pre-therapy. Noting that the first problem of PC counseling is to establish psychological contact, Prouty focused on these processes in individuals who are "contact impaired" (Prouty, 1998, p. 389)—those who are labeled schizophrenic and mentally challenged. This interesting theory presents a detailed description of the types of reflections that are helpful in establishing contact (e.g., situational, facial, word-for-word, body). Further, Prouty distinguished among three kinds of contact characteristic of successful pre-therapy: reality, affective, and communicative contacts.

Another interesting approach that situates itself within the PC camp is Motivational Interviewing (MI; Miller, 1983). Developed primarily for use with individuals who abuse substances, MI combines the unconditional acceptance and empathic stance of PC with a sort of Socratic questioning designed to help individuals become motivated to change (Hettema, Steele, & Miller, 2005). Oddly enough, MI also sounds a little like Solution Focused Therapy (see Chapter 14), for in exploring the client's thoughts and feelings, the MI counselor "seeks to evoke...'change talk'—expressions of the client's desire, ability, reasons, and need for change—and responds with reflective listening"(Hettema et al., 2005, p. 92; quotes in original). It is a short-term approach designed to enhance commitment to change and it usually consists of one to two sessions.

Daryl is a traditional PC therapist and will simply try to provide the right conditions for Richard. He will unconditionally accept Richard and strive to understand Richard's experience and communicate this to him. Therapist congruence is also important to Daryl, so he will attempt to be genuine and in the moment with Richard.

EVALUATION OF THE THEORY

PC theory has been one of the most influential theories in the field of counseling and psychotherapy. It can be seen as forming the basis for most approaches to counseling, because almost every approach to therapy acknowledges the impact of the therapeutic relationship on counseling outcome. Beginning counselors are taught good listening skills and are often drilled in responses that convey active listening and empathy (e.g., Egan, 2006; Hill, 2004; Ivey & Ivey, 2007).

Despite his impact on the profession, Rogers has also been criticized for wearing "rose-colored glasses"; his view of people is characterized as overly positive and ignorant of the "darker side of human nature" (Coleman, 1988, p. 23). Seager (2003) argues that "unconditional positive regard is impossible in any human relationship" (p. 401). From a scientific perspective, most of Rogers' theory rests on his observations of client reports of thoughts, feelings, and behaviors. Some research suggests that we sometimes don't know the causes of our behavior (Kirsch & Lynn, 1999) and that we are self-serving in our perceptions or unrealistically positive in our views of ourselves (Taylor & Brown, 1988). These questions relate to a more basic concern about whether people can accurately report on their own processes (Nye, 1986). Psychoanalytic theorists, of course, would shout an emphatic no! Because Rogers claimed to base his theory on the reports of his clients, these critics would say that he was on shaky ground, scientifically.

A second set of criticisms relates to the methods of PC counseling. Combs (1988) argued that PC therapists neglect the important educational role of the counselor because it is inconsistent with PC ideology. He noted that quite often counselors become impatient with the slow pace and nondirectiveness of PC theory. They often feel a need to add tools drawn from other approaches or in other ways attempt to accelerate the process of therapy. In my experience teaching this approach, I have similarly found that students struggle with the concept of trusting the client's growth tendencies; instead, they want to "do something."

The activity level of the therapist is directly tied to arguments about whether PC theory's necessary and sufficient conditions are really that: sufficient implies that all one has to do is be empathic, congruent, and provide unconditional positive regard, and the client will get better. Tudor and Worrall (2006), recent writers in the PC realm, state flatly that "Rogers' therapeutic conditions are neither necessary nor sufficient" (p. 10). Citing empirical data that suggests that many variables, and most especially the resources of the client, influence the outcome of therapy, Tudor and Worrall conclude that "the conditions are intrinsically helpful and often implicated in therapeutic growth" (p. 20).

QUALITIES OF THE THEORY

Precision and Testability. Rogers was a pioneer of research on the psychotherapy process, and he and his associates generated many studies testing PC theory. Despite this legacy, disagreements abound over how to measure PC constructs, which bears directly on the testability of the theory (Beutler, Machado, & Neufeldt, 1994; Hill & Corbett, 1993). In early research, congruence, for instance, was measured by differentials in adjective sorts of clients and experts (e.g., the client description was assumed to be of the distorted, incongruent self, whereas the observing experts could discern the more realistic self-experience of the client). However, it could be argued that this approach does not adequately capture the internal processes that create incongruence; observation by others, even experts, will not yield an accurate picture of an individual's self-experience because this can only be experienced by the individual. Other early efforts to measure empathy, unconditional regard, and congruence seemed successful because raters could generally agree on what they were observing (Rogers et al., 1967). However, the reports of raters, clients, and therapist were sometimes found to be discrepant, as they were in the Wisconsin Schizophrenia Study (Rogers et al., 1967, see Box 5.2).

PC theory provides clear and simple predictions. For example, PC theory predicts that if clients receive empathy and unconditional positive regard from a congruent therapist, they will change in favorable directions. However, the theory has been criticized as imprecise because the predictions derived are too general (Lietaer, 1990). For instance, it is possible that the core conditions are differentially effective depending on the stage of counseling—they might be much more important in the early rather than later stages (Lietaer, 1990). Few predictions are offered about the other constructs of the theory, except in general ways (e.g., if parents are not accepting of children, children will develop conditions of worth).

Empirical Validity. PC theory has received a good deal of research attention. Most of these efforts have focused on the predictions about therapy rather than those derived from the personality theory. In general, research has supported PC theory, but Rogers' core conditions are considered necessary but not sufficient.

RESEARCH SUPPORT

Outcome Research. Over the years, many reviews of the outcome effects of PC have appeared. In their classic meta-analytic study of psychotherapy approaches, Smith, Glass, and Miller (1980) found that PC counseling produced average effect sizes, meaning that it fell among a group of therapies that produced client change (including Adlerian therapy, behavior modification, transactional analysis, and psychodynamic therapy), but that PC did not produce as much change as some kinds of cognitive therapy.

Bozarth, Zimring, and Tausch (2001) present a traditional summary review of PC research, breaking it into four time periods and describing research within each. They maintain that recent common factors research that emphasizes the power of the therapeutic relationship and the resources of the client in producing positive outcomes (see Chapter 1) supports PC theory's basic assumptions. They conclude that "the clear message of five decades of research identifies the relationship of the client and therapist in combination with the resources of the client (extratherapeutic variables) . . . respectively account for 30% and 40% of the variance in successful psychotherapy" (p. 168).

Greenberg, Elliott, and Lietaer (1994) meta-analysis of studies of experiential-humanistic psychotherapies demonstrated that clients in PC therapy showed significant change from pre- to post-therapy, and that these changes were comparable to those found in other therapeutic approaches. However, this review covered treatments that included elements beyond those specified in PC counseling (e.g., active interventions such as therapeutic dialogues and directed experiencing) because very few large-scale studies of "pure" PC therapy have been conducted. Similarly, Elliot (2002) conducted a meta-analysis of 99 studies of humanistic therapies and reported that overall, clients demonstrated significant amounts of change. These gains were found to be maintained for up to a year. Again, this analysis was of a set of studies that included a number of approaches that can be called humanistic, such as person-centered therapy or the emotion-focused hybrid approaches developed recently (e.g., process-experiential or emotionally focused therapies for couples). In this regard, the research on Process Experiential Therapy reviewed in Chapter 7 is relevant to PC theory, too.

In two major studies that included PC treatment groups (Grawe, Caspar, & Ambuhl, 1990; Stuhr & Meyer, 1991), PC therapy was found to be as effective as broad spectrum behavior therapy and psychodynamic therapy. DiLorento (1971) compared the effectiveness of Person-centered therapy, Rational Emotive therapy, and systematic desensitization for the treatment of interpersonal anxiety, and found that all three groups improved compared to a no-treatment control. An interesting aspect of this study was that the systematic desensitization showed more general anxiety reduction than the other groups, but when examining interpersonal activity outside of treatment, the Rational Emotive therapy group fared best, followed by the systematic desensitization group and then the Person-centered group.

A recent, large-scale study that included PC counseling was conducted by Stiles, Barkham, Twigg, Mellor-Clark, and Cooper (2006). They compared the outcomes of over 1,300 clients in the UK who received either PC, psychodynamic, or cognitive-behavioral therapy, and found no differences in the effectiveness of these three approaches. Note that this study more resembled an effectiveness rather than a controlled clinical trial project (see Chapter 1) so it could be criticized for its lack of random assignment to treatment and checks of treatment fidelity.

An interesting case study was presented by Goodman, Morgan, Juringa, and Brown (2004). The case was part of a larger study (an RCT) that compared the effectiveness of manualized PC and cognitive-behavioral therapies with families of the emergency workers who died in the 2001 World Trade Center attacks. Goodman et al. described the case of a 15-year-old young woman and her mother, who participated in 16 sessions of PC therapy. Both the young woman and her mother reported improvement across time, and objective measures collected at a posttesting session demonstrated a decrease in posttraumatic traumatic stress symptoms. However, global functioning, as rated by an independent clinician at posttest, showed little change from pretreatment assessment, although this rating did show a decided drop at mid-treatment and a return to pretreatment levels at posttest.

Studies of Motivational Interviewing (MI) can be seen as relevant to PC theory as it is practiced in the United States currently. Recall that MI was one of the therapeutic approaches used in Project Match (see Chapter 1). Hettema et al. (2005) conducted a meta-analysis of 72 studies of MI and found effect sizes were generally positive but they varied across samples and therapists, and decreased rapidly over follow-up periods of up to 12 months. For example, they report that the average effect size right after treatment is 0.77, which is strong. However, over a year, the effect size drops to 0.11. It is interesting that effect sizes for MI were stronger in minority as compared to white client samples (Hettema et al., 2005).

Theory-Testing Research. Much energy has been devoted to testing the theoretical propositions of PC theory, at least those pertaining to the necessary and sufficient conditions. Rogers was the first investigator to systematically use recordings and transcripts of counseling sessions to understand the counseling process. Although this research is, of course, dated, I will briefly summarize a few examples of Rogers' and his colleagues' early efforts.

At the University of Chicago Counseling Center, Rogers and his colleagues designed an intensive study of clients in counseling that exemplified some of the most important tenets of experimental design. Twenty-nine clients and a matched control group (no treatment) were assessed, and audio recordings and other measures were gathered. Raskin (1952) reported his test of the locus of evaluation hypothesis on 10 of these cases. PC theory predicts that the locus of evaluation should shift from external (based on others' perceptions) to internal (based on the client's own perceptions) over the course of therapy. Using ratings made of client statements of evaluation, Raskin demonstrated that the shift along the internal—external dimension among the clients was significant and in the predicted direction.

That is, clients were rated as having made judgments based more on their own values at the end of counseling compared to the beginning. Using the same 10 cases, Bergman (1951) studied counselors' responses to client requests for evaluation by the counselor (e.g., requests for advice, evaluation of progress, etc.). After classifying counselor responses to these requests, Bergman demonstrated that when the counselor responded with reflection of feeling, clients were more likely to continue significant self-exploration than when counselors chose other responses (Bergman, 1951).

Rogers and his associates conducted many other studies of the process of counseling over the years, and most supported the basic tenets of PC theory. Of particular interest were Barrett-Lennard's efforts to operationalize the core conditions by creating the Barrett-Lennard Relationship Inventory (Barrett-Lennard, 1959). This study was Barrett-Lennard's doctoral dissertation and produced a measure that is still used in research today. Rogers argued, with some justification, that the fact that these conditions could be reliably measured was, in itself, support for the theory (Rogers, 1967).

Early studies conducted by other investigators also supported PC theory. Truax and Carkhuff (1965) experimentally manipulated levels of empathy and unconditional positive regard in a small sample (three clients) case study. Their examinations of levels of client experiencing supported PC predictions—clients' levels of experiencing appeared to decrease in tandem with the decrease in therapist conditions. The Wisconsin Project (see Box 5.2) provided a wealth of data on person-centered theory and supported the contention that the level of the PC therapeutic conditions (e.g., empathy, congruence, and unconditioned positive regard) was related to client outcome (Rogers, 1967; van der Veen, 1967). In nontherapy contexts, Cramer (1988, 1994) demonstrated that individuals' levels of self-esteem were related to having a close friend who provided unconditional acceptance, empathy, and congruence.

Later research focusing on Rogers' statement of the necessary and sufficient conditions generally finds that these conditions are correlated with client outcome but are not sufficient. Patterson (1984), a well-known advocate of PC therapy, reviewed nine major review articles on the conditions, and concluded that we can be fairly certain that they are necessary, but not as positive that they are sufficient. Greenberg and colleagues (1994) indicated that, broadly construed, therapist facilitativeness was related to client outcome. Beutler, Machado, and Neufeldt (1994) suggested that empathy, congruence, and unconditional positive regard were aspects of the therapeutic relationship (going beyond the notion of these as therapist characteristics) and that ample evidence existed for the impact of the therapeutic relationship on client outcomes. Most researchers in psychotherapy would probably agree that one of the safest conclusions that we can make about psychotherapy is that the relationship is essential to client progress. Therefore, in some ways, PC theory is one of the best-supported theories of psychotherapy in existence.

The support for the impact of the therapeutic relationship, however, can also be seen as only weak support for PC theory because this effect is seen across theoretical orientations (Beutler et al., 1994). Worse, arguments about how to operationally define the constructs in PC theory further weaken the empirical support for the theory—that is, researchers disagree about how best to measure empathy, unconditional positive regard, and congruence (Greenberg et al., 1994; Hill & Corbett, 1993). Nonetheless, Klein, Michels, Kolden, and Chisholm-Stockard (2001) reported that of 77 studies they reviewed, 34% demonstrated a positive relationship between therapist congruence and client outcome. None of the studies they reviewed showed negative relationships; where results were not positive, the relationship between congruence and outcome was simply nonexistent.

By far the most popular and controversial construct has been empathy. There is much disagreement about how to define, operationalize, and measure this important PC construct (Duan & Hill, 1996; Hill & Corbett, 1993). Generally, when research has attempted to relate empathy to outcome, these efforts have produced results supportive of PC theory (Bachelor, 1988; Barrett-Lennard, 1986). For example, Greenberg, Elliott, Watson, and Bohart (2001) reported that ratings of empathy from clients, counselors, and independent observers all correlated with client outcomes. The strongest relationship was found between client ratings and outcome. Bohart, Elliott, Greenberg, and Watson (2002) meta-analyzed 47 studies of empathy and outcome, finding an effect size of 32, considered a medium effect and comparable to effect size estimates for outcome and the therapeutic alliance. However, in evaluating all of this research, we should probably heed Beutler and colleagues' (1994) warning that because the definitional problems are so intense, conclusions can only be drawn cautiously from the research on empathy and outcome (Hill & Corbett, 1993).

ISSUES OF INDIVIDUAL AND CULTURAL DIVERSITY

PC theory has been both villainized and praised in addressing its utility with individuals from diverse backgrounds. Like many theories of counseling, PC theory can be criticized for placing too much emphasis on the individual and paying relatively little attention to family and cultural effects on people's lives and behaviors (Holdstock, 1990; McDougall, 2002; Poyrazli, 2003; Spangenberg, 2003). Sue, Ivey, and Pedersen (1996) noted that "many psychologists fail to realize that the majority of societies and cultures in the world have a more collectivistic notion of identity; they do not define the psychosocial unit of operation as the individual" (p. 5). Values such as duty to family and cultural groups are largely neglected given the strong emphasis on the internal locus of evaluation prized by PC therapists (Usher, 1989).

Poyrazli (2003) flatly states that "despite its popularity, Rogerian therapy clashes with and is inappropriate for Turkish culture" (p. 111). She cites most of the major problems noticed by others in PC theory: emphasis on individualism and emotional expression, disregard of the power of the family, and the lack of structure and authoritative stance on the part of the counselor. Similar to other critics, however, Poyrazli cites the utility of the core conditions in working with Turkish clients. Spangenberg (2003) agrees that these conditions are useful in working with South African clients and notes that successful PC counseling with these clients would focus on the client in the context of family, community, and culture. In contrast to Poyrazli, Spangenberg sees the nondirectiveness of the PC counselor as respectful to the client, and cautions therapists not to succumb to the temptation to give advice and suggestions without providing the opportunity to process them.

The stress on individualism in PC theory can lead to an attitude that the person must change, not the environment, organization, or society in which he exists. The notion that an individual can actualize without the recognition that sometimes social structures oppress is seen as detrimental to women, racial, and ethnic minorities, and individuals who are gay, lesbian, or bisexual.

Chantler (2005) joins in these kinds of criticisms of PC theory, and suggests an extension of the concept of conditions of worth to include "racialised and gendered conditions of worth"

(p. 254). In doing so, the internalization of societal stereotypes and the often negative impact that they have would be recognized. Chantler also advises counselors who are of dominant group backgrounds working in an enlightened PC mode to examine their own lives for the effects of privilege and how these factors influence their work with clients. Consistent with feminist theory, Chantler emphasizes the issue of socially-conferred power, particularly when counseling those of backgrounds other than the dominant group. She points out that although PC therapists attempt to create a symmetrical therapeutic relationship, "the desire to equalize counseling relationships does not mean that they will be equal" (p. 253).

Clients from cultures other than white European may expect and desire more guidance from the counselor than is provided by traditional PC therapists. MacDougall (2002) suggested that this lack of direction may produce frustration for these clients, and suggested that PC counselors consider alternative behaviors such as giving advice and making suggestions.

Sue and colleagues (1996) also noted that the emphasis on self-disclosure in psychological theory can be problematic for clients from non-European cultures. Clearly, self-disclosure is a cornerstone of PC theory, and clients from cultures that do not value such disclosure (such as Asian individuals) may not respond well to this approach. Also, clients who for good reasons mistrust "majority" individuals may also be reluctant to invest in PC counseling. Insight is highly valued in the PC approach; individuals from cultures or groups other than European and of lower socioeconomic status may not share this value. The latter clients, particularly, may be more concerned with concrete life problems (Sue & Sue, 2003). Sue and Sue, for example, note that many Asian elders believe that thinking about something too much can create problems (p. 110).

PC theory does have some strengths that are relevant to working with clients who are of diverse origins. The assumption that the client, rather than the therapist, determines the goals of counseling avoids the imposition of culturally-based notions of the healthy personality (Usher, 1989). In fact, Rogers probably would have argued that the PC credo of trusting the individual would create an atmosphere of respect for clients' culturally-based values and personal history. Essentially, the PC counselor wants to walk in the client's world. Freire, Koller, Piason, and da Silva (2005) provided an example of such work in their description of the process and outcomes of using a PC approach with 98 lower socioeconomic status, neglected children and adolescents in Brazil. At the publication of Friere et al.'s report, 98 clients had participated in this ongoing program attending a range of 1–39 sessions (average was 12). Initially, the clients in this project were puzzled by the nondirective approach, but Friere et al. report that they quickly began to learn to use the unique relationship to their benefits. Improvements in interpersonal, emotional, and academic functioning were noted by these authors. However, no data are presented to support these contentions and it should be noted that this study in no way approached the standards of controlled outcome studies.

The valuing of real, egalitarian relationships in this approach is consistent with the values of a feminist approach to counseling (Waterhouse, 1993). However, feminists point out that PC theory can be seen as ignoring the social and political context in which women reside (Chantler, 2005; Waterhouse, 1993). The emphasis on autonomy and individual responsibility for change ignores the fact that social roles and norms often prevent women from realizing their potential and can result in blaming women for their problems. According to Waterhouse (1993), "there is within the Rogerian perspective a strong faith in the transformative powers of counselling which is at best overambitious and at worst reckless and irresponsible" (p. 62). Further, the construct of empathy is problematic—to empathize with a women or members of other historically oppressed groups requires not just awareness in the here and now, but also an understanding of the historical influences on current social contexts.

From a GLBT perspective, many of the criticisms and strengths elaborated here apply. The total acceptance of the client by the counselor would be a positive. However, GLBT advocates would also criticize the theory for ignoring cultural and historical influences that contribute to discrimination and prejudice. The conditions of worth construct might need to be broadened to include societal conditions of worth. Lemoire and Chen (2005) emphasized this latter idea in their discussion of the use of PC counseling with GLBT adolescents. Allowing that the core conditions provided by the therapist create a safety situation in which the adolescent can explore his sexual identity, Lemoire and Chen also note that at least three elements need to be added to PC counseling when working with this group: deliberate validation of the adolescent's sexual identity, discussion of risks and benefits associated with disclosure of sexual identity, and socialization into the GLBT community in ways appropriate to the ages of clients.

Toward the end of his life, Rogers became much more involved politically, conducting large encounter groups with individuals from conflicting social groups (such as in South Africa and South America), suggesting a greater awareness of group and social factors in human behavior. In his book *On Personal Power*, Rogers discussed the utility of the PC approach with a wide variety of people, including African Americans; gay, lesbian, and bisexual individuals; Chicanos; Filipinos; and many others. He acknowledged that "minority group members feel tremendous rage and bitterness towards whites. . . . Rage needs to be *heard*. This does not mean that it simply needs to be listened to. It needs to be accepted, taken within and understood empathically. . . . To achieve this kind of empathic listening the white needs to listen to his own feelings too, his feelings of anger and resentment at 'unjust' accusations" (1977, pp. 133–134; quotes and italics in original). However, some writers maintain that these experiences with diverse cultures had little influence on Rogers' thinking because he did not fully recognize the implications of cultural norms of interdependence and community (Holdstock, 1990).

Long-time PC advocate Patterson (2000) opines that the recent emphasis on cultural diversity leads to an excessively technique-oriented position in which counselors modify what they do on the basis of the client's background. Arguing that this stance is also detrimental because it only emphasizes differences between people, he says "this approach only ignores the fact that we are rapidly becoming one world, with rapid communication and increasing interrelations among persons from varying cultures, leading to increasing homogeneity and a worldview representing the common humanity that binds all human beings together as one species" (2000, p. 310).

THE CASE STUDY

Richard presents with depressive and anxiety symptoms, probably very common among the clients with whom Rogers worked as he was developing his theory. The theory accounts particularly well for anxiety and is generally useful in understanding individuals who have difficulty processing and expressing emotion. Richard is a member of a culture (Caucasian) that values individual choice and striving for betterment of the person, values that are consistent with the PC approach. Once Richard gets past his hesitance to discuss and experience emotion, he might be quite comfortable with this approach and its goals.

Summary

Person-centered therapy begins with an optimistic view of people. Humans are seen as growthful beings that attempt to maximize their potential. We inherently move toward experiences that contribute to our growth and away from those that don't, following our actualizing tendency, which is, in turn, guided by the organismic valuing process.

Part of actualization of the organism is the development of the self, which adopts part of the actualizing tendency. The urge to self-actualize can create problems, however, when it runs into the need for positive regard. In wanting the love of others, we may internalize conditions that brand aspects of the self as worthy or bad; these conditions of worth may be counter to the self-actualizing tendency. Once an individual internalizes conditions of worth, he is incongruent; he has a discrepancy between self and experience. He denies or distorts aspects of his experience that do not fit the conditions of worth.

PC counselors do not diagnose or assess. They simply provide the right atmosphere and trust the client to lead the way. Therapist congruence, empathy, and unconditional positive regard are the necessary and sufficient conditions for client change. Given these conditions, the client will progress from a state of incongruence to one of congruence and become fully functioning.

PC theory has been criticized for being simplistic and oblivious to the true qualities of human nature. Outcome research supports the theory, but theory-testing research is less convincing. The core conditions are likely to be necessary but not sufficient, according to the data.

The individualistic emphasis within PC theory can be detrimental to clients who have experienced oppression. The lack of attention to familial and cultural factors in PC theory may be problematic in dealing with clients from other cultures. On the other hand, PC theory's trust in the individual to know what is needed can be helpful in working with clients from diverse backgrounds.

Visit Chapter 5 on the Companion Website at **www.prenhall.com/murdock** for chapter-specific resources and self-assessments.

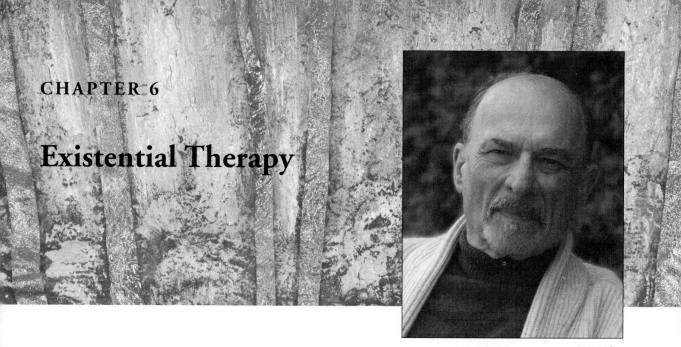

CHAPTER 6

Existential Therapy

Irvin Yalom

Helen is a 43-year-old Caucasian woman who presents for counseling due to problems in her marriage. Helen holds an MFA in Playwriting from Yale University. She and her husband Steve have three children, a 10-year-old boy named Luke, a 12-year-old girl named Grace, and a 14-year-old boy named Charlie. Helen met Steve, 48, while she was attending Yale and he was working in New York City as a bond trader.

Helen grew up in suburban Chicago, the third of five children. Helen's family had the appearance of the "perfect" family. Dad was a very successful surgeon, but not involved in the children's lives on a daily basis. Mom was loving and steady yet also somewhat reserved; she was perhaps more concerned with what others thought than she would have liked to admit. In some ways the family environment was one of benign neglect—the children behaved well and so no one thought there could possibly be anything wrong. In fact, two of Helen's sisters had eating disorders and her brother has battled an alcohol addiction off and on.

Steve and Helen lived in New York City after they married. Helen had an administrative job with a theatre and wrote some at night, although she stopped writing when they had their son Charlie. They had plenty of money, but Steve began to gamble during a period when his work was not going as well as he would have liked. Helen was 8 months pregnant when she learned that Steve had gambled away large amounts of money, including most of their savings.

Helen was devastated, but having grown up in a family where you stick it out no matter what, she immediately began looking for treatment for Steve and housing options for their young family. Unable to deal with the strain, Helen called on her parents for assistance in spite of the fact that she believes that they never truly accepted Steve. They suggested she look in the Chicago area because it would have job options for Steve and perhaps less pressure than New York City. Helen's parents offered financial assistance in the

179

form of a down payment on a house and although it was never stated, it was understood that it was for a house in Chicago. The family moved and has lived in the same house now for 10 years.

On a recent trip to New York with some friends, Helen ran into a former professor from Yale. He asked about her work and she was pleased, but also embarrassed that she's done nothing, although in her mind this is no great loss because she isn't all that talented. He reminded her that she won a competition during graduate school and shared a couple of things faculty members said about her in which they praised her talent and insight. He is divorced, 8 years older than Helen, and very handsome.

He asked her to meet him for a drink and gave her his business card. She didn't call him, but kept the card and did not tell Steve about the encounter. Having survived a crisis in her marriage she now feels resigned to the humdrum existence of a woman whose husband does not support her career ambitions and has never really confronted his own demons.

Helen is a "good girl," a thoughtful woman and a good mother, who has no interest in destroying her family by having an affair. However, she is troubled deeply by the way she feels right now, that her husband can "do no right" and her fear that this is a permanent state for the rest of her marriage. She is surprised by the fact that for 10 years she has endured the crisis caused by her husband's gambling without its sounding the death knell of their marriage. Yet, out of the blue, she bumps into a former professor who displays interest in her and in her work and her reaction to this—her interest in him, irritation that her husband doesn't do the same thing, worry about the aimlessness she is feeling now that her children are older—brings her to a place where she decides to seek help.

BACKGROUND

Existential approaches to psychotherapy (ET) are more philosophy than pragmatics; more attitude than specific theoretical orientation. ET's roots are in existential philosophy, or the study of being and phenomenology, which emphasizes that all we can really know is our own experience (Cooper, 2003). The ideas of many are represented in ET, yet they hang together quite well, as Fischer, McElwain, and DuBoise (2000) so aptly pointed out when they asserted that "existential psychology is an approach of like-minded persons looking for correctives to determinism, materialism, and realism" (p. 245). Therapists of many stripes probably employ ET ideas, at least occasionally, and some writers contend that therapists often draw on existential ideas without conscious recognition that they are doing so (Norcross, 1987).

Norcross (1987) warns us that "existential therapy's process is frequently ill-defined and widely misunderstood" (p. 43). You may believe that this is a less-than-promising start to your study of ET, but I am hopeful that things will soon get clearer. This may help: Yalom (an important existential therapist) defines ET as "a dynamic approach to therapy which focuses on concerns that are rooted in the individual's existence" (1980, p. 5). There seem to be two general orientations within the ET school. The first is the Continental or European, rooted in an analytic orientation (although not exactly accepting the content of psychoanalytic theory), that tends to emphasize the limitations and tragedy of the human condition (Yalom, 1980). The second arose in the United States in the 1960s, and emphasizes human potential and encounter. It is closely related to the humanistic school exemplified by the work of Carl Rogers, James Bugental, and Abraham Maslow. In Box 6.1, the views of Carl Rogers and Rollo May exemplify these differences.

The major writers in ET are numerous, and who you consider important depends on how far back you want to go historically. Most sources trace the approach back to the founder of existential philosophy, Soren Kierkegaard (1813–1855), and acknowledge other existential philosophers, including Friedrich Nietzsche, Martin Buber, Martin Heidegger, and Jean-Paul Sartre (Fischer et al., 2000). Contributors who are specifically concerned with psychotherapy include James Bugental, Emmy van Deurzen-Smith, Victor Frankl, Eric Fromm, R. D. Laing, Rollo May, and Ernesto Spinelli. A particularly moving contribution to ET is Frankl's book *Man's Search for Meaning* (first published in 1946) in which Frankl describes his experiences in the Nazi concentration camps and how these experiences contributed to his theory of logotherapy. You can read a section of Frankl's book in Box 6.2.

Box 6.1

Humans are Basically Good—and Evil:
Views from Two Existentialists

In the early 1980s, Carl Rogers wrote an article praising Rollo May's work, and acknowledged May's contributions to the humanistic movement. In this article, Rogers also pointed out a fundamental philosophical difference between the two men, a difference that centered on the question: Does the nature of the human individual inherently include evil?

Rogers believed that individuals were inherently good, and that they would always choose to actualize the self, given the necessary conditions. In Rogers' view, evil or destructive behavior was not consistent with the goal of self-actualization. To explain phenomena like senseless violence, the looming arms race of the 1970s and 80s, antisocial behaviors, and other manifestations of seemingly evil behavior, Rogers (1982) pointed to cultural influences as the primary factors in promoting evil. Rogers said that humans were "essentially constructive in their fundamental nature, but damaged by their experience" (p. 8).

May's (1982) response to Rogers was to note the obvious, that culture is made of individuals. To assign blame for the evil in the world to the group is to ignore the conscious actions of the individual members of the group. May accepted that evil was a part of the individual; it was inherent in the human condition that individuals must understand and balance both good and evil in themselves. May viewed Rogers' position as naïve and possibly a disservice to clients, and he illustrated his point by directly addressing person-centered counseling.

To May, it was of fundamental importance for the client to be able to take a stand against the therapist. He maintained that person-centered therapy took away this opportunity by overemphasizing the goodness of client and counselor. May wrote, ". . . client-centered therapists did not (or could not) deal with the angry, hostile, negative—that is, evil—feelings of the clients" (1982, p. 15). Essentially, there is a tendency to be too nice, almost naïve, and that this stance robs the client of independence. Further, the therapist's anger toward a client can be an important tool in helping clients understand how their behaviors affect their relationships in general. May was clear on this issue when he wrote:

> This means that aspects of evil—anger, hostility against the therapist, destructiveness—need to be brought out in therapy. Personal autonomy occurs not by avoiding evil, but by directly confronting it. Therapists need to be able to perceive and admit their own evil—hostility, aggression, anger—if they are to be able to see and accept these experiences in clients. (1982, p. 17)

May believed that failing to accept and confront the reality of evil was a significant error of the humanistic movement and a denial that could have potentially dire consequences for the world. May believed that people may be lulled to inaction by the belief that individuals are only good; that by not acknowledging their capacity to choose between good and evil actions, individuals will end up doing nothing. In May's view, if evil is to gain strength and ultimately triumph in the world, it will be through the inaction of individuals. Stressing our agency in the world, May wrote:

> In my experience it is this polarity, this dialectical interaction, this oscillation between positive and negative that gives the dynamic and the depth to human life. Life, to me, is not a requirement to live out a preordained pattern of goodness, but a challenge coming down through the centuries out of the fact that each of us can throw the lever toward good or toward evil. (1982, p. 19)

Contributed by Sean Comeau

Box 6.2

An Excerpt from Frankl's *Man's Search for Meaning*

Let us first ask ourselves what should be understood by "a tragic optimism." In brief it means that one is, and remains, optimistic in spite of the "tragic traid," as it is called in logotheraphy, a traid which consists of those aspects of human existence which may be circumscribed by: (1) pain; (2) guilt; and (3) death. This chapter, in fact, raises the question, How is it possible to say yes to life in spite of all that? How, to pose the question differently, can life retain its potential meaning in spite of its tragic aspects? After all, "saying yes to life in spite of everything," to use the phrase in which the title of a German book of mine is couched, presupposes that life is potentially meaningful under any conditions, even those which are most miserable. And this in turn presupposes the human capacity to creatively turn life's negative aspects into something positive or constructive. In other words, what matters is to make the best of any given situation. "The best," however, is that which in Latin is called *optimum*—hence the reason I speak of a tragic optimism, that is, an optimism in the face of tragedy and in view of the human potential which at its best always allows for: (1) turning suffering into a human achievement and accomplishment; (2) deriving from guilt the opportunity to change oneself for the better; and (3) deriving from life's transitoriness an incentive to take responsible action.[1]

It must be kept in mind, however, that optimism is not anything to be commanded or ordered. One cannot even force oneself to be optimistic indiscriminately, against all odds, against all hope. And what is true for hope is also true for the other two components of the triad inasmuch as faith and love cannot be commanded or ordered either.

To the European, it is a characteristic of the American culture that, again and again, one is commanded and ordered to "be happy." But happiness cannot be pursued; it must ensue. One must have a reason to "be happy." Once the reason is found, however, one becomes happy automatically. As we see, a human being is not one in pursuit of happiness but rather in search of a reason to become happy, last but not least, through actualizing the potential meaning inherent and dormant in a given situation.

This need for a reason is similar in another specifically human phenomenon—laughter. If you want anyone to laugh you have to provide him with a reason, e.g., you have to tell him a joke. In no way is it possible to evoke real laughter by urging him, or having him urge himself, to laugh. Doing so would be the same as urging people posed in front of a camera to say "cheese," only to find that in the finished photographs their faces are frozen in artificial smiles.

Frankl V. E. (1984) *Man's Search for Meaning*, NY: Pocket Books.

---

[1]This chapter is based on a lecture I presented at the Third World Congress of Logotherapy, Regensburg University, West Germany, June 1983.

Perhaps the most coherent and readable formulation of existential theory, at least for the purposes of doing counseling, is that presented by Irvin Yalom. For this reason, this chapter draws heavily from Yalom's work, with the ideas of other writers occasionally inserted. Yalom, a psychiatrist, is well known for his 1980 book, *Existential Psychotherapy*, but also for his work as group therapist (Yalom, & Leszcz, 2005; Lieberman, Yalom, & Miles, 1973). He is also an entertaining writer of fiction that is based on the psychotherapy process, in such books as *When Nietzsche Wept* (1991), which involves the interesting characters Sigmund Freud, his mentor Joseph Bauer, and the existential philosopher Friederich Nietzsche. A particularly notable book for therapists is a compilation of tips for psychotherapists, called *The Gift of Therapy* (2003). Yalom's webpage, is, of course, www.yalom.com .

Other resources in existential psychotherapy are the International Society for Existential Psychology and Psychotherapy, which can be found on the Web at http://www.existentialpsychology.org/ . The society's official journal is the *International Journal for Existential Psychology and Psychotherapy*, which debuted in July 2004. A second organization of interest is the Society for Existential Analysis http://www.existentialanalysis.co.uk/index.htm .

BASIC PHILOSOPHY

The basic philosophy of ET theorists is that humans are free, responsible for their own lives, and have the potential for self-actualization (Norcross, 1987). It can sometimes appear to be a rather gloomy approach. Cooper (2003) reports that when asked what ET is, he sometimes resorts to "it's similar to person centred therapy. . . only more miserable!" (p. 1). Randall (2001) suggests that underlying ET is a philosophy that "the life of each human being is a finite drama enacted in a hostile or indifferent universe; that the purpose of life is not at all given, but must be selected afresh by each individual through conscious acts of willfulness tempered by responsibility, and that no matter how close a person may feel toward another, each ultimately must face life alone" (p. 260). Frankl (1984) adds "to live is to suffer, to survive is to find meaning in the suffering" (p. 11).

On the other hand, ET theorists recognize the human capacity for creativity and love. Frankl (1984) wrote that "love is the ultimate and the highest goal to which man can aspire . . . *the salvation of man is through love and in love* (p. 57; italics in original).

Lars, Helen's ET counselor approaches her with the attitude that she is a free, responsible being who has the potential to grow and flourish. Helen may seem stuck right now, but her distress and sadness are signs of the potential within her to be creative and loving.

HUMAN MOTIVATION

Frankl (1984) contended that the principal motivation of human beings is the search for meaning and most ET theorists would agree. However, there is some disagreement about the source of this meaning. For Frankl, meaning is inherent in each individual—each individual has an ultimate, true calling—and it is the task of the individual to discover it (Cooper, 2003). For other ET theorists, meaning is created; there is no discovery involved.

Frankl maintained that we discover life meaning through three routes: "(1) by creating a work or doing a deed; (2) by experiencing something or encountering someone; and (3) by the attitude we take toward unavoidable suffering" (p. 133). Despite statements like the one above, some accuse Frankl of implicitly endorsing a religious aspect to meaning (Yalom, 1980).

Proponents of ET generally accept the idea of the unconscious and the dynamic nature of psychological functioning, but the content of the unconscious is not instinctual drives, as Freud proposed (May & Yalom, 2005). Instead, what is relegated to the unconscious is the true nature of our existence: that we are finite beings alone in a meaningless world (Cooper, 2003).

Lars wonders about Helen's search for meaning. He guesses that in the past, she has found meaning through her writing, her marriage, and raising her children. Lars guesses that the vague sense of anxiety that Helen is experiencing stems from her sense of mortality, which is just beneath the surface of awareness right now.

CENTRAL CONSTRUCTS

MODES OF BEING

ET theory is focused on the *being* of humans. ET theorists recognize distinct ways of being although they often use different names for them and the classic terms are in German (Bauman & Waldo, 1998; van Deurzen-Smith, 1997). The first is Umwelt, or being in the physical world. Mitwelt is being in relation to others, the social/interpersonal world, and

Eigenwelt refers to the inner psychological world (being in one's subjective experience). Truly authentic existence means attending to all realms. However, we typically have one or two ways of being with which we are most comfortable (van Duerzen-Smith, 1997).

Helen appears to be functioning primarily in the mitwelt—or at least attending to that aspect of her being at the expense of Umwelt and Eigenwelt. She has spent much time worrying about her family until the recent encounter with her former professor. She is tempted to enter the Eigenwelt, but her early training in her family of origin leads her to be uncomfortable with a self-focused orientation.

ANXIETY

ET theorists assume that everyone experiences anxiety; indeed May and Yalom (2005) argued that "anxiety arises from our personal need to survive, to preserve our being, and to assert our being" (p. 271). Certain kinds of anxiety, for example that associated with the awareness of one's finiteness are normal, and critical in determining psychological life, as we shall soon see. This kind of anxiety, called *existential anxiety* by some, is a significant feeling of disease that is not accompanied by any of the usual psychological symptoms (Bauman & Waldo, 1998). For these theorists, anxiety is not to be banished or avoided; it is a critical element in coming to terms with our lives (van Deurzen, 2006).

May and Yalom (2005) distinguished between normal and neurotic anxiety. Normal anxiety fits events and makes sense. It is not threatening enough to engage repressive processes. Normal anxiety also serves as a signal that we need to attend to some situation that evoked it. Existential anxiety is one form of normal anxiety. In contrast, neurotic anxiety seems exaggerated for the person's situation. It is destructive and paralyzing, and tends to be repressed.

Lars notes Helen's clear sense of loss of purpose and unrest. Clearly, she is becoming aware of her existential anxiety, which he thinks stems from her sense of finiteness.

THE ULTIMATE CONCERNS

Yalom (1980) identified four existential themes of human existence: death, freedom, isolation, and meaninglessness (May & Yalom, 2005; Yalom, 1980).

Death. The ultimate concern, "death itches all the time," according to Yalom (1980, p. 29). We humans have a great propensity to avoid really facing the idea of our own mortality, but when we are able to, we experience the ultimate terror. As a result, much of our psychological life is built around avoiding truly facing our fates: death and the anxiety that it triggers are the source of most psychological dysfunction. However, the awareness of death gives meaning to life (Strasser & Strasser, 1997).

Freedom. From an ET perspective, an essential aspect of human existence is freedom—the notion, according to Yalom that "the individual is entirely responsible for—that is, the author of—his or her own world, life design, choices, and actions" (1980, p. 9). May and

Yalom (2005) point out the terrifying consequences of accepting one's freedom: if we are totally free to choose and act, then we must recognize that "there is no ground beneath us: there is only an abyss, a void, nothingness" (p. 280). Ultimately, freedom implies responsibility for ourselves; our actions, but also our failures to act.

Awareness of our freedom implies responsibility to choose. Even if we are not aware of it, we are constantly making choices and our actions reflect these (Norcross, 1987). The reality of freedom, choice, and responsibility brings to us the notion of *existential guilt*: guilt that we experience about possibilities unfulfilled. Existential guilt is unavoidable, because every time we make a choice we are discarding other possibilities (Cooper, 2003).

What if one is trapped in a situation and there is really no way out? Frankl (1984) has the answer; as we know, his thoughts were highly influenced by his experience in the holocaust. He wrote movingly about prisoners in the concentration camps that gave their last food away to others, saying that "they offer sufficient proof that everything can be taken from a man but one thing: the last of the human freedoms—to choose one's attitude in any given set of circumstances, to choose one's own way" (p. 86).

Meaninglessness. Most ETs accept that human existence does not come with built-in meaning (Strasser & Strasser, 1997). Frankl would be the exception to this philosophy, as described above; however, he believed that each individual's meaning was unique and is found only as a result of a difficult search and perhaps unavoidable suffering.

Isolation. We are always and ultimately alone, according to ET theorists. If one accepts one's mortality, freedom, and responsibility to create meaning, the realization of our isolation is unavoidable. People deal with aloneness in many ways, but it presents quite a dilemma, for "trying too hard to achieve security through merger may result in damage to the self; still, abandoning the effort to connect at all leads to emptiness" (Randall, 2001, p. 261).

Helen, Lars thinks, is struggling with all of these concerns simultaneously. She is probably the least aware of her death anxiety, but it is surely the font for her discontent in the other areas of ultimate concern. Helen feels trapped in her current situation and yet guilty for feeling this way. Her sense of meaning has been for a long time invested in raising her children and although she verbalizes her sense of self-worth tied to this aspect of her existence, now she finds that something is missing. She now recalls the sense of meaning and purpose she found in her work as a playwright. Lars think that because of these realizations, Helen probably feels isolated from others and a vague sense of guilt.

Defenses

No matter how hard we try to avoid it, awareness of ultimate concerns is possible. When we become aware of one of these issues, we experience anxiety. The result of anxiety is inevitably, defense (Yalom, 1980). According to Yalom (1980) there are two major defenses that we use to ward off the awareness of death: specialness and the notion of the ultimate rescuer. If we are special, death does not apply to us as it does to others. If we have a magical rescuer, he or she or it will save us from the possibility of nonexistence.

Lars thinks that Helen's sense of specialness is not as prominent as her belief in the rescuer. Her disappointment with her husband and her surge of discontent after meeting her former professor would support this hypothesis.

THEORY OF THE PERSON AND DEVELOPMENT OF THE INDIVIDUAL

ET counselors are not interested in theories of personality because of their orientation toward the essential issues of human existence. They would contend that each individual has the choice, on a moment-to-moment basis, to determine who they are. Theories of personality and development are contrary to the notions of ET because they are based on normative patterns and therefore do not capture the unique experience of the individual client. In addition, the ET therapist is more interested in the client's present experience than her past. However, some ET theorists recognize the developmental sequence from attachment to separation or individuation as inherently tied to the existential dilemma of aloneness (Yalom, 1980). Thus, neoanalytic ideas such as those presented in Chapter 3 would fit with the ET perspective.

Lars is more interested in understanding Helen from her perspective than through any scheme describing personality types. He does, however, recognize the influence of Helen's early environment in the beliefs and ideals she holds as a woman, mother, and spouse.

HEALTH AND DYSFUNCTION

A good definition of health from an ET perspective would be *authentic* (Maddi, 2005). Authenticity involves courage and determination; it involves the willingness to face our own anxiety about not being (Cooper, 2003). Health, in this view, is to live with as little neurotic anxiety as possible, but also to be able to deal with the anxiety that is surely unavoidable as part of being human. Being authentic means to not deceive oneself; such deception is known as acting in bad faith (Sartre, 1956, cited in Yoder, 1981).

For Yalom (1980), the major source of psychological dysfunction is the awareness of death. He proposes that instead of the psychoanalytic notion that the surfacing of instinctual drives leading to anxiety, and then to defense and dysfunction, that the correct sequence is the following: the awareness of ultimate concerns (particularly death) raises anxiety, which then triggers the defense mechanisms. More simply put, people "fall into despair as a result of a confrontation with harsh facts of the human condition—the 'givens' of experience" (Yalom, 2002, p. xvi). In dealing with the notion of our own deaths, we rely mostly on two important defense mechanisms, described earlier, feeling special and believing in an ultimate rescuer (May & Yalom, 2005, p. 283). Yalom links the defense of specialness to paranoia, and, not surprisingly, narcicissm.

The belief in an ultimate rescuer can also lead to dysfunction, and according to Yalom, it is a less effective defense than specialness. Investing oneself in the ultimate rescuer can cause the loss of self and a lifestyle that is restricted. This defense is also more likely to break down in the face of personal illness, or sometimes, when a special other is threatened.

Another way of looking at psychological dysfunction was presented by Bugental and Bracke (1987). They argued that popular culture in recent years has encouraged emptiness and narcissism by focusing on individual achievement without a sense of purpose or meaning. We experience emptiness because of this lack of meaning, which stems partially from the loss of connection associated with current lifestyles and norms. We define ourselves through the eyes of others, and "are seduced into search for direction, completion, and meaning by seeking more *things*, desperately fabricating a fashionable appearance, and looking almost exclusively to others . . . to define ourselves (Bugental & Bracke, 1987, p. 29, italics in original). In their version, the healthy person has a "centered awareness of being" (p. 29), which involves searching inwardly for an authentic self.

Maddi (2005) goes even further, to identify three types of meaninglessness: vegetativeness, nihilism, and adventurousness (p. 108). The most severe form is vegetativeness, in which the individual has virtually no sense of life meaning. Nihilism involves feelings of disgust and anger, because the individual, paradoxically, finds meaning in insisting that life has no meaning. The least severe form of dysfunction is adventurousness. In this presentation, the client is prone to take severe risks to establish life meaning, such as in gambling, substance abuse, or physical adventures. Maddi maintains that "many respected industrialists and professionals fall into this category, regardless of the socially acceptable nature of their activity" (p. 108).

Frankl (1984) explicitly contrasted "traditional" neuroses and existential neurosis. Traditional or psychogenic neuroses have their origins in the psychological processes identified by other theorists. Frankl is much more interested in what he called noogenic neurosis, difficulties related to existential frustration, or the lack of life meaning. Logotherapy, Frankl's approach, derives its name from the word logos, which means meaning.

Spinelli (2001) presented an existential take on psychosis. Arguing that we have no definitive proof for biological explanations for these client presentations, Spinelli suggests abandoning traditional diagnosis in favor of understanding the meaning of the experiences of severely disturbed clients. He identifies two types of clients in this regard: one who is frightened by her mental turmoil and the second who adopts the experiences as truth. The latter client is more difficult to help than the former, according to Spinelli.

Lars speculates on Helen's recounting of her current experience. She clearly presents a sense of aimlessness, a feeling that her existence is "humdrum." These elements add up to meaninglessness. At present, Helen is not very authentic, because she refuses to face up to her existential tasks and have the courage to live without self-deception. However, that she comes to counseling suggests that she is moving in the right direction—with some support she will likely begin to confront her sense of despair and the reality of her finite existence. Helen does not seem to be very centered right now; she lives more according to the needs of others and neglects her own very difficult feelings. She seems a little vegetative, yet Lars sees movement starting to build.

NATURE OF THERAPY

Assessment

ET therapists don't do much formal assessment; most would agree that to assess and diagnose creates distance between client and counselor, interfering with authentic encounter necessary for effective therapy.

Lars does his best to get to know Helen, to enter her world while maintaining his own authenticity.

Overview of the Therapeutic Atmosphere

ET is an experiential approach and is focused intently on the immediate subjective experience of client and therapist (Schulenberg, 2003). Because this approach is very philosophical, you might expect the ET counselor to act like your stereotypic philosopher: thoughtful, passive, turned inward. You would be wrong: ET therapists are quite active in their relationships with clients (Fischer et al., 2000).

As active as they are, ET therapists do not attempt to give clients solutions to their problems (Yalom & Bugental, 1997). In fact, they are more likely to challenge clients, encouraging them to have the courage to face the ultimate concerns (Cooper, 2003). As van Deurzen puts it, "an attitude of openness is encouraged and clients are not mollycoddled, though treated with respect, care and understanding" (2006, p. 283).

For Yalom, ET does not fit in a short-term model. He typically sees clients for several years, and sometimes twice a week. However, he readily acknowledges that many therapists practice in conditions under which longer-term psychotherapy is not possible. There is, in fact, at least one time-limited model of ET in existence (Strasser & Strasser, 1997).

Lars begins the counseling relationship with Helen with a sure sense of who he is and a ready energy to devote to the process. He is unsure what is to come, but welcomes the challenge and has faith in Helen to be able to handle it.

Roles of Client and Counselor

The therapist in the ET tradition has been described as a consultant who has a very real, deep caring for the client (Bugenthal & Kleiner, 1993). The therapist also attempts to demystify the counseling process and relate authentically to the client. Part of relating authentically is for the counselor to have attended to his own existential issues, for as van Deurzen-Smith points out, the counselor should not be "existentially lazy" (1997, p. 195). The therapist who has accomplished this existential scrutiny will not hide behind authority or therapeutic neutrality and will treat the client as an equal.

Walsh and McElwain (2001) emphasize that the client and counselor have a mutual investment and risk in the therapeutic encounter. Similarly, Spinelli (1997) sees therapy as a challenge for both therapist and client. He maintains that the therapist must be an active participant, not an observer of the process, and thereby risks having his values and beliefs shaken by experiences with clients. The client is challenged to clarify the nature of herself in all aspects. Spinelli describes an attitude of "un-knowing" on the part of the therapist that facilitates the therapeutic relationship as the "therapist's willingness to explore the world of the client in a fashion that seeks not only to remain accessible to, and respectful of, the client's unique way of being-in-the-world, but also to be receptive to the challenges to the therapist's own biases and assumptions (be they personal or professional, or both) that the exploration may well provide" (p. 8).

Lars engages in the relationship with Helen relying on an attitude of un-knowing and the acknowledgement that what he brings to the relationship will only be evident if he is as authentic as he can possibly be. He is prepared to care deeply about Helen and to feel challenged by the paths of exploration she chooses and the likely sense of suffering and pain that will emerge.

GOALS

Perhaps the simplest statement of the goal of ET comes from Norcross, who opined that "the purpose of psychotherapy is to set people free: free of symptoms and free to be aware and to experience one's possibilities" (1987, p. 48). A more detailed description comes from van Deurzen-Smith:

> The aim of existential counseling is to clarify, reflect upon, and understand life. Problems in living are confronted and life's possibilities and boundaries are explored. Existential counseling does not set out to cure people in the tradition of the medical model. Clients are considered to be not ill bu sick of life or clumsy at living. When people are confused and lost the last thing they need is to be treated as ill or incompetent. What they need is some assistance in surveying the terrain and in deciding on the right route so that they can again find their way. (1988, p. 20)

ET counselors want to help the client live an authentic life, which involves accepting the ultimate concerns of being; most importantly, the inevitability of our own deaths (Strasser & Strasser, 1997).

Lars hopes that Helen, ultimately, can find her way out of her current "stuckness" into authentic experiencing. She must accept her own sense of freedom and the responsibility that is hers alone for what she does with this freedom. Lars believes that Helen will acknowledge her limited existence and the aloneness that will first catapult her into existential terror. However, eventually, Lars is certain that Helen will find her way out of the abyss by examining her current existence and moving forward to develop new meaning in her life.

PROCESS OF THERAPY

Bugental and Kleiner (1993) presented the following basic principles of ET:

1. An existential orientation recognizes that psychological distresses overlie deeper (and often implicit) existential issues
2. An existential orientation maintains primary regard for the unique individuality and humanness of each client
3. An existential orientation gives central attention to the client's own beingness, awareness, or subjectivity
4. An existential orientation emphasizes the atemporality—the lived present—of subjective life, and thus all other time frames are seen chiefly in relation to the immediate (pp. 105–106).

Fischer et al. (2000) pointed to three general themes that can be seen in all contemporary ET approaches: relationship, understanding, and flexibility (p. 248). The therapist must engage in the relationship and attend to its nuances. Understanding means the counselor's sincere attempt to enter into the client's world. The idea of the uniqueness of the individual leads to the conclusion that the therapist must be flexible in approaching clients and may need to change approach or orientation across or within sessions (Walsh & McElwain, 2002).

Although ET therapists always keep their versions of the ultimate concerns in mind, Yalom reminds us that these concerns are not in the forefront for all clients, or for a particular client at all times. He warns us that "therapy should not be theory-driven but relationship-driven" (2002, p. xviii).

All ET therapists see the relationship as an existential encounter, which should be authentic and trusting. Bugental writes about *presence*, or the quality of being fully engaged in the moment (Bugental & Bracke, 1992). For the best therapy, both therapist and client need to be fully present (Cooper, 2003).

Some proponents of the ET approach take an interpersonal approach, seeing the client's pattern of interpersonal relationships as reflective of her stance toward self, others, and the world, or in other words, her way of being in the world (Spinelli, 2002). This orientation would translate to a focus on the therapeutic relationship as an indicator of the client's selfhood. The relationship between therapist and client often becomes the center of therapy. Spinelli (2002) suggests that ET approaches are distinctly different from others in their focus on the here-and-now relationship of therapist and client, the experience of being "us," as he puts it (p. 113).

Bugental and Kleiner (1993) identified four stages of the therapy process: Developing the alliance, deepening the client's concern, inner exploration, and disclosing and working through the resistance (pp. 107–108). In this view, resistance results from the individual's efforts to shield herself from the ultimate threat of nonbeing. The therapist's job is to do his best to understand the client as a unique individual who exists in the world (Norcross, 1987).

Spinelli (1997) presents an interesting perspective on transference and countertransference. He maintains that labeling events in these terms allows the therapist to escape the essence of the real encounter by locating them in the past. Instead, these *resonances*, as he calls them, should be viewed as evidence of the "values, beliefs and emotions that present themselves in the *current encounter between therapist and client*" (p. 37, italics in original).

Lars anticipates that his encounter with Helen will change both of them. He attempts to enter her world as best he can, staying present in the moment and true to himself. However, Lars anticipates that there are times that he will get off track, distracted, or will experience emotions that are connected with their encounter. When this happens, Lars will try to be authentic in dealing with these experiences.

THERAPEUTIC TECHNIQUES

Van Deurzen (2006) opines "the existential approach is in principle against techniques, as these might hamper human interaction at a deep, direct and real level" (p. 283). Other ET writers accept that although for the most part ETs do not advocate any specific techniques, they do tend to draw from a wide array of interventions found in existing counseling approaches (Fischer et al., 2000); Yalom (1980; May & Yalom, 2005) would advocate that any intervention that helps the client gain awareness of the anxiety associated with the four ultimate concerns is fair game. I will present a few techniques mentioned most often by ET advocates below, with emphasis on how they might be used to address ET goals.

ATTENTION TO NONVERBAL BEHAVIOR

Because the emphasis in ET is on awareness of one's being, ET counselors are very interested in observing the client's nonverbal expression and calling their attention to it (Cooper, 2003).

Lars observes Helen for nonverbal signs of her current state. He notes that she clasps her hands across her body and asks her to notice this and try to describe what she is experiencing. Helen responds that she is feeling isolated and alone, and the clasp of her hands is a way of soothing herself.

SELF-DISCLOSURE

It is quite common for ET practitioners to share their personal reactions with their clients (Fischer et al., 2000). Stemming from the ET value that the counselor must be authentic and present, self-disclosure is seen as deepening the therapeutic encounter. The counselor can disclose in one of two ways: about the process of therapy (i.e., the client-counselor relationship) or about the therapist's own existential struggles (Colledge, 2002).

Lars is willing to open himself to Helen, should the moment arise. For instance, he might respond to the feeling that he is distant from Helen and express his real wish to more fully encounter her. Lars might also reveal some aspect of his own search for life meaning.

PARADOXICAL INTENTION

One of the best known ET techniques, paradoxical intention, originated with Frankl (1984). Used mainly for what Frankl terms neurotic fear (as compared to the realistic fear of unbeing), it involves encouraging the client to "go with" a troublesome symptom or problem and experience it deliberately (Cooper, 2003). By facing and experiencing whatever it is we greatly fear allows us to engage the unique human capacity to laugh at ourselves and thereby gain distance from our symptoms. Fischer (1991) adds that practicing the symptom allows the client and the therapist to understand its meaning to the client.

Because Helen does not report a specific, traditional symptom, paradoxical intention may not be a good choice, thinks Lars. However, he does consider asking Helen to deliberately experience "humdrum" to more fully explore this sense of stuckness.

DEREFLECTION

Another strategy offered by Frankl, dereflection, consists of directing the client to turn her attention out to the world. It is meant to combat the tendency that Frankl saw in some distressed individuals to focus too intently on internal processes (Cooper, 2003).

Lars observes that Helen does not seem excessively self-focused at this time. Rather, she seems more intent on meeting the needs of others, and this is a long-time pattern for her. Lars concludes that using dereflection is not advisable but is always open to the possibility that it might be useful later on in therapy.

DREAM ANALYSIS

Yalom (1980) is a big fan of dream analysis. Rather than looking for unconscious conflicts between psychic entities as a psychoanalytic therapist would, however, the ET therapist is looking for manifestations of the client's issues around the four ultimate concerns.

Helen relates a dream to Lars about being swept away by a river. Her family watches from the banks, passively. The college professor is also on the banks, but seems to be upset and follows her progress closely. Together, Lars and Helen explore the meaning of this dream, finding that it symbolizes her feelings of powerless and the state of her relationships with her family. The professor is the only hope, the dream seems to say. He may be the ultimate rescuer; however, it is likely that on a deeper level, the professor-figure is a reflection of a part of Helen that wants to take action to find new sources of meaning in her life.

BRACKETING

The ET counselor must learn to suspend her own beliefs and biases in favor of fully understanding the client's world (Strasser & Strasser, 1997). This process is called bracketing.

Lars works hard to clear his mind of his own beliefs and values when he encounters Helen. However, he is aware that this is not entirely possible, so he brackets his material but remains aware that it is there without focusing on it.

GUIDED FANTASY

Yalom describes using imagery to increase death awareness (1980, p. 175). The client is asked to meditate on her death in some way; picturing her funeral, write her obituary, speculate on where, how, when.

Lars considers having Helen contemplate her death. She is at first very afraid of this exercise but goes on to paint a vivid picture. She cries as she connects with the feelings of aloneness.

EVALUATION OF THE THEORY

ET is criticized on a number of counts. First, it is not really a cohesive theory of psychotherapy—it seems more a collection of components of existential philosophy upon which to base a technically eclectic practice. The very diversity of viewpoints makes it difficult to form a coherent sense of ET. A second criticism is that writers in this area are often difficult to read. They tend to use abstract terms, and sometimes, convoluted language and rationales. For English-speaking readers, the borrowing of terms from German is often difficult.

According to Cooper (2003), ET suffers from something akin to the paradox of relativism: if everything is individual and unique, how can we theorize about the givens of human existence? How can one advise authenticity and courage? If everything is subjective, isn't this a philosophy of "anything goes" (p. 31)?

QUALITIES OF THEORY

Precision and Testability. You have probably divined by now that the ET approach is not very testable because of its philosophical nature and variations in theoretical structures across theorists within this camp. However, a recent line of research in social psychology explores Terror Management Theory, or the ways in which humans avoid evidence of their mortality. In Box 6.3, I provide a brief summary of this line of theory and research.

Box 6.3

Terror Management Theory: Existential Theory in an Experimental Paradigm

Despite claims by many that existential theory could not be studied in traditional scientific paradigms, in the early 1980s, three graduate students decided to try. Sheldon Soloman, Jeff Greenberg, and Tom Pyszczynski, reviewing the current state of social psychology, concluded that it was quite elegant in describing *how* we function, but lacking in explanation about *why*. Soloman et al. (2004) identified two critical questions that were neglected by mainstream psychology:

1. Why are people so intensely concerned with their self-esteem?
2. Why do people cling so tenaciously to their own cultural beliefs and have such a difficult time coexisting with others different from themselves? (p. 14)

They set out to study these issues, developing what they later named terror management theory (TMT). Early research efforts found a less-than-warm reception from their social psychology colleagues, but they were not dissuaded. Based partially in evolutionary theory, Soloman et al. postulated that because humans are self-aware, we are also aware of our own mortality. To compensate for the resulting terror, we developed culture. Culture gives us a sense of self-worth (we are valuable members of a meaningful venture), safety and security, symbolic immortality through preserving cultural artifacts and traditions (e.g., art and science), and protecting children. Sometimes culture implies religion, which assures us of the "real" immortality of an afterlife.

The need for self-esteem, in this view, is universal (p. 17). Self-esteem is connected to culture, for it is derived through membership in the meaningful culture and adherence to cultural rules. However, the existence of other cultural groups who have different values is inherently threatening: to acknowledge the validity of beliefs at odds with our own is to perceive that ours is not the true, protective cloak that protects us from mortality. Thus, two essential processes protect us from the terror of death: (a) belief in our cultural world views, which leads to (b) self-esteem attained through meeting our culture's standards.

Soloman et al. set out to test their theory, and a particularly interesting aspect of this research is that involving the *mortality salience* (MS) hypothesis: "if cultural worldviews and self-esteem provide beliefs about the nature of reality that function to assuage anxiety associated with the awareness of death, then asking people to ponder their own mortality should increase the need for the protection provided by such beliefs" (p. 20). MS interventions, for example, should produce positive affect for those similar to us (who hold the same beliefs) and denigration of those who are different. Typical MS interventions ask participants to write down feelings invoked by thoughts of their own deaths.

Terror management hypotheses have since been confirmed in a series of studies. For example, Greenberg et al. (1990) asked participants who were Christian to evaluate target individuals who were either Christian or Jewish after receiving or not receiving an MS intervention. They found that these Christian participants reported more positive reactions to the Christian target and more negative reactions to the Jewish target when they had received the MS intervention (these effects are called "worldview defenses"). No such differences were found in the control (no MS intervention) condition. Subsequent studies confirmed these attitudinal effects, and found behavioral differences too. Other research has demonstrated that MS interventions create activity directed at bolstering self-esteem and that relatively high self-esteem appears to reduce the need to enact worldview defenses.

So, terror management is alive and well, if you believe Soloman et al.'s research (but you would have to be of a culture that values such scientific activity, according to the theory). You might want to give these ideas some thought the next time you are facing a client of a different worldview.

Empirical Validity. ET folks are not too enthusiastic about traditional empirical research. According to Norcross (1987), this reluctance has to do with the perception among ET proponents that the reductionistic and deterministic nature of empirical study is contrary to the basic philosophy of ET. Further, the general lack of structure and clarity of ET as a theoretical orientation contributes to the difficulty.

RESEARCH SUPPORT

Outcome Research. Elliot (2001) conducted a meta-analysis of 99 studies of humanistic therapies and reported that overall, clients demonstrated significant amounts of change. These gains were found to be maintained for up to a year. However, most of the studies included in the meta-analysis were of person-centered therapy or the emotion-focused hybrid approaches developed recently (e.g., process-experiential or emotionally focused therapies for couples).

Lantz and his colleagues have reported on the outcomes of ET therapy with a number of different client problems. For example, Lantz and Raiz (2004) presented a 5-year study of ET therapy with 29 older adult couples. They found significant improvement during therapy on the Purpose in Life Test (Crumbaugh & Maholick, 1964) and on perceptions of the couples' relationships. Lanz and Gregoire (2000a) studied couples dealing with breast cancer who were seen in ET therapy over a 20-year period. This study of 27 couples revealed eight common themes in these couples' lives: mindfulness of being, loss of control, recollection and grief, guilt and abandonment, communication disruptions, why us?, anger at God, anger at medical personnel (due to perceived coldness and distance), and worries about future sexual performance. Eighteen of the couples provided 3 measurements on the Purpose in Life Test and a measure of relationship functioning. Overall these couples showed improvement over the course of therapy, and maintained these changes at follow-up. Similarly, positive outcomes were reported with couples in which one member was a veteran of the Vietnam War (Lantz & Gregoire, 2000b). In evaluating Lantz's research, however, it is important to note that these are not controlled outcome studies (with standardized intervention and control groups), so conclusions from these should be treated carefully.

Theory-Testing Research. ET theorists generally advocate case study or qualitative approaches to research, although Yalom (1980) reviews research from general psychology that he asserts supports ET. Schneider (2003) also notes that support for ET can be found in common factors research that looks at the therapeutic alliance, empathy, genuineness and in research on process-experiential therapy (Elliot, Watson, Goldman, & Greenberg, 2004; see Chapter 7, "Gestalt Therapy," for a discussion of this approach and research results). Walsh and McElwain (2002) came to similar conclusions after reviewing research that they saw as relevant to ET, although it is not explicitly seated in existential principles. For example, they cited research based in the constructivistic notions about the role of narrative in human lives that links storytelling and a sense of life meaning is also offered as evidence in support of ET. As I noted earlier, terror management theory explores some hypotheses developed from existential theory.

Norcross (1987) conducted a survey of ET therapists to determine what they did in practice, which can loosely be construed as a test of ET theory. Three hundred and nineteen psychologists responded to a survey that identified 14 components of practice activity. The top-ranked intervention for ET counselors was "Rogerian skills," meaning empathy and warmth, followed closely by therapist authenticity. Lowest ranked were flooding and psychological testing. ET proponents also reported using more relationship-building skills, attention to nonverbal behavior, and self-disclosure than psychoalanalytic and behavioral respondents in this sample.

ISSUES OF INDIVIDUAL AND CULTURAL DIVERSITY

ET is seen as very useful with a wide range of clients. Burlin and Guzzetta (1977) contend that the themes of ET are particularly relevant for women. For example, the ET value that "people are subjects, not objects" encourages women to discover value within themselves rather than through the culturally endorsed dimension of physical attractiveness (p. 262). Likewise, Vontress (1985) sees ET as viable for use across cultures. He writes that "although it is important to consider specific cultures and their impact on individuals socialized in them, it is more useful to become fully aware of the human condition. As members of the same species, individual members of Homo sapiens face conspecific and culture specific problems simultaneously" (p. 211).

However, for others, the emphasis on individualism in ET theory is problematic in considering people from cultures other than the white, Western European variety. A particular problem might arise in cases where the client is from one of the groups who have historically experienced oppression (e.g. gay/lesbian, African American, Native American)—they might find the emphasis on free will and choice to be counter to their views of the world. However, Frankl (1984) would contend that even if there is no choice, meaning can be found in suffering.

THE CASE STUDY

The case of Helen was relatively easily conceptualized from an ET perspective. She is at a stage in her life in which she is reevaluating meaning, which fits perfectly with ET assumptions. Because she is from a social situation where she has the means and support to engage in such reflection, the application of ET theory was fairly straightforward.

Summary

ET theory is grounded in philosophy more than perhaps any other theory of counseling. Its advocates unite in the contention that humans are motivated to seek meaning in life. Yalom (1980) presents the four ultimate concerns of life: death, freedom, isolation, and meaninglessness. Psychological health is seen in authentic living and awareness and acceptance of our plight as human beings.

ET therapy is seen as an encounter between two beings, focused on the present. The relationship between therapist and client is central and is often the vehicle for interventions, such as when the therapist self-discloses to the client. Very few specific techniques are identified in this approach.

ET theory is criticized for being difficult to read and understand and its diverse nature makes it difficult to test directly in traditional scientific paradigms. Case study or qualitative research is often used along with drawing supportive information from the more general studies of psychotherapy or psychological functioning. ET is a flexible approach, so it is often characterized as helpful to a wide range of clients. However, its emphasis on freedom and individual responsibility may not fit with the worldview of clients who are members of groups that have been oppressed.

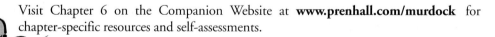

Visit Chapter 6 on the Companion Website at **www.prenhall.com/murdock** for chapter-specific resources and self-assessments.

CHAPTER 7

Gestalt Therapy

Fritz Perls

Jessica is a 30-year-old African American woman who works as a police officer. She is physically fit, verbal, and appears open to counseling. Jessica has a 5-year-old son, Dale, from a previous marriage. Jessica and Dale have had no contact with Dale's father for several years.

Jessica seeks counseling because she is troubled in her current relationship with Randy, with whom she has been living for 2 years. Recently, the couple had a serious fight involving physical contact. Jessica had been trimming Randy's hair, and she moved his head too abruptly. Randy became angry and Jessica apologized. Randy remained agitated and got up, threatening to leave their apartment. Jessica, who feared that Randy would not return, took Randy's car keys. Randy reacted by locking the door, closing the blinds, and grabbing Jessica by the neck, shoving her against a wall. Randy then retreated to the bedroom. The couple did not speak about the incident afterward, and they have not discussed it since then. This altercation was the fourth episode of violence in Jessica's relationship with Randy.

Jessica is the oldest in a family of four children. Her parents divorced when Jessica was 12, and her mother remarried shortly afterward. She has two step-siblings as a result of this marriage, but she is not close to them. Jessica reports a "normal" childhood and some emotional turmoil as a teenager (in reaction to the divorce), but overall, says the household in which she lived was relatively calm. Jessica characterizes her mother as distant and businesslike, and reports that she has difficulty relating to her.

Jessica had a positive relationship with her biological father, who has not remarried, up until she decided to become a police officer. Her biological father reacted very negatively when Jessica told him, saying, "Cops are pigs. If you become a cop, I never want to see you again." Jessica pursued her wishes despite this reaction and has spoken with her father only three times in the last 8 years.

Jessica admits that she is afraid of Randy when he gets angry, but that otherwise they have a good relationship. Jessica seems to take responsibility for anything that goes wrong in her relationship. Randy sees no real problem with the violent incidents in the past and does not want to come to counseling. According to Jessica, he is very much in charge of their relationship, specifying how and when things get done around their apartment. Randy and Jessica's son Dale generally get along, but are not close.

Jessica wants to learn how to create a better relationship with Randy so that they do not get into as many fights. She sees herself as responsible for many of the problems in the relationship. Jessica thinks that if she tries harder to meet Randy's expectations, things will get better.

BACKGROUND

Gestalt Therapy (GT) is in some ways a difficult topic to approach. Historical descriptions of GT often center on the practice of the flamboyant and controversial Fritz Perls (1893–1970). Perls is captured well by his statement in his autobiography, written when he was 76: "I believe that I am the best therapist for any type of neurosis in the States, maybe in the world. How is this for megalomania?" (Perls, 1969b, p. 228).

Others have contributed to the theory and practice of GT, including Perls' wife, Laura, and the theory has evolved considerably from the approach he developed. Often, writers comment on "Perlism," which refers to Perls' distinctive style of doing therapy: showy, confrontive, and typically in a very public workshop format (Parlett & Hemming, 1996a). Insiders speak of "splits" within the GT community, "East and West Coast New York and Cleveland Gestalt Therapy, Gestalt Therapy with the empty chair and Gestalt Therapy face to face, Gestalt Therapy and body work, Gestalt Therapy and psychoanalysis, Gestalt Therapy of the early Perls and Gestalt Therapy of the later, etc., etc." (Friedman, 2003, p. 60). Modern variants are generally less confrontive and more attentive to the therapeutic relationship. Practitioners of these styles of GT may look more like traditional psychoanalysts than did Perls at the end of his career. In this chapter, I will attempt to convey the approach as it is practiced currently, but also describe the defining features of Perls' approach to GT.

Probably because Perls was a very colorful character and prone to providing showy public demonstrations of GT, the credit (or blame) for the theory is usually placed with him. He was a very controversial figure, a self-confessed "dirty old man" (Perls, 1969b), which prompted Clarkson and Mackewn (1993) to comment,

> Who Perls was depends upon whom you speak with, and when. To some he was a hero, to others a bastard; to some cruel, to others tender; to some generous, to others the world's biggest taker; to some a genius, to others a near-illiterate non-intellectual; to some he seemed sociable and happy, to others lonely and poor at making genuine contact with the people around him; to some he was a beautiful sensuous man, to others an ugly toad, a dirty lecherous old man; to some a narcissistic exhibitionist, to others a shy, withdrawn introvert too proud to ask for love. (p. 30)

Perls was initially trained in classic psychoanalysis, and his first theoretical attempts replaced Freud's sexual drive with the hunger drive (Harman, 1990). In *Ego, Hunger, and Aggression* (1942), Perls' first book, he attempted to integrate these ideas with traditional psychoanalytic theory. Aspects of the "oral metaphor" can be seen in later GT theory's emphasis on assimilating (or digesting) experience and the rejection of introjection, or swallowing whole. Perls' subsequent writings retained some of the flavor of psychoanalytic theory, but progressively diverged both in theory and technique.

A major influence on Perls' thought was Gestalt psychology, a branch of perceptual psychology that explored how humans create meaning out of perceptual stimuli. The influence of this approach can be seen in the ideas about the holistic nature of human experience and the primacy of figure–ground relationships (see the section on needs later in this chapter). As GT theory evolved, however, the influence of the purely perceptual Gestalt theory diminished. Perls acknowledged that he was not wholly committed to classic Gestalt theory because he was uncomfortable with the traditional scientific approach used by these theorists. "The academic Gestaltists of course never accepted me," he wrote (1969b, p. 62).

GT theory was also shaped by Perls' background in theater, his stints in Reichian body therapy and Rolfing, and existentialist and Zen philosophy. Reich, who believed that psychic energy, including emotion, was stored in the body, was Perls' analyst for 2 years (from 1931 to 1933).

Born to a progressive Jewish family in 1893, Perls grew up in a suburb of Berlin, Germany. He was the youngest of three children; his mother was devoted to her children, whereas his father was more distant emotionally and physically (traveling for business) and reportedly had numerous extramarital affairs (Clarkson & Mackewn, 1993). Fritz was closer to his mother than to his father until about age 10, when his relationships with both parents, along with his scholastic performance, deteriorated. Rebellious throughout his adolescence, he was expelled from school once, but managed to find a second school that affirmed his independence, from which he graduated. Throughout his adolescence he pursued theater work, and his emphasis on nonverbal behavior in GT counseling is said to stem from these experiences (Clarkson & Mackewn, 1993).

After serving in World War I, Perls received his medical degree in 1920. He began his practice of medicine as a neuropsychiatrist (Clarkson & Mackewn, 1993). At age 31, still living at home with his mother, Perls began psychoanalysis with Karen Horney. Although brief, this analysis started Perls on the road to becoming an orthodox analyst, despite a very negative experience with his second analyst, who said almost nothing during sessions and scraped his feet on the floor to signal the end of sessions (Perls, 1969b). In 1926 he moved to Frankfurt, Germany, and it was there that he became familiar with Gestalt psychology. After Perls completed his training analysis, he established himself as a psychoanalyst and practiced in Berlin from 1928 to 1933.

According to Clarkson and Mackewn, the existentialist influences in Gestalt Therapy came by way of Laura Posner Perls, who had studied with the well-known phenomenologists Buber and Husserl. Laura and Fritz met in 1926 and married in 1929. They had two children, Renate and Steve.

Fritz and Laura left Berlin in 1933 as Hitler was appointed chancellor of Germany (Clarkson & Mackewn, 1993). They ended up in South Africa, where they established the South African Institute for Psychoanalysis. During this period Perls returned to Europe for a conference, hoping to meet Sigmund Freud. He was disappointed when his work was poorly received and Freud paid him little attention. Shortly thereafter, the International Psychoanalytic Association decreed that analysts who had not served as training analysts in Europe could not be recognized as such in other parts of the world. This invalidation of Perls' work in South Africa was a powerful event in Perls' development.

After World War II, in which Perls served as a physician in the South African army, Perls moved to America, followed a year later by Laura and their children (in 1947). Settling in

New York, the couple established a practice and eventually established the Gestalt Institute of New York. The participants in the institute were diverse people with wide-ranging interests and strong personalities. During this time period, Perls first encountered Eastern religion and psychodrama, a form of psychotherapy invented by Jacob Moreno that required the client to act out life situations.

What many consider to be the foundation text of Gestalt Therapy, *Gestalt Therapy: Excitement and Growth in Human Personality* (Perls, Hefferline, & Goodman, 1951), was a result of the vigorous and lively discussions among the early members of the Gestalt Institute. According to Parlett and Hemming (1996a), the book originated from a 50-page manuscript that Perls asked Goodman to transform into a book. Goodman, described as a "quirky, brilliant thinker" (p. 91), took the challenge and ran with it; some authors refer to the work as Goodman's (Wheeler, 1991). The exercises in awareness in the first half of the book were contributed by Hefferline, who used them with his university students. The book is often referred to as "Perls, Hefferline, and Goodman," and its merits are still the subject of debate. All acknowledge that the basic elements of the GT approach were in the book (e.g., holism, the phenomenological approach, experiments), but it has been characterized both as dense and unreadable and as multilayered and deeply meaningful, like poetry (Parlett & Hemming, 1996a).

Fritz Perls was diagnosed with a heart condition in 1956 and moved by himself to Miami, Florida, at age 63. Tension had arisen in Fritz and Laura's relationship, and although they never divorced, they never lived together again for any significant period (Clarkson & Mackewn, 1993). It was in Miami that Fritz became the therapist, and then lover, of Marty Fromm. This relationship, needless to say, was a controversial one, labeled "irresponsible and unethical" by Clarkson and Mackewn (1993, p. 23). Perls characterized his relationship with Fromm as the most important in his life. It ended when Fromm fell in love with a younger man (Perls, 1969b).

Moving to the West Coast in 1960, Perls became affiliated with the Esalen Institute in Big Sur, California, in 1964. He was in poor physical health at the time. Ida Rolf eventually treated Perls with her approach, which emphasized breaking down chronic tension through deep muscle massage. Perls responded favorably, perhaps further supporting his conviction that many psychological dynamics are translated into physical problems.

Esalen became famous in the 1960s as a center of the human potential movement. It was known for the freewheeling styles of teachers and participants, including sexual encounters and drug use. At Esalen, Perls was exposed to many well-known individuals, including Rollo May, Virginia Satir, and Abraham Maslow (Clarkson & Mackewn, 1993). He began the workshop tradition for which he is well known at Esalen in which he demonstrated Gestalt Therapy on stage in front of large crowds. *Gestalt Therapy Verbatim*, consisting largely of edited transcripts of Perls' workshops, was published in 1969 (Perls, 1969a). An interesting account of Perls' and others' antics at Esalen, which still operates, is found in Anderson's (2004) *The Upstart Spring*.

From Easlen, Perls moved on to start a Gestalt community at Cowichan Lake, Vancouver Island, Canada, in 1969. According to reports, Perls was happy there, leading training sessions and working on several other books. Rather quickly, however, his health declined, and he died of a heart attack after surgery in March 1970.

Miller, in his introduction to *Gestalt Therapy Verbatim*, pointed out that GT was a product of the 1960s, which he described as "outrageously playful, promiscuous, utopian, rebellious; the mood of the sixties was alternatively good-humored and angry, and somehow managed to be at once sophisticated and naïve" (Miller, 1989, p. 19). Over the years of his professional career, Perls' philosophy evolved from traditional conservative psychoanalysis to the freedom-loving, spectacular approach of GT, rebelling against authority and emphasizing a return to innocence. Perls himself, and GT, became icons of the hippie generation (Crocker, 1999), which rejected traditional norms in favor of experiments in living, the most prominent of which were drug use and "free" sex. To catch some of the flavor of GT, read the "Gestalt Prayer" shown in Box 7.1. I remember seeing the prayer on a poster, done up in psychedelic colors against a black background so that it would be cool under black lights. According to Anderson (2004), the last line was often left off, because it was too gloomy. What people in the '60s and '70s resonated to was the "do your own thing" message.

Second- and third-generation students of Gestalt Therapy such as Erving Polster, Miriam Polster, Isadore Fromm, and Gary Yontef continue to practice and promote the approach. You can read a selection about the therapist's tasks in Box 7.2, written by Joen Fagan. These later versions have promoted a more moderate form of GT than the confrontive, stagey "Perlism" (Parlett & Hemming, 1996a, p. 95; Rice & Greenberg, 1992). Wagner-Moore (2004) describes "modern Gestalt Therapy" as "a gentler, 'Rogerian-ized' version" (p. 183). However, one of the confusing things about GT theory is that although there are core principles and a broad sense of method, there is little orthodox doctrine about how these are put into action (Parlett & Hemming, 1996a). A survey of 225 attendees at the American Association of Gestalt Therapy's second international conference in 1997 revealed that GT is largely defined by how it is practiced (i.e., spontaneous, authentic, creative, alive, a process as compared to content orientation) rather than by its theory (Bowman, 1998, p. 105).

Miller (1989) observed that "Gestalt Therapy remains on the margins of the therapeutic establishment where it no longer generates much heat or controversy; most psychotherapists have heard of it, but relatively few know very much about it" (p. 20). Despite this rather grim assessment, there still seems to be significant activity around this theoretical orientation, particularly in Europe. Yontef and Jacobs (2000) reported that there is a GT institute in every major U.S. city and many other countries in the world. Parlett and Hemming (1996b) suggested that GT in Great Britain has raised eyebrows by becoming almost too establishment! In the United States and Canada, Process Experiential Psychotherapy

---

Box 7.1

The Gestalt Prayer

I do my thing, and you do your thing.
I am not in this world to live up to your expectations.
And you are not in this world to live up to mine.
You are you, I am I,
And if by chance we find each other, it's beautiful.
If not, it can't be helped.

From F. S. Perls, (1969). *Gestalt Therapy Verbatim.* Reprinted by permission of the Gestalt Journal Press.

Box 7.2

The Tasks of the Therapist Gestalt Therapy

PATTERNING

The therapist is first of all a perceiver and constructor of patterns. As soon as he is informed of a symptom or a request for change, and begins listening to and observing a patient and responding to him, he begins a process that I refer to as *patterning*. While *diagnosis* is a more common term, it has the disadvantage of provoking the analogy of the medical model and implying that the purpose of the process is arriving at a specific label. A better analogy for the process of patterning is that of artistic creation, involving sometimes cognitive, sometimes perceptual and intuitive skills in interaction with the material and demands of the environment as, for example, in the creation of a mobile, in which a variety of pieces or systems are interconnected into an overall unity and balance.

As the therapist begins his contact with the patient requesting help, he has available a body of theory which is largely cognitive in nature, a background of past experience, and a number of awarenesses and personal responses derived from the ongoing interaction that have large emotional and intuitive components. From these, which may be given varying degrees of importance by a specific therapist, he begins to form an understanding of the interaction of events and systems that result in a given life style that supports a given symptom pattern. *Events* refers to the things that have happened or do happen to the patient; *systems* includes all those interlocking events that interact on a specific level of existence, such as biological systems, self-perception systems, family systems, etc. The patient is visualized as a focal point of many systems, including the cellular, historical, economic, etc. The more the therapist can specify the entire interaction, or be sensitive to the possible effects of systems he is not directly concerned with (such as the neurological), or intuit the connecting points between systems where the most strain exists, the more effective he can be in producing change. He can act on a level and at a point that promises the most positive change in symptoms or conflicts at the least cost of effort, and where the least disruptive change will occur to other systems.

An example may clarify some of the above description. A mother refers her son whose increasing stomach distress causes him frequently to stay home from school. The therapist shortly begins to accumulate information of various sorts. He learns that: the boy also has stomachaches that keep him from going to camp or from visiting relatives; the mother has few interests outside the home; the father does not like his job and also has frequent illnesses; the mother and father have intercourse very infrequently; the boy has average intelligence; the grandmother is very interested in his becoming a doctor; the other children tease him for being a sissy; his teacher is considered strict; the school system has a new superintendent who has made many changes, etc. The therapist observes that the boy waits for his mother to answer for him; that his voice is weak when he does answer; and so on through a long list of responses, observations, and experiments in which the therapist obtains some sort of assessment of the abilities of the boy and his family to respond to varying suggestions and pressures. Through these processes a picture emerges with increasing clarity. The boy, his stomach, his family, his peer group, the school, the school system, and the community come into focus with varying degrees of explicitness.

The Gestalt contribution to patterning involves a de-emphasis on cognitive theory and provides extensive assistance with the therapist's own awareness. Enright, in chapters 8 and 21, describes this process in detail, emphasizing the clues to underlying events and life styles that can be uncovered by awareness of the person's movements, tones, expressions, word choice, etc., and suggesting some appropriate techniques for exploration. Much of Gestalt patterning is worked out in the therapy process itself rather than by history-taking or interviewing. The meanings that result, as in dream work, are very different from the more traditional analytic interpretive approaches where certain meanings are specified in advance by theory or predicted from the patient's previous history. Of course, past events of much importance do arise from the process of exploring posture, gestures, and dreams. However, the Gestalt therapist is not interested in the historical reconstruction of the patient's life, nor in weighing the effects of various environmental forces, nor in focusing upon one specific behavior such as communication style. Rather, he is interested in a global way in the point of contact between the various systems available for observation. The interactions between a person and his body, between his words and his tone of voice, between his posture and the person he is talking to, between himself and the group he is a member of are the focal points. The Gestalt therapist does not hypothesize nor make inferences about other systems that he cannot observe, though he may ask the patient to reenact *his* perceptions of them, as in a dialogue with his father, for example. Most Gestalt procedures are designed to bear upon the point of intersection, and the nature of the other system is viewed as less important than how the patient perceives or reacts to it.

In other words, the patterning emphasis in Gestalt Therapy is on the process of interaction itself, including the patient's skills in fostering and risking interaction, or blocking awareness and change. Since these are skills of importance in the intersection of any systems from the biological through the social, the Gestalt therapist sees himself as preparing the individual to interact more effectively in all aspects of life. Perls's ideas concerning a therapeutic community, which he is presently formulating, represent a possible extension of Gestalt thinking to a more extensive system.

Fagan, J. (1970). The tasks of the therapist. In J. Fagan and I. L. Shepherd (Eds.) *Gestalt therapy now* (pp. 88-106). Palo Alto, CA: Science and Behavior Books.

(see Box 7.3 for a description), which combines Gestalt and Person-Centered theories, is considered a respected theoretical development. Enough supportive research on this approach has accumulated for it to be referred to as evidence-based experiential psychotherapy (Elliot, Watson, Goldman, & Greenberg, 2004; Greenberg & Rice, 1997).

I am pleased to invite you to watch the work of a contemporary Gestalt therapist, Shelley Stelmach, on the *Theories in Action* DVD. Other sources of current information on GT include a number of organizations and journals, such as the Gestalt page (www.gestalt.org). This site is a joint project of the *Gestalt Journal* and the International Gestalt Therapy Association. That the International Association held its first annual conference in 2002 demonstrates that Gestalt Therapy is still of interest among practicing therapists. An electronic journal, *Gestalt!*, can be found at www.g-g.org/, and two other English-language GT journals are *Gestalt Review* and *British Gestalt Journal*. The Association

Box 7.3

Emotion Focused Therapy: The Process-Experiential Approach

A recent approach, Process Experiential Therapy (PET) also known as Emotion Focused Therapy, fuses aspects of the Person-Centered (PC) Gestalt, and existential approaches. PET is based on the assumption that human emotions are adaptive signals that tell us what is important and prepare us for action. Dysfunction results from problems in symbolizing experience, and accompanying distorted emotional processing of the experience. Here you surely see the influence of PC and GT versions of psychological dysfunction. The goal of therapy in this approach is to help clients learn new ways of processing emotion that lead to different meanings and more adaptive coping strategies. The therapist in PET first strives to create a therapeutic climate similar to that in PC therapy in order to evoke and understand client emotional experience. Once the relationship is established, the therapist can then use interventions that help reprocess the emotions; among these are chair dialogs similar to those used in GT.

PET emphasizes the importance of a collaborative therapy relationship and the power of the therapist's empathic prizing of the client in creating a situation in which clients can productively explore their experiences. Techniques in PET include a set that is similar to PC theory (focusing, systematic evocative unfolding, narrative retelling, and meaning creation) and dialogs reminiscent of Gestalt Therapy (two-chair and empty chair). Focusing, systematic evocative unfolding, narrative retelling and meaning creation are all interventions that support client exploration of feelings and the transformation of these feelings in ways that promote effective client responses to them. In two-chair dialog, clients experience aspects of themselves as they shift between two chairs. Two types of dialogs are identified: those between conflicting aspects of the self and those between the experiencing self and an aspect of the self that is blocking the expression of emotions or needs. Resolution of the conflict generally requires the two aspects to be accepted by the client so that they can work together.

Adapted from "Humanistic Approaches" by N. L. Murdock and D. C. Wang (in press), in H. E. A. Tinsley & S. Lease (Eds.) *Encyclopedia of Counseling*, Thousand Oaks, CA: Sage. Reprinted by permission.

for the Advancement of GT is an organization that includes professionals and laypeople dedicated to "governing itself through adherence to Gestalt Therapy principles enacted at an organizational level" (Yontef & Jacobs, 2000).

BASIC PHILOSOPHY

Gestalt Therapy (GT) theorists begin with the notion that humans are growth oriented. A very basic value is holism (Yontef & Jacobs, 2005): humans can't be separated from their environments, nor can they be divided into parts (such as body and mind). Physical and psychological functioning are inherently related; thoughts, feelings, and physical sensations are all a part of a unified being. GT theorists often use the term *organism* to convey the inseparable psychological and physical aspects of human nature; the process of being in touch with one's experience (defined in the broadest sense) is known as *organismic self-regulation* (Yontef & Jacobs, 2005).

GT is a humanistic/existential approach, and as such, it emphasizes individual choice and responsibility (Clarkson, 1989). In fact, GT theorists sometimes use the term *response-ability* to reinforce this perspective (Perls, 1970a). One can see the GT view of humans as neutral. Perls seemed to see humans as simply another form of biological life, yet the emphasis in the theory on growth and actualization would seem to support a positive view of human nature (Clarkson, 1989). According to GT theory, all organisms have an innate tendency to grow toward fulfillment and actualization (Crocker, 1999). GT is "a growth-oriented approach in which we are not focusing on a cure, pathology and cure, but on the growth process" (Edward Smith, cited in Harman, 1990, p. 19).

An important aspect of the GT mentality is an emphasis on creativity, spontaneity, and resisting conformity to convention (Tillet, 1994). It is expected that healthy behavior will sometimes be in conflict with societal norms (Perls, 1970a). Perls wrote, "Society has undergone a process that has moved it so far from healthy functioning, natural functioning, that our needs and the needs of society and the needs of nature do not fit together any more. Again and again we come into such conflict until it becomes doubtful whether a healthy and fully sane and honest person can exist in our insane society" (1970a, p. 16).

Paralleling developments in psychoanalysis, GT theorists of late have placed great emphasis on the inherent relatedness of the human condition (Yontef & Jacobs, 2005). In contrast to Perls' versions of GT, contemporary GT theorists focus more on the role of interdependence in human life.

Enrico is Jessica's GT counselor. He begins his work with her from the premise that she is a growing organism living an existence embedded in the environment. Jessica has the potential to grow in creative ways, actualizing herself in relationship to the world around her. She has the capacity to accept responsibility for herself and make choices that are true to her actualization. Yet, Enrico notes that allowing Jessica's true potential to surface may be contrary to some commonly accepted social rules.

HUMAN MOTIVATION

Human behavior is motivated by the drive to satisfy needs. Both biological and psychological needs are important. Although GT theory does not present a specific list of needs, biological needs are clearly important, and further reading of GT literature suggests that one very important need is interaction with other human beings (Hycner, 1987).

Another way to look at motivation from a GT perspective is to see humans as striving to regulate the organism so that it can grow. The goal of the process of self-regulation is harmony with the environment, maturity, or actualization. Self-regulation involves the process of discriminating what is good and bad for the organism, which should lead toward acceptance of the good and rejection of the bad (Rice & Greenberg, 1992). The tendency to self-regulate is innate, and humans adapt easily to the changing environment (Crocker, 1999).

Enrico sees Jessica as striving to meet her needs so that she can grow and mature. She gravitates toward experiences that maximize her growth, including wanting contact with other people. Jessica strives to adapt to her environment in a harmonious way.

CENTRAL CONSTRUCTS

CONTACT

Contact is the central feature of life, according to GT. It is defined as meeting the environment, which can be either external to the person or aspects of the self. Seeing, hearing, touching, moving, talking, smelling, and tasting are all ways of contacting the environment (Polster & Polster, 1990). Healthy contact results in *assimilation* of novel elements (i.e., things not already a part of the organism) and hence, growth (Perls et al., 1951). Following contact, the organism withdraws for a period of rest to "digest" the results of the contact (Crocker, 1999). Assimilation involves aggression and destruction, which are natural processes essential to making new experiences part of the organism, thereby creating growth (Perls et al., 1951). As a result, Gestalt therapists see aggression as a natural and healthy part of life, rather than as an antisocial behavior.

Effective contact is essential to life, because it is necessary to the satisfaction of needs. Contact can occur in a fully aware state, such as when we deliberately touch someone else, or in the sort of automatic mode that we use in most of our daily living. An example of the latter kind of contact is breathing, during which we make contact with the environment.

The individual makes contact with the environment at the *contact boundary* (Yontef, 1995). An important aspect of the contact boundary is the differentiation between self and other. The "I–thou or I–it contact" is essential in establishment of the I (Yontef, 1995, p. 263). Yontef and Jacobs (2005) note that the contact boundary should be recognized as having two functions: to connect one to others, but also to allow us to be separate from them.

Jessica is able to make basic contact with her environment. She is healthy, indicating that she obtains the basic substances she needs. Enrico observes that she has a number of relationships, indicating that she is able to establish some kind of contact with other human beings. Jessica appears to have a sense of self; Enrico has a hunch that that sense varies from relationship to relationship.

NEEDS

Life is a process of need satisfaction (Rice & Greenberg, 1992). GT theorists use the notion of Gestalt, a German word roughly meaning "whole" or "pattern" (Crocker, 1999) to describe this process. A Gestalt has a *figure*, or feature that stands out, and a *ground*, which is the rest of experience (i.e., the background). In perceptual terms, the figure is clear and compelling to our attention, and everything else becomes ground. Look at the picture shown in Figure 7.1. What you make of this picture depends on what features become figural to you. If you are able to shift your attention, you will see that two different perceptions of this drawing are possible (a young woman and an old woman). Figure 7.2 illustrates another basic aspect of the GT theory of perception—the fact that we strive to integrate pieces into a complete Gestalt (Do you see the horse and rider?).

In GT theory, a need is an incomplete Gestalt that emerges into the organism's awareness; it becomes figure, and the rest of experience becomes ground. Think about how difficult it would be to concentrate on this paragraph if you were very hungry. Your mind would probably keep drifting to images of pizza! Once a need has become figural, the person

FIGURE 7.1. A Figure-Ground Exercise.

FIGURE 7.2. A Perceptual Integration Task.

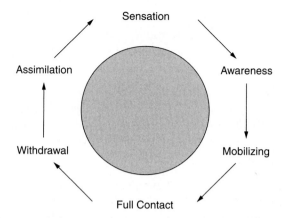

FIGURE 7.3. The Cycle of Awareness.

then initiates behavior aimed at meeting the need. When the organism is successful at sat-isfying the need, the Gestalt is completed and it is said to be destroyed (Wallen, 1970); the need becomes background rather than figural (Wagner-Moore, 2004). Very quickly, another incomplete Gestalt emerges to take its place. Whatever need is most urgent to the organism at a given time becomes figure (Yontef, 1995). It is important to note that *awareness* (of the need) is critical to this cycle.

The continual process of need emergence, satisfaction, and Gestalt destruction is the essence of life. Healthy growth requires this natural rhythm of figure–ground cycles. In fact, GT theorists like to draw pictures of the *cycle of experience,* and Clarkson (1989) ac-knowledged that everybody seems to have their own version of the cycle and name for it. It is in this spirit that I have created Figure 7.3.

Enrico makes some very basic observations in his early interactions with Jessica. He sees that Jessica is aware of the environment around her; he assumes that the degree to which she is aware varies from situation to situation. She appears to be meeting physiological needs ad-equately. Enrico tries to deduce current needs from Jessica's presentation and wonders if one thing that is figure *for her is a need to be loved. Her work and relationships with intimates other than Randy seem to be* ground *at present.*

POLARITIES

GT emphasizes the holistic nature of human functioning, and this allows the recognition of the power of polarities. If something exists, the opposite must as well; for instance, light im-plies dark, and right creates left (Perls, 1969a). Other relevant polarities are life and death, good cop and bad cop, passive and aggressive, and masculine and feminine (Levitsky & Perls, 1970). Perls maintained that Freud partly described one of the most important polarities when he acknowledged the superego. However, Freud did not label the other end of the dimension, which Perls called the infraego (Perls, 1969a). More commonly, Perls called this polarity top dog and underdog. Contemporary GT theorists would add connection/separation to the list of important polarities (Yontef & Jacobs, 2005).

Polarities are a natural part of life, and we have within our psyche both ends of the polarities. However, sometimes we don't want to accept one end of the polarity so we rigidify them into dichotomies and reject one end of the continuum (Yontef & Jacobs, 2000).

Enrico suspects that Jessica can recognize a number of polarities operating in her experience. Some particularly critical polarities seem to be bad–good and strong–weak. In her relationship with Randy, she seems to reject the strong part of the strong-weak polarity.

CONTACT DISTURBANCE

When the cycle of awareness is disrupted, problems are seen at the contact boundary. Perls and colleagues (1951) identified some basic ways that contact is interrupted; these processes are called **contact disturbances** or **boundary problems**. They are also sometimes called **resistances** (to awareness). Traditional GT practitioners deem these ways of operating dysfunctional if used chronically and inappropriately (Perls et al., 1951). For example, in discussing introjection, or the swallowing whole of experience, Perls and colleagues declared, "On this point we differ with Freud. He held that some introjections are healthy . . . but in this he was obviously failing to make the distinction between introjection and assimilation" (1951, p. 190). Other GT theorists maintain that these defenses should be seen as styles of contact and are sometimes adaptive and even healthy (O'Leary, 1997; Wheeler, 1991).

The most primitive contact disturbance is *introjection*, or taking in experience or food without digesting it. Infants survive by introjection of food, and the introjection of the attitudes and values of parents is to some extent an unavoidable feature of early childhood (Polster & Polster, 1973). For the infant, the only alternative to introjection is vomiting or spitting out, by which the infant deprives itself of nourishment. Once the child develops teeth and can bite and chew, she is able to digest and assimilate both physically and psychologically (Clarkson, 1989). For example, we often operate on the basis of shoulds that are dictated by society—a sure sign of introjection (Rice & Greenberg, 1992). You *should* be nice, quiet, and obey the rules! The problem, according to GT theory, is that we have not really considered whether these are our own values, or in the typical GT way of saying it, we have not chewed them up, digested them, and then assimilated them. They are foreign, alien things that sit in our stomachs.

The counterpart to introjection is *projection*, in which an unwanted part of the self is expelled into the environment. According to Perls and colleagues, we are aware of the impulse but can't cope with it, so we conclude that it has to come from outside of us. A good example of projection is seen when we avoid the experience of our own hate for someone by believing that they hate *us*. Projection can be based on introjection because the "shouldn't" that prompts the projection is probably an introject (Polster & Polster, 1973). A less dysfunctional view of projection is that it is essential to empathy. Empathy involves identifying with the others' experience, and one way to do that is to use one's own experience as a guide (Parlett & Hemming, 1996b).

Confluence is similar to introjection, except that it refers to a complete loss of self in which the individual cannot separate herself from the environment (Perls et al., 1951). Yontef and Jacobs (2005) point out that confluence occurs when the individual is unable to withdraw when it is appropriate to do so. An individual in confluence with another person has trouble expressing her own beliefs and values. A good example of confluence might be a kid who becomes a gang member and adopts the identity (self) of the gang. As with all of the boundary disturbances, confluence can be healthy, particularly in intimate relationships. O'Leary (1997) maintained that empathy represents healthy confluence, which she defines as aware or deliberate confluence.

In *retroflection* the unacceptable impulse is turned toward the self, such as when John tenses his muscles to resist slapping someone. For this reason, GT counselors are often interested in the physical expressions of their clients as clues to where awareness has been interrupted. Retroflection can be healthy because it is sometimes dangerous to express our impulses (such as hitting someone); the extent to which the retroflection is adaptive depends on whether the individual has a rational reason for restraining the impulse (Perls et al., 1951). Awareness is the key to understanding healthy retroflection. Unaware, chronic retroflection is, according to Perls and colleagues (1951), equivalent to repression and therefore neurotic.

Various writers have identified several other defenses or contact disruptions (Yontef, 1995). An individual can *isolate* herself, losing contact with both the environment and the self. Although withdrawal can be healthy at times (e.g., to avoid bad things), persistent isolation is dysfunctional (Yontef, 1995; Yontef & Jacobs, 2005). In *deflection* the impulse is blunted or dampened, such as when Kathy smiles to soften the expression of her anger (Yontef, 1995). Deflection is also seen when we avoid or interrupt interaction with another person (O'Leary, 1992).

Jessica seems to be demonstrating several interruptions to contact. Enrico thinks that she has introjected cultural values that mandate that women can't be assertive and angry. She also appears to be very critical of herself, suggesting retroflected feelings that might have originally been directed at Randy. Allowing Randy to control the household may be evidence that she is in confluence with him.

THEORY OF THE PERSON AND DEVELOPMENT OF THE INDIVIDUAL

Originally, Perls revised the developmental theory of psychoanalysis, shifting the focus from the sexual instincts to the hunger instinct (Clarkson, 1989). Infants progress from sucking to biting; development culminates with the ability to chew food thoroughly so that it can be digested and assimilated. Perls and his followers later de-emphasized this model, although elements of it can be seen in the descriptions of the process of need satisfaction as destructive, and the use of eating-related metaphors (e.g., introjection as swallowing whole).

Current GT has relatively little developmental or personality theory (Miller, 1989). Miller (1989) maintained that the anti-intellectual bias of GT (largely a product of the 1960s influences) is responsible for this indifference to the why of behavior. Perls himself said, "*Why* and *because* are dirty words in Gestalt Therapy" (1969a, p. 44; italics in original).

Even though they lack an elaborate theory, GT theorists acknowledge the importance of childhood events. According to Perls, "Maturation is the development from environmental support to self-support" (1970a, p. 17). To grow healthfully, children need support from the environment, as well as love and respect (Yontef, 1995). Events in childhood that are related to the frustration of need satisfaction can live on in adulthood and create trouble for the individual (see the later discussion of unfinished business). Perls noted that children need to learn to deal with frustration and overcome it, thereby increasing their independence. He said, "In the process of growing up, there are two choices. The child either grows up and learns to overcome frustration, or it is spoiled" (1969a, p. 32).

The self is simply the organism at the contact boundary, yet it is seen as an active transformer of experiences. The self is "the artist of life. It is only a small factor in the total organism/environment interaction, but it plays the crucial role of finding and making the meanings that we grow by" (Perls et al., 1951, p. 235).

Jessica has developed from needing complete environmental support to a level of self-support that allows her to function adequately as an adult in her community. However, Enrico suspects that some early childhood experiences of need frustration are still plaguing her.

HEALTH AND DYSFUNCTION

Healthy people are those who live in harmony with the environment, according to GT theory. The process of self-regulation guides the individual to be aware of shifting needs of the organism, which then organize behavior (Yontef & Jacobs, 2005). The organism simply follows its natural tendencies to self-regulate, taking in what is good for it, digesting it, and then assimilating it (Clarkson, 1989).

The healthy individual recognizes her interconnection with the environment, so although she is self-supporting, she strikes a balance between taking care of herself and attending to the needs of other people and her community (Mackewn, 1997). *Creative adjustment* is a term used by GT counselors to describe this balance between changing the environment to meet the needs of the organism and changing the organism to fit the environment (Yontef & Jacobs, 2005).

Healthy contact with the environment results in a "clear bright figure freely energized from an empty background" (Perls et al., 1951, p. 255). In Yontef and Jacob's (2005) terms, "good health has the characteristics of a good Gestalt. The good Gestalt describes a perceptual field organized with clarity and good form" (p. 312). It is clear which need is most important, and the person can then attend to it, and the bright shiny need is satisfied. Once the need is satisfied, the Gestalt is closed and another figure emerges.

Health can also be described as living an authentic existence (Yontef, 1995). "Since unfinished business does not pile up, he is free to do and be quite fully and intensely whatever he is doing or being, and people around him often report a sense of his being much more *with* them when he is with them" (Enright, 1970, p. 120; italics in original). The healthy individual is spontaneous, emotionally responsive, and expressive and can make direct interpersonal contact with others and relate authentically. She takes responsibility for the choices she makes in life and the meaning she makes of those experiences (Mackewn, 1997).

Dysfunction in GT counseling is called "dis-ease" to emphasize the view that the person is not in harmony with the environment (Clarkson, 1989, p. 41). Neurosis is seen as a "growth disorder" that results from the interruption of the cycle of awareness (Perls, 1969a). Wagner-Moore (2004) identifies a rather narrow view of this process—that all disruptions are due to a failure to be aware of a need—and a second, broader view associated with the contemporary GT theorists. In this enlarged view, disruption of the cycle of awareness can also happen when the need or goal is in awareness but the person acts, but fails to satisfy the need.

When the continuous process of Gestalt formation and destruction has failed in some way, the result is **unfinished business** because the need that is not met hangs around to bother the person (Clarkson, 1989). Significant unmet needs organize the person's perception and behavior, interfering with the healthy processes of awareness and contact (Mackewn, 1997). The person does not clearly perceive her current needs and may appear confused or uncertain of what she wants. She may also display stereotypic or rigid behavior, signaling that her behavior is governed not by the organismic search for homeostasis but by the unfulfilled need (Clarkson, 1989).

GT counselors recognize that dysfunctional behavior was a creative adjustment made in an earlier difficult situation (usually childhood) that is no longer functional in the present (Yontef & Jacobs, 2005). Probably these behaviors protected the organism from injury or pain or somehow allowed a limited form of need satisfaction in what was then an emergency. Unfortunately, the use of this *neurotic self-regulation* in the present prevents the person from responding spontaneously and creatively to the environment as it now is. Healthy organismic self-regulation is replaced by the will to control experience instead of accepting it (Yontef & Jacobs, 2005).

Perls contended that modern society (defined as the kind existing in the United States or other Western European countries) contributes a great deal to the development of unhealthy functioning (1969a). Western culture encourages people to artificially separate mind and body (Clarkson & Mackewn, 1993). Social norms often punish aggressive behavior, which according to GT theorists is a normal and helpful kind of human behavior. Other "shoulds" are introjected at early life stages, and these are not necessarily in alignment with healthy organismic self-regulation.

If we focus on our experience long enough, we will eventually come across something uncomfortable or unpleasant. We inherently want to avoid such experience, so we interrupt our awareness of the now (Perls, 1970a). Many times what we don't want to experience is our own cruelty or aggression, and we disown the experience rather than tolerate it in our awareness. Society doesn't help by encouraging us to reject these experiences. By interrupting our experience, according to Perls, we reveal ourselves as frightened children who instead of assuming adult responsibilities retreat into phony social roles. "These phony roles are meant to mobilize the environment for support instead of mobilizing one's own potential. We manipulate the environment by being helpless, by playing stupid, asking questions, wheedling, flattering" (Perls, 1970a, p. 18).

If the client can get past the phony roles, she might be able to observe the *impasse*, the point where she is stuck. She no longer has support from the environment but does not have sufficient self-support to function adequately (Perls, 1969a). Mackewn (1997) characterized the impasse as the point where growth and resistance to growth are in a deadlock. Yontef and Jacobs (2005) describe the experience of impasse as one of terror. We avoid prolonged contact with our impasses because they force us to "take existential responsibility for our own stuckness and our ability to choose to experience things differently and we have often not had sufficient environmental or self support to face these choices. . . we are paralysed by the fear of the unknown" (Mackewn, 1997, p. 171).

GT theorists don't spend much energy discussing what might be called traditional forms of dysfunction, such as depression, anxiety, and so forth. They recognize emotions as signals to the self about unmet needs or danger (Cole, 1998). An exception to this position is that anxiety is seen as resulting from two possible processes. The first process is cognitive. Anxiety is "futurizing"—failing to remain centered in the present (Yontef & Jacobs, 2005, p. 315). Perls, in his characteristically flamboyant way, called anxiety "stage fright" (Perls, 1969a). Anxiety can also be created through faulty breathing. When an individual becomes aroused, deep breathing is required. If the individual breathes shallowly and quickly, she is likely to experience symptoms that feel like an anxiety attack (e.g., hyperventilation; Yontef & Jacobs, 2005).

Jessica is not optimizing her integration with her environment. She has interrupted contact and appears to be carrying around some unfinished business, with associated behavior patterns. Enrico guesses that her early experiences with her withholding mother may have created an unfulfilled need for love for Jessica. She responded, he thinks, by burying her need because to allow it into awareness was painful. Jessica learned to deny her needs and feelings in intimate relationships through this early solution. Her experience with her father about becoming a police officer is another piece of unfinished business. Jessica felt close to her father, yet she has almost completely isolated herself from this relationship in recent years.

Jessica's relationship with Randy is problematic because she is denying aspects of her experience in it by using old patterns of defense. She is not experiencing some very vivid feelings that she has about how she and Randy relate, probably because she has introjected the societal rule that girls and women should be "nice." Further, her experiences with her mother and father—that uncompleted need for love and acceptance—are active in her relationship with Randy. Instead of experiencing and expressing her feelings and needs, she retroflects her dissatisfaction to herself, becoming critical of her own behavior in the relationship. She also shows confluence with Randy in her failure to assert her own needs and wants.

NATURE OF THERAPY

ASSESSMENT

No formal assessment is used in GT, although Yontef (1995) noted that nothing in the theory absolutely forbids it. More generally, the GT counselor is the assessment tool, using his powers of observation to assess how the individual functions in her life. The Gestalt therapist sees assessment and treatment as an integrated process that attends to all aspects of the individual's experience (physiology, ethnicity, social context, family relationships, and so forth). The GT counselor looks most specifically at the individual's patterns of contact with the environment, level of awareness, and how much support she has, both environmental and personal (Yontef, 1995). Enright (1970) observed that the Gestalt therapist tells the client to "sit down and start living, then note(s) where and how he fails" (p. 113).

Traditional diagnosis is also rejected by hard-line GT advocates based on the humanistic idea that labeling people is dehumanizing (Clarkson, 1989). Others take the position that diagnostic terminology helps in communication with other professionals and can facilitate therapy (Yontef, 1995; Yontef & Jacobs, 2005). Melnick and Nevis (1998) advocate the use of diagnosis, pointing out that, among other things, it can reduce anxiety in the therapist by allowing him to distance a bit and allow the client's figure to emerge. The process of diagnosing gives the therapist something to do while waiting. Melnick and Nevis' system for understanding DSM-IVTR diagnosis uses the cycle of experience as a conceptual basis. For example, they see borderline personality disorder as originating in the very beginning of the cycle; the individual simply can't manage the sensory input. Their conceptualization leads to the caution that awareness-heightening interventions should not be used for these clients (e.g., empty chair, confrontation). They go on to describe specific phobia as connected to problems in mobilization, histrionic personality disorder as related to the contact phase and posttraumatic stress disorder as a function of demobilization (or assimilation in my Figure 7.3).

The most common assessment/diagnostic question used in GT counseling is, "What do you experience right now?" (Yontef, 1995, p. 272). That is, the Gestalt therapist is most interested in assessing the client's current state of awareness (Parlett & Hemming, 1996b).

Enrico greets Jessica and simply asks why she came in. He listens and observes her closely as she relates her story about the fight with Randy. As she talks, he notes her tone of voice and physical reactions. Jessica pauses in her narrative, and Enrico inquires, "What are you experiencing right now?" Jessica stiffens and looks surprised. She then tentatively begins to describe her feelings of anxiety about being in therapy, her fear of Randy, and a feeling of being alone.

OVERVIEW OF THE THERAPEUTIC ATMOSPHERE

The essence of GT counseling is observed in the therapist's emphasis on the immediate experience of the client. A famous GT slogan is "I and Thou, Here and Now," which Perls borrowed from the philosopher Buber (Yontef & Jacobs, 2000). Polster and Polster (1973) maintained that "the therapeutic experience is not merely a preparatory event, but a valid moment per se, needing no external referent to confirm its inherent relevance to the patient's life" (p. 5).

The dictate to remain in the present does *not* mean that the past or the future is never the subject of therapy; it means that these are examined as they are experienced in the present (Parlett & Hemming, 1996b). Laura Perls, reacting to the misperception that Gestalt Therapy does not deal with the past or future, wrote, "The past is ever present in our total life experience, our memories, nostalgia, or resentment, and particularly in our habits and hang-ups, in all the unfinished business, the fixed gestalten. The future is present in our preparations and beginnings, in expectation and hope, or dread and despair" (1992, p. 52).

Traditional Gestalt therapists are very suspicious of intellectual activities because they tend to lead to *talking about* rather than experiencing and acting. Another famous Perlism is "Lose your mind and come to your senses" (Perls, 1970a, p. 38). Seeking intellectual understanding (asking the *why* question) is avoiding life. GT counselors tend to believe that "In modern life we suffer from too many explanations. . . . Perls' Gestalt Therapy gave up on explanations; it became impatient for something to happen. Happening, after all, is the best explanation" (Miller, 1989, p.12). Emphasizing action rather than talking often leads to the construction of experiments in awareness, in which the counselor asks the client to actively experience some disowned aspect of her life in the session (Zinker, 1977).

Because experiencing the unfinished situation in the therapy session arouses anxiety, Perls characterized therapy as a "safe emergency" (Perls et al., 1951, p. 286). The reexperiencing of the rejected experience in the safe environment of counseling allows the completion of the Gestalt and, thus, the assimilation of the experience. An important consideration is the balance between support from the counselor (safety) and the therapeutic emergency (risk). The client is not allowed to stay in "safe but infertile territory," but neither is she exposed to experiences too threatening (Polster & Polster, 1990, p. 104).

The current approach to GT counseling is more moderate than what Perls presented. Support of the client is considered very important and GT counselors tend to emphasize the building and exploration of the here-and-now relationship between therapist and client more than did Perls and are less rejecting of the intellectual elements of counseling (Rice & Greenberg, 1992; Yontef, 1995). The Gestalt therapist strives to create an authentic contact with the client, a true encounter (Rice & Greenberg, 1992). According to Wagner-Moore (2004), the contemporary GT views the therapeutic relationship as a critical aspect of therapy and is less likely than GTs of the 1970s to use the techniques stereotypically associated with the approach. Yontef and Jacobs add that good therapy involves a fluid back-and-forth shifting on the therapist's part from attention to the client's process to focus on the relationship between therapist and client.

The GT counselor is active, directing the client's attention to various aspects of her experience (Rice & Greenberg, 1992). Empathic reflection is used to help the client become aware of her experience (Yontef, 1995). The GT counselor often proposes experiments that are designed to help the client heighten awareness (Crocker, 1998). At the same time, a primary task of the therapist is observation in the interest of discovering where the client has interrupted her experience (Rice & Greenberg, 1992).

GT counseling can be either short or long term (Yontef & Jacobs, 2000). Although Perls maintained that group psychotherapy using the "hot seat" method (discussed later) was superior to all other forms of counseling, contemporary Gestalt therapists disagree, practicing individual, couples, family, group, and organizational GT (Polster & Polster, 1973; Wheeler & Backman, 1994).

Enrico endeavors to help Jessica stay in the here and now without sacrificing his support of her. He makes observations about how he feels in relation to her in an honest, open way. He asks many how and what questions and no why questions. Enrico encourages Jessica to reveal her present experience as she talks about her relationship with Randy. If she brings up her father, mother, or family, Enrico will encourage Jessica to explore her feelings about them as they are present in the here and now.

ROLES OF CLIENT AND COUNSELOR

As is the case with Albert Ellis and Rational Emotive Behavior Therapy, the role of the counselor in GT often gets confused with the person of Fritz Perls. In Perls' version of GT counseling, the role of the counselor was to frustrate the client's avoidance of self-support (Perls, 1970a). The client was often confronted with her attempts to get the counselor to take care of her and her reluctance to be authentic. One of Perls' favorite labels was "phony" (Nelson-Jones, 2000). Clearly, confrontation was the hallmark of Perls' approach to GT

(Yontef & Jacobs, 2000). Friedman (2003) commented that the therapist in this version was something of a stage director or coach, and related that Laura Perls maintained that in interacting with clients in this way, Fritz Perls "turned away from the patient" (p. 63). Although this extreme approach is probably not used by many GT counselors currently, the extent to which confrontation is used varies greatly among GT practitioners.

In more recent versions of GT, the abrasive style of Perls is softened. GT counselors are expected to be authentic and transparent in their relationships with their clients. This approach is sometimes called dialogic or relational GT (Yontef & Jacobs, 2000).

Gestalt therapists are admonished to stay in touch with their own experiences in counseling, using such awareness as diagnostic tools (Mackewn, 1997). "Exclude nothing; dismiss nothing as irrelevant. What is your body doing involuntarily in the presence of this other person? Are your muscles tightening up or relating and opening? Does your attention wander or is your interest riveted? If you begin to daydream, *when* do you do so and *what* are you daydreaming?" (Mackewn, 1997, p. 47; italics in original). To maintain this level of awareness, a Gestalt therapist must have a significant emotional commitment, according to Clarkson (1989). Candidates should undergo personal psychotherapy, similar to the training analyses of psychoanalysts, only from a GT counselor, of course. "Gestalt Therapy is not an approach which can be applied by people who are themselves largely unaware of their own contact style or bodily experience" (Parlett & Hemming, 1996b, p. 207).

The client in GT counseling is expected to engage actively in the process of self-discovery (Rice & Greenberg, 1992). She is a student who is learning to test what is offered in therapy, to see if it fits (Yontef, 1995). The Gestalt therapist respects the client's expression of disagreement (and even better, anger) with the therapist because it demonstrates self-support. The last thing the GT counselor wants is the client to introject the values or opinions of the therapist.

Enrico is a moderate GT counselor. His first goal is to connect with Jessica in an authentic relationship. Enrico observes Jessica as she talks about her experience and also pays attention to his responses to her (e.g., he has a fantasy of her in her police uniform that quickly alternates with an image of a small child). Enrico also notices that his muscles are tensing and that he has impulses to rescue Jessica.

Jessica, eager for the therapist's help, openly discloses about her situation. She is willing to engage with Enrico. Jessica has a little difficulty expressing her own wants and preferences in counseling, but Enrico helps her stay with her experience until she is able to experience her needs.

GOALS

The one big goal in GT is awareness. Perls said, *"Awareness per se—by and of itself—can be curative"* (1969a, p. 16; italics in original). Yontef (1995) pointed out that, really, there are two kinds of awareness: "microawareness (i.e., awareness of a particular content area) and awareness of the awareness process" (p. 275). The point is that, although the Gestalt therapist wants the client to be aware of a current situation in therapy, he is also interested in the client understanding the process or event of awareness so that she can apply it to other situations. An added benefit of this kind of awareness is that it promotes taking responsibility for behaviors enacted when one has awareness (Yontef, 1995). Parlett and Hemming

(1996b) described the goal of GT a little differently, saying that the process should "promote self-support sufficient for the person to live a life of freedom and choice (thus increasing his or her 'response-ability')" (p. 205).

Awareness will ultimately result in the growth of the individual, for increased awareness will result in better harmony with the environment and enhancement of the organism through assimilation of needed things. Thus, a goal of GT could be said to be growth. In fact, many Gestalt therapists maintain that people come to counseling not for remediation, but for the facilitative aspects of GT. Polster and Polster (1973) emphasized the growth orientation of GT counseling when they said "therapy is too good to be limited to the sick" (p. 7).

Enrico hopes to help Jessica become aware of the unfinished business she is carrying around. He'd like to help her recognize the ways she avoids contact with the environment and aspects of herself. Enrico has no predetermined ideas about what she should do about her situation or relationships; he'd like her to become aware so that she can decide for herself. Ideally, Jessica will come to value awareness and responsibility in her life, taking these tools out of therapy to use in future life experiences.

PROCESS OF THERAPY

GT counseling has three central elements: relationship, awareness, and experiment (Clarkson, 1989). According to Yontef and Jacobs (2005) the method of GT is engagement, whether that is between therapist and client or between client and aspects of her experience. The first step is for the GT counselor client to establish an authentic *relationship*. This relationship is often the medium through which awareness is explored. For example, the client's desire to be dependent on the therapist can be brought up explicitly, with the client living and describing this experience in the session. *Awareness*, of course, is critical because interruptions in the awareness process are what bring the client to counseling.

Experiments in awareness are often used in GT counseling. Mackewn (1997) explained that experiments are intended to help clients try things out in the safe environment of counseling. She identified several goals of the experiment, including (a) increased awareness of the self and how it relates to others, (b) the integration of cognition and body experience, and (c) helping the client reach the impasse and experience it. The client and counselor should agree on, or even construct together, the experiment (Zinker, 1977).

Levitsky and Perls (1970, pp. 140–144) described the rules and games of Gestalt Therapy. The games will be described later in the discussions of the various techniques. The most critical rules are (a) staying in the now; (b) I and thou, or the emphasis on aware and authentic communication; (c) using "I" not "it" language, or taking responsibility for all statements; and (d) asking no questions—because they are seen as asking something of the counselor and therefore as aspects of the client's passivity or laziness. The client is urged to turn questions into statements. Clients in therapy groups are expected to follow the "no gossip" rule: one must speak directly to any person present, not about them.

An aspect of GT that sets it apart from other approaches is its emphasis on physical or body sensation and functioning as a critical aspect of human existence. Unfinished business is often seen in the body of the client. Thus, Parlett and Hemming (1996b) suggested that in GT counseling "the body is regarded as a source of wisdom, a provider of organismic truth" (p. 200).

Gestalt therapists refer to the "paradoxical theory of change" (Yontef & Fuhr, 2005, p. 82). By this term, they mean that the more you try to change, the more you stay the same. Change is, instead, accomplished by becoming aware of and accepting who you are. The Gestalt therapist needs to be aware of this dictate so that he will not align with aspects of the client that pressure the client for change. Perls and colleagues (1951) recommended that the GT counselor adopt a stance of *creative indifference* toward his work. This somewhat confusing term does not mean that the counselor is truly indifferent to the client, only that he is not intensely invested in some particular outcome or process in therapy (Mackewn, 1997).

Contemporary Gestalt therapists are prone to referencing the "field," a somewhat vague construct that includes everything that is around and goes on between the client and counselor (Parlett, 2005). The notion of field suggests that the therapist is an integral part of the therapy, not a detached observer. Further, according to Parlett, the field has inherent structure, which should be examined in therapy. These ideas connect to the relational emphasis in current GT theory—the therapist and client both have input into the here-and-now situation and to this they must attend (Parlett, 2005). Another important implication of the field perspective is that, similar to family systems theorists, GT therapists are aware that any change in the field will affect the rest of it (Yontef, 2005).

Client resistance is not to be fought, eliminated, or overcome in GT counseling. Instead, resistances are identified as the energy of the organism placed in service of protecting the person from an experience that might be harmful (Yontef & Jacobs, 2000). Typically, these behaviors stem from adaptive responses to past experience, as described earlier (i.e., neurotic adaptation). Instead of overcoming it, the GT counselor wants the client to experience the resistance, encourage it, bring it to the center of awareness. In this way, resistances, which are ways of avoiding meaningful contact, can be used to resolve unfinished business (Enright, 1970).

Although Gestalt therapists will acknowledge transference and countertransference, they see these phenomena differently from the way traditional psychoanalysts would see them (Mackewn, 1997). Transference is not seen as purely the client's distorted way of perceiving the world, although it is seen as a clue to how the client habitually structures experience. Gestalt therapists acknowledge that we do bring the past into current situations, particularly when we carry around unfinished business. However, GT theory distinguishes itself by instructing that the therapist's input to the interaction is considered, too, and the GT counselor needs to be ready to examine his contributions to the situation. The therapist must be open to being changed in the therapeutic encounter, and ready to admit to being wrong (Yontef & Jacobs, 2005).

Two kinds of countertransference are identified in GT theory (Mackewn, 1997). *Proactive* countertransference is when the counselor's unfinished business is activated while in relationship with the client. The GT counselor must be alert to this event and be able to set these responses aside (termed "bracketing") to be dealt with in supervision or personal therapy (Mackewn, 1997, p. 95). *Reactive* countertransference is when the GT counselor responds to the client's transference behavior. These responses are taken as data for the analysis of the interaction of client and counselor in the here and now.

Contemporary GT theorists have begun to discuss the role of shame in the therapeutic relationship and its outcomes (Yontef, 2005). According to Yontef and Fuhr, the client comes to therapy primed for shame because she feels bad about herself and needing to ask for help makes the situation worse. The counselor must be alert to anything in the field that will exacerbate shame, and most importantly, take responsibility for anything he does that contributes to it (Yontef, 2005).

Enrico focuses on the three elements of GT counseling with Jessica. It is relatively easy to establish a relationship with her, but Enrico is sensitive, at first, to the relatively superficial level of their contact. As time goes on, the relationship becomes more authentic.

Awareness is always central for Enrico. He endeavors to be aware of his own experience in relation to Jessica, and everything he does in counseling is directed toward helping Jessica become aware of her experience. For example, when she is talking about her mother, Enrico notices that she assumes a rather flat tone of voice. Enrico asks Jessica if she is aware of how her voice has changed.

Enrico is sure that he will devise some experiments for Jessica to try out in session, assuming that she agrees to them. He is not adamant about reciting the rules of therapy with Jessica, although he does encourage her to use "I" language. He also attends to her physical presence, noting that when she talks about her fight with Randy, she seems to shrink into her chair and crosses her arms across her chest. He asks her if she is aware of these sensations.

Enrico sees Jessica resist contact around her feelings for her mother and father. When he asks questions, attempting to get Jessica to experience these in the session, he notes that she becomes more closed physically and less responsive verbally. Attempting to explore the resistance, Enrico asks Jessica to become aware of how she is feeling, physically and emotionally. If she still shows a need to protect herself, Enrico accepts this as a sign of Jessica's strength and helps her verbalize this to him.

Enrico notes no proactive countertransference, although he is aware that this could happen. He has recently returned to Gestalt Therapy to explore some of his own interruptions. He will be vigilant in looking for signs that his own issues are intruding on his interactions with Jessica.

Noting that he experiences Jessica as wanting him to direct and support her, Enrico decides that this is reactive transference. He finds ways to share this awareness with Jessica.

THERAPEUTIC TECHNIQUES

GT has often been perceived as synonymous with its techniques, particularly dialogue techniques or the "empty chair" (discussed later). Current Gestalt theorists and therapists reject this perspective, saying, "Techniques are only a part of the therapy; Gestalt Therapy theory would also encompass the dialog between therapist and patient" (E. Polster, cited in Hycner, 1987, p. 31). In reality, GT counselors are technically eclectic; any technique that fosters awareness is considered acceptable (Enright, 1970). Melnick and Nevis (2005) comment that "Our goal is to support uncertainty. We create the conditions for growth to occur without having any commitment to a specific outcome" (p. 107). For this reason, GT techniques can be broadly construed as *experiments* that happen to take many forms.

As I noted earlier, toward the end of his career, Perls began to work increasingly with groups and thought that individual therapy was becoming obsolete (Perls, 1970a). During the late 1960s, Perls did most of his work in large training workshops for professionals, in which he would invite members of the audience to participate as his clients. Essentially, he was really doing one-session individual counseling with the client in front of an audience. The client would assume the "hot seat," and Perls would create various exercises in awareness. Other Gestalt therapists used a more traditional group therapy format (Leiberman, Yalom, & Miles, 1973), but integrated GT techniques and games into these groups. What follows are descriptions of some of the techniques used in both individual and group counseling; many are applicable to couples and family therapy, too.

THERAPIST SELF-DISCLOSURE

Often, the Gestalt therapist, attending closely to his experience, will disclose his awareness to the client (Yontef & Jacobs, 2000). "Sometimes the therapist is bored, confused, amused, angered, amazed, sexually aroused, frightened, cornered, interrupted, overwhelmed and on and on. All of these reactions say something about both the patient and the therapist and they comprise much of the vital data of the therapy experience" (Polster & Polster, 1973, p. 18). The GT counselor authentically discloses an experience, and then the client and counselor discuss it in the immediacy of the relationship.

Enrico decides to disclose his alternating images of Jessica as a child and police officer to her. She bursts into tears, saying that she feels like the child in the moment. Enrico replies that he feels like taking care of her.

DIALOGUES

In the interest of increasing awareness and finishing unfinished business, GT counselors often ask the client to create a conversation, or dialogue, in the counseling session. These dialogues can be (a) among parts of the self, (b) with the therapist, and (c) with some other individual in the client's life, past or present (Hycner, 1987). Dialogues are also created between the "splits" or polarities in the client's personality (Levitsky & Perls, 1970).

Historically, one well-known dialogue is top dog and underdog (Levitsky & Perls, 1970). In this experiment, the client plays two parts of herself, the critical, demanding top dog and the whiny, excuse-using underdog. These are the end points of a critical polarity inherent to humans, and according to Perls, we use the conflict between the top dog and underdog as a way of torturing ourselves (Perls, 1969a). In top-dog–underdog dialogue, the client alternates between playing the two poles. She bosses like the top dog and whines like the underdog. The goal of the dialogue is to have these two aspects of the self listen to each other. Ultimately, full expression of these aspects of the self will result in their integration (Miller, 1989). That is, the two aspects will no longer be "split off" from each other, but integrated as parts of the personality. Most modern GT therapists would likely reject this version of dialog as outdated. They favor splitting off the harsh, judgmental, inner critic into one chair, and the person experiencing the self into the other (Kellogg, 2004). If the critic is the introjection of someone from the past (such as a parent), this can be noted and emphasized with the client—what she's dealing with is *her* version of the parent, not actually the "real" one.

A contemporary perspective on dialog is presented by Elliot, Watson, Goldman, and Greenberg (2004). Dialog is an important feature of their hybrid approach, Process Experiential Therapy (see Box 7.3 for a brief description) that combines aspects of Person-Centered and Gestalt Therapy. They differentiate between two-chair and empty chair dialog. Two-chair dialogs are aimed at healing split aspects of the self, whereas empty chair dialogs are interventions for unfinished business. Anything or anyone can be put in the empty chair, and the client talks to the entity. Often, the client is asked to play the part of the person or projection in the chair and switches seats as she does this enactment. Sometimes the GT counselor plays the entity in the empty chair. This approach has many uses from the GT perspective, including creating a situation in which unfinished business can be completed with significant others, helping the client to resolve internal conflicts, or allowing the client to experiment with behavior that is very threatening and scary (Crocker, 1999).

Enrico asks Jessica if she'd like to talk to her mother, guessing that Jessica has unfinished business with Mom about love and belonging. Hesitant at first, Jessica agrees to try the experiment.

> Enrico: *Tell your mom what you're experiencing right now.*
> Jessica: *I wish I could get close to you.*
> E: *What are your feelings?*
> J: *I am sad. I'm angry. I want to hurt you.*
> E: *Say that again.*
> J: *I'm ANGRY!!*

PLAYING THE PROJECTION

To increase the experience of disowned parts of the self, the GT counselor might ask the client to play the role of the projection (Sapp, 1997). For instance, if the client sees someone as angry and hateful toward her, the therapist might ask her to act out an angry and hateful person. The therapist could then ask the client if she could find these qualities in herself (Levitsky & Perls, 1970).

Because Jessica does not seem to be projecting, Enrico decides that playing the projection is not a technique he will use.

EXAGGERATION

If the client appears to be unaware of some (typically nonverbal) aspect of her experience, the GT counselor guides her through the process of exaggerating the movement (Levitsky & Perls, 1970). Often, the original expression of the client is incomplete or stunted; the therapist helps her make the movement more authentic. The client might be wiggling her leg. The astute GT counselor asks her to exaggerate the wiggle, attempting to get the client to increase her awareness of this expression and create meaning. This technique can also be used with client statements—the counselor hears the client glossing over something she says and asks her to repeat it, perhaps more forcefully.

When Jessica talks about her mother, Enrico notices that she hunches up her shoulders. He asks Jessica if she notices this. Jessica says "not really," so Enrico asks her to exaggerate the tension and describe what it is like. Jessica reports that she is protecting herself from psychological blows from her mother.

REVERSALS

Recognizing that observable behavior is sometimes the opposite of underlying impulses (i.e., the opposite end of a polarity), the GT counselor directs the client to act the reverse (Levitsky & Perls, 1970). For instance, a shy client could be asked to play the extrovert.

Enrico has observed (from watching her dialogue with him in the empty chair) that Jessica is passive in her relationship with Randy, always trying to please him. He asks Jessica to put Randy back in the chair and play the bossy, bitchy, overbearing woman.

DREAM WORK

Perls called the dream the "royal road to integration" (Perls, 1970b); in fact, dreams are the most spontaneous form of human expression (Perls, 1970b). Despite the allusion to Freud's position on dreams ("the royal road to the unconscious"), the way dreams are handled in GT is very different from the way they are handled in traditional psychoanalysis.

In GT dream work, the client takes on the role of the parts of the dream, giving each its own speech and experiences. Perls insisted that the client "play" all of the objects and persons in the dream, giving them voice and action, because this represents experiencing aspects of the self symbolized in the dream elements (Perls, 1970b). Most likely, these aspects are ones that the client has disowned or represent important people in the client's life (Staemmler, 2004). Kellog (2004) notes that the aspects of the dream may represent important polarities for the individual; dreamwork is another way to help the client integrate these.

Jessica dreams that she is a gardener. She has her hoe and her spade and gardening gloves. She gleefully plants flowers and vegetables and watches them grow.

Enrico asks Jessica to play the parts in the dream. First she is the hoe, turning up the soil. Then she is the spade, moving things around, carrying soil to where it belongs. The gloves protect. Flowers and plants struggle against soil and emerge into sunlight.

WORKING WITH POLARITIES

GT counselors are aware of what is present in the client's presentation, but are often more interested in what is missing (Parlett & Hemming, 1996b). Likely, the client has repressed or "disowned" one aspect of the self, which tends to be one end point of a polarity. Examples of polarities identified in GT theory are messy–tidy, strong–weak, love–hate, dependent–responsible. The Gestalt therapist brings the polarities to the client's attention, often using less toxic language for them (Parlett & Hemming, 1996b). Clients can also ask to play the polarity similar to the way in which playing the projection is used. That is, the client is asked to take the role of each of the ends of the polarity identified as critical for her.

One of Jessica's key polarities appears to be strong–weak. She is a tough, strong police officer, yet a weak, dependent person in her relationship. Enrico decides to have Jessica play both of these polarities to help her increase her awareness of this split.

AWARENESS TRAINING OR BODYWORK

In one sense, all GT counseling is awareness training. In a more specific sense, GT counselors work with their clients to become more aware of their physical sensations, because these are often clues to aspects of experiences blocked out of awareness. The client might be asked to attend closely to any body sensation that the counselor thinks important—breathing, tone of voice, physical gesture, and so on.

Enrico notices that Jessica clenches her fist when she talks about Randy. He asks that she attend to this motion and experience what the tensing is like. He might even ask her to "play" her fist.

MAKING THE ROUNDS

If a group therapist notices that a client seems to be focused on a particular theme, she might ask the client to "make the rounds" of the group by saying a sentence to each group member that expresses the theme (Daniels, 2003; Levitsky & Perls, 1970). The client is to add something specific about each person as well. For example, if the client says that the group scares him, the GT counselor would ask him to say to each of the other group members "you scare me" and then add an extra phrase pertinent to that individual. Nonverbal expression could be used in this way, too; for example, a client might touch each member of the group as a way of making contact.

If Jessica was working in group, she might be asked to make the rounds saying "I am afraid that you will reject me because . . ." and then finish the sentence to fit each of the members.

TAKING RESPONSIBILITY

The client is asked to follow her statements with this phrase: "I take responsibility for it" (Levitsky & Perls, 1970). For example, if Bob is in a quandary about his life circumstances, he would be asked to follow his remark "I don't know what to do" with "and I take responsibility for it."

Jessica could be asked to use the phrase "I take responsibility" in her interactions with Enrico. He thinks he might remind her to use it every time she uses "it" language. So when she says it is hard to express her feelings to Randy, Enrico will ask her to say, "I find it difficult to express how I feel, and I take responsibility for it."

EVALUATION OF THE THEORY

Responses to GT are numerous and rarely moderate! Crocker (1999) commented that GT had a reputation as "an intrinsically rude and confrontational method, lacking in both gentleness and a respect for clients, and practiced by people with questionable moral standards" (p. 7). GT has also been characterized as "wild, uncontrolled, undisciplined—in a word, dangerous" (Smith, 1991, p. 62). These criticisms seem to stem from two sources. First, the approach is highly identified with Perls and his confrontive, abrasive approach. GT in the classic form overemphasized the individualistic. Moreover, Perls acted unethically and was sometimes abusive (Clarkson & Mackewn, 1993). However, a second issue was that after being captivated by Perls' charismatic style, many insufficiently trained people put on their Gestalt therapist hats and created havoc (Parlatt & Hemming, 1996a).

A second reason that GT is thought to be wild and dangerous seems to be connected to its adoption of the rebellious, antiauthoritarian stance of the mid- to late 1960s. Numerous people who had little background in psychology or the formal education typically associated with the profession of psychotherapy were "trained" as Gestalt therapists (Sapp, 1997).

This reaction also seems to be the result of GT's emphasis on raw experiencing and lack of structure. Modern Gestalt therapists are careful to explain that "the experiment is not simply a facile technique to be applied indiscriminately" and to caution counselors to provide support in conjunction with challenge (Polster & Polster, 1990, p. 104).

The lack of supporting theory is also seen as a failing of GT; the approach is seen as little more than a collection of gimmicky techniques, the most notorious of which is the empty- or two-chair dialogue (Miller, 1989; Wagner-Moore, 2004). Miriam Polster (cited in Hycner, 1987) argued that the excessive reliance on technique is seen only among inexperienced or narrow-minded GT counselors.

QUALITIES OF THE THEORY

Precision and Testability. Gestalt theory (the perception theory) was based on well-constructed laboratory research. The constructs of GT theory diverge from classic Gestalt theory, and some are very difficult to operationalize. They are difficult to define (e.g., contact) and observe, partly because they are so broad (e.g., awareness). At the same time, some success has been found by Greenberg and associates in operationalizing particular GT techniques such as chair dialogues (Elliot et al., 2004; Greenberg, Rice, Rennie, & Toukmanian, 1991; see Box 7.3 and the discussion of research in the following sections).

Empirical Validity. Although fewer studies on the outcome of GT counseling have been conducted compared to other theoretical approaches, support for the effectiveness of the therapy is evident (Strumpfel, 2004). Less support exists for the theoretical structure on which GT counseling rests, possibly because it is so difficult to operationalize. Again, the exception to this generalization is the research of Greenberg and associates on Process Experiential Therapy (Elliot et al., 2004).

RESEARCH SUPPORT

Outcome Research. Outcome research on GT exists, but not to the extent that it does for other theoretical approaches (e.g., cognitive or behavior therapy). In their early, classic study of encounter groups, Leiberman, Yalom, and Miles (1973) examined the outcomes of group leaders. Two GT leaders were included in this study. These two leaders produced very different outcomes, although they were characterized similarly as active, energizing leaders. One leader produced the highest number of casualties (participants who were negatively affected by the group experience) among all of the leaders, whereas the second GT leader had no casualties. The second leader tended to produce mild to moderate change among members. Yontef (1995) maintained that the first leader did not follow the principles of GT; he was "abrasive, insensitive, and charismatic rather than dialogic and experimental" (p. 290).

Elliott (2001) conducted a meta-analysis addressing humanistic therapy, which included seven studies of GT as well as investigations of client-centered, process experiential, and emotionally focused therapy. He located 86 studies and found an overall effect size (average change) of 1.06, suggesting that the average client in humanistic therapy improved from the 50th to the 85th percentile on outcome, compared to pretreatment measures. This study also demonstrated no significant differences in effectiveness between humanistic and nonhumanistic approaches and that humanistic psychotherapy was superior to no-treatment conditions. The seven GT studies produced an effect size similar to that found for the entire group of humanistic therapies. An earlier meta-analysis of 38 studies conduced by Bretz, Heekerens, and Schmitz (1994) found similar results.

Strumpfel and Goldman (2001) reviewed huge amounts of research on GT, including studies conducted in Europe, and document impressive support for the approach. For example, they described an Austrian study that included 431 outpatients, citing improvement rates of over 70 percent (Schigl, 1998, cited in Strumpfel and Goldman). This was an effectiveness study modeled on the Consumer Reports study (Seligman, 1995, see Chapter 1), so did not involve all the trappings of a randomly controlled clinical trial.

Individual studies of GT outcome are of varied sophistication and quality. Johnson and Smith (1997) studied snake-phobic university students, randomly assigning them to Gestalt empty-chair dialogue (ECD), systematic desensitization, or no treatment. On objective measures of phobia, both the ECD and systematic desensitization groups improved in comparison to the control participants. O'Leary, Sheedy, O'Sullivan, and Thoresen conducted a randomized study comparing GT group therapy and a no-treatment (assessment only) control group with older adults. Comparing these rather small groups (21 in the control group and 22 in the two GT treatment groups), they found that at the end of the treatment, those in the GT groups reported expressing more anger and having less control over it. At first glance, this might look like a scary finding, but then recall that one indicator of health in a GT model is to experience and express emotions freely. Thus, O'Leary et al. interpreted this finding as an indication that the clients in the therapy group were possibly living more in the present because the treatment had allowed them the opportunity to deal with unfinished business.

An interesting study tested the effects of Gestalt group therapy with hospitalized schizophrenics in Israel (Serok & Zemet, 1983). Matched pairs (on age, sex, and education) of patients were randomly assigned to 10 sessions of GT group treatment or a no-treatment control group. Using two indexes of reality testing derived from the Rorschach inkblot test, Serok and Zemet found that clients in Gestalt group therapy showed improved reality testing compared to those who received no treatment. Some researchers would question the psychometric validity of the Rorschach (an ambiguous set of stimuli for which scoring is difficult). Because the Rorschach was the only measure of reality testing used, Serok and Zemet's results could be called into question.

Elliot, Greenberg, and colleagues (Elliot et al., 2004; Greenberg et al., 1991; Paivio & Greenberg, 1995) have established a respected research program that investigates Process-Experiential Therapy (PET), also known as Emotion-Focused Therapy. Although not directly intended to test GT outcomes and theory, these investigations are still relevant to our understanding of GT. In a recent summary, they summarize their program of research that looks at both process and outcomes in PET (Elliot et al., 2004). They describe a number of outcome studies, three of which were true randomized clinical trials, using either wait list, no treatment, or comparison group controls (e.g., Greenberg, Goldman, & Angus, 2001; Greenberg & Watson, 1998; Watson et al., 2003). For example, Watson et al. compared PET to cognitive-behavioral treatment for depression and found both treatments to result in reduced levels of depression and increases in the use of adaptive coping styles. In other studies reviewed by Eliot et al. (2004), the results were similar, demonstrating significant empirical support for this variant of GT theory. However, to their credit, Elliot et al. (2004) do point out that this research is conducted almost entirely by advocates of PET, warning that allegiance effects could play a part in the process (see Chapter 1).

Theory-Testing Research. Some of the PET research directly assesses the effects of chair dialog (ECD) on client outcome, and other studies combine elements of theory-relevant testing and outcome assessment, so it does not fit neatly into my research categories. I present it here because it does seem to be some of the only research that bears directly on the theory of GT. Greenberg and his colleagues have conducted quite a bit of research on this approach, finding supportive results, so I will only sample a few studies in the following section. Interested readers can consult Elliot et al. (2004) for further detail.

Greenberg and Dompierre (1981) compared the effects of one session of ECD and one session of empathic reflection on 16 psychotherapy clients. Each client received both interventions. Results indicated that ECD produced deeper levels of emotional experiencing and more client-perceived changes in awareness, progress, and conflict resolution than did the empathic reflection. Although supportive of GT theory, the measurements used in this early study were somewhat primitive.

Looking at the process of conflict resolution more closely, Greenberg and Foerster (1996) examined the performances of 22 clients who were rated as successful or unsuccessful in resolving unfinished business using ECD. In a detailed study of these ECDs, Greenberg and Foerster found that successful resolution was more likely to be accompanied by intense emotional expression, need expression, and positive expressions about the "other" in the dialogue (whether it was self or someone else). These findings would seem to support the GT assumption that increased experiencing or awareness is necessary for the resolution of dysfunction (unfinished business).

Paivio and Greenberg (1995) studied the effects of treatment containing ECD compared to a group educational experience that introduced information about unfinished business. Seventeen clients (recruited via newspaper advertisements) completed each intervention. Pretests and posttests on symptom variables as well as measures of unfinished business were administered to both groups, and the ECD group was followed up at 4 months and 1 year. Significant differences were found between the groups on a number of the symptom measures; most significantly, the ECD group reported more resolution of unfinished business than did the group experience group. This finding supports the utility of ECD interventions and is indirectly supportive of GT theory.

However, we must keep two other considerations in mind when reviewing these results. First, the individual counseling sessions used ECD in only 53% of the sessions. Thus, it is difficult to directly link the use of this strategy to symptom change. A related concern is that the ECD group and the educational group differed in the number of sessions and, of course, the level of individual attention and support received. Thus, differences between the groups could be attributable to the very different kinds of treatment received rather than any specific effects of ECD.

Field and Horowitz (1998) studied the use of ECD in resolving grief following the loss of a spouse. Participants completed a dialogue, and then self-rated the amount of unresolved grief they had felt during the dialogue. The degree of resolution was related to symptoms 6 months and 14 months after the study. That is, participants who indicated less resolution showed higher levels of depression, avoidance of the grief, and intrusive memories than those who had more fully resolved their grief.

Tyson and Range (1987) found that ECD had no specific effects on mild depression. They compared a no-treatment control group to three other treatment groups. Two treatment groups engaged in dialogues; the difference between the two was that in one group, the dialogues were personally relevant, and in the other, they were enactments of Shakespeare's plays. In a third treatment group, affective expression was encouraged but no dialogues took place. Analyses of pre-, post-, and follow-up measures of depression indicated that all of the groups, including the control, improved over time. Tyson and Range concluded that their study demonstrated that mild depression dissipated over time whether it was treated or not. However, several other explanations of the findings can be offered, including the brevity of the treatments (weekly for 4 weeks) and the small number of participants in each of the experimental conditions (about 10 in each), which can lead to low statistical power to detect differences. Also, it is possible that ECD is more effective when conflict is present than for mild depression.

Other research bearing on GT has attempted to explore boundary or contact disturbances. For example, Mills (1997) attempted to develop a self-report scale to measure projection, introjection, retroflection, confluence, and deflection. Unfortunately, these efforts have not been very successful (Caffaro, 1991; Mills, 1997). A question that can be raised in this area is whether individuals can rate their own contact disturbance styles, as is assumed by these kinds of investigations. Still other investigators have attempted to create a method for rating the quality of contact in an interpersonal relationship, but the reliability and range of the ratings seriously hampered the usefulness of this attempt (Leonsky, Kaplan, & Kaplan, 1986).

ISSUES OF INDIVIDUAL AND CULTURAL DIVERSITY

Many critics have pointed to the individualistic bias of GT. Saner (1989) opined that "most American Gestalt Therapy theorists and practitioners are unaware of being influenced by culture values or fixed gestalten best described as individualism or individualistic neurosis. My claim is that the contemporary form of Gestalt Therapy made-in-U.S.A. is not universally valid and needs theoretical and methodological revisions in order to be truly cross-culturally valid and meaningful" (p. 59). Similarly, Wagner-Moore (2004) noted this bias, attributing it to the personality of Perls emerging in his theory.

Mackewn (1997) maintained that because GT counselors strive to understand the person in the environment and explore the client's awareness, the approach is well suited to working with clients from all walks of life. "Gestalt's insistence upon the fact that the individual cannot be understood in isolation but only as a part of their historical and social context means that in theory at least we have the capacity to take into account and attend to cultural difference, historical background and social perspectives" (Mackewn, 1997, pp. 50–51). However, Kareem and Littlewood (1992) differed in their review of the applicability of GT counseling; they pointed out the inherent biases introduced by the origins of the theory in Jewish Western culture. They recommended that the counselor address cultural issues with the client if they seem relevant to the progress of therapy.

The emphasis in GT on verbal, emotional, and behavioral expressiveness is counter to the values of many cultural groups (Sue & Sue, 2003). Traditional Hispanic/Latino and Asian individuals may see the control of emotions and behavior as signs of wisdom. Also, GT's emphasis on self-disclosure may be in opposition to these groups' values. At the same time, GT's disavowal of insight may be consistent for individuals who want action, such as individuals from lower socioeconomic status. The relative lack of focus on content and the ambiguous structure of GT, on the other hand, may be disconcerting to clients of diverse cultural backgrounds, such as Hispanic/Latino clients (Sue & Sue, 2003).

GT writers have paid attention to the issues of individuals who are gay, lesbian, or bisexual (GLB). Curtis (1994) and Singer (1994) presented chapters on GT with gay and lesbian couples. Singer provided a good description of issues specific to gay couples, while also acknowledging that GT counseling with a gay couple is not that different from GT counseling with a straight couple. Curtis discussed critical issues for lesbians, such as the strong heterosexist bias in most cultures, and applied GT constructs to issues likely to emerge with lesbian clients in counseling, such as shame.

Enns (1987) presented a feminist perspective on GT. She maintained that GT is in many ways consistent with a feminist orientation because it emphasizes awareness and personal power. In this system, women can be encouraged to become aware of parts of themselves that are culturally discouraged (e.g., intense feelings of anger). GT can also support women as they go against existing norms in defining themselves separately from others. At the same time, the emphasis on responsibility and individuality found in GT can be problematic. Enns pointed out that "the singular focus of Gestalt Therapy replaces the old 'shoulds' with a new and potentially dangerous 'should': 'I must be fully autonomous, self-reliant and self-determining'" (p. 94). This kind of approach neglects the role of environmental factors at best, and at worst, characterizes the examination of these factors as intellectualizing or making excuses (p. 94).

Enns (1987) also highlighted GT's neglect of the fundamental interrelatedness of humans. Autonomy in the GT model looks very much like a male value, counter to the female valuing of relationships that is discussed by many feminist writers. At the same time, women traditionally equate their self-worth with gaining and maintaining the love and approval of others. GT's support for growth and personal responsibility may help female clients find their worth in themselves rather than in others' perceptions of them.

Fernbacher (2005) argues that the emphasis on awareness in GT is facilitative in working with clients from diverse backgrounds provided that the therapist is aware of his own process. She also points to the field theory construct of GT as promoting the understanding of the client and counselor as indivisible from their contexts (e.g., culture, society, political systems). However, Fernbacher also cautions that the heavy reliance on nonverbal observation and intervention in GT calls for attention to differences across individuals to understand the meaning and impact of these expressions.

THE CASE STUDY

Jessica presents with troubled feelings about her relationship, for which she blames herself. This internalization fits well with a GT approach because it suggests that she is denying her personal dissatisfaction with the encounter. She has lost contact with her aggression and anger, as well as her need for love. Jessica's history also seems to be amenable to a GT viewpoint, especially her unfulfilling relationships with her parents.

Potential problems with a GT approach to Jessica would seem to involve her feelings of responsibility for the relationship with Randy. Women are taught by Western culture to take care of relationships, and so insisting that she violate these cultural rules could create difficulty for her. That Jessica is African American could also be a factor in employing a GT framework because the emphasis on individualism may be counter to the more collectivistic approach of African American culture.

Summary

GT counseling is an existential/humanistic approach to human functioning. Individuals are seen as functioning holistically and striving to meet needs such as physical and emotional support. Needs are met through contact with the environment in an unending cycle of need emergence, activity by the individual aimed at satisfying the need, need satisfaction, and disappearance of the need. Contact with the environment is sometimes scary or painful so we sometimes avoid contact by introjecting, projecting, deflecting, retroflecting, or moving into confluence. When we avoid contact and needs go unmet, we create unfinished business, holes in the personality, and psychic splits. Our awareness of the environment (which includes the self) is disrupted and contributes to further dysfunction.

GT counseling is conceptualized as an encounter between two individuals. No formal assessment or diagnosis is used. The counselor is to be authentic in the relationship and will self-disclose if it seems helpful. The goal of GT is to support the client so that she can freely experience herself and her environment. Numerous techniques are employed, and most GT counseling involves some form of experiment in awareness.

GT has been faulted for its extreme emphasis on individual responsibility. This orientation may lead to problems in using this approach with individuals who are from cultures that are more relationship or group oriented. Outcome research supports GT as a viable approach to psychotherapy, and some research supports the link between increased experiencing and client progress.

Visit Chapter 7 on the Companion Website at **www.prenhall.com/murdock** for chapter-specific resources and self-assessments.

B. F. Skinner

CHAPTER 8

Behavior Therapy

Shirley is a 79-year-old single Caucasian female. She has been married twice; both husbands are deceased. Shirley has no children and no surviving relatives. Shirley does not work; she lives on social security and income from pensions.

Shirley was ordered to come to counseling by the municipal court because she has been caught shoplifting on multiple occasions. Mandated counseling was assigned as an alternative to traditional sentencing after she was recently arrested. Based on her description of the incident that brought her to counseling, it appears that Shirley was an ineffective thief. She did not check to see if she was watched; instead, she just grabbed some items and headed out the door of the department store.

Shirley was a last-born child, raised in Chicago. She describes a very unhappy relationship with her mother, whom she characterized as unloving, harsh, and domineering. She describes a good relationship with her father, although she resented that he never stepped in to protect her from her mother. Shirley graduated from college with a degree in finance and was one of the few women working in business in the 1940s. She describes herself as very successful at her job managing investments, despite being in a male-dominated career. Her first husband was a military officer. After they married, Shirley left her job and moved with her husband through a number of assignments across the United States and Southeast Asia. Shirley's second husband owned an auto parts store. During this marriage, Shirley focused on her role as a homemaker and was involved in volunteer work in her community. Shirley portrays both of her marriages as very happy and rewarding.

Currently, Shirley reports being involved in community service with the elderly, helping out at a senior citizens' center about once a week. She no longer drives a car, instead relying on the bus for transportation. Shirley lives alone in an apartment and reports that she has few social contacts outside of her volunteer work.

As she reluctantly discusses her shoplifting, Shirley says that she has recurrent obsessive thoughts about stealing when she is in a store. She describes a feeling of anxiety that does not subside until she has stolen something and left the store. Shirley immediately feels guilty about her actions. She says that she never steals anything particular; it does not matter what she takes. Shirley reports that she first began to steal things when she was in her 40s, after the death of her mother. Her first husband knew about the shoplifting, but she was better able to control it back then. Her second husband apparently never knew about it. Shirley has never experienced legal difficulties as a result of her stealing until recently.

Shirley is unhappy about being referred to counseling. She believes that she is the only one who can prevent her "compulsive stealing" as she terms it, and that therapy can do little to help her. Shirley is extremely embarrassed to see a counselor and expresses a good deal of shame about her behavior.

BACKGROUND

Behavior Therapy (BT) is actually a cluster of models and techniques that involve several different perspectives on human learning. In this chapter, I will review the models and techniques of traditional BT, but will also include techniques based on what is generally called Cognitive-Behavior Therapy. The term *Cognitive-Behavior Therapy* can be a confusing one; it is sometimes used to refer to a behavioral approach that includes the appreciation for, and modification of, cognitive influences on behavior. Other times, it is used to refer to any of the cognitive approaches (such as Rational Emotive Behavior Therapy and Cognitive Therapy, Chapters 9 and 10). Most therapists in the behavioral tradition today would acknowledge the influences of cognition, yet there are still a few hard-core advocates of BT who maintain that the target of change should be behavior, and behavior only (for example, the classical applied behavior analysts, see the following sections). However, out there in the "real world" of practice, you will mostly see a pragmatic approach that blends aspects of the material in this chapter along with assumptions and interventions more closely resembling Cognitive Therapy and Rational Emotive Behavior Therapy.

What the BT approaches share is the commitment to a scientific approach that is concerned with "the application of principles broadly derived from psychological research (across experimental, social, cognitive, and developmental psychology), rejecting a traditional intrapsychic or disease model of disordered behavior, and with an emphasis on the empirical evaluation of treatment effectiveness" (Glass & Arnkoff, 1992, p. 609). Others add that Behavior Therapy is characterized by a concern with current causes of behavior rather than those rooted in the individual's history (Franks & Barbrack, 1990).

Because BT has such a long history, many influences, and many influencers, a comprehensive historical perspective is beyond the scope of this chapter. What follows are snapshots of important figures in BT; readers who would like a more complete review should consult Glass and Arnkoff (1992) or Kazdin (1978).

Behavior Therapy was developed very much in reaction to the psychoanalytic model, and therefore early Behavior Therapy emphasized observable behaviors rather than internal events or client history (Goldfried & Davison, 1994). As Franks and Barbrack (1990) put it, "Behavior therapy began in the late 1950s as an antimentalistic, somewhat blinkered alternative to the prevailing disease-oriented model of psychodynamic psychotherapy" (p. 551).

Contemporary forms of BT are more flexible in admitting cognitive and emotive factors in the explanation of human activity. Fishman and Franks (1997) noted that "with the exception of traditional applied behavior analysis, prevailing behavioral approaches all embrace the use of cognitive mediational concepts, and, to greater or lesser degrees, all emphasize the integration of principles derived from traditional learning theory and conditioning with those stemming from cognitive and social psychology" (p. 144). In contrast, read the statement of the Association for Behavior Analysis International (ABAI) that "behavior analysts make the assumption that all behavior is the product of two kinds of variables: biological and environmental" (ABAI, n.d., *Understanding behavior analysis*). Thoughts and feelings (those things that folks commonly see as the causes of behaviors) are merely other behaviors to be counted.

The most distant origins of Behavior Therapy are usually located with Russian scientist Ivan Pavlov and his experiments on classical conditioning. In studying the eating behavior of dogs, Pavlov discovered that pairing food, which resulted in the dogs salivating, with a bell eventually resulted in the dogs salivating in response to the bell only. This model will be explained more fully in a later section.

Joseph Wolpe used this classical conditioning model as the basis for his approach to the understanding and treatment of anxiety, which he called reciprocal inhibition (more on this model later). Fishman and Franks (1997) noted that the important technique spawned by the theory of reciprocal inhibition, systematic desensitization, was the first real alternative to the psychoanalytic approaches in vogue in the 1940s and 1950s.

Most sources trace the beginnings of American behaviorism to John B. Watson and his 1913 *Psychological Review* article, "Psychology as a Behaviorist Views It." Watson, who had been influenced by Pavlov's work, was vehement about erasing "mentalism" from psychology, thereby eliminating the study of consciousness as a viable approach to understanding human behavior (Glass & Arnkoff, 1992). Watson and his graduate student (and later, second wife) Rosalie Rayner applied Pavlov's ideas about conditioning to create conditioned fear in their famous report about Little Albert (see Box 8.1; Watson & Rayner, 1920/2000). Later, Watson's student, Mary Cover Jones (1924, 1960a), used these ideas to eliminate fear in a 3-year-old boy, Peter (see Box 8.2). It is also interesting that Jones (1924/1960b) acknowledged the usefulness of observational learning in her discussion of eliminating children's fears.

Box 8.1

The Story of Little Albert

John B. Watson was a famous behaviorist. In 1920 he and his graduate student, Rosalie Rayner, decided to see if they could create human fear through conditioning principles that Watson had outlined in an earlier article (Watson & Morgan, 1917). They chose as their subject of study Little Albert, an 11-month-old infant whom they described as "stolid and unemotional" (Watson & Rayner, 1920/2000, p. 313).

Watson and Rayner presented to Albert a white rat. When Albert touched the rat, a loud noise was made by banging a steel bar with a hammer. Albert immediately showed signs of distress and on the second pairing, began to cry. Seven subsequent pairings were conducted, and it was clear that the presentation of the rat produced a strong reaction, so that on the last trial Albert "*raised himself on all fours and began to crawl away so rapidly that he was caught with difficulty before reaching the edge of the table*" (p. 314; italics in original).

Watson and Rayner also tested whether the conditioned emotional response would transfer to other stimuli. They presented Albert with a rabbit, dog, sealskin coat, cotton wool, and a Santa Claus mask. All of these presentations evoked responses from Albert, as did Watson's hair. Albert's reactions were similar 5 days later. Finally, the researchers looked at the effect of time on the conditioning, finding that 31 days later the fear reactions still persisted, without any further pairing of the noise and stimuli.

Unfortunately for Albert, he was mysteriously removed from the hospital a day after the tests of persistence were made. Watson and Rayner never had the chance to decondition him, although they speculated that pairing feared objects with food or sexual stimulation, or simply repeatedly presenting the feared stimuli until habituation would cause the "fatigue" of the reflex.

True to his behaviorist ideology, Watson (and Rayner) took on the Freudian perspective in the report's discussion. "The Freudians twenty years from now, unless their hypotheses change, when they come to analyze Albert's fear of a sealskin coat—assuming that he comes to analysis at that age—will probably tease from him the recital of a dream which upon their analysis will show that Albert at three years of age attempted to play with the pubic hair of the mother and was scolded violently for it" (p. 317). Rilling (2000) presented another view of the Little Albert study, arguing that Watson was really attempting to scientifically verify Freud's ideas about transference, but to make the construct more general, rather than specific to sexual emotions. In fact, Watson and Rayner clearly stated, "Emotional disturbances in adults cannot be traced back to sex alone" (p. 317). The result was that, instead of defeating psychoanalytic ideas, Watson actually supported them.

Box 8.2

Mary Cover Jones: A Pioneer in Eliminating Fear in Children

Mary Cover Jones was a graduate student who worked with John B. Watson, the American founder of Behavior Therapy. In two articles, she described her work, which was based on Watson and Rayner's (1920/2000) study of fear in infants (the Little Albert study; see Box 8.1). In an article published in the *Journal of Experimental Psychology* (1924/1960a) Jones relates her efforts to eliminate fear in children, fear that had presumably been classically conditioned.

Jones selected 70 children from a group in an institution that we might call day care. These children were in this institution temporarily because they could not be cared for in their homes (e.g., a parent was ill, a mother worked). Jones selected kids who showed "a marked degree of fear under conditions normally evoking positive (pleasant) or mildly negative (unpleasant) responses" (Jones, 1924/1960a, p. 39). The children's fears included such things as being left alone, loud sounds, and the sudden presentation of animals (rats, rabbits, snakes).

Jones tested a number of techniques in a case study format. For example, she found that "verbal appeal," which consisted of talking about the feared object in a pleasant way, did not work. "Social repression" in which the feared object was presented to a child in the presence of other children, was equally ineffective. Presaging Bandura's (1969) ideas, Jones did find that social imitation showed promise as an intervention for fear. However, Jones maintained that the best method of eliminating fear was direct conditioning, which she detailed in a separate article, "A Laboratory Study of Fear: The Case of Peter" (Jones, 1924/1960b).

Peter was a 2-year-old boy who demonstrated fears very similar to Little Albert's—of a rat, fur coat, rabbit, cotton wool, and other white furry objects. After presenting a white rat to Peter (whereupon he screamed and fell over), Jones observed the following reactions in a subsequent testing period:

Play-room and crib	Selected toys, got into crib without protest
White ball rolled in	Picked it up and held it
Fur rug hung over crib	Cried until it was removed
Fur coat hung over crib	Cried until it was removed
Cotton	Whimpered, withdrew, cried
Hat with feathers	Cried
Blue woolly sweater	Looked, turned away, no fear
White toy rabbit of rough cloth	No interest, no fear
Wooden doll	No interest, no fear

(Jones, 1924/1960b, p. 46.)

Jones used two kinds of conditioning with Peter and reported that his fear was completely eliminated and that he even showed signs of affection toward a rabbit at the end of the study. In the first stage of conditioning, Peter was exposed to the rabbit in the presence of other children who were not afraid of it. Gradually, situations were introduced that required Peter to be closer to the rabbit. In a second stage of the procedure, a rabbit in a cage was brought as close as possible to Peter while he was eating, without disturbing his eating. Presumably, the rabbit was brought closer and closer every day.

Jones reported extinction of the fear behavior, not only of the rabbit, but also in response to the white cotton, fur coat, and the other objects to which he initially reacted. Peter also seemed to be less fearful of new animals or unfamiliar situations. Although his fears appeared to be gone, Jones reported that Peter returned to a rather diminished and discouraging home environment, in which his mother used fear to control his behavior ("Come inside Peter, someone might steal you!" Jones, 1924/1960b, p. 51). Unfortunately, we have no further information about the fate of Peter.

The second model of learning, the operant model, originated with the work of E. L. Thorndike, who studied the behavior of cats. He would put cats in a puzzle box and entice them to figure out how to get out of the box by placing food outside. Thorndike noticed that in repeated trials the cats became faster and faster at getting out of the box.

From his observations he formulated the law of effect, which proposed that behavior is learned through its consequences (Kazdin, 2001).

B. F. Skinner is probably the most famous name associated with the operant approach, which is sometimes called radical behaviorism or applied behavior analysis. The focus of this approach is on the consequences of behavior. Skinner, who performed most of his research with laboratory animals (rats and pigeons), was not particularly interested in applying his science of behavior to developing intervention techniques for people, although he recognized the potential to do so (Spiegler & Guevremont, 2003). In fact, Skinner and his colleagues were credited with the first use of the term *behavior therapy* in a report on using conditioning principles with hospitalized schizophrenics (Glass & Arnkoff, 1992). However, Skinner was more interested in broad applications of his work, such as in his novel *Walden Two*, in which he describes a community based on behavioral principles (Skinner, 1976). Others went on to apply the principles outlined by Skinner to working with psychological dysfunction, such as Ayllon and Azrin, who developed the notion of token economies (Glass & Arnkoff, 1992). You can read some of Skinner's views in the sections from *Beyond Freedom and Dignity* in Box 8.3.

A third force in behavior therapy came from the work of Albert Bandura, who recognized the power of observation in learning (Spiegler & Guevremont, 2003). Bandura developed social learning theory (1969, 1974), which emphasizes the role of social events such as the observation of others in learning. The individual who demonstrates a behavior is called the model, and hence, this approach is sometimes referred to as modeling theory.

Box 8.3

An Excerpt from Skinner's *Beyond Freedom and Dignity*

ALMOST ALL LIVING THINGS act to free themselves from harmful contacts. A kind of freedom is achieved by the relatively simple forms of behavior called reflexes. A person sneezes and frees his respiratory passages from irritating substances. He vomits and frees his stomach from indigestible or poisonous food. He pulls back his hand and frees it from a sharp or hot object. More elaborate forms of behavior have similar effects. When confined, people struggle ("in rage") and break free. When in danger they flee from or attack its source. Behavior of this kind presumably evolved because of its survival value; it is as much a part of what we call the human genetic endowment as breathing, sweating, or digesting food. And through conditioning similar behavior may be acquired with respect to novel objects which could have played no role in evolution. These are no doubt minor instances of the struggle to be free, but they are significant. We do not attribute them to any love of freedom; they are simply forms of behavior which have proved useful in reducing various threats to the individual and hence to the species in the course of evolution.

A much more important role is played by behavior which weakens harmful stimuli in another way. It is not acquired in the form of conditioned reflexes, but as the product of a different process called operant conditioning. When a bit of behavior is followed by a certain kind of consequence, it is more likely to occur again, and a consequence having this effect is called a reinforcer. Food, for example, is a reinforcer to a hungry organism; anything the organism does that is followed by the receipt of food is more likely to be done again whenever the organism is hungry. Some stimuli are called negative reinforcers; any response which reduces the intensity of such a stimulus—or ends it—is more likely to be emitted when the stimulus recurs. Thus, if a person escapes from a hot sun when he moves under cover, he is more likely to move under cover when the sun is again hot. The reduction in temperature reinforces the behavior it is "contingent upon"—that is, the behavior it follows. Operant conditioning also occurs when a person simply avoids a hot sun—when, roughly speaking, he escapes from the threat of a hot sun.

Negative reinforcers are called aversive in the sense that they are the things organisms "turn away from." The term suggests a spatial separation—moving or running away from something—but the essential relation is temporal. In a standard apparatus used to study the process in the laboratory, an arbitrary response simply weakens an aversive stimulus or brings it to an end. A great deal of physical technology is the result of this kind of struggle for freedom. Over the centuries, in erratic ways, men have constructed a world in which they are relatively free of many kinds of threatening or harmful stimuli—extremes of temperature, sources of infection, hard labor, danger, and even those minor aversive stimuli called discomfort.

Escape and avoidance play a much more important role in the struggle for freedom when the aversive conditions are generated by other people. Other people can be aversive without, so to speak, trying: they can be rude, dangerous, contagious, or annoying, and one escapes from them or avoids them accordingly. They may also be "intentionally" aversive—that is, they may treat other people aversively because of what follows. Thus, a slave driver induces a slave to work by whipping him when he stops; by resuming work the slave escapes from the whipping (and incidentally reinforces the slave driver's behavior in using the whip). A parent nags a child until the child performs a task; by performing the task the child escapes nagging (and reinforces the parent's behavior). The blackmailer threatens exposure unless the victim pays; by paying, the victim escapes from the threat (and reinforces the practice). A teacher threatens corporal punishment or failure until his students pay attention; by paying attention the students escape from the threat of punishment (and reinforce the teacher for threatening it). In one form or another intentional aversive control is the pattern of most social coordination—in ethics, religion, government, economics, education, psychotherapy, and family life.

A person escapes from or avoids aversive treatment by behaving in ways which reinforce those who treated him aversively until he did so, but he may escape in other ways. For example, he may simply move out of range. A person may escape from slavery, emigrate or defect from a government, desert from an army, become an apostate from a religion, play truant, leave home, or drop out of a culture as a hobo, hermit, or hippie. Such behavior is as much a product of the aversive conditions as the behavior the conditions were designed to evoke. The latter can be guaranteed only by sharpening the contingencies or by using stronger aversive stimuli.

Another anomalous mode of escape is to attack those who arrange aversive conditions and weaken or destroy their power. We may attack those who crowd us or annoy us, as we attack the weeds in our garden, but again the struggle for freedom is mainly directed toward intentional controllers—toward those who treat others aversively in order to induce them to behave in particular ways. Thus, a child may stand up to his parents, a citizen may overthrow a government, a communicant may reform a religion, a student may attack a teacher or vandalize a school, and a dropout may work to destroy a culture.

It is possible that man's genetic endowment supports this kind of struggle for freedom: when treated aversively people tend to act aggressively or to be reinforced by signs of having worked aggressive damage. Both tendencies should have had evolutionary advantages, and they can easily be demonstrated. If two organisms which have been coexisting peacefully receive painful shocks, they immediately exhibit characteristic patterns of aggression toward each other. The aggressive behavior is not necessarily directed toward the actual source of stimulation; it may be "displaced " toward any convenient person or object. Vandalism and riots are often forms of undirected or misdirected aggression. An organism which has received a painful shock will also, if possible, act to gain access to another organism toward which it can act aggressively. The extent to which human aggression exemplifies innate tendencies is not clear, and many of the ways in which people attack and thus weaken or destroy the power of intentional controllers are quite obviously learned.

Excepted from *Beyond Freedom and Dignity* by B. F. Skinner, 1971. New York: Bantam/Vintage.

Recognizing the power of observation was a revolution because it turned our attention to cognitive processes in learning. Bandura discovered that his participants could learn a behavior through observation and then, placed in the same situation, refuse to perform it. This finding led to the assumption that the learning is stored cognitively in some way (Kazdin, 2001). In current applications, modeling is typically combined with other behavioral techniques, such as when a counselor models a desired social skill as a prelude to teaching it to the client (Kazdin, 2001). The label *Social Cognitive Theory* is often used to describe the current version of social learning theory (Wilson, 2005).

It is difficult to discuss the history of BT without pointing to the influence of Hans Eysenck and his wildly controversial study of psychotherapy, which I reviewed in Chapter 1. Psychotherapy was the term that Eysenck, a classical conditioning behaviorist, used to refer to approaches other than behavioral, and he expended a great deal of energy attempting to discredit the former and promote the latter. A particularly rabble-rousing quote from Eysenck is the following: "Learning theory does not postulate any such 'unconscious causes,' but regards neurotic symptoms as simple learned habits; there is no neurosis underlying the symptom, but merely the symptom itself. *Get rid of the symptom and you have eliminated the neurosis*" (1960, p. 9; italics in original).

Behavior Therapy is still a vital approach, and the prominent professional association of these counselors is the Association for Behavioral and Cognitive Therapies (ABCT), which was until 2005 known as the American Association of Behavior Therapy, formed in 1966 (the name change should tell you something). The *Behavior Therapist* is the official journal of the ABCT. An organization for the applied behavior analysts is the Association for Behavior Analysis International (http://www.abainternational.org/).

The first journal exclusively devoted to Behavior Therapy was originated by Eysenck and Rachman, *Behavior Research and Therapy*, and the first to promote operant principles was the *Journal of Applied Behavior Analysis*, which debuted in 1968 (Glass & Arnkoff, 1992). There are many journals devoted to Behavior Therapy, including *Advances in Behavior Research and Therapy* and *Behavior Modification*. Division 25 of the American Psychological Association is the Division of Behavior Analysis, and has a homepage at www.apa.org/divisions/div25. In testimony to its historical roots, Division 25 sponsors a B. F. Skinner award for new research on a yearly basis.

Hayes, Luoma, Bond, Masuda, and Lillis (2006) identify a third wave of BT approaches that are cognitively-oriented, but focus more on the context and function of thought than the specific content of it (as does, for example classic Cognitive Therapy, see Chapter 10). That is, these approaches, particularly Acceptance and Commitment Therapy, look at the situation in which thoughts occur and the effects of the thoughts in terms of behavior and beyond, to life satisfaction. These most recent developments in BT are interesting in that they are much more attentive to the therapeutic relationship than traditional BT (Lejuez et al., 2006). I provide brief descriptions of three newer BT approaches in Box 8.4, Functional Analytic Psychotherapy, Acceptance and Commitment Therapy, and Dialectical Behavior Therapy.

Box 8.4

NOUVEAU BEHAVIOR THERAPY

Recent versions of Behavior Therapy have presented some unusual twists and turns when compared to traditional approaches. Here I will describe three of these newer approaches.

DIALECTICAL BEHAVIOR THERAPY (DBT)

Developed by Linehan (1993), DBT was originally oriented to dealing with clients who present with fairly severe levels of dysfunction (e.g., self-injurious behavior, borderline personality disorder). Combining BT, cognitive therapy techniques, and elements of Zen Buddhist philosophy, DBT is an intensive approach, including weekly individual sessions, group skills training, and frequent telephone consultation. In the context of a warm, accepting relationship, clients are allowed to vent about and tolerate their negative feelings, which the therapist validates. The goal is for the client to approach life with a more balanced, dialectical process. Like ACT (described next), DBT incorporates the principles of mindfulness and acceptance into its philosophy and treatment. DBT therapists also teach their clients emotional regulation skills, which are critical for clients with significant levels of dysfunction (Robins & Chapman, 2004).

Two aspects of DBT are particularly interesting: contingency management and reciprocal communication. In contingency management, the therapist uses her approval, warmth, and caring to reinforce desired client behavior in sessions, and "breaks" from the relationship are sometimes used as punishers (Lejuez et al., 2006). Reciprocal communication refers to the use of therapist self-disclosure (often about the therapeutic relationship) and irreverent communication, which is described as "reframing something the patient says in an unorthodox way or adopting the opposite level of intensity of the patient" (Lejuez et al., 2006, p. 462). For example, Lejuez et al. describe responding to a client who complains about role-playing with "Great, I assume that all of your interpersonal relationships have improved?" (p. 462).

ACCEPTANCE AND COMMITMENT THERAPY (ACT)

Based on the notion (and experimental findings) that avoiding unwanted thoughts, feelings, and physiological experiences can create worse problems, ACT is a behaviorally-oriented approach that encourages clients to simply accept and observe these (Bach & Hayes, 2002). Once the client stops trying to banish these experiences, he or she can focus on overt behaviors directed at desired outcomes. Thus the acronym ACT also stands for Accept, Choose, and Take Action (Hayes, Strosahl, & Wilson, 1999). Based on an elaborate underlying theory of cognitive process (Relational Frame Theory), proponents of ACT (particularly its founder, Stephen Hayes) have generated volumes of literature, much of it empirical, supporting the approach.

The overall goal of ACT is to increase psychological flexibility (Hayes et al., 2006). What is unusual about ACT is that it draws from ancient spiritual traditions in its emphasis on acceptance and mindfulness (Hayes, 2002). Clients are taught to observe their thoughts and accept them as just that—something that happens that need not be true! For example, you might teach a client to think "I am having the thought that I am from another planet" rather than "I am from another planet." This loosening of thoughts allows the client the freedom to concentrate on life values and make a commitment to actions that advance toward these goals. Techniques used in ACT include basic behavioral techniques (for the committed action part) but some that look more like Buddhist rituals (e.g., passively observing thought, repeating a thought out loud).

FUNCTIONAL ANALYTIC PSYCHOTHERAPY

Functional Analytic Psychotherapy (FAP), developed by Kohlenberg and Tsai, is Behavior Therapy that puts the focus on the therapeutic relationship. In this approach, the assumption is made that "all people act (do, think, feel, see, know, follow instructions, etc.) because of the contingencies of reinforcement they have experienced in past relationships" (Kohlenberg & Tsai, 1995, p. 638). Therefore, the FAP therapist is happiest when she can operate on material produced by the client in the therapy session, which FAP advocates call clinically relevant behavior (CRB; Hopko & Hopko, 1999). There are three types of CRBs: *problem* behavior, behavioral *improvements* that are observed in session and client *interpretations* of behavior (which indicate client understanding of the contingencies and consequences associated with behaviors). The FAP therapist is to watch for each of these, and provide reinforcement when the last two occur and either fail to reinforce or punish the first (problem behavior). Sometimes they even evoke these behaviors (Hopko & Hopko, 1999). Because many clients present with relationship problems and it is assumed that contingencies reside in relationships, many times FAP therapists focus on the actual client-therapist relationship as it occurs in the counseling session.

BASIC PHILOSOPHY

Because contemporary BT is more of a general orientation than a specific theoretical approach, the assumptions behind the orientation are helpful in understanding how it is currently practiced (Antony & Roemer, 2003). Martell (2007) outlined eight basic principles of Behavior Therapy; these are listed in Box 8.5. I will present here a general overview of the philosophy of the approach, which will touch on these principles.

Behaviorists tend to take a neutral view of human nature. Although they recognize genetic influences, ultimately, they believe behavior is determined by the environment, so to rate humans as inherently "good" or "bad" is useless (Skinner, 1971).

Behavior therapists tend to emphasize, as you might expect, behavioral descriptions of people rather than trait descriptions (Spiegler & Guevremont, 2003). They are more likely to describe how someone talks (e.g., she speaks very precisely) than to characterize using trait description (she's snotty). At the extremes, BTs would rather discuss behavior disorders or problems in living than traditional diagnostic categories because the latter are imprecise and involve trait language (Wilson, 2005). However, a review of BT resources will demonstrate that traditional diagnostic categories are often used for organizational purposes.

Early behaviorists, such as Ullmann and Krasner (1965), pointed out that traditional approaches to behavior change were based on what they called the "medical model" (p. 2). In this approach, also called the disease model, a person experiencing psychological difficulties is viewed as sick or diseased, and the sickness results from some underlying causal factor or mechanism inside the individual (such as repressed conflicts). What needs to be changed, then, is the underlying cause, not the symptom. If you don't treat the cause, you get more symptoms, perhaps different ones, but symptoms just the same; this process is called symptom substitution. Taking a medical approach to psychological dysfunction

---

Box 8.5

The Principles of Behavioral Therapy

1. Behavior, whether public or private, is strengthened or weakened by its consequences.
2. Behaviors that are rewarded are increased; those that are punished will decrease.
3. The approach is functional rather than structural.
4. Neutral stimuli, paired with positive or negative environmental stimuli, can take on the properties of the environment in which they are presented and be conditioned to be positive or negative.
5. Behaviorism is antimentalist.
6. Behavior therapy is data driven and empirically based.
7. Changes clients make in therapy must generalize to their day-to-day lives.
8. Insight alone is not beneficial to a client.

From "*Behavioral Therapy*" by C. R. Martell, in A. Rochlen, ed., *Applying Counseling Theory: An On-line, Case Based Approach*, pp. 143–156, 2007. Upper Saddle River, NJ: Prentice Hall.

leads to a "doctor knows best" attitude because the real causes of behavior can't be seen. Diagnosis becomes central in the medical model, which should then guide treatment.

In stark contrast to the medical model, BT adopts the psychological or learning model of dysfunctional behavior, which focuses on overt behavior, and in the case of cognitive behaviorists, cognition, too. In this model, the symptom is the focus of attention, rather than the assumed underlying causal factor(s). Behavior is seen as simply behavior, which gets defined as pathological because it deviates from social norms (Bandura, 1969). BT counselors see themselves as *scientists* who rely on the results of experimental studies of learning to help their clients. They do not search for deep, hidden causes of behavior; it is not necessary to know the origins of a problem to solve it (Wilson, 2005). In fact, some of these folks do not like to use the term Behavior Therapy, instead preferring alternatives such as behavior modification or the environmental analysis of behavior (Sherman, 1973).

Historically, a controversy within the ranks of behavior therapists has centered on the roles of cognition and emotion in human behavior. These arguments allow the identification of several varieties of Behavior Therapy, ranging from radical behaviorism to cognitive behavior modification. Radical behaviorism, rooted in the ideas of Watson and Skinner, would totally exclude cognitive or otherwise inferred processes from *causal* explanations of behavior (Goldfried & Davison, 1994). That is, although these theorists recognize that thoughts and feelings exist, they do not see them as determinants of behavior, instead seeing only the environment as critical. A more moderate position is the one presented by Martell (2007) that "behaviorists do not accept that there is a mind apart from the body" (p. 147). At the extremes, these theorists adhere to an "outer model of psychopathology" and accuse cognitively oriented behavior therapists of adopting the medical model because they pay attention to events inside people that cannot be observed directly (Reitman, 1997, p. 342). The contemporary version of radical behaviorism is generally known as applied behavior analysis.

On the other end of the spectrum fall the cognitive behavior therapists and social learning theorists, who allow for the influence of internal events such as cognition and imagery in understanding and changing behavior. Most behavior therapists today probably fall into the cognitive behavioral camp; in fact, as early as 1983, a sample of members of ABCT reported that a majority of them used cognitive techniques (Gochman, Allgood, & Geer, 1983). In fact, Craighead (1990) reported that 69% of respondents to an ABCT membership survey characterized themselves as cognitive behavioral in orientation. Last and Hersen (1994) noted that "the importance of cognitions in mediating maladaptive behavioral and emotional responses is now accepted by most *practicing* behavior therapists" (1994, p. 8; italics added). For these reasons, my presentation of the principles of Behavior Therapy will rely mostly on classic discussions of the theory; readers should keep in mind that current practices are pragmatic and integrative (Martell, 2007).

JaNelle is the behavior therapist who accepts Shirley as her client. She is a moderate behavior therapist who, at times, attends to cognitive processes. Approaching Shirley with a neutral attitude, JaNelle assumes that Shirley's behavior is mostly environmentally determined. She is aware that some therapists (and indeed, some behavior therapists) would associate Shirley's behavior with a DSM-IV diagnosis of obsessive-compulsive disorder. JaNelle prefers to simply describe the behavior and look for the elements that support it. JaNelle is also interested in the cognitions that Shirley has at the times when the problem behavior occurs.

HUMAN MOTIVATION

Behaviorists see humans as motivated to adapt to the environment. Adaptation in this view means survival; thus, our behavior is in service of obtaining things that help us survive, which then become valuable to us, or reinforcing, and away from behaviors or experiences that don't promote survival, which become aversive experiences. According to Skinner (1971), "the process of operant conditioning presumably evolved when those organisms which were more sensitively affected by the consequences of their behavior were better able to adjust to the environment and survive" (p. 114). On a more general level, Wolpe (1990) defined adaptive behavior as that which "actually results in satisfying the individual's needs, brings him or her relief from pain, discomfort, or danger, or avoids undue expenditure of energy" (p. 8).

JaNelle sees Shirley's behavior simply as the most recent way she has adapted to the environment. Shirley seeks positive stimulation and avoids aversive situations. In this way, Shirley is seeking the resources she needs to survive and moving away from experiences that might be harmful. Unfortunately, Shirley's behavior has become maladaptive for her because it places her in opposition to society. Getting resources (i.e., items from the store) is adaptive in some ways, but social rules have determined that Shirley's behavior is dysfunctional.

CENTRAL CONSTRUCTS

To understand contemporary BT, it is helpful to know the three major models of learning: **classical**, or Pavlovian; **operant**, or Skinnerian; and **observational**, or modeling. The first two approaches generate a distinct set of techniques, whereas the theory of observational learning is generally applied as a way to enhance operant and classical interventions through adding attention to cognitive and social influences on behavior (Bandura, 1969). Although the distinctions between the models can be fuzzy and the connections between models and techniques not as simple as one would like, I present the models because a basic understanding of learning principles is helpful in many situations.

CLASSICAL CONDITIONING

Classical conditioning is thought to be an involuntary, reflexive process (Ullmann & Krasner, 1965). In this model, a relation between a stimulus and response that is presumably "wired in" for evolutionary reasons gets associated with a new stimulus, which can then elicit the response. For Pavlov, this sequence had to do with a bell, food, and dog saliva. We could diagram this relation in humans as follows:

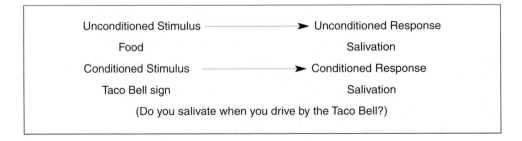

Unconditioned Stimulus ┈┈┈┈┈┈▶ Unconditioned Response
Food   Salivation

Conditioned Stimulus ┈┈┈┈┈┈▶ Conditioned Response
Taco Bell sign   Salivation

(Do you salivate when you drive by the Taco Bell?)

This classical conditioning model is the basis of Wolpe's approach to changing dysfunctional behavior, which he called *reciprocal inhibition* (Wolpe, 1960, 1990). Wolpe reasoned that anxiety is a dysfunctional behavior when it occurs in circumstances in which there is no objective threat to the person (Wolpe, 1960). The idea is that anxiety (the unconditioned stimulus, or UCS) gets conditioned to some stimulus that is normally not anxiety provoking (the conditioned stimulus, or CS). In other instances, anxiety is a natural and adaptive response, or the "autonomic response pattern or patterns that are characteristically part of the given organism's response to noxious stimulation" (Wolpe, 1960, p. 88).

A little green garden snake, for example, is not really an occasion for a major anxiety attack because it is not harmful to me (provided I have correctly identified it). So why do I jump and scream when I see one of these little critters? Using a classical conditioning model, we would see the snake as a conditioned stimulus, having been paired with some other natural event that was indeed threatening or noxious, the unconditioned stimulus. That other event (and we often don't know what it is) is what originally evoked the anxiety. The snake now evokes anxiety because of its earlier association with the unconditioned stimulus.

The association between a conditioned stimulus and a conditioned response can be weakened or eliminated by repeated presentation of the CS in the absence of the UCS, a process called *extinction* (Wolpe, 1990). For example, Pavlov could repeatedly ring his bell and never present food to the dog. Eventually, the dog will stop responding with salivation when the bell rings because it hasn't gotten any food in a long time—the salivation response is extinguished. Some BT techniques are based on the principle of extinction, such as when an individual is made to sit in a room with a garden snake until her anxiety goes away.

Because Shirley's problem behavior involves anxiety, JaNelle considers the possibility that classical conditioning is involved. Somehow, anxiety has been associated with being in a store for Shirley, and it disappears when she steals something and leaves the store. JaNelle wonders if Shirley has somehow associated being in a store with a truly threatening situation that would logically lead to anxiety. Perhaps she experienced a life-threatening event in a store in some distant past. In terms of intervention, it does not matter how or when the original conditioning occurred, except that JaNelle needs to be sure that the anxiety is conditioned to the store, not something else. For example, the problem could be more general. Shirley might experience anxiety every time she leaves her home. JaNelle knows that she needs to explore this issue with Shirley, as well as the abrupt cessation of the anxiety that she experiences upon leaving the store.

OPERANT CONDITIONING

Developed most elegantly by B. F. Skinner, the operant learning model starts with the idea that behavior is maintained by its consequences. The term *operant* is used because it emphasizes that behavior operates on the environment to produce consequences that, ideally, contribute to the person's adaptation (Nye, 1986; Skinner, 1953), in contrast to respondent (classically conditioned) learning, in which the behavior considered is seen as sort of automatic.

In the operant model, behavior is said to be *contingent upon* its consequences (Skinner, 1971). *Reinforcement* is the formal term for consequences that maintain a given behavior. That is, reinforcers are consequences that *increase* the probability that a behavior will occur. Whether a particular event is reinforcing is a function of an "individual's biological endowment, learning history, and current situation" (Milan, 1990, p. 71). To take a simple example, some people like salty foods, and others like sweet foods. The reinforcement value of potato chips is higher for me than that of chocolate.

Two kinds of reinforcers can be distinguished—positive and negative (Skinner, 1953). **Positive reinforcers** increase the likelihood of a behavior occurring because something good is presented following the appearance of the desired behavior. **Negative reinforcers** increase the probability of behavior through the removal of aversive stimuli. Keep in mind here that the terms *positive* and *negative* are not used in the ways we typically use them. In Behavior Therapy language, *positive* refers to the *addition* of something that causes behavior to increase, whereas *negative* refers to the *removal* of something *resulting in an increase* in behavior (Nye, 1986). When Mom pats little Johnny on the head after he does a cartwheel, she has employed positive reinforcement. When Dad gives Laura a cookie to stop her tantrum, Dad's cookie-giving behavior is *negatively* reinforced; it terminated an aversive stimulus (the tantrum). Note that Laura's tantrum behavior is positively reinforced, assuming that she likes cookies and has not just eaten a truckload of them. Box 8.6 gives another example of positive and negative reinforcement.

Box 8.6

Behavior Modification in Humans and Felines

I have a cat. His name is Skat, also known as the Cat from Hell. Skat the Cat is, like most cats, used to going where he wants to when he wants to. Skat is equally comfortable roaming the neighborhood or sleeping on my feet.

Sometimes Skat the Cat wants inside when he is in fact outside. He is not very patient, and one way of demonstrating this is through screen-scratching behavior. Clearly, someone, sometime must have let him in the house following screen-scratching behavior, thereby positively reinforcing his screen-scratching behavior (it was not me, of course). As a good student of behavior modification, I would never positively reinforce screen-scratching behavior, yet because some visitor(s) have, this behavior is on an intermittent schedule of reinforcement with a *very* long interval. The intermittent schedule thus accounts for Scat's persistence in the behavior—he has been known to keep it up for hours . . . despite it being 3 a.m.

What is my response to Skat's behavior? I consider screen-scratching an aversive stimulus, so my first impulse is to yell at him. This behavior on my part, as you might guess, is extinguished very quickly, because it produces no change in the noxious stimulus. I could opt for an extinction approach (i.e., never opening the door), but because he is apparently on a long-interval intermittent schedule, it would take a very long time and many screen replacements to extinguish his behavior. Chasing him away is even more aversive to me because I must get out of bed in the middle of the night to do so. Also, Skat might just find my chasing him a positive reinforcer! "Hey look! I got Mom out of bed and all upset! This is fun! Maybe I can get her to do it again!"

One night I had a glass of water at hand and, perhaps vaguely remembering some observed relationship between Skat's behavior and the experience of getting wet, decided to throw the water thorough the screen. Bingo! Skat was gone . . . and my water-throwing behavior was *negatively* reinforced. The noxious stimulus of screen scratching was terminated as a result of my water-throwing behavior. The next time he appeared at the screen, guess what I did? (I threw the water, of course.)

But what of Skat's behavior? Because screen scratching was immediately followed by a consequence that decreased the probability of that behavior, we conclude that he experienced punishment. Now we know that punishment merely suppresses behavior and could have some other problematic consequences, such as avoidance, but Skat likes inside and food too much to avoid me altogether. Instead, he substituted another behavior for screen scratching, a very loud meow. Choosing the lesser of two evils, I now immediately let him inside when he yowls (thus positively reinforcing the yowling behavior). Every now and then he delicately puts a few claws on the screen to show me that he has not forgotten his power and then yowls. Mostly, though, we are satisfied with the contingencies we have established.

Reinforcers come in all shapes and forms. The most basic reinforcers are food and sex, because they relate to the evolutionary goals of survival and reproduction (Nye, 1986). Skinner (1953) called these *primary* reinforcers. Many things are reinforcers because they have been historically linked with survival. Skinner (1971) gives the example of a person moving out of the hot sun into the shade. The behavior of moving is reinforced by the reduction in temperature that follows it, which is presumably good for the organism's survival.

Unfortunately for neophyte behavior modifiers, though, what is reinforcing to one person may not be to another. The power of a given reinforcer can also vary across time. Many things affect whether a given consequence is reinforcing; for example, food is not reinforcing just after a big gourmet meal. Too much of a good thing is called *satiation;* the power of a reinforcer is decreased in these circumstances (Skinner, 1953). To get around the problem of all things not being reinforcing across persons or time, BT theorists have referred to the notion of *establishing operations* (Lejuez, Hopko, Levin, Gholkar, & Collins, 2006). Establishing operations are defined as "environmental events, operations, or stimulus conditions that affect an organism's behavior by altering the reinforcing or punishing effectiveness of other environmental events and the frequency of occurrence of that part of the organism's repertoire" (Lejuez et al., p. 457).

Many things become positively reinforcing because they are associated with gaining desired outcomes; they are not the desired consequence itself. These *conditioned reinforcers* become reinforcing because they tend to occur at about the same time that reinforcement occurs (almost in a classical conditioning sense; Reynolds, 1968; Skinner, 1953). Some stimuli occur in the presence of many kinds of reinforcers, and these stimuli become *generalized.* Money is a good example of a generalized conditioned reinforcer. The paper or metal substance is not in itself positively reinforcing, but it becomes so because it is associated with getting reinforcing things (food, clothes, or other things that support survival). Attention from others is a conditioned reinforcement, presumably because babies have to get someone's attention to get things that meet survival needs, such as food or clothing

(Ullmann & Krasner, 1965). Manipulating the environment is a generalized reinforcement because many kinds of reinforcers only occur following such behavior (Skinner, 1953).

Sometimes a stimulus in the environment signals that a given contingency is operative. This is called a *discriminative stimulus*, and you can think of it as a stoplight of sorts. When the light is green, a behavior such as walking across the street will result in reinforcement (getting to where one wants to go). When the light is red, it is a signal that behavior will not be reinforced (i.e., you could get hit by a car and smushed, which would be considered punishment, I think). As we all know, however, a traffic light is not truly a discriminative stimulus because if you are careful, you can still walk across the street on a red light and receive the reinforcer of getting to the other side. Perhaps a better example would be a light on a drawbridge. If you go against the red light, you will not be reinforced; instead, you are probably punished unless you are a very good swimmer!

When behavior becomes controlled by discriminative stimuli, it is said to be under stimulus control. Discriminative stimuli can become conditioned reinforcers, as in the case of money. The acquisition of money becomes reinforcing because it signals that the behavior of giving money to others gets us desired things (food, swimming pools, shoes; Ullmann & Krasner, 1965).

Once a discriminative stimulus is established, *generalization* can occur, and the reinforced behavior will appear in situations in which a stimulus similar to the discriminative stimulus is present. For example, if Laura receives cookies from Dad when she throws a temper tantrum, Dad becomes a discriminative stimulus for tantrum behavior. Laura also may begin to show tantrum behavior in the presence of other male adults, or in the presence of adults in general.

Extinction is said to occur when the reinforcement maintaining behavior is removed and a response becomes less frequent and finally disappears (Skinner, 1953). The behavior is extinguished because the contingencies supporting it are no longer in effect. An important thing to know about extinction, however, is that early in the process, "emotional behaviors" may occur, such as anger or frustration (Skinner, 1953, p. 69). Also, the target behavior may intensify (i.e., increase in frequency or strength) under extinction conditions (Sherman, 1973). For example, Sam exhibits loving behavior toward Sally, one form of which is calling her daily and visiting her in the evenings. She reinforces him by cooking his dinner and allowing sexual contact. However, Sally suddenly decides that she no longer desires relationship behaviors with Sam and discontinues reinforcing his loving behaviors. At first, his phone calling behavior intensifies; he calls her hourly and drives by her house every night. He probably displays some emotional behavior, such as anger or sadness. If Sally continues to ignore Sam, the calling and driving by behavior will eventually decrease and then disappear.

Reinforcements can be given after every response (called *continuous* reinforcement) or after some responses and not others (*intermittent* reinforcement). Resistance of the target behavior to extinction varies depending on the schedule of reinforcement (Skinner, 1953). Behavior reinforced intermittently is extremely resistant to extinction, whereas continuous schedules produce much less resistance. In the laboratory, behavior can be maintained in pigeons on a one-in-ten-thousand response schedule (Skinner, 1953). My cat's screen-scratching behavior is clearly on an intermittent schedule, with long intervals between reinforcements (see Box 8.6).

Punishment is the opposite of reinforcement; a punisher is anything that reduces the probability of a behavior occurring. For example, if I lock myself out of my house in the middle of January, I am strongly punished for this behavior because it results in (for me) an extremely aversive event (exposure to cold weather). It is unlikely that I will repeat this behavior, for sure.

Operant behavior is behavior that the organism freely emits. However, a desired behavior can be created by a process called *shaping*, in which responses that gradually more closely resemble the desired behavior are reinforced in a progression.

JaNelle wonders if operant learning could account for Shirley's stealing behavior. From that perspective, stealing behavior would be reinforced by something. Normally, JaNelle might guess that the stealing behavior is reinforced by what Shirley acquires as a result. However, Shirley has indicated that she does not steal any particular object, which suggests that the objects themselves are not reinforcing. JaNelle guesses that the cessation of anxiety is highly negatively reinforcing to Shirley, so that leaving the store becomes a highly reinforced behavior. It is possible that on an earlier occasion, Shirley experienced anxiety while in a store and resorted to a previously learned behavior of picking something up in a wild, almost random attempt to decrease her anxiety. She then fled the store. In a chaining process, the anxiety reduction reinforced the leaving the store behavior, which then became a conditioned reinforcer that reinforced the stealing behavior.

OBSERVATIONAL LEARNING

The idea that people can learn by viewing the behavior of others was developed by Bandura (1969, 1974). Also called social learning theory (Bandura, 1969), this approach incorporates the cognitive aspects of learning because what is learned through observation and later performed must be retained somehow, presumably in the brain. Observational learning plays a large part in the acquisition of new behaviors; it is much more efficient to learn a behavior vicariously than to randomly emit behaviors to be shaped by the environment (Bandura, 1969).

Consider learning to bowl. You've never bowled before, and your buddies drag you to the bowling alley. Trying to be a good sport, you put on your bowling shoes and take to the lanes. Almost automatically the first thing you do is watch someone else bowl. If one of your buddies is a teacher-type, she may take you through the process of a turn by showing you step by step how to wind up, move forward, and release the ball. Your buddy is the model. You learn the basic fundamentals without ever picking up the ball. Of course, you may need some practice to bowl a perfect game.

Both dysfunctional and functional behavior can be learned through modeling. For example, a phobia can be acquired by watching someone else experience an anxiety-provoking event (Bandura, 1969; Wolpe, 1990). This phenomenon is called *vicarious* conditioning.

Modeling theory combines with operant theory readily because the consequences of the modeled behavior *for the model* influence the observer's behavior as well (Bandura, 1969). If, for example, Mary sees other children praised for speaking up in class, she would be more likely to speak herself (provided she values the teacher's positive reinforcement). Likewise, punished behavior can be learned observationally and displayed when the punishment contingencies are not known to be in effect. Bandura (1969) pointed out that role-playing interventions often involve modeling because the client first observes the behavior on the part of the counselor before performing it.

JaNelle wonders if modeling plays a role in Shirley's behavior. Certainly, aspects of the stealing behavior could have been learned through modeling, but the observation that Shirley is not a successful thief would suggest otherwise. Had Shirley observed a good thief, she might have learned to be inconspicuous in her behavior and to hide the object stolen!

THEORY OF THE PERSON AND DEVELOPMENT OF THE INDIVIDUAL

Behaviorists are not interested in personality theory or developmental stages. They attend to a client's past using the construct of a *learning* history. Reynolds (1968) maintained that understanding reinforcement contingencies operative in an individual's past makes it possible to implement different contingencies in the present and, thus, to change behavior. Ferster (1983) provided a detailed discussion of how depressed individuals develop faulty and diminished behavioral repertoires. According to his view, disruptions in reinforcement occur when the mother fails to notice subtle changes in the child that might lead to activity and thus does not reinforce these, to give one example. The child, therefore, does not learn as many behaviors as might the child of a more observant parent.

Other BT theorists are less reluctant to discuss childhood events. They maintain that it is simply more efficient to study the current conditions of a behavior to be changed.

JaNelle is not very interested in Shirley's childhood. She is, however, interested in the history of the stealing behavior and asks Shirley to recount how it first started. Shirley remembers being in a store shortly after her mother's death and getting panicky. She grabbed the first thing she saw (a really nice fountain pen) and left the store immediately. Afterwards, she felt very guilty and ashamed, as well as fearful of returning to the store because they might catch her.

HEALTH AND DYSFUNCTION

In the behavioral tradition, psychological health is seen as adaptive behavior. Adaptive behavior is that which promotes the survival of the person. All behavior is learned.

Psychological dysfunction is maladaptive behavior, and it arises from the same processes as adaptive behavior—namely, it is learned (Ullman & Krasner, 1965). The "so-called symptom is the problem" (Sherman, 1973, p. 18). Whether a behavior is considered dysfunctional is dependent on whether it is adaptive or maladaptive for a given situation (Sherman, 1973). Behavior is not considered to be equivalent to mental illness or psychopathology as in the medical model.

A classical conditioning perspective portrays psychological dysfunction as resulting from faulty conditioning of anxiety (or fear; the terms are used interchangeably) to behaviors (Wolpe, 1990). Essentially, fear is an unconditioned response that gets associated with a previously neutral conditioned stimulus (Wolpe, 1990). Although he did acknowledge that some behavior was unrelated to anxiety (e.g, nail-biting, extreme stinginess, nocturnal enuresis, 1990, p. 9), for Wolpe, the majority of neurotic behavior is, in essence, simply habit learned in anxiety-provoking settings. Wolpe (1990) saw schizophrenia, antisocial personality disorder, and drug addictions as primarily biological in nature, although conditioning procedures could be used to alter some behavior patterns in these presentations.

Wolpe defined neuroses as "persistent maladaptive learned habits in which the foremost feature is anxiety" (1990, p. 23). These habits can be established in a variety of ways. First, neurosis can be based on simple classical conditioning, in which anxiety is aroused by a threatening situation, and some stimulus in the situation is associated with the anxiety. This association can be established in one trial if the situation is traumatic enough. For example, the anxiety in a battle situation can become conditioned to the sound of gunfire, or sirens. The individual knows that the *sounds* of gunfire or sirens are not immediately threatening, but becomes anxious nonetheless when she hears them in a nonbattle situation.

Fear can also be vicariously conditioned, according to Wolpe (1990). Observing someone else's extreme fear response to a stimulus might result in the observer acquiring a classically conditioned fear of that stimulus. If, Danny, as a child, observed his mother reacting very fearfully to the sight of a Doberman pinscher, he might develop the same neurotic fear.

In a similar process, neurotic fears can be brought about by misinformation (Wolpe, 1990). The old fear of masturbation causing blindness is a good example of this neurotic mechanism.

Although the classical conditioning approach appears to focus heavily on anxiety and the maladaptive behavior associated with it, Wolpe (1992) maintained that many forms of depression were based in anxiety as well. In fact, he estimated that 60% of depressions were neurotic, which in his view meant anxiety based.

JaNelle considers the possibility that Shirley's anxiety in stores is classically conditioned somehow. When she asks Shirley about the history of her anxiety in stores, Shirley relates that she doesn't remember anything in particular triggering the anxiety. She just started to get panicky while in a store one day. Although it is interesting that Shirley mentions that the attacks started shortly after the death of her mother, JaNelle does not consider this information particularly useful.

From an operant perspective, dysfunctional behavior is maintained by contingencies of reinforcement (Iwata, Kahng, Wallace, & Lindberg, 2000). Sherman (1973) suggested two broad classifications of maladaptive behavior, surplus and deficiency. *Surplus* behaviors are inappropriate or ineffective for a given situation. *Deficiency* problems occur when individuals fail to learn behaviors appropriate to situations. From this perspective, surplus behaviors would be viewed as maladaptive responses maintained by existing environmental reinforcers. Deficiency problems would involve a lack of desirable behaviors—the individual just never learned them. A deficit in behavior can also result when the contingencies in a situation punish or simply do not reinforce the behavior.

A social learning perspective fits with the operant perspective because dysfunctional behavior can be learned, maintained, and suppressed by observations of models. If the individual is not exposed to the right models, she will not learn certain behaviors deemed important to a given cultural group, for example. If a child were never exposed to a dinner in which multiple forks are used, for instance, she would not know what to do when faced with a formal place setting.

Operant theorists sometimes discuss maladaptive behaviors using general classifications, such as when they theorize about social skills deficits or depression. Operant theorists view depression as stemming from problems in the person's range of actions, or what is called the behavioral repertoire. Ferster (1983) conceptualized depression as resulting from an overuse of passive behaviors and decreased incidence of adaptive, active behavior. Consequently, the depressed person receives little positive reinforcement from her environment (Ferster, 1983). Additionally, the depressed person has distorted perceptions of the environment, including faulty perceptions of the self (negative self-concept) and overblown ideas about her responsibility for events (excessive self-blame). These distortions lead to further reductions in positive reinforcement. Ferster, in fact, proposed that depressed people have "(1) a limited view of the world, (2) a 'lousy' view of the world, and (3) an unchanging view of the world" (1983, p. 379). You will discover that this triad sounds a lot like that proposed in Beck's Cognitive Therapy (Chapter 10).

Still other behaviorists point out that depression can result when an individual perceives no control over the world, or more accurately, when she perceives that there are no contingencies between her behaviors and outcomes. This "helplessness" view of depression suggests that the critical factor in affective states is "the person's perception of his [sic] ability to control the world" (Goldfried & Davison, 1994, p. 234; Seligman, 1975).

Social skills deficits, from an operant perspective, could be the result of faulty learning (i.e., the individual was reinforced for behaviors deemed socially inappropriate) or a simple lack of behaviors (i.e., the individual never learned social behaviors). Some social behaviors might have been punished.

JaNelle thinks that Shirley's stealing behavior may be reinforced by the cessation of anxiety; that is, the stealing is negatively reinforced. When she enters a store, Shirley becomes anxious and then steals something so that she has to exit the store, thereby escaping the anxiety.

NATURE OF THERAPY

ASSESSMENT

Assessment is very important in BT. It is seen as a scientific process that focuses on "what the client *does* rather than the traits the client *has*" (Glass & Arnkoff, 1992, p. 599; italics in original). Both formal and informal assessment are used, but behaviorists are most emphatic that they are *not* doing personality assessment or looking for underlying causes of symptoms. Kuehnel and Liberman (1986) pointed out that a behavioral assessment should include client strengths as well as deficits. BT counselors also look for sources of reinforcement that can be used to facilitate behaviors.

Formal diagnosis (e.g., DSM-IV) is not consistent with the BT model because it is based on a medical model and thus far from a functional analysis of an individual's behavior. However, BT counselors are likely to use formal diagnoses for pragmatic reasons, such as when required by third-party payers or when working within a medical treatment setting (Watson & Gross, 1999).

In BT, assessment is closely linked to intervention, and it focuses on the individual's current behavior, with specific attention paid to antecedents and consequences (Last & Hersen, 1994).

Some BT counselors would add organismic variables such as cognitions and physiological factors (Goldfried & Davison, 1994). A *baseline*, or frequency count of the target behavior over time, is often established so that change in behavior can be clearly documented (Kazdin, 2001).

A more global term for what BT counselors do before they intervene is functional analysis (Antony & Roemer, 2003). The actual assessment phase is followed by the creation of hypotheses about the conditions maintaining the behavior of interest. Baseline patterns established in earlier phases of assessment may suggest hypotheses about what is controlling the behavior (Kazdin, 2001, p. 104).

A variety of methods can be used to assess behavior in BT counseling. The most theoretically pure form of assessment is direct observation of the client by independent, trained raters across various life situations (Goldfried & Davison, 1994). Clearly, this is an expensive and cumbersome form of assessment, and it is rarely used except perhaps in institutional settings. Even in institutional settings, samples are used (for instance, a 10-minute observation taken eight times per day). Instead, BT counselors more often use their own observations (e.g., in-session role-play or imagery techniques), those of the client's significant others, or simply the client's self-report.

The simplest and most cost-effective assessment method is the informal assessment, which involves interviewing the client (Kazdin, 2001). More structure can be added by using existing structured interview guidelines, such as the Anxiety Disorders Interview Schedule (DiNardo, Brown, & Barlow, 1994). Some behaviors can be assessed through role-play scenarios, such as social skills. The therapists can then either simply observe, or record the presence or absence of targeted behaviors.

Behavior therapists often ask clients to log the frequency of a behavior between counseling sessions, a technique called self-monitoring. There are three potential problems with self-monitoring. First, there is the question of whether the client can accurately and honestly monitor her behavior. Second, monitoring may disrupt normal routines, causing the client to become aggravated. Third, behavior has been known to change when monitored—most notably, unwanted behavior tends to decrease (Spiegler & Guevremont, 2003).

Formal assessment in BT often involves the use of standardized instruments or symptom checklists. Wolpe (1990), for instance, was adamant that the use of the Willoughby Neuroticism Questionnaire and the Fear Survey Schedule is essential in Behavior Therapy. He said "failure to use these instruments is a serious deprivation of data, parallel to a physicians' nonuse of the electrocardiogram in suspected heart disease" (1990, p. xi).

Behavioral checklists and surveys are often used in cognitive behavior forms of BT (Spiegler & Guevremont, 2003). Clients might be asked to complete the Beck Depression Inventory (Beck, Ward, Mendelson, & Erbaugh, 1961), the Reinforcement Survey Schedule (Cautela & Kastenbaum, 1967), or the Test Anxiety Behavior Scale (Suinn, 1969). Many other such inventories exist.

JaNelle begins with a simple interview approach with Shirley. She asks a lot of questions about Shirley's current situation, including her living situation, social activities, and financial supports. Shirley reports that although she enjoys her community service, she wishes she had more friends with whom to spend off-hours. JaNelle thinks that an assessment of Shirley's social skills, with some focus on assertive behavior, is warranted. To start, JaNelle closely observes as she and Shirley interact. She notes that Shirley seems a little shy at times, avoiding eye contact and speaking very softly.

Gently, JaNelle asks Shirley about the incident that got her to counseling. Initially reluctant, Shirley responds to JaNelle's approach and tells JaNelle about the recent incident. She admits that this behavior happens about on a weekly basis. JaNelle asks many specific questions about these incidents, attempting to gain a step-by-step picture of Shirley's behavior. She considers a live observation of Shirley's stealing behavior, but then decides to have her role-play the behavior in the counseling session.

OVERVIEW OF THE THERAPEUTIC ATMOSPHERE

Behavior therapists assume that behavior is predictable from antecedents, organismic variables, and consequences, so "clinical interaction constitutes a form of experiment" (Goldfried & Davison, 1994, p. 4). This emphasis on the scientific approach in BT has led, at times, to significant disagreement about the nature of, or necessity for, the relationship in Behavior Therapy. At one extreme, Eysenck (1960) dismissed the transference-based relationship of psychoanalysis, saying, "behavior therapy has no need of this adjunct, nor does it admit that the evidence for its existence is remotely adequate at the present time. . . . In certain cases, of course, personal relationships may be required in order to provide a necessary step on the generalization gradient; but this is not always true" (p. 19).

In contrast, others emphasize that the therapeutic relationship is essential to BT. For example, Wolpe (1985) maintained that "trust, positive regard, and serious acceptance of the patient are part and parcel of behavior therapy practice" (p. 127). As Goldfried and Davison put it, "a tough-minded approach to conceptualizing human problems in no way precludes a warm, genuine, or empathic interaction with clients" (1994, p. 7). Last and Hersen (1994) added that it would be asking a great deal of a client to do all of the self-monitoring and practicing required in Behavior Therapy in the absence of a good therapeutic relationship.

Most contemporary behavior therapists see a good relationship as important in producing good client outcome (Antony & Roemer, 2003; Keijsers, Schaap, & Hoogduin, 2000). The BT counselor has the potential to reinforce the client for desired behavior (Goldfried & Davison, 1994). In what might be seen as a surprising development, recent adaptations to the BT approach have emphasized the therapeutic relationship as the "primary vehicle for therapeutic change" (Lejuez et al., 2006, p. 458; see also Box 8.4). In what sounds very much like a return to classic analytic thought, these behaviorists maintain that the counselor must form a close and genuine attachment with the client (using positive reinforcement to strengthen the alliance, and closely observe the client's interpersonal behavior. In the case of Dialectical Behavior Therapy (DBT), counselors engage in *reciprocal communication*, which can include self-disclosure. Although self-disclosure is not unheard of in traditional BT, DBT therapists may go as far as to disclose their feelings and reactions to the client's interpersonal behavior in the therapy setting (Lejuez et al., 2006). Of course, BTs are careful to ensure that such disclosure is in the interests of the client, not the counselor. DBT practitioners also use "irreverent communication", or the use of exaggerated or unorthodox ways of responding to the client (Lejuez et al., p. 462).

Because Shirley does not really believe that she belongs in counseling, JaNelle knows that it is essential that she establish some kind of rapport with her. JaNelle tries to be supportive, genuine, and caring in her interactions with Shirley.

ROLES OF CLIENT AND COUNSELOR

The counseling relationship in Behavior Therapy is collaborative, and the client is seen as a cotherapist (Sweet, 1984). The counselor is a model for the client (Goldfried & Davison, 1994) and takes the role of a consultant, who is teaching the client the skills necessary to be her own behavior therapist (Sweet, 1984).

The client in BT is just that, a client rather than a patient (Sweet, 1984). The client is expected to contribute actively to the BT assessment and goal setting and to complete her homework faithfully. She is a learner of the knowledge presented by the teacher/counselor.

JaNelle approaches Shirley as a collaborator, acknowledging that Shirley has not voluntarily come to counseling. She offers herself as a consultant to Shirley, suggesting that she has some ideas that might help Shirley better her life conditions. If Shirley accepts this offer, JaNelle will expect Shirley to be a partner in BT counseling, participating in goal setting and homework assignments.

GOALS

The goal in BT is simple—reduce or eliminate maladaptive behavior and teach or increase the incidence of adaptive responses. Picking behaviors to modify sounds easier than it really is. Traditionally, BT has targeted very specific behaviors such as smoking, weight gain or loss, and specific phobias. These behaviors are easily observable and quantifiable. However, clients often present much more complicated pictures and often do not present their concerns in terms of specific, observable behaviors. For example, many clients come to counseling saying that they want to get rid of their depression, or that they are unhappy with their relationships.

Spiegler and Guevremont (2003, p. 56) presented the "*dead person rule:* never ask a client to do something a dead person can do." Only dead people can avoid behaving altogether, so it is generally better to prescribe behavior than to try to delete it. For example, it would be better for Robert to ask Steve to pick up his clothes after his shower than to admonish "don't leave your clothes on the bathroom floor."

The increasing recognition within the ranks of BT counselors that client problems are usually not as simple as we would wish has led to new considerations about selecting behavioral goals (Marsh, 1985; Thompson & Williams, 1985). Target behaviors in modern BT include cognitions and emotions, and it is important that the targets involve some "*significant* aspect of the client's overall functioning" (Marsh, 1985, p. 66; italics in original). In other words, the BT counselor should be aware that the traditional, specific targets of BT may not coincide with the desired outcomes of the client.

Thompson and Williams (1985) presented an even more radical view in observing that "behavioral therapists, simply because of the ease of their available technology, often treat rather than think" (p. 48). They argued that behavior therapists need to accept that some client problems are existential in nature, requiring a different perspective, one that admits the possibility of "*long-term therapy* and focusing on the therapeutic *relationship*" (p. 49, italics in original).

Shirley and JaNelle set two goals for counseling: decrease anxiety that seems to be connected to stealing behavior, and increase social skills, particularly assertive behavior. They also agree that some problem solving around Shirley's desire to have more social contact in her life would be helpful.

The specific goals they establish are as follows: (a) Shirley will be able to enter a department store and purchase an item (or just browse) without stealing anything. (b) Shirley will learn new social behaviors, including increased eye contact and voice volume. (c) Shirley will increase her social contacts (outside of her volunteer work) to at least three times per week.

PROCESS OF THERAPY

BT practitioners see therapy as composed of two distinct phases: assessment and intervention (Wolpe, 1990). After the therapist has performed a functional analysis of the client's behavior and specified a target behavior or behaviors, it is time to intervene. At an early point in this process, the client is oriented to BT, which usually consists of giving her a brief explanation of how the BT counselor views problems and interventions (Wolpe, 1990). Goldfried and Davison (1994) were very clear that the client's expectations about therapy are important to assess and address because misconceptions can get in the way of treatment. Clients may expect detailed explorations of childhood events, dream analysis, or free association. The BT counselor should be empathic about the client's reasons for these assumptions, but should not necessarily accede to them (Goldfried & Davison, 1994). The counselor can listen to client history empathically, while also inserting comments to help the client redefine the problem in behavioral terms. In essence, the behavior therapist teaches the client the behavioral model.

BT counselors see the first session of counseling as critical. It has four goals: "(1) establishing rapport with the client, (2) understanding the client's problem and selecting a target behavior, (3) gathering data about maintaining conditions, and (4) educating the client about the behavioral approach to treatment and issues of confidentiality" (Spiegler & Guevremont, 2003, p, 83). At the end of this session, the client and counselor may create a written therapeutic contract (Goldfried & Davison, 1994). The contract typically contains information about fees, cancellations, frequency of sessions, and other procedural details. It also outlines the expectations for the client's and counselor's behavior both within and outside of the counseling sessions (such as the expectation that the client will complete homework between sessions).

When clients behave in ways that suggest resistance to BT, the fault is laid squarely at the feet of the BT counselor. In discussing this issue, Goldfried and Davison (1994) maintained that "*the client is never wrong*. If one truly accepts the assumption that behavior is lawful—whether it be deviant or nondeviant—then *any* difficulties occurring during the course of therapy should more appropriately be traced to the therapist's inadequate or incomplete evaluation of the case" (p. 17; italics in original). What other therapists (particularly of a psychoanalytic persuasion) would call transference and countertransference, the BT calls stimulus generalization (Beach, 2005). The person of the therapist, for example in the case of "transference" is similar to a stimulus person in another realm or time of the client's life, and she responds to the therapist in the same way that she responded to the previous person.

JaNelle explains the basics of BT to Shirley. She explains that Shirley's anxiety and stealing behavior are learned and can be unlearned if Shirley is willing to work on it. Shirley, the reluctant client, is not very happy about the ordeal of therapy, but she grudgingly agrees that getting rid of her stealing behavior might be a good thing.

JaNelle also talks to Shirley about the social isolation she experiences and her desire to increase social contact. Describing assertiveness training, JaNelle asks if Shirley would like to consider addressing this issue. Shirley and JaNelle agree on goals for counseling, which are (a) to decrease or eliminate the stealing behavior and (b) to increase Shirley's social contracts through learning new social skills. JaNelle gives Shirley a written contract that states these goals, the duties of both parties, and the expected outcomes of counseling.

THERAPEUTIC TECHNIQUES

A variety of techniques are used in BT counseling. The majority of these techniques focus on overt behavior, but some, to some extent, focus on internal events like cognition (Wolpe, 1990). Some of these techniques are implemented by the counselor, and others are taught to the client so that she can use them on her own. Many of the techniques presented have cognitive aspects.

RELAXATION TRAINING

The basis for several other techniques in BT (e.g, systematic desensitization), progressive relaxation training is also thought to be therapeutic by itself (Goldfried & Davison, 1994; E. Jacobson, 1929). Goldfried and Davison (1994) described two types of relaxation training. One approach alternates between tensing and relaxing specific groups of muscles, one at a time. For example, the counselor might begin by having the client tense her right hand, then relax it and study the difference. After several repetitions of this sequence, the therapist might then direct the client to tense her arm, and so forth, progressing through all of the various major muscle groups in the body. It is important that clients practice their relaxation training, so in the past, they were given audiotaped instructions to use at home between sessions. Nowadays iPods and podcasts might be used for this purpose.

The second approach to relaxation training, relaxation by letting go (Goldfried & Davison, 1994), is really an advanced form of the tensing–relaxing procedure. After clients have learned how to do the first version, they either spontaneously, or are encouraged to, simply relax progressive muscle groupings without the tensing part.

JaNelle teaches Shirley progressive relaxation training, beginning by giving her an introduction about the process and why it is helpful. She then guides Shirley through a complete relaxation session. Shirley takes home an audiotape so that she can practice.

Flooding

Flooding, typically used with phobias, involves prolonged exposure to a feared or aversive stimulus (Marshall & Gauthier, 1983). This technique is also sometimes called exposure therapy. The idea is to reduce or eliminate completely the distress associated with the unpleasant stimulus. Traditionally, flooding is done *in vivo*—involving real exposure to the feared stimulus. However, when it is not possible to use an in vivo approach, imaginal flooding can be used. For example, a client who obsesses about maintaining a clean house can be exposed to a very dirty house using imagery.

Although some consider flooding to be a risky technique because it exposes clients to feared stimuli, Marshall and Gauthier (1983) maintained that it is no more so than other behavioral techniques. They identified several critical considerations in the success of flooding techniques, including an accurate assessment and conceptualization by the therapist, proper client preparation, and involvement of the client's significant others. The counselor must also be ready to deal with the real distress experienced by the client, because terminating the exposure too soon may result in failure of the technique, or even worsening of the anxiety (Marshall & Gauthier, 1983). Sometimes it is important to add skills training to BT when flooding is used (Marshall & Gauthier, 1983). For example, imaginal or in vivo flooding can be used with a client who is fearful of public speaking, but it might also be a good idea to teach the client some public speaking skills.

Depending on Shirley's preferences, either in vivo or imaginal flooding could be used to extinguish Shirley's anxiety connected with being in stores. If she refuses an in vivo visit to the store, JaNelle can attempt to use imagery to recreate the experience in the counseling session.

Exposure Therapy

Used widely for phobias fears, and compulsive behavior, this technique requires that the client encounter the anxiety-provoking stimulus and not respond as she typically does (Foa & Franklin, 1999). Similar to flooding, exposure can be done imaginally or in vivo (Emmelkamp, 2004). Sometimes, the therapist even accompanies the client in these situations to make sure the response is prevented. In other instances, a significant other is recruited to help with the procedure. I once had a client who had a light switch compulsion. On his own, he discovered the technique of "just not doing it." Even though he was anxious, he would refrain from touching the light switches in his home. He was doing self-directed exposure and response prevention. This technique was very successful for him; his light-switching behavior was virtually eliminated.

Exposure therapy is also used to intervene when clients show symptoms of posttraumatic stress disorder (PTSD). Although this technique is theoretically based in extinction, Massad and Hulsey (2006) warn that the prudent BT therapist should know that exposure does not eliminate underlying conditioning in associations established by trauma; it merely weakens them. Thus, they suggest that exposure therapy take place in conditions that are as similar as possible to the situation in which the original learning occurred.

JaNelle thinks that exposure and response prevention is a potentially useful technique for Shirley. Shirley will have to enter a store, experience her anxiety, and refrain from stealing anything. JaNelle begins by taking a "field trip" with Shirley. She and Shirley enter numerous stores, and JaNelle makes sure that Shirley does not take anything.

SYSTEMATIC DESENSITIZATION

This technique evolved from Wolpe's idea that if a response that is incompatible with anxiety (or other undesirable behavior) can be produced in the presence of a stimulus classically conditioned to fear, the fear will become disassociated with the stimulus (Wolpe, 1990). He called this process *reciprocal inhibition* because one response (anxiety) is inhibited by a presumably opposite one. Deep muscle relaxation is the response most often used in systematic desensitization (Spiegler & Guevremont, 2003). However, other responses, such as pleasant imagery, humor, and sexual arousal, have been used in this procedure, along with drugs (tranquilizers) and carbon dioxide inhalation.

The first steps in systematic desensitization are (a) teaching the client progressive relaxation procedures and (b) constructing an anxiety hierarchy to be used in the procedure (Wolpe, 1960). Progressive relaxation, as described earlier, consists of teaching the client to alternatively contract and relax muscle groups in the body, progressing from one part of the body to another.

The anxiety (or fear) hierarchy is a list of situations that evoke fear in the client, ranked from least to most threatening, on a 1 to 100 scale. Goldfried and Davison (1994) recommended that jumps between items are ideally 10 points or less; if a gap is more than 10, at least one additional item should be constructed to bridge the gap. Hierarchies are usually composed of 12 to 24 items.

Once these tasks have been accomplished, the actual desensitization procedure begins. The client is relaxed and is instructed to imagine the item or scene lowest on her fear hierarchy. If she experiences anxiety, she signals, usually by raising one finger. The counselor then helps the client get back to the relaxed state. The idea is to keep the level of anxiety relatively low, so that it is counteracted by the relaxation (Sherman, 1973). The item is then presented again until the client can visualize the scene for 10 to 15 seconds without anxiety (Goldfried & Davison, 1994). Then the client is asked to visualize the next item on the hierarchy. Wolpe (1960) maintained that two to four items could be presented per counseling session and that it usually took between 10 and 30 sessions to get to the highest items on the hierarchy without disturbance.

JaNelle decides that systematic desensitization would be ideal for Shirley's anxiety episodes connected with her stealing behavior. She explains the procedure to Shirley, and they work on Shirley's anxiety hierarchy. As expected, Shirley's most feared image is of being in a store by herself. This scene she rates as a 100. The remainder of Shirley's hierarchy is shown in Figure 8.1.

---

100 Standing in a store by herself
95 Walking through the door of the store
90 Getting off the bus near the store
80 Riding the bus to the store
75 Getting on the bus to go to the store
65 Walking to the bus stop
55 Leaving her apartment to go the store
50 Looking at an item she has stolen
40 Telling someone she is going to the store
30 Thinking about going to a store

FIGURE 8.1. Shirley's hierarchy of anxiety.

JaNelle begins the procedure in the next session, asking Shirley to relax and taking her through a progressive relaxation sequence. She then asks Shirley to imagine being in her apartment and thinking about going to a store. Immediately, Shirley's finger shoots up, and JaNelle asks her to again relax and to "wipe the picture out of your mind." JaNelle presents the image repeatedly until Shirley no longer indicates anxiety, and then progresses to the next item in the hierarchy.

AVERSIVE TECHNIQUES

Aversive techniques are considered a last resort in BT (Wolpe, 1990). Sometimes called *aversive counterconditioning*, these techniques consist of pairing some noxious stimulus with an unwanted emotional reaction. The most commonly used aversive stimuli are electric shock or nausea-inducing drugs.

As you might guess, these techniques have been the subject of controversy. One "problem" to which these techniques were applied was homosexuality. In the 1960s, there was a flurry of interest in changing sexual orientation, and many times this was approached by showing clients same-sex erotic stimuli (e.g., photographs) while administering shock. The shock was terminated when heterosexual erotic materials were presented (Haldeman, 1994). Of course, the ethics of such treatment were eventually questioned, even when used with men who voluntarily sought such treatment. The ethical issues, arguments about whether these techniques really produced aversion, and lack of support for their effectiveness resulted in their abandonment in the 1970s (Haldeman, 1994; LoPiccolo, 1990).

Aversive techniques have also been employed to treat alcoholism (Wilson, 1987). Mostly, these approaches have used nausea-inducing drugs, although shock has also been used. Concerns about the usefulness of these interventions beyond traditional interventions for problem drinking have also been raised (Wilson, 1987).

One problem that seems to justify aversive techniques is self-injurious behavior (SIB). Often seen in developmentally disabled individuals, these individuals often place their lives in danger by banging their heads or performing other dangerous behaviors. A pad is attached to the client's arm or leg, and shock is delivered upon the occurrence of an unwanted behavior. A detailed review of the necessity for such procedures, often by government regulatory committees, is typically required to begin such a program (e.g., Nord, Wieseler, & Hanson, 1991).

JaNelle does not think that aversive techniques are advised in Shirley's case. After all, they are techniques of last resort, and Shirley is a reluctant client.

"BLOW-UP" TECHNIQUE OR PARADOXICAL INTENTION

Lazarus (1996) described the blow-up technique, in which clients are encouraged to actively practice, and even elaborate on, their symptoms. Lazarus described the technique as particularly helpful for clients who are plagued by obsessive thoughts. The client would be encouraged to dwell on the thoughts and images, taking them to their most disastrous conclusion, much as in implosive therapy. I infer that the behaviorist rationale behind these techniques is to disconnect the problematic behavior from its discriminative stimulus.

Frankl (1963) also advocated prescribing the symptom, which he called *paradoxical intention*. Emphasizing the humorous element of the approach, Frankl would encourage his clients to be the world's best at their symptoms!

JaNelle considers the use of a modified paradoxical technique with Shirley. She could have Shirley study how to become a better shoplifter. Shirley could go to stores and watch for other shoplifters and see how they perform. She could also write her findings down, creating a manual about how to be a better shoplifter. If she were able to go to the store and look for other shoplifters rather than getting anxious and stealing, Shirley might find that her anxiety decreases. JaNelle could accompany her on these outings. Shirley might also be engaged by the humorous bent of JaNelle's prescriptions, thus reducing some of the anxiety around the behaviors. Another application of this technique would be to have Shirley imagine the worst possible outcome of her stealing behavior—being taken off to jail, tried in court, and placed in prison.

SHAPING

The process of teaching a new behavior is called shaping. First, the BT counselor gets the client to respond in some way, usually by using verbal prompts. Modeling can also be used in this stage. The therapist can demonstrate the behavior, or the client could watch a videotape. After the initial response is established, the therapist will reinforce only responses that move a step closer to the desired response (Sherman, 1974).

Shaping could be used to address Shirley's social skills deficits, JaNelle thinks. She plans to model eye contact and appropriate voice tone for Shirley and then praise her when she attempts these behaviors. At first, Shirley's attempts will be tentative, but JaNelle will reinforce them and coach Shirley to improve them. She will then reinforce Shirley's improved behaviors.

REINFORCEMENT

The BT counselor can use positive and negative reinforcement to increase the occurrence of a desired behavior. For instance, praising the client for completing an assigned homework activity would tend to increase the probability of homework getting done. Negative reinforcement is probably used less often because it is difficult to find a situation in which a negative stimulus could be discontinued on the appearance of a desired behavior. An important source of reinforcement in BT is the counselor's verbal responses to her, which Beach (2005) calls *verbal conditioning*. He opines that the therapist must be alert in the counseling situation to the kind of verbal behavior she is reinforcing—for instance differentially reinforcing verbalizations about problems (by "uh hming" every time the client speaks of these and not responding to nonproblematic or successful behavior) might make the client's situation worse (Beach, 2005).

Often, clients are taught to self-reinforce. If the client, for example, went to the gym and worked out, she would reward herself with a hot bath or a low-fat ice cream sundae.

Another example of self-reinforcement is seen in stress inoculation training (Meichenbaum, 1977). Clients are taught to use coping cognitions in stressful situations and then to self-reinforce their successful use through covert verbal statements ("Hey, I did a great job getting through that!").

JaNelle thinks that positive reinforcement would be a good technique to use with Shirley. She praises Shirley for coming to counseling and reinforces Shirley's discussions of her life with attention and head nods. JaNelle will use positive reinforcement to teach Shirley assertive skills and will reinforce her for completing homework assignments. She will also use positive reinforcement when Shirley survives an in vivo experience in a store.

DIFFERENTIAL REINFORCEMENT

This technique, sometimes called *differential reinforcement of other* behavior (DRO), consists of reinforcing one behavior (a desired one) and subjecting an undesired behavior to extinction at the same time (Milan, 1990). Any behavior other than the target response can be reinforced during a specified time interval, or a response incompatible to the undesirable behavior is reinforced (Nemeroll & Karoly, 1991). For instance, if Mother wants Hillary to watch less TV, she could reinforce Hillary for reading a book or playing outside of the home or almost any behavior other than watching TV.

JaNelle is not quite sure about how to use DRO with Shirley. She supposes that she could go to a store with Shirley and reinforce her for walking through the store without stopping. She could also reinforce her for talking to a salesperson.

EXTINCTION

Extinction involves removing a reinforcement that is maintaining a behavior. A very common example is when parental attention is reinforcing a child's tantrum behavior. The parent simply does not respond to the tantrum. When using extinction procedures in isolation, it is important to be sure one can tolerate the possible intensification in the target behavior that might result when the intervention is first implemented (Sherman, 1973). For the parent tolerating a tantrum, this can be a very stressful experience, you can guess!

For Shirley, applying extinction to her stealing behavior would mean virtually the same thing as in vivo exposure, because JaNelle thinks that the stealing is partly maintained by the anxiety reduction Shirley experiences. However, operant extinction would require that Shirley perform a very difficult behavior—picking up an item in the store and not leaving the store.

Punishment

Punishment, remember, is when the consequences of an event are linked to a decrease in or disappearance of the behavior. For the purposes of intervention, two kinds of punishment can be identified (Milan, 1990; Skinner, 1953). First, and most familiar to us, an aversive event can be applied following the undesirable behavior, which is sometimes called punishment by *contingent stimulation* (Milan, 1990). Spanking a kid falls under this category.

A second kind of punishment results when a desirable set of conditions is terminated when an unwanted behavior occurs. For instance, Dad can turn off Liza's favorite television show if she is slapping her little brother. Because this kind of punishment can be seen as the termination of a positive reinforcer, it is referred to as *punishment by contingent withdrawal* (Milan, 1990). A similar procedure is *response cost*, in which an individual is required to surrender something reinforcing, such as when you pay a fine at the bank for bouncing a check.

Time out from reinforcement is another form of punishment, in which positive reinforcers are removed for a specified period of time. A familiar example of this procedure is seen in classrooms, when a child displaying disruptive behavior is removed to a time-out room. The critical element is that all sources of reinforcement are unavailable to the child (Kazdin, 2001). Usually, the access to reinforcers is only removed for a short period of time (e.g., a minute or two) because longer intervals do not increase the effectiveness of the time-out intervention (Kazdin, 2001).

Punishment as a behavior change technique has drawbacks. First, because punishment only suppresses behavior, such behavior is likely to reappear when the contingencies are no longer in effect (Skinner, 1971). Also, humans are motivated to escape or avoid aversive conditions, so punishment can create these behaviors; the best way to avoid punishment is to avoid the punisher. Punishment can also result in aversive emotional states, such as shame, anger, frustration, anxiety, or depression (Milan, 1990). Individuals may resort to dysfunctional behaviors to avoid these aversive states, such as refusing to think about the punished behaviors (e.g., "repression") or engaging in risky behaviors such as drinking alcohol or doing drugs to blunt these feelings (Milan, 1990). Finally, these negative feelings may become associated with the agents of punishment, such as parents, school, or law enforcement officials (Kazdin, 2001). Consider also that using punishment models the use of aggressive behavior. For these reasons, punishment should be a last resort and used very carefully (Kazdin, 2001).

If punishment must be used, it should be immediate to the undesired behavior. A consistent, continuous schedule is most effective, rather than intermittent punishment (Kazdin, 2001).

JaNelle doubts that punishment would work for Shirley's stealing behavior, unless Shirley would agree to self-punish. In a sense, she already does that by making herself feel guilty and ashamed after she steals, and this has not been effective in deterring her behavior. Getting arrested can be seen as a punishment, but not one that is likely to happen every time, making it an ineffective punisher.

Assertiveness Training

In Wolpe's view, assertive behaviors are called for when the client is experiencing dysfunctional anxiety in interpersonal situations. Assertive behavior is defined as "socially appropriate verbal and motor expression of any emotion other than anxiety" (Wolpe, 1990, p. 135). Wolpe thought that anxiety got (classically) conditioned to social responding, and through reciprocal inhibition, assertive responding should compete with the anxiety and weaken the conditioning. Assertiveness training involves teaching the client to express the resentment that she experiences in interpersonal relationships because anger, for example, is thought to inhibit the expression of anxiety (Wolpe, 1960).

Other BT theorists would probably take an operant (i.e., skills deficit) view in using this technique. The assertive behavior is modeled for the client, or she could be verbally prompted to perform the behavior. The behavior therapist then shapes the client's behavior, reinforcing better and better assertiveness responses. Primarily, the behavior therapist could use praise as the reinforcer, unless she was working with a child, in which case other kinds of reinforcers might work (such as candy).

Assertiveness training is perfect for Shirley. JaNelle will teach her to make eye contact, speak with more volume, and ask for things she wants. For example, JaNelle will help Shirley practice asking a fellow volunteer to go out to a movie or dinner with her.

STIMULUS CONTROL

Many behaviors are under the control of a set of stimuli. As noted earlier, these stimuli are termed discriminative stimuli. The most commonly used examples of these types of behavior are cigarette smoking and eating. People who smoke tend to have specific triggers for smoking behavior, such as finishing a big meal. If you eat popcorn in bed at night, just getting in bed may cause you to feel an urge to eat. In fact, it is thought that overweight individuals often eat in response to cues in the environment rather than in response to hunger.

Once the discriminative stimuli associated with a behavior have been clearly specified (and there usually are more than one), the environment can be manipulated to either produce, increase, or reduce the behavior. Typically, the behavior therapist teaches the client how this process works and helps the clients to identify discriminative stimuli or the lack thereof (Kazdin, 2001). The client is then charged with putting the program into place. Sometimes, the BT counselor would even help the client make the desired changes in the environment.

If a stimulus is controlling an unwanted behavior, the client is usually urged to avoid the stimulus at first. A gradual approach to the stimulus is then developed so that the client can resist performing the behavior (Kazdin, 2001). In other cases, the client might need to associate a behavior with one or more stimuli to get it under control. For example, if Julie has a problem with eating too much too often, it might be helpful for her to limit eating only to full meals at a set table. She would not be allowed to eat while watching television or in any other location.

JaNelle decides that Shirley's stealing behavior is cued by the stimulus of a department store. Shirley reports that she rarely steals at the grocery store, or in other kinds of stores. JaNelle decides that to extinguish the association between store and stealing, Shirley will avoid the department store for a while. She is assigned the task of going to the grocery store once a day for a week. The first day she is to only walk into the store and immediately walk out. The second day she is to walk down one aisle and then out of the store. After each of these forays, she is to positively reinforce herself in some way. A gradual progression in the amount of time she spends in the grocery store is prescribed until she reports no anxiety or impulses to steal. JaNelle then transfers this program to the department store.

COVERT CONDITIONING

Covert conditioning procedures employ imagery in the service of changing behavior. The term *covert* is used because the client imagines rather than really experiences the behavior to be changed, along with the consequences of maintaining it (Cautela, 1994). In addition, the manipulation of consequences to change the imagined behavior is covert.

Cautela (1994, p. 3) identified a number of covert conditioning procedures that can be used (e.g., sensitization, extinction, covert positive reinforcement, covert negative reinforcement, response cost); most of these are simply applications of BT techniques using imagery.

The *self-control triad* or procedure is a more complex intervention consisting of three steps. First, the client mentally shouts "stop" when a target behavior occurs. She then takes a deep breath, exhales, and relaxes (Step 2). Step 3 is to imagine a pleasant scene, which is seen as aiding the relaxation and also as self-reinforcement (Kearney, 1994).

A general outline of covert conditioning is as follows (Cautela, 1994): The client's ability to image is checked; if necessary, imagery exercises are assigned. The client is then asked to imagine the scene of the target behavior. In the case of covert positive reinforcement, for instance, the client is asked to imagine successful behavior. Once this scene is clear to the client (she indicates by some signal, such as raising a finger), the counselor instructs the client to imagine a pleasant scene (the reinforcer). This sequence is repeated a number of times in the session, and it is also assigned as homework, using a specially prepared audiotape.

Covert conditioning could be used to extinguish Shirley's anxiety associated with department stores through using covert desensitization. JaNelle would guide Shirley through an imaginary sequence of going into the store, staying there while the anxiety becomes intense, and then leaving the store without taking anything. Reinforcement could also be added; after Shirley imagines a successful trip to the store, she would imagine a pleasant scene.

MODELING

Modeling is a flexible technique that often is combined with other kinds of interventions. The most basic form of modeling is simple observation, in which the client watches a model perform a target behavior (Rosenthal & Steffek, 1991). The model will typically progress through harder and harder tasks. For example, if a client is afraid of heights, she might observe a model standing on a step-stool and so on, until the model is looking over the balcony rail of a 20-story hotel.

Another version of modeling is participant guidance (Rosenthal & Steffek, 1991). In this approach, the client actually practices the target behavior after the model has demonstrated it. The model coaches the client through successively more difficult behaviors.

The counselor often serves as a model for the client, demonstrating problem solving or social skills. In assertiveness training, for example, the counselor might first model assertive skills for a client in a role-play.

JaNelle uses modeling to help Shirley learn new social skills. She demonstrates appropriate vocal tone and eye contact, and then asks Shirley to practice these in the counseling session. Together, JaNelle and Shirley identify situations in which Shirley might have behavioral deficits and then generate new responses for Shirley. JaNelle first models these behaviors, and then Shirley tries them out for herself.

JaNelle considers using modeling as an initial step in desensitizing Shirley to department stores. She could videotape a model entering a store, choosing an item to buy, purchasing it, and then leaving the store. Shirley could watch the videotape between counseling sessions until she could do so without experiencing anxiety.

BEHAVIORAL SELF-CONTROL

Not really a specific technique, behavioral self-control refers to teaching the client to apply behavioral techniques to herself. Kanfer and Karoly (1972) pointed out that in using this approach, the client must really commit to the process and her designated goals. They specified factors that promote "intention statement making" (p. 411; e.g., these statements are more likely when the client is experiencing the negative effects of behavior or when positive reinforcement is available) and those that decrease the likelihood of these statements (e.g., when the person is likely to receive punishment for making the statements or the probability of punishment is high for failure).

Almost any of the behavioral techniques described earlier can be used in a behavioral self-control model. You might remember the television ad campaign in which the celebrity model (Larry Hagman) snapped a rubber band around his wrist when he experienced the urge for a cigarette. This is an example of an aversive self-control procedures (based either in aversive counterconditioning or punishment). A few other examples of ways in which the behavioral self-control approach is used include teaching the client stimulus control procedures.

In cognitive behavior approaches, therapists teach clients coping cognitions to use while in the midst of the flooding experiences. The client first rehearses these statements, uses these statements out loud, and then fades to private rehearsal of the thoughts (Meichenbaum, 1977).

EVALUATION OF THE THEORY

Behavior Therapy has evoked a great deal of controversy over the years, comparable to that associated with psychoanalytic theory. Behavior therapists have been accused of being cold-hearted because of their scientific approach and language (Goldfried & Davison, 1994). The emphasis on prediction and control of behavior has led to accusations that Behavior Therapy denies the rights and freedom of clients (Franks & Barbrack, 1990), and that it ignores the importance of emotion in human behavior. As Sweet (1984) put it, "Behavior Therapy is viewed as the cold and mechanical application of techniques, previously tested on sub-human species, and often delivered in a dangerous and impersonal fashion" (p. 254).

Behavioral approaches are seen as simplistic and fit for interventions for discrete, narrowly defined problems, such as phobias. The first applications of Behavior Therapy were with extremely dysfunctional clients (e.g., mentally challenged or psychotic), so its utility for a wider range of clients was questioned (Franks & Barbrack, 1990).

BT is criticized for its emphasis on observable behavior at the expense of thought and feeling. However, as we have seen, most behavior therapists today attend to cognition and other inferred events as important aspects of human behavior (Goldfried & Davison, 1994). Neglect of the client's past is also cited as a weakness of behavioral approaches, to which the behaviorists would retort that reinforcement (learning) histories are very important in understanding the client's current presentation.

Behavior therapists are also said to ignore the role of interpersonal relationships in the generation and maintenance of psychological dysfunction (Marshall & Gauthier, 1983). For example, Marshall and Gauthier (1983) suggested that failures in BT procedures could result when improvement results in decreased dependence of the client on family members or other significant others.

QUALITIES OF THE THEORY

Precision and Testability. BT theorists maintain that theirs is the most scientific approach, because it is rooted in "established principles and paradigms of learning" (Wolpe, 1997, p. 633). Certainly, it is very precise to count behaviors following the institution of a reinforcer and observe changes from baseline rates of behavior. If one is studying nodding behavior, clearly this behavior can be operationalized fairly easily. The complex behaviors involved in client presentations and in the counseling process, however, are not as easily specified and targeted.

Arguments abound about the exact definition of some BT terms, such as *reinforcement.* Some critics assert that the definition of reinforcement is circular: What is a reinforcement? Something that makes behavior increase. Why did that behavior increase? Because it was reinforced. The classical conditioning model has also been criticized, particularly by advocates of social learning theory (Bandura, 1969). They maintain that the effects of classical conditioning procedures are simply that the person builds a mental image that affects her behaviors rather than establishing a relatively permanent conditioned reflex. Still other authors note that attempts to tie BT techniques to the principles of learning from experimental laboratory study are fruitless and that these very principles (e.g., reinforcement) are questionable as explanations for *learning* even though they can at times predict *performance* (Breger & McGaugh, 1973; Jacobson, 1997).

Empirical Validity. Overall, BT has received support from outcome research. It is important to note, though, that many studies test cognitive Behavior Theory (in a multitude of forms) rather than pure BT (if such a thing really exists). As I noted earlier, the validity of the theoretical bases of BT is much less clear.

RESEARCH SUPPORT

Outcome Research. The literature on the efficacy of BT is enormous (Emmelkamp, 2004). Numerous outcome studies have supported the efficacy of BT, although the evidence to support the claims for the superiority of the approach over others is not as robust. I shall review a few meta-analyses and then several studies that provide examples of research testing BT. However, because of the sheer amount of research relevant to BT, it is impossible to provide a comprehensive summary.

Butler, Chapman, Forman, and Beck (2006) reviewed 16 meta-analyses on outcome studies of cognitive-behavioral therapy (CBT). They found that CBT was effective over a wide range of dysfunction and that BT was as effective as CBT in the treatment of adults who were depressed or displaying signs of obsession and compulsion. Earlier, simple meta-analyses had found similar results, beginning with Smith and Glass (1977) who suggested a slight superiority for behavioral and cognitive behavioral approaches. However, these effects tend to disappear when methodological variables are controlled (Smith, Glass, & Miller, 1980). These methodological issues involve the reactivity of the measures used—how responsive the outcome measures are to the demands of the experimental situation (Lambert & Ogles, 2004). Behaviorally oriented studies generally use measures that are more susceptible to these influences. Also, when allegiance effects are controlled (i.e., the theoretical allegiance of the study's authors), differences between approaches tend to disappear (Wampold, 2001). In another meta-analysis, Shapiro and Shapiro (1982) found evidence that cognitive therapy was superior to systematic desensitization. However, later meta-analyses found no differences between the approaches, and the data suggest that the effects can be accounted for by researcher allegiance (Berman, Miller, & Massman, 1985; Miller & Berman, 1983; Robinson, Berman, & Neimeyer, 1990). In a more recent meta-analysis of 277 treatment comparisons, Wampold and colleagues (1997) specifically tested for variations in efficacy among theoretical orientations and also found no significant differences.

For those who argue that meta-analysis is comparing apples and oranges, exemplar studies can be informative. As early as 1975, the Temple Study (Sloane, Staples, Criston, Yorkston, Whipple, 1975) reported no differences in efficacy between BT and psychoanalytically oriented therapy, but both produced more improvement than a wait-list control group. More fully described in Chapter 1, this study is still considered to be one of the most methodologically sound in the psychotherapy outcome literature (Lambert & Bergin, 1994). The NIMH Collaborative Treatment of Depression study compared cognitive-behavior therapy (Beck's approach; see Chapter 10), interpersonal psychotherapy, placebo-clinical management, and psychopharmacological treatment with clinical management and found no differences in outcomes across the four conditions (Elkin et al., 1989).

BT has been shown to be effective with a wide range of client problems. Exposure therapy has loads of empirical support (Emmelkamp, 2004). For example, Rothbaum et al. (2006) described an interesting study comparing the use of virtual reality exposure (VE), traditional in-vivo exposure and a control treatment for fear of flying. They found that VE and traditional exposure produced similar good results—76% of the clients in these treatments agreed to go on a posttreatment flight compared to 20% of control participants. Other examples of the success of exposure therapy can be readily found in the literature.

Other research has tested the effectiveness of BT and CBT (cognitive-behavior therapy) with other symptom constellations and have found positive results. Emmelkamp (2004) reports that the literature supports the use of BT for anxiety disorders and depression. However, he notes that interventions for sexual dysfunction have been little studied in the last decade and that there are doubts about the effectiveness of BT interventions in this sphere.

A recent meta-analysis of studies of substance use disorders (e.g., drugs, alchohol, and tobacco) demonstrated that contingency management procedures (the general term for manipulating reinforcers and punishers) produced positive results (Prendergast, Podus, Finney, Greenwell, & Roll, 2006). Benton and Schroeder (1990) presented a meta-analysis of 27 studies that assessed the effects of social skills training with schizophrenic clients. They found strong evidence for improvement on what they called behavioral indexes (such as self-rated assertiveness and discharge rates) and moderate effects for relapse rates. Similarly, Zimmerman, Favrod, Trieu, and Pomini (2004) used a meta-analytic technique and determined that CBT interventions were useful as adjuncts to psychotropic medications in reducing hallucinations and delusions among clients diagnosed as schizophrenic.

Theory-Testing Research. Discussing the role of theory in BT is difficult because BT is not a theory per se; it is more a collection of techniques said to be based on theories of learning. If you consider only research testing behavioral interventions (rather than that testing basic learning theory), it is difficult to separate theory-testing research from outcome research. Most investigations are focused on the effects of a given technique on the incidence of a target behavior. Very few attempt to test the assumed mechanisms underlying the technique (this evidence is assumed based on the original, nonclinical research). Although outcome research could be cited as indirect support for the model of learning underlying the technique, it is clearly indirect, at best.

As I noted earlier, the theoretical formulations of BT as models of learning has been questioned (Breger & McGaugh, 1973). For example, some discussion has centered on Wolpe's reciprocal inhibition explanation for the effects of systematic desensitization (1990). Recall that Wolpe thought that pairing an incompatible state (e.g., relaxation) with the undesirable one (e.g., anxiety) would cause deconditioning. Because research seems to show that relaxation is not necessary, Wolpe's causal scheme is undermined (Emmelkamp, 1990). Similarly, studies of flooding indicate that low levels of anxiety are as effective as high levels of anxiety in producing extinction, which is contrary to conditioning theory, which would predict that the high levels of anxiety are necessary. Finally, Steketee and Cleere (1990) maintained that there was not good support for the acquisition of anxiety-related dysfunction via the pairing of a neutral object with a stimulus that naturally evokes fear. However, the fact that exposure and response prevention seem to help when fear avoidance responses are present would seem to support a hypothesis that these behaviors are maintained by avoidance conditioning.

Wadden and Bell (1990) concluded that there is virtually no empirical support for a behavioral model of obesity. For example, one prediction of the behavioral model of obesity is that obese people are more responsive to environmental cues for eating (discriminative stimuli) than are nonobese individuals. This hypothesis led to the institution of stimulus control programs for weight reduction. However, Wadden and Bell maintained that there is no solid evidence that obese individuals are more sensitive than nonobese individuals to external cues. At the same time, BT for obesity has been shown to produce clinically significant weight loss (Wadden & Bell, 1990).

Dismantling studies, in which BT techniques are broken down into component parts and administered separately or in combination, are one attempt to answer the question about the specific effects of BT techniques. Clear answers to the specific effects question might be seen as evidence of the validity of BT theory; however, they do not constitute direct tests of theoretical predictions.

Some BT researchers would point to single-subject intensive case studies as providing evidence for the theoretical underpinnings of BT. Historically, these designs have been used quite often in BT studies. A baseline is established on a target behavior, an intervention is made (e.g., instituting reinforcement or extinction), and then the intervention is withdrawn. Changes in behavior with the presentation and withdrawal of the intervention are thought to be evidence of the validity of behavioral techniques. Again, these types of study can demonstrate relationships between interventions and performance of a given behavior, but they provide little evidence for the theoretical foundations of BT.

ISSUES OF INDIVIDUAL AND CULTURAL DIVERSITY

Hoffman (2006) notes that because culture shapes our perceptions of the environment and how we seek to understand it, it will surely influence how clients respond to cognitive and Behavior Therapy. Several characteristics of BT make it an attractive approach to use with clients from diverse backgrounds. First, the structure inherent in BT would appeal to clients from Asian backgrounds, as would the relative de-emphasis on expression of emotion (Sue & Sue, 2003). In addition, African American clients might respond positively to the collaborative nature of the therapeutic relationship once they have established that the counselor is trustworthy. However, clients from Asian or Hispanic/Latino backgrounds may expect a more formal approach from the counselor because of the emphasis on hierarchy found in these cultures. The concrete and immediate nature of the BT approach would fit well for American Indians and Alaskan Natives because they tend to be present oriented (Sue & Sue, 2003). On the other hand, the future orientation implicit in the BT emphasis on goal setting could create discomfort.

Spiegler and Guevremont (2003) discuss issues of diversity relative to BT and maintain that its emphasis on the role of the environment in problematic behavior is particularly suitable to clients who are of diverse backgrounds. Interventions are specifically designed for individual clients and can be tailored to fit the client's background and current circumstances.

Chambless (1986) maintained that African American clients would respond more positively to Behavior Therapy's active, directive, and problem-focused approach (p. 7) than they would to traditional, more passive approaches to counseling. She argued that BT avoids the pitfall of many counseling approaches that blame the victim for psychological problems, presumably because in BT, causal factors are located in the environment. For clients who are members of traditionally oppressed groups, such as African Americans, Latinos/Latinas, or Asians, this approach may be a relief.

Some aspects of Behavior Therapy are compatible with feminist values. Initially, feminists reacted positively to the behavioral principle that learning is a function of environmental factors, seeing this as a departure from traditional approaches that blame the individual for his or her problems (Kantrowitz & Ballou, 1992; Worell & Remer, 2003). Behavior Therapy's emphasis on self-help and encouraging client self-direction are consistent with feminist philosophy (Hunter & Kelso, 1985). An emphasis on skills development and Behavior Therapy's goal of giving the client more control over the environment is consistent with feminist ideology.

At the same time, the behaviorists can be criticized for ignoring the sociopolitical context of their clients' lives. Kantrowitz and Ballou (1992) argued that defining health as behavior that is adaptive is problematic. Who decides what is adaptive? They maintained that the norms of the dominant social group (i.e., white males) define adaptiveness, which is an unfair, biased standard, particularly for women and other historically oppressed groups. The broader issue underlying the controversy about definitions of health is probably control—that is, is it OK for a behavior therapist to "engineer" changes in clients' behavior without taking serious note of social or cultural forces that are very powerful (Ivey, D'Andrea, Ivey, & Simek-Morgan, 2002)? Clients who are facing prejudice and discrimination would likely feel misunderstood if these issues were not addressed as part of the counseling process. Further, BT's emphasis on a rational, scientific approach to human behavior is a reflection of White, male, European values, which are not appropriate for women and members of other ethnic or cultural groups (Kantrowitz & Ballou, 1992).

Hunter and Kelso (1985) noted that in a review of 100 articles in which Behavior Therapy was used with female clients, many goals were addressed (weight loss, depression, sexual problems, etc.), yet very little attention was paid to the social environment of the clients. Thus, feminists urge behavior therapists to take a social learning perspective with their clients, studying and respecting the social roles that constrain women. Reinforcers within the client's culture that could be damaging (i.e., those that support submissive, self-deprecating behavior) should also be addressed (Hunter & Kelso, 1985).

Collins and McNair (1986) pointed out that although Behavior Therapy emphasizes the environmental determinants of behavior, interventions most often target individual behavior. This bias can be seen as supporting the oppressive forces in society that affect women and individuals from non-Caucasian cultures, lower socioeconomic status, and of diverse sexual orientations and ablener. They specifically point to the use of skills-training interventions with women and argue that treating the woman rather than the culture reinforces traditional sex-role behavior, such as when parent training focuses primarily on the roles of mothers and children. Further, Collins and McNair suggested that the more active coping strategies of minority women could be deemed maladaptive by therapists who endorse traditional sex-role stereotypes. However, others argue that recent versions of behaviorism are much more attuned to environmental aspects of client presentations than were earlier versions (Spiegleman & Guevremont, 2003).

In the late 1960s BT as a profession supported the use of conditioning procedures to change the sexual orientations of homosexuals (Glass & Arnkoff, 1992). However, in 1974, the president of AABT, Gerald Davidson, declared in his presidential address that it was unethical to continue these attempts (Davidson, 1976). According to Glass and Arnkoff (1992), Davidson's plea was one of several that prompted the elimination of homosexuality as a diagnostic category in the *Diagnostic and Statistical Manual of the American Psychiatric Association.*

THE CASE STUDY

The story of Shirley is, in many ways, an ideal fit for the BT approach. Her primary problem behavior, the shoplifting, is fairly specific, and BT approaches are easily applied. It is less clear that BT approaches will directly affect Shirley's loneliness, although it does seem to make some sense that increasing Shirley's social contacts would help to some degree with this problem. However, if Shirley's loneliness is associated with feelings that are not addressed by increased social contacts, such as mourning, this approach might be less useful.

Summary

BT counseling rests on a psychological model that emphasizes the learned nature of behaviors, whether they be adaptive or maladaptive. Three general models of learning are identified (classical, operant, and social learning), although the validity of these models and their direct connections to some techniques can be questioned. A variety of techniques are associated with BT, and most have been found to be effective.

BT counseling has been the target of criticism and controversy. The traditional approach to BT emphasizes behaviors and their environmental rather than personal determinants. This emphasis, less common today, may lead to less attention to emotional and cognitive factors in behavior.

In some ways, BT seems to be an approach that is applicable to a range of clients, if carefully applied. Some client groups may respond favorably to the problem-focused, direct techniques used in BT. However, BT's lack of attention to societal norms that influence behavior in ways that discriminate against some groups is a potential pitfall associated with this approach.

Visit Chapter 8 on the Companion Website at **www.prenhall.com/murdock** for chapter-specific resources and self-assessments.

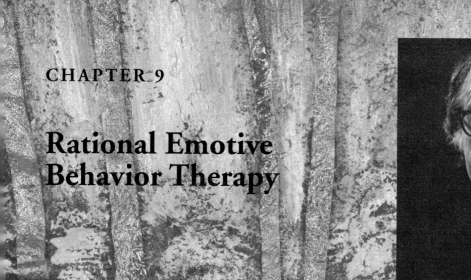

CHAPTER 9

Rational Emotive Behavior Therapy

Albert Ellis

Alan is a 27-year-old Caucasian male. He works in a warehouse managing workers who move stock. Alan is married to Teresa, an Asian woman who is 30 years old. The only child of devout Catholic parents, Alan is a committed Catholic, as is Teresa. Teresa and Alan are active in their church, and most of their social activity is church related. Alan's parents live in another city 2 hours away, and Teresa's live on the West Coast. The couple has no children.

Alan comes to counseling because he is anxiety ridden and showing some repetitive, anxiety-driven behavior. He reports that when he leaves a room in his home, he has to return several times to be certain that he has turned off the lights. Sometimes he flips the light switch; other times he just looks at it. Alan is also troubled by the worry that he has run over someone with his car on his way home from work and frequently gets back in his car and retraces his route to make sure he has not. Most troubling to Alan is disturbing mental imagery of a religious nature that he believes he cannot control. Alan is hesitant to describe these images, but he says they involve the Virgin Mary and sexual content.

Alan reports that he has had variants of these symptoms for at least 5 years. He recalls being almost immobilized by his fears shortly before he and Teresa married. Alan went to counseling at that time and found some relief from his symptoms but says that his anxiety was still bothersome. Since that time, Alan has experienced brief periods of compulsive behavior, but of the least disturbing kind, such as checking the light switches. He became more concerned when the religious images began about a month ago, along with the worries about hitting someone with his car.

When he comes to counseling, Alan appears uncomfortable and nervous. He speaks quickly and softly and seems motivated, but is at a loss about what to do about his symptoms.

BACKGROUND

The colorful and flamboyant Albert Ellis (1913–2007) thought up Rational Emotive Behavior Therapy (REBT). Ellis, a sex therapist who retrained as a psychoanalyst, freely admits that he developed his theory out of his frustration with the passive, slow methods of psychoanalysis (Ellis, 1994a). He also acknowledges that REBT is a product of the "personal anti-neurosis campaign" of his youth (Ellis, 1997a, p. 76; see Box 9.1). I shall begin this chapter with a quote that will give you a good flavor of Ellis: recently, he wrote:

> "Why did I (really) become a psychotherapist? In a word, because I primarily wanted to help myself become a much less anxious and happier individual. Oh, yes, I wanted to help other people, too, and I wanted to help the world be a better place, with healthier and happier people who fought like hell to create better, better conditions. But I *really* and *primarily* wanted to help me, me, me! (2004, p. 73; italics in the original)

REBT was first known as rational therapy. In 1961 Ellis renamed his theory Rational Emotive Therapy to emphasize the emotional elements of the approach (Ellis, 1994a). The *B* was added in 1991 to acknowledge the behavioral element that Ellis maintains has always been crucial to RET but had not been widely recognized. Using the term *rational*, Ellis said, was a mistake because *rational* implies an absolute criterion and no such criterion exists (Ellis, 1999c). If

---

Box 9.1

REBT Therapist Heal Thyself!

Young Al Ellis had a fear of girls. When he was 19, he decided to do something about it. He had already conquered his fear of public speaking—in his own words, "Shit, I said to myself. If in vivo desensitization is good enough for little children, it's good enough for me. I'll try it with my terror of public speaking. If I fail, I fail. If I die of discomfort, I die! Too damned bad!" (Ellis, 1997a, p. 71). With this experiment, the technique now known as shame attacking was born . . . and was found to be successful.

Ellis then decided to apply this technique to his girl phobia. He lived, at the time, near the Bronx Botanical Gardens and frequented this beautiful park often but flirted with girls only in fantasy. Telling himself "do, don't stew" (p. 72), Ellis assigned himself the homework to go to the gardens every day in July, find women sitting alone on benches, sit down beside them, and talk—for one whole minute! Ellis carried out his assignment with 130 women that month, and to his great surprise, not one screamed, threw up, or called the police. Ever the scientist, Ellis reported that "30 of them waltzed away. They rejected me before I even got going! But, I said to myself, strongly, 'that's okay. That leaves me a sample of an even hundred—good for research purposes!' " (p. 72).

Of the first hundred, Ellis managed to make one date, but then she didn't show up. Ellis persisted and reported that of the second hundred women he talked to, he got three dates. He claims that this first expedition into REBT was entirely successful, so that forevermore, he can talk to women any place, any time.

he had to name the theory today, Ellis would call the approach cognitive-emotive-Behavior Therapy, except that cognitive therapy and cognitive-Behavior Therapy got there first.

Albert Ellis was born in Pittsburgh, Pennsylvania, in 1913, the oldest of three children. He was raised in New York City. Ellis's early childhood experience was characterized by "benign neglect"; his father was a salesperson who traveled a good deal, and his mother seemed uninterested in parenting (Yankura & Dryden, 1994, p. 2). His parents divorced when Ellis was 12. After that, his father was rarely seen and did not support the family financially.

Ellis experienced a number of physical maladies in his early years that required periods of hospitalization and reduced activity during convalescent periods at home (Yankura & Dryden, 1994). At age 12, Ellis launched his writing career, and around age 16, he began devouring books and articles about philosophy and psychology, which set the stage for the development of his theory.

As a child and young adult, Ellis was shy and socially avoidant. Ellis's voracious reading habits served him well when at the age of 19 he decided to overcome his fear of public speaking (Ellis, 1997a). He had read the early works of several behaviorists who advocated in vivo desensitization (Mary Cover Jones and John Watson; see Chapter 8) and assigned himself the task of giving many public speeches. Ellis found, to his surprise, that he actually began to enjoy public speaking (Ellis, 1997a). Subsequently, he applied this desensitization technique to his anxiety about relating to women (see Box 9.1).

After receiving his bachelor's degree in business administration, Ellis went to work at a succession of jobs, planning to support himself with these while becoming a professional writer. He wrote voluminously during this time, but had little success getting published. At the same time, he was extensively reading and studying many resources on sex to produce his manuscript *The Case for Sexual Promiscuity* (Yankura & Dryden, 1994). He became somewhat of an authority on sex among his friends and associates, and even started a small consulting practice (Blau, 1998). At the age of 28, Ellis entered Columbia University, training as a marriage, family, and sex therapist, eventually earning his master's and Ph.D. degrees in clinical psychology.

Working in his first job, Ellis increasingly became aware of the weaknesses of the authoritative, advice-giving approach he was taught in graduate school. Ellis embarked on a course of traditional psychoanalytic study, complete with a training analysis and supervised practice. He learned to use the psychoanalytic couch, dream analysis, and transference neurosis in his work. Anticipating that this "depth" therapy would create more profound change in his clients, Ellis was disappointed to find that the results did not meet his expectations. His clients simply did not change in the profound ways promised by psychoanalytic theory. Becoming skeptical about the efficacy of traditional psychoanalysis, Ellis began experimenting with variants of psychoanalytic theory, such as those proposed by Harry Stack Sullivan, Karen Horney, and Otto Rank. Ellis found these approaches much more to his liking because, although they used psychoanalytic theory, they dispensed with the slow, laborious methods such as free association and dream analysis.

Although these variants of psychoanalysis seemed to create client change more quickly than standard psychoanalysis, Ellis still found himself dissatisfied with the results of his therapy. He began to experiment with a fusion of psychoanalytic and Behavior Therapy and became convinced that insight alone was not enough to "cure" his clients—behavioral change was needed, too (Ellis, 1994a). In 1954 Ellis began to integrate his knowledge of behaviorism, philosophy, and psychology, and by January 1955 he began practicing Rational Therapy (RT; Ellis, 1992a). He presented his first paper on RT at the American Psychological Association (APA) annual convention in 1956. In 1959 he founded the Institute for Rational-Emotive Therapy (Ellis, 1992a) and in 1962 published his landmark book, *Reason and Emotion in Psychotherapy.*

These events marked the beginning of Ellis's long and controversial career. He is known for his no-nonsense style and his free use of profanity in professional contexts. His early career took place in a psychological community largely dominated by psychoanalysis and conservative attitudes about sex; Ellis's ideas ran counter to both of these cultures. In fact, Ellis's first idea for his doctoral dissertation about love among college women was not approved because the faculty thought it was too controversial (Yankura & Dryden, 1994). The profession of psychology was not very accepting of his Rational Emotive Therapy, either; Ellis reported that "its strong cognitive component horrified almost everyone except the Adlerians" (1992a, p. 9). Eventually, however, Ellis's persistence paid off, and his contributions have been recognized by several professional organizations (American Counseling Association; American Humanist Association). In 1985 he was awarded the APA's award for distinguished professional contribution to knowledge. Today, REBT is international in its influence and is generally considered one of the major approaches to psychotherapy (Smith 1982; Yankura & Dryden, 1994).

A close study of REBT theory will reveal similarities to the ideas of the intellectual descendents of Sigmund Freud. Ellis acknowledges the influence of Alfred Adler, Karen Horney, Harry Stack Sullivan, and Otto Rank on his work, along with the existential philosophers (Heidegger, Kierkegaard, Buber, Sartre, and others). He also recognizes the contributions of Will Schutz and Fritz Perls and the 1960s encounter movement (Ellis, 1994a). Ellis is also unflinchingly critical of other theorists. The following quote illustrates Ellis's distinctive style: "I could fairly easily see that Socrates was something of a sophist. That Plato was often a silly idealist. That Kant courageously threw out God and then cravenly brought him in the back door. That Freud was an arrant overgeneralizer. That Jung was a brilliant but sloppily mystical thinker. That Wilhelm Reich was pretty psychotic. That Carl Rogers was a nice fellow, but an FFB—a fearful fucking baby" (Ellis, 1997a, p. 70).

Ellis is probably the most prolific psychologist of the 20th century. He has published over 800 articles and more than 70 books. For many years, on Friday nights Ellis conducted a demonstration of REBT at the Albert Ellis Institute. Admission was five dollars, and one might even be one of the lucky two individuals chosen to serve as the demonstration client for Ellis in the session. Even in his 80s, he maintained an 80-hour work week schedule, conducting individual and group REBT and REBT supervision, lecturing, and of course writing. In August 2000, at the age of 87, he and Aaron Beck staged a debate on their approaches at the APA convention. The event drew an overflow crowd who were delighted with the repartee between the two giants and particularly with Ellis's lively presentation.

Albert Ellis passed away in July 2007. His work, however, will be continued on at the Albert Ellis Institute, founded by Ellis in 1955 (www.rebt.org). *Rational Living,* the first REBT journal, was first published by the institute in 1966; in 1983 it became the *Journal of Rational Emotive Therapy,* and then in 1988 became the *Journal of Rational-Emotive & Cognitive-Behavior Therapy* (Neenan & Dryden, 1996). Read a section from Ellis' 2005 book *The Myth of Self-Esteem* in Box 9.2.

Box 9.2

An Except from Ellis's *The Myth of Self Esteem*

Is Self-Esteem a Sickness?

Is self-esteem a sickness? That's according to the way you define it. In the usual way it is defined by people and by psychologists, I'd say that it is probably the greatest emotional disturbance known to man and woman: Even greater than hating other people, which seems somewhat worse, but is perhaps a little better.

Why does hating and damning other people seem worse than self-esteem, which almost always leads to self-hatred? Well, it obviously results in fighting, acting against, war, and genocide. Pretty dramatic! While self-hatred produces more subtle results—like despising yourself but not necessarily committing suicide. *Living* with your self-lambasting.

Let me spend some time trying to clearly define self-esteem and self-disesteem. This won't be easy, since definitions have been vague and overlapping for the past century. But for the purposes of this book, here goes!

Self-esteem: You rate your self, your being, your personality, your essence, your totality, in terms of two main goals: (1) Your achieving success or effectiveness in your accomplishments. Your school, your work, your projects. When you succeed in getting what you want (and avoiding what you don't want), you say *that* is good. Great! But you also rate yourself and say, "I am a good person for succeeding!" When you fail to satisfy your achievement goals, you say, "That is bad; and *I* am bad."

(2) When your goal is relating well to other people and you actually relate well and win their approval, if you tie up your relating to your self-esteem—your worth as a *person*—then you tell yourself, "*That* is good!" and also, "I am a good and worthy person!" If you fail to win the approval of significant others, you then rate your *effort* and your *self* as *un*worthy.

That seems quite clear—and clearly gets you into trouble. As a fallible human, you can't help failing at work and at love, so your self-esteem is at best temporary. Even when it is high, you are in real danger of failing next time and of plummeting down again. Worse yet, since you know this after awhile, and you know that your worth as a person *depends* on your success, you make yourself anxious about important achievements—and, very likely, your anxiety interferes with your performances and makes you more likely to fail.

Rotten go! Your need for self-esteem makes you less likely to achieve it and more anxious when you do. Unless, of course, you are perfect—which is highly unlikely.

Realizing this some centuries ago, some philosophers—Asian and Greek and Roman, among others—invented self-acceptance. They said you could constructively *choose* to always have what is called unconditional self-acceptance (USA) by merely strongly *deciding* to have it—and keep it. Simple!

To achieve USA, you still pick an important goal—such as work or love—and you evaluate its achievement as good or bad, successful or unsuccessful. But—watch it now!—you refuse to rate or measure your self, your being, as "good" or "bad." You realize, along with a modern philosopher, Alfred Korzybski, that your performance is *part* of you, but certainly not *all* of you. You did it and are largely *responsible* for it. But it is a single performance, can easily change (be better or worse) tomorrow, and is always—yes, always—one ever-changing *aspect* of you. As Korzybski said, you *are* not your behavior. You are that and thousands of other behaviors—good, bad, and indifferent.

So you accurately tell yourself, "I did that desirable or undesirable act. It certainly did not do itself! I did it with my little hatchet; and I will—because of my talents and fallibilities—do many more desirable and undesirable behaviors. But I *am* not my acts—just a *person* who behaves well and badly."

Period. You evaluate the efficacy of your thoughts, feelings, and actions; but you don't rate or measure your *total* self or efficacy. In fact, you can't—because you are a *changeable* individual. You are not *static*. You grow, develop, progress—and retrogress. Why? Because you do.

Is this the only way you can get unconditional self-acceptance? No. You can get it indirectly, by convincing yourself that somebody gives it to you gratuitously—say God, your fairy godmother, your mother, a therapist, or someone else. But, first of all, you would have to *prove* that that spirit or person gives you USA. Otherwise, you really give it to yourself—which, fortunately, you can do. Instead of saying that God (or the devil!) gave you USA, why not merely say that you did? That's more honest! You *saw* that conditional self-acceptance (CSA) wouldn't work, so you *decided* to give USA to yourself *un*conditionally. Why not?

Excerpted from *The Myth of Self-Esteem* by A. Ellis; 2005. New York: Prometheus. Used with permission.

BASIC PHILOSOPHY

REBT can be summarized in one sentence by Ellis's paraphrase of Epictetus, the stoic philosopher: "It's never the events that happen that make us disturbed, but our view of them" (2005a, p. 259). This assumption lies at the heart of REBT theory, that people can control their own thoughts, feelings, and behaviors. When his clients say someone "made" them feel a certain way, Ellis has been known to reply "That's really impossible. No one can make you feel almost anything—except with a baseball bat" (2002, p. 110).

Ellis sees his theory as constructivist—by this he emphasizes the individual's creation of his reality and the fact that the individual's perception of reality is the deciding factor in determining behavior, not some externally validated reality (Ellis, 1998a). In his later writings, Ellis is inclined to say that philosophically, REBT has much in common with Tibetan Buddhism (2005a).

Ellis is best characterized as a soft determinist (Ziegler, 2000). Individuals have some choice in their lives, but inherited or innate potentials also exert substantial influence. In fact, Ellis once wrote that he thought that about 80% of the variability in human behavior was attributable to biological factors, leaving only 20% to environmental influence (Ellis, 1979a, p. 17). If so much of behavior is biologically determined, one might wonder if it makes any sense at all to attempt behavior change. Ellis would reply that innate characteristics can be changed—it is just very difficult, requiring much use of the REBT tactic of PYA (push your ass; Ellis, 1998b).

REBT theory is fairly neutral in terms of human nature. Humans are neither essentially evil nor actualizing; in fact, REBT advocates would probably acknowledge that there is a little of God and the devil in all of us. Ellis identified two powerful human tendencies, the "innate tendency to take their strong desires and preferences . . . and to make them, construct them into absolutistic musts" and the "propensity to be strongly proactive: to be motivated and impelled to constructively change things for the better" (Ellis, 1994a, pp. 14–15). Thus, human beings are biologically programmed to be both irrational and rational, self-actualizing and self-defeating (Barnard, Ellis, & Terjesen, 2006; Ellis, 2005b).

In REBT, people are seen as responsible for their behavior; they can easily determine if that behavior is "bad" or "good," self- and society-serving or self- and society-defeating. The standard for good and bad is a consensual one based on community standards (Ellis, 1994a). A centerpiece of REBT theory is that the behavior should never be equated with the person—one's *behavior* can be said to be bad, but not the person behaving (Ellis, 2005). "People's intrinsic *value or worth* cannot really be measured, because their *being* includes their *becoming*. They are a *process* with an ever-changing present and *future*. Therefore, how can we ever rate *them* while they are still alive and changing?" (Ellis, 1994a, p. 188; italics in original).

Raphael is Alan's REBT counselor. He greets Alan and asks him what brings him in. Raphael is thinking that Alan is, like himself, only human, likely to have both strengths and weaknesses. Alan will probably show some signs of irrationality. At other times, Raphael will discern very forward-moving, productive aspects of Alan. What Raphael keeps most in mind is that the world is as Alan currently views it.

HUMAN MOTIVATION

REBT counselors assume that people have the overall goals of "surviving and being reasonably happy (a) when alone, (b) socially, with other people, (c) intimately relating to a few selected people, (d) gathering information and education, (e) working productively, and (f) having recreational interests, such as art, music, literature, philosophy, entertainment, and sports" (Ellis, 1994a, p. 18). Ellis believes that humans should be long-range hedonists, implying that the basic human motivation is to obtain pleasure and avoid pain.

Raphael sees Alan as a person in search of survival and happiness. Raphael notes that Alan is currently involved in behavior directed toward satisfying intrinsic human goals. He seeks (and has established) social and intimate relationships in that he has a partner, Teresa, and friends at work as well as at his church. He and Teresa play on the church softball team. Alan mostly works productively, but lately his anxiety is getting in the way. He also finds that his anxiety leads to socially avoidant behavior, and he has been spending more time at home.

CENTRAL CONSTRUCTS

ABCs

REBT counseling is as simple as ABC. The A stands for the antecedent event or activating experience, or something that happens to us that we find relevant. Sometimes the *A* refers to adversity (Ellis, 1999d). The *A*, in fact, can stand for almost anything. As can be thoughts, fantasies, emotions, or other people; it is whatever the person is upset about (Wolfe, 2007).

The *C* is the consequence, or what we normally think of as the result of the *A*. *C*s can be emotional events (sadness, happiness, anxiety, depression) or behaviors (persisting at a task, avoidance, compulsive behavior). *C*s can take the form of healthy emotions (such as sadness or happiness) or unhealthy emotions (depression, anxiety, or rage; Ellis, 1999a).

If you have had the good fortune to be exposed to Ellis, Epictetus, or some other rational emotive behavior therapist, you know that what makes the difference in experiencing healthy or unhealthy emotions is what you think about the *A* event. *A* is not directly connected to C, but instead is filtered through *B*, our belief about *A* (Bernard et al., 2006).

An important, but conceptually difficult aspect of REBT is that even though the ABC model seems very straightforward (i.e., *A* activates *B* and then *B* causes *C*, or $A \times B = C$; Ellis, 1999d), Ellis is clear that emotions, beliefs, and behaviors interact (Ellis, 1994a). That is, feelings usually involve cognitive components and vice versa. Behaviors are intertwined with thinking and feeling. Let's assume that I believe very strongly that the world must be fair and just. When someone cuts in front of me in line at the grocery store (an *A*), I am likely to perceive this slight as much more catastrophic than someone who does not hold the same belief. The *A* becomes much more negatively valenced based on my *B* system. Another example of the interrelatedness of human experience is that extremely powerful or unusual *A*s (a hurricane, for example) can cause *C*s (Ellis & Dryden, 1997).

Raphael begins to identify some of the As, Bs, and Cs of Alan's presentation. The Cs are what brings him to counseling, so Raphael starts by looking at them: anxiety, unwanted repetitive checking behavior (of light switches and his path home from work), and disturbing imagery. The As of Alan's situation seem less clear. Alan reports that prior to his repetitive behavior, he has thoughts and images associated with danger that seem to trigger it, simple sentences like, "Something bad might happen if I leave the lights on," or "I might have run someone over." The C of experiencing religious imagery is also an A event because it is connected to the Cs of anxiety, shame, and guilt. It is less clear where the images themselves come from.

BELIEFS

Beliefs are simple, declarative sentences we say to ourselves, or images and symbols that have special meaning to us. Collectively, our beliefs form our life philosophies, which then "run—and ruin! most of our lives" (Ellis, 1994a, p. 46).

There are two kinds of beliefs, according to REBT theory, rational beliefs (rBs) and irrational beliefs (iBs). On a descriptive level, rational beliefs are those that express preferences and wishes. *Rational* in REBT language means "effectively self helping" (Ellis, 1994a, p.25); rational beliefs are ones that help people achieve their goals. They generally lead to mild to moderate emotions (Bernard et al., 2006). Despite what might seem to be a straightforward assumption, REBT writers are careful to note that rational beliefs don't have to be logical or supported by empirical evidence.

Dryden and Neenan (2006) identify four kinds of rational beliefs: "flexible preferences, anti-awfulizing beliefs, high frustration tolerance beliefs, and acceptance beliefs" (p. 2). These will make much more sense to you after you read the sections on irrational beliefs next.

Irrational beliefs are rigid, demanding musts or shoulds (Bernard et al., 2006). They are usually illogical and unrealistic, but not always. Depending on which source you consult, various classifications of irrational beliefs can be found, so I will here present Ellis' (1994a) classic three categories of irrational beliefs or *musturbatory* headings:

1. *Self-demandingness.* "I, myself, absolutely must, under practically all conditions and at all times, perform well (or outstandingly well!) and win the approval (or complete love!) of significant others. If I fail in these important—and sacred!—respects, that is *awful* and I am a *bad, incompetent, unworthy person*, who will probably *always* fail and who *deserves* to suffer."

2. *Other-demandingness.* "You, significant people with whom I relate or associate, *absolutely must*, under practically all conditions and at all times, treat me nicely, considerately, and fairly. Otherwise, it is *terrible* and you are *rotten, bad, unworthy people* who will *always* treat me badly and who do not *deserve* a good life and should be severely punished for acting so abominably to noble me!"

3. *World-demandingness.* "The conditions under which I live (my environment, the ecology, the economic and political conditions) *absolutely must*, at practically all times, be favorable, safe, hassle-free, and quickly and easily enjoyable, and if they are not that way it's *awful* and *horrible*, and I *can't stand it.* I can't ever enjoy myself *at all.* My life is impossible and hardly worth living!"

(From *Reason and Emotion in Psychotherapy* [rev. ed.] by Albert Ellis. Copyright © 1994 by Birch Lane Press. All rights reserved. Reprinted by permission of Citadel Press/Kensington Publishing Corp. www.kensingtonbooks.com)

When people rely on irrational thinking a lot (or musturbate, in Ellis's terms), they can fall into other kinds of thinking that are thought to be derivatives of the musts. These irrational conclusions are (a) awfulizing, or seeing things as much more than bad; (b) I-can't-stand-it-itis, or low frustration tolerance (LFT), the belief that bad things should never happen and I can't stand it if they do; (c) damnation, or rating ourselves, others, or the world as absolutely, totally horrible (see the discussion on human worth ratings); and (d) allness or overgeneralization (Bernard & DiGiuseppe, 1989; Ellis & Dryden, 1997).

We are not always aware of our iBs because they can operate on both conscious and unconscious levels (Ellis, 1994a). Because humans are in the habit of hanging on to their iBs, they tend to repeat these again and again to themselves. Eventually, they are transformed into basic (irrational) philosophies that feel like the truth sent from on high (Ellis, 1994a). These dysfunctional basic philosophies are then reinforced in a number of ways. They lead to strong negative emotions, which makes them feel true. They use circular reasoning

(If I fail, I am bad. I failed, therefore I'm bad). They tend to be pre- or unconscious, which leads to little explicit examination of them (Ellis, 1994a).

Raphael thinks that Alan's iBs are fairly easy to guess, although Alan might not consciously think about them. Raphael thinks that Alan seems to have some kind of extreme belief around the light switches: "If I don't turn off all light switches, some disaster will happen and that would be awful!" Similarly, he might be thinking, "I absolutely must *not* ever *hit anyone with my car. If I did that, it would be* terrible *and I would be an absolutely* rotten *person!" Although Raphael is wondering what the imagery is about, he suspects that Alan is also telling himself that he should* never *have images such as these, and the fact that he does make him an* unworthy worm, *a definite no-goodnik! Underlying these specific beliefs is Alan's adoption of the three musts, and most particularly the first—I* must *be perfect. Because he has such difficult symptoms that sometimes seem to cause other people to treat him badly, Alan probably harbors the other two musts as well—others* must *treat me well, and the world* must *be an easy place to live or I just can't stand it. Clearly, Alan is awfulizing, rating himself as worthless, and is beset by low frustration tolerance. He sees himself as all bad because of the symptoms he experiences.*

GOALS (*G*s)

According to REBT, people have goals (*G*s) that they carry with them, and the most important *A*s happen when those goals are thwarted. We all have the general goals to survive and be happy, but these are translated into more specific subgoals that we share with other people (for instance, the desire for a successful career), or some goals may be idiosyncratic. One common goal is to be loved (Ellis, 1995a). When we receive information that indicates that someone important is unhappy with us, the goal of being loved is blocked, and we experience an antecedent event. Other specific goals mentioned by Ellis are to be comfortable and successful (Ellis, 1995a). "We naturally want love, power, freedom and fun—for they often add to our enjoying of life and help us survive" (Ellis, 1999d, p. 8).

Alan's goal of being reasonably happy is threatened by his compulsive behavior. He has to interrupt his normal life rhythms to check the light switches, and he can never relax at home, because he must go back and check to see if he has hit anyone with his car. The anxiety and depression he experiences also interfere with his goal to be comfortable and successful. He is having difficulty at work because of his anxious, compulsive behavior, Raphael discovers. His coworkers sometimes react to his apparent discomfort and anxiety, and he sometimes checks and rechecks small details of their work. Raphael also suspects that Alan's goals to be accepted by others and loved by his wife are also frustrated to some extent because his sometimes odd, anxious behavior puts others off, and Teresa is getting quite frustrated with his "checking" behavior (the light switches and retracing his route home from work). He is most concerned about the strife in his relationship with Teresa. (Raphael wonders, as an aside, if Teresa is experiencing some I-can't-stand-it-itis about Alan's behaviors). Raphael also knows that Alan's religion is very important to him and guesses that the imagery Alan reports creates a perception that Alan can't possibly achieve his goals of being worthwhile in the eyes of God and his church.

HUMAN WORTH RATINGS AND USA

In REBT, global human worth ratings—that is, seeing yourself or someone else as an all-good or all-bad person—are a no-no. The person and the behavior must be separated—one can behave badly, but that does not make one a bad person (a rotten person [RP] or a worm; Ellis, 1999b). Ellis (2005a) opined "So you accurately tell yourself, 'I did that desirable or undesirable act. It certainly did not do itself! I did it with my little hatchet; and I will—because of my talents and fallibilities—do many more desirable and undesirable behaviors. But I *am* not my acts—just a *person* who behaves well and badly' " (p. 15; italics in original).

Instead of making global judgments of worth, individuals should work toward unconditional self-acceptance, or USA (Ellis, 2004a). USA can be achieved in one of two ways. One option is to fight your natural tendencies to self-evaluate and instead choose to see yourself as a good person just because you are alive and human (Ellis, 1999e).

The problem with viewing yourself as inherently good is that it is definitional—anyone could come along and disagree with your definition of yourself and say that you are a worm. You have no way of proving that your assertion is right. Also, "you, alas, are a fallible and often screwed-up human" (Ellis, 1999e, p. 54) so you would be constantly confronted with your own imperfection. The better option to global goodness is to refuse to make such evaluations of the self at all. Simply evaluate your behavior, thoughts, and feelings as good or bad according to the standard of rationality (i.e., whether they help you achieve your goals; Ellis, 1999b).

This REBT rule applies to our self-ratings as well as to our appraisals of others. Ellis maintains that it is best to practice UAO, too, or unconditional acceptance of others (Ellis, 2004b). Because others are human too, they will most certainly treat you badly and may even believe that you *deserve* to be treated that way! UAO, then, involves applying the same standards to others that you apply to yourself—hate the behavior, not the person. Similarly, Ellis (2004a) argues that unconditional life-acceptance (ULA) is necessary to achieve a state of minimal disturbance.

Alan is rating himself as a worthless human being particularly because of the uncomfortable religious images he experiences that he feels he cannot control. He does not unconditionally accept himself. Because he has experienced the anxiety and repetitive behavior for a long time, he tells Raphael that he believes that there is something wrong with him; he is a 100% bad person. He also sees most other people as uncaring and mean because they would not accept him and his dysfunctional behavior.

SECONDARY DISTURBANCES

It's bad enough that we create our own unwanted negative feelings and behaviors (*C*s). What's worse is that, according to REBT, we go even further and believe that we "*must not* think crookedly, *must not* have disturbed feelings, *must not* have dysfunctional behaviors" (Ellis, 1999b, p. 81). When we have an upsetting ABC experience, then we treat the *C*s as activating experiences themselves (*A2*s) and then get all wound up with *B*s about them. Ellis calls these kinds of upsets secondary disturbances because they come in response to the first ABC sequence, which we have mishandled by relying on an iB in response to *A*1. Then we create more trouble by adding an iB in response to *A*2 (or the original *C*). When we tell ourselves that we *must not* have lousy thinking, or get anxious, or whatever, we are creating secondary disturbance or symptom stress (Ellis, 1999b).

For example, if my mother yells at me (*A*1), I can respond with the rB "Well, I'd rather she didn't do that, but it does not make me or her a rotten person." This sequence might result in some annoyance or mild discomfort on my part, a healthy negative emotion. Alternately, I might respond with the iB "She *must* not yell at me—I can't stand it and she is a rotten person!" In this second case, the *C* would probably be anger, and even some angry behavior (such as shouting back at Mom). If I shout, then I have created an *A*2 because I immediately respond with the iB that "I must be perfect at all times, absolutely never lose my cool or be mean to anyone or I am a *worm*!" I have then constructed the secondary disturbance, *C*2, that is shame, guilt, or depression.

Ellis (1999b) also noted that clients can even create *tertiary disturbances* that have to do with musting about doing well in therapy and expecting that the counselor will help perfectly, significantly, and quickly! These tertiary disturbances need to be discovered and disputed while, or even before, the counseling addresses the primary or secondary ones.

Raphael thinks that Alan is evidencing significant secondary disturbances. When he gets anxious and performs his compulsive behavior (C1 and also A2), he tells himself that he must not be like this (iB2), and he absolutely should not ever act in such silly, immature ways (iB2). Further, life should not be so difficult—he just can't stand how hard it is to live (iB2). These Bs are likely creating feelings of rage and depression (C2s).

THEORY OF THE PERSON AND DEVELOPMENT OF THE INDIVIDUAL

REBT does not present a personality theory; nor does it offer a detailed developmental discussion. As noted earlier, REBT postulates that humans are a product of both inherited influences and environmental teaching. Ellis does not discuss any developmental progression; at one point he called Freud's psychosexual stages figments of his (Freud's) obsessive need for perfection.

Biological influences include things such as individual differences in the tendency to think irrationally, react emotionally, and conversely, to grow and actualize. Tendencies toward behavior (such as compulsive behaviors) can also be innately determined (Ellis, 1994b, 1997b).

The most important environmental influences are other people. We absorb rules, standards of behavior, and goals from those around us, including parents, siblings, teachers, peers, and religious or political groups (Ellis, 1995a). "You, like almost all people, are a born 'musturbator' and will almost inevitably take parental, societal and personal rules and foolishly make them into imperatives. So most—not all—of your profound musturbation is self-constructed, self-repeated, self-learned" (Ellis, 1995a, p. 4). Of course, we don't have to internalize these rules, but it is our human nature to tend to do so.

When her parents, for example, tell Julie that she should be getting better grades, they really mean, according to Ellis (1995a), that it would be *preferable* if she got all As. Most parents then proceed with business as usual and still love Julie even if she gets all C grades. Because she is born with a twisted little human mind, Julie takes the preferential "you should" and turns it into an absolute demand that runs something like this: "I absolutely *must* get all As and be perfect. It will be positively *horrible* if I don't, and I will be a *worthless, rotten worm.*"

Much of this construction of musts and shoulds happens when we are children and have immature (bad, rigid, crooked) thinking processes (Ellis, 1995a). We then carry these irrational ideas into adulthood, constantly reindoctrinating ourselves without really realizing what we are doing.

Raphael and Alan don't spend a lot of time discussing Alan's childhood or how he got to be how he is today. Raphael knows that although some of Alan's behaviors and beliefs probably originated early in his life, some things about Alan may be the result of biological influences.

HEALTH AND DYSFUNCTION

In the REBT view, healthy people are those who rely mostly on rational beliefs in their daily lives. Healthy folks tend to use strong preferential thinking rather than absolutistic musts and shoulds (Dryden, 1996). Unconditional self-acceptance is characteristic of healthy individuals because they take responsibility for their psychological functioning and choose to accept themselves even with all of their imperfections. They will still have the inclination to awfulize, should, musturbate, and do all of those other things associated with the human tendency to be irrational, but mostly they will defeat these tendencies (Ellis, 1995a).

Healthy people have healthy basic philosophies that value flexibility and open-mindedness and oppose bigotry (Ellis, 1994a). Relativistic thinking and desiring (as opposed to absolutely needing) is a core characteristic of psychological health. Self-interest is a primary value because healthy people realize that "if they do not primarily take care of themselves, who else will?" (Ellis, 1985, p. 108). However, they balance self-interest with social interest because most of them also want to live happily in a social group. If they act in ways counter to the group's good, they are not likely to create an environment in which they can live happily.

Acceptance, or USA (rather than damnation), is an important characteristic of the healthy person, in the sense of accepting one's and others' human fallibility and the fact that life is complicated and sometimes influenced by factors outside of one's control. However, acceptance does not mean resignation; healthy people actively change their worlds when they can (Ellis & Dryden, 1997). In fact, Ellis (1999d) argued that the REBT counselor's job is not only to help clients deal with iBs around social injustice, but also to encourage them to work to change these unhealthy As.

Healthy people endorse the philosophy of REBT. The values in the REBT philosophy include long-range hedonism, self-interest, social interest, self-direction, tolerance of others, the acceptance of life's ambiguity and uncertainty, flexibility and openness and change, and the value of scientific thinking (Ellis, 2005a). Commitment to something outside of one's self is important, whether that commitment is to people, things, or ideas. REBT also emphasizes risk taking, nonperfectionism, and nonutopianism (Ellis, 1985, p. 110).

Dysfunction from an REBT perspective is, most simply, operating in the world on the basis of irrational beliefs or, more globally, on the basis of an irrational philosophical system. Ellis (2003) wrote "I have stubbornly insisted that human disturbance is contributed to by environmental pressures, including our childhood upbringing, but that its most important and vital source originates in our innate tendency to indulge in crooked thinking" (p. 205).

People who experience life difficulties have taken their preferences and elevated them to absolute demands. "Anxious, depressed, and enraged people have many dysfunctional ideas or irrational beliefs by which they largely create their neurotic disturbances; and as the theory of REBT holds, these beliefs almost always seem to consist of or be derived from unrealistically, illogically, and rigidly raising their nondisturbing wishes and preferences into godlike absolutist musts, shoulds, demands, and commands (Ellis, 1999a, p. 477). They awfulize, engage in damnation, and have textbook cases of I-can't-stand-it-itis.

"The three main neurotic processes may be seen as 1) self downing (damning oneself for poor performances and rejection; 2) hostility and rage (damning others for poor performances and unkind reactions); and 3) LFT (low frustration tolerance; damning things and the world for poor, dislikable conditions)" (Ellis, 1999a, p. 479). *Sacredizing* is an important contributor to neurosis (Ellis, 1999b). Sacredizing is when one makes something one deems important an absolute must and insists that because it is *so* important, it *absolutely must* be obtained, achieved, or so forth. Sacredizing is to be distinguished from *importantizing*, which is the healthier form of making something a priority in one's life. In other words, it is OK to importantize anything, as long as you don't sacredize it (Ellis, 1999b).

In the most specific sense, psychological dysfunction originates when a person experiences an activating event or adversity that frustrates the attainment of a goal. This experience engages the irrational belief system, with its shoulds, demands, musts, and so forth. The result is the unwanted *C*, an unhealthy emotion or behavior. Worse, the person, perceiving the negative *C*, then turns *it* into an *A*, which spurs iBs about how one should not have symptoms, feel bad, and so forth, creating a negative secondary *C*.

Ellis acknowledged that severe psychological dysfunction, such as personality disorders, profound depression, obsessive-compulsive disorder, or psychosis, likely stems from the joint influence of traumatizing early experience and innate, organic deficits (Ellis, 2002). Individuals who display these syndromes probably are inherently more emotionally reactive and behaviorally disorganized than "nice normal neurotics" (Ellis, 1997b, p. 198). They may experience more frustration and criticism in life because of their sometimes odd behavior (Ellis, 1994b). Even worse, individuals with severe dysfunction tend to create severe secondary disturbances about their very real deficits. They easily develop severe low frustration tolerance (LFT), insisting that "my symptoms *must* not be so upsetting and handicapping." They self-down about having such deficits (Ellis, 1994b). These problems tend to make individuals with these kinds of dysfunction VDCs (very difficult customers; Ellis, 1994b, 1997b).

Raphael thinks that some of Alan's thoughts and behaviors stem from biological tendencies, such as the propensity toward anxiety and compulsive behaviors. Alan might even be seen as having obsessive-compulsive disorder (OCD). Alan's tendencies to be anxious, reactive, and compulsive are likely to be partly biologically rooted. Raphael has identified the irrational beliefs that Alan connects with light switches, running people over with his car, and the scary sexual religious imagery. Raphael can also see how Alan responds to events in his life with thought processes that are self-defeating. He is self-downing. With the recent resurgence of his compulsive behavior, Alan seems to be holding beliefs such as, "I must not be flawed like this! I can't stand it that I am not perfect in every way! Further, when I am like this, everyone disapproves of me. I'll never be loved and accepted by everyone, and that is really intolerable! I can't stand this anxiety or the rejection of others! I am a rotten, flawed human, and I will never lose these symptoms, and therefore I can never have a happy life or the love of those important to me. This is just too hard!" Clearly, Alan is showing both ego and discomfort disturbance; he downs himself for his anxiety, compulsive behavior, and images. He believes that he can't stand the pain and trouble in his life.

NATURE OF THERAPY

ASSESSMENT

REBT rejects the traditional (medical) model of assessment, in which clients are subjected to a lengthy comprehensive assessment procedure prior to therapy (DiGiuseppe, 1995a). Instead, REBT counselors see assessment as a continuous process throughout the counseling experience (Ellis & MacLaren, 2005). Despite this ideological stance, DiGiuseppe (1991a) reported that clients at the Albert Ellis Institute complete a formal assessment battery that includes traditional assessment instruments (e.g., Millon Clinical Multiaxial Inventory II and the Beck Depression Inventory, among others). Several of these instruments are used every 4 weeks for progress reviews. However, DiGiuseppe (1991a) emphasized that the first task of the therapist is forming a relationship with the client, not diagnosis.

In addition to standardized assessment, REBT therapists use several structured techniques that are directed at assessing clients' belief structures. These more formal techniques, sometimes called vivid REBT, are discussed later in the context of the assessment of specific iBs.

Informal assessment involves simply asking what brings the client to therapy. The counselor then listens for *A*s, *B*s, and *C*s, as well as other characteristics deemed relevant to REBT treatment, such as cognitive flexibility, problem-solving skill, and indicators of secondary emotional disturbance (DiGiuseppe, 1995a). The *C* is usually explored first because it is what gets the client to counseling. After the client and counselor agree on the most important *C*, it is time to get to *A*. Finally, the counselor assesses *B* (Ellis & MacLaren, 2005).

Advocates of REBT do acknowledge that it is sometimes difficult to determine what iBs the client is holding because iBs are often not immediately available to conscious reflection (Ellis, 1994a). When the client is simply asked what he is thinking (in conjunction with an *A* or *C*), he will usually report automatic thoughts or inferences (DiGiuseppe, 1995a) rather than the core iBs.

Although the counselor can proceed to dispute these thoughts, this is not the most efficient route. Instead, the REBT therapist uses *inference chaining* to get to the core beliefs (DiGuiseppe, 1995a). In this procedure, the counselor asks the client to assume that the thought or inference is true and then asks, "Then what?" or "That would mean . . .". The client's response is then followed by further questioning, until the process reveals a *C* (an emotional or behavioral problem). At this point, the counselor then asks why, to further elaborate on the *A*'s properties (Dryden, 1995a).

For example, Larry does not like to dance in public, but his girlfriend Pam wants to go out and boogie. Their relationship is deteriorating because of this argument, and Larry asks his REBT counselor to help. The following might be a typical assessment dialogue:

Larry: *I just can't go out dancing. (an A)*
Louise: *Why?*
Larry: *Because I'd be petrified. (a C)*

Louise: *What would you be petrified about?*
Larry: *That other people would watch me dance. (an inference)*
Louise: *If that happens, then what?*
Larry: *They'd see what a terrible dancer I am. (inference)*
Louise: *And if other people saw that you were a terrible dancer?*
Larry: *They'd laugh at me. (inference)*
Louise: *And if they laughed?*
Larry: *That would be absolutely awful. (an iB)*
Louise: *What would be awful about the laughing?*
Larry: *I'd feel really stupid. (an iB connected to a C—embarrassment)*

In this example, the counselor has clearly gotten to a part of the problem—Larry is awfulizing about looking bad in public. However, she has not yet really helped Larry to see the core underlying belief, which is probably "I absolutely must be perfect" (i.e., "I must never appear stupid or imperfect") or "Others must always approve of me." Further questioning would reveal this more significant philosophical idea. As this example illustrates, clients also have iBs about inferences (e.g, the inference that others seeing Larry dance would laugh is connected with the idea that it would be awful) that contribute to emotional upset; these should be assessed along with the ultimate, core iB (Dryden, 1995a). This example also illustrates that the inferences clients make can be faulty—who knows if folks watching Larry would laugh? They might instead applaud and cheer!

Some clients have difficulty labeling emotional experience or relating emotions to *A* events. Dryden (1995b) recommended the use of vivid methods in these cases, when the traditional dialogic methods of assessment are ineffective. Vivid assessment can take any of a number of forms. First, the counselor can try using language that is much more emotional and colorful than normal. Guided imagery about *A* events might help the client experience more fully his emotions and cognitions. Clients can be asked to bring photographs or mementos that relate to the problem situation into sessions. Finally, Dryden (1995b) described the *interpersonal nightmare technique,* in which the client is asked to write a brief script, as if for a play, about his most feared event. The script can be audiotaped and then played for the client in the counseling session, and the counselor and client can examine the beliefs revealed.

Dryden (1995b) also described riskier techniques that involve either recreating the problem situation in the counseling session (rational emotive problem solving, REPS; Kanus & Wessler, 1976) or in vivo assessment. In REPS, for example, the therapist might criticize the client, recreating the behavior of a critical other. As Dryden noted, this technique can be very difficult for the client, and the counselor must be careful to fully assess the client's reaction to it. If the client finds the approach negative, the counselor should immediately explain his rationale for using it.

In vivo assessment involves a field trip. Client and counselor actually take the assessment process out of the office and into the setting most relevant to the problem. A client with an animal phobia, for instance, might be taken to the zoo or an animal shelter. Again, the counselor must be very careful to monitor the effects of this technique on the client.

Raphael decides not to use formal, standardized testing with Alan. Instead, he proceeds by asking Alan what is bringing him in, and then looks for the As, Bs, and Cs. Raphael has guessed quite a few of Alan's irrational beliefs. The As of the situation are less clear. Some perception of threat seems to set off Alan's irrational beliefs about checking light switches and driving in his car. The As could be thoughts, seeing light switches, or images of hitting someone with his car. Another explanation could be that Alan is simply biologically predisposed to anxiety, which then sets off his belief system, so that the anxiety is acting like a secondary C. The Cs for Alan include anxiety, repetitive behavior, depression, shame, guilt, and probably some anger, although Alan is not expressing that directly.

Raphael might use some imagery assessment around Alan's repetitive behavior to see what he is thinking before and during this behavior. This approach would provide clues to the specific content of Alan's beliefs. Inference chaining might be useful around the light-switching behavior, creating a dialogue such as the following:

R: *So you get the notion to go back and check to see if the switch is off, that you might have left it on. (the A)*
A: *Yes.*
R: *Why do you think you have to check to see?*
A: *Because I become unsure if I did it.*
R: *What if you didn't turn off the switch?*
A: *Something bad would happen. (inference)*
R: *What kind of bad?*
A: *I don't know. Just something bad. Maybe the house would burn down. (inference)*
R: *And if it did?*
A: *It would be awful, terrible, and it would be my fault. (iB resulting in C, anxiety, compulsive behavior)*

It would be risky, but Raphael could use the interpersonal nightmare technique to explore Alan's fears about hitting someone with his car. This kind of assessment could also be done in vivo, but if Raphael chooses this approach, he would probably blend it with the use of some coping statements (discussed later) to help Alan through the experience.

OVERVIEW OF THE THERAPEUTIC ATMOSPHERE

REBT counseling is distinctive in its active, directive nature. Ellis wrote, "If the therapist is namby-pamby, is Boy Scout-ish or Girl Scout-ish, as lots of therapists are, I doubt whether the therapist will be too helpful. Unless you use your own personality traits and have a good deal of push and drive to help your many unpushing clients, you will not greatly help those who are pushing very hotly in the wrong direction" (Ellis, 1992b, p. 95).

The authoritative stance of the counselor in REBT is combined with unconditional acceptance of the client (Wolfe, 2007). Ellis added that "unlike Rogerians, moreover, they actively, forcefully teach their clients to *accept themselves* unconditionally (1995a, p. 16; italics in original). The counselor is encouraging and supportive of the client and projects confidence that the client can change his ways (Ellis, 1994a; Garfield, 1995). The REBT counselor often uses humor with clients because one of the major reasons they are clients is that they take themselves, their problems, and the world too seriously (Ellis & Dryden, 1997). However, Dryden and Neenan (2006) caution that the REBT therapist needs to be interpersonally flexible, willing to be formal or informal, self-disclosing or not, and humerous or unfunny depending on what most promotes the therapeutic relationship.

As in most current approaches, the therapeutic alliance is considered important in REBT work (Bernard et al., 2006). The REBT counselor uses active listening and empathic responding, conveying unconditional acceptance of the client. Although Ellis recognizes the value of the therapeutic relationship, he also cautioned that, depending on the relationship, too much emphasis on it can lead to clients *feeling* better, not *getting* better (i.e., changing their behaviors; Ellis, 1996a). Also, he warned that a very close relationship can be damaging for clients who tend to be dependent. The REBT counselor avoids letting the client get into lengthy descriptions of *A*s, because he is not very interested in history, seeing it as "sidetracking" (Ellis, 1979c, p. 95). Likewise, allowing the client to wallow in *C*s is considered nonproductive. The real deal is to guide the client back to the source of the *C*s, the iBs.

Although Ellis claims that REBT is more efficient than other therapeutic approaches, whether it is a brief approach is questionable. Ellis is fond of saying that "poor Sigmund Freud was born and reared with a propensity for *in*efficiency, while I seem to have been born and reared with a gene for efficiency" (1996a, p. 4; italics in original). Despite this humorous claim, no evidence has been presented indicating the average number of sessions of REBT clients. Ellis (1996a) maintained that most normal neurotic clients are helped within 20 sessions.

Raphael is an energetic, active counselor, who demonstrates respect and acceptance of Alan. He approaches the relationship in a straightforward, honest way and expects Alan to do the same. Raphael responds empathically to Alan's presentation and conveys understanding of Alan's discomfort about his bothersome and scary symptoms.

ROLES OF CLIENT AND COUNSELOR

An interesting quandary arises when attempting to describe the role of the counselor in REBT: it seems that even more than other approaches, it is easy to confuse the role of the therapist with the personality of Albert Ellis (Garfield, 1995). Ellis's distinctive confrontive and directive style threatens to become the "manual" for how to do REBT, and he believes that a softer, more indirect approach is probably an ineffective approach. "If therapists are honest, direct, and active they are likely to achieve better results with most clients more of the time. But not with all!" (Ellis, 1994a, p. 54). Ellis (2005b) characterizes a warm relationship as preferable, but not essential to therapy. However, he does emphasize USA on the part of the therapist for the client.

You don't have to mimic Albert Ellis to be a REBT therapist. As long as you know the theory, you can implement it with a softer style. Wolfe (2007) goes so far to say that "you definitely don't have to use an exhortative voice tone or four-letter words in order to be a good REBT practitioner" (p. 188).

First and foremost, the REBT counselor is an active teacher (Ellis, 2005a). The therapist must teach the client to identify iBs because most clients want to think that *A* causes *C* (Ellis & MacLauren, 1998).

The REBT client is a student of the counselor, but needs to be a very involved and energetic one. Clients have to work hard in REBT. Although Ellis believes that we can change our ways of thinking, emoting, and behaving, "*only hard work and practice* will correct irrational beliefs—and keep them corrected (Ellis, 2005b, p. 168, italics in original)

Raphael approaches Alan as a friendly teacher, an expert on the ABCs. Alan responds well to this structured approach and works hard as the REBT student.

GOALS

REBT has two major goals: (a) to eliminate irrational thinking and thereby the associated dysfunctional emotions and behaviors and (b) to teach the client REBT philosophy.

At the simplest level, the goal of REBT is to help clients change irrational beliefs into rational beliefs. "REBT holds that showing disturbed people that they are profound musturbators is most probably the most important thing a therapist can do to help them" (Ellis, 1999b, p. 80). Ellis maintains that you can change your *A*s, *B*s, or *C*s. However, he warns that *A*s are sometimes difficult to change because we have little control over them. Sometimes it is impossible to change a *C* unless we change our *B* first (Ellis, 1994a, p. 22).

Beliefs, therefore, are the target of many REBT interventions. However, the REBT therapist also wants the client to learn unconditional self acceptance, high frustration tolerance, and unconditional acceptance of others (Bernard et al., 2006). Further, the REBT counselor strives to help clients change their dysfunctional basic philosophies. Ellis wrote, "Moreover, if you radically modify some of your basic musturbatory attitudes, and thus make a *profound philosophical change*, REBT hypothesizes that you can thereby change *many* of your self-defeating feelings and behaviors as well as your negative, antiempirical automatic thoughts, keep them healthfully changed, and actually make yourself less disturb*able*" (Ellis, 1994a, p. 23; italics in original). Ideally, the REBT client adopts the philosophy of the healthy person described earlier.

To change their philosophies, clients need to accomplish three major objectives: "(1) Acknowledge that they mainly are responsible for their own disturbed thoughts, feelings and actions, and stop copping out by blaming their parents, their culture, or their environment. (2) Clearly see how they are thinking, feeling, and behaving when they needlessly upset themselves. (3) Work hard, forcefully, and persistently to change their neurotic cognitions, emotions and performances" (Ellis, 1985, pp. 110–111).

Finally, clients in REBT are expected not just to feel better, but to get better, too. The REBT client must have insight into the ABCs of life, but also must work to behave differently (Ellis & MacLaren, 2005).

Raphael's goals for Alan could be stated in several ways. First, he hopes to help Alan combat his specific iBs and change them into more rational beliefs. It would be particularly important to work with the secondary disturbance Alan harbors because without addressing this aspect of Alan's distress, a new philosophy is unobtainable. Alan really needs to change how he thinks about life because it is possible that he will always experience some kinds of symptoms (anxiety, a tendency to obsess). He will need to develop a philosophy that emphasizes the need to accept himself (with his symptoms), work hard to defeat his irrational tendencies, accept others, and accept the ambiguity of human existence.

Raphael also wants behavior change for Alan. In the best case, Alan will be able to fight off his urges to engage in the repetitive behaviors.

PROCESS OF THERAPY

REBT follows an ABCDE model. *D* stands for dispute. The client's faulty beliefs and philosophies must be disputed so that he will give them up. When the client surrenders his iBs, then he will experience a new effect, or *E*. The *E* element also stands for effective new philosophy if therapy is really successful (Ellis, 1995a; Ellis & Dryden, 1997).

There are two kinds of REBT: general, or *inelegant*, and preferential, or *elegant*. Inelegant REBT consists of using cognitive behavioral interventions common to other forms of cognitive therapy to help the client solve problems (Ellis, 2005b). Inelegant REBT often focuses on the client's inferences that result from iBs; for instance, the therapist might confront the validity of the client's statement that everyone would laugh at him if he danced poorly.

Elegant, or preferential, REBT, in contrast, is aimed at the shoulds, musts, and I-can't-stand-its of the client. The therapist helps the client adopt a more functional basic philosophy, the REBT philosophy (Ellis, 2005b). In elegant REBT, therapists teach clients about the difference between preferences and musts, and the goal is to "arrange, for the rest of their lives, that they rarely (not never) change their preferences to grandiose demands and thereby make themselves significantly less upsettable" (Ellis, 1995b, p. 71). Clients, in essence, learn to be their own REBT therapists. One outcome of elegant REBT is that clients make a serious commitment to something outside of themselves, such as family, work, or a political cause (Ellis, 1991).

Wolfe (2007) maintained that the first task of the therapist is usually to help the client to reduce his emotional disturbance. She sounds a little un-REBT-like when she writes that the second phase of therapy should address self-actualization. However, what she means by self-actualization essentially involves setting short- and long-term goals that involve cognitive, emotive and behavioral changes, all of which are consistent with an REBT philosophy.

Client resistance is seen as stemming from several influences. Sometimes, clients resist because they believe that the therapist is mistaken (Ellis, 2002). However, another way to look at resistance is that it is simply difficult to change. For instance, Ellis (2002) suggests that some clients may hold beliefs such as "It's not only hard for me to change, but it's *too* hard! It absolutely *should not be* that hard! How awful! I guess I'd better give up trying to do so!" (p. 27; italics in original). Ellis calls clients who resist REBT (and other therapies, too) difficult customers (DCs; Ellis, 1987). The most important source of resistance is the innate human tendency to think irrationally, to be short-range hedonists "obsessed with the pleasures of the moment rather than of the future" (1987, p. 365).

Other sources of client resistance include the client's embarrassment about the problems he is experiencing, unwillingness to give up secondary gains resulting from symptoms, the client's belief that he must punish himself, and perfectionism/grandiosity (Ellis, 2002). Transference-like phenomena, such as client–therapist mismatching, traditional client transference in the psychoanalytic sense, or genuine attraction between client and therapist can also feed resistance. Finally, clients are also known to resist out of rebellion and reactance or hopelessness, or in response to a judgmental, moralistic therapist.

Not surprisingly, Wolfe (2007) indicated that coutertransference is a direct function of therapist cognition. She recommends disputing irrational beliefs ("I can't stand it when my client drones on and on"), even resorting to using the REBT self-help form, shown in Box 9.5. Ellis (2001) presented a similar view, but also pointed out that countertransference can have both rational (i.e., helpful) and irrational aspects. The desire and motivation of the counselor to help the client, for example, can be beneficial in therapy. In contrast, Ellis (2001) described a case in which his own low frustration tolerance (and attraction to the client) got in the way of therapy. If you really want to be a good REBT counselor, you should carefully read Ellis' (2003) article, "How to Deal With Your Most Difficult Client—You," in which he describes particular irrational beliefs to which therapists are susceptible. For instance, do you believe that you absolutely must be successful with most of your clients most of the time? If so, you have some disputing to do.

Raphael knows that he needs to dispute Alan's irrational thinking and to help Alan learn to do this as well. The D *will lead to* E, *a new effect (less anxiety, shame, and anger), as well as a new effective philosophy. At first, the focus of counseling will be on Alan's symptoms, and the duo will work to modify the iBs that lead to the dysfunctional emotions and compulsive behaviors. An elegant solution will involve Raphael helping Alan to adopt a philosophy of self-tolerance, long-range hedonism, self-interest, social interest, self-direction, tolerance of others, acceptance of life's ambiguity and uncertainty, flexibility and openness to change, and the value of scientific thinking. Raphael will encourage Alan's commitment to his partner and church.*

If Alan seems reluctant to accept the task of therapy, Raphael will look for the sources of this resistance. Raphael will examine his own behavior, but also test the hypothesis that Alan is embarrassed about his situation or that he feels hopeless or that he can't change. Low frustration tolerance could also be creating Alan's unwillingness to work, or he might be punishing himself for his awful thoughts that are in violation of his religious values.

THERAPEUTIC TECHNIQUES

The major technique used in REBT is *D*, or disputing. Albert Ellis typically begins using disputation very quickly. However, other REBT counselors would argue that teaching comes before disputing. Wolfe (2007) suggested that the first task of the therapist is teaching the client about REBT—what is expected of client and therapist and the general process of the therapy. Resources exist that can be given to the client to read, such as Grieger's (1989) client guide. For some clients, it is also useful to directly teach the ABCs, *D*s, and *E*s. The therapist patiently teaches the client how to identify *A*s, search out *B*s (most likely iBs), and then link these to *C*s. Ultimately, the client learns to dispute his iBs to reach *E*, the new effective philosophy. Dryden and Neenan (2006) emphasize that the client should be taught how to generalize what he learns in counseling, so that it can be applied to new situations without resorting to the company of an REBT therapist.

In REBT, techniques, are usually divided into three categories: cognitive, emotive, and behavioral (Ellis & MacLaren, 2005). In the sections following, I review a selection of these.

Disputing

Cognitive disputes often begin with asking the client to assume that the *A* is true (Dryden & Neenan, 2006). For instance, Larry's therapist would say, "So, let's assume that if you dance in public, others will laugh at you." Even if the *A* is very illogical, the counselor should avoid challenging it in the interest of getting to the beliefs beyond the *A*.

Dryden (1994) cautioned that counselors should be sensitive in their use of disputing techniques, particularly when the client is presenting a very traumatic experience, such as rape or other forms of physical or sexual abuse. "Your first task is to be empathic and your second task is to explain to her that you need to join together to help her give up her additional disturbance, but not her healthy upset" (Dryden, 1994, p. 57).

Ellis and MacLaren (2005) identify four kinds of disputing: functional, empirical, logical, and philosophic. Cognitive disputing can be accomplished through a Socratic approach, in which the therapists asks the client questions, or through the presentation of mini-lectures about the ABC process (Yankura & Dryden, 1994).

Pragmatic, or *functional, disputes* attempt to detach the client from his beliefs by emphasizing the consequences of the belief. The idea in this dispute is to show the client that the belief is interfering with the accomplishment of life goals (Ellis & MacLaren, 2005). The client is asked what will happen if he continues to hold the belief. Jim's counselor asks him, "Well, as long as you think that every time you screw something up you are a *really rotten* worm, what feelings are you likely to have, and how often? Because we know you're human and you *will* screw up!"

Empirical, or *realistic, disputing* involves asking the client what evidence supports his beliefs. Usually, iBs are counter to reality (defined as the social consensus on which we operate most of the time; Ellis, 1996a). For example, Lisa might be asked, "What evidence is there to support your belief that because Steve dumped you, you are a failure, a rotten person?"

Logical disputation focuses on the faulty logic of the client's iBs. The counselor asks the client if his belief is consistent or logical. Kathy's therapist might ask her, "Does it follow logically that if you fail one test in one class that you will always fail tests?" An example cited by Beal and colleagues (1996) is amusing: "I would very much like to win the Kentucky Lottery. If I did, I might win 10 million dollars. Wow, I would never have to work again. Now, because I very much *want* to win the lottery, does it follow logically that I *must* win the lottery?" (p. 217, italics in original).

Philosophical disputes focus on life satisfaction (Ellis & MacLaren, 2005). Sometimes, the client is so immersed in problems that he loses sight of the bigger issues in existence. To a client who believes that she is fat and ugly, the therapist might say "I realize that you are very unhappy with your weight. Do you suppose that there might be other things in your life that are meaningful and important?"

Raphael uses all of the disputing methods with Alan. He asks Alan what evidence exists that if the house burns down it is his fault and he is worthless? Where is it written that if he can't stop flipping light switches, he is a reprehensible worm?

Logical disputes include Does it logically follow that if he has these disturbing images he is a totally worthless person? If a friend had these beliefs, would Alan find them reasonable? Yes, it might be preferable to banish those disturbing images, but does that mean he absolutely has to or he can't live a meaningful life? Pragmatic disputes are What do you do to yourself by continuing to believe that it would be absolutely the end of the world and your existence if you did hit someone with your car on the way home from work? Where is it going to get you if you continue to believe that you must always be perfect?

BIBLIOTHERAPY

Clients in REBT are very often assigned readings, and very often these are Ellis' writings in various forms. One of Ellis' books was written specifically for the general public rather than clients or therapists, *How to Make Yourself Happy and Remarkably Less Disturbable* (1999e; see Box 9.3).

Alan likes to read, so Raphael loans him a copy of How to Make Yourself Happy. *He encourages Alan to go to the website of the Albert Ellis Institute and look at the materials there. On a weekly basis, Raphael asks Alan what he has learned from his studies.*

Box 9.3

Positive Thinking the REBT Way: The Five Self-Starting Beliefs

In his 1999 book, *How to Make Yourself Happy and Remarkably Less Disturbable*, Albert Ellis argued, as he has many times, that you *can* change if you want to. It just takes work and practice, and the right attitude. Always the proponent of self-help, Ellis recommended the following beliefs as the keys to happiness:

1. Because I am mainly a self-disturber, I can definitely stop disturbing myself.
2. I definitely can reduce my irrational thinking that sparks my emotional and behavioral problems.
3. Although I am distinctly fallible and easily disturbable, I also have the ability to think, feel, and act differently and thus to reduce my disturbances.
4. My emotional upsets include thoughts, feelings, and actions that I can observe and change.
5. Reducing my upsetness almost always requires persistent work and effort.

PROSELYTIZING

Albert Ellis wants you to become a disciple! Clients are often told to go out and spread the word, to try to help friends and relatives work on their iBs (Ellis, 2002). The idea behind this approach is that sometimes identifying and analyzing someone else's problem is easier than identifying and analyzing your own. Of course, you must warn your client that others may not uniformly respond positively. I guess then you have created a shame-attacking exercise (discussed later).

Raphael encourages Alan to try to help his wife or friends in his social group at church with their difficulties if the opportunity arises. For instance, if it is not a really "hot" topic, Alan might address Teresa's idea that she can't stand *his (Alan's) repetitive behavior.*

RECORDING THERAPY SESSIONS

Clients are often given tapes of their therapy sessions to study between appointments (Ellis & MacLaren, 2005). Several things are helpful about this approach. Clients don't usually remember all that happened during their sessions, so tape review can reveal aspects they've forgotten. Reviewing tapes also gives clients the chance to really listen to how they think, and they might become more objective about their situations as a result.

Alan routinely takes his counseling tapes home for review. He says that it helps him practice his changed thinking and philosophy. Sometimes Alan even plays these tapes for Teresa.

REFRAMING

Reframing involves helping clients see things a little differently. For example, clients can be encouraged to view *A*s as challenges rather than pains in the you-know-what (Ellis & MacLaren, 2005). Self-criticism can be reframed as self-help, but of course, this requires that the client be much less dogmatic about it.

Raphael encourages Alan to understand his "checking" behavior as an effort to keep himself and Teresa safe. Of course, this is a drastic way of doing so, but the reframe may help both Alan and Teresa to relax a little about the symptom.

STOP AND MONITOR

Because some clients have great difficulty noticing their cognitions, it is sometimes helpful to have them place cues in the environment. Every time the client notices the cue, he is to stop and observe his thoughts at that moment (Ellis & MacLaren, 2005). Cues can be anything—a string around a finger or a yellow sticky on a computer monitor.

Alan decides to wear a ring on his right hand that he has not worn in years. Every time he glances at the ring, he observes and records his thoughts. He can then analyze them for faulty beliefs. When they can, Raphael and Alan also use the thought log in their sessions to track the sequences leading up to Alan's repetitive behavior or the disturbing imagery.

RATIONAL COPING STATEMENTS

As clients dispute their iBs, they create Es, effective new philosophies. Part of the Es are rational coping statements, which are sentences the client constructs that he should review and practice as part of working to change his ways (Ellis, 1995b). An example of a rational coping statement might be, "I never absolutely need what I want. I only, only prefer it and can live reasonably happily even if I am deprived of it" (Ellis, 1995a, p. 19). Ellis (2002) cautions that these mantras should be kept realistic, checked against what happens in the world, and revised as necessary.

Raphael teaches Alan rational coping statements to use. He asks Alan to restrain his repetitive behavior and talk himself through his discomfort saying something like "If I forgot to turn off the light switch, something could happen. It is unlikely, but if something bad happened, I can deal with it. It won't be absolutely terrible or awful, and I won't be a terrible and awful person." Similar statements could be developed about driving home from work and the troubling images. Alan could practice these statements first using imaginal techniques, and then in vivo.

RATIONAL EMOTIVE IMAGERY

Rational emotive imagery (REI) (Maultsby & Ellis, 1974) is an important emotional disputation technique (Yankura & Dryden, 1994). In REI, the client is asked to close his eyes and conjure up the terrible, awful, dysfunctional emotion that has been targeted in collaboration with the counselor. When the client has fully achieved the emotional experience, he signals the counselor, who then instructs the client to change the feeling into a healthy negative emotion. After the client has achieved this transformation, he is asked to gradually return to the therapy situation. He is asked how he feels now, and how he managed to change from the unhealthy to healthy feelings. A bonus in this technique is that the client can learn to distinguish between healthy and unhealthy emotions if the therapist allows the client to pick the second emotion (the therapist just insists on a healthy emotion and lets the client choose it).

Raphael and Alan start with the light switch behavior. Alan closes his eyes and tries to feel the anxiety that would result if he did not check the switches after leaving a room. When he indicates that he is fully experiencing this emotion, Raphael asks him to change it to a healthier emotion. Alan has great difficulty doing this. At first, he does not know what emotion to turn to. Raphael suggests concern. After Alan has made the emotional transformation, Raphael asks him to open his eyes. They talk about what Alan did to change his feeling of anxiety to concern, and Alan reports that he changed his thoughts; for example, he changed the thought "Something terrible is going to happen, and it will be all my fault. Because I did not keep the terrible thing from happening, I am imperfect and a terrible, horrible person" to "Something terrible could happen. If it does, it does not mean that I am worthless because I did not prevent it. I would like to prevent terrible things from happening, but I don't absolutely have to, and sometimes I can't. This failure does not make me a rotten person." He also reported thinking that the connection between light switches and awful events was probably not based in reality.

Flamboyant Therapist Actions

This intervention can be verbal or nonverbal. Ellis used this one often, in a verbal mode, either by swearing (and thereby modeling that he is not affected by what others think of him) or in the choice of language used (terms such as *rotten person, worm, no-goodnick*, and so forth). Nonverbal flamboyance is even more dramatic. The therapist could proceed to stand on his head in session and then ask the client to evaluate the behavior. When the client indicates that this stunt is a little weird (or stupid), the therapist can then respond with, "Well, does that make me a weird or stupid person?"

Raphael, in the midst of a discussion with Alan about his embarrassing need to check light switches, jumps to his feet and proceeds to turn in circles until he is so dizzy he can hardly stand. All the while he is singing, "Take me out to the ballgame." Alan, at first, is shocked, and then begins to laugh at Raphael. When Raphael, exhausted and dizzy, is able to talk again, he and Alan discuss what happened, with Raphael modeling rational thinking and emphasizing that maybe his behavior is silly, but that doesn't make him a stupid or worthless person.

Humor

REBT counselors believe in having some fun . . . gently (DiGiuseppe, 1995b; Ellis, 2005b). One must never make fun of the client, only of his silly behavior or thinking. Ellis devised some REBT tunes just for this purpose (Ellis & MacLaren, 2005; see also Box 9.4).

Raphael will have to be careful using humor with Alan because he is clearly very sensitive about his troubles. He could gently jest with Alan about the light switch issue (How many times does he do it? Is it a particular switch or one of a certain color? Would he like to work on the switch in Raphael's office?). However, Raphael would have to be certain that he and Alan had a solid relationship before trying anything like this.

Forceful Coping Statements and Taped Disputing

Rational coping statements can be made into an emotive technique by having the client state them forcefully, maybe even yelling them at full volume (Ellis & MacLaren, 2005). Forceful coping statements and forceful disputing statements can also be recorded for the client to listen to between sessions.

Raphael will encourage Alan to practically shout at himself when he has the thought that he might not have turned off the lights and something bad could happen, "I'd rather prevent something bad from happening, but I am not worthless if something bad does happen!" If he has an experience in which he believes that others disapprove, he should forcefully tell himself, "I'd rather that others accept me, but if they don't, I can stand it and I am OK!" I don't have to be perfect; I am a fallible human being." Alan can tape these statements and listen to them every morning before going to work.

Box 9.4

Sing Along with Albert Ellis

Perfect Rationality
(Tune: "Funiculi, Funicula" by Luigi Denza)

Some think the world must have a right direction,
And so do I—and so do I!
Some think that, with the slightest imperfection
They can't get by—and so do I!
For I, I have to prove I'm superhuman,
And better far than people are!
To show I have miraculous acumen—
And always rate among the Great!
Perfect, perfect rationality
Is, of course, the only thing for me!
How can I ever think of being
If I must live fallibly?
Rationality must be a perfect thing for me!

Love Me, Love Me, Only Me!
(Tune: "Yankee Doodle Dandy")

Love me, love me, only me
Or I'll die without you!
Make your love a guarantee
So I can never doubt you!
Love me, love me totally—really, really try dear;
But if you demand love, too
I'll hate you till I die, dear!
Love me, love me all the time
Thoroughly and wholly!
Life turns into slushy slime
'Less you love me solely!
Love me with great tenderness
With no ifs or buts, dear.
If you love me somewhat less,
I'll hate your goddamned guts, dear!

You for Me and Me for Me
(Tune: "Tea for Two" by Vincent Youmans)

Picture you upon my knee
Just you for me, and me for me!
And then you'll see

How happy I will be, dear!
Though you beseech me
You never will reach me—
For I am autistic
As any real mystic!
And only relate to
Myself with a great to-do, dear!
If you dare to try to care
You'll see my caring soon will wear,
For I can't pair and make our sharing fair!
If you want a family,
We'll both agree you'll baby me—
Then you'll see how happy I will be!

I Wish I Were Not Crazy!
(Tune: "Dixie" by Dan Emmett)

Oh, I wish I were really put together—
Smooth and fine as patent leather!
Oh, how great to be rated innately sedate!
But I'm afraid that I was fated
To be rather aberrated—
Oh, how sad to be mad as my Mom and my Dad!
Oh, I wish I were not crazy! Hooray! Hooray!
I wish my mind were less inclined
To be the kind that's hazy!
I could, of course, agree to be less crazy—
But I, alas, am just too goddamned lazy!

ROLE-PLAYING

Role-playing is used in several ways in REBT. Wolfe (2007) indicates that role playing can be used to problem solve around the practical problems that bring clients to therapy (e.g., how to assertively express one's feelings). Role-playing can also be used to assess irrational beliefs by asking the client to enact the situations that elicit dysfunctional consequences. Rational role reversal is useful after the client has learned something about disputing iBs. The client takes the counselor role and disputes the therapist's iBs. For best effect, the therapist should play a naive client, presenting a problem that is close to the client's (Dryden, 1995b). If it seems as though the client might respond well, the therapist can humorously overdo the whiny thing: "Oh poor little miserable me. Everyone should be nice to me because I am such a wimp!"

Raphael could play the client and have Alan dispute his iBs about light switches and being frightened about driving. He could also present as a client feeling guilty about having "bad" thoughts in some context.

RATIONAL–IRRATIONAL DIALOGUES

Dryden (1995c) described several techniques under this heading, all of which involve interchanges based on iBs and rBs. In the zigzag approach, the client lists a rational belief, and then attacks the rB with an irrational belief. A rational defense is then formulated, which is attacked via irrational belief. This process continues until the client has exhausted his irrational attacks. This technique is called zigzag because it is typically done on paper with the client filling in blocks like the ones shown in Figure 9.1. The same kind of dialogue can be done with two-chair role-playing. One chair is the rational chair, the other the irrational, and the client moves back and forth between them.

REINFORCEMENTS AND PENALTIES

REBT therapists often assign reinforcements that are self-administered when the client completes a "work" task (Ellis & MacLaren, 1998). Likewise, penalties are things the client doesn't like doing, and they are activated if the client does not complete his task. For example, if Jenny completes her shame attacking assignment of making funny faces at people in the mall, she can then go eat at fast food heaven (Jenny loves french fries). If she fails to do her homework, she has to spend an hour cleaning her basement (a task that she hates).

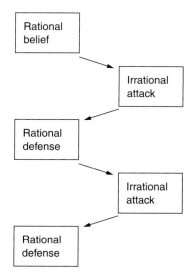

FIGURE 9.1. Zigzag Dialogue Form.
Source: Adapted from *Brief Rational Emotive Behavior Therapy* (p. 152) by W. Dryden, 1995, New York: John Wiley & Sons, Limited. Copyright © 1995 John Wiley & Sons Limited. Reproduced with permission.

Raphael tells Alan that if he goes without touching a light switch one evening, the next day he gets to play computer solitaire for 20 minutes. If he checks the light switches, no solitaire the next day at all.

SKILL TRAINING

Sometimes even if clients have all the right beliefs, they still have skill deficits that hinder their pursuit of their goals. REBT therapists would not hesitate to teach their clients assertive behavior or other social or interpersonal skills (Ellis, 2005b). In fact, this technique would fit well in the second stage of therapy, in which client and therapist might be working on life enhancement.

Because Alan sometimes feels awkward in social situations, Raphael decides to teach him some interpersonal communication skills. They role-play common social situations and devise responses for Alan. These listening and response skills should also help in his relationship with Teresa.

IN VIVO DESENSITIZATION

Borrowed from Behavior Therapy, in vivo desensitization is simply asking the client to experience the feared situation. Typically, forceful cognitive coping and dispute statements are employed (Dryden & Yankura, 1993). Basically similar to a technique called "staying in a difficult situation," repetition is important—the client must encounter the stressor repeatedly (somewhat like Ellis and his 130 encounters with women). This technique is often used with phobias, and it could also be used in an imaginal approach if the in vivo version is too threatening. The client would simply visit the feared situation in fantasy and rehearse disputes and coping statements verbally.

Alan is the perfect candidate for in vivo desensitization. Raphael asks him to simply deny the urge to turn off light switches. He explains that Alan will experience anxiety, but that he can talk himself through it using his rational coping statements. Raphael also requests that Alan not retrace his route home from work, using the same rationale and strategies.

ACTING ON RATIONAL BELIEFS

This technique is similar to the "as if" technique used in Individual Psychology therapy. Reasoning that we often spend a lot of time on iBs, it makes sense to have the client act on the basis of rBs developed in conjunction with the counselor (Ellis & MacLaren, 2005).

Alan is to act as though he truly believes that if he is not perfect, that is simply too bad, not a total catastrophe. If the house burns down, that is tough luck. Alan is to proceed with his life as if he believed that he would not be totally worthless if he did not prevent this event from happening. The next time he experiences a disturbing image, Alan is to behave as if it doesn't make him a no-good, evil person, simply one who has some faults.

HOMEWORK

REBT counselors almost always give clients homework (Dryden, 1994). Tasks are devised that fit the client's problems and may include techniques described here, such as shame attacking exercises or bibliotherapy. Another frequently used homework assignment is the REBT self-help form, shown in Box 9.5 (from Ellis & MacLaren, 2005). The client is instructed to complete the form daily, and then counselor and client review the results in the next counseling session.

Raphael would give Alan homework such as monitoring his thoughts, particularly during difficult situations. He might use the REBT self-help form with Alan to get him to chart and dispute his iBs. In fact, almost anything directed at Alan's beliefs could be used for homework.

SHAME ATTACKING

Shame attacking (Ellis, 2002) is a notorious REBT technique that Ellis used on himself before he ever knew what he was doing (see Box 9.1)! The client is instructed to go out and do something dreadfully embarrassing. We can think of lots of examples, such as standing backward in an elevator or singing "My Way" while standing in line in a burger joint. It is best, however, if the shame attacking behavior directly relates to the client's situation. The rationale for this technique is that the client will discover that he won't die of embarrassment, that it is not *absolutely 100% worse than bad* if others think he is weird. Rational coping statements can also (and maybe had better) be combined with this task.

Raphael devises a shame attacking exercise for Alan. He instructs Alan to stop at every stop sign on his way home stick his head out the car window, and yell, "Did I run over anything yet?" If Alan can see the humor in this task, it might be quite successful. Raphael must be careful in assigning it, though, so he devises a few less risky shame attacking exercises first. Alan could tell his buddies about his light switch thing, and even demonstrate for them. He and Teresa could take turns switching lights on and off in their living room for a designated period of time.

EVALUATION OF THE THEORY

REBT has evoked a great deal of controversy over the years. Some of the controversy is probably attributable to the personality of Albert Ellis—but of course he would not care if you did not like him or agree with his opinions! Ellis' use of salty language and liberal attitudes about sex may offend some, and if therapists adopt his style in blueprint manner, they'd better be ready for these kinds of criticisms (Garfield, 1995, p. 114).

On the most general level, REBT has been accused of being too intellectual, making it less useful for clients below certain levels of education and intelligence (Ellis, 1990; Garfield, 1989). Ellis himself specified that clients should be over the age of 8 and of average intelligence (Ellis, 1985). The emphasis on cognition in REBT, in the views of some, inappropriately de-emphasizes the role of client history, emotion, and the client–counselor relationship (Ellis, 1990). Lazarus (1989) also pointed to an over-reliance on cognitive disputation at the expense of other techniques.

Box 9.5

Rational Emotive Behavior Therapy (REBT) Self-Help Form

A (ACTIVATING EVENTS OR ADVERSITIES)

- Briefly summarize the situation you are disturbed about (what would a camera see?).
- An *A* can be *internal* or *external, real* or *imagined.*
- An *A* can be an event in the *past, present,* or *future.*

IBs (IRRATIONAL BELIEFS)   **D (DISPUTING IBs)**

To identify IBs, look for:
- Dogmatic Demands (musts, absolutes, shoulds)
- Awfulizing (It's awful, terrible, horrible)
- Low Frustration Tolerance (I can't stand it)
- Self/Other Rating (I'm/he/she is bad, worthless)

To dispute, ask youself:
- Where is holding this belief getting me? Is it *helpful* or *self-defeating?*
- Where is the evidence to support the existence of my irrational belief? Is it *consistent with social reality?*
- Is my belief *logical?* Does it follow from my preferences?
- Is it really *awful* (as bad as it could be)?
- Can I really not *stand* it?

C (CONSEQUENCES)

Major unhealthy negative **emotions:**

Major self-defeating **behaviors:**

Unhealthy negative emotions include:
- Anxiety
- Shame/ Embarrassment
- Depression
- Hurt
- Rage
- Jealousy
- Low Frustration Tolerance
- Guilt

E (EFFECTIVE NEW PHILOSOPHIES)

E (EFFECTIVE EMOTIONS AND BEHAVIORS)

New healthy
negative emotions:

New constructive
behaviors:

To think more rationally, strive for:
- Non-Dogmatic Preferences (wishes, wants, desires)
- Evaluating Badness (it's bad, unfortunate)
- High Frustration Tolerance (I don't like it, but I can stand it)
- Not Globally Rating Self or Others (I—and others—are fallible human beings)

Healthy negative emotions include:
- Disappointment
- Concern
- Annoyance
- Sadness
- Regret
- Frustration

Weinrach (1996) discussed several shortcomings of REBT theory. He believes that the theory has neglected to attend to cultural differences that affect definitions of rationality and the conduct of counseling. He pointed out that sometimes what is labeled rational could be counter to values from cultures other than the Westernized European American (for instance, when the avoidance of the disapproval of parents or other family members seems to drive emotions and behavior is deemed irrational). Weinrach lamented that some REBT counselors have inadequate interpersonal skills, being more "tough minded than tender-minded" (Weinrach, 1996, p. 68). Neenan and Dryden (2000) add that REBT is often criticized because REBT therapists talk too much and, worse, put words in clients' mouths (p. 48). These criticisms are consistent with the idea that REBT is authoritarian (Kleiner, 1979).

The concept of long-range hedonism has been seen as problematic by numerous authors. At the least, this philosophy can lead to ignoring the interrelatedness of human existence; at its worst, it could promote very effective sociopathy (Weinrach, 1996; Wessler 1996; Woolfolk & Sass, 1989). Finally, Weinrach noted that REBT promises more than it can deliver—that presentations of the theory fail to note that REBT may not be the best approach for some clients or problems. Noting that "there is hardly a topic in the area of counseling, psychotherapy, REBT or CBT about which Ellis has not written, spoken or sung," Weinrach found this "anything you can do I can do better" ideology self-defeating (Weinrach, 1996, p. 72).

Ellis energetically defends his theory against all critics at any opportunity (Ellis, 1979b, 1989, 1996b). He acknowledges the need for attention to cultural issues in REBT, but maintains that the theory is flexible enough to apply across cultures. Long-term hedonism is not a harmful philosophy; it requires social interest and cooperation because to survive and be happy, people typically choose to live in social groups (Ellis, 1989).

The strengths of REBT lie in its simple, clear-cut theory and method (Mahoney, Lyddon, & Alford, 1989). These qualities are probably appreciated by clients and therapists alike (Garfield, 1989). REBT also sanctions a wide variety of techniques, so its flexibility allows the counselor to meet many different kinds of client presentations. Although there are no data to support the brevity of REBT, Ellis maintains that it takes less time than other forms of Cognitive-Behavior Therapy. Ellis's activity and professional visibility lent energy and credence to the theory (Mahoney et al., 1989).

QUALITIES OF THE THEORY

Precision and Testability. Although on the surface, REBT offers some fairly simple and precise predictions (e.g., irrational beliefs should lead to psychological dysfunction), many have identified problems with the testability of REBT theory.

First of all, defining exactly what happens in REBT is difficult (Haaga & Davison, 1989). As I noted earlier, Ellis distinguished between two types of REBT, elegant and inelegant, and the latter is equated with all other forms of cognitive-Behavior Therapy. However, these two interventions would be difficult to separate and assess because the former certainly contains a great deal of the latter. In addition, a concrete description of the elements of elegant, or preferential, REBT has not been offered.

Haaga and Davidson (1993) pointed out that it is difficult to define that key term in REBT, *irrational belief.* In his many writings, Ellis gave numerous definitions of the iB, creating much confusion about the construct. The term *irrational* is not used as it typically is (i.e., to mean illogical or unreasonable; Oei, Hansen, & Miller, 1993). In his later writings,

Ellis defined irrational beliefs as those that lead to unproductive outcomes (Ellis, 1994a; Wessler, 1996). Oei and colleagues (1993) pointed out that this definition is circular, and further, that using this definition would force researchers to wait to observe an individual's outcomes to get any research done.

Ziegler (1999) and Wessler (1996) pointed out that a big challenge to REBT theory is the formulation of clear-cut hypotheses about its central constructs—antecedent events, cognition, emotion, and other consequences. The problem here is that over the years that he has been refining his theory, Ellis became more and more emphatic that *A*s, *B*s, and *C*s overlap significantly and are mutually influential. Bond and Dryden labeled this the "interdependence principle" (1996, p. 30). Because thoughts, feelings, and behaviors blend together, it is impossible to precisely measure any one of the primary constructs of the theory (Bond & Dryden, 1996; Smith, 1989). For instance, the major measures of irrational belief used in research, the Rational Behavior Inventory (RBI) and the Irrational Beliefs Test (IBT), seem to measure beliefs and emotions simultaneously (Zurawski & Smith, 1987).

Empirical Validity. Many studies report positive findings for REBT. However, the value of these findings is often suspect because of questions regarding the operationalization of variables (most particularly, iBs; Zurawski & Smith, 1987). However, it is fairly well established that REBT is generally efficacious (David, Szentagotai, Eva, & Macavei, 2005; Oei et al., 1993) even if the exact mechanisms that lead to change are not specifiable. Indeed, Haaga and Davison (1989) commented that "RET cannot be considered a treatment of choice for any disorder. On the other hand, there is little evidence that RET would be contraindicated for any type of patient" (p. 494).

RESEARCH SUPPORT

Outcome Research. Although REBT has not been used in the major psychotherapy outcome studies, many studies have addressed the outcomes of REBT. For the most part, the findings have been supportive, but methodological problems often complicate the interpretation of results. Using standard summary review format, McGovern and Silverman (1986) concluded, for example, that their review of research published between 1977 and 1982 provided significant support for REBT theory. A similar review by Silverman, McCarthy, and McGovern (1992) found that 49 out of 89 studies they reviewed favored REBT over other approaches, and that many not included in the favorable 49 showed no differences between REBT and comparison approaches. In all of these reviews, results varied widely based on the types of outcome measures used. It seems relatively clear that studies employing measures of rationality, and to a smaller extent, transient anxiety, produce more positive results, whereas those using more stable (theoretically) measures (self-esteem or self-concept; Silverman et al., 1992) show weaker effects. In contrast, in a comparison of drug treatment alone and REBT in combination with it, Macaskill and Macaskill (1996) found that combination treatment was superior for depressed individuals who had high levels of cognitive dysfunction. Although this study used a small sample (20 clients), it employed a wide range of outcome measures, including some that could be considered less reactive.

Hajzler and Bernard (1991) reviewed 21 studies that investigated the outcomes of rational emotive education (REE), an educational approach that involves teaching the principles of

REBT to students in classroom settings. The outcome measures used in the 21 studies in-cluded measures of irrationality, self-esteem, internal versus external locus of control, and anxiety. The most robust finding supported the hypothesis that REE decreased irrationality; the results for outcome on other indexes were less convincing. Hajzler and Bernard generally concluded that their review supported the effectiveness of REE; however, questions remain about the validity of the measures commonly used to assess irrationality.

Several meta-analyses have been completed on studies of REBT. Gonzales et al. (2004) analyzed 19 studies of REBT with children and adolescents, finding a moderate effect size (0.50). Extrapolating, this value means that the average treatment client scored better than 69% of the control group. Lyons and Woods (1991) reviewed 70 studies of outcome and found that REBT was effective in comparison to baseline or control conditions, but not significantly different from cognitive behavior modification or Behavior Therapy. In se-lecting the studies they used, Lyons and Woods only required that the treatment group have "elements of RET" (p. 358), thus illustrating one of the major problems with research on REBT—defining the treatment.

Engles, Garnefski, and Diekstra (1993) used more stringent selection criteria, reviewing 28 studies (covering the period from 1971 to 1987) that tested interventions that were specifically described as rational or rational–emotive. Their meta-analysis found results very similar to those of Lyons and Woods (1991). Clients receiving REBT were better off than those in control or placebo groups, but REBT was found to be no different in efficacy when compared to other kinds of psychological intervention (e.g., systematic desensitization or combinations of REBT and specific behavioral elements). Further, no differences in effec-tiveness were found across client problem types or types of outcome measured. Two obser-vations suggest caution when evaluating Engles and colleagues' results: (a) the small sample size of many of the studies may have reduced the power to detect significant differences be-tween treatments, and (b) the client sample across the studies was biased towards the YAVIS (young, attractive, verbal, intelligent, and social) client and milder levels of disturbance. Soloman and Haaga (1995) questioned whether meta-analytic results can be generalized to the routine practice of REBT and noted several other methodological limitations of the re-search (such as a lack of follow-up studies and documentation of attrition rates) reviewed by Engles and colleagues and Lyons and Woods (1991).

Gossette and O'Brien (1992) presented one very negative view of the efficacy of REBT. These authors reviewed comparisons of REBT with wait-list, placebo, or other treatment groups and concluded that "RET has little or no practical benefit for either children or adults, normal or troubled" (p. 20). Even though they found evidence for changes in irra-tional beliefs and, to a somewhat lesser extent, reductions in self-reported emotional dis-turbance, Gossette and O'Brien maintained that these observations paled in the light of the lack of behavioral changes demonstrated in studies of REBT. They explained that the observed changes could be attributed to the verbal training (conditioning) inherent in REBT, which can be "conceptualized as a rather crudely designed verbal training history, in which forceful punitive pressures await 'irrational' statements, while only relatively weak positive reinforcement follows espousal of 'rational' statements" (p. 19).

Three observations can be made about the Gossette and O'Brien (1992) review. First, it was published in the *Journal of Behavior Therapy and Experimental Psychiatry*. Presumably, the authors are behaviorists and thus may have an ideological stake in defeating REBT, much in the same way that REBT theorists may overpromote the approach. Second, a large number of comparisons in Gossette and O'Brien's review were obtained from dissertation research, which they maintained was probably as good as or better than published research because of the detailed description of treatments and the overriding faculty supervision provided in these efforts. However, it could be countered that dissertation research mostly goes unpublished because it does not meet the prevailing methodological standards of the profession. Further, Gossette and O'Brien did not take into account sample sizes, power levels, or other method-ological characteristics of the studies they reviewed, and rather than using meta-analysis, they used a simple count of the number of significant results obtained across studies. Notice that many of these criticisms could be applied to the other reviews of REBT research.

Finally, an interesting outcome project was described by Ellis and Joffe (2002), in which the opinions of Ellis' Friday-night session participant-clients were summarized (see the Background section for a description of these sessions). After collecting data for a few years (with at 40% response rate), Ellis and Joffe randomly selected the responses of 100 volun-teers and found that whereas no clients reported these sessions to be not helpful, 19% responded that they were somewhat helpful and 78% thought that they were very helpful. Although this study has all kinds of obvious flaws and bias, I find it to be an aspect of Ellis history that is difficult to leave out.

Theory-Testing Research. Most of the research that bears on REBT theory has focused on the important REBT proposition that cognitive processes lead to emotional distress. Many of these studies have used nonexperimental methods; most simply measure the relation-ships between some theoretically important measure (unconditional self acceptance, irra-tional beliefs, frustration tolerance) with some measure of psychological distress. I will briefly review a few of these.

Davies (2006) reported on a study of the relations between unconditional self-acceptance and irrational beliefs. Using both the IBT and a short version of the General Attitudes and Belief Scale (GABS), Davies found support for REBT theory. Chamber-lain and Haaga (2001) found that after controlling for initial levels of self-esteem, USA was related to low propensity for depression and found that participants higher in USA were more objective in evaluating their performances (on a speech) than individuals lower in USA and less likely to denigrate individuals who evaluated their speeches poorly. However, at issue in these studies is the measure of USA; it is found to be corre-lated with self-esteem (around the 0.5 level) which questions whether the construct is really being accurately measured.

Macavei (2005) compared the beliefs of depressed, mildly depressed and nondistressed groups, and found that the groups differed in expected ways on various dimensions of irrationality. These results were seen as supporting REBT theory, but questions about instrumentation and statistical analyses compromise the degree to which we can be certain about this conclusion. In contrast, Jones and Trower (2004) tested competing hypotheses from REBT and Cognitive Therapy about anger, finding more evidence to support CT than REBT.

Harrington (2006) developed a multidimensional measure of frustration intolerance, the Frustration Discomfort Scale (FDS), which contains subscales for emotional intolerance, dis-comfort intolerance, entitlement, and achievement. He then assessed the relationship between scores on this scale and depression, anxiety and anger in a clinical sample. As would be predicted by REBT theory, frustration intolerance was positively related to psychological distress, even after statistically controlling for negative affect and self-esteem. Subscales on the FDS were uniquely related to the various measures of dysfunction: anxiety was most related to emotional intolerance, discomfort intolerance to depressed mood, and entitlement to anger.

The trouble with all of these studies is their nonexperimental nature. Because no manipulations are used, cognitive processes could be causing the psychological distress, as predicted by theory, or the other way around. Another possibility is that the measures are tapping the same global process or that an unknown, third variable could be responsible for the relationships found. Across these studies, there is wide variation in attempts to capture the last possibility by using measures of other constructs.

Further controversy centers on the nature of the measures used to assess the endorsement of iBs. As early as 1987, Zurawski and Smith cast doubt on much of the literature supporting REBT when they found that two often-used measures of iBs (the IBT and the Rational Behavior Inventory, RBI; Shorkey & Whiteman, 1977) seemed to be tapping the same thing as measures of general negative affectivity. These concerns prompted the construction of the General Attitude and Belief Scale (GABS; DiGiuseppe, Leaf, Exner, & Robin, 1988, cited in David et al., 2005). Bernard (1998) tested the psychometric properties of this measure and found them to be acceptable. Scores on the measure differentiated between those from individuals receiving couples counseling and individuals who were not, presumably supporting the REBT assertion that irrational beliefs are associated with psychological distress. However, a review of the items on the GABS suggests that there still may be some confounding between irrationality and emotionality (e.g., "it is awful and terrible to be treated unfairly by people in my life" for example, Bernard, 1988, p. 189).

However, this study, as well as others that simply correlate irrational beliefs and distress, are not good tests of REBT theory, according to Szetagotai and Kallay (2006). For one thing, this method leaves out the A (activating event), an essential component of the theory. Secondly, these authors point out that low levels of irrational belief do not necessarily correspond to high levels of rational belief.

Other tests of REBT theory have attempted to experimentally manipulate beliefs. For example, Cramer and Buckland (1995) had participants read and repeat rational or irrational statements, and then assessed state anxiety and levels of irrational beliefs. They found that participants in the rational beliefs condition reported lower levels of anxiety than those in the irrational condition; scores on the Irrational Beliefs Scale (Malouff & Schutte, 1986) followed the same pattern. One problem with studies that use experimental manipulations is possible demand characteristics—that is, cues that lead participants to figure out what the experimenter expects. Typically, participants obey these messages. Although Cramer and Buckland attempted to control for this problem, it is not clear that they were successful. Similarly, Harris, Davies, and Dryden (2006) randomly assigned participants to one of three conditions (rational belief, irrational belief, or irrelevant belief) and then subjected them to a stressful situation. They found that participants who held irrational beliefs showed more anxiety and concern than did the other groups, and also showed marked increases in blood pressure from pre- to posttest. A difficulty, however, with this research is that it appears that the groups were possibly different on blood pressure readings at pretest, making conclusions based on pre- and post-changes suspect. Also, this study would be subject to the guessing effect described previously.

Smith, Houston, and Zurawski (1984) assessed participants' endorsements of irrational beliefs (via the Irrational Belief Test), and then exposed them to stressful or nonstressful interviews, and afterwards, measured psychological and physiological distress. Results suggested that only cognitive variables (preoccupation with cognitive processes, denigration of self or one's performance) were related to endorsement of iBs, and that further, a measure of fear of negative evaluation (FNE) was more powerful than iBs in predicting emotional distress. These findings led Smith and colleagues to suggest that "it could be argued that this model is a useful metaphor but an inaccurate theory. Emotionally distressed persons may behave *as if* they endorsed various irrational beliefs" (1984, p. 200; italics in original).

In a comprehensive review, Smith and Allred (1986) concluded that at best, method and measurement problems may have created a situation in which REBT has not been adequately tested. However, they also noted that "it may also be, however, that RET provides an effective intervention but a misleading account of maladjustment and the process of change. The ABCD framework may be a useful metaphor but an inaccurate theory" (p. 82).

David et al. (2005) came to the opposite conclusion, arguing that there was significant evidence in support of REBT theory and outcome. These disparate conclusions are likely due to a number of factors, including research published between Smith and Allred's review and David et al.'s. On the other hand, my assessment of the sophistication of REBT research is that although it has improved somewhat, methodological rigor is still very much lacking in many of published studies.

Given the conflicting results found in tests of REBT theory, it is probably safest to remain unconvinced of the validity of the REBT predictions about beliefs and emotions. Thus, Oei and colleagues (1993) concluded that although REBT is "an effective therapeutic intervention for a variety of target problems, there is no evidence to show that improvement in RET is due to changing irrational beliefs to rational beliefs" (p. 199).

ISSUES OF INDIVIDUAL AND CULTURAL DIVERSITY

Ellis claimed that he was the "first prominent psychologist to advocate gay liberation" (1992a, p.10). He did, in fact, write the preface to a classic book on homosexuality (Corey's 1951 *The Homosexual in America*) at a time when this subject was very taboo. Ellis's history of sexual liberalism as well as REBT's emphasis on tolerance of self and others would lead him and his advocates to argue that REBT does not perpetuate bias based on sexual orientation.

Writing on the issue of multiculturalism, Ellis (2002) acknowledges that "therapists, like all humans, easily succumb to narrow-mindedness and intolerance" (p. 203). Still, he continues by adding that the emphasis on USA and UOA in REBT practice promotes openness to cultural difference.

On a theoretical level, the importance placed on personal responsibility and assumption that problems reside within the person (in the form of iBs) in REBT can lead to an underemphasis on the role of social or cultural factors in people's lives. Groups who are the targets of negative stereotypes and oppression, such as women, ethnic minorities, and gay, lesbian, or bisexual (GLB) individuals, are greatly affected by these biased attitudes and prejudicial behavior, and to tell them to change the ways they think about these influences would appear to be detrimental to their functioning, if not discriminatory. REBT's assumption that the world is not fair (inherent in the third musturbatory attitude) could be seen as acceptance of prejudicial attitudes and discrimination in behavior. Ellis, of course, would maintain that REBT teaches clients to see the situation as bad, not awful, and that it is very appropriate to encourage clients to change the *A*s through working for social justice (Ellis, 1999d). Ellis (2005b) says it this way: "clients can unconditionally accept themselves and other individuals and can achieve high frustration tolerance when faced with life adversities. . . . and most multicultural issues involve bias and intolerance— which REBT particularly works against" (p. 195).

Robin and DiGiuseppe (1997) maintained that REBT is an appropriate intervention for clients from all cultures. Citing REBT's empirical base, they argued that REBT does not need to rely on constructs that are essentially untested, such as those found in more construct-laden theory (e.g., psychoanalysis) that are liable to be culturally biased. They further argued that REBT's stoic philosophical values of tolerance and acceptance are compatible across such diverse cultures as Western European, Asian, and Native American. Acknowledging that the empiricist perspective of REBT is not compatible with some foundational cultural values (for instance, those that emphasize spirituality), Robin and DiGiuseppe asserted that it is still helpful and culturally respectful to point out the *B–C* connection and allow clients the choice of whether to use the information. They recommended that when working with clients from non-Western cultures, the counselor do two things: (a) tell the client about his expectations for therapy and (b) find out what the client's expectations are.

REBT is active, directive, and short term, which is consistent with the expectations of clients from many non-Western cultures (Sue & Sue, 2003; Wolfe, 2007). Still, Ellis (2005a) recognized that indirect methods are more effective with some clients, and points to the use of stories, fables, and parables of examples of suitable interventions in these situations. Chen (1995) contended that the values underlying REBT (the emphasis on logical thinking, cognitive control of emotion, the counselor as teacher, and the active directive nature of therapy) are very consistent with those of the Chinese culture, so that REBT may be better than other theories for use with this cultural group. Disputing methods, however, probably need to be modified because the confrontive approach could create negative reactions in Chinese clients, who, although comfortable with the student role, become distressed about not knowing the answer to the teacher's questions. Instead, Chen recommended using didactic disputing, in which therapists provide clients with more alternatives. Also, emotive techniques should be used cautiously because of the normative Chinese reluctance to express feeling.

As with most of the other major theoretical approaches, REBT focuses on the individual. Healthy people are independent and autonomous. These values may clash with those of cultures that are more collectivistic (e.g., some Asian and Hispanic/Latino/Latina groups) and those to whom spirituality is very important and that downplay the importance of individuality (Sue & Sue, 2003). If the counselor does not recognize these biases, clients who are collectivistic can be labeled as dependent, immature, and fused with family or others (Sue, Ivey, & Pedersen, 1996).

REBT, again because it mostly locates problems and the responsibility for change within the person (i.e., cognitions), can be accused of being sexist as well. Women are devalued by our cultural norms, and to buy into these and to tell women to "deal with it and stop whining" is to ignore very real factors that influence women's mental health. Wolfe (1986) argued that the goals of REBT are consistent with feminist ideals for a number of reasons. REBT targets and disputes the shoulds, musts, and "love-slobbism" that are the basis of sex-role stereotypes (p. 401). An emphasis on personal responsibility and autonomy in determining the goals of therapy and the encouragement of assertiveness are also supportive of feminist values. Wolfe also maintained that REBT encourages women (and others) to fight for *A*-changes, or changes in the societal conditions that keep women and other groups down (1986, p. 401).

THE CASE STUDY

In many ways, the case of Alan is ripe for the application of REBT. Anxiety is central in REBT theory, and the cognitive behavioral slant of the approach seems helpful in working with Alan's behavioral disturbances. Alan shows symptoms of obsessive-compulsive disorder (OCD), about which Ellis theorized (1994b, 1997b). Alan's ABCs seem to be fairly easy to identify, although changing some of them might be tough (e.g., the images). A puzzle presented by this case is the origin of the religious/sexual images. Other approaches might attempt to locate the source of these troubling mental pictures, but the REBT therapist would more likely see them as connected to biological deficits inherent in OCD.

Summary

Rational Emotive Behavior Therapy starts with the premise that life events (*A*s) don't cause emotions (*C*s). Beliefs about the events (irrational *B*s or rational *B*s) are what link the *A*s and *C*s. Humans are innately predisposed to think both rationally and irrationally, and these tendencies can extend to color an individual's life philosophy. That is, healthy people tend to think in terms of preferences, whereas dysfunctional people think in terms of demands. Healthy people have rational life philosophies that include tolerance for self and others, acceptance of uncertainty, rational self and community interest, and an understanding of how one makes oneself disturbed. Dysfunctional people harbor many irrational beliefs that include musts, low frustration tolerance, and self-downing thoughts. They think in terms of absolutes and are conditional in their acceptance of self and others.

REBT follows an ABCDE model. After the ABCs are identified, the REBT counselor disputes the irrational beliefs to help the client achieve a new effect or an effective new philosophy. Cognitive, behavioral, and emotive techniques are applied in a teacher–student model. The therapist, typically active and directive, is unconditionally accepting of the client. He teaches the client the ABC model without focusing too much on the *A*s or *C*s.

REBT has been criticized for being too intellectual and ignoring emotions and significant events in clients' past. The emphasis on rationality, independence, and self-determination may be inconsistent with the experiences of clients from cultures other than those of Western European origins, those who are not heterosexual, or women. The idea that the world is not fair and we can't expect it to be may convey a tolerance of discrimination and oppression.

Research evidence supports the effectiveness of REBT. Studies attempting to test the theoretical assumptions of REBT are less supportive.

Visit Chapter 9 on the Companion Website at **www.prenhall.com/murdock** for chapter-specific resources and self-assessments.

Aaron T. Beck

CHAPTER 10

Cognitive Therapy

Steve is a 38-year-old Caucasian male. He lives in a residential treatment facility for recovering substance abusers and participates in a work-therapy program sponsored by a local hospital.

Steve is the only child of an upper-middle-class family. He characterizes his family life as "swell," like "Beaver Cleaver." Steve reports that his father was a great provider but that their relationship was distant. His relationship with his mother was similar.

When he was in third grade, Steve was sent to a private military academy. In seventh grade, he switched to public school, but was subsequently expelled for "acting up" (he wore a bikini to school one day). After he was expelled, Steve reentered the military academy, from which he eventually graduated.

When Steve was 11, his parents separated, and then divorced. Steve lived with his mother, who remarried when he was 17. He remembers his mother as being very sad about the divorce, but that she "put up a strong front," assuring him that "things would be all right."

After graduating from the military academy, Steve entered the navy, where he served for 4 years. After his discharge, he was working in an auto body shop when he discovered blood in his urine. He reports that his father sent him to the Mayo Clinic, where he was found to have a lesion on his left renal tube. Steve reports that his first episode of depression occurred at this time and that his first episode of mania occurred shortly thereafter. After seeing a psychiatrist, he was diagnosed as bipolar and treated with lithium.

In 1990 Steve was engaged to be married. Around that time he was involved in an automobile accident that resulted in the death of the driver of the other vehicle involved. Steve reports that he does not remember the accident because he was intoxicated (alcohol) but that the police determined that the accident was the other driver's fault. Nonetheless, he was charged with manslaughter, placed on probation, and ordered to pay $10,000 in *restitution. During this period, Steve's father was supportive, but his grandparents told him that his mother had announced to friends and family that she had "disowned" Steve.*

After these events, Steve's fiancée presented him with the ultimatum that if he drank alcohol again she would leave him. He reports that he stopped drinking easily. A year later, Steve's fiancée left him, and he resumed drinking. About 4 months later, Steve admitted himself voluntarily to the local Veteran's Administration Alcohol and Drug Abuse Treatment Unit. Steve has subsequently relapsed and returned to treatment twice. He is currently medicated with antabuse and lithium.

Steve is in counseling as part of his participation in the work-therapy program. He says that he is too immature and that he sacrifices self- and others' respect when he "acts out." Steve reports that he basically accepts himself as he is, but that sometimes he imagines his parents' point of view—their son is an "alcoholic and a manic-depressive" and this frightens and saddens him. He sometimes gets depressed about his situation. Steve tells his counselor that he wants to get back on his feet, get a good job, and become self-supporting.

BACKGROUND

The proper title Cognitive Therapy (CT) is typically reserved for the theoretical structure developed by Aaron T. Beck, beginning in the late 1960s. The development of this theory can roughly be divided into two phases: the period of schematic processing (pre-1990) and a newer variant of the theory that was proposed beginning in the mid-1990s (what I call the "modal" perspective; Beck, 1996, 1999; Clark & Beck, 1999). I will review both variants of the theory because the older theory has received significant research support and attention in clinical circles. Although the newer theory is an extension of the earlier version, it has received far less critical and empirical attention.

Before I proceed to further background, it is worth noting that in practice, the distinctions between Behavior Therapy (Chapter 8), Rational Emotive Behavior Therapy (Chapter 9), and Cognitive Therapy (Chapter 10) can get really blurry, at least if you are someone other than Judith or Tim Beck (see next paragraph). In fact, the term Cognitive Therapy is often used as a general label for a number of systems that emphasize the role of cognition in dysfunction and intervention. These approaches are also generally known as *Cognitive-Behavior Therapy*, and include Rational Emotive Behavior Therapy, problem solving, self-instructional training, and coping skills approaches (Arnkoff & Glass, 1995). In the real world, many therapists use a combination of techniques from all three approaches. However, if you follow the writings of the Becks, you will see that there is a very clear pure version of CT; you can watch Dr. Jennifer D. Lundgren do classic Cognitive Therapy with Helen on the *Theories in Action* DVD.

Aaron Temkin Beck was the son of Russian immigrants. According to Weishaar (1993), Lizzie Temkin, his mother, wanted to be a physician, but this was unheard of in the early 1900s. Lizzie married Harry Beck, a commercial printer with socialist leanings, and Aaron Beck was the youngest of their five children (born in 1921). The family was Jewish and very devoted to their religion.

Two of Beck's siblings died as children, leading to significant depression in his mother that abated only with Aaron's birth. As a result, Beck was overprotected by his mother (Weishaar, 1993). Beck almost died during his seventh year from sepsis that resulted from an infected broken bone. According to Weishaar (1993), this prolonged illness, hospitalization, and surgery resulted in Beck developing anxieties and phobias. He also had difficulties because of missed school and was held back a year in the first grade. He thought he was dumb and that others thought so, too. These beliefs challenged Aaron to work hard, and he became an excellent student, graduating first in his high school class. During this period he acquired his nickname, Tim (for Temkin, his middle name), which is used by his close friends and wife (Weishaar, 1993).

Beck put himself through college at Brown, delivering papers and working as a door-to-door salesperson (Weishaar, 1993). He majored in English and political science, and a consult with a career counselor suggested that he should be a YMCA counselor! Warned about quota systems enforced against Jews, Beck still applied to medical school at Yale and received his MD in 1946. According to Weishaar, Beck admitted that his anxiety was one reason why he chose medical school—he wanted to defeat his blood-injury phobia. He acknowledged other fears as well, such as of abandonment, public speaking, and heights (Weishaar, 1993, p. 13).

After flirting with a career in neurology, he turned his attention to psychiatry and was classically trained as a psychoanalyst. Early in his career Beck was engaged in the science of psychotherapy, attempting to test Freud's hypothesis that depression was anger turned inward. Instead he found that depressed individuals sought the approval of others (Arnkoff & Glass, 1995). A subsequent series of studies investigating the construct of masochism in depression more clearly revealed that a distinguishing characteristic of depression seemed to be pessimism and negativity rather than masochism (Clark & Beck, 1999). At about the same time, Beck's clinical work was informing his theoretical development. He began to notice that his clients had thoughts during free association that they did not report (Beck, 1997a). Most of these thoughts had to do with the analytic relationship (worries about what the therapist thought of the client, for example), and they were closely associated with the client's current emotional state. Beck turned his attention to these thoughts (later labeled automatic thoughts) along with what he called the internal communication system, and Cognitive Therapy was launched (Beck, 1997b).

Beck acknowledges the contributions of other psychologists to his system, but maintains that he learned very little from existing theories of psychotherapy. Among the influences Beck recognizes are the philosopher Kant, and cognitive theorists Magna Arnold, George Kelley, and Albert Bandura. He characterized Albert Ellis as a pioneer whose ideas provided support for his (Beck's) break from traditional psychoanalytic ideas (Beck, 1991). Beck even uses the famous Epictetus quote usually associated with Ellis's REBT in his well-known 1976 book, *Cognitive Therapy and the Emotional Disorders* ("Men are not moved by things but the views which they take of them" Epictetus, cited in Beck, 1976, p. 47).

Beck is a prolific writer and researcher, having published hundreds of journal articles and many books. Both the medical and psychological communities have recognized his work. In 1989 Beck was awarded the American Psychological Association's Distinguished Scientific Award for the Applications of Psychology. He has also received the Association for the Advancement of Behavior Therapy Lifetime Achievement Award (1998) and the American Psychological Society James McKeen Cattell Fellow Award in Applied Psychology (1993). Beck is currently Professor Emeritus of Psychiatry at the School of Medicine at the University of Pennsylvania.

Beck founded the Beck Institute for Cognitive Therapy and Research in 1994. You can view its website at www.beckinstitute.org. Other websites of interest include the International

Association for Cognitive Psychotherapy at http://www.cognitivetherapyassociation.org, which publishes the *Journal of Cognitive Therapy: An International Quarterly.*

Beck's daughter, Judith, is a psychologist and cognitive therapist.[1] She is currently director of the Beck Institute. Judith's books *Cognitive Therapy: Basics and Beyond* (1995) and *Cognitive Therapy for Challenging Problems* (2005) present structured, easy-to-follow guidelines for the conduct of CT. If you want to try the CT approach to that diet you've been putting off, you could acquire Judith Beck's 2007 book, *The Beck Diet Solution.* Read a selection from *Basics and Beyond* in Box 10.1.

Box 10.1

Judith Beck on Automatic Thoughts

Automatic thoughts are a stream of thinking that coexists with a more manifest stream of thought (Beck, 1964). These thoughts are not peculiar to people with psychological distress; they are an experience common to us all. *Most of the time we are barely aware of these thoughts, though with just a little training we can easily bring these thoughts into consciousness.* When we become aware of our thoughts, we may automatically do a reality check if we are not suffering from psychological dysfunction.

A reader of this text, for example, while focusing on the content of this chapter, may have the automatic thought, "I don't understand this," and feel slightly anxious. He may, however, spontaneously (i.e., without conscious awareness) respond to the thought in a productive way: "I *do* understand *some* of it; let me just reread this section again."

This kind of automatic reality testing and responding to negative thoughts is a common experience. People who are in distress, however, may not engage in this kind of critical examination. Cognitive therapy teaches them tools to evaluate their thoughts in a conscious, structured way, especially when they are upset.

Sally, for example, when she is reading an economics chapter, has the same thought as the reader above. "I don't understand this." Her thinking becomes even more extreme, however: "And I'll *never* understand it." She accepts these thoughts as correct and feels quite sad. After learning tools of cognitive therapy, however, she is able to use her negative emotion as a cue to look for, identify, and evaluate her thoughts and thereby develop a more adaptive response: "Wait a minute, it's not necessarily true that I'll never understand this. I am having some trouble now. But if I reread it or come back to it when I'm fresher, I may understand it more. Anyway, understanding it isn't crucial to my survival, and I can ask someone else to explain it to me if need be."

Although automatic thoughts seem to pop up spontaneously, they become fairly predictable once the patient's underlying beliefs are identified. The cognitive therapist is concerned with identifying those thoughts that are dysfunctional, that is, those that distort reality, that are emotionally distressing and/or interfere with the patient's ability to reach her goals. Dysfunctional automatic thoughts are almost always negative unless the patient is manic or hypomanic, has a narcissistic personality disorder, or is a substance abuser.

---

[1]To minimize confusion, where I reference Aaron T. Beck's work, no initials are used.

Automatic thoughts are usually *quite brief*, and the patient is often more aware of the *emotion* she feels as a result of the thought than of the thought itself. Sitting in session, for example, a patient may be somewhat aware of feeling anxious, sad, irritated, or embarrassed but unaware of her automatic thoughts until her therapist questions her.

The emotion the patient feels is logically connected to the content of the automatic thought. For example, Sally thinks, "I'm such a dope. I don't really understand what [my therapist] is saying," and feels sad. Another time she thinks, "He's watching the clock. I'm just another case to him," and feels slightly angry. When she has the thoughts, "What if this therapy doesn't work? What will I do next?" Sally feels anxious.

Automatic thoughts are often in "shorthand" form but can be easily spelled out when the therapist asks for the *meaning* of the thought. For example, "Oh, no!" may be translated as "[My therapist] is going to give me too much homework." "Damn!" may be the expression of an idea such as "I left my appointment book at home and I can't schedule another appointment with my therapist today; I'm so stupid."

Automatic thoughts may be in *verbal form, visual form* (images), or both. In addition to her verbal automatic thought ("Oh, no!") Sally had an image of herself, alone at her desk late at night, toiling over her therapy homework (see Chapter 13 for a description of automatic thoughts in image form).

Automatic thoughts can be evaluated according to their *validity* and their *utility. The most common type of automatic thought is distorted in some way and occurs despite objective evidence to the contrary. A second type of automatic thought is accurate, but the conclusion the patient draws may be distorted.* For example, "I didn't do what I promised [my roommate]" is a valid thought, but the conclusion "Therefore, I'm a bad person," is not.

A third type of automatic thought is also accurate but decidedly dysfunctional. For example, Sally was studying for an exam and thought, "It's going to take me hours to finish this. I'll be up until 3:00 a.m." This thought was undoubtedly accurate, but it increased her anxiety and decreased her concentration and motivation. A reasonable response to this thought would address its *utility.* "It's true it will take a long time to finish this, but I can do it; I've done it before. Dwelling on how long it will take makes me feel miserable, and I won't concentrate as well. It'll probably take even longer to finish. It would be better to concentrate on finishing one part at a time and giving myself credit for having finished it." Evaluating the validity and/or utility of automatic thoughts and adaptively responding to them generally produces a positive shift in affect.

To summarize, automatic thoughts coexist with a more manifest stream of thoughts, arise spontaneously, and are not based on reflection or deliberation. People are usually more aware of the associated emotion but, with a little training, they can become aware of their thinking. The thoughts relevant to personal problems are associated with *specific* emotions, depending on their content and meaning. They are often brief and fleeting, in shorthand form, and may occur in verbal and/or imaginal form. People usually accept their automatic thoughts as true, without reflection or evaluation. Identifying, evaluating, and responding to automatic thoughts (in a more adaptive way) usually produces a positive shift in affect.

Excerpted from *Cognitive Therapy: Basics and Beyond* by J. S. Beck, 1995. New York: Guilford.

BASIC PHILOSOPHY

CT theory generally takes a neutral position on the properties of human nature. When the overall qualities of human existence are discussed at all, it is from an evolutionary perspective, which portrays humans simply as organisms adapting to the environment.

Alford and Beck (1997a) characterize CT theory as constructivist because it recognizes that a critical aspect of human existence is the creation of meaning from experiences. Unlike radical constructivist approaches (those that recognize no single objective reality), however, CT assumes both an external, objective reality and a personal, subjective, phenomenological one (Clark & Beck, 1999).

Beck would like to see his theory as the great integrator—that is, the "one" psychological theory that can explain all others (Alford & Beck, 1997a). One point in his favor is that the roots of the theory lie in both behavioral and psychoanalytic approaches. The behavioral roots of CT theory are evident in the techniques used in intervention, and in earlier versions of the theory that placed little emphasis on processes out of awareness. Beck wrote:

> The cognitive model was in part derivative from and in part a reaction against classical psychoanalysis. The derivative components consisted of the emphasis on meanings, the role of symbols and the generalization of reaction patterns across diverse situations . . . The "reaction against" consisted of eschewing the predominately motivational model, the notion of an unconscious cauldron of taboo drives defended against by repression and other mechanisms of defense, and the critical importance attached to the psychosexual stages of development. (Beck, 1991, p. 192)

Recently, CT theorists have begun to discuss the childhood origins of core beliefs, seeming to parallel psychoanalytic notions of the origins of dysfunction (Padesky, 2004). Also, current versions of CT theory pay much attention to cognitive processes that are not fully in awareness (e.g., automatic thoughts, cognitive schemas; these are discussed later) and are in this way reminiscent of Freud's ideas about the unconscious determinants of behavior.

A final point to note about CT theory is that it is mostly a theory of psychological dysfunction. Because it originated as a theory of depression (Beck, Rush, Shaw, & Emery, 1979) and also because it has been intimately tied to therapeutic practice, this theory tends to focus on the dynamics of psychological maladjustment rather than on healthy functioning.

Mia is Steve's counselor, and she follows a Cognitive Therapy approach. Assuming that Steve is a human like any other, she begins her work with him without any preconceived notions about his goodness or badness; he is simply a person striving to make sense of his environment. His behavior, in Mia's view, is in response to his current perceptions of his environment, which are tied to his early learning. She seeks to understand the way he thinks about things and how his cognitive process is related to his current situation.

HUMAN MOTIVATION

CT theory is probably best characterized as an adaptive theory. Beck draws on evolutionary theory to locate the motivation for human behavior in two major evolutionary goals: survival and reproduction (Beck, Freeman, Davis, and Associates, 2004). Cognitive processes evolved to enhance adaptation to the environment, and hence, survival (Clark & Beck,

1999). Humans struggle to comprehend the world and assign meaning to life events so that they can develop effective adaptive strategies (Alford & Beck, 1997a). "Cognition is implicated in controlling or directing behavior so as to maximize positive consequences (both short-term and long-term)" (Alford & Beck, 1997a, p. 64). The basic needs of humans are thought to be preservation, reproduction, dominance, and sociability (Clark & Beck, 1999, p. 67).

Mia assumes that Steve's situation is a result of many influences, but at the most basic level, he is struggling to adapt to his environment. He seeks positive consequences (survival, social contact, dominance or control of his situation, and intimate relationships). Mia looks at Steve's ways of construing the world in order to understand how his meanings relate to his behavior and feelings.

CENTRAL CONSTRUCTS

THE COGNITIVE MODEL

Simply put, the cognitive model, which is the foundation of CT, proposes that our emotions and behavior are the product of our *perceptions* of situations (J. S. Beck, 1995). "The cognitive view of behavior assigns primary importance to the self-evident fact that people *think*" (Kovacs & Beck, 1978, p. 525; italics in original). Cognition, in this model, means both the process and content of thinking, or how you think and what you think (Kovacs & Beck, 1978). Three levels of cognitive processing are seen in humans: the automatic or preconscious, the conscious, and the metacognitive (Alford & Beck, 1997a). The automatic level consists of thoughts and other cognitive organizations that are based in survival processes (see the later discussion of modes) that are largely out of awareness. The conscious level is what we normally think of as thinking, and the metacognitive level refers to our ability to think about our thought processes.

Of primary importance to Mia is how Steve thinks about things. She is also interested in the content of his thinking, and is aware that some of his thoughts might not be very accessible to him at present. Steve's emotions and behaviors are clues to his thought processes.

SCHEMAS

Schemas (sometimes also called schemata) are cognitive structures that organize the barrage of information with which we are constantly confronted (Beck & Emery, 2005). They help us create meaning out of what otherwise would be a bewildering array of stimuli, both internal and external. Schemas are the most basic unit of psychological function. Beck compares them to electrons in that they are theoretically critical elements that can only be indirectly observed (Alford & Beck, 1997b, p. 282). A formal definition of schemas is provided by Clark and Beck (1999): "Schemas are relatively enduring internal structures of stored generic or prototypical features of stimuli, ideas, or experience that are used to organize new information in a meaningful way thereby determining how phenomena are perceived and conceptualized" (p. 79).

Schemas can be dormant or active. To intuitively understand schematic processing, simply think of the word *librarian*. I am certain that you almost instantly came up with a set of images or words associated with the term. Further, if I told you someone was a

TABLE 10.1
EXAMPLES OF ADAPTIVE AND MALADAPTIVE SCHEMAS

Adaptive	Maladaptive
No matter what happens, I can manage somehow.	I must be perfect to be accepted.
If I work at something, I can master it.	If I choose to do something, I must succeed.
I'm a survivor.	I'm a fake.
Others can trust me.	Without a woman, I'm nothing.
I'm lovable.	I'm stupid.
People respect me.	People can't be trusted.
I like challenge.	The world is frightening.

Adapted from "Cognitive Therapy" by J. H. Wright and A. T. Beck, 1996, in R. E. Hales & S. C. Yudofsky (Eds.), *The American Psychiatric Press Synopsis of Psychiatry* (p. 1015). © 1996 American Psychiatric Press. www.appi.org. Reprinted with permission.

librarian, you'd be expecting the person to display those qualities. Your "librarian" schema is activated and is influencing how you respond to information.

Schemas influence the selection, encoding, and retrieval of information in the cognitive system. They contain general knowledge, core beliefs, and emotional elements relevant to a particular domain of experience (Reinecke & Freeman, 2003). If your librarian schema is activated, you are likely to observe features of someone that are consistent with your librarian schema, and you may have great difficulty recalling features that are inconsistent with the schema. You might also feel some emotion stemming from your past experience with librarians (did you get yelled at for talking in the library when you were a kid?). Some schemas are more easily activated than are others because they are broader, have more elements, and apply to more situations (i.e., are more complex; Clark & Beck, 1999). Adaptive and maladaptive schemas can be distinguished, as shown in Table 10.1. Box 10.2 illustrates an important schema dynamic, stereotype threat.

Box 10.2

The Power of Schemas

As you have read, schemas are the most basic unit of thinking and are developed either through personal experience with the world or through vicarious learning (watching what others do). Schemas are formed very early in life, even as early as infancy. When we experience new events, we store away information about those events for future use. For example, when Alexandra pets the family cat she discovers that the cat is soft, warm, and purrs. The next time Alexandra encounters a cat out in the environment, her "cat schema," which contains information about cats being soft, warm, and purring will automatically be activated. Although schemas are the basic unit of thinking they can be quite complex. Each schema that we hold is based on one or more core beliefs about the world. So as you can imagine, if we hold faulty core beliefs about something, we are also going to activate faulty schemas that effect behavior. If Alexandra had been scratched by her family cat, she might then hold a core belief that all cats want to hurt her, which then would activate a negative cat schema that includes scratching and danger each time she sees a cat. As you can see, schemas can be very powerful and can be accurate or inaccurate based on the experience the individual has in the world.

Another example of the power of schemas is a dynamic called stereotype threat. Stereotype threat can be defined as anxiety aroused by the prospective risk of believing and confirming a negative stereotype about yourself because you belong to a group that has been negatively stereotyped. The threat then interferes with performance on tasks relevant to the stereotypic behavior. Although there are many examples of stereotypes that society has come to accept and advocate a troubling one in particular is that females (innately) have poorer math skills than males. A study done by Keller (2002) showed that when males and females were given a math test, they performed relatively equally. However, when students were informed before the test of the stereotype that males typically scored higher than females, the females performed more poorly than males.

Similar results were found when Steele and Aronson (1995) examined racial stereotypes with White and African American students on intelligence tests. In this study it was found that if African American students were primed with a racial stereotype about test performance before taking the test, they did more poorly than White students on the test. However, if the African American students were not reminded of the racial stereotype before taking the test, no differences in performance were observed.

Another example of stereotype threat that has been documented in the literature by Koenig and Eagly (2005) addresses the common stereotype that women are more socially sensitive than men. In this experiment, men who were warned that the test they were taking tapped this social skill and that women were generally superior in this domain, scored lower compared to men who were told that the test measured information processing.

In light of this information, what schemas do you have, and how might then affect you?

Contributed by April L. Connery.

Mia's CT perspective tells her that Steve is surely harboring some maladaptive schemas. These schemas are influencing how he sees the world, including what he pays attention to and how he behaves and feels. Mia thinks that Steve probably operates, at times, from schemas such as, "I'm a fake and a failure" but also from some manic schemas that are grandiose ("I am strong and powerful and can get away with a lot. I should take advantage of this. I can drink and act up and why not?").

BELIEFS

As just noted, beliefs are important components of schema, and as critical targets of Cognitive Therapy, are discussed extensively. Judith Beck (2005) distinguished between two kinds of cognitions that are important in CT: core beliefs, and assumptions, roles and attitudes. Our schemas contain our **core beliefs**, which are the most basic beliefs we hold, and are thought to be the hardest to modify. They tend to be overgeneralized and absolute, and are usually self-referent (Clark & Beck, 1999). Assumptions, rules and attitudes, also known as **intermediate beliefs**, are situated between core beliefs and automatic thoughts (J. S. Beck, 2005; Clark & Beck, 1999). These beliefs include "should" and "must" beliefs as well as conditional beliefs that are influential in creating meaning from experience. An example of an assumption might be, "If I don't get an A in my Theories of Counseling course, then I am dumb." The intermediate beliefs also include rules or coping strategies used by individuals in reaction to other beliefs (J. S. Beck, 2005). These coping strategies are largely automatic and can be clearly distinguished from other forms of problem solving or coping responses. For example, an individual could hold the core belief "I am a failure" which is connected to and the rule "I must get all As." A coping strategy would be, "I will achieve perfection in all of my coursework so that I get As." Clark and Beck (1999) added the most specific form of schema, the **simple schema**. Simple schemas deal with physical objects or very distinct, simple ideas, such as dogs, books, computers, and so forth.

As she begins her work with Steve, Mia looks carefully for evidence of his core beliefs and associated attitudes, rules, and assumptions. Because he does not appear to be psychotic, his simple schemas are intact. She thinks that some core beliefs may be, "I'm a goof-off and therefore nobody loves me" and paradoxically, "I am cool and can do what I want." Steve may bounce back and forth between these beliefs and associated schematic processing.

Steve's intermediate beliefs are linked to his core beliefs and schemas. Mia discovers that Steve thinks that he should please people so that they will love him and that that will make him worthwhile. When his manic schemas are activated, he probably thinks that the world must be good to him and allow him anything he wants. If it doesn't, he gets angry.

AUTOMATIC THOUGHTS

Automatic thoughts (ATs) are a normal feature of our cognitive process (J. S. Beck, 1995). They are swift, evaluative statements or images that exist alongside our more conscious thoughts. ATs tend to occur in shorthand rather than in full sentence form and often seem to just pop up out of nowhere (hence their name). Depending on their content, these thoughts can be functional or distressing, but in either case, they tend to be reasonable to the thinker (Beck, 1976). Usually, we are not particularly aware of our ATs we are more likely to be aware of the emotion associated with them. In reality, ATs are the result of our core and intermediate beliefs. They are thought to be easier to change than intermediate or core beliefs (J. S. Beck, 1995).

Judith Beck (1995) identified three general types of automatic thought. First are the distorted thoughts that are contrary to available objective evidence ("I never do *anything* right!"). Most ATs are of this type. A second type of ATs can be accurate, but the conclusion drawn is distorted ("I upset my boyfriend. Now he'll never love me again!"). A third type of ATs is accurate but dysfunctional (p. 77). This kind of thought either contributes to a reluctance to approach a task or increases anxiety so that focus and concentration are disrupted. For example, I could have the automatic thought, "It's going to take a *long time* to finish this book!" This thought is true, but it may decrease my motivation to write, or it may distract me from my current writing activity because it definitely increases my anxiety.

Mia is interested in the automatic thoughts that might influence Steve's behavior. Probably he has some negative ATs, such as "I'm worthless," "Life is too hard," "I must not disappoint others," "I am not loved," and so forth. His drinking behavior is probably accompanied by thoughts such as, "What the hell," "I can handle it," "No use in trying to quit," and "I can't stand it without a drink." If he is in a manic swing, his ATs are things like, "I am great," "Others can't touch me," and "People had better be nice to me."

MODES

To more fully capture the complexity of human behavior, Beck proposed the concept of the mode, which is defined as "networks of cognitive, affective, motivational, and behavioral schemas that compose personality and interpret ongoing situations" (Beck & Weishaar, 2005, p. 239). Modal information processing is largely automatic and global, that is, schema-driven, particularly in the primal modes described later. Like schemas, modes are either active or dormant; when activated, modes tend to dominate behavior in a rather automatic way.

The **conscious control system** can override modal processing (Beck, 1996). This system is responsible for metacognition and intentional behavior, such as that based on personal goals and values. Logical reasoning and long-term planning are also products of the conscious control system.

CT proposes three major mode categories: primal, constructive, and minor. **Primal** modes are the most basic kinds of operation and function to meet the evolutionary goals of survival, procreation, and sociability (Beck & Clark, 1997). Because they are so basic to survival, they operate rapidly and automatically. Thinking in the primal modes is distorted and rigid (Beck & Weishaar, 2005). Clark and Beck (1999) identified four primal modes, although other sources seem to suggest others. For example, in their revised treatise on anxiety disorder, Beck and Emery (2004) stated that modes are "designed to consummate certain adaptational principles relevant to survival, maintenance, breeding, self-enhancement, and so on. Thus, we have a depressive mode, a narcissistic mode, a hostility mode, a fear (or danger) mode, an erotic mode, and so on" (p. 59). According to what I identify as one of the earliest formulations of modal theory (Clark & Beck, 1999), the four primal modes are threat, loss or deprivation, victim, and self-enhancement. Each mode contains a cluster of schemas: cognitive–conceptual, affective, physiological, motivational, and behavioral. A description of these modes is shown in Table 10.2. The first three modes (threat, loss, and victim) evolved to protect the organism against threats to survival. The self-enhancement mode works in the opposite manner to the first three modes to enhance the survival and adaptation of the person.

Beck (1996) argued that primary modes are not inherently dysfunctional because they serve to enhance human survival. For example, it is very adaptive to mobilize the organism to fight or flee in the face of threat. Unfortunately for us, our environment has

TABLE 10.2
THE FOUR PRIMAL MODES

Mode	Characteristics
Threat	Perception of threat
	Feelings of anxiety or anger
	Physiological arousal
Loss	Perception of possible or actual loss of vital resources
	Feelings of dysphoria (depression) or sadness
	Fatigue or physiological deactivation
Victim	Perception of injustice or offense against the self and self-interests
	Feelings of anger
	Physiological activation
Self-enhancement	Perception of achieved or anticipated personal gain
	Feelings of happiness
	Physiological activation

Adapted from D. A. Clark & A. T. Beck (1999), *Scientific Foundations of Cognitive Theory and Therapy of Depression* (pp. 89–91). Copyright © 1999 by John Wiley & Sons, Inc. This material is used by permission of John Wiley & Sons, Inc.

changed a bit from that in which the primary modes evolved, causing a "mismatch" at times in which modal behavior is not necessarily the best strategy to deal with the complex situations we encounter (Beck, 1996). Even what we think of as positive modes (self-enhancement) can become exaggerated, as in mania (or bipolar disorder), and are therefore dysfunctional.

The second class of modes is termed the **constructive** modes (Clark & Beck, 1999). These modes are developed primarily through life experience and serve to increase the life resources available to the individual. They are associated with positive emotions and adaptive characteristics and include (a) the capacity for intimacy, (b) personal mastery, (c) creativity, and (d) independence. As you can observe from Table 10.2, one of the primal modes is constructive as well, the self-enhancement mode.

The **minor** modes are the third category of thinking and tend to be under more conscious control than the other modes. They tend to be narrowly focused on situations and include everyday activities such as reading, writing, social interaction, and athletic or recreational activities (Clark & Beck 1999).

Mia listens very carefully to Steve. She thinks that he operates out of several of the primal modes that periodically dominate his cognition and behavior. First, his feelings about his parents and perhaps some of his drinking behavior seem to flow from a loss mode because he sometimes drinks because he is depressed or upset. He is unhappy with his irresponsible behavior, indicating a poor self-concept associated with the loss mode, as well as weak constructive modes. At other times Steve shows overactivation of the self-enhancement mode in his manic behavior. During these episodes he is likely to be hyperactive, show irrational positive emotion, and have an inflated view of himself and his capacities. Steve's drinking can also occur when he is functioning in a manic fashion, because the grandiose schemas associated with this mode include thoughts of invincibility. When he fails or the world does not treat him as he wishes, his victim mode is activated. At these times, he can become angry and aggressive.

It is evident to Mia that Steve is able to use his conscious control system sometimes to override his activated primal modes. The operation of this system is what gets him to treatment after he has relapsed into substance use. It is also what helps him evaluate his acting-out behavior and set goals for the future.

THEORY OF THE PERSON AND DEVELOPMENT OF THE INDIVIDUAL

In discussing human development, CT theorists conceptualize human functioning as the product of learning and genetics. Drawing on literature in developmental psychology, Beck and his associates start with the notion that certain personality tendencies can be genetic in origin, such as sensitivity to rejection by others or dependency (Beck et al., 2004).

As children, we strive to make sense of our environments (including our selves and others) and organize this information into schemata (J. S. Beck, 2005). The tendency to create meaning through the use of schemas is thought to be innate (Clark & Beck, 1999). Based on the amounts of positive and negative experiences we have, we develop corresponding views of ourselves and the world. A kid who gets a lot of glowing feedback will develop a positive set of schemata about himself and the world and will therefore be less likely to develop faulty cognitive processes. Modal theory (Beck, 1996) replaces the construct of schemas with that of **protoschemas**, which are innate patterns that interact with experience to develop the modes.

Previous versions of CT theory did not elaborate a theory of personality. More recently, two general dispositions have been identified, autonomy and sociotropy (Beck, 1997b; Beck and Weishaar, 2004). Individuals who are high in sociotrophy find their self-worth in relations with others. Autonomous individuals emphasize mastery and independence and build self-esteem through achievement and control (Clark & Beck, 1999). Different kinds of life experiences, then, will differentially affect individuals who are oriented toward one dimension or the other. For example, an interpersonal conflict would have much different ramifications for a sociotrophic than for an autonomous individual. Beck and his associates, however, acknowledge that pure types are relatively rare: most people display tendencies of both sociotrophy and autonomy (Beck & Weishaar, 2004).

Under normal circumstances, we tend to operate via simple schematic processing and with our conscious control system (Beck, 1996). We cruise along, using minor modes to attend to everyday activities. These schemas are activated and have some cognitive, affective (usually mild), and behavioral effects, but these effects dissipate quickly. Occasionally (or often, if you are dysfunctional), information is present that matches an **orienting schema** that is linked to a primal mode. When a match is made, the primal mode is activated; the cognitive, affective, behavioral, and physiological systems or schemas are energized; and primary modal processing is seen (Beck, 1996). The kinds of behavior, affect, and cognition observed will depend on whether the primary mode activated is one of the constructive modes or one of the defensive or protective modes.

Steve appears to be more sociotrophic than autonomous in his orientation. Mia thinks that his early experiences in his family resulted in the formation of schemas emphasizing the value of the love of others. He likely grew up wanting close relationships with his parents, but never achieved these. He may also have experienced the loss of these relationships because of his parents' conditional acceptance of his behavior. Steve's cognition and behavior suggest that as he matured, the loss primal mode may have been very alive, and so even now, this mode and accompanying schemas are sensitive and easily activated. Also, it appears that early on, his self-enhancement primal mode was hyperactive, as evidenced by his acting-out behavior at school.

HEALTH AND DYSFUNCTION

"Contrary to common belief among clinicians, the cognitive approach to depression and psychopathology does *not* assume that a well-adjusted individual is one who thinks logically and solves problems rationally" (Kovacs & Beck, 1978, p. 528; italics in original). Presumably, people can function with illogical beliefs and irrational thoughts as long as they are not creating dysfunction. For example, one of my clients, Alex, believed that he was a flexible person. It was my observation that his cognitive and behavioral flexibility was limited. Alex had also received feedback from others to this effect. Fortunately, Alex did not see flexibility as crucial to his self-worth, so this inaccurate (i.e., not consensually validated) belief was not dysfunctional for him.

Although CT theorists don't spend a lot of time discussing healthy psychological functioning, it appears that the CT version of health would include information processing that allows the individual to meet his goals of survival, reproduction, and sociability. We can infer that healthy folks don't rely on a lot of primary mode processing and don't show a lot of distorted thinking. The constructive modes of processing are more in evidence, and the individual is able to use the conscious control system to moderate schematic processing. The healthy person probably has fairly good problem-solving skills, too.

In viewing dysfunction, Beck and his collaborators have emphasized an interactive view. For instance, Beck and Weishaar (2005) contend that "psychological distress is ultimately caused by many innate, biological, developmental and environmental factors interacting with one another, and so there is no single 'cause' of psychopathology" (p. 246). However, the focus in most of CT theory is, predictably, cognition. J. S. Beck (2004) writes "the cognitivist assumes that the individual's primary problem has to do with his construction of reality. The remedy lies in modifying the cognitive set. The psychological modification then produces biochemical changes that in turn can influence cognitions further" (p. 200). Despite this strong statement, Beck does allow that pharmacological interventions can cause cognitive-neurochemical change. Writing specifically about depression, Young, Beck, and Weinberger (1993) put it this way: "The pharmacotherapist intervenes at the biochemical level; the cognitive therapist intervenes at the cognitive, affective, and behavioral levels. Our experience suggests that when we change depressive cognitions, we simultaneously change the characteristic mood, behavior, and (we presume) biochemistry of depression. The exact mechanism of change, however, remains a target of considerable investigation and debate" (p. 241).

Very early in his theoretical journey, Beck (1976) identified a number of cognitive problems that are characteristic of depressed individuals (see Figure 10.1). These **cognitive distortions** remain important theoretical constructs in CT theory. Each of the problems outlined in Figure 10.1 is followed by an example of Steve's cognitive distortions. Because much of Beck's early thinking was oriented to depression, another useful concept is the **cognitive triad**, which refers to the depressive's negative views of the self, the world, and the future (Kovacs & Beck, 1978).

Distorted thinking results from faulty schemas and their associated core beliefs. Young and colleagues (1993) described the "deepest" type of schemas, the early maladaptive schemas (p. 242). These cognitive structures develop very early in life as a result of interactions with the surrounding environment, most notably those with significant others. After the schema is created, it can be activated by environmental or internal events, and information processing becomes selective—information that is consistent with the schema is admitted to awareness, whereas inconsistent information is distorted or rejected. In this way, the maladaptive schema is maintained.

These schemas are resistant to change, connected to significant emotional responses, and if examined by the client, perceived as absolute truths (Young et al., 1993). A client would simply say, "That's just the way I am!" An example of such a schema might be called the rotten person schema. This person would be totally convinced that he can't do anything right and that others hate him. J. S. Beck (2005) identifies three broad categories of negative core self-beliefs that would be seen in a rotten person schema: helplessness, unlovability, and worthlessness.

Beck and colleges, over the years, have identified specific ways of thinking and perceiving that are characteristic of various psychological dysfunctions. Beck calls this idea the **cognitive specificity principle** (Beck, 2005). In anxiety disorders, for example, the individual is hypervigilant, focused on signs of danger or threat (Beck & Emery, 2005). Automatic thoughts of threat and harm come easily and often. Other examples of dysfunction-specific beliefs are seen in drug-abusing clients who harbor "need" beliefs such as, "I can't stand the boredom without my drug" (Beck, 1993). Individuals who display bipolar disorder are thought to have both depressive beliefs and beliefs such as, "I have exceptional powers and should use them" (Beck, 1993).

The idea of cognitive specificity allows the extension of CT theory to various kinds of psychological dysfunction. Much attention has been paid to anxiety disorders, including panic disorder (Beck & Emery, 2005). Other conceptualizations have focused on eating disorders (Edgette & Prout, 1989), substance abuse (Beck, Wright, Newman, & Liese, 1993), and even schizophrenia (Beck & Rector, 2000; 2005).

The revision of CT proposed by Beck (Beck, 1996; Clark & Beck, 1999) locates the source of psychological dysfunction in overactive primal modes (Beck, 1996). We are all born with the protoschemas for primal modes. Through experience, the primal modes are constructed and endowed with energy (or "charged"; Beck, 1996, p. 8). A series of experiences relevant to a specific mode will result in the mode being fully activated and operative. As Beck explains it, "A particular mode is generally silent or latent at first, but through successive relevant experiences can receive incremental charges until it reaches the threshold for full activation. In some psychopathological conditions—for example, recurrent depression—the mode is chronically but subliminally charged so that it can become fully activated after a comparatively minor stressful event (the kindling phenomenon)" (Beck, 1996, p. 8).

1. All or nothing thinking (black-and-white, polarized, or dichotomous thinking). Life is seen in rigid categories; no shades of gray are allowed. *Steve believes that he must be perfect in the eyes of important others to maintain self-respect.*

2. Catastrophizing (fortune telling). The future is viewed as a disaster; other kinds of outcomes are not considered as even remote possibilities. *Steve is sure that the future holds nothing but gloom; he will never get a job he likes nor regain his relationship with his mother.*

3. Disqualifying or discounting the positive. Good stuff just does not count! *Steve downplays his previous successes. He does not acknowledge that, despite his slips, he has been able to get himself to treatment and is currently doing well in the work-therapy program.*

4. Emotional reasoning. Because of the emotional investment in an idea, it is seen as true, regardless of discrepant information. *Steve is deeply hurt by his mother's disowning him and feels certain that she is right; he is worthless.*

5. Labeling. A global rating is made (of self or other). *Although Steve says he accepts himself, his reports that he worries about the opinion of his parents suggest that he may not be as self-accepting as he says he is. He may be rating himself negatively, which would be consistent with his early experience.*

6. Magnification/minimization. Negative information is highlighted; positive information is ignored or minimized. This kind of thinking is the opposite of wearing rose-colored glasses. *If Steve makes a mistake at work, he worries terribly that he'll be perceived as a bad worker and get fired. He does not attend to the things he does well at work.*

7. Mental filter (selective abstraction). One negative detail is attended to, resulting in a conclusion that does not consider other factors in a situation. *Steve's supervisor was curt with him, and Steve concludes that his supervisor is angry or unhappy with him. He does not consider that his supervisor has many other demands on her, and that she was brisk with other workers as well.*

8. Mind reading. Need this one be described? *Steve believes he knows exactly what his mother and father think of him.*

9. Overgeneralization. The conclusion (usually negative) becomes larger than is justified by an event. *Because Steve has not succeeded in staying "dry" previously, he concludes that he will never be able to achieve his goal of sobriety.*

10. Personalization. Another person's behavior is attributed to oneself without considering alternative explanations. *Steve's supervisor announces a new rule at work—anyone who gets angry must leave for one hour. Steve assumes that the rule was made in response to his outbursts and feels depressed.*

11. Should and must statements. Rigid rules for life, which, if not met, create a catastrophe. *Steve believes that he must be perfect so that others will love him. Others must not show disapproval of him.*

12. Tunnel vision. A narrow focus on the negatives. *Steve sees his life in terms of his immature behavior, substance abuse, and cycles of mania and depression. He fails to recognize his strength in getting help and trying to turn his life around. He also ignores his successes in his current working environment.*

FIGURE 10.1. Cognitive Distortions.
Adapted from *Cognitive Therapy: Basics and Beyond* (p. 119) by J. S. Beck, 1995, New York: The Guilford Press. Adapted with permission.

TABLE 10.3
MODES AND DIAGNOSTIC CATEGORIES: PRIMAL SYSTEMS

Disorder	Cognitive Features	Affective Features	Behavioral Impulse	Physiological Activation
Specific phobia	Specific danger	Anxiety	Escape or avoid	Autonomic nervous system
General fear	Generalized danger	Anxiety	Escape, avoid, inhibit	Autonomic nervous system
Hostility	Threatened, wronged	Anger	Punish	Autonomic nervous system
Depression	Loss	Sad	Regress	Parasympathetic activation

Adapted from "Beyond Belief: A Theory of Modes, Personality, and Psychopathology," in
P. M. Salkovskis (Ed.), *Frontiers of Cognitive Therapy*, 1996, New York: The Guilford Press.

According to Beck, the various categories of psychological dysfunction (as classified in the *DSM*-IV, for example) can be understood in terms of the specific primal mode involved and the characteristic "goal" of the mode (1996, p. 8). For example, in depression, the loss threatens the organism's livelihood, and the behavioral inactivation so common to depression represents a means of preserving the organism. Further, depression is typically accompanied by a weak constructive mode, so the individual probably has poor self-concept and a decreased ability to think constructively (Beck, 1996). Table 10.3 shows Beck's (1996) conceptualization of the psychological disorders and associated modal functioning. Note that Beck includes hostility among these because he believes that it is needed to account for excessive violence and homicide.

Recently, CT theorists have become interested in the struggle to work with clients diagnosed as having personality disorders. Although she doesn't invoke modal theory, J. S. Beck (2005) notes that "cognitive therapists view the development of Axis II disorders as the result of an interaction between individuals' genetic predispositions toward certain personality traits and their early experiences. A histrionic patient, for example, may have been born with a flair for the dramatic" (p. 41).

Mia thinks that Steve's most active schema is the depressogenic schema. He shows the negative triad in his dim view of himself, his perception that others don't like or approve of him, and his perception that the world is difficult and the future is uncertain or negative. Mia guesses that although Steve's loss mode is somewhat active at present, it is not fully charged because he evidences mild to intermittent and moderate, rather than severe, depression. Because of Steve's apparent sociotropic orientation, Mia will be on the lookout for interpersonal situations that could set off more extreme modal processing.

Steve's loss primal mode was probably sensitized by his early experiences with his parents. They were distant in their interactions with him, and he interpreted the distance as rejection based on his inadequacy and bad behavior. The victim mode might be relevant to Steve's situation as well because he sometimes sees himself as the scapegoat of an unfair world (for instance, in the automobile accident). Steve may also have been born with genetic tendencies toward passive, depressive types of behavior.

When Steve's loss mode is activated, he withdraws and drinks to escape. He shows evidence of cognitive distortion in this situation ("it's no use; I can't do anything right; why bother to try to stop drinking when the world is so awful"), low motivation, and behavioral inactivation. If Steve's victim mode is also activated by his perception of some injustice, he may feel threatened and angry, too. At these times, he may seem energized by the anger.

Occasionally, Steve enters a manic phase that results from activation of the self-enhancement mode. At these times, he may drink because he believes himself invincible. He acts out because he has an exaggerated sense of his power. If his victim mode becomes activated at the same time, he may physically attack the person or entity perceived to be threatening him. When the manic mode is active, he probably has automatic thoughts such as, "what the hell," "one drink is fine," and "everyone loves me."

NATURE OF THERAPY

ASSESSMENT

Both formal and informal assessment is used in CT. Newman and Beck (1990) strongly encouraged a formal comprehensive diagnostic evaluation for three reasons: (a) to fully understand the psychological picture of the client, (b) to determine if any organic syndrome is involved, and (c) to assess the need for medication or hospitalization. Ultimately, the goal of the assessment is a structured cognitive case conceptualization (J. S. Beck, 1995, 2005; Persons & Tompkins, 1997). Often, a special session (i.e., intake) is used for assessment prior to the official start of counseling (J. S. Beck, 1995). The initial evaluation generally results in a formal *DSM*-IV diagnosis.

Formal assessment in CT often involves using standardized self-report inventories such as the Beck Depression Inventory (BDI; Beck, Ward, Mendelson, & Erbaugh, 1961), the Beck Anxiety Inventory (BAI; Beck, Epstein, Brown, & Steer, 1988), the Automatic Thought Questionnaire (ATQ; Hollon & Kendall, 1980), or the Dysfunctional Attitude Scale (DAS; Weissman & Beck, 1978), which measures schema-related core beliefs and assumptions. The latest of these tools seems to be the Beck Cognitive Insight Scale (Beck, Baruch, Balter, Steer, & Warman, 2004). Numerous other instruments have been constructed for cognitive assessment; an excellent review of these and their psychometric properties is presented by Blankstein and Segal (2001). These instruments are often used intermittently throughout counseling to assess progress (Persons & Tompkins, 1997).

CT counselors are most interested in assessing their clients' thoughts, and they do this continually throughout therapy. The simplest way to make this assessment is to simply ask the client, "what was going through your mind?" either in reference to a mood change in session, or in helping clients reconstruct situations outside of therapy. As I noted earlier, the Dysfunctional Attitude Scale or Automatic Thought Questionnaire can also be used for this purpose.

Cognitive assessment leads to a formal treatment plan. In the first session of CT, the client is asked to establish goals; the therapist helps the client to make these specific and concrete. The CT counselor then takes each problem or goal and analyzes it from a CT perspective (J. S. Beck, 1995; 2005). J. S. Beck's recent writings emphasize the creation of a formal cognitive conceptualization for each client, using a format she specifies in her recent book (2005).

Mia gives Steve the Beck Depression Inventory to assess his current level of dysphoria. She finds that he is moderately depressed. She also spends time in the first (and later sessions) helping Steve identify his cognitions, first his automatic thoughts, and later his core beliefs. She considers using the Dysfunctional Attitude Scale to assess his core beliefs and assumptions.

OVERVIEW OF THE THERAPEUTIC ATMOSPHERE

Advocates of CT agree that it is structured, active, collaborative, and psychoeducational (Reinecke & Freeman, 2003). Cognitive, behavioral, and imaginal techniques are used.

CT is characterized by a collaborative relationship between client and counselor (Beck & Emery, 2004). Cognitive therapists recognize the importance of the therapeutic relationship, sounding much like person-centered theorists in their emphasis on warmth, genuineness, trust, and respect (Newman & Beck, 1990). J. S. Beck (2005) and Beck and Emery (2005), however, note that the therapist must be alert to signs from the client that the nature of the relationship needs to be modified. For example, highly sociotropic clients might need more warmth from the therapist than would those lower on this dimension (Beck & Emery, 2005).

The CT relationship is seen as different from other counseling relationships because it emphasizes a scientific approach (Beck, 1997a); the relationship is said to be based on **collaborative empiricism** (Beck & Weishaar, 2005). Client and counselor are co-investigators in the scientific study of the client's difficulties (Reincke & Freeman, 2003). The client's schemas, beliefs, and automatic thoughts are treated as hypotheses to be tested by the two scientists (Young et al., 1993). Evidence is gathered and experiments are designed and conducted to test the hypotheses.

Alford and Beck (1997c) discussed the role of interpersonal support in CT. They maintained that the therapist must create "responsible dependency" in the client; the client is not to become passive in the relationship (p. 107). Support in CT means support of the efforts of the client to learn and implement the CT model in his life. The therapist makes genuine efforts to understand the client and accepts the client in the sense that all client cognitions, feelings, and behaviors are openly examined for their advantages and disadvantages (Alford & Beck, 1997c). However, the cognitive therapist does not accept certain client actions and goals when they are considered antisocial (e.g., illegal acts, abuse of others).

Beck (1976) calls CT a common-sense therapy that simply helps the client apply problem-solving techniques that he has used in the past to correct the current faulty thought processes. CT is typically a short-term intervention, ranging from 10 to 20 sessions (Wright & Beck, 1996). For more severe problems (e.g., personality disorders), CT can be longer, but it is still considered a comparatively brief approach to these dysfunctions. Booster sessions are often scheduled after formal termination to help prevent relapse (J. S. Beck, 1995).

Mia approaches Steve in a friendly, warm way. She is accepting of him and sometimes responds empathically to his description of his troubles, hopes, and dreams. Mia attempts to build a relationship based on the idea that she and Steve will look at how he views the world, testing out the conclusions he draws and determining their relationship to his feelings and behavior. Mia expects that if Steve becomes engaged in their scientific counseling project, he will be in therapy for about 6 months. However, the length of Steve's counseling will likely depend on what goals he sets.

ROLES OF CLIENT AND COUNSELOR

In CT, the counselor is an expert who teaches the client about Cognitive Theory (Alford & Beck, 1997c). In this way, the relationship somewhat resembles that of doctor-patient. Judith Beck characterized the cognitive therapist as simultaneously caring, collaborative, and competent (1995, p. 304). The counselor typically is very active, particularly early in the therapy process (Wright & Beck, 1996). Cognitive therapists ask their clients a lot of questions and are very likely to assign tasks related to the clients' identified problems.

Initially, the client is a student who is expected to work hard to learn about CT. He is expected to devote energy to examining his thought process, and to complete homework assignments. At the same time, the client is a collaborator in the counseling process whose direct input is always solicited in setting session agendas and selecting homework assignments (Wright & Beck, 1996). As therapy progresses, the client is expected to take more and more responsibility for what happens in counseling sessions, developing CT explanations for his feelings and behaviors, setting the session agenda, and developing homework tasks. In essence, the client becomes an expert on how CT theory applies to him (Alford & Beck, 1997c).

Mia takes a straightforward, educative approach with Steve. She explains the cognitive model to him in the first session, attempting to get him to understand and accept the system and engage collaboratively with her in the process of CT. She gives Steve a pad of paper and a pen and encourages him to take notes about the model. Mia is very aware that it will be important to establish a good working relationship with Steve because he is a sociotropic type who is sensitive to the evaluations of others. She is supportive of his efforts to learn and apply the model.

If Steve responds well to Mia's invitation to participate, he will become a good student of CT. Steve will work in tandem with Mia to identify his cognitive processes and to understand how they relate to his feelings and behavior. He will follow Mia's instructions in his sessions and complete his homework assignments. The two will engage in collaborative empiricism, testing Steve's ideas in a CT model.

GOALS

The goals of CT are to identify and change faulty information processing and to modify beliefs that support psychological dysfunction to ones that are more adaptive (Beck & Weishaar, 2005). Typically, a good deal of this work focuses on the client's automatic thoughts (J. S. Beck, 2005). Through addressing automatic thoughts, basic beliefs or schemas are sometimes accessed, but significant change in these deeper structures may require longer-term therapy than is typical in CT. A broader goal of CT is to teach clients problem-solving strategies that they can use across situations.

Altering faulty core beliefs and the associated schematic change, although difficult, should prevent relapses (Young et al., 1993). The idea is to get the individual to operate based on reflective, constructive processes through the use of the conscious control system, or metacognition, rather than primitive schemas (Beck & Clark, 1997). The dysfunctional modes need to be deactivated and the more adaptive modes need to be built (Beck & Weishaar, 2005). Modifying the content of the modes is yet another way to achieve more adaptive behavior, which is achieved through addressing core beliefs and schemas.

Steve is harboring some faulty beliefs that need to be modified. Mia helps him identify his automatic thoughts (ATs) first, and then replace them with more functional beliefs. For instance, the AT that "no one loves me" needs to be replaced with something less drastic.

Mia is sure that Steve's self-enhancement primal mode needs to be strengthened. This process will be tricky because Mia is aware that sometimes Steve's functioning based in this mode gets exaggerated (when he is manic). Steve will need to learn to use his conscious control system to discriminate between these two states. Mia decides that Steve needs to find ways to deactivate or de-energize his primal loss and victim modes and to use his conscious control system to interrupt this modal processing when it occurs. Mia targets Steve's problematic ATs and intermediate beliefs as a way to start this process. Later in therapy, he can begin to examine his core beliefs, schemas, and primal mode content and process.

PROCESS OF THERAPY

CT can be seen as moving through three general stages (Dobson & Shaw, 1988). In early sessions, behavioral activation is important. Once the client has some energy, the focus turns to specific automatic thoughts and their relationship to emotion and behavior. Finally (and some clients never get to this stage), the work turns to the more complex level of schematic processing.

In the first session of therapy, three goals are considered critical: establishing the working relationship, goal setting, and socializing the client (Newman & Beck, 1990). Young and colleagues (1993) added that rapport is enhanced and the client's suffering reduced if the therapist can create some quick symptom relief in the first meeting. Judith Beck agreed, writing that "one of the best ways to strengthen the therapeutic alliance is to help patients solve their problems and improve their mood" (2005, p. 67).

Socialization involves directly teaching the cognitive model. A second important part of the educative process is teaching the client about the structure of counseling sessions. Each CT session can be partitioned into seven segments (J. S. Beck, 1995): (a) brief update, (b) bridge from the previous session, (c) setting the agenda, (d) review of homework, (e) discussion of the issues, (f) devising new homework, and (g) summary and feedback (p. 25). Although most of these segments are easily understood given their labels, two deserve extra comment. In the "bridging" stage, the counselor checks to see if the client understood what happened in the previous session. The summary and feedback segment includes the therapist's summary of the session, but also the opportunity for the client to evaluate the session. According to Judith Beck, the CT counselor is likely to ask the client, "Is there anything I said today that bothered you? Anything you think I got wrong?" (1995, p. 58).

Guided discovery describes the process of CT (Beck & Weishaar, 2005). The therapist has an idea (based on her cognitive conceptualization) about where she wants the client to end up, and through her questioning helps the client to get there (Beck, 1997a). Persons and Tompkins (1997) put it another way: "The goal here is for the patient to discover the answers she needs, guided by the therapist" (p. 328). Along the way, the therapist checks with the client often to see if they are in agreement on the goals and activities of the counseling (Persons & Tompkins, 1997). In Judith Beck's (1995) model, the counselor asks for the client's feedback at the end of each therapy session.

As counseling progresses, the counselor takes less responsibility and the client more for what happens in sessions. The therapist begins to take on an advisory role as the client conducts therapy (Young et al., 1993). Ultimately, the aim of the cognitive therapist is to help the client become his own counselor (Newman & Beck, 1990). Clients are even encouraged to conduct their own "self-therapy" sessions, following proper CT structure, after therapy terminates (J. S. Beck, 1995).

Although CT therapists recognize the existence of transference, the goal in CT is to keep these reactions to a minimum through the use of collaborative empiricism (Wright & Beck, 1996). If client transference does appear, it is treated like any other hypothesis—client and therapist explore the cognitive process around it and the evidence that supports or refutes it.

Beck and his colleagues (Beck, Freeman, & Associates, 1990) discussed client resistance under the heading of problems in collaboration. They suggested many possible reasons for noncompliance. Among these are lack of collaborative skills on the part of the client or counselor, client factors (stress, beliefs about change), client and therapist dysfunctional beliefs match (e.g., the therapist and client both believe the situation to be hopeless), poor socialization of the client, mistiming of interventions, and unclear or unrealistic therapy goals. J. S. Beck (2005) emphasized that it is important for the therapist to be attuned to the client's reactions in therapy, and to correspondingly modify her style to match the proclivities of the client. For example, she maintains that many clients like counselor-self disclosure, but some may wonder "why is this therapist wasting my time telling me about his problems?"

In her book on *Challenging Problems* (2005), J. S. Beck discusses difficulties in the therapeutic alliance, recognizing that these can stem from therapist errors or when the client's beliefs affect the alliance. When the problem is found to be the client's belief system, the therapist needs to determine whether it is a specific belief about the therapist or one about people and the world in general. For example, the client might harbor the core belief of helplessness, feel vulnerable, and avoid bonding with the therapist, or be overly protective and defensive. The therapist can then intervene with standard CT techniques. Reinecke and Freeman (2003) note that "the cognitive construct of schema activation is similar to the psychodynamic construct of transference" (p. 241)—that is, there are times when the client behaves in ways similar to those he employs outside of therapy. If this happens, the CT therapist does not attempt to deepen and elaborate upon the transference, but instead tries to help the client to become more aware of these reactions and change them (Reinecke & Freeman, 2003).

J. S. Beck also discusses therapists' dysfunctional reactions to clients and identifies a number of ways in which these can be addressed, such as attending to the competence of the therapist, assessing one's expectations for clients (are they too high or low?) giving feedback and setting limits, and practicing good self-care. In extreme cases, the client may be referred to a different therapist (J. S. Beck, 2005).

Mia and Steve begin their work with Steve learning the relationships among thoughts, feelings, and behaviors (the cognitive model). Mia asks Steve what he wants to get out of counseling, and he replies that he wants to get his life together and get a good job. Mia explores what "getting his life together" means. Steve lists the following (a) staying abstinent, (b) acting in more mature ways, (c) being less depressed and lethargic (which is also connected with his drinking), (d) establishing a better relationship with his parents, (e) feeling better about himself (despite his initial presentation of self-acceptance), and (f) getting a job.

Mia struggles to get Steve to be specific about his difficulties. She asks him what "acting out" and "immature" behavior are. He gives several examples: He yells at coworkers when he is frustrated. He has walked off the job when unhappy with how things were going (for example, when his supervisor is dissatisfied with his performance). He pouts when he does not get his way in group discussions at the residence facility where he lives.

Although his current level of depression is not as severe as it has been in the past, Steve would like to work on ways to deal with possible intensifications of depression in the future. He and Mia decide that setting some goals about depression would be appropriate.

Mia and Steve establish the following treatment plan:

1. *Develop strategies to help Steve stay abstinent from drinking. Identify situations that trigger drinking (those that activate the loss mode, primarily). Evaluate dysfunctional beliefs and automatic thoughts associated with drinking.*

2. *Help Steve identify and evaluate beliefs and thoughts about himself and his relationships with others, including his parents. Work on ways to improve these relationships.*

3. *Problem-solve about "acting-out" behavior. Identify beliefs and automatic thoughts associated with situations in which he feels criticized (i.e., the victim mode is operative). Construct alternative strategies to use in these situations.*

4. *Examine Steve's depression. Identify and evaluate cognitive structure and processes that are active when he is depressed (the depressogenic schema and associated beliefs and automatic thoughts).*

5. *Develop job-search behaviors and implement them. Examine cognitions around these behaviors.*

Mia's cognitive case conceptualization is shown in Figure 10.2, which guides her work with Steve. She helps him with his struggles, asking questions that orient his explorations (guided discovery). Mia gently encourages Steve to take responsibility for choosing topics to put on the agenda, and to take the lead in applying the cognitive model. In each session, they follow the steps of the CT model: (a) Steve gives a brief update on his situation. (b) Mia and Steve relate the previous session to the present. (c) Mia and Steve set the agenda. (d) They review the homework. (e) They discuss the issues on the agenda. (f) They construct new homework. (g) Mia summarizes the session and asks for Steve's feedback—how he felt about the session. Both Steve and Mia offer input.

THERAPEUTIC TECHNIQUES

Beck advocates the flexible use of techniques; almost any ethical technique that attacks dysfunctional thought is appropriate if the counselor and client agree on its use (Newman & Beck, 1990). "Cognitive therapy is highly eclectic, but not theoretically 'neutral'" (Alford & Beck, 1997a, p. 90). Techniques are selected to serve the overall conceptualization developed via cognitive theory (Alford & Beck, 1997a).

Techniques can be selected from other psychotherapeutic approaches, provided that the following criteria are met: (1) The methods are consistent with cognitive therapy principles and are logically related to the theory of therapeutic change; (2) the choice of techniques is based on a comprehensive case conceptualization that takes into account the patient's characteristics (introspective capacity, problem-solving abilities, etc.); (3) collaborative empiricism and guided discovery are employed; and (4) the standard interview structure is

Client: <u>Steve</u>	**Counselor:** <u>Mia</u> **Date:** <u>6-12-06'</u>
Presenting Problems	Alcohol use, immature behavior, acting out, sadness/depression, unsatisfactory relationships.
Relevant History	Difficulty in school ("acting up"), family turmoil (distant parents, parental divorce), diagnosis of bipolar disorder at age 25, serious automobile accident, alcohol problems resulting in multiple courses of inpatient treatment, breakup of significant relationship.
Modes, Core Beliefs, and Schemas	Loss, victim, overactive self-enhancement modes. Self-schema negative ("I am worthless"). Believes that the world is generally hostile and unforgiving ("Others won't treat me well anyway"). Values the approval of others but doubts that he will get it ("I must be loved. Others disapprove of me.").
Conditional Beliefs	"If I don't keep my parents happy, then I am worthless. If others don't treat me well, they are evil and the world is a rotten place. If I am not perfect at work, I am a failure."
Situational Factors	When others criticize, interactions with parents, perceived failure of any kind.
Automatic Thoughts and Beliefs	*Associated with loss mode:* "No one loves me; I'm a failure and worthless; I must be perfect; I must not get angry; it's no use; I can't do anything right." *Associated with victim mode:* "Others are mean to me; others won't give me a break." *Associated with self-enhancement mode:* "I'm invincible; others can go to hell."
Emotions	Sadness and depression, anger and irritation in work environment, exhilaration in manic phases.
Behaviors	When depressed, becomes lethargic and may drink. In victim mode, can behave angrily and disrespectfully to others. Social/assertiveness skills weak?
Integration/Cognitive Construction of Current Presentation	Bipolar tendencies may be partly biological in origin. They are associated with loss, victim, and self-enhancement modes. Negative self-schema is a function of sociotrophic tendencies combined with early family environment and relationship with parents. Primal modes were also shaped by these factors. Different modes, when activated, are associated with emotions, behaviors, and cognitions as indicated earlier. Alcohol use appears in either loss or self-enhancement modes.

FIGURE 10.2. CT Case Formulation for Steve.

followed, unless there are factors that argue strongly against the standard format. (Alford & Beck, 1997a p. 91)

Both cognitive and behavioral techniques are used in CT. A general term for anything that changes client cognitive structure is **cognitive restructuring**. Behavioral techniques are used in the interest of behavioral activation (i.e., to get a severely depressed client moving as in activity scheduling) or to teach new skills (such as assertion or problem-solving training). **Homework** is considered essential in CT, and many of the techniques described in this section can be transformed into homework assignments (Beck & Emery, 2005).

The majority of presentations of CT focus on modifying or eliminating schemas, core beliefs, and automatic thoughts (e.g., Leahy, J. S. Beck, & Beck, 2005; J. S. Beck, 1995; 2005). Beck and Weishaar (2005) identified 3 ways to deal with dysfunctional modes: "(1) deactivating them, (2) modifying their content and structure, and (3) constructing more adaptive modes to neutralize them" (p. 240). According to Beck (1996), corrective information from the counselor activates a "safety" mode that contains more functional beliefs (p. 16). Basic cognitive-behavioral interventions that emphasize mastery and pleasure build or strengthen adaptive modes (Beck, 1996). Other interventions are oriented toward deactivating the protective primal modes. Routes to modal change include changing the appraisal of the situation (e.g., from dangerous to benign), distraction, and reassurance from the counselor (i.e., corrective information leads to change in how the client interprets the situation). The most significant change in primal modes, however, is through changing the underlying beliefs in the mode, the rules the individual uses to interpret the world. This belief change results in activation of adaptive modes and deactivation of dysfunctional modes (Beck & Weishaar, 2005). For example, a client who initially interprets a rapid heartbeat as the sign of an impending heart attack changes two beliefs: (a) that rapid heartbeat always leads to heart attack and (b) that he is a good candidate for a heart attack (when he has very few risk factors).

Following are descriptions of some of the techniques typically used in CT.

QUESTIONING

One of the most prominent techniques in CT is questioning. In fact, one of the most basic interventions in CT is to ask the client, "What was going through your mind right now?" when the counselor notices a change in the client's affective state (Newman & Beck, 1990). The idea is that emotions are good indicators of the presence of automatic thoughts.

Socratic questioning refers to the strategy of asking leading questions so that the client comes to the Cognitive Therapy conclusion (Beck & Emery, 2005). A favorite question of cognitive therapists is, "Where is the evidence for this thought/belief?" It is the counselor's job to devise questions that help clients alter their current views to "a state of inquisitiveness and curiosity" (Wright & Beck, 1996, p. 1021).

Six types of questions are considered effective in helping clients test automatic thoughts (J. S. Beck, 1995, p. 109): "(1) What is the evidence? (2) Is there an alternative explanation? (3) What is the worst that could happen? Could I live through it? What is the best that could happen? What is the most realistic outcome? (4) What's the effect of my believing the automatic thought? What could be the effect of changing my thinking? (5) What should I do about it? (6) What would I tell _____ [a friend] if he or she was in the same situation?"

Mia asks Steve about what goes through his head when he gets mad at work. He reports, after some consideration, that sometimes he thinks, "they are mean" and "they hate me." At other times he thinks, "I screwed up" or "I can't do this job." Mia asks Steve what evidence he has that others hate him and are mean. He replies that they criticize his performance on the job. "Do you deserve the criticism?" asks Mia. "Well, yes," Steve replies, "I did screw up." "But does that automatically mean that they hate you?" Mia asks. "Well, I guess not," replies Steve. Mia then follows with "What's the effect of thinking that people at work are mean and hate you?" Steve acknowledges that his belief leads to easily triggered anger and subsequent "immature" behavior. Afterward, he finds himself depressed.

DOWNWARD ARROW

This technique is used to identify core beliefs. It is so-named because the therapist starts by examining thoughts relatively close to the "surface" and proceeds downward to core beliefs. First, a key automatic thought is identified that the counselor thinks is related to a core belief. The counselor then asks the client what this thought means, assuming it is true. Repeating this question for each client response will eventually lead to the core belief. Judith Beck (1995) noted that asking the client what the thought means *to* the client often leads to an intermediate belief, whereas asking what the thought means *about* the client leads to a core belief (p. 145).

Mia asks Steve to examine the belief that his parents think he is an alcoholic manic-depressive. She directs Steve to assume this is true and asks him what it means to him. Steve divulges that it means that his parents think badly of him. "OK, so assume that's true," Mia says, "What does that mean, that they might think badly of you?" Steve replies, "Well, it means that I am a failure as a person and worthless." Mia and Steve have identified a dysfunctional core belief or schema.

THOUGHT RECORDING

Cognitive therapists almost always instruct clients in some form of thought recording (Wright & Beck, 1996). One commonly used instrument is the Dysfunctional Thoughts Record (DTR), which is shown in Table 10.4 (J. S. Beck, 1995). The counselor gives the client the DTR to take home, asking him to record various occurrences of ATs between counseling sessions. At the next session, counselor and client review the DTR, evaluate the client's responses to the ATs, and work on alternatives, if necessary.

Steve records his automatic thought that occurred after disagreeing with a coworker, Sue. Thinking "she hates me" leads to Steve's sadness. Mia and Steve review the form and find that Steve did not really convince himself with the adaptive response he devised, although he did feel less sad. Mia and Steve work to find a response that will help Steve further reduce the sadness or eliminate it entirely.

BEHAVIORAL EXPERIMENTS

Behavioral experiments are assignments that are tailored to a specific belief. The therapist and client design a task or activity that challenges a faulty cognition (Beck & Emery, 2005). For example, Nancy, who believes that she has no fun in life, is asked to pick one activity that might possibly be fun, such as going to the zoo. She is asked to go to the zoo

TABLE 10.4
STEVE'S DYSFUNCTIONAL THOUGHT RECORD

Date/Time	Situation	Automatic Thoughts	Emotions	Adaptive Response	Outcome
	1. What event, image, or recollection led to the emotion?	1. What thoughts/ images?	1. What emotion did you feel?	1. (optional) What cognitive distortion did you make?	1. How much do you now believe your AT?
	2. Any physical sensations?	2. How much did you believe them?	2. How intense? (0–100%)	2. Use questions at bottom to form a response to the AT.	2. What emotions do you feel now? How intense? (0–100%)
				3. How much do you believe the response? (0–100%)	3. What will you do (or did you do)?
6/19/06	1. Disagreed with coworker	1. She hates me	1. Sad	1. Magnification? Overgeneralization? (not sure)	1. 40%
			2. 80%	2. Just because I disagreed with Sue doesn't necessarily mean she hates me	2. Still sad, but less
				3. 70%	3. Nothing

Questions to consider about AT: (1) What is the evidence that the AT is true? (2) Is there an alternative explanation? (3) What's the worst that could happen? (4) What's the effect of my believing the AT? (5) What should I do about it? (6) If _____ [a friend] was in the situation, what would I tell him/her?

From *Cognitive Therapy: Basics and Beyond* (p. 126) by J. S. Beck, 1995, New York: Guilford. © 1995 by The Guilford Press. Adapted with permission.

and report what happens. If she has fun, then her belief is disconfirmed. If she doesn't have any fun, then the thoughts she has at the zoo can be examined.

Mia and Steve develop a behavioral experiment for him that tests his belief that "it's no use; I can't do anything right." They identify something that would be "right"—he could negotiate a conflict in his living situation without getting so angry that he "blows up." For example, Steve wants to be able to see a certain show on TV, but is afraid to ask the others in the residence about it (the TV is communal). Mia and Steve work on strategies to help Steve ask this question.

ACTIVITY SCHEDULING

When clients are very depressed or for other reasons have low motivation, it is often helpful to have them create a daily schedule, on paper, to follow between therapy sessions (Newman & Beck, 1990). The counselor may ask the client to simply keep a record of daily activities at first to establish baseline information. After reviewing these data, the client and counselor then work together to fill in the blocks of an activity chart, which lists the days of the week across the top and hours along the left side (J. S. Beck, 1995). Part of recording daily activities often involves rating each on a scale of 1 to 10 for mastery and pleasure (Beck & Weishaar, 2005). This technique is sometimes called mastery and pleasure therapy, particularly when activities are developed to create successful outcomes (Beck, 1976).

Because Steve is in the work-therapy program, he does not need to activity schedule during the week. However, he does admit that he has difficulties on the weekends. Mia and Steve develop a schedule for Saturdays that includes important errands that Steve would like to accomplish (go shopping, for example) along with some fun activities (watch a Little League baseball game). Specific times are set up for the activities, and Steve is to record his completion of each, along with ratings of mastery and pleasure.

GRADED TASKS

When a client faces what seems to be an overwhelming task, the counselor and client can work to make it less intimidating by breaking it down into smaller steps. This procedure is called creating a graded task assignment (Beck & Weishaar, 2005). Concrete steps are formulated to reach the agreed-upon goal, and the client then works on the steps one at a time, focusing on the achievement of each. The first steps devised should be relatively easy so that the client is not overwhelmed and, ideally, experiences some initial success (Freeman, Schrodt, Gilson, & Ludgate, 1993). In fact, Beck also called this technique success therapy (Beck, 1976, p. 272). Self- and therapist reinforcement are important in this process.

Mia and Steve examine Steve's goal to get a job. Because this is an intimidating task for Steve, they break it down into a number of steps using the graded task approach. The first step is to have Steve read a good reference book on job searching. Next, Steve constructs his resume and brings it to Mia for review. Steve decides he wants to go into the restaurant industry, so he and Mia problem solve about how to get a job there given his lack of background. They decide that he should have lunch in a moderately priced restaurant and try to engage in some chitchat with one or two staff members about how to get a job. These steps are just a beginning, but Steve and Mia write them down, and as he tackles each, they examine his cognitions about them. Mia is careful to praise Steve when he accomplishes his task for the week, and she makes sure that Steve does something nice for himself, too.

ASSERTIVENESS TRAINING

Borrowed from behaviorism, assertiveness training involves teaching clients skills that support their rights without violating the rights of others. Role-play is frequently used in assertiveness training, along with simple, concrete teaching of information about rights and responsibility.

Mia teaches Steve about assertive behavior. She suggests that he read a book on assertiveness training. Together, Mia and Steve decide that assertiveness training is in order for Steve because it should help his relationships at work and in the residential facility. He notes that his immature behavior is not assertive because it is either passive (he walks out) or aggressive (he gets angry and yells). They generate a list of problem situations and examine Steve's thoughts, feelings, and behaviors while in the situations. They then generate alternative assertive behaviors to replace Steve's previously passive or aggressive ones. Mia helps Steve rehearse these new behaviors in session.

PROBLEM SOLVING

Problem-solving techniques involve identifying and clarifying the problem, generating alternatives, evaluating the alternatives, implementing an alternative, and then assessing the utility of the new approach (Newman & Beck, 1990). In CT, this approach is often used to evaluate dysfunctional beliefs, such as when the benefits and costs of maintaining a given belief are explored.

Steve and Mia problem solve around his desire to remain abstinent from alcohol. One thing they decide is that when Steve gets depressed, he is likely to drink. They examine his cognitions and behaviors and devise alternative responses to use when Steve notices that he is down.

IMAGERY

When a client is having difficulty identifying automatic thoughts, the counselor can resort to using imagery or role-playing to vividly conjure up the problem situation (Wright & Beck, 1996). Because these techniques are likely to evoke the emotions associated with the problematic situations, they should help the client identify cognitions associated with the feelings. The **turn-off technique** can be used to help clients learn that they can control images (Beck & Emery, 2005). In this technique, the therapist and client think up a way to sharply disrupt the image, such as clapping his hands or blowing a whistle. Images can also facilitate the development of adaptive cognitions, and then the client can practice this in session or as homework.

Steve wants to work on feeling good about his interactions with his parents. He is terrified to contact his mother because he has heard that she has "disowned" him. Mia helps Steve imagine making a phone call to his mom, and they examine his thoughts and responses.

ROLE PLAYING AND OTHER BEHAVIORALLY-ORIENTED TECHNIQUES

Also known as behavioral rehearsal, role playing can be used to help the client practice behaviors useful in social situations (Beck & Weishaar, 2005). Exposure is also used in CT, particularly with clients who present with anxiety-related problems (Beck & Emery, 2005). Typically, a graded approach is used, in which the client takes baby steps toward the feared situation or object. Self-instruction can be added to exposure: the client uses a prepared set of self-coaching statements to help the client cope with the stress of confronting the feared situation (Beck & Emery, 2005).

Mia and Steve role-play the telephone call to his mother. Mia plays mom; Steve practices what he will say, using adaptive thoughts rather than negative automatic ones.

EVALUATION OF THE THEORY

Cognitive Therapy has evoked criticism from many fronts. Early on, it was attacked by the behaviorists and psychoanalysts alike (Arnkoff & Glass, 1995). Behaviorists thought that cognition was superfluous to behavior change. According to Meichenbaum (1993), a subgroup of behavioral therapists threatened to throw the "cognitivists" out of the Association for Advancement Behavior Therapy. Psychoanalytic folk tend to dismiss CT as surface oriented, dealing with symptoms rather than the important issues. Behaviorists, at least, seem to have changed their opinions; in a 1990 survey 69% of the members of the American Association of Behavior Therapy reported that they use cognitive techniques (Craighead, 1990).

On first examination, CT appears relatively simple to use. It provides clear explanations for problems and allows the use of a wide variety of techniques (Arnkoff & Glass, 1995). However, counselors may find that identifying cognitions, particularly automatic thoughts, is not as simple as it may seem.

Paradoxically, a common criticism of CT is that it is too simple and mechanistic. It is said to ignore the client's emotions and history in favor of the client's thinking. Others accuse CT theory of ignoring environmental influences and the effects of individuals' attempts to cope with their situations (Coyne & Gotlib, 1986). CT theorists respond to these criticisms by pointing out that the client's early experiences are seen as very important in determining schemas and core beliefs (Beck et al., 2004; Beck & Weishaar, 2005). The relative sensitivity of modes to activation (which determines the degree of dysfunction) is also linked to early experience.

A strength of CT is that Beck and his associates have continually evaluated, modified, and advanced the theory. Loads of outcome research supports this approach (for a recent summary, see Beck, 2005 or Leahy, 2004). The modal perspective is an interesting addition to CT theory, although it makes the theory sound a lot more psychoanalytic. I personally find the addition of recent constructs such as modes, personality types, and so on, confusing because it is not clear how they relate to earlier CT theory. Depending on which source you consult, the modes and personality types might or might not be discussed. For example, J. S. Beck is silent about modal processing. Also, the specific modes hypothesized by the theory seem to change depending upon what source you consult.

QUALITIES OF THE THEORY

Precision and Testability. To his credit, Beck was one of the leaders in the development of treatment manuals; Beck, Rush, and colleagues (1979) presented the first treatment manual for CT (it should come as no surprise that the behaviorists developed the very first manuals). The presence of treatment manuals makes the testing of CT outcome easier and more valid. There is a massive amount of data that tests the outcome of CT, but despite the theory's apparent simplicity, the testability of CT is debated. Coyne and Gotlib (1986) argued that the CT constructs were difficult to test, calling them "slippery and indeterminate" (1986, p. 697). In addition, Oei and Free (1995) suggested that measurement problems plagued CT theory in that the standard measures of cognitive dysfunction (the ATQ and the DAS) might be assessing general psychological dysfunction rather than cognitive distortion specifically. Hayes, Luoma, Bond, Masuda, and Lillis (2006) maintained that although there is much research on CT, the link between cognitive change and improvement is not well established (more on this later).

Empirical Validity. Cognitive Therapy is perhaps the most well-researched counseling approach in existence, with an overwhelming amount of empirical support for its effectiveness with a variety of client problems (Beck, 2005; Leahy, 2004). However, evidence for the theoretical assumptions and structure is less impressive.

RESEARCH SUPPORT

Outcome Research. Outcome research has uniformly supported CT. Hundreds of studies have examined the efficacy of CT, probably because it was one of the earliest manualized treatments and also because good outcome measures exist, particularly for depression (e.g., the Beck Depression Inventory and the Hamilton Depression Rating Scale).

Numerous studies have tested the efficacy of CT with various diagnostic categories. For the most part, CT has been found to be as effective as other treatments, more effective than no-treatment controls, and in some cases more effective than placebo control groups. Not surprisingly, a significant amount of this research has focused on depression. One of the best known trials of CT is the NIMH treatment of depression study, summarized in Chapter 1. As you may recall, the results of the NIMH study were disappointing because the treatment approaches (CT and interpersonal therapy) did not produce improvement relative to the placebo group.

Meta-analytic studies have generally supported the efficacy of CT. Butler, Chapman, Forman, and Beck (2006) reviewed 16 meta-analyses on outcome studies of cognitive-behavioral therapy (CBT). They found that CBT was effective over a wide range of dysfunction, including depression, anxiety, posttraumatic stress disorder, anger, chronic pain, and marital distress. Dobson (1989) conducted a meta-analysis of 28 studies of depression, each of which used Beck's treatment manual and the Beck Depression Inventory (BDI) as the outcome measure. When compared to no-treatment or wait-list control groups, CT achieved an effect size of 2.15, which is large by psychotherapy outcome standards and indicates that the average client in CT was better off than 98% of the control clients. Dobson also reported that CT was more effective than behavior therapy or pharmacotherapy, although the effect sizes were much smaller (about 0.50). A comparison of CT and placebo treatment was not included in this study. Reinecke, Ryan, and DuBois (1998) found that CT was effective in interventions for depression among adolescent clients.

Because depression is commonly treated with antidepressant medication, investigators in this area have been interested in the relative efficacy of CT and drug treatment. A meta-analysis addressing this question examined studies published between 1977 and 1997, including 48 trials consisting of 2,765 clients (Gloaguen, Cottraux, Cucherat, & Blackburn, 1998). In all of these studies, the outcome measure was the BDI. Gloaguen and colleagues found that CT produced better results than waiting lists, placebo treatments, and antidepressant drug treatment. Comparisons with a set of "other" therapies also showed CT to be more effective. However, CT was found to produce about the same amount of change as Behavior Therapy.

Studies documenting the superiority of CT to other approaches, however, must be viewed with caution. Some evidence suggests that studies conduced by proponents of a given approach tend to show results favorable to that approach. Robinson, Berman, and Neimeyer (1990) examined the effects of investigator allegiance and found this state of affairs true for studies of depression. When allegiance was *not* controlled, cognitive, cognitive behavioral, and behavioral approaches appeared to produce better outcomes than other approaches (labeled *general verbal therapy* by these investigators). However, when investigator allegiance was controlled, these effects disappeared. In addition, as a group, all therapies did not significantly improve on the effects of placebo treatments. When comparing psychotherapy to pharmacological treatments, Robinson and colleagues also found investigator effects: an initial apparent superiority of psychotherapy disappeared once allegiance effects were taken into account. Gaffan, Tsaousis, and Kemp-Wheeler (1995) replicated this effect, but found less evidence of allegiance effects in a set of more recently published studies that were not included in Robinson et al.'s analyses. Similarly, Wampold and colleagues (1997) meta-analyzed 277 treatment comparisons, specifically testing for variations in efficacy among theoretical orientations, and also found no significant differences.

Although fewer studies are available, CT appears to be effective for anxiety disorders, including generalized anxiety, panic disorder, agoraphobia, and social phobia (Chambless & Gillis, 1993; Clark & Ehlers, 1993; Gould, Buckminster, Pollack, Otto, & Yap, 1997; Wenzel, Sharp, Brown, Greenberg, & Beck, 2006). However, it should be noted that in many cases these trials involved treatments that combined pure CT with standard behavioral techniques, such as relaxation training, desensitization, or biofeedback. It is not clear that CT is effective for these disorders (particularly agoraphobia) on its own, nor that it is superior to behavioral approaches. An interesting finding from Wenzel, Sharp, Brown, et al. (2006) was that beliefs specific to panic decreased over CT treatment, which would seem to partially support the cognitive conceptualization of anxiety disorders proposed by Beck and Emery (2005; 1985). Earlier, Chambless and Gillis (1993) had found similar results, but also noted that cognitive changes are produced by approaches other than CT, so these results can not be construed as robust support for CT theory.

Beck and his colleagues are also very interested in suicidal behavior (Beck, 2005). An example of a recent study that assessed the effects of CT in reducing repeated suicide attempts was reported by Brown et al. (2005). In this randomized controlled trial of CT and treatment as usual (TAU) with clients who had been evaluated at a hospital for attempted suicide, those who received CT were less likely to reattempt and had lower rates of self-reported depression at a 6-month follow-up compared to the TAU clients. CT clients also reported less hopelessness than the TAU clients. Although this study attests to the effectiveness of CT, only cautious conclusions about the relative superiority of CT over TAU can be drawn, however, because of the differences in the ways that CT and TAU are administered. Chapter 1 discusses some of the issues involved in TAU-treatment comparisons.

Studies of CT with a wide range of diagnostic categories have been reported. Abramowitz (1997) reviewed interventions for Obsessive Compulsive Disorder (OCD) and concluded that CT was found to be as effective as the behavioral treatment exposure and response prevention (ERP), considered to be the "gold standard" for OCD. In a few studies, CT was found to be superior to ERP, leading Abramowitz to speculate that both approaches lead to the disconfirmation of dysfunctional beliefs associated with OCD.

Clark (2004) opined that the results comparing ERP and CT were inconclusive, writing "at this time, there is no evidence that adding a cognitive component to ERP produces significantly more symptomatic improvement than ERP alone" (p. 175). However, Clark maintains that there may be some subtypes of OCD that respond better to CT than ERP (e.g., obsessional ruminative) but comparative data are scarce. Similarly, Pretzer and Beck (2004) summarized the research the effectiveness of CT for clients diagnosed as personality disordered, and concluded that positive evidence existed. In one such study, Brown et al. (2004) found that CT was effective for clients diagnosed as borderline personality disorder in an open trial study (i.e., not a randomized clinical trial). Rector (2004) presents evidence that CT is helpful in treating schizophrenia.

Jamison and Scogin (1995) took an interesting approach when they tested the effectiveness of cognitive bibliotherapy with adults. Participants read David Burns' book *Feeling Good* (1980). Half of the participants served in a delayed bibliotherapy group as controls. Using multiple outcome measures (including the BDI and the observer-rated Hamilton Rating Scale for Depression), these investigators demonstrated that therapists are not absolutely necessary! Moreover, the significant changes in depression observed at posttest were maintained at a 3-month follow-up.

Jakes and Rhodes (2003) reported on an interesting small N study of solution focused and cognitive-behavioral strategies with clients who had delusions. Five clients were intensively studied at baseline (no treatment) and as they were then treated with a solution focused and 2 CT interventions (Schema-Focused Cognitive Therapy and Cognitive Therapy focused on challenging the delusion) in that order. They observed that these clients (who were diagnosed with chronic psychosis as well as delusion for at least 1 year) responded positively to treatment in terms of decrease in negative beliefs about the self, as would be predicted by CT theory. However, because this was a multiple case study design, we must be cautious in drawing causal inferences from its results.

Research has also looked at whether CT helps clients retain the gains made in counseling. Hollon, Shelton, and Davis (1993) reported that in four major clinical trials of CT, clients receiving CT alone or in combination with antidepressants showed lower rates of relapse (i.e., return of symptoms) than those treated with psychopharmacological methods only. Hensley, Nadiga, and Uhlenhuth (2004) compared 5 trials of the long-term effects of CT vs. antidepressant medication (tricyclic antidepressants), finding that CT was superior in terms of preventing relapse. van Oppen et al. (2005) found that clients diagnosed as Obsessive Compulsive Disorder maintained their outcomes 5 years after treatment, but there was no difference between groups receiving CT and exposure treatment alone and those receiving psychological treatment plus antidepressant medication. However, they cautioned that because there are very few good studies of the long-term effects of CT and other therapies, strong statements about prevention effects associated with CT should be avoided at present.

Theory-Testing Research. Overall, research support for the validity of CT theory is mixed. Much of the controversy has focused on the CT model of depression. In the 1980s Coyne and Gotlib (1983, 1986) declared that the evidence for the causal role of cognitions in depression was unconvincing, and they criticized CT theory for its neglect of environmental factors and individual coping strategies. They added that "the modal depressed patient is probably a woman with marital difficulties, and glib attempts to reduce her problems to a matter of distorted cognitions have potentially pernicious social implications" (1986, pp. 703–704).

Haaga, Dyck, and Ernst (1991) also reviewed the evidence relevant to the CT theory of depression and distinguished between CT's *descriptive* theory of depression (that depressives are a certain way) and its *causal* theory of depression (that cognitions cause depression). Depressed individuals, according to theory, are thought to display more negativity, which involves their views of self, the world, and the future (the cognitive triad), as well as other biases or distortions in information processing when compared to nondepressed people. In addition, CT theory predicts that positive thoughts are practically nonexistent in depressed individuals. Further, the cognitive triad should be evident in all types of depression, and in all depressed people. The degree of negative thinking should be positively associated with the severity of noncognitive depressive features (e.g., somatic symptoms, depressed mood). Finally, the cognitive specificity hypothesis implies that depressed individuals should show different cognitive patterns than individuals displaying other types of psychological dysfunction.

In reviewing evidence relevant to the descriptive model, Haaga and colleagues (1991) found support for the negativity hypothesis, the cognitive triad, and bias in information processing. Individuals who are depressed seem to display more negative thoughts than people who are not depressed do, and this effect extends to views of the self, world, and future. Evidence for the other hypotheses was weaker and often was compromised by methodological problems or theoretical fuzziness. For instance, the elements of the cognitive triad seem to be overlapping—the negative view of the world seems to emphasize self-related aspects.

Evidence for the causal model of CT (that cognitions cause depression) is less convincing (Bieling & Kuyken, 2003; Hayes et al., 2006). Controversy has long been evident, and still is, around the issues of what is generally known as the diathesis-stress model, which is the fancy name for the idea that both cognitive vulnerability (i.e., activation of negative cognitive systems) and an external stressor are required to produce dysfunction. Early on, Hagga and colleagues (1991) asserted that no single study has completely tested the proposed relationships among personality dimensions (sociotrophy and autonomy), dysfunctional beliefs, stress, and depression. Haaga and colleagues concluded, "We thus find little convincing support for causal hypotheses of cognitive theory, but at the same time, it would be premature to abandon them" (p. 231). More recently, Zuroff, Mongrain, and Santor (2004) reviewed the literature specific to sociotrophy and autonomy, and concluded that the picture was less bleak, and that there was merit in continuing to investigate the diathesis-stress model. An attempt to perform such research is represented by Dozois and Backs-Dermott's (2000) study of sociotrophy and negative outcomes. This was an experimental study in which participants listened to an audiotape depicting an interpersonal rejection and then completed checklists of self-relevant adjectives and a reaction time task. Consistent with predictions, participants high in sociotrophy showed more negative reactions than those low in sociotrophy. Studying more generalized dysfunctional attitudes in an experimental design, Abela and D'Alessandro (2003) found some support for the model in that such attitudes predicted depression for students who had received negative feedback on a college admissions decision. Although the experimental nature of these designs appears to be a far cry from actual depressive processes in the "real world," nonetheless the study yields some support for CT theory. Using a longitudinal design, Grazioli and Terry (2000) found similar results in studying postpartum depression.

Oei and Free (1995) looked at the role of outcome research in validating CT theory more closely and found that cognitive change occurs in depressed individuals who engage in CT therapy. However, this evidence is not considered as particularly supportive of CT theory because the same kind of change is documented among individuals in other psychological therapies as well as in psychopharmacological treatment and wait-list groups. In explaining these findings, Oei and Free offered the circular process model, which suggests that the changes in biological processes induced by drug treatment create changes in cognition (reduced negative thinking). The process is reversed in verbal therapy; change in cognition leads to biochemical change. Even if research data existed that supported the second hypothesis, the fact that these changes occur in other therapies still suggests a general process found in counseling rather than one specific to CT theory. In contrast, Beevers and Miller (2005) used a longitudinal design, and found that the relationship between cognitions and depressions was weaker for clients who had completed Cognitive Therapy than family therapy (in both cases, pharmacological interventions were used).

Recent research in treatment contexts also provides some evidence for the hypothesized links between cognition and dysfunction. Wenzel, Sharp, Sokol, and Beck (2006) demonstrated that individuals completing a trial of CT for panic disorder differed in the degree of attentional fixation depending on their treatment outcomes. Clients who still met the criteria for panic disorder at the end of treatment showed higher levels of fixation than those who no longer could be diagnosed. Because attentional fixation is considered to be a theoretically predicted element of panic disorder, this research can be seen as supportive of CT. However, this study is probably subject to the same criticisms that Oei and Free offered. In a study of postpartum women, Evans, Hernon, Lewis, Araya, and Wolke (2005) documented that women who had the most negative self-schemas were more likely to become depressed after childbirth when compared to women with less negative schemas. Once again, because of the design of this study, causal conclusions are risky, although the longitudinal design makes it somewhat more convincing than would a cross-sectional method.

In summary, research generally supports the effectiveness of CT with a wide variety of clients. However, claims of its superiority to other treatments are less convincing. Although some evidence has suggested support for the theoretical propositions of CT, it is extremely difficult to really test the underlying assumptions of the CT model.

ISSUES OF INDIVIDUAL AND CULTURAL DIVERSITY

Hoffman (2006) noted that an individual's culture will influence how he or she perceives the world, including one's own behavior, and thus, interventions should take this into account. Drawing on literature from social psychology, Hoffman suggests that individuals from non-Western culture are more likely to accept contradictory thoughts or ideas than are westerners. For example, explaining anxiety as worry about an upcoming job-related presentation rather than as a sign of an impending heart attack might be acceptable to a client from a Western culture. This client could pick the first rather than the second explanation. In contrast, a non-Western client might be much more comfortable in holding both explanations simultaneously. Differences such as this one clearly could have some important implications for cognitive restructuring efforts.

Other Western-based principles of CT conflict with the values and norms of other cultures. CT assumes that the individual is largely responsible for his own fate; this individualistic outlook may clash with collectivistic values such as those found in some Asian, Hispanic/Latino/Latina, or American Indian cultures. Clients who are highly spiritual may not respond well to the emphasis on individual choice and control because they believe in the influence of higher powers in human activity. At the same time, Ivey, D'Andrea, Ivey, and Simek-Morgan (2002) argued that the structure and clarity of CT may appeal to minority clients. Chen's (1995) comments about the consistency of REBT values (emphasis on logical thinking, cognitive control of emotion, counselor as teacher, and the active directive nature of therapy) and Chinese culture probably apply to CT as well. There seems to be much agreement that CT can be adapted to a wide range of client diversity (Hays & Iwamasa, 2006).

Scorzelli and Reinke-Scorzelli (1994) collected data that illustrated the problem with the individualistic stance of CT. They surveyed a group of graduate students in India about the fit of CT (REBT and CT) with their culture. Most of the students were female and identified Hindusim as their primary religion. About 87% of these students judged that CT was inconsistent with their cultural values, most prominently with the belief in karma, that one's destiny is fixed. These students also saw CT as conflicting with values such as obedience to family and other cultural values, including sex role expectations.

In contrast, Wong, Kim, Zane, Kim, and Huang (2003) found that for clients who were identified with Asian culture, CT was viewed as more credible than time-limited psychodynamic therapy. In this study, Asian clients who varied in ethnic identity were exposed to treatment rationales for depression based on the two approaches. Asian participants who identified more strongly with Western culture did not differ in their reactions to the two rationales, whereas those lower in Western identity responded more favorably to the CT rationale. Also, individuals with more independent self-construals (as compared to those who were more interdependent) evaluated CT more favorably. Wong and colleagues suggested that the emphasis on individual control in CT was responsible for both of these effects. Clients who are less Anglo in their orientations (presumably more identified with Asian culture) prefer interventions that stress individual adaptation to unchanging extrapersonal factors. Independence, which is thought to be relatively unrelated to cultural identity, would fit well with the individual focus of CT.

Davis and Padesky (1989) suggested that the collaborative nature of the CT relationship promoted the egalitarianism that is important when working with female clients. Encouraging the client to evaluate therapy sessions, set the counseling agenda, and giving the client the opportunity to discuss diagnoses, should empower women who may have experienced cultural pressure to be passive and submissive to men. On the other hand, the presentation of the counselor as an expert, almost in the doctor–patient mode, would seem to contradict the egalitarian spirit endorsed by Davis and Padesky.

Clients who are stigmatized by society may also develop negative self-schemas as a result of cultural pressure. Individuals who are gay, lesbian, bisexual, or transgender (GLBT) or members of groups who have been the subject of prejudice or discrimination would seem particularly vulnerable in this respect. Although the sensitive cognitive therapist could help modify a client's self-schema, this intervention would not immunize the client from social pressures (Davis & Padesky, 1989). The therapist would also have to direct attention toward helping the client deal with cultural disapproval.

In general, the neglect of environmental factors and influences in CT theory may be problematic when working with culturally and individually diverse individuals. People who have experienced prejudice, discrimination, and oppression might have more difficulty locating the sources of their discomfort solely in their cognitive processes.

THE CASE STUDY

Aspects of Steve's presentation fit well with a CT approach, and others do not. Steve is a Caucasian male, so cultural issues may not be paramount. The classic client for CT is one with prominent depression. Although Steve does report some depression, it does not seem severe. However, CT has been applied to a variety of client dysfunctions, including substance abuse, which is clearly a central issue for Steve. In fact, Steve is not reporting a lot of affect in general and seems to be more focused on changing his life situation. Thus, the problem-focused CT approach works well for him.

Beck's modal view describes Steve's manic behavior as hyperactivation of the self-enhancement mode. Thus, his diagnosis of bipolar disorder is captured by activity in the loss and self-enhancement modes. Mia hypothesized that his victim mode was also active, which raises the question about how many modes are likely to be sensitized for a given person.

Summary

CT proposes the cognitive model of therapy: our behaviors and feelings are a result of our cognitive process and structures. Specifically, clients' automatic thoughts, intermediate beliefs, and core schemas are associated with depression, anxiety, and a variety of other kinds of psychological dysfunction. Automatic thoughts are brief, telegraphic statements or images that are related to core beliefs or schemas. Beliefs and schemas are more elaborate structures that sometimes function outside of our everyday awareness. Schemas are complex cognitive structures that aid in the organization of experience and can influence the ways we interpret events. One important schema is the depressogenic schema, which features the cognitive triad of a negative view of self, world, and future.

Cognitive therapists help clients by engaging them in collaborative empiricism—the process of examining their thoughts, assumptions, and beliefs as hypotheses rather than truths. The cognitive therapist is an expert and the client a learner who is expected to take increasing responsibility for counseling as he learns the system. Both cognitive and behavioral techniques are used in CT, and clients are almost always given homework.

CT has the strength of being relatively straightforward and structured. It is probably appealing to clients who expect the therapist to be an expert. The efficacy of CT is well established; however, the support for the theoretical predictions of CT is less impressive.

Concerns can also be raised that CT's emphasis on internal process and individual responsibility may clash with the views and values of clients who are from non-Western European cultures, female, or of GLBT orientation or in other ways diverse (physically challenged, for instance). However, the collaborative relationship found in CT can be empowering to clients who are members of groups that have been historically subject to oppression.

Visit Chapter 10 on the Companion Website at **www.prenhall.com/murdock** for chapter-specific resources and self-assessments.

For ease of expression, throughout this chapter references to Beck (without initials) will refer to Aaron Beck's authorship.

William Glasser

CHAPTER 11

Reality Therapy

Donald is a 31-year-old male Caucasian who is currently living alone. He and his wife are separated, and he has recently been fired from a job as a financial advisor. Donald reports that he is experiencing financial stress but does not want to take "just any old job." He has a history of frequent job changes.

Donald's appearance is neat and appropriate. He speaks very quickly and appears agitated. His manner is somewhat grandiose. Donald appeared to have difficulty making eye contact with his female counselor and becomes extremely anxious when asked to talk about his feelings.

Donald says that he has no close friends but that he is active in community service (e.g., a volunteer group at a local hospital). He reports that he gets along well in these situations by carefully presenting an image that he wants others to see. In his spare time Donald likes to read magazines and watch movies. His favorite topics are mystery and science fiction.

Donald was raised in a large family with three brothers and several step-siblings. His father was violent when he was young and was imprisoned for some time. Donald does not know why his father was in prison. His mother filed for divorce while his father was in prison and remarried soon after. After his father was released from prison, Donald went to live with him. At the time, his father was self-employed, but Donald does not know in what kind of business or work. Donald expressed resentment when talking about his mother and sees her as being weak and a Valium addict. He says that his father is his idol.

Donald's current marriage is his second. He divorced his first wife after catching her in bed with another woman. Donald's present relationship has lasted 4 years. His wife, Tammy, moved out about a month ago, saying that she no longer loved or respected Donald. He wants very much for his wife to come back to their relationship.

Donald is seeking counseling because of his job loss and marital difficulties. He believes he functions well in other aspects of his life. He says that physically he is OK, but he does

352

complain of weariness, occasional nausea, and a "tired" back and tense neck muscles that cause "migraines."

Donald says that he feels addicted to excitement and tends to move from job to job for this reason. He is an impulsive spender, and his spending habits are part of the conflict with his wife, Tammy. Donald sees himself as a superficial person who is unable to share his feelings with his wife and unable to sustain relationships. He says that he feels like a failure and that there is something wrong with him and he wants to know what it is.

BACKGROUND

William Glasser developed Reality Therapy (RT) out of his dissatisfaction with traditional psychoanalytic theory. Glasser, a son of immigrant parents, was born in 1925 and grew up in Cleveland, Ohio, during the Depression years. He described himself as very shy as a young person, certain that he did not measure up to other people. A first-generation college student, Glasser obtained his bachelor's degree in engineering and worked for a year afterward as a chemical engineer (Wubbolding, 2000).

Realizing that he was unhappy in his job, Glasser wanted to go to medical school, but thought that his poor grades as an undergraduate would prevent his admission. Instead, Glasser obtained his master's degree in clinical psychology from Case Western Reserve University in 1948 and began work toward his doctorate. In the meantime, he was persuaded by one of his psychology professors to apply for medical school and was admitted as one of six or seven students who did not have the usual qualifications to be admitted to Case Western's program (Wubbolding, 2000). Glasser survived medical school and was board certified in psychiatry in 1961 (Howatt, 2001).

Howatt (2001) related an interesting story about the early origins of Glasser's conviction that people choose their behaviors. During his psychiatric residency at an inpatient veteran's unit, Glasser decided to conduct a quick study to determine if his ideas were on target. Knowing that the clients on the ward loved pinball, he moved all of the pinball games into one area and decreed that "no crazy behavior" was allowed in this area (Howatt, 2001, p. 8). Clients could hallucinate, yell at invisible people, or engage in other nutty behavior anywhere else, but if they did so in the game area, they would be asked to leave. What happened? Most of the clients were able to abide by the rule, suggesting that they chose to play games over acting crazy.

Also during his psychiatric residency, Glasser became a consultant to the Ventura School, a state institution for troubled girls. The best-selling book *Reality Therapy* (Glasser, 1965) is based on Glasser's experiences in this school. RT principles were the basis for the conduct of this school: punishment was eschewed, and relationships among the girls were nurtured (Glasser, 1965).

Glasser closed his practice in 1986 in favor of teaching and writing about RT. His best known book is probably *Reality Therapy* (1965). His most recent books are *Unhappy Teenagers: A Way for Parents and Teachers to Reach Them* (2002) and *Warning: Psychiatry Can Be Hazardous to Your Mental Health* (2003). The best description of the most recent version of Glasser's theory is found in *Counseling with Choice Theory: The New Reality Therapy* (Glasser, 2000a). You can read part of the first chapter in this book in Box 11.1.

Box 11.1

An Exercpt from Glasser's *Choice Theory*

Suppose you could ask all the people in the world who are not hungry, sick, or poor, people who seem to have a lot to live for, to give you an honest answer to the question, "How are you?" Millions would say, "I'm miserable." If asked why, almost all of them would blame someone else for their misery—lovers, wives, husbands, exes, children, parents, teachers, students, or people they work with. There is hardly a person alive who hasn't been heard saying, "You're driving me crazy. . . . That really upsets me. . . . Don't you have any consideration for how I feel? . . . You make me so mad, I can't see straight." It never crosses their minds that they are choosing the misery they are complaining about.

Choice theory explains that, for all practical purposes, we choose everything we do, including the misery we feel. Other people can neither make us miserable nor make us happy. All we can get from them or give to them is information. But by itself, information cannot make us do or feel anything. It goes into our brains, where we process it and then decide what to do. As I explain in great detail in this book, we choose all our actions and thoughts and, indirectly, almost all our feelings and much of our physiology. As bad as you may feel, much of what goes on in your body when you are in pain or sick is the indirect result of the actions and thoughts you choose or have chosen every day of your life.

I also show how and why we make these painful, even crazy, choices and how we can make better ones. Choice theory teaches that we are much more in control of our lives than we realize. Unfortunately, much of that control is not effective. For example, you choose to feel upset with your child, then you choose to yell and threaten, and things get worse, not better. Taking more effective control means making better choices as you relate to your children and everyone else. You can learn through choice theory how people actually function: how we combine what is written in our genes with what we learn as we live our lives.

The best way to learn choice theory is to focus on why we choose the common miseries that we believe just happen to us. When we are depressed, we believe that we have no control over our suffering, that we are victims of an imbalance in our neuro-chemistry and hence that we need brain drugs, such as Prozac, to get our chemistry back into balance. Little of this belief is true. We have a lot of control over our suffering. We are rarely the victims of what happened to us in the past, and, as will be explained in Chapter 4, our brain chemistry is normal for what we are choosing to do. Brain drugs may make us feel better, but they do not solve the problems that led us to choose to feel miserable.

The seeds of almost all our unhappiness are planted early in our lives when we begin to encounter people who have discovered not only what is right for them—but also, unfortunately, what is right for us. Armed with this discovery and following a destructive tradition that has dominated our thinking for thousands of years, these people feel obligated to try to force us to do what they know is right. Our choice of how we resist that force is, by far, the greatest source of human misery. Choice theory challenges this ancient I-know-what's-right-for-you tradition. This entire book is an attempt to answer the all-important question that almost all of us continually ask ourselves when we are unhappy: How can I figure out how to be free to live my life the way I want to live it and still get along well with the people I need?

From the perspective of forty years of psychiatric practice, it has become apparent to me that all unhappy people have the same problem: They are unable to get along well with the people they want to get along well with. I have had many counseling successes, but I keep hearing my mentor, Dr. G. L. Harrington, the most skillful psychiatrist I've ever known, saying, "If all the professionals in our field suddenly disappeared, the world would hardly note their absence." He was not disparaging what we do. He was saying that if the goal of psychiatrists is to reduce the misery rampant in the world and to help human beings get along with each other, their efforts have hardly scratched the surface.

To begin to approach that goal, we need a new psychology that can help us get closer to each other than most of us are able to do now. The psychology must be easy to understand, so it can be taught to anyone who wants to learn it. And it must be easy to use once we understand it. Our present psychology has failed. We do not know how to get along with each other any better than we ever have. Indeed, the psychology we have embraced tends to drive us apart. In the area of marriage alone, it is clear that the use of this traditional psychology has failed.

I call this universal psychology that destroys relationships because it destroys personal freedom external control psychology. The control can be as slight as a disapproving glance or as forceful as a threat to our lives. But whatever it is, it is an attempt to force us to do what we may not want to do. We end up believing that other people can actually make us feel the way we feel or do the things we do. This belief takes away the personal freedom we all need and want.

Excerpted from *Choice Theory: A New Psychology of Personal Freedom.* 1998. New York: Harper Collins. Reprinted with permission.

In 1967 Glasser established the Institute for Reality Therapy, known since 1996 as the William Glasser Institute. The institute can be found on the World Wide Web at www.wglasser.com. The title "Reality Therapy Certified" is earned by completing an intensive training program with the institute (Wubbolding, 2000). Currently, over 5,000 people hold this title worldwide. RT is internationally known and practiced, with RT counselors active in many countries around the world (e.g., Norway, Sweden, Australia, Hong Kong). The *International Journal of Reality Therapy* was initiated in 1981 and is still published.

Glasser is known for his public demonstrations of RT. He often does counseling sessions for professional audiences. Currently, Glasser still lectures, writes, and consults on RT. He is married to his second wife, Carleen, who is active in the RT community (his first wife, Naomi, died in 1992).

Glasser radically revised RT theory in 1996 to emphasize the importance of relationships. He also changed the name of the theory underlying RT from control theory to choice theory (Wubbolding, 2000). I will present the revised version of RT in this chapter.

BASIC PHILOSOPHY

RT theorists believe that the essential nature of humans is positive (Glasser & Wubbolding, 1995). They are careful to point out, however, that they are not naive in their approach;

although humans can be altruistic, forgiving, loving, and productive, they also "can be beguiled, bedeviled and bewildered. . . . Our actions can be hesitant, halting and horrifying to others. . . . We can be selfish, self-absorbed, self-indulgent and self-aggrandizing" (Wubbolding & Brickell, 1998, p. 48).

RT is a social constructivist theory. Glasser acknowledges the existence of a "real world" that is defined by consensual agreement. At the same time, he recognizes that total objectivity is a figment of our imaginations; it could only exist if we all had the same values or levels of need (Glasser, 1998).

RT theory places people firmly in the driver's seat—they choose their own behaviors. The belief that folks are helpless in the face of forces outside of them is an element of what Glasser calls external control theory (Wubbolding, 2007).

Recently, Glasser has challenged the traditional psychiatric community, criticizing the trend toward understanding mental illness within a biological model. "What alarms me the most is the present direction of psychiatry, *to replace psychology altogether with the pseudoscience of brain chemistry*" (Glasser, n.d., p. 2; italics in original). Counselors who take this view are oblivious to the idea that "they are staring at the brains of lonely people engaged in a wide variety of unsuccessful attempts to get connected to another human being" (Glasser, n.d., p. 2). Glasser (2003) criticizes the psychiatric community on the grounds that "there is no longer any concerted effort . . . to establish a doctor-patient relationship and counsel you about what's on your mind. You are told that the mental illness is caused by an imbalance in your brain chemistry that can only be corrected with drugs" (p. 2). Further, Glasser, maintains that prescribed psychotropic medications have the potential to be harmful and that the emphasis on biological causation of psychological distress creates the situation in which "*when you are diagnosed with a mental illness there is nothing you can do to help yourself*" (2003, p. 3; italics in original). Glasser (2004), who claims to have never prescribed a psychotropic drug, sees the solution to this dilemma is choice theory, which you will read about later.

Mei Ling is Donald's RT counselor. Her basic orientation toward Donald is that he is a person who has the potential to take charge of his life. Over their time together, Mei Ling is confident that she will see the goodness in Donald, as well as aspects of his behavior that may seem less desirable. However, Mei Ling realizes that the way Donald sees the world will be a major factor in how he behaves and that she needs to understand this in order to help him.

HUMAN MOTIVATION

The most obvious human motivation is to maximize pleasure and minimize pain (Glasser, 1998). The source of these feelings of pleasure or pain is the satisfaction (or nonsatisfaction) of basic needs. The basic needs are survival, love and belonging, power, freedom, and fun (Glasser, 2004). When we manage to get a need satisfied, we feel really good. When we experience a need that is unmet, we feel lousy. The gap between what we want and what we have is the most concrete motivator of our behavior (Wubbolding, et al., 2004).

Donald seems to be currently in pain, which suggests that he has not managed to satisfy some of his needs. Mei Ling knows that to help Donald, he must discover which of Donald's needs are unmet and help him to satisfy them.

CENTRAL CONSTRUCTS

Basic Needs

The five basic human needs—survival, love and belonging, power, freedom, and fun—are innate and universal (Glasser & Wubbolding, 1995). As a part of being human, we inherit the ability to remember the behaviors that made us feel good or bad (i.e., that satisfied or did not satisfy needs), and these memories guide our future choices of behavior (Glasser, 1998). It is interesting that Glasser (2004) sees only humans having the need for power; other mammals do not, in his view.

All of our behavior represents our best effort, at the time, to satisfy needs (Glasser, 1998). Individuals meet their needs in different ways, and the specific people or things that they identify as need-satisfying are sometimes called *wants* (Wubbolding, 2000). For example, I may have a need for power that is to some extent satisfied by the sense of accomplishment derived from writing this book and possibly helping people help others. Finishing the book becomes, for me, a want that helps to satisfy a need.

Love and belonging is the most important need. The need to give and receive love extends to family, friends, and intimate partners (Peterson, 2000). Glasser distinguishes among love, belonging, and friendship and cautions that sex, sometimes involved in love, is not synonymous with it (Glasser, 1998).

Most people have no difficulty fulfilling belonging needs through friendships; the process is fairly easy. Love is much more difficult to find, and Glasser maintains that this is because we tend to believe we "own" our lovers, and are therefore more likely to use external control psychology (discussed later) in these relationships (Glasser, 1998).

The need for fun is satisfied through play (Peterson, 2000), but it is also related to the capacity of humans to learn. Glasser (2002) wrote "having fun, which produces a very good feeling, is our genetic reward for learning" (p. 20). The need for fun is one of the most easily satisfied needs because it can be fulfilled in many ways (Glasser, 1998). Glasser observed that successful relationships satisfy the need for fun because they involve learning and laughter (which is one sign you are having fun).

Wanting power for the sake of power, rather than as a way to survive, is unique to humans, according to Glasser (2004). People inherently want to feel important and to have their importance recognized by others (Peterson, 2000). Power needs are also satisfied by getting our way, telling others what to do (and watching them do it), being right, getting more stuff, and punishing others when they are "wrong" (Glasser, 1998). This controlling aspect of our power need often leads us to try to coerce others.

Other ways of satisfying power needs are less malevolent, such as doing things for the good of others. The good feelings we get from a job well done result from the satisfaction of power needs. We will work hard for the recognition that satisfies our power needs (Glasser, 2002). Power needs also lead us to want others to listen to us; if we are ignored by important others, we feel powerless, and that is painful.

The need for freedom is satisfied when we believe that we have control of our lives (Peterson, 2000). We are most concerned with freedom needs when they are threatened (Glasser, 1998). Freedom to make choices is an important aspect of this need, although we sometimes forget we have this power.

The relationships among the needs are complex. Sometimes several needs can be satisfied simultaneously, as when relationships satisfy needs for love and fun. On the other hand, fulfilling our need for love and belonging is often complicated by our need for power (Glasser, 2002). "Power destroys love," wrote Glasser, (1998, p. 42) because nobody likes to be bossed around. In Box 11.2, I summarize Glasser's ideas about two types of personalities that are troublesome in relationships.

Our basic survival need for sex may lead us to unloving sex, which deprives us of satisfaction of love and belonging needs. Freedom and belonging needs can conflict in relationships in which partners have different levels of these needs yet seek to satisfy both simultaneously. Successful relationships are those in which partners negotiate so that needs are satisfied by both partners.

Donald's presenting problems suggest to Mei Ling that Donald is failing to satisfy a number of his needs. Love and belonging needs seem to be central in that he wants to reconnect with Tammy. Power needs also seem to be important; for example, Donald says that his job loss is upsetting. Impulsive spending, Mei Ling knows, can also be a way to satisfy power, fun, and

---

Box 11.2

The Two Personalities Unsuitable for Long-Term Significant Relationships: The Sociopath and the Workless

Glasser (1998) maintains that most individuals have significant needs for love, loving sex, and belonging. However, he does recognize that two kinds of individuals are not very successful in committed, long-term relationships: sociopaths and the workless.

Sociopaths seem to care only about power and freedom. Glasser maintains that they are likely to be male because he thinks males genetically have lower needs for love and belonging and higher needs for power than females. According to Glasser, the sociopath will tell a woman that "he's been looking all his life for a woman like you, and that's true. But you have not been looking for a man like him" (1998, p. 107). He is out to get what he can and does not care about his victim, exiting as soon as she expresses any belonging needs. A sure sign of a sociopath is that he has no friends.

The *workless* individual is more puzzling on first glance. Male workless types seem more prevalent in our society, but this may be because it is still more acceptable for a woman to be unemployed than it is for a man. Workless people seem to have low needs for survival and high needs for power. They have some belonging needs (compatible with their power needs), which lead them to want to talk about themselves and how wonderful they are. The prominent dynamic is the mismatch between their strong needs for power and the lack of energy to institute the power strivings that is the result of the low survival need.

Adapted from *Choice Theory: A New Psychology of Personal Freedom*, in 1st ed by W. Glasser, 1998. New York: HarperCollins.

freedom needs. In the context of his relationship with Tammy, this spending is probably an attempt to satisfy freedom needs. Donald's tendency to move from job to job may also be related to his need for freedom. Mei Ling also suspects that Donald's power needs have been tempting him to try to control Tammy's behavior and therefore play a part in the troubled relationship.

QUALITY WORLD

The quality world refers to a place in our brain where we store images of need-fulfilling things or people (Glasser & Wubbolding, 1995). Because they satisfy needs, these people or objects make us feel good. The construction of the quality world begins shortly after we are born, and it is revised continuously over our lifetimes. Images that we maintain in our quality worlds are those of individuals we want to be with, things that we want to possess, experiences we desire, and beliefs or ideas that guide our lives (Glasser, 1998, p. 45).

For the most part, we consciously choose to put these people or objects in our quality worlds, with the exception of our parents or other primary caretakers, who are there by the time we are aware of them (Glasser, 1998). Glasser (2002) goes so far to say that your mother is the first person that you put in your quality world because she is the source of food and love. Parents also put their children in their quality worlds almost automatically, and Glasser maintained that "parents and children are stuck in each other's quality worlds forever" (1998, p. 195). Sometimes we put unrealistic pictures in our quality worlds, such as a young man carrying an image of himself as a professional football player when he is a benchwarmer on his high school team.

We can remove images from our quality world, but doing so can be a painful process. The kid who desperately wants to be a pro football player will have difficulty coming to terms with the loss of that image of himself. Removing people from our quality worlds is particularly difficult, such as when a significant intimate relationship ends. However, when a person or object is repeatedly experienced as contrary to our needs, he, she, or it is banished (Glasser, 1998).

Donald's quality world probably includes his father, Tammy, spending money, and the objects obtained by spending. Mystery and science fiction magazines and movies are there as well because they satisfy his fun need. These people, things, and behaviors contribute to the satisfaction of Donald's needs, making him feel good. Mei Ling is not sure whether Donald's mother is in his quality world. The hostility he expresses about her suggests that she may have repeatedly denied his needs for love and belonging as a child. As a result, Donald may have engaged in the painful process of removing a parent from his quality world.

TOTAL BEHAVIOR

The term *total behavior* is used to accentuate the multidimensional nature of human behavior. All behavior is composed of four components: acting, thinking, feeling, and physiology (Glasser, 2000b, p. 3). Glasser used the image of a front-wheel-drive car to explain the relationships among these components. The front two wheels are thinking and acting, and the rear wheels are feeling and physiology. Steering the car is accomplished through changing the direction of the front wheels, and the rear wheels generally follow. This image makes two points: (a) acting and thinking are more under our control than feeling and physiology and (b) feelings and physiology can be influenced by acting and thinking (Glasser, 2002).

Mei Ling knows that Donald's total behavior is composed of his actions, thoughts, feelings, and physical sensations or state. The way he thinks about his situation has great influence on how he feels, as does his behavior. He may be thinking that Tammy should obey his wishes and come back to their marriage. Thinking this way connects to anger and then depression and loneliness. He behaves in a depressed way, gets fired from work, and feels even more depressed. So Donald's actions are sitting at home, his thinking is that he is worthless, his feeling is depression or anger, and his physiology is that his neck and head ache.

CHOICE THEORY

Choice theory is the ideological basis for RT. The 10 axioms of choice theory are listed in Box 11.3. The most important tenet of choice theory is that "we choose *everything* we do, including the misery we feel" (Glasser, 1998, p. 3; italics in original). We therefore have control over our own behavior, but *we cannot control the behavior of others*. We can only give others information.

Choice theory is contrasted with external control psychology, which rests on the premise that human existence is controlled by the environment (including other people;

Box 11.3

The Ten Axioms of Choice Theory

1. The only person whose behavior we can control is our own.
2. All we can give or get from other people is information.
3. All long-lasting psychological problems are relationship problems.
4. The problem relationship is always part of our present lives.
5. What happened in the past that was painful has a great deal to do with what we are today, but revisiting this painful past can contribute little or nothing to what we need to do now—improve an important, present relationship.
6. We are driven by five genetic needs: survival, love and belonging, power, freedom, and fun.
7. We can satisfy these needs only by satisfying a picture or pictures in our quality worlds.
8. All we can do from birth to death is behave. All behavior is total behavior and is made up of four inseparable components: acting, thinking, feeling, and physiology.
9. All total behavior is designated by verbs . . . and named by the component that is most recognizable.
10. All total behavior is chosen, but we have direct control over only the acting and thinking components. We can, however, control our feelings and physiology indirectly through how we choose to act and think.

Wubbolding, 2007). "The simple operational premise of the external control psychology the world uses is: Punish the people who are doing wrong, so they will do what we say is right; then reward them, so they keep doing what we want them to do" (Glasser, 1998, p. 5).

External control psychology persists because it is sometimes effective—those who have the power to control others sometimes get what they seek. Those who are powerless are aware that external control sometimes does work, and they hope to one day employ it. Also, those who are controlled (a) believe that they have no choice other than to submit (wrong) and (b) are aware that fighting would likely make the situation worse (often right; Glasser, 1998).

Three basic beliefs underlie external control psychology: (a) my behavior is controlled by external factors; (b) I can make other people do what I want them to do and they can do the same to me; and (c) it is my obligation to punish and reward others depending on whether they meet my standards for behavior (Glasser, 1998, p. 16). The *seven deadly habits* of external control psychology are criticizing, blaming, complaining, nagging, threatening, and punishing or rewarding to control (Glasser, 2000b, p. 6). Contrast these to the "seven connecting habits: caring, trusting listening, supporting, negotiating, befriending, and encouraging" (Glasser, 2002, p. 14).

Glasser is adamant in his assertion that living by the principles of external control psychology is a major mistake. He warns:

> This psychology is a terrible plague that invades every part of our lives. It destroys our happiness, our health, our marriages, our families, our ability to get an education, and our willingness to do high-quality work. It is the cause of most of the violence, crime, drug abuse, and unloving sex that are pervasive in our society. (1998, p. 7)

Donald, who is having trouble with a significant relationship, has likely fallen into believing external control psychology. It is possible that others have used external control psychology to try to influence his behavior as well. He blames others for his situation and feelings rather than realizing that he has choices. He feels bad because Tammy left. However, he resents that she tried to make him spend less money when they were together. They probably used the seven deadly habits on each other. Donald is feeling inadequate because those *&%$# at work fired him for no reason. He is sitting around because he is depressed and deserves better than just any old job. Donald sees himself as a superficial person who is "unable" to relate to others and believes that something is definitely wrong with him.

Mei Ling believes that if Donald would adopt choice theory, he would realize that all of his behavior is chosen, and he can make better choices. No magical entity can make him depressed, addicted to excitement, or in general a faulty human being. Further, he can't control others' behaviors, and trying to do so is simply frustrating and drives them away. When others try to control his behavior, he gets mad and uncooperative, such as at work.

THEORY OF THE PERSON AND DEVELOPMENT OF THE INDIVIDUAL

According to RT, "personality" is based on the relative strengths of a person's basic needs (Glasser, 1998). Glasser maintained that the relative strength of the needs is fixed at birth; thus, personality does not change. For example, Irene's strong need for freedom makes her seem like a very different person from Casey, who is much less interested in freedom and more interested in love and belonging. These two individuals may have difficulty negotiating a relationship because of the differences in their needs. They might be able work out some compromises. However, when two people in a relationship have high needs for power, negotiation is more difficult because negotiation implies that one person has to give in.

RT does not have a formal theory of personality development. However, Glasser admitted that the "seeds of almost all our unhappiness are planted early in our lives when we begin to encounter people who have discovered not only what is right for them—but also, unfortunately, what is right for us" (Glasser, 1998, p. 4). This kind of behavior on the part of parents or other powerful people (the use of external control theory) leads to poor relationships characterized by mistrust of the child on the part of the parents. This mistrust will affect future relationships (Glasser 1998). An extreme example of this process is seen with abused children. If you can't be safe with your parents, how can you be safe with others? Children who are abused never learn to trust their parents, and as a result, have great difficulties establishing relationships in general (Glasser, 1998). Using external control theory with children also prevents them from learning to be responsible for their own choices.

Emphasizing the need to use choice theory rather than external control theory with kids, Glasser had a great deal to say about parenting as well as our current educational practices (Glasser, 1968, 1990, 1998, 2002). He maintained that the early experience of trust is critical in healthy development because "learning to trust is crucial to learning how to satisfy our needs" (1998, p. 219). Choice theory parents reject the use of punishment and instead give their kids massive amounts of love, which is not conditional on behavior. Parents should evaluate their own behaviors based on whether they bring more closeness with their children, not on their need to be "right," which is an expression of power needs and an endorsement of external control theory. According to Glasser, this criterion ("will this choice bring me closer to this important other?") is helpful in any relationship.

However, Glasser does concede that the parent must at times hold her ground because a child is not ready to handle making a choice. For example, the decision about going to school is not negotiable for an 8-year-old. On the other hand, as soon as you determine that it is safe to allow the child to be around the home without direct supervision (but with parents or other responsible adults present), you can allow him to choose his bedtime. The child will learn responsibility through experiencing the consequences of his choice about how much sleep he needs. Of course, waking-up time is not negotiable because he must attend school.

Donald seems to be relatively high in his needs for power and freedom. His movement from job to job and compulsive spending are probably choices meant to meet these needs. He also shows interest in relationships, suggesting relatively high belonging needs. Donald's survival and fun needs seem weaker. Mei Ling wonders whether Donald's characterization of himself as being addicted to excitement is related to his need for fun or power.

Donald clearly carries with him some issues around trust that stem from his relationships with his parents. Although his father appears to be in Donald's quality world, the violence Donald reported (and may have experienced) could have influenced his views of relationships and his level of trust in others. Clearly, he has great difficulties relating to his mother, and Mei Ling is uncertain about whether Donald's mother is in his quality world. Because Donald's parents divorced, Mei Ling guesses that they both probably endorsed external control theory because this kind of separation suggests an escalation of freedom needs that may have occurred in response to the attempt by the parties to control each other.

Donald's history of relationships is probably related to how he behaves in his current relationships. He demonstrates a need for love and belonging but may be trying to force Tammy into his version of their relationship in an attempt to satisfy his freedom and power needs. Also, Mei Ling suspects that Tammy has tried to use external control theory on Donald and force him to change his behaviors through punishment (yelling, criticizing, leaving) and reward.

HEALTH AND DYSFUNCTION

Healthy people, from the RT perspective, are advocates of choice theory. They are happy because they have found ways to satisfy their needs without violating the rights of others (Glasser, 2000b); most important, they have satisfying personal relationships.

Originally, the source of dysfunction in RT theory was seen as the failure to satisfy one's needs. Glasser contended that "when we are unable to figure out how to satisfy one or more of the five basic needs built into our genetic structure that are the source of all human motivation, we sometime choose to behave in ways that are currently labeled mental illness" (2000b, p. 1).

Glasser's revision of RT theory makes the matter simpler: dysfunction happens when an individual feels disconnnected from others and, as a result, chooses painful and destructive behavior (2000b, p. 4). As Glasser put it, "I believe that *there is only one basic psychological problem. Either a person suffers from a present unsatisfying relationship or he or she has no satisfying relationships at all*" (Glasser, n.d., p. 1; italics in original).

We are always in the business of choosing behavior aimed at satisfying our needs. To more clearly emphasize the power of humans to choose their psychological dysfunctions, the suffix *ing* is added to traditional behavioral labels. Depression, for example, becomes *depressing* (Glasser, 1998). You don't have a headache, you are *headaching*. These choices are simply the *best alternatives we perceive at a given time;* clients are not to be criticized for their choices.

We make bad choices for three reasons:

1. When we get lonely because we don't have the relationships we need, our first response is to get angry. Choosing funky behavior like depression restrains the anger, which is important because we realize that expressing it might further damage what relationships we do have.
2. People learn that choosing such behavior, particularly depression, is an effective way to get help. Also, depressing (or other maladaptive behavior) is much more functional than angering—civilization would not have survived if we all acted on our initial anger.
3. Choosing to depress avoids tougher alternatives—like facing problems and risking rejection (Glasser, 2000b, p. 5).

The typical RT diagnosis is *unhappy person.* "All unhappy people have the same problem: They are unable to get along well with the people they want to get along well with" (Glasser, 1998, p. 5). Further, "barring grinding poverty, incurable illness, or living under tyranny, unhappiness is the only human problem" (Glasser, 2002, p. 2). This kind of unhappiness can lead people down two distinct roads (Glasser, 1998). The first road is the obvious one—an unhappy person tries to find relationships that are satisfying so that he can be happy again. The second option is seen when the unhappy person decides to give up on relationships altogether. He tries to find happiness or pleasure without relationships, which, according to

Glasser, is impossible. These individuals often replace pictures of people in their quality worlds with other sources of pleasure such as drugs, unloving sex, and violence.

Even psychotic behavior is seen as our bad choices in attempting to meet needs. Glasser wrote,

> But when we are unhappy we are capable of bizarre and unrealistic creativity as commonly seen and labeled schizophrenia, bipolar disorder, obsessive compulsive disorder, relentless phobia, disabling panic attacks or clinical depression. But as much as these creative symptoms, which include hallucinations, delusions, obsessions, compulsions, disabling fear and severe depression, appear to be beyond the client's control—they seem to materialize as if they are happening to him or her—they are not. (Glasser, 2000b, p. 4)

Donald is clearly displaying unhappiness that stems from an unsatisfactory relationship with his wife, Tammy. He is lonely because he fails to connect in other life relationships— for instance, he has no close friends. Mei Ling knows that he is in pain because his love and belonging needs are going unmet. He has chosen to depress about this situation, and also appears to be headaching as well. Donald's depressing behavior is probably also a bid to establish a relationship with others or to get Tammy to continue to attend to him. Underneath the depression is the angering resulting from the dissatisfaction he experiences.

Mei Ling guesses that Donald's job loss resulted from his depressing behavior. He was ineffective on his job and listless with his clients, and missed a lot of days at work. These behaviors compromised Donald's ability to satisfy his power needs through work accomplishments. His freedom needs are unmet because he can't spend money because he doesn't have any.

NATURE OF THERAPY

ASSESSMENT

No assessment is used in RT counseling, other than figuring out what relationship(s) is (are) problematic. Given his views on traditional psychiatric approaches, it is probably no surprise that Glasser does not advocate the use of formal diagnosis except for insurance purposes (Corey, 2001). "I strongly believe that all psychiatric diagnoses—usually thought of as mental illnesses—are not only wrong, they are harmful to the people so labeled" (Glasser, n.d., p. 1).

Mei Ling would not use any formal assessment with Donald. She would simply try to understand what relationship or lack thereof was related to his troubles (i.e., his loss of the relationship with Tammy). Mei Ling diagnoses Donald as an unhappy person.

OVERVIEW OF THE THERAPEUTIC ATMOSPHERE

The client–therapist relationship is very important in RT. Ultimately, the RT counselor wants to become a picture in the client's quality world (Wubbolding, 2000). The counseling relationship can also be seen as a way of meeting the client's love and belonging needs. Further, the therapist approaches the client with the confidence that he can learn to better satisfy his needs, and this confidence becomes part of the client's view of himself (Wubbolding et al., 2004).

To achieve the quality relationship needed in RT, the counselor displays empathy, genuineness, and positive regard (Wubbolding & Brickell, 1998). The RT counselor is straightforward and, as a way of being genuine, has the option of self-disclosing to the client (Wubbolding, 2000). Although some might call the RT counselor confrontational, Glasser said that "reality therapists are among the least pushy of all people" (1992b, p. 282). He meant that RT counselors, while directly addressing the client's current choices, take great care to avoid using external control theory with their clients, encouraging them instead to make their own choices.

RT is very active, focused on behavior and thinking. It is firmly centered in the present (Wubbolding, 2007). Wubbolding (2000) devised the acronym ABCDE to describe the RT relationship, which stands for "Always Be Courteous, Determined, and Enthusiastic" (p. 93).

Glasser sees RT as short term in nature; most clients need 10 sessions or so (Glasser, n.d.). However, Glasser cautioned that the length of counseling is ultimately determined by how quickly the therapist can establish a good relationship with the client (Glasser, 2000a).

Mei Ling will work hard to enter Donald's world and to genuinely relate to him. She will appreciate him as a human being, working hard to convey this positive regard in an unconditional way. Her enthusiasm and determination will give Donald hope that he can change his life. Mei Ling will be honest and direct in asking Donald about his current situation.

Roles of Client and Counselor

RT counselors ask lots of questions and challenge the client to evaluate his behavior (Wubbolding, 2000). Because the counselor is directive, the relationship can resemble one of doctor–patient. The counselor is an expert on choice theory and human behavior, and the client is there to receive this knowledge. Clients in RT are often taught the principles of choice theory, necessitating the use of the teacher–student role. However, the RT counselor's rejection of external control theory makes the client the expert in the sense that he is the only one who can determine what is right for him. The client must accept responsibility in the counseling sessions, because he must evaluate his current situation and decide if and how he will institute change.

Wubbolding and Brickell (1998) suggested that the effective RT counselor needs to have a positive view of human nature, energy, and the ability to see the bright side of situations. They also added that the RT counselor must have "some degree of mental health" (p. 47).

Mei Ling is energetic and active in her sessions with Donald. She teaches him about choice theory and points out the ways external control theory can be detrimental to human relationships. Mei Ling expects Donald to listen to her ideas, but accepts that he may disagree or decide not to put them into action. She appreciates his ability to evaluate and choose for himself and does not pressure him to do things her way. At the same time, Mei Ling expects that Donald will take some responsibility for what happens in counseling sessions.

Goals

RT counselors are interested in helping their clients make better choices that are helpful to them and don't interfere or hurt others (Glasser, 2000a). Ultimately, the reality therapist teaches the client to reconnect in the critical relationship(s) that is central to the client's discomfort or establish new, more satisfying relationships (Glasser, 2000b). As a part of counseling, the client learns about bad choices, and in the ideal RT, he learns choice theory so that he can use it in future situations (Glasser, 1998). Thus, the client learns to take responsibility for his choices and make more effective choices that will reestablish effective, satisfying relationships. Wubbolding (2007) further clarifies that the RT counselor can help the client determine specific wants related to the basic needs.

Changing feelings is a goal of interest to most clients. RT counselors believe that feelings can be changed only by making more effective acting and thinking choices (Glasser, 2000b). According to Glasser, "when we want to stop choosing a painful behavior like depressing [we must] (1) change what we want, (2) change what we are doing, or (3) change both" (1998, p. 71).

Mei Ling will help Donald evaluate his current situation and decide if he would like to invest in his relationship with Tammy by changing his way of relating to her. If he decides to attempt to regain his relationship with Tammy, Donald needs to choose behavior other than depressing. He should use the criterion of closeness to choose his new behaviors—that is, he should always ask himself, "Will this behavior bring me closer to Tammy or not?" Mei Ling reminds Donald that despite his new choices, Tammy might still choose to end their relationship. Donald needs to begin thinking in terms of how he could change his thoughts and actions, not in terms of how Tammy should be, act, think, or feel differently. It is possible that if Donald chooses behaviors based on choice theory, Tammy would feel less coerced and more loved and be more able to relate to Donald.

PROCESS OF THERAPY

RT is present oriented, and RT counselors see dwelling on the past as a bad thing. Glasser rejects "the idea that people can only be helped by endless visiting and revisiting past misery" (Glasser, n.d., p. 1). RT counselors engage in no faultfinding or blaming. The emphasis is on what to do now and how the client can make new choices (Wubbolding, 2000).

Good reality therapists should let go of the past and help the client get to work on the present interpersonal relationship problem (Glasser, n.d.). Bad therapists view clients as helpless in the face of their circumstances, and are therefore unlikely to help them.

The RT counselor doesn't like to spend a lot of time talking about symptoms the client is choosing because doing so allows the client to avoid the real problem, the major unsatisfying relationship (Glasser, 2000b, p. 9). There is no sense in devoting a lot of time to stuff the client can't control (the behavior of others, or the past). If the client protests that these externals are important, the therapist is likely to tell the client that there is no guarantee that life is fair; the only sure thing is that you are the only person you can change.

Wubbolding (2000, 2007) presents the acronym WDEP to describe the counseling process. The RT counselor helps clients explore *wants*, describe the *direction* of their lives and what they are currently *doing*. Most important, the therapist helps the client self-*evaluate* by asking if his current actions are effective. Clients are then helped to make simple and attainable action *plans*. Once the plan is made, the RT counselor accepts no excuses for not following through on the plan. If one plan doesn't work, another is tried—there is no perfect plan (Glasser, 1992a).

RT counselors do not relate to psychoanalytically based constructs such as transference and countertransference. The reality therapist should just be herself. Any talk about transference is simply the client and counselor avoiding responsibility for the current relationship. According to Corey (2001), Glasser says that Freud created transference to avoid getting personally involved with his clients.

Fuller and Fuller (1999, pp. 309–317) presented an eight-step approach to RT. Not all of these steps are truly stages; instead, some are cautions or admonitions to the counselor.

Step 1: Involvement. The counselor makes friends with the lonely client.

Step 2: Focus on Present Behavior. Counselor and client describe what the client is doing now.

Step 3: Value Judgment. Client and counselor work to evaluate the client's current choices.

Step 4: Planning Responsible Behavior. Plans should be reasonable, specific, and positive.

Step 5: Commitment to the Plan. The counselor asks the client, "Will you do it or do you want to make another plan?"

Step 6: Accept No Excuses. The client is not punished if he does not follow the plan, but the counselor doesn't listen to why either. The counselor asks, "When will you do it?"

Step 7: Do Not Punish. RT counselors believe in allowing the consequences of the client's behavior to happen rather than imposing negative outcomes, or punishment. In fact, all of the seven deadly habits of external control theory are forbidden.

Step 8: Never Give Up. RT counselors always endeavor to send the message that the problem can be solved, even if it takes many tries.

Adapted from "Reality Therapy Approaches" by G. B. Fuller and D. L. Fuller. In H. T. Prout & D. T. Brown (Eds.), *Counseling and Psychotherapy with Children and Adolescents.* Copyright © 1999 John Wiley & Sons, Inc. This material is used by permission of John Wiley & Sons, Inc.

After she is sure that she has established a good relationship with Donald, Mei Ling focuses on the current situation and asks him to describe what he is currently doing. She asks him if his current behavior is getting him what he wants. Donald, with a little squirming and discomfort, acknowledges that his current situation is not the best, and that he'd like things to be different. Mei Ling teaches Donald that the only thing he can change is his own behavior and proceeds to help Donald look at new choices and develop a plan to better meet his needs. If he decides to pursue his relationship with Tammy, Mei Ling helps him develop a plan to choose different behaviors in relating to her. Alternatively, Donald may decide that trying to recapture the relationship is futile, and Mei Ling will then help him plan to go through the painful process of removing Tammy from his quality world and, eventually, establish new relationships.

No matter what Donald does, Mei Ling will not give up on him. If he tries to talk to Tammy and blows up, Mei Ling will not criticize this behavior. She will only ask how Donald wishes to be the next time he talks to Tammy.

THERAPEUTIC TECHNIQUES

Unlike some other approaches, RT does not identify a host of techniques available to the counselor. The practice of RT is more aptly described as a process of discussion leading to the identification of (a) the client's current need-related behavior that is problematic and (b) ways in which more functional behavior can be chosen that still meets the client's needs. With that said, I will present several interventions that have been discussed by reality therapists.

QUESTIONING

RT counselors are quite likely to ask the client a lot of questions. Howatt (2001, p. 9) identified four that are commonly used: (a) What do you want or what do you really want? (b) What are you doing? (c) What is your plan? and (d) What will happen if you continue to do what you are doing? Another key question is, "Is what you are now choosing to do (your actions and thoughts) getting you what you want?" (Glasser, 1992a, p. 277). The reality therapist is very interested in being specific rather than general (Glasser, 1992a). Choices made need to be described in detail so that the client can evaluate them.

Questions are aimed at identifying needs and current behavior, and they serve to reinforce the client's choice in maintaining it. The last two questions are intended to help clients self-evaluate. The general motive of the therapist is to help the client develop a simple plan to take charge of his life.

One further question is of great importance to RT counselors. The RT counselor almost always asks the client what is going right in his life (Wubbolding, 2000). This question builds hope and identifies client strengths that might be used to make new choices.

Mei Ling asks Donald if his current behavior is getting him what he wants. Donald acknowledges that he is unhappy and that he wants a new job and to fix his relationship with Tammy. In response to Mei Ling's question, he reports that he is not doing much of anything and that if he continues, he'll go to the poorhouse and never get Tammy back.

Mei Ling guides Donald through a specific, detailed description of his current functioning. She asks what his plans are to be different. Donald says that he will do two things over the next week: call Tammy and ask her out for a date, and start to explore job options. Mei Ling insists that Donald create a more specific plan to look at job opportunities.

BIBLIOTHERAPY

Clients in RT are often encouraged to read books, particularly Glasser's books. *Choice Theory* (Glasser, 1998) is the most general of these. Glasser has written other books directed toward understanding relationships and working with kids (Glasser, 2002; Glasser & Glasser, 2000).

Mei Ling gives Donald the books Choice Theory *and* Getting Together and Staying Together. *Donald jokes that he likes science fiction better, but he agrees to read one of them prior to the next counseling session.*

DOING THE UNEXPECTED

Rather than a specific technique, doing the unexpected is an admonition to be creative in helping clients assume responsibility for their lives. Under this heading, a reality therapist would consider using paradoxical techniques that require the client to perform the symptom. If the client can perform the symptom, he acknowledges his choice and control. If he doesn't perform the symptom, the problem is solved. For example, a child could be given the choice to cry now or wait until later (Glasser, 1998).

REFRAMING

Reframing is a paradoxical approach that involves helping the client find a different perspective on his situation. For instance, compulsive client behavior could be reframed as "careful and deliberate."

Mei Ling reframes Donald's "addiction to excitement" as energy that he could use in his work. She could prescribe this behavior by having him visit 15 potential places of employment in one day.

HUMOR

RT counselors are likely to poke fun at themselves and, carefully, at the client's problem. For example, in Glasser's (2000a) fantasy RT with Jerry, the Melvin Udall client, the client's girlfriend spontaneously adapts the tune "Ring around the Mulberry Bush" to describe Jerry's compulsive behaviors: "This is the way he locks the door, locks the door, locks the door" (p. 96). Jerry's problem becomes funny while at the same time his control of the behavior is emphasized.

Mei Ling gently teases Donald about his shopping "addiction." Referring to his "black belt in shopping," she suggests that the perfect job for Donald would be as a buyer for a department store, or better yet, as a personal shopper for a very rich person.

SELF-DISCLOSURE

RT counselors are encouraged to be warm and human, and one way to do that is to disclose to the client. Wubbolding (2000) maintained that disclosing some relevant information about yourself is a great path to a closer relationship with your client. I would add that self-disclosure needs to be used carefully to ensure that the relationship stays focused on the client, rather than on the therapist.

Mei Ling considers how to use self-disclosure with Donald. She is very careful in her approach and decides simply to tell him that she thinks that relationships are one of the best and worst things we have to experience in life. She does not reveal her own struggles specifically. She could self-disclose more specifically about her attempts to set up an exercise program, particularly about the things that helped her.

METAPHORS

Adopting and using the client's own metaphors can be very helpful in conveying understanding of the client's perceptions of his world. For example, a client may say that she feels like the lamb being taken to the lions when she goes to work. The RT counselor might then ask what the lamb could do to seem less tasty to the lions, or better, what the lamb could do to befriend the lions.

Donald uses the image of a slug in describing himself. He is lethargic and slow moving, has little motivation, and very rarely has fun (he maintains that slugs have no fun in life). Mei

Ling thinks about this image briefly and then decides that Donald is close, but not quite, because he is really a caterpillar that is going to turn into a butterfly (and butterflies do indeed have fun). He is simply going into his cocoon right now. Mei Ling begins to ask Donald what he can do to (a) make the best cocoon and (b) become the best butterfly.

PHYSICAL ACTIVITY AND MEDITATION

Glasser and reality therapists have long endorsed the benefits of physical activity. In his book *Positive Addiction* (1976), Glasser identified running as a very common form of positive addiction, but other activities can induce this state, too. The key component of positively addicting activities is the mental one; these activities induce an extremely pleasurable trancelike state. Glasser believes that this mental state allows the mind to "spin free," and the result is a joining of mind and body that leads to unusual levels of performance and creativity (Glasser, 1976). It is not easy to get to the level of positive addiction; it takes at least 6 months of daily running, for instance.

Glasser maintained that meditation is the second most common way of achieving positive addiction (Glasser, 1976). As is the case with exercise, not all meditators achieve the truly addicting mental state.

Donald does not think he can focus long enough to meditate, so Mei Ling encourages Donald to think of some form of physical activity that he could tolerate. Donald says that he used to like boxing. Mei Ling asks Donald if he could find a way to do some boxing, and he agrees that he could start by visiting some gyms over the next week.

ALLOWING OR IMPOSING CONSEQUENCES

The typical consequence of problem behavior is the temporary loss of freedom or a privilege (Fuller & Fuller, 1999). The distinction between consequences and punishment may seem fuzzy at times (Wubbolding, 2000) so this approach must be used carefully. Advocates of RT say that the attitude of the one who allows consequences is critical. Mistakes should be seen as chances to learn; the individual has been told about the rules and what happens when they are broken (Fuller & Fuller, 1999). Punishment embodies the opposites of those characteristics and is often delivered in an angry way, whereas consequences are imparted in a friendly manner, according to Fuller and Fuller (1999). The most effective consequences are probably those that happen naturally, such as being too sleepy because you stayed up too late the night before. Second best are consequences based on social rules. An example of the latter would be when a disruptive child is removed from the classroom to a special room and is helped to evaluate her behavior.

Donald has already experienced the consequences of his depressing in that he lost his job. He can also see that his spending behavior has some undesirable consequences (having no money, hurting his relationship with Tammy).

EVALUATION OF THE THEORY

RT has the great strength of being relatively simple and easy to understand. Glasser, particularly, writes in a friendly, commonsense manner that can be quite entertaining to read.

He also devotes a great deal of attention to illustrating his ideas using client case studies or applying his ideas to characters in popular movies and books.

Critics have charged that RT is too simple, or simplistic. Although commonly used language was deliberately chosen to make RT easy to understand, its advocates warn that this simplicity is deceptive when it comes to putting the theory into action (Glasser & Wubbolding, 1995; Wubbolding & Brickell, 2000). Glasser argued that "the fact that what we do is relatively clear-cut and understandable does not make it easy. It takes a skilled counselor to persuade clients that they are choosing what they are complaining about or doing and further, to persuade them that it is to their benefit to choose a more effective total behavior" (Glasser, 1992a. Copyright 1992 by J. K. Zeig. (Ed.), *The Evolution of Psychotherapy: The Second Conference* [pp. 270–278]. Reproduced by permission of Routledge/Taylor & Francis Books, Inc.).

RT is often faulted for ignoring social influences on behavior (Zeig, 1992). RT does not seem to take these phenomena into account. Glasser would probably say that going along with the crowd is more a result of a failure to wake up and make choices than to any magical power of social forces.

Qualities of the Theory

Precision and Testability. Operationalizing some RT constructs—the quality world, for instance—would seem quite difficult. This set of photos could never be observed directly, and it would seem difficult to devise a way to clearly observe its effects on behavior. Other aspects of RT seem to be general assumptions that are not amenable to empirical tests, such as the idea that we choose our behavior.

Empirical Validity. Research has not been the strong point of reality therapy. The propositions of the theory are not often directly tested, and outcome research is sketchy at best. Sansone (1998) reported that only 9% of the articles in the *International Journal of Reality Therapy* were research related.

Research Support

Outcome Research. Outcome studies of RT counseling exist and are supportive of the theory's effectiveness. Radtke, Sapp, and Farrell (1997) conducted a meta-analysis of 21 RT studies and found a medium effect size. The studies included in the analysis varied widely in methodological sophistication, sample sizes, treatment characteristics, and presenting concerns of participants. Many are school based, suggesting that there is some evidence for the effectiveness of RT in these settings, but far fewer studies support the utility of RT as an approach to counseling more generally.

Wubbolding (2000) presented a traditional review (that is, not meta-analytic), a long list of outcome studies, which varied considerably in quality. Many were case studies, either of individuals or of schools implementing RT principles. Generally, the results were favorable to RT. However, few if any of these studies approached the highest standards of methodology generally accepted in the study of therapy outcome (random assignment to more than one condition, treatment vs. control group comparisons, checks on therapist adherence, etc.).

Many studies attempt to assess the effect of RT on self-concept. For example, Peterson, Chang, and Collins (1998) tested the efficacy of RT among Taiwanese university students. They randomly assigned students to instruction about choice theory, group RT therapy, or a no-treatment control group. Using self-concept as the outcome measure, Peterson and colleagues found that the RT groups did not differ, but were better off than the no-treatment group. Fuller and Fuller (1999) reviewed a number of other studies that implemented some kind of RT treatment (and these varied greatly) and found inconsistent results in affecting self-concept. Overall, Fuller and Fuller concluded that the results of research on RT were mixed. This conclusion is not surprising given the typical lengths of the interventions studied (8 weeks of group RT, for example). Such brief interventions are not likely to have a serious impact on such a global, psychologically powerful construct as self-concept.

Other studies have looked at the effects of RT interventions on a variety of outcome variables. These studies also varied in methodological sophistication. Loyd (2005) looked at the effects of giving high school students five sessions of teaching about RT. In this quasi-experimental study done in the school, students who learned about RT reported higher levels of satisfaction of power, freedom, and fun needs after treatment (in comparison to a control group who did not receive the intervention), but not in belonging needs. However, the lack of random assignment of students to treatment conditions somewhat compromises this study, as does the lack of psychometric information on the measure of needs. A similar method was used by Kim (2006) to study the effects of a RT bullying prevention program on 16 fifth and sixth graders. Although differences were found in self-responsibility and frequency of victimization in the expected direction, pretreatment differences on these variables and design concerns decreases confidence in the results of this study. Likewise, Lawrence (2004) assessed the effects of RT group intervention (in comparison to a support group control condition) for individuals with developmental disabilities. He found that scores on self-determination were significantly higher for the treatment group than for the control group.

Kim (2002) evaluated the effects of an 8-week RT intervention program on fifth graders' locus of control and social responsibility. This study is notable because although there were only two groups in the study, control and treatment (and they were very small groups of 12 and 13), students were randomly selected and assigned to groups. Analysis of changes in the variables from pretest to posttest verified that the RT treatment group changed in the expected directions and the control group did not. Thus, this very small study supports the effectiveness of RT at least for these two measures.

Most of the research on RT is published in the *International Journal of Reality Therapy*, which raises some question about the objectivity of the review process applied to the manuscripts. A critical analysis of the RT literature suggests that many of these studies violate traditional tenets of experimental design such as the absence of random assignment to treatment versus control, or comparison conditions. In addition, the length or amount of treatment administered is often too limited to expect changes in such variables as self-concept or locus of control. These problems probably contribute to the mixed results found in RT research.

Theory-Testing Research. Reports of direct tests of RT theory are few and far between. Instead, RT proponents argue that research not specifically conducted as a test of RT theory provides support for their approach. For instance, Sansone (1998) maintained that

Deci's (1995) research on self-determination theory supports RT theory because it confirms the idea that intrinsic motivation is a powerful and lasting determinant of behavior in comparison to extrinsic motivation.

LaFond (2000) described the development of an instrument intended to measure the relative intensity of an individual's basic needs. Called the Choice Theory Basic Needs Scale, this instrument may spur the theory-testing research that is badly needed to support RT. Data from LaFond's study did lend some support to RT's need theory in that analyses documented the predicted five-factor structure corresponding to the five basic needs. Unfortunately, LaFond found that psychometric analyses indicated that many of the items of the scale need to be revised before its utility can be fully assessed and that the concurrent validity data she collected (correlation with a measure of marital satisfaction) were weak. Harvey and Retter (1995) also developed a measure of basic needs for use with children, the Basic Needs Survey, which showed adequate retest reliability. However, they provided no validity information for this measure.

ISSUES OF INDIVIDUAL AND CULTURAL DIVERSITY

Most RT writings seem to have a heavy emphasis on heterosexuality, and particularly married heterosexuality. Glasser's book, *Counseling with Choice Theory* (2000a) presents cases that deal exclusively with heterosexual couples. The book Glasser wrote with his wife Carleen, *Getting Together and Staying Together* (Glasser & Glasser, 2000) is subtitled *Solving the Mystery of Marriage.* In the core RT literature, discussions of relationships seem to focus on marital relationships with little acknowledgment that other types of relationships exist. Although the emphasis on heterosexual relationships does not, in itself, equate with an inherent bias, it is important to note these leanings in light of the theory's significant emphasis on relationship over other aspects of human functioning. Recognition of other forms of relationships, including those involving gay, lesbian, bisexual and transgender (GLBT) individuals, would broaden this theory's appeal.

The assumption that humans have choice is subject to criticism from the perspectives of cultural minorities, women, GLBT individuals, and other groups that have been the targets of oppression and mistreatment by the white male establishment (Ballou, 2006; Linnenberg, 2006). In fact, members of these groups have been forced to behave in certain ways under the threat of punishment or even physical harm; Glasser would agree and would characterize these events as perfect examples of the use of external control theory. For example, external control theory was clearly demonstrated when in the 1960s the choices of African Americans were limited when it came to dining, riding the bus, or even drinking from public water fountains.

RT theorists would respond by saying that individuals cannot control the environment, only how they react to it (Howatt, 2001; Tham, 2001). Individuals can choose how they respond to adverse circumstances, and those choices will determine how well they function psychologically. For example, in an article in which she describes teaching choice theory to Albanian women, Tham (2001) maintained that these women found the ideas useful, despite the perception that, for Albanians, freedom of choice seems like an illusion. Wubbolding (2007) points out that "seeing clients, especially minorities, as victims disempowers them, demeans them, and condemns them to a mental state characterized by self-talk such as "I can't because they won't let me." Reality therapists believe that no matter what people have suffered they need not remain in the position of victim" (p. 203).

The needs identified in RT theory could be seen as culturally bound (especially, for instance, power and freedom). Facing these criticisms, its advocates would argue that there are many ways to meet needs, and the way in which an individual does this is not dictated by RT, but by the individual's own quality world. The quality world is influenced by the person's culture, and the good RT counselor respects these choices (Sanchez, 1998; Wubbolding et al., 1998). A brief review of the RT literature seems to support this sensitivity to issues of diversity among RT proponents (Mickel & Boone, 2001; Sanchez, 1998). For example, Wubbolding and colleagues (1998) endorsed the cultural competencies of the Association for Multicultural Counseling and Development (Arrendondo et al., 1996) for RT counselors and further elaborated on ethical issues relevant to the applications of RT in a diverse world.

Other evidence suggests that RT may be a very acceptable approach for some diverse clients (Wubbolding et al., 2004). For example, Okonji, Ososkie, and Pulos (1996) reported that a sample of African American adolescents (Job Corps participants) responded more favorably to a videotape sample of RT counseling than to one depicting person-centered counseling, particularly when the counselor was an African American male. However, it is always risky to draw conclusions based on one research study. Also, these clients did not actually experience RT counseling; they only watched it.

Wubbolding et al. (2004) suggested that in working with clients from other than the Western European cultures, a safe therapeutic relationship becomes critical, writing that "clients unfamiliar with the nature of counseling and who see it as foreign to them can be helped when they realize that the reality therapist is genuinely empathic and concerned about their welfare and committed to assisting them" (p. 223). Wubbolding (2000) detailed other modifications to RT that are necessary with diverse clients. For example, he suggested that RT counselors working with clients of Japanese heritage should use gentle, indirect questioning styles. They should also recognize that the individualistic values of Western society are inappropriate for these clients; evaluation of life is more commonly based on family or community well-being. Wubbolding (2000) performed this kind of analysis for clients from other diverse groups, such as African Americans, Puerto Ricans, and Koreans. He mentioned differences in perspectives based on spirituality as well. However, Wubbolding is silent on the issue of sexual orientation.

Sanchez, Perez-Prado, and Cadavid (1998) discussed the application of RT to Puerto Rican clients. They identified specific elements of Puerto Rican culture that are critical in working with clients of this origin, including *respeto* (respect), *dignidad* (dignity), and *personalismo* (personalism). Sanchez and colleagues maintained that these and other characteristics of Puerto Rican culture were essential aspects of the quality worlds of these individuals, and to sensitively conduct RT with them, counselors needed to understand and account for these differences.

THE CASE STUDY

Donald's presentation fits with the RT assumption that relationships are the core of psychological dysfunction. His grandiose presentation and addiction to excitement might seem less consistent with RT assumptions, but, conceptualized as ways to meet power or fun needs, this inconsistency seems less troubling. Generally, the details of Donald's presentation are easily understood through choice theory—he is angering, depressing, and generally making bad behavior choices.

Summary

Reality therapy is based on the assumption that people are motivated to meet their basic needs of survival, love and belonging, fun, freedom, and power. The most important of these needs is that for love and belonging. Each individual constructs his quality world, which is a mental collection of need-satisfying people, experiences, and objects. Behavior represents the best effort of the individual at a given time to meet his needs.

Psychological dysfunction results when we make bad choices. At the root of all problems is a key relationship—the individual is having difficulty satisfying love and belonging needs. When these needs are frustrated, the person becomes angry, but typically turns to other behaviors because angering behavior can have very severe consequences. Dysfunctional behavior, particularly depressing, usually gets the person attention from others and allows the person to avoid trying other behaviors that might be riskier.

The RT counselor is first interested in establishing a warm, empathic relationship with the client. She avoids blaming or criticizing the client, instead helping the client to examine his current behavior in light of what he really wants. Together, the client and counselor formulate a plan for the client to choose different ways to meet his needs.

Very little research exists that directly tests RT theory. The outcome research that has appeared, for the most part, does not meet the current methodological standards for empirical validation. RT has been characterized as simplistic and culturally bound. The assumption that all behavior is chosen has been the target of criticism because it ignores the fact that social and environmental factors influence behavior. The writings of RT theorists seem to ignore GLBT relationships in favor of an emphasis on traditional marriage relationships.

 Visit Chapter 11 on the Companion Website at **www.prenhall.com/murdock** for chapter-specific resources and self-assessments.

CHAPTER 12

Feminist Therapy

Susan is a 30-year-old Korean American women who is recently divorced from her husband of 2 years. She is a full-time student beginning her third year of medical school and lives with her mother. Susan arrives for sessions neatly dressed, usually in hospital scrubs. She generally appears younger than her stated age, demonstrates poor eye contact, and shows very little emotion.

Susan was referred for counseling following an incident in which she verbally confronted another student during class and was asked to leave the classroom. The counselor at the medical school who referred her suggested that she may have difficulty managing and appropriately expressing anger; Susan does not agree that this is a problem. She says that she was justified in her anger because the other student, a man, had called her "crazy."

Susan is adopted. She has no knowledge of her biological parents. Susan's adoptive father is Caucasian; her adoptive mother is Asian. She is an only child. Her father, who died 2 years ago, had a history of alcohol abuse. Initially, Susan reported having "basically a good childhood." She described her mother as "the disciplinarian, hard working and loving." She further stated that although her father abused alcohol, this was not a stressor; she "adored him" and he "was very good to her." In later counseling sessions, Susan described her home life growing up as uncomfortable; her mother and father argued frequently. She further disclosed feelings of resentment and guilt related to her father's alcohol abuse.

Susan reported having problems with interpersonal relationships for many years. Her ex-husband, who lives in another city, recently told her that she should seek counseling because she has difficulty letting go of relationships. She agreed with his assessment, characterizing herself as "codependent." Susan reports a lack of self-confidence, feelings of numbness during conflict, insecurity with authority figures, and a desire to avoid uncomfortable situations.

Susan provided an example of her difficulty with relationships in describing a long-term female friend. Susan and her friend Leah met during their first year of high school, and they immediately became friends, studying together, shopping, having lunch together, and so forth. Susan described her relationship with Leah as "very close right from the begin-ning," saying that they were "practically inseparable." They decided to pursue careers in medicine, attended the same college, and now are in medical school together. Susan reported that Leah was always very protective of her and that when Susan had a problem with another acquaintance or family member, Leah was there to defend her.

Susan recalled a time when she was dating a man and believed that he was cheating on her. She discussed her suspicions with Leah, who convinced her that the two of them should slash the tires on his car and spray paint the windshield to "teach him a lesson." Susan and Leah went through with their plan and vowed never to disclose what they had done. Susan reported that they engaged in other activities similar to this one throughout the years and that she felt "somewhat guilty" about some of the things they have done to other people. Susan further reported currently feeling "smothered" by Leah; she would like to pursue friendships with other people. However, Susan reports being unable to end her friendship with Leah because she feels it is necessary to remain loyal to her.

With men, Susan says she is unable to express her feelings when she senses disagreement, and describes herself as fearing abandonment. She says these kinds of things happened in the relationship with her ex-husband. Susan reports that a previous significant relationship was physically abusive. She felt responsible for the abuse because she was, at times, verbally abusive toward the man. During the abuse she would feel calm, and when it was over, she would simply leave the situation. She had great difficulty ending this relationship because of her feelings of loyalty to this man.

Susan comes to counseling somewhat reluctantly (mostly because the counselor at school suggested it), although she recognizes her difficulties with relationships. She says that she'd like to work on her "temper" and her feelings of abandonment.

Note: In tribute to the egalitarian spirit of feminist therapy, the image I chose for this chapter is intended to represent the many diverse contributors to this theoretical approach.

BACKGROUND

Traditionally, psychotherapy has let women down. The same is true for members of dis-empowered groups. Created by the mainstream to serve the mainstream, psychotherapy has failed marginalized people in fundamental ways. This is not to say women and other minority-group members have never received help or felt more able to cope after coun-selling or therapy but, rather, that therapy they received made little attempt to address the root causes of their problems. In focusing narrowly on the personal and individual, which mainstream psychotherapists insist is their domain, they ignore the big picture and miss the point. A therapy which fails to address power issues in people's lives works, automatically, to reinforce oppression. (McLellan, 1999, p. 325)

Feminist therapy (FT) is a rather different approach to counseling; it is more a philosoph-ical approach than a specific theory and technique (Wyche & Rice, 1997). The preceding quote is a good illustration of the ideology of a radical feminist approach to counseling. However, feminist philosophy spans an ideological continuum that ranges from radical to more conservative positions. These variations of feminist philosophy will be described later in the chapter. If you'd like to see a feminist therapist in action, watch Dr. Linda Moore work with Helen on the *Theories in Action DVD*. You can also read part of an article by prominent feminist therapist Laura Brown in Box 12.1.

Box 12.1

Still Subversive? Where Is the Evidence?

Is feminist practice still subversive? Is this practice still viable as an approach to psychotherapy after all these years? Not only in my opinion are the answers to both of these questions in the affirmative, but I would also like to argue that what feminist practice brings to the table has become more salient and increasingly necessary for the soul of psychological practice in the twenty-first century. Let us discuss, beginning with the hoary old feminist cliché about the personal being political, why and how I see that maxim applying to the evidence of the power of feminist therapy.

Feminist therapy continues to be one of the few approaches to practice that owns and names the politics of the realities affecting us all, client and therapist, student and teacher, researcher and participant, and makes that political analysis central to theory. Other postmodern therapies such as Narrative and Constructivist models join feminist practice in disowning the notions of objective truth claims and diagnostic labels. Feminist practice also converges with person-centered therapies around the importance of meeting clients where they are and valuing the client's voice in the therapeutic discourse. Feminist practice, however, continues to be one of only a handful of therapy domains in which therapists are called upon to acknowledge as central the politics of practice and the impact on practice of the politics of gender, power, and social location on the lives and work of all of us. Feminist practice is joined by liberation psychology (Almeida, 2003; Aron & Corne, 1994), which has been brilliantly synthesized with feminist insights by Comas-Diaz (2000). Yet in the textbooks on systems of psychotherapy studied by our beginning students (Corey, 2004; Prochaska & Norcross, 2003) when liberatory perspectives are included at all, feminist practice stands alone representing the call to acknowledgment of political realities in the psychotherapy office.

When feminist therapists speak of the politics of the personal, we speak of the experiences of power and powerlessness in people's lives, experiences that interact with the bodies and biologies we bring into the world to create distress, resilience, dysfunction, and competence. Foregrounding power and its absence as a central issue in the efficacy of psychotherapy seems particularly necessary today, speaking as I did in Washington, DC not far from places where people with the power to do so are attempting to legislate away from me rights that, as a lesbian citizen of the United States, I have not yet attained. I write this revision a week after Hurricane Katrina came to the Gulf Coast, exemplifying that powerlessness is the defining element in the terrible trauma affecting the poor, the people of color, the old, and the very young who were left behind as waters rose.

Foregrounding the corrosive effects of powerlessness, as feminist therapy has always done by focusing on how to bring "power to the powerless," and as Adrienne Smith and Ruth Siegel described two decades ago in their chapter in The Handbook of Feminist Therapy (Smith & Siegel, 1985), seems to gain new urgency at a moment in U.S. history when the hope of empowerment seems to be drifting ever further out of reach for most ordinary people. Feminist therapy, speaking out loud about power, disrupts the trance of despair that has become so common in today's culture. Feminist therapy requires its practitioners to think in a complex and nuanced manner about how power and powerlessness are roots of distress. Failing to do so, feminist practice ceases to fulfill its mission and loses its subversive potentials.

This insistence on the personal being political, and the political being deeply and intimately personal, is especially meaningful when we look at what we are teaching our next generations about the nature of the work of psychologists. Students in training to become practitioners are learning that their tasks are to offer empirically supported treatments for disorders that are in turn defined by the DSM. Clinicians are to do this because: (a) it is the wave of the future in health care—everyone (meaning physicians) is doing evidence-based practice and so should we, particularly given our heritage of being based in the science of psychology (Task Force, 1995) and (b) managed care requires these treatments of psychotherapists, thus providing empirically supported treatments is required to make a living. Resistance is futile; we are being assimilated and should stop injuring ourselves by fighting back.

This discourse of constraints on practice, our powerlessness to resist these trends, and the anxieties that these constraints create in our next generation permeated some of the questions that my students raised with their peers and me. How can they call themselves feminist therapists when we still have such a small base of randomized clinical trials supporting feminist practice as efficacious? If feminist therapists are critical of, and generally rejecting of DSM diagnostic categories, how can they bill for their services (or more salient and immediate in their lives, how will they pass their clinical competency exams if feminists do not give DSM diagnoses)? In addition, what managed care company will pay for feminist therapy (an important question for someone who is graduating from school with over $100,000 in student loan debt)?

Feminist practice and theory steps in at this juncture to be subversive to the dominant discourse and I hope a little reassuring to our next generation. We have both evidence and a diagnostic strategy, both of which give feminist therapists powerful tools. They are different sorts of evidence, and radically different ways of conceptualizing pain and dysfunction, but they are not absent.

Excerpted from "Still Subversive . . ." by L. S. Brown (pp. 15–24) 2006. *Psychology of Women Quarterly*, 30.

Feminist therapy developed out of deep dissatisfaction with traditional approaches to psychotherapy (Gilbert, 1980), the emergence of a psychology of women and gender, and the feminist movements of the 1960s and 1970s (Contratto & Rossier, 2005; Evans, Kincade, Marbley, & Seem, 2005; Worell & Johnson, 2001). In her book *Subversive Dialogs*, Laura Brown (1994) defined feminist therapy in the following way:

> Feminist therapy is the practice of therapy informed by feminist political philosophy and analysis, grounded in the multicultural feminist scholarship on the psychology of women and gender. This approach leads both therapist and client toward strategies and solutions advancing feminist resistance, transformation, and social change in daily personal life and in relationships with the social, emotional, and political environment. (pp. 21–22)

No one individual developed FT; rather, it emerged from the application of feminist political philosophy (Brown, 1994). It is considered a grassroots phenomenon

(Brown & Liss-Levinson, 1981), and its proponents generally eschew the idea of "experts" (Brown, 1994). Feminism in counseling actually has a long history, beginning with Alfred Adler, who recognized the cultural effects on women's behavior (but who still saw women as needing to adjust to the role of mother). Another early feminist was Karen Horney, a psychoanalyst who rejected the idea of penis envy and substituted the woman's envy of men's privileged, power-wielding position in society (Forisha, 1981; Nutt, 1979). Many writers and therapists are currently active in the FT world, and producing a list of them here would surely lead to leaving someone out, not to mention the fact that creating such a list would be contrary to the egalitarian principles of FT.

Numerous organizations are devoted to feminist psychology, psychotherapy, and the psychology of women. The American Psychological Association (APA) established the Committee on Women in Psychology in the 1970s, and this committee initiated the APA Task Force on Sex Bias and Sex Role Stereotyping in Psychotherapeutic Practice. Division 17 of the APA, the Society of Counseling Psychology, established a Committee on Women and produced *Principles Concerning Psychotherapy of Women* (APA, 1979; Fitzgerald & Nutt, 1986) which have been recently revised as the *Guidelines for Psychological Practice with Girls and Women* (APA, 2007). Division 35 of the APA is the Society for the Psychology of Women, which sponsors the journal *Psychology of Women Quarterly*. Division 35 can be found online at www.apa.org/divisions/div35. In 1993, Division 35 was instrumental in holding the first National Conference on Education and Training in Feminist Practice, which produced the Core Tenets of Feminist Therapy shown in Box 12.2 (Worell & Johnson, 1997).

The Association of Women in Psychology (AWP) emerged in 1969 as a parallel organization to the American Psychological Association. The AWP was instrumental in the creation of Division 35 of the APA. Its members picketed the APA board of directors meeting at the 1969 convention to argue for its creation (www.apa.org/divs/div35). AWP created the first Feminist Therapy Roster in 1971 (Brown & Liss-Levinson, 1981).

Another famous hotbed of feminism is Wellesley College, which sponsors the Wellesley Centers for Women (www.wcwonline.org). The Stone Center, a well-known feminist think tank, is also at Wellesley, as is the Jean Baker Miller Training Institute, which produces research and training centered on the relational model of women's development (see the section "Theory of the Person and Development of the Individual").

Box 12.2

Core Tenets of Feminist Therapy

1. Feminist therapy recognizes that being female always occurs in a cultural, social, political, economic, and historical context and affects development across the life span.
2. Feminist therapy focuses on the cultural, social, political, economic, and historical factors of wom[e]n's lives as well as intrapsychic factors across the life span.
3. Feminist therapy includes an analysis of power and its relationship to the multiple ways women are oppressed; factors such as gender, race, class, ethnicity, sexual orientation, age and ablebodiness, singly or in combination, can be the basis for oppression.

4. Feminist therapy acknowledges that violence against women, overt and covert, is emotionally, physically, and spiritually damaging.

5. Feminist therapy acknowledges that misogyny exists in all women's lives and is emotionally, physically, and spiritually damaging.

6. Feminist therapy's primary focus is on strengths rather than deficits. Therefore, women's behaviors are seen as understandable efforts to respond adaptively to oppressive occurrences.

7. Feminist therapy is committed to social change that supports equality forever.

8. Feminist therapy is based on the constant and explicit monitoring of the power balance between therapist and client and pays attention to the potential abuse and misuse of power within the therapeutic relationship.

9. Feminist therapy strives toward an egalitarian and nonauthoritarian relationship based on mutual respect.

10. Feminist therapy is a collaborative process in which the therapist and client establish the goals, direction, and pace of therapy.

11. Feminist therapy helps girls and women understand how they have incorporated societal beliefs and values. The therapist works collaboratively with them to challenge and transform those constructs that are destructive to the self and helps them create their own perspectives.

12. Feminist therapy empowers girls and women to recognize, claim, and embrace their individual and collective power as girls and women.

13. Feminist therapy expands girls' and women's alternatives, options, and choices across the life span.

14. Feminist therapy is a demystification process that validates and affirms the shared and diverse experiences of girls' and women's lives.

15. Feminist therapy involves appropriate types of self-disclosure. However, because self-disclosure may be harmful, it must be both value and theory driven and always in the client's best interest. Therapists must develop methods of continually monitoring their level of self-awareness.

16. Feminist therapists are committed to continually monitoring their own biases, distortions, and limitations, especially with respect to cultural, social, political, economic, and historical aspects of girl's and women's experiences.

From *Shaping the Future of Feminist Psychology* (p. 69) by K. F. Wyche & J. K. Rice, 1997. Copyright © 1997 by the American Psychological Association. Reprinted with permission.

BASIC PHILOSOPHY

Feminism is, according to Laura Brown (1994), "the collection of political philosophies that aims to overthrow patriarchy and end inequities based on gender through cultural transformation and radical social change" (p. 19). Patriarchy refers to the pervasive norms of most cultures that favor men over women, give them power automatically (i.e., male privilege, particularly white male privilege) while at the same time devaluing women and keeping them in subordinate positions. This political perspective translates into a core belief for feminist therapists that the ultimate cause of psychological dysfunction resides in the oppression of the individual by society (McLellan, 1999). Women, particularly, are expected to adhere to a rigid set of expectations, and both overadherence and deviation from these behaviors are labeled mental illness (Chesler, 1972).

Feminists, and feminist therapists, tend to be activists and are pretty noisy about it. For example, Laura Brown, the self-proclaimed subversive (as in the title of her book *Subversive Dialogs* [2002]) evaluates the current state of feminism in this way:

> the most subversive thing that feminist practice still brings to the table after all these years is a belief that the civilization we know as racist, sexist, heterosexist, classist, neglectful, colonizing, occupying, and violent is the problem, for which feminist activisim in and outside of the therapy office, the classroom and the lab, is one solution. (2006, p. 22)

Mary Ballou (2005) calls attention to the hegemony of the medical model, traditional science, health insurance industry, professional associations, and licensing boards (p. 202). She sees the dominance of these institutions as well as the increasing conservative political swing in our current lives as limiting the visions of therapists, feminist or otherwise, in their efforts to understand and help others. So given even these limited examples, you can see that FT writers are not shy in their critical evaluations of the current state of our world.

Feminists are always aware of power differentials and are attentive to features of human interaction that promote such differentials (Gilbert & Rader, 2007). One important influence is language; how we speak is assumed to both reflect and influence our views of the world. Thus, you will *not* hear a feminist using the pronouns *he* or *him* to refer to both sexes. More subtly, feminists argue that those traditionally in power (men) typically are referred to by their last names, whereas women and children are called by their first names. As a consequence, feminist writers often use both first and last names in their references to others' writings. To be true to FT ideology, I will use both names in the first reference to writers in this chapter (other than in parenthetical references).

Feminist theory, which forms the basis of FT counseling, encompasses a wide range of perspectives. Next I will review some feminist philosophies, but you should keep in mind that the boundaries between these categories are not as distinct as you might gather from my presentation of them. Complicating matters, different writers sometimes use different terms when apparently referring to a similar feminist stance. For example, one variant of feminism, woman of color feminism, can be enacted from liberal, radical, or cultural feminist perspectives. For the most part, the feminist stances vary primarily in the degree to which they (a) emphasize unique qualities of women, (b) advocate the rejection of masculine, or patriarchal, models, and (c) integrate issues of culture and class into their viewpoints. For a more detailed review of these philosophies and their histories, read Carolyn Zerbe Enns' (2004) book, *Feminist Theory and Feminist Psychotherapies* or Laura Brown's *Subversive Dialogs* (1994).

Liberal feminists emphasize women's equality within a rational framework (Worell & Johnson, 2001). Also called reformist feminists, advocates of this perspective emphasize equality of women and men and tend to focus on changing legal structures and interventions to promote access for women. Betty Friedan, who identified "the problem that has no name" (i.e., the malaise of the traditional 1960s "housewife"), can be seen as a liberal feminist because she meant by this phrase that women were blocked from reaching their potentials, and that the patriarchal society did not want to discuss these issues (Friedan, 1963). Friedan was instrumental in establishing the National Organization for Women (NOW), which worked for the passage of the Equal Rights Amendment (ERA) to the U.S. Constitution. The ERA, of course, failed, but other initiatives did not (such as paid maternity leave and the right of women to control reproduction). The liberal position is criticized by other feminists for encouraging women to become members of the male club and, by doing so, denying the paternalism in societal structures. It is dangerous, in this view, to teach women to be "more like men" because this view inherently assumes that women are deficient (Brown, 1994, p. 54).

Radical and social change (or *socialist*) feminists are those who see oppression based on gender as the most fundamental and stubborn form of injustice and seek to eliminate all forms of male domination (Enns, 2004; Worell & Johnson, 2001). Socialist feminists, who base their arguments on Marxism, add that capitalism is a second major factor in the oppression of women and would prefer communal living environments that would emphasize equality of work roles for men and women (Enns, 2004). Radical and socialist feminists point to the many ways that society represses women, including violence and harassment and restricting their reproductive rights. The liberal feminists' efforts to promote women into positions of power in society are seen by these feminists as tokenism (Brown, 2000) because this practice is more likely to change the woman to fit male norms than to change the patriarchal, capitalist system. Nothing less than abolishing patriarchal systems is acceptable to the radical and socialist feminists, so they are likely to advocate separatism, or the refusal to participate in institutions that perpetuate the patriarchy. For instance, engaging in all-women events, businesses, and consciousness-raising groups is seen as refusing to conform to male-favoring cultural values (Enns, 1997). *Lesbian* feminists would add heterosexism to the list of cultural dominations, defining this bias as the heteropatriarchy (Brown, 1994; Worell & Remer, 2004).

Cultural feminists revere women's unique qualities such as relatedness and cooperation. They tend to emphasize the differences between men and women in such values (Moradi et al., 2002). Unlike radical and socialist feminists, who are critical of norms of femininity, cultural feminists celebrate what they would see as qualities unique to women (e.g., connectedness, cooperation; Worell & Remer, 2004).

Woman of color feminism, or *womanism*, is a reaction to mainstream feminism's neglect of the experiences of women of color, or to put it a little more bluntly, the racism inherent in early feminism. These feminists reject the primacy of gender as a category of oppression, arguing that the gender interacts with race, social class, and other categories in affecting individuals' lives (Evans et al., 2005). Although some authors equate womanist with Black feminism, Enns (2004) points out that this term is also used more broadly, to refer to one who loves all things woman. Some woman of color feminists prefer the term *colonization* to *oppression* as a way of emphasizing that people of color are pressured to adopt the values and norms of white, Eurocentric culture (Comas-Diaz, 1994, p. 288). Lillian Comas-Diaz argued that "colonized individuals are not only exploited and victimized for the benefit of the colonial power, but also serve as the quintessential scapegoats" (p. 289). Much as other feminists might emphasize examining one's internalized sexism, woman of color feminists advocate distinguishing between internal and external colonization (Comas-Diaz, 1994). Supporters of this orientation sometimes see men and women of the same race or ethnicity as more similar to each other than women from different ethnicities. This position is probably the most widely endorsed in recent years (Moradi et al., 2002; Wyche & Rice, 1997).

Another FT ideology is labeled *postmodern* feminism (Brown, 2000; Enns, 2004). Postmodernists reject the idea that there is one real, objective truth out there in the world. Instead, postmodernists contend that reality is constructed in relationships and that truth is often determined by who is in power. Some versions of lesbian/queer feminism can be classified as falling into postmodernist approaches. Finally, Enns (2004) describes *third-wave* feminism, a postmodern approach that although appreciating the contributions of earlier feminisms, struggles to deal with the backlash against feminism and to push for further progress in combating violence, problems in health care, and economic and environmental concerns.

Postmodernism is difficult to describe, because within it are views that vary from mild to radical on the notion of whether there is a reality to be comprehended. Among the postmodernist approaches are those who view radical relativism (i.e., the view that there is no one reality only shifting views) as problematic because it would disallow statements about historical (and present) oppression of women and other marginalized individuals. Social constructivists adopt this perspective so that problematic constructions of gender, race, and so forth, can be addressed (Enns, 2004). The point of all postmodernists, as I see it, is to emphasize that we and our clients can bring many ideas in to counseling that we treat as "truth" that can be profitably considered as products of social reality training (Hare-Mustin, 1994).

Chandra, Susan's feminist therapist, is first aware that Susan is a woman and of Asian heritage in a culture infused with the values of European men. Characterizing herself as a womanist feminist in the broadest sense, who also respects the contributions of radical and cultural feminisms, Chandra recognizes that Susan's female sex and Korean heritage will likely have a significant impact on who she is and how she operates in the world, and how the world reacts to her. Chandra assumes that Susan experiences the power disparity in mainstream culture, and that the behavior that others label "dysfunctional" is a reaction to these inequities.

HUMAN MOTIVATION

FT counselors don't spend a lot of time discussing human motivation—they are too busy intervening. According to Mary Brabeck and Laura Brown (1997), the lack of theory in FT can be partly attributed to the fact that FT developed in the field rather than within the confines of academia.

In considering motivation, FT counselors might draw their views from an existing theory of human behavior, provided that it was not sexist. Nancy Chodorow modified classic psychoanalytic theory to eliminate the "penis envy" bias (Chodorow, 1978, 1989). She focused on the role of mothering in child development and particularly on the individuation of boys and girls. Modern versions of psychoanalytic theory such as attachment theory have received feminist criticism, as has the evolutionary perspective (Contratto, 2002). Ultimately, the issue of motivation partly turns on the question of the origins of sex differences (if they exist), which is a controversy far from settled as you will see from the following discussion under development.

Another way of addressing motivation might be to adopt a system associated with humanistic (e.g., Gestalt or Person-Centered) orientation because an actualization perspective is compatible with a feminist orientation (Enns, 1997). However, Person-Centered Theory, for example, has been faulted for its lack of attention to the social factors that contribute to the development of the self. Also, the emphasis placed on individualism in humanistic/existential approaches is reflective of traditional American values (rugged individualism or the John Wayne syndrome) and can obscure commonalties in women's experiences in the oppressive culture (Enns, 2004).

Chandra sees Susan as motivated to grow to her full potential as a human. An advocate of humanism, Chandra views Susan from a positive perspective but is careful to attend to social influences that are significant in Susan's life.

CENTRAL CONSTRUCTS

Gender

No matter what FT ideology one adopts, gender, considered the social manifestation of sex, is a critical construct. Feminist therapists use the term *sex* when biological differences are the subject (such as anatomical ones). *Gender* is the term used to emphasize that differences between men and women are more than the product of biology and that social learning and social context are important influences on what our cultures define as "male" and "female" (Yoder, 2003). As you might suspect, liberal feminist therapists are adamant that gender is a construction of culture and that most apparent psychological differences between men and women are a product of societal influence rather than biological sex (Gilbert & Scher, 1999). I have friends who are parents who are convinced that raising boys is different from raising girls. Boys are active and aggressive and girls are sweet and compliant—you know, the "boys will be boys" phenomenon. Liberal feminists would point out that many of these behaviors are known to be differentially reinforced by parents when children are very young (Paludi, 2002). Female and male infants are treated very differently from one another from very early on. Baby boys wear blue and girls, pink; boys are given toy trucks or tool kits, and girls are given dolls or kitchen sets.

Cultural and to some extent radical and socialist feminists are more likely to see gender differences as inherent to the sexes. This position is sometimes called the *essentialist* stance (Brown, 1994). For instance, the traditional female emphasis on relationships is to be celebrated, not to be treated as an artifact of socialization (Enns, 2004).

Janice Yoder (2003) presents an integrationist perspective on these arguments. Noting that although biology seems to be more "basic" than environment and so more immutable, she asserts that research is amassing that experience can affect physiology. She writes "I believe that as the flexibility of biology becomes more and more acknowledged, feminist psychologists will find it useful to let go of the presumed distinction between sex and gender, nature and nurture. This opens the door to regarding *sex and gender as inseparable and intertwined* so that a holistic understanding of women and men, girls and boys, will include biology (sex) and what our culture makes of our biological sex (i.e., gender)" (2003, p. 17; italics in original).

In any case, all feminist therapists recognize that society has devalued women and the qualities typically associated with them. Power and gender are therefore tightly bound in most cultures in the world (Brown, 1994).

Chandra works to identify multiple influences on who Susan is now. Some of the important factors are her biological sex, family background, social class, and the fact that she is Korean. Chandra does not know how much each of these factors influences Susan, but she guesses that gender is a powerful influence. Susan has probably been reinforced for exhibiting traditionally "female" behaviors and punished for displaying traditionally "male" behaviors.

THE PERSONAL IS POLITICAL

In contrast to traditional psychological theory, which tends to focus on internal determinants of behavior, this basic principle of FT emphasizes that women's experiences are connected to factors external to them, embedded in social norms and traditions (Enns, 2004). FT theorists are very conscious of the traditional gender imbalance in society, which dictates that power and status are bestowed on men. Women's problems are seen as resulting from social, political, and legal systems that oppress and disempower women (Worell & Johnson, 2001). Feminists believe that the "personal experience is the lived version of political reality" (Brown, 1994, p. 50). In other words, the distress of the individual woman (the personal) is a function of the social and political rules and norms of the culture in which she lives (the political).

Chandra assumes that the difficulties Susan brings to counseling are a product of factors in her environment and especially the cultural context in which she was raised and now exists. She suffers from society's disempowerment of women, and some of her current behavior is likely in reaction to these very real feelings of helplessness. For example, her low self-confidence is surely influenced by the societal devaluing of women.

THEORY OF THE PERSON
AND DEVELOPMENT OF THE INDIVIDUAL

There are a number of ways of examining personality and development from the FT perspective. First, the FT approach attends closely to theory and research on sex differences. Liberal feminists assume that males and females do not differ in any important psychological ways at birth (Brown & Liss-Levinson, 1981). Subsequent experiences in the social environment are thought to account for any later observable differences.

What is the outcome of this lifelong process of learning to be a gendered person? Stereotypically, men are thought to be independent, assertive, competitive, unemotional, and invested in their careers. Women are seen as emotional, relationship oriented, passive, and willing to put others' (particularly men's) needs before theirs. Men are dominant, and women are submissive. Men are career and work oriented; women are family and child oriented.

Arguments over the "reality" of gender differences began as early as 1914 and have continued to this day (Hyde, 2005). Alice Eagly (1995) maintained that enough evidence existed to conclude that there are real sex differences and in the directions indicated by stereotypes (for instance, women are more relationship oriented than men; men are more independent and controlling than women).

In contrast, in a recent review, Janet Shibley Hyde (2005) looked at 46 meta-analyses of such differences and found that 78% of these differences were in zero to small range. The categories she reviewed included ones in which differences are traditionally expected, such as math and verbal ability; in these latter two cases, differences again were small or nonexistent. Three general areas did show moderate or large differences: motor performance, some sexual behaviors/attitudes (but not sexual satisfaction), and aggression, particularly physical aggression. Surely of interest to many feminists is Hyde's assertion that the reported difference in relationality between men and women (women are nurturers and men are not) is not supported by the data. Yoder (2003) also summarized a large body of these difference-testing efforts and she concludes that it is frustrating that so much research has been done with so little agreement about the results. She noted that the really important question in this debate is, what causes the differences? It is not enough to know that men and women are from different planets—we need to look at the workings of the spaceships in which they fly around.

Evidence exists that children are treated differently based on their sex, giving rise to the opinion that this learning, termed sex-role socialization, is responsible for observed differences in the behaviors of men and women. Cultures endorse clear values of what it means to be a male or a female, and parents, peers, and teachers tend to treat children accordingly. Yoder (2003) summarized this research as well. For example, parents are likely to describe their male and female children differently (e.g., girls are more delicate); parental preferences for toys appear to be sex-consistent as well (although it is noted that overall "boy" toys are more fun than "girl" toys, so parents sometimes will cross boundaries here). Berk (2007) noted that parents' reactions to violations of stereotypical behavior are more negative for boys than for girls and the same pattern appears among children's peers. Yoder's (2003) summary also demonstrates that boys and girls are treated differently by their teachers; for example, boys get more attention and corrective feedback, whereas girls are generally advised to not fuss about mistakes. Finally, the media, although somewhat more balanced than in the past, still depicts males in more prominent and dominant roles than females. Perhaps you've noticed that many cartoon characters are male (think about the Road Runner and Scooby Doo). Shannon Davis (2003) content analyzed cartoons and found that major characters were more likely to be male, and they were more likely to be depicted in an occupational setting. Lots of central characters in popular movies for kids are typically male (think *Harry Potter* and *Star Wars*). So, the next time someone tries to tell you that our society is now gender-neutral, you can tell them to spend a Saturday morning watching television or to go to a kid's movie.

A second perspective on development is offered by Jean Baker Miller of the Stone Center at Wellesley College. The Stone Center is known for its studies of women's issues and feminist intervention. Miller (1991) proposed a model of feminine development that could be loosely called "self-in-relation." Although initially developed to explain the experiences of girls and women, the model has been broadened to include all human experience (Jordan & Hartling, 2002). Both boys and girls first develop a sense of self that is tied to relationships because parents (most likely mothers) are continually attending to the infant's well-being. The infant learns to attend to the caretaker's emotional state, but the link of relationship to self largely disappears for boys as they develop because they are encouraged to become active and separate from mom. In contrast, girls are encouraged to maintain their focus on the feelings of others. The girl's sense of self-esteem thus becomes linked to maintaining relationships. Miller wrote about the Oedipal conflict in girls: "We may ask whether one reason that people, beginning with Freud, have had such trouble delineating this stage in girls is that it may not exist. There is no major crisis of 'cutting off' anything, and especially relationships" (1991; p. 18). However, at this stage, girls likely get the message, based on cultural beliefs, that they should turn their relationship focus to men (check out the cartoon).

In adolescence, boys are encouraged to explore and expand their sense of self. Girls, however, are taught to contract their identities because achievement and sexuality are not acceptable. These natural strivings are diverted to relationships, so that a girl's sense of who she is and how she achieves is once again linked to relationships. Thus, Miller described very different paths to adult identity for men and women, which produce values and characteristics consistent with traditional roles.

Another perspective on female development is Feminist Identity Development Theory (FIDT; Downing & Roush, 1985; Moradi, et al., 2002). In this model, women are thought to traverse five stages in the journey to a feminist identity. It is important to note that women can recycle through the progression multiple times (Downing & Roush, 1985). The first stage is *passive acceptance*, in which women accept the status quo, not recognizing or denying oppression and discrimination. They tend to endorse traditional gender roles and gender-based (patriarchal) power structures.

Women move into the *revelation* stage, according to Downing and Roush, when they experience either positive feminist experiences (e.g., consciousness-raising groups) or adverse experiences that seem gender related (e.g., divorce, denial of a credit application). A primary characteristic of women in this stage of identity development is anger at the sexist society and at themselves for their participation in the system.

The third stage of FIDT is *embeddedness–emanation*, and it is composed of two phases. In the first phase, embeddedness, women tend to immerse themselves in women's culture, adopt feminist ideology wholesale, and become involved in very close relationships with female friends. However, because most women are involved with men on a daily, if not intimate, basis, they realize that uncritical adherence to feminist theory and the associated anger may not be the most productive stance to take. They move on to the emanation phase, becoming more relativistic and flexible, but are still tentative in their relationships with men.

Even more flexible perceptions of life are evident as women move into the *synthesis* stage. Their reactions to men are less "automatic," and they are more flexible in their evaluations of life events and therefore less likely to attribute sexism.

Few women reach the final stage of FIDT, *active commitment*. The hallmark of this stage is the energy devoted to eliminating all forms of oppression through social change action.

STONE SOUP © 2002 Jan Eliot. Reprinted with permission of UNIVERSAL PRESS SYNDICATE. All rights reserved.

Chandra sees evidence of sex-role socialization in Susan's behavior, but also notes that some of her behavior is contrary to stereotypical norms. The angry outbursts, for example, are not within the traditional female role of being sweet and nice. On the other hand, low self-confidence, worries about abandonment, and loyalty to relationships (even "bad" ones) are embodiments of the stereotypically feminine woman. Chandra guesses that Susan's parents reinforced these behaviors as unwitting agents of the paternalitic society. In addition, the world in which Susan grew up is fraught with sexism and oppression. Susan complies to some extent with these pressures, feeling insecure and helpless. Occasionally, though, her anger comes through, and she acts in ways contrary to traditional roles. This behavior tends to get her in trouble with others, even the authorities. Susan may be in the passive acceptance or the revelation stage of feminist identity development, but she clearly is not in the embeddedness–emanation stage.

HEALTH AND DYSFUNCTION

An important aspect of the FT approach is its critique of traditional approaches to psychological dysfunction and intervention (Ballou & Brown, 2002, Worrel & Remer, 2003). A powerful statement was offered by Phyllis Chesler in her classic book *Women and Madness* (1972):

> What we consider "madness," whether it appears in women or in men, is either the acting out of the devalued female role or the total or partial rejection of one's sex-role stereotype. Women who fully act out the conditioned female role are clinically viewed as "neurotic" or "psychotic." When and if they are hospitalized, it is for predominantly female behaviors such as "depression," "suicide attempts," "anxiety neuroses," "paranoia," or "promiscuity." Women who reject or are ambivalent about the female role frighten both themselves and society so much that their ostracism and self-destructiveness probably begin very early. Such women are also assured of a psychiatric label and, if they are hospitalized, it is for less "female" behaviors, such as "schizophrenia," "lesbianism," or "promiscuity." (p. 56)

FT theorists charge that society devalues traits and behaviors that are typically associated with women, labeling them as unhealthy in comparison to male-associated traits (Worell & Johnson, 2001). Thus, the standard of health resides in male qualities, such as independence, competition, assertiveness, objectivity, and activity (Chesler, 1972). Also, both Chesler and more recent FT writers recognize that gender is not the only influence on perception; qualities and behaviors stereotypically associated with women from nonwhite, non–middle-class backgrounds are deemed dysfunctional by traditional psychotherapeutic approaches. Generally, society views the problems of women as stemming from internal factors (i.e., something is wrong with her) rather than from social and cultural inequality (Worell & Johnson, 2001).

Traditional diagnostic categories, such as those found in the *Diagnostic and Statistical Manual of Mental Disorders* (*DSM*-IV-TR) are also the targets of FT criticism. Feminists see as problematic the assumption that every form of distress is abnormal, when in fact, it is often a normal response to the problems inherent in an oppressive society (Brown, 2000). For example, the proposed diagnosis masochistic personality disorder (a.k.a. self-defeating personality disorder) was rejected by feminists because many women in abusive relationships display the characteristics of this category. Pathologizing this behavior ignores the adaptive value of passive or pacifying behavior in abusive relationships (Enns, 2000). This disorder was eventually removed from the *DSM*-IV.

Equally reprehensible is the late luteal phase dysphoric disorder, which is also known as premenstrual dysphoric disorder. Critics contend that the patriarchal psychiatric community makes women's hormones a source of mental disorders while at the same time ignoring the influence of hormones on men (Tavris, 1993). Terry Kupers (1997) suggested that an analogous disorder in men be named pathological arrhythmicity (p. 345). Because of the controversy around premenstrual dysphoric disorder, it is included only in the appendix of *DSM*-IV, among disorders in need of further study (Ross, Frances, & Widiger, 1997). Others have provided critiques of the personality disorders, such as histrionic, dependent, and borderline personality disorders (Kaplan, 1983; Kupers, 1997; Walsh, 1997). An interesting perspective on the common label "codependent" is described in Box 12.3.

FT sees psychological distress, or "dis-ease," as a communication about unjust systems (Brabeck & Brown, 1997, p. 28). Symptoms are seen as normal responses to oppressive environmental conditions (Enns, 2004). They are signs of health and strength because they are attempts to resist patriarchy. Consequently, feminist therapists focus on clients' strengths, not dysfunction (Wyche & Rice, 1997). They see human behavior as resulting from a complex combination of factors, both internal (biological and psychological) and external to the person. The latter set of variables, the social context, is considered critical to understanding individual experience.

Box 12.3

Codependent, Female, or Simply Low Power?

Laura Brown and other feminists have critically examined a term we all seem to love to throw around, *codependent*. The term was coined in the late 1980s to recognize that alcoholics were part of a system, and that those around them, the codependents, shared some responsibility for the drinking behavior. By protecting the alcoholic from the consequences of his or her abuse, the codependent *enabled* the drinking behavior. Typically, the codependent was a white, middle-aged wife of a white male alcoholic. Based on this conceptualization, the focus of intervention became both the alcoholic's and codependent's behaviors. Since that time, the term has been used in a much broader way. Feminists have taken exception to this term. Here I present some of their views, based mostly on the writings of Laura Brown and Kay Leigh Hagan.

There are many definitions of codependency, but most commonly, these definitions carry a common thread of descriptions of relationship dynamics of the codependent and significant others. Some of the characteristics offered are as follows:

1. Sacrificing one's needs for those of others
2. A sense of powerlessness
3. Gaining self-worth through being needed by others
4. Low self-esteem
5. Avoidance of conflict

The problem, according to Laura Brown (1994), is that no attempt is made to take social and cultural factors into account in understanding the "codependent's" behaviors. She pointed out that women in a sexist society are awarded responsibility for taking care of the emotions of men, and that codependent behavior very much resembles the expected heterosexual female behavior. The woman's sense of failure in the relationship may indeed cause significant personal feelings of guilt and shame, but again, this dynamic is based on the cultural rules rather than on some defect in the individual. Also, this "diagnosis" is likely to be racist because the behaviors described are very typical for individuals in cultures of color.

Kay Hagan (1993) began her dissection of the term by linking codependency and family dysfunction. Dysfunctional families are characterized as oppressive; they have rigid rules, discourage honest expression of feelings, and emphasize perfection among the members. These qualities might logically result in low self-esteem and other characteristics associated with codependency. However, she noted, "Most American families might qualify as dysfunctional in that they practice similar oppressive rules whether or not a chemical addiction is present" (p. 31). Thus, codependency really becomes a convenient label for submissive roles inculcated by traditional Western family life. "The oppressive rules of the patriarchal family system train us to accept and expect the paradigm of dominance and subordination. Even the most benign of patriarchal families operates in a manner that cultivates the characteristics of *codependency*, a term that is much more acceptable than *internalized oppression*, which might encourage us to question authority or even to rock the boat" (p. 32; italics in original).

Another way of saying it is that behaviors labeled as codependent very much resemble those of individuals in low-power groups toward the powerful (Brown, 1994). The behavior of the subordinate group members will look like overattentiveness, mindreading, enabling, and so forth. In reality, this approach is adaptive; it helps the individual survive because survival is dependent on the rules and desires of the powerful.

Nowadays, the term *codependent* is used very globally to describe anyone who seems dependent, or "addicted," to relationships. Unfortunately, Brown maintained, because of the description's resemblance to stereotypical female roles, thousands of women adopt the diagnosis. Sadly, the term has become a stigma associated with addiction and disease, when the set of behaviors it describes appear to be those that are adaptive for members of a low-power group. One can also see the use of this term as one more instance of blaming women (wives) for their partners' problems.

> Codependency is no accident, nor is it a disease or an individual character disorder afflicting us in a random manner, as popular self-help books and current therapeutic treatment would have us believe. A society of dominance trains the oppressed to be subordinate so that dominance may continue. For women this conditioning begins when we are born and extends throughout our lives via our family models, the images we see in the media, and interactions with institutions infused with male dominance. When we do not recognize the relationship codependency has to the culture, we risk falling prey to another aspect of our training in which we accept personal responsibility and blame for having somehow developed "unhealthy intimacy patterns." In a culture of dominance, the oppressed is always at fault.

From Kay L. Hagan [1993], *Fugitive Information: Essays from a Feminist Hothead*, p. 34. New York: HarperCollins. Reprinted with permission of the author.

For example, depression is diagnosed more often in women than in men. Yoder (2003) pointed to several possible explanations for this finding, all of which are linked with low self-esteem. Is it possible that women get depressed more often than men because characteristics that are deemed typically female (e.g., orienting toward relationship, cooperating rather than competing) are devalued by society? Yet another explanation focuses on the discrimination women face. Achievement behaviors are typically less acceptable in women than in men. Think for a moment about an aggressive woman. Is she evaluated differently from a man labeled aggressive? The stress of maintaining multiple roles is also exacerbated for women. When was the last time you heard anyone ask whether a man could "have it all," meaning a successful career and family life?

Not surprisingly, FT theorists are also interested in the development of eating disorders, and have advanced several hypotheses about these types of behavior (Enns, 2004). For an individual client, a combination of these factors might be operative, which include the cultural pressure of the thin body as ideal, body control as a way to gain power from a powerless position, ways of coping with achievement-related anxiety, and remaining small to avoid threatening men.

The origins of the feminist movement lie in the establishment of battered women's shelters and rape crisis centers in the 1960s. Thus, feminist therapists are especially attentive to problems that are more likely to affect women than men and problems that are linked with patriarchal cultural norms, and particularly with physical, sexual, and emotional violence.

Susan appears to be experiencing some distress associated with the pressure to maintain traditional female roles and behaviors. Chandra will not use any formal diagnostic system to understand her presentation because she believes these to be androcentric. Instead of seeing Susan as "dysfunctional," Chandra sees Susan's strengths in expressing herself when treated badly by others (the guy in class) and in her persistent attempts to care for others. That Susan is pursuing a traditionally male-dominated career is not lost on Chandra, either.

Chandra wonders what effects Susan's experiences with her alcoholic father have had on her perceptions of the nature of women and men. Her struggles in relationships with men are probably connected in some way because she likely learned very early that men can't be trusted. Susan has been the object of both verbal and physical abuse by men, and the effects of these traumas cannot be ignored.

NATURE OF THERAPY

ASSESSMENT

FT counselors are unlikely to use formal assessment methods. In fact, radical feminist therapists would completely reject formal assessment and diagnostic systems, seeing them as rooted in the patriarchal system that controls access to services and reinforces hierarchical systems within society (Enns, 1995). Other FT counselors, most likely liberal feminists, might use traditional diagnosis if it is a means to provide services to their clients.

Judith Worell and Pam Remer (2003) point out that traditional approaches to diagnosis and assessment minimize the effects of environment and culture. Further, as noted earlier, traditional approaches compare women's behavior to a male standard. Carolyn Enns (2000) gave the examples of "women have low self-esteem" as compared to "men are more conceited than women" (p. 619). Traditional approaches may also support the notion that differences between women and men are biological in nature. Just think for a minute about the popular book *Men Are from Mars, Women Are from Venus* (Gray, 1992). Not only are women and men unalterably different, but they are possibly different kinds of life forms!

Laura Brown (1993) proposed an alternative, a biopsychosocial model of distress, with emphasis on the social. This model emphasized the strengths of the client while also acknowledging the influences of culture, such as political forces and traditional social structures (e.g., heterosexuality, notions about "normal" families). As for traditional diagnosis, Brown (2006) contends that although *DSM*-IV labels are sometimes used by FT counselors, it is in the context of a much more detailed and broader approach that includes the factors above and an awareness of the therapists' own input into the process.

Chandra does no formal assessment or diagnosis with Susan. She sees these systems as confining and limiting, probably distorting the role of cultural norms in Susan's current distress.

OVERVIEW OF THE THERAPEUTIC ATMOSPHERE

Traditional approaches to psychotherapy are assumed to maintain the androcentric, patriarchal status quo by assisting women to "adjust" rather than to challenge stereotypes and oppression (Worell & Johnson, 2001). In Phyllis Chesler's words, "For most women the (middle-class-oriented) psychotherapeutic encounter is just one more instance of an unequal relationship, just one more opportunity to be rewarded for expressing distress and to be 'helped' by being (expertly) dominated" (1972, p. 108).

Marecek and Kravetz (1998) suggested that, in fact, the feminist therapist is really in a dilemma because she is supporting an enterprise that focuses on the self apart from history and culture, assumes free choice, and assumes that individualism is realistic and to be desired. Feminist therapists who see therapy as a patriarchal, class-bound system that simply perpetuates the status quo advocate consciousness-raising groups and social action instead of traditional psychotherapy (Enns, 1995). Laura Brown (1994), on the other hand, carefully considered the merger of feminist politics and therapy and concluded that feminist therapy is not an oxymoron.

Some FT counselors argue that therapy is best done in groups because this approach minimizes power differentials between therapist and clients (Enns, 1995). Worell and Remer (2003) add that groups allow women to become empowered through helping heal each other and collectively engaging in efforts to promote social change.

Chandra has given a great deal of thought to the feasibility of feminist therapy. She has examined her own beliefs about what counseling is about, and blends an empowerment approach with a relational one. She seeks to help Susan accept her "feminine" tendencies, while at the same time accepting her own power as a person.

Roles of Client and Counselor

One thing all FT theorists agree on: the promotion of an egalitarian relationship between therapist and client is essential to FT. Because of the therapist's professional qualifications, an inherent power imbalance in therapy is assumed; the counselor must acknowledge this imbalance and discuss it with the client (Enns, 2004). That the counselor determines the time and place of meetings and that clients pay counselors for their time means that *egalitarian* does not mean *totally equal*. At the same time, the client and counselor are assumed to be equally expert (Enns, 2004; Gilbert, 1980). The client is an expert on herself, and the therapist owns her professional knowledge and expertise. The therapist's power is temporary and lies in knowledge of the change process and assisting client empowerment (Brown, 2000).

Brown (2000) pointed out that "the empowerment of the client, is not, after all, the disempowerment of the therapist" (p. 372). She suggested that one of the ways in which feminist therapists use power is to remind clients of their own power. Also, feminist therapists see power in the ability to nurture and care and to listen calmly to the terrifyingly painful stories of their clients (Brown, 2000).

Part of the client's power stems from her willingness to enter the therapy relationship. Acknowledging this temporary form of dependency represents resistance to the patriarchal dictate that dependency needs be expressed only indirectly or in socially sanctioned ways (Brown, 2000). Further, the client is seen as possessing unique knowledge of herself (Enns, 1995). Feminist therapists emphasize that the client has the power to define herself within a personal and cultural context (Brown, 2000).

Chandra discloses her own sense of power to Susan, saying that she will do her best to help Susan find her own way in life. Emphasizing Susan's strengths and struggles, Chandra lets her know that she respects Susan's willingness to come for help. Chandra also lets Susan know that she (Susan) is the expert on her life and that she expects Susan to contribute this expertise to the counseling process.

Goals

The most important objective of FT is simple: to empower clients (Gilbert & Rader, 2007). FT counselors work to help clients accept their personal power in life and to teach them the difference between power within and coercive power, or power over others (Enns, 2007). They do not encourage the client to adjust to circumstances, unless the client has carefully explored her options and freely chooses to do so. Thus, an important part of empowering the client is the therapist's acceptance of the client's goals. However, the therapist helps the client explore a wide range of life possibilities.

Laura Brown (2000) offered a more radical view when she argued that "each act of feminist therapy must have as a goal the uncovering of the presence of the patriarchy as a source of distress, in order to name, undermine, resist, and subvert such oppressive influences" (p. 367). Woman of color feminists see the development of *conscientizacao*, or critical consciousness, as the goal of counseling (Comas-Diaz, 1994). Increasing the client's awareness of colonization and accompanying internalized racism leads them to be aware of their location in society and consciously criticize social norms and structures. They take action in the environment aimed at transformation.

Chandra is committed to helping Susan find her way in life and helping her recognize that she has the personal power to do so. Part of her task is to help Susan look at the forces in her life that both support and hinder her journey, particularly societal attitudes and structures that keep women and individuals of non-Caucasian cultures oppressed. These are Chandra's general goals; she also is very careful to discover what Susan's goals are, make these clear and concrete, and devise ways to reach them.

Susan wants to "get the world off her back." Chandra empathizes with Susan and supports Susan's goal.

PROCESS OF THERAPY

The principles of feminist therapy, as developed by the 1993 National Conference on Education and Training in Feminist Practice (Worell & Johnson, 1997) are shown in Box 12.2.

FT counselors believe that value-free counseling is impossible (Enns, 2004). Therefore, the FT counselor must be aware of her own values and beliefs, particularly those that involve sex, gender, race, and class. Yet another important realization is that we are embedded in a heterosexist culture (Enns, 2000). Some feminist therapists will directly communicate their feminist perspective to their clients; others hesitate to use the term *feminist* because of the stereotypes associated with it. Most important, however, is that the FT counselor not impose her value system on clients (Enns, 2004).

One important way the feminist therapist attempts to enhance equality and collaboration with her clients is to give the client information about FT counseling and request the client's informed consent (Enns, 2000). The *therapy contract* was developed first by feminist therapists and has since been widely adopted by adherents of other theoretical orientations (Brown, 1994). Contracting involves the client and therapist in a collaborative process of determining the goals and pace of the counseling process. The FT counselor explains her approach to helping, the costs and benefits of counseling, the roles of client and counselor, and other features of the process that she deems relevant (Enns, 2004). These points, along with agreed-upon goals, may be put in writing or handled more informally.

One intent of informed consent and contracting is to *demystify* the therapeutic process. To make the FT process accessible to the client, FT counselors avoid jargon. Another way to demystify the therapy process is the careful use of self-disclosure on the part of the therapist (Wyche & Rice, 1997). Such disclosure is meant to emphasize the shared experiences of client and counselor, and of all women and to equalize power in the relationship (Worell & Remer, 2003). However, the counselor must be careful not to discount the very significant effects of other factors associated with oppression, such as race, sexual identity, and ableness.

In FT, resistance is defined as the person's healthy attempt to defeat oppression (Brabeck & Brown, 1997). In fact, Laura Brown (1994) endorsed teaching clients resistance to the patriarchy as one aspect of FT. Client feelings about or reactions to the therapist and therapy are not typically labeled as "transference" and considered problematic. Instead, FT counselors welcome client feedback about the process, and especially, expressions of anger because women are taught to supress such expression (Worell and Remer, 2003).

The question often arises whether men can be feminist therapists, and if FT is appropriate for men. Box 12.4 presents a perspective on this question. Radical feminists would answer emphatically no! In 1994, Laura Brown, for example, suggested that although men could not truly be feminist therapists, they could be profeminist and antisexist in their approaches to counseling. However, she has since come to see this position as "essentialist and problematic" (Brown, 2006, p. 20). She now asserts that "if one can think as a feminist, think about gender, power, and social location, and if gender is socially constructed, then neither the biology or the gender of the person thinking like a feminist in the therapist position ought to matter" (p. 20). Espin (1994) argued that the best therapy for women of color is "ethno-specific," which means that the therapist is of the same ethnic or racial background as the client (p. 275).

Chandra and Susan develop a therapy contract, in writing, which specifies the goals that they have jointly developed. The contract is written in everyday language and includes the following agreements and goals:

1. *Susan and Chandra will actively work toward a useful therapy relationship with input from both parties.*
2. *The role of social and political factors in Susan's distress will be explored.*
3. *Susan and Chandra will explore Susan's thoughts and feelings about relationships, with the goal of helping Susan assume her own power in relationships so that her rights are not violated.*
4. *Susan and Chandra will explore the sources of Susan's anger, with special attention to its roots in social structures, attitudes, or practices that contribute to it.*

Box 12.4

Can Men be Feminist Therapists?

At first glance, the terms *feminist* and *male* seem to be contradictory. However, recent discussions of feminist therapy suggest that men, too, can adopt feminist perspectives that inform their counseling behaviors.

Szymanski, Baird, and Kornman (2002) decided to find out what these feminist male therapists were like. They surveyed 91 male counselors, finding that 18 of these counselors self-identified as feminists. They found that feminist male counselors differed from nonfeminist counselors on attitudes toward the women's movement and gender-role attitudes. They also endorsed counseling behaviors associated with feminist therapy. Self-identified feminist male counselors were more liberal in their gender-role attitudes, more positive toward the women's movement, and more likely to endorse therapy interventions such as establishing egalitarian relationships with clients and emphasizing the social construction of gender. Basically, these male therapists looked very much like female feminist therapists!

THERAPEUTIC TECHNIQUES

FT has few unique techniques. Any technique or approach is acceptable if it is used in a gender-fair way (Enns, 1995). Some therapists adopt and modify traditional counseling theories to fit feminist principles. Thus, there are psychodynamic, Jungian, and cognitive-behavioral approaches to FT (Enns, 1995). In this section I present several techniques that are the most closely identified with FT.

GENDER-ROLE ANALYSIS

Gender-role analysis is practically synonymous with FT. Clients are supported in a personal examination of cultural rules about female and male behavior and how these relate to client distress (Worell & Remer, 2003). Socialization processes are discussed in terms of how they relate to the client's current behaviors in the interest of detoxifying them. For example, what might be labeled "dependent" behavior can be construed as behavior that is powerfully reinforced by our society as being appropriate to the female role (Philpot, Brooks, Lusterman, & Nutt, 1997). The client is helped to understand the origins of her behaviors in social norms and oppressive environments, and the possible consequences of changing them (Enns, 2004).

Chandra is very interested in Susan's belief that she has trouble letting go of relationships. She guides Susan through an analysis of this characterization and its potential roots in an exaggeration of traditional sex roles that are reinforced by the dominant culture. Chandra and Susan also explore the values of Susan's adoptive mother, who was raised in a very traditional society. How these influences shaped Susan's view of herself and her behavior are examined in an attempt to depathologize Susan's behavior and move the locus of the problem to the political realm.

SELF-DISCLOSURE

Another approach to equalizing power imbalances in FT is for the therapist to use self-disclosure (Enns, 2004). Wyche and Rice (1997) suggested that there is no current consensus on the use of this technique. As noted earlier, therapist self-disclosure is helpful in demystifying the counseling process and in emphasizing the shared experiences of women. Any self-disclosure by the therapist must be in the interests of the client rather than to satisfy any need of the therapist (Wyche & Rice, 1997).

Chandra considers whether disclosure on her part would be helpful to Susan. She decides that because Susan doesn't seem to have a sense of community with other women, some disclosure is appropriate. Briefly, Chandra speaks of her struggles with autonomy in a world that gives power to males. Susan reacts positively to this disclosure and goes on to a productive examination of her own experiences.

ASSERTIVENESS TRAINING

Popular in the 1970s, assertiveness training teaches the pursuit of one's rights without violating the rights of others (Jakubowski, 1977a). Assertiveness is distinguished from aggression, which involves the violation of others' rights, and nonassertiveness, which is allowing one's own rights to be violated. Patricia Jakubowski, a well-known writer in this area, commented that assertiveness "is a direct, honest, and appropriate expression of one's thoughts, feelings, and beliefs" (1977a, p. 147). Respect for self and other is an important element of assertive behavior. You might have noticed that nonassertive behavior fits the stereotypical female behaviors such as putting the needs of others first, withholding opinions, and "being nice."

Assertiveness training was developed to teach women to abandon their culturally approved nonassertive behaviors. Most often, assertiveness training was conducted in groups (and typically, women-only groups), although it can be used in individual counseling as well. Jakubowski (1977b) identified four components of assertiveness training: (a) teaching the distinctions among assertive, nonassertive, and aggressive behavior and helping clients observe their own behaviors; (b) teaching clients a philosophy that respects individual rights and supports assertive behavior; (c) removing or reducing the salience of factors that inhibit assertive behavior; and (d) teaching assertive skills through practice (p. 169). A combination of teaching and group discussion is used to teach clients the differences among assertive, aggressive, and nonassertive behavior as well as to promote basic assertive philosophy. Many Behavior Therapy techniques are used in assertiveness training, including role-playing and self-observation. Systematic desensitization is sometimes used to reduce the anxiety around the new behaviors (Jakubowski, 1977b).

Chandra decides to work with Susan on increasing her assertive behavior and decreasing the angry, aggressive behavior that she occasionally displays. However, Chandra is very aware that Susan's anger is a form of strength and stems from her resistance to confining societal norms. For this reason, Chandra does not want to take Susan's anger away; it is a valid and healthy emotion. Susan and Chandra role-play situations in which Susan is likely to be nonassertive as well as those in which she is prone to anger.

EVALUATION OF THE THEORY

Criticisms of FT come from both within and outside of the women's movement. Most of you are probably familiar with the so-called backlash against feminism: feminists are man-haters engaged in male bashing. FT can also be criticized for being a political stance rather than a theory of therapy. The diversity of views within FT leads to the charge that it is not clear what FT actually is, beyond a set of beliefs.

Radical feminists reject FT because *any* kind of therapy is a tool of the patriarchal, oppressive society (Chesler, 1972). Cultural feminists charge that FT is based on the experiences of white, middle-class women and therefore neglects discrimination and disempowerment based on race, social class, sexual orientation, and other factors (Alleyne, 1998).

Sharon Baron Spiegel (1979) questioned the usefulness of a special, separate set of principles for counseling women. Arguing that such an approach was not yet justified empirically, she pointed out that other client characteristics could be more important than gender (e.g., social class). Developing separate sets of principles for the various groupings of clients could prove divisive to the profession of counseling, according to Spiegel. Also, nonsexist values and knowledge about women's experience is important for men, too. Spiegel advocated a generalist model for counseling that adopts nonsexist values, but that does not replace one set of biases with another.

QUALITIES OF THE THEORY

Precision and Testability. FT is not very testable in terms of a theory of human behavior. It does rely on volumes of research on sex roles and gender issues, however. Aspects of FT can and have been operationalized, such as assertiveness training, gender-role analysis, and therapist self-disclosure. However, some of these activities are not unique to FT.

Empirical Validity. Outcome research on FT as a counseling approach is sparse. The basic tenets of the approach, such as sex-role issues and socialization, are empirically supported.

RESEARCH SUPPORT

Very little research has been conducted on the actual practice or outcome of FT. Because of its philosophical basis and tendency to be technically eclectic, it is difficult for proponents to agree upon what exactly constitutes the theory of FT. This situation, of course, is a major factor in the lack of research bearing directly on the theory and practice of FT (Murray, 2006). For these reasons, I will present a broad selection of research relevant to the FT approach, and in doing so, will dispense with my usual distinction between outcome and theory-testing research.

Some of its proponents would argue that FT is not unique—it is simply good therapy (Worell & Johnson, 2001). Nonetheless, Worell and Johnson maintained that FT is an identifiable approach, basing their arguments on a series of survey studies of therapists and clients. Using an instrument called the Therapy with Women Scale (based on the principles in Box 12.2), differences in philosophy and goals can be documented between feminist and nonfeminist therapists (Worell & Johnson, 2001). Important factors underlying these differences were (a) affirming the client, (b) women-centered activism, (c) the use of self-disclosure, (d) adopting a gender-role perspective, and (e) an egalitarian stance. In contrast, Andrea Chester and Diane Bretherton (2001) found less agreement about the essential elements of FT in their sample of Australian feminist therapists. In their research, the largest area of agreement was that FT involved woman-centered concerns (e.g., sociopolitical analysis of problems, understanding sex-role stereotypes, critique of the patriarchy), with 85% of their sample listing these issues as essential to FT.

Looking at client perceptions, Gail Hackett and Carolyn Enns (Enns & Hackett, 1990; Hackett, Enns, & Zetzer, 1992) demonstrated that feminist therapists are perceived positively by samples of college students. In Enns and Hackett's (1990) study, college women who were either feminist or not viewed either liberal feminist, radical feminist, or humanistic-nonfeminist counselors on videotape. The researchers also varied the type of problem for which participants were judging the acceptability of the counselor. Somewhat surprisingly, Enns and Hackett found that all participants, regardless of attitudes, preferred the feminist counselors to the nonfeminist counselors when career decision making, sexual harassment, or assault was the issue. Using a similar method, Hackett and colleagues varied the mode of presentation of the counselor (videotape or written materials) and found no effect of presentation. Overall, the liberal FT counselor was perceived more favorably than nonsexist or radical FT counselors. Of course, the generalizability of the results of these studies beyond college women is risky.

Jill Rader and Lucia Albino Gilbert (2005) attempted to test whether counselors who identified as feminist exemplified their orientations in terms of egalitarianism, here defined as power sharing and collaboration. Forty-two female therapists were recruited, and 34 clients of these therapists participated as well (some of the clients recruited did not return their materials). Nineteen of the therapists identified themselves as feminists; interestingly, when clients were asked if their therapists were feminists, their identifications matched their therapists' about 50% of the time. The study confirmed the centrality of egalitarianism to FT: power sharing was reported more frequently by therapists identifying as feminist and also by the clients of these therapists, when compared to therapists who did not identify as feminist. Another interesting aspect of this study was that when all of the therapists were asked if they used the behaviors considered characteristic of FT (similar to those identified in Box 12.2), no differences were found between the groups of therapists, mainly because all of them reported that they consistently acted in those ways with their clients.

Some of the research that is relevant to FT focused on the effectiveness of consciousness-raising groups and assertiveness training. This research is dated and can be criticized on a number of methodological grounds (Enns, 1993). In one study of actual FT, Ronald Mancoske and colleagues (Mancoske, Standifer, & Cauley, 1994) produced somewhat disappointing results for advocates of FT. Groups of battered women were offered either grief counseling or feminist counseling (after crisis intervention). Clients in FT did not show statistically significant improvement, whereas the clients who underwent grief counseling did. However, this study used a very small sample of clients (20 per group), and two therapists (the study's authors) conducted all of the therapy groups. These factors (plus the lack of definition of the approaches) very likely limited the power of the study to find significant differences.

Studies of feminist identity development theory (FIDT) indirectly address FT because it is often used as the basis for thinking about women in counseling. Several measures of FIDT have been developed, but unfortunately, although some psychometric data on these scales are supportive, other data do not confirm the proposed stage structure built into the instruments (Moradi & Subich, 2002a). One study suggested that an often-used measure (the Feminist Identity Development Scale; Bargad & Hyde, 1991) produces a different factor structure when used with other than traditional white Caucasian female groups (Flores, Carfubba, & Good, 2006).

Given the measurement problems, then the results of studies of FIDT should be viewed cautiously. One study related to the feminist therapy behaviors of women psychotherapists (Juntunen, Atkinson, Reyes, & Gutierrez, 1994) found that revelation stage attitudes were the best predictor of whether a therapist self-identified as a feminist therapist. Further, therapists who had high scores on synthesis and revelation attitudes and low scores on passive acceptance endorsed more feminist therapy behaviors than did those with the opposite pattern.

Studies of feminist identity development and psychological distress have produced inconsistent results. For instance, Bonnie Moradi and Linda Mezydlo Subich (2002b) looked at the relationships among the stage of feminist identity development, experience with sexist events, and psychological symptoms. Passive acceptance attitudes, which these researchers conceptualized as evidence that the participant was denying the existence of sexism, were related to greater occurrence of symptoms given the occurrence of sexist events over the past year. Natalie Sabik and Tracy Tylka (2006) also examined the relations between FIDT and perceived sexist events, but they were interested in dysfunctional eating patterns. Only Synthesis and Active Commitment attitudes predicted problematic eating (that is, women lower on these scales tended to score high on disordered eating), and these attitudes explained some of the relationship between experiencing sexist events and the eating issues. Ann Fischer and Glen Good studied FIDT, anger, and psychological symptoms, and found that only the identity stage of Revelation related to symptoms. Anger was associated with Revelation attitudes but not with the other FIDT stages, and except for Revelation, did not explain the relationship between FIDT and distress, contrary to Fischer and Good's expectations. However, the authors noted that the anger measured was general, not specific to the patriarchy or other relevant targets. Kendra Saunders and Susan Kashubeck-West (2006) found that feminist identity was related to self-reported psychological well-being: Active Commitment positively, and Revelation negatively. That is, women who scored higher on Active Commitment reported higher levels of well-being than women lower on this dimension and women higher on Revelation reported lower levels of psychological well-being compared to women lower on Revelation attitudes.

In a study that bears on feminist identity and intervention, Rachel Peterson and colleagues tested whether teaching female college students feminist views on body image could affect their levels of body satisfaction and feminist identity (Peterson, Tantleff-Dunn, & Bedwell, 2005). Participants were pre- and posttested, and then exposed to a 15-minute audiotape of traditional psychoeducation about body image, a feminist intervention, or no intervention. No effects of treatment were observed on body image dissatisfaction but the feminist intervention did appear to create change in satisfaction with appearance (without going into tedious detail, these two measures were different in content and form). Although participants showed increased self-identification as feminists when compared to the other two groups, only one effect of intervention was observed for feminist identity: contrary to hypothesis, participants in the feminist intervention group decreased in their Active Commitment scores. Peterson et al. speculated that simply completing the FIDT may have made them realize how inactive they really were, thus causing a decline in the scores at posttest.

Before you read the next paragraph, look at Box 12.5.

Much research has focused on whether counselors are sexist. The "grandmother" of this line of investigation was a study conducted by Inge Broverman and her colleagues (Broverman, Broverman, Clarkson, Rosenkrantz, & Vogel, 1970). They asked practicing therapists to describe a healthy man, a healthy woman, and a healthy person, sex unspecified. To the horror of many, they found that the qualities of the healthy person most resembled the qualities of the healthy male. Healthy women were rated lower on qualities such as independence, adventurousness, aggression, and competitiveness than were men. In addition, healthy women were seen as easier to influence, more excitable, and submissive in comparison to men. As you might guess, this study incited great controversy.

Broverman and colleagues' study has been criticized for a number of reasons (Phillips & Gilroy, 1985; Widiger & Settle, 1987). On a most basic level, the study could be faulted because the counselor participants were rating hypothetical individuals, not responding to a "real" client. Also, Widiger and Settle (1987) provided convincing evidence that the findings of Broverman and colleagues could be almost entirely attributed to characteristics of

---

Box 12.5

Consider the following adjectives:

Independent

Assertive

Strong

Confident

Do these words describe a male or a female? Are they healthy qualities or not? Here are some more words to consider:

Passive

Easily excited by minor events

Dependent

Cautious

Ask yourself what picture came to mind as you read these words.

These are some of the adjectives presented in the famous study of sexism among counselors conducted by Broverman, Broverman, Clarkson, Rosenkrantz, and Vogel in 1970.

---

the method used. Subsequent studies have been inconsistent in their findings, and are now somewhat dated. Since *overt* sexism in society is thought to be decreasing (Campbell, Shellenberg, & Senn, 1997), it would seem that counselors would be unlikely to respond in sexist ways to research stimuli. Whether this evenhandedness is a result of a true change in attitudes or "underground sexism" is up for debate. Also, a few studies have suggested that sexism may still exist among therapists (Fowers, Applegate, Tredinnick, & Slusher, 1996; Turner & Turner, 1991).

ISSUES OF INDIVIDUAL AND CULTURAL DIVERSITY

It would seem obvious that FT is a good approach to use with women. However, some radical feminists would object to using a liberal FT approach because they would see it as upholding the patriarchal status quo. A major bedrock of early FT, assertiveness training, for example, has been criticized as based on a model that views stereotypically female behavior as deficient (Fodor, 1985).

FT is grounded in sensitivity to oppression, so it can be considered to be very appropriate for use with individuals from diverse backgrounds. Earlier versions of FT, based on White, middle-class experience, have been accused of racism, but contemporary feminist therapists recognize the influence of other important dimensions on the experiences of women, such as class, age, ableness, sexual orientation, and race/ethnicity (Brown, Riepe, & Coffey, 2005). Feminism recognizes the heteropatriarchy, and lesbian feminism is an alternative for women who are lesbian. Indeed, feminist scholars have always attended to issues relevant in theory and practice with lesbian and bisexual women (Brown et al., 2005). Increasing attention to issues of diversity have resulted in explorations of the implication of feminism for African American (Williams, 2005), Latina (Lijtmaer, 1998), biracial (Nishimura, 2004), and Japanese (Matsuyuki, 1998) clients, among others. However, some critics of FT continue to remind us of the White female bias present in FT (Espin, 1993).

The question always arises about the appropriateness of FT for male clients. Some feminist therapists argue that it is very helpful for men to examine the social aspects of their existence, particularly for the privileged White male. These types of concerns, along with the recognition that men experience significant gender-role conflict, have prompted the development of gender-aware or gender-sensitive therapy (Good, Gilbert, & Scher, 1990; Philpot et al., 1997). These approaches integrate feminist principles with a broad examination of gender. Men in gender-aware therapy are encouraged to explore the ramifications of traditional male roles, develop stronger interpersonal skills, and decrease their emphasis on career and work aspects of identity.

THE CASE STUDY

Susan seems to be an ideal client for FT. She is engaged in the pursuit of a traditionally male-dominated career. However, the adoption of this career goal may be partly a result of the norm of Asian culture that values scholastic achievement above all. Susan reports relationship difficulties that seem to involve both extreme expressions of femininity and violations of the cultural norms that women should not be angry or aggressive. These characteristics would predict a good fit with FT. She has also been the victim of abuse, an injustice that lies at the heart of the feminist movement.

Susan's Asian heritage raises questions about applying FT. If her adoptive mother heavily reinforced the "proper" characteristics of women in the Asian culture, ignoring this influence would be a serious mistake. The goals of empowerment and liberation may be in conflict with Susan's culturally linked values. However, in other ways, Susan seems to be fairly acculturated to the United States, if the adoption of her nontraditional career goal is any indication.

Summary

Feminist therapy is more of a philosophical approach to working with clients than a defined theoretical structure. Feminist therapists are attentive to the norms of society that confer power and status on men and oppress women. The social pressure to conform to stereotypical notions of what it means to be a man or woman are seen as important influences on how people behave. Feminist therapists also recognize the effects of social class, race/ethnicity, ableness, and sexual orientation on individuals' lives; individuals who are not of the "majority" on these dimensions are subject to oppression by society.

FT counselors believe that the personal is political and that women's (and other oppressed groups') struggles are the result of societal structures and norms that are disparaging of women and celebratory of men. The norm for "healthy person" is based on stereotypically male qualities (e.g., rational, independent, and so forth), whereas traditionally female qualities are seen as less valuable (e.g., emotionality and connectedness).

Women are damned if they do and damned if they don't—social penalties are imposed for expressions of female traits and masculine traits by women.

Feminist therapists approach counseling with an egalitarian attitude, recognizing that true equality will not exist in the therapy relationship. They attempt to recognize and minimize power imbalances in therapy by forming therapy contracts and demystifying the therapy process. The goal of FT is empowering the client so that she can achieve her life goals. Few techniques are specific to FT, although one very closely tied to this approach is the analysis of social roles.

FT has been criticized for being anti-male and for being a political stance rather than a theoretical system. Radical feminists may totally disagree with doing FT at all. Because of the emphasis within FT on societal power imbalances and oppression, it is likely to be a valuable approach for individuals who are of diverse backgrounds.

Visit Chapter 12 on the Companion Website at **www.prenhall.com/murdock** for chapter-specific resources and self-assessments.

CHAPTER 13

Family Systems Theory

Virginia Satir

Jean and Derril, mother and son, come to counseling because Jean is concerned about Derril's angry behavior. Jean is African American and Derril is of multiracial heritage; his father is Caucasian. Derril, age 12, is Jean's only son with his father, Al, but she has a daughter from a previous relationship who is 20 years old and married with children. Jean is 42 years old, currently single, and not dating anyone.

Jean and Al, Derril's father, were married for about 6 years. They divorced 2 years ago. Last year Al moved in with a woman who has three children. Derril lives with his mother, but spends Sunday mornings at church with his father. He reports having no real desire to see his father and says that he does not get along with his father's girlfriend or her kids. Jean and Al divorced because of severe relationship conflict, which often resulted in physical abuse of Jean. On some occasions, Derril stepped in to interrupt the abuse. Currently, Jean and Al are on speaking terms, but do not appear to get along well. She reports feeling uncomfortable if she is alone with Al.

Jean has a bachelor's degree in business and works as an administrator in a government agency. Her family lives in the immediate vicinity, but although they used to spend a lot of time together, they recently have not done so. Jean says she has few friends. She does not spend much time with her daughter, although Derril sometimes spends the night with the daughter and her children. Both Jean and Derril report that they spend much of their time together.

Derril's behavior became increasingly troublesome, according to Jean, after his father moved in with his girlfriend. The incident that actually brought Jean and Derril into counseling involved an altercation with the security guard at school. Derril reportedly was "talking back" to the officer and became more and more angry as the guard "got in his face." The security guard eventually shoved Derril against a locker. As a result of this incident, Derril was suspended from school for 10 days.

More recently, Derril's problematic behavior appears to have become less severe, but something seems to happen about every other week. For example, Jean reported that Derril was expelled from the extended day program at school because he slapped a boy who was "talking about his mama." Jean says that she is not sure how to handle such behavior and that she is afraid of the way her son treats women and adults. She says that Derril has no respect for his elders, and that she has been unable to find any way to change his behavior.

BACKGROUND

At first glance, it might seem a little strange to include a chapter on family systems (FS) theory in a book otherwise devoted to theories focused primarily on individuals. Even if it weren't my favorite set of theories, though, I'd still include this chapter for several reasons. First, family systems theory is considered one of the major schools of counseling and psychotherapy. Second, an FS approach can be used with individual clients; family systems theorists believe that they can best understand the individual through understanding his experiences as a member of the family. Opinions vary as to whether doing FS therapy without the complete family group is effective, however.

I will review four major approaches to family systems intervention in this chapter: structural, strategic, the family systems theory of Murray Bowen, and the existential/humanistic approach of Virginia Satir. There are others, including the most recent additions, the constructivist theorists, such as the Narrative and Solution-Focused approaches, described in Chapters 14 and 15. Nichols (2006) classifies these two approaches as the wave of the future. However, they also acknowledge that family therapists readily borrow from various approaches so I have chosen to present the four approaches in this chapter because they are the historical bedrocks of FS theory and still influence many counselors currently. In this chapter, I will describe the "classic" versions of these approaches for the most part. However, most therapists probably draw from one or more of these approaches in their day-to-day work, integrating these ideas in a social constructivist framework. Because there is much to cover in the four approaches I have chosen, I will use an abbreviated form of the structure similar to that I used to present the neoanalytic theories in Chapter 3.

On the *Theories in Action* DVD, you can watch Dr. Paul Anderson do family systems therapy with the client Helen. Although Dr. Anderson's style is primarily Bowenian (see Section on Bowen theory later in this chapter), he draws from other systemic approaches, too.

A detailed history of family therapy and FS theory is beyond the scope of this chapter. Interested readers should consult Nichols (2006) or Guerin and Chabot (1995). A fascinating read is Simon's (1992) book, *One on One*, which reprints interviews with the leaders of the family therapy movement, including Jay Haley, Cloe Madanes, Salvador Minuchin, and Virginia Satir.

The professional community in family therapy is very active. Not all family counselors are family systems advocates, but I think it is safe to say that the majority probably incorporate some knowledge of systems in their work. More so than advocates of other theoretical perspectives, it seems, family systems therapists have a wide variety of professional affiliations. They may identify themselves as psychologists, professional counselors, social workers, or simply as couples/family therapists. One of the major organizations for family systems adherents is the American Association of Marriage and Family Therapists (AAMFT), which can be found at www.aamft.org. AAMFT publishes the *Journal of Marital and Family Therapy and the Family Therapy Magazine*. The American Psychological Association has a division of Family Psychology (43), which publishes a newsletter, *The Family Psychologist*, and has an official APA journal, *The Journal of Family Psychology*. Perhaps the most prestigious FS journal is *Family Process*, founded in 1967. The first editor of *Family Process* was Jay Haley, and the board of directors of the Family Process Institute, which publishes the journal, reads like a family systems who's who, including Peggy Papp, Salvador Minuchin, Virginia Satir, Don Jackson, and Gregory Bateson, among others. Murray Bowen was the first president of the American Family Therapy Academy, an organization of teachers, researchers, and practitioners devoted to family systems issues. This organization can be found at www.afta.org.

Before I begin my description of the four family systems approaches, I will highlight some important ideas shared by family systems theorists. First and foremost is the conceptualization of the *family as a system*. From this perspective, a family is seen as a system defined as a group of interrelated people "*plus the way they function*" (Nichols, 2006, p. 374; my italics). Family systems theorists are adamant that the best way to approach helping individuals is to see them in context, as a part of a larger system, and they tend to focus on the relationships among individuals who are members of the system (Becvar & Becvar, 2006).

For family systems theorists, the family is interconnected, and influences on one part of the system will affect other parts. The image of a mobile is helpful to illustrate this idea. Imagine that you have a mobile that consists of two sailboats, three speedboats and a cruise ship. All of the elements of the mobile are connected by a common supporting structure from which they hang. If you touch one of the sailboats, it floats in the direction of the cruise ship. At the same time, your touching the sailboat causes the speedboats to chase the sailboat. Much like the mobile, argue the FS theorists, moving one member of a family in any way will create movement in other parts of the system. Also note that there is no clear start or finish to the sequence of movements in the mobile—the cruise ship is not leading the sailboats; it could just as easily seem to be pursuing the speedboats. Note also that factors other than your fingers can influence this system's elements individually and as a group and that the influence of other factors (such as the social context of the system) can differentially influence its elements. For instance, a sharp breeze might cause all of the boats to move, but the sailboats might be more responsive than the cruise ship.

Consider this a common situation from the human sphere: when a child is acting out, we often observe that on the surface the parents are calm and intent on helping their child. If the child is "fixed," however, all of the sudden the parents begin to have serious battles. In FS terms, one of two things is happening here: the friction between the parents is either diffused by or channeled into the acting-out kid. When the pressure is released by the disappearance of the symptom, the conflict between the parents becomes clear.

Most families present with an individual who has been labeled by them as the "one with the problem." Because systems theorists resist the idea of problems within individuals, most FS therapists call this person the *identified patient* (IP).

Systems thinking leads to the attitude that the causes of a given behavior or problem are irrelevant because the system is an interlocking chain of events. Designating one event as causal to another is silly. Doing so is kind of like asking whether the chicken or the egg came first. Systems theorists use the term *circular causality* to describe this view of interaction. Contrast this circular view with a typical linear view of behavior A (of the IP) *causing* behavior B (parent's rage, grief, etc.). For example, Amy, an adolescent girl, likes to dress in a style reminiscent of Britney Spears (or Cher, for you older folks). Her mom shrieks that Amy looks horrible in these clothes. Does Amy back down and wear golf shirts and chinos? Of course not. She continues to favor her usual provocative things, and even manages to acquire more extreme examples, or perhaps even threatens to shave her head. Mom yells more, and so on. Did Amy cause the mom's yelling in the first place? Unlikely, say the systems theorists. Mom's focus on Amy may have led in the first place to her attempts to individuate by dressing like her peers. In this simple case, it is clearly difficult to say who caused what, and that is the point that the systems theorists want you to get. For this reason, FS therapists usually are more interested in the *process*, or how things happen in a family, than the *content* (the what) of the happenings (Becvar & Becvar, 2006).

Systems can be open or closed (Nichols & Schwartz, 2006). Open systems are those in which the parts are interactive and information flows into and out of the system easily. Closed systems don't allow information in or out, and this impermeability leads to rigidity and thus the inability to change and adjust with the environment.

Another important quality of systems that family therapy theorists emphasized is homeostasis—that is, the idea that systems tend to self-regulate and, therefore, to resist change. Even more important, this view implies that if you change one member in isolation, when they return to the system, the system will attempt to get the individual to change back. Nichols (2006) suggested that early in the history of systems theory, this tendency was overemphasized, causing theorists and therapists to overlook the inherent flexibility and growth displayed by families.

The Satir Approach

OVERVIEW

Although most refer to this approach as the Satir approach, Satir herself called her system the human validation process model. Virginia Satir (1916–1988) began her career as a family therapist when she enrolled in the master's degree program at the School of Social Service Administration at the University of Chicago in 1941 (McLendon & Davis, 2002). One of the original group of researchers at the Mental Research Institute (MRI) when it began in 1959, Satir published her influential book, *Conjoint Family Therapy* in 1967. Prior to her move to MRI, she had been seeing families in independent practice, and then directed the formation of a family therapy training program at the Illinois State Psychiatric Institute (Nichols, 2006). It is an interesting tidbit that she had also been reading the works of Murray Bowen and had met him in 1958 (Brothers, 2000).

Satir left MRI formally in 1964. For quite some time, she had been involved in the interesting things going on at the Esalen Institute in Big Sur, California, then one of the hotbeds of the human potential movement (Anderson, 2004; McLendon & Davis, 2002). Many leaders of the movement came through Esalen at that time, including Fritz Perls. As a result, Satir's ideas became more experiential and humanistic than those of the other family therapy schools and incorporated attention to emotional and physical experience into her work. Satir emphasized the uniqueness of people and that "contact with the self and the other was a sacred, spiritual event" (Haber, 2002, p. 23).

From a professional/theoretical standpoint, Satir's ideas became less influential in the 1970s, and she eventually moved away from the family therapy profession (Nichols & Schwartz, 2001). A pivotal public debate in 1974 truly seemed to alienate Satir from mainstream family therapy. During this debate, Salvador Minuchin criticized her humanistic stance. Nichols and Schwartz (2001) summarized it this way:

> Minuchin argued that it (family therapy) was a science that required skills rather than just warmth and faith, and that the main job was to fix broken families. Satir stuck to her belief in the healing power of love, and spoke out for the salvation of humankind through family therapy. It turned out that Minuchin was speaking for the field. (pp. 174–175)

According to Gurman and Fraenkel (2002), Satir felt "unappreciated and marginalized by the newer waves of (male) family systems engineers" (p. 215).

Satir was renowned as a therapist adept at moving large groups while demonstrating her work. Her 1972 book *Peoplemaking*, according to McLendon and Davis (2002) "became a household guide to healthy family living" (p. 177). Satir was as naturally charismatic as Minuchin, and that is really saying something.

In 1977, Satir created Avanta, an educational organization, now international in scope and still functioning. It can be found at http://www.avanta.net/. In 2006, The Satir Institute of the Pacific (satirpacific.org) launched a new journal, *The Satir Journal: Transformational Systemic Therapy*.

CENTRAL CONSTRUCTS

SELF-ESTEEM

The cornerstone of Satir's approach is self-esteem or self-worth. In Box 13.1 you can read Satir's manifesto about self-esteem. Self-esteem is defined as the degree to which the individual values himself regardless of the opinions of others (Satir & Baldwin, 1983). Loving the self is a precondition for loving others (Satir, 1988). People with low self-worth are anxious and uncertain about themselves and overly concerned with others' evaluations of them.

Low self-esteem is thought to be catching. Satir and Baldwin (1983) asserted that "often a person with low self-esteem selects to marry another person with low self-esteem. Their relationship is based on a disregard of inner feelings, and any stress tends to augment their feelings of low self-esteem. Children growing up in that environment usually have low self-worth" (p. 195).

Parents who have good self-esteem are able to teach what they already know (Satir, 1988). Parents who have shaky senses of self-worth cannot teach what they don't have. However, one can learn self-esteem even as an adult, if one is willing.

For Satir, self-esteem resides in the acknowledgment of the uniqueness and worth of each individual. She wrote, "You are a member of the human race, and as such, *you are a miracle*. Furthermore, you are a "one of a kind" miracle" (Satir, 1978, p. 9; italics and quotes in original).

Alice considers herself to be a proponent of Satir's approach. As she begins her relationship with Derril and Jean, she assumes that they are unique individuals with great potential.

Box 13.1
===

My Declaration of Self-Esteem

I am me.

In all the world, there is no one else exactly like me. There are persons who have some parts like me, but no one adds up exactly like me. Therefore, everything that comes out of me is authentically mine because I alone choose it.

I own everything about me—my body, including everything it does; my mind, including all its thoughts and ideas; my eyes, including the images of all they behold; my feelings, whatever they may be—anger, joy, frustration, love, disappointment, excitement; my mouth, and all the words that come out of it, polite, sweet, or rough, correct or incorrect; my voice, loud or soft; and all my actions, whether they be to others or to myself.

I own my fantasies, my dreams, my hopes, my fears.

I own all my triumphs and successes, all my failures and mistakes.

Because I own all of me, I can become intimately acquainted with me. By so doing I can love me and be friendly with me in all my parts. I can then make it possible for all of me to work in my best interests.

I know there are aspects about myself that puzzle me, and other aspects I do not know. But as long as I am friendly and loving to myself, I can courageously and hopefully look for the solutions to the puzzles and for ways to find out more about me.

However I look and sound, whatever I say and do, and whatever I think and feel at a given moment in time is me. This is authentic and represents where I am at that moment in time.

When I review later how I looked and sounded, what I said and did, and how I thought and felt, some parts may turn out to be unfitting. I can discard that which is unfitting, and keep that which proved fitting, and invent something new for that which I discarded.

I can see, hear, feel, think, say, and do. I have the tools to survive, to be close to others, to be productive, and to make sense and order out of the world of people and things outside of me.

I own me, and therefore I can engineer me.

I am me and I am okay.

Reprinted with permission from *Making Contact* by Virginia Satir. Copyright © 1976 by Virginia Satir, Celestial Arts, Berkeley, CA. Available from your local bookseller, by calling Ten Speed Press at 800-841-2665, or by visiting us online at www.tenspeed.com.

Because they are experiencing life difficulties, she suspects that both of them have low self-esteem. Likely Jean and Al have difficulty talking about their own feelings and respecting those of others. It appears to Alice that Derril has learned some of this orientation from his parents.

Self Mandala

Satir maintained that human essence has eight aspects: the body, thoughts, feelings, senses, relationships, context, nutrition, and soul (Satir, 1988). None of these parts functions independently. Attention to each of these spheres is critical for individuals' health, both psychological and physiological.

Alice sees her clients as multifaceted. In this case, she notes that Derril and Jean are very preoccupied with thoughts and feelings and seem to neglect attention to other important areas of the self. She thinks that it might help Derril and Jean to focus on body, senses, context, nutrition, and soul.

Communication

For Satir, the process and outcome of communication is critical to family life (Satir, 1967). We must be able to communicate with others to survive. Functional communication is clear, complete, and assertive. Congruent communication refers to communication in which verbal and nonverbal messages match; in incongruent communications, they don't (Brothers, 2000). Metacommunication (i.e., communication about communication) can affirm or disqualify a message, and often conveys something about the relationship between interactants.

At the most basic level, a communication between two individuals is a request for validation of one by the other. If Tammy's supervisor is acting unpredictably, Tammy wants me, her friend, to validate her experience by saying, "That woman is impossible!"

When individuals are stressed, they usually resort to one of four problematic patterns of communication (Satir, 1972): *placating, blaming, computing,* and *distracting* (p. 59). In all cases, these stances are the product of low self-esteem and are attempts to cover up vulnerability. All of us usually can communicate in these modes, but we usually have a preferred stance (Satir & Baldwin, 1983).

The *placator* is the "yes person," who is always trying to get others to approve of him. He ingratiates and apologizes. He communicates in whiny tones. To experience this stance, Satir recommended that you get down on one knee, stretch one hand out in begging fashion, and stretch your neck and head upward.

The *blamer* is the bossy dictator. She has a loud, shrill voice and is tense and tight. The stance of the blamer is one hand on hip, with the other forming the pointing finger.

Computers analyze everything and show very little feeling about anything. Sometimes referred to as the "superreasonable" (Brothers, 2000), these folks are sensible and rational, but distant and cool to others. Physically, the computer is stiff and still, as though she has a long metal rod running from the base of the spine to the nape of the neck.

The *distractor* is the buzzbrain. He makes no sense, has a singsong voice, and never addresses a point directly. Satir provided the image of a lopsided spinning top, with arms, body, and mouth moving almost randomly, going in many directions at once.

Healthy folks, contended Satir, operate from the stance of *leveling*. This person communicates coherently, and body, words, and vocal tone all fit together. Another term for healthy communication that Satir used is *congruent*. One who is congruent and levels has high self-esteem and thus has no need to hide; communication is free and honest. Of all of the stances, "only the leveling one has any chance to heal ruptures, break impasses, or build bridges between people" (Satir, 1972, p. 73).

Alice watches Jean and Derril interact in the counseling session. It seems clear to Alice that Jean and Derril are taking a blaming stance in relation to each other a lot of the time. In talking with Jean, Alice decides that Jean and Al probably take this stance in relation to each other as well. However, every now and then, Alice observes authentic, caring interchanges between Jean and Derril, signs of the very real connection that sustains both of them.

Alice senses many messages in the communication that she observes between Jean and Derril. Jean tells Derril to respect others with a very bossy tone of voice that is not respectful to him. Derril says he wants to act like a grown man, but something in the way he says this conveys that he is not really convinced that he can.

PRIMARY TRIAD

The concept of the triangle is an important one in all family systems theories. A triangle is any grouping of three family members, or for that matter, any three people. Satir labels the mother-father-child triangle the *primary triad*, and this relationship is the most important influence on an individual's life functioning (Satir, Banmen, Gerber, & Gomori, 1991). Children learn from the primary triad how to cope with the world, the nature of relationships (whether one can trust others), and how to understand communication.

Inconsistencies in communication (i.e., discrepancies between verbal and nonverbal channels) are inevitable in the family, and how children interpret these is an important form of early learning. For example, if Mom comes home from work mad, she may say nothing's wrong. Little Kevin, however, picks up on the nonverbal message of anger. If the confused kid mistakenly thinks Mom's anger is his fault, his self-worth is likely to be undermined. According to Satir, it would be better for Mom to simply explain that she had a rotten day at work and that the boss is a jerk.

It is the nature of triangles that one person often feels excluded from the relationship of the other two. How the child interprets the occasional exclusion from the parental dyad is critical. If Mary believes that she is being rejected, she is likely to develop low self-worth.

The child's ideas about personal power are also formed in relation to the primary triad (Satir & Baldwin, 1983). Parental interactions demonstrate power operations. Also, kids often learn that they can persuade one parent to take their side against the other parent. This pattern is often seen when one parent disciplines the child and the other breaks in to rescue him.

Satir emphasized that although many theories of family life seem to promote the negative aspects of the triangle, it is important to remember that the power of the triangle can be positive, too (Satir & Baldwin, 1983). Much support can be gained from the three-person configuration. If the three parties in the triad have good self-esteem, they can work together to use the resources in the relationships.

Alice concludes that the primary triad is critical in understanding Jean, Derril, and Al. Derril learned much about relationships from watching Jean and Al—mostly that blaming and arguing are what relationships are made of. Power is often expressed in verbal interaction, and occasionally physical force is used.

Alice wonders if Derril felt very excluded by his parents. It is hard to be in contact with two people who are alternating between fighting and the silent treatment. There are also some signs that Derril is caught between his mother and father in that Jean seems to want Derril to side with her against Al. Derril admits that his parents' physical confrontations frightened him very much. He would try to yell at them to stop, until the one day he intervened and prevented his father from hitting his mother.

Alice guesses that Derril's response to the years of exposure to this triangle has affected his relationship with both parents and his self-esteem. He has learned that the most powerful communications are ones that are shouted and angry, and that physical force bolsters verbal anger. Derril has also learned that to have influence with others (and thus, be worthwhile) one presents a noisy, blaming front, rather than communicating in an authentic leveling way.

FAMILY RULES

The rules by which a family operates can be overt or covert. For example, the rule for Debbie's bedtime is 8:00. The covert rule might be that she could stretch it to 8:30 by whining a lot. More serious examples of covert rules are found in troubled families, such as when there is a rule not to speak of Auntie Mame's drinking.

Rules should be doable, or as Satir put it, "humanly possible" (Satir & Baldwin, 1983, p. 202). She gave the example of a rule that members must *always* be happy. Abiding by this rule is clearly impossible and leads members to conceal their feelings, resulting in isolation and emotional distance. In addition, if one is not happy, one is bad and disobedient; this assessment can lead to low self-worth.

Flexibility and age appropriateness are also important to family rules. As children grow, families must adjust the rules to match. For instance, a bedtime of 7:00 P.M. might be OK for a 6-year-old, but would be silly for a 12-year-old.

Rules should also allow for diversity among members' ways of operating in the world, and also should allow for members to share information freely. Family secrets are a no-no in the Satir approach. Feelings and opinions should also be accepted, including the expression of intimacy and anger (Satir & Baldwin, 1983).

The rules in Derril's family are not immediately evident to Alice, except that anger is power, but dangerous. Jean struggles to teach Derril not to express anger, yet she often does so herself in relationship to Derril, and clearly did so with Al. When Jean or Derril expresses anger, it is in a volatile rather than leveling manner, and it gets them into trouble.

The rules around Derril's role in the family seem unclear, or at the least, inconsistent. He is asked to take a lot of responsibility in the home and is assigned many household tasks (e.g., cleaning, laundry, taking out the garbage, and mowing the lawn). He also feels free to comment on his mother's appearance, critiquing her clothing choices on a daily basis.

On the other hand, Jean seems at times to treat Derril as younger than he is. She keeps him close to her, much as one would an 8-year-old child. She addresses him more as a child than as a young man entering adolescence.

THEORY OF THE PERSON
AND DEVELOPMENT OF THE INDIVIDUAL

Satir proposed no formal theory of personality or personality development. She did see life as a journey, describing five basic life stages: conception to birth, birth to puberty, puberty to adulthood, adulthood to senior status, and senior status to death (1988, p. 306).

Families are the crucibles of individuals. According to Satir, adults are "people makers" (1972, p. 3), and the parents are "the architects of the family" (1988, p. 141). Four dimensions of family are important: the individual self-esteem of the members, communication patterns, the rules of the family, and its relation to society (Satir, 1972).

Seven dimensions or processes are essential to becoming fully human (Satir, 1988): differentiation (distinguishing between self and others), relationships (knowing how to connect with self and others), autonomy (how to rely on self), self-esteem (feeling worthwhile), power (using personal power to direct one's own behavior), productivity (demonstrating competence), and loving (p. 307). Satir particularly emphasized the human need for love, saying, "I believe in love—in loving and in being loved. I think that love, including sexual love, is the most rewarding and fulfilling feeling any human being can experience. Without loving and being loved, the human soul and spirit curdle and die" (1988, p. 141).

Alice has assessed this family's self-esteem, communication, and rules. She would describe Jean and Derril's relationship to society as guarded and protective. She thinks that Derril and Jean are both facing growth in the areas of differentiation and relationships. Derril is learning how to be autonomous and to find his personal power. It is clear that these two share a deep connection and love for each other, but that sometimes it is hard to express.

HEALTH AND DYSFUNCTION

Satir, because she was a humanist, had something to say about healthy human beings. In her view, "all human beings carry with them all the resources they need to flourish" (Satir & Baldwin, 1983, p. 208). Behavior is motivated by good intentions and represents the best that the individual knows (Woods & Martin, 1984). Brothers (2000) wrote of Satir, "utterly convinced that no evil people exist, she was passionately devoted to showing how the "evil"—the destructiveness—lay, instead, in the process between people" (p. 5; quotes in original).

The healthy person is open and honest with self and others, takes risks and is creative, and can change and accommodate to new situations (Satir, 1972). Playful, loving, and authentic, the healthy person stands on his own and can "love deeply and fight fairly" (p. 3). As described earlier, self-worth is very prominent in Satir's view of people. Satir et al. (1991) point to congruence and high self-esteem as major indicators of psychological health.

In the healthy, or nurturing, family, communication is open, individual self-worth is strong, and rules are flexible and humane and can change if appropriate. For the most part, communication is congruent, although Satir recognized that nobody, no family, was perfect (Satir, 1975). Further, the healthy family's connection to society is open and hopeful (Satir, 1972, p. 4).

Just the opposite is true in dysfunctional or troubled families. Communication is fuzzy, and self-esteem is low. These families are fearful in relationship to society and can be blaming or placating in response. Family rules tend to be set in stone and inhuman. Family members are not friends.

In Satir's system, symptoms are signs that communication is faulty or rules are dysfunctional, and these things are blocking one or more family members' growth (Satir & Baldwin, 1983). When individuals are stressed beyond their capacities, they become fearful and develop primitive methods of survival that are their best attempts to cope (Haber, 2002). That is why Satir said that the problem is not the problem; coping is the problem (cited in Haber, 2002, p. 28).

Alice thinks that Derril is doing his best to grow, to differentiate from his mother and become an adult. At the same time, Jean is struggling to be the best parent that she can. These two are having great difficulty communicating at times and talk to each other in blaming, disrespectful ways. These problems in communication seem to replicate those between Jean and Derril's father. Jean is feeling as though she is losing control of Derril, and resorts to yelling and blaming as ways of trying to get him to behave. She also seems to alternate the rules of their relationship, sometimes treating Derril as a much younger child and sometimes as her partner.

Alice thinks that Derril's angry behavior is no real surprise given what he observed in his family, between his parents. He watched two individuals whom he loved attack each other angrily. Alice thinks that Jean and Al were so quick to take offense at each other's behavior because they had very weak senses of self-worth. They also did not know how to manage conflict in ways other than yelling, labeling, and blaming.

Jean often has very little to say about Derril that is positive. In counseling sessions, she criticizes him almost continuously. At the same time, she calls him her "baby" and her "hope." These communications are very inconsistent. Alice thinks that without really recognizing it, Derril and his mother are both suffering from the lack of genuine love, mostly because they have difficulty expressing it.

NATURE OF THERAPY

Assessment

A counselor practicing the Satir approach relies greatly on her powers of observation to perform critical assessments of the family. She observes the relationships among individuals to gauge communication patterns. Self-presentations of members can give information about self-esteem (Satir & Baldwin, 1983), and interactions among family members can yield information about covert and overt family rules.

In *Conjoint Family Therapy*, Satir (1967) discussed the use of formal diagnosis, warning about the tendency to treat individuals solely in terms of such labels. The therapist can tell the client, "You are behaving now with behavior which I, as a clinician, label 'schizophrenia.' But this label only applies *at this time, in this place*, and *in this context*. Future times, places, and contexts may show something quite different" (Satir, 1967, p. 103; emphasis in original).

Alice carefully observes Jean and Derril as they interact in the counseling session. Jean berates Derril for his lack of respect; Alice notes Derril's sulky response. Sometimes Derril will resort to blaming Jean for his behavior. Both seem to be using these styles to cover up vul-nerability that results from shaky senses of self-worth. At other times, Jean expresses her love for her son and her concern that he will get into big trouble.

Overview of the Therapeutic Atmosphere and Roles of Client and Counselor

Satir believed that anyone can change at any point in his life (Satir, 1988). This positive out-look leads to a therapeutic approach that is optimistic, warm, and positive. A primary concern for Satir was to create a safe environment in which all clients feel valued (Loeschen, 1998).

Humanistic approaches typically emphasize the use of the therapist's person in coun-seling, and Satir was masterful in this respect. The use of the self of the therapist is therefore considered critical to this approach (Satir, 2000). What sometimes makes the implementation of the approach difficult is that, like Ellis and Rational Emotive Behavior Therapy, for example, the person of Satir is practically synonymous with her therapeutic approach.

A prime criterion for the therapist following Satir is that she must be in touch with and accepting of herself, which allows her to be authentic in the session. The therapist must take a nonjudgmental and genuine approach while responding to the overt and covert communications of the family (Satir & Baldwin, 1983).

In Satir's approach, the therapist is characterized as a resource person (Satir, 1967, p. 67). Although Satir recognized the therapist as an expert, she is not "God, parent, or judge" (p. 67). A certain amount of humility is required to be a good family therapist. However, the counselor *is* an experienced observer and a model for functional communi-cation. The teacher role is essential to Satir's approach because families need to learn to communicate more effectively.

According to Woods and Martin (1984), Satir's approach can be summarized in four elements (p. 8):

1. The warmth and acceptance of Carl Rogers
2. The strong experiential here-and-now techniques reminiscent of Fritz Perls
3. The "detective" genius of Satir
4. The comfortable, humanistic presence of Satir

Alice tries to be authentic in her relationship with Jean and Derril. She knows that she is an imperfect human being, but she has had good training and has devoted a lot of energy to self-exploration. Alice sees the strength in Jean and Derril and is optimistic about the out-come of the counseling. She is accepting and warm in her relationship with Jean and Derril.

Goals

Therapy is essentially an "experientially based educational program for families in pain" (Woods & Martin, 1984, p. 8). There are a number of interlocking goals of this approach; they center on releasing the blocked potential of families and engaging the healing powers of the client (Satir, 2000). One important goal of therapy is to enhance the self-esteem of family members (Woods & Martin, 1984). As members become more aware of themselves and others, they become more congruent and authentic. Communication becomes clearer and more functional (Satir, 1967).

Alice intends to help Jean and Derril grow, to acknowledge their strengths, uniqueness, and individuality. She hopes that they gain in self-worth. She expects that their ways of communicating with each other and those outside of their relationship will change and become more like the leveling or congruent communication described by the theory.

PROCESS OF THERAPY

Satir tended to emphasize the process of therapy over its content (Woods & Martin, 1984). She believed that the major curative element in therapy is changing how the family relates and giving them new experiences in the counseling relationship. What they are actually talking or arguing about is not as important as is *how* they are doing it.

Satir's approach generally involves three stages of counseling (Satir & Baldwin, 1983, p. 209). Families can cycle through the stages many times before they leave counseling, although as I outline the stages, it will become apparent that stage 1 is different after the first cycle. The following is a summary of the stages based on Satir and Baldwin's (1983) description.

Stage 1. Contact. Families who come to therapy are in pain. The counselor's first job is to attempt to create an atmosphere of hope and trust. Every family member is greeted and acknowledged as an important member of the group. As the therapist works to make the family comfortable, she is also gathering information by observing family patterns. According to Satir and Baldwin, the therapist's main goal is to "make manifest for family members what she has observed and to make explicit what family members often know implicitly" (p. 213). Sometimes, but not always, a specific therapy contract is established.

Stage 2. Chaos. The second stage of therapy appears when one family member ventures into risky territory. The therapist helps the individual to reveal hurt, pain, and/or anger that has previously remained hidden. The therapist also helps the client to stay in the present (rather than focusing on past fears or uncertainty about the future). Also, the therapist must support other members of the family if necessary. Often, the family feels stuck and hopeless.

Stage 3. Integration. When the family finds a way to move on the issue that created the chaos, stage 3 begins. The family develops new ways of being, and some closure is gained on the pivotal issue.

Alice anticipates that she, Jean, and Derril will journey through the three stages of therapy. Initially, they get to know each other in the first stage, and Alice may point out the ways that Jean and Derril relate to each other (blaming, disrespectful). After a while, Alice is confident that either Derril or Jean will take the risk to reveal the hurt, pain, and anger they are hiding behind the bossy exterior. No matter who risks, this sequence of events will be very scary for both clients. The one who risks has taken a big leap into unknown territory, but the other will have to tolerate a different experience of the risk taker, as vulnerable. Alice is certain that eventually this pair will find a way out of the chaos.

THERAPEUTIC TECHNIQUES

Describing specific techniques in Satir's approach is somewhat difficult because of her emphasis on uniqueness and also the experiential bent characteristic of this theory. Satir was adept at devising experiences for the family that changed the way they experienced life. I will attempt to describe experiences that Satir and others have most commonly used in their work with clients.

FAMILY SCULPTING

Satir's emphasis on the integration of the physical, intellectual, and emotional led to the development of sculpting, which involves having family members physically take positions that exemplify the family's interactions. Most commonly, family members would take the poses reflective of one or more of the four communication types (e.g., blaming, appeasing, computing, or distracting) and Satir would help them explore their thoughts, emotions, and physiological reactions (Haber, 2002). Placing members higher or lower than one another can denote power relation (Satir et al., 1991), such as when a superreasonable parent is asked to stand on a chair. Somewhat reminiscent of Gestalt Therapy, the therapist then directs questions to the various members, such as, "What are you feeling right now? What body feelings do you have? Can you exaggerate that movement?" However, sculpting is not restricted to posturing the communication stances.

Family members can be used as sculptors (Satir et al., 1991). One member of the family, a creative adolescent, say, can be asked to place family members in positions that resemble his view of the family atmosphere. In this approach, the sculptor is asked to give commentary on what he is doing.

Alice asks Jean and Derril to assume the pose of blamers, facing each other. She asks them to exaggerate their accusing vocal tones and to shake their fingers really hard at each other. Then she asks them to change how they talk and try to relax their bodies. Afterwards, Alice, Jean, and Derril talk about how it felt to be in the various positions, and how it felt to change.

FAMILY STRESS BALLET

In the family stress ballet, an extension of sculpting, the family is asked to move in ways that illustrate their experience. The therapist can direct the movement or simply observe what families choose to do (Satir & Baldwin, 1983).

Alice asks Jean and Derril to act out what happens when Derril comes home after getting in trouble at school. Jean immediately takes the blamer pose, and Derril alternates between blaming others and going silent. They move in a dance around each other with tense bodies and shrill voices. Alice then asks them to talk about how this ballet felt.

COMMUNICATION ANALYSIS

Satir spent a lot of time examining family communication and creating experiences that promoted healthy communication, including support and validation of each individual in the family (Woods & Martin, 1984). Family members are encouraged to express their feelings and respect these communications.

Alice asks Jean and Derril to talk about respect. Alice notes that Jean does not seem very validating of Derril during this discussion; she accuses him, demanding that he always show respect for his mother! Derril responds by getting mad and then quiet. Alice intervenes and asks Jean to describe her experience during this conversation, and to own her frustrations rather than accusing Derril. Once Jean communicates in a congruent way about her feelings and what she'd like in her relationship with Derril, Derril is asked to respond in a different way to his mother. In this interaction, Alice emphasizes that it is essential to express anger, but that it must be done through owning it rather than laying it at the feet of the other person.

THERAPIST COMMUNICATIONS

Therapists in the Satir tradition are very deliberate in their use of language. Reframing can be used to help families view things in a different light. Humor can also be used to the same end. Metaphors are often employed. One well-known metaphor is the notion of the "pot" when discussing self-worth (Satir, 1988). The pot can be full or close to empty, boiling or calm.

In talking about the recent incident in which one of his peers reportedly dissed Derril's mother, Alice reframes Derril's reaction as a way of caring for his mother. She asks if there might be some less active ways that he could have used to demonstrate his caring.

Another way Alice intervenes is around the issue of respect. She points out that a strong value in this family is respect. Derril is only trying to get respect in his own world by reacting when someone gets in his face. She uses a metaphor of the bull and red flag to describe Derril's behavior, but then also applies this metaphor to Jean's interactions with Derril.

TOUCH

One of Satir's trademarks was that she often physically connected with her clients (Nichols, 2002). Of course, care must be taken when using touch so that the client's boundaries are not violated. Satir often began her work with families by taking every member's hand, and in this way established her special contact with each of them (Satir & Baldwin, 1983).

Alice greets Jean and Derril with a firm handshake. She is not afraid to touch Jean or Derril in her work with them, such as when she wishes to be particularly supportive or when she is helping them make family sculptures.

FAMILY THERMOMETER

In her revision of the classic *Peoplemaking* (1988), Satir described the construction of the family thermometer. Five themes are discussed by the family in this process: appreciation, negatives of life, puzzles, new information, and hopes and wishes (pp. 190–191). Families are encouraged to physically construct the thermometer and hang it in the home to remind them that they should periodically take readings on each of the themes.

The family thermometer is perfect for Derril and Jean, because it offers an opportunity to discuss many things they have not ever touched on, and some areas that are tricky. For instance, in the hopes and wishes zone, Derril admits that when his mother calls him her hope he feels very pressured and scared. Derril and Jean discuss this issue in a careful way with Alice as their guide.

PARTS PARTY

Really a group technique, the parts party (Satir et al., 1991) requires at least 10 people. The client is the host and identifies between 6 and 10 people who are either attractive or repulsive to him; these should be individuals who are readily recognizable to most people (e.g., Martin Luther King, Hillary Clinton, John Travolta). The rest of the group is asked to play these parts and interact, with the counselor (the guide) observing and directing the interaction. The players must understand the qualities of their respective roles *as the client/host perceives them.* The parts meet and interact (and sometimes conflict), and can be asked to change how they deal with each other. Finally, the host is asked to ceremoniously accept each of the parts, while verbalizing his feelings.

A parts party doesn't seem to be efficient or particularly helpful with Derril and Jean. Alice thus decides to bypass this intervention.

Structural Therapy

OVERVIEW

The name most associated with Structural Family Therapy is Salvador Minuchin. His book *Families & Family Therapy* (1974) is considered a classic in the field, and Nichols (2002) contended that Structural Family Therapy "owned" the profession of family therapy in the 1970s. You can read some of the first chapter of this book in Box 13.2. Minuchin is a charismatic figure who uses his personal qualities to boost his impact in working with families. In fact, some argue that the power of Minuchin's theory can be attributed more to his personality than to the system per se (Nichols, 2002). Minuchin freely acknowledges the influence of his person in his work; he says that over time "my style has grown softer, and more effective. I feel free to use my compassion and humor in joining with families. I have learned to use my life experiences and my fellow feeling for families as part of the therapeutic processes. Having made my share of mistakes in my life, I don't expect my patients to be perfect" (Minuchin & Fishman, 1981, p. 289).

Quite the colorful guy, Minuchin is the son of Russian Jewish immigrants who were transplanted to Argentina. He was ambivalent about Argentina as his psychological home and aligned himself more with Zionism (Simon, 1992). In 1943 Minuchin was arrested in a student protest of Argentinean dictator Juan Peron. Minuchin served in the Israeli army for two years during that country's struggles for independence.

After he earned his medical degree, Minuchin began work at the Wiltwyck Center, a school for troubled inner-city youths. Here Minuchin, in league with his able colleagues, began to think about family therapy in his work with poor African American families. He eventually wrote his influential book *Families of the Slums* (Minuchin, Montalvo, Gurney, Rosman, & Schumer, 1967).

Box 13.2

An Except from Minuchin's *Families and Family Therapy*

Robert Smith, his wife, his twelve-year-old son, and his father-in-law are sitting with me for their first consultation with a family therapist. Mr. Smith is the identified patient. He has been hospitalized twice in the past seven years for agitated depression and has recently requested rehospitalization.

Minuchin: *What is the problem? . . . So who wants to start?*
Mr. Smith: *I think it's my problem. I'm the one that has the problem . . .*
Minuchin: *Don't be so sure. Never be so sure.*
Mr. Smith: *Well . . . I'm the one that was in the hospital and everything.*
Minuchin: *Yeah, that doesn't, still, tell me it is your problem. Okay, go ahead. What is your problem?*
Mr. Smith: *Just nervous, upset all the time . . . seem to be never relaxed . . . I get uptight, and I asked them to put me in the hospital . . .*
Minuchin: *Do you think that you are the problem?*
Mr. Smith: *Oh, I kind of think so. I don't know if it is caused by anybody, but I'm the one that has the problem.*
Minuchin: *. . . Let's follow your line of thinking. If it would be caused by somebody or something outside of yourself, what would you say your problem is?*
Mr. Smith: *You know, I'd be very surprised.*
Minuchin: *Let's think in the family. Who makes you upset?*
Mr. Smith: *I don't think anybody in the family makes me upset.*
Minuchin: *Let me ask your wife. Okay?*

The consultation that began with this exchange was the beginning of a new approach to the problem of Mr. Smith. Instead of focusing on the individual, the therapist focused on the person within his family. The therapist's statement, "Don't be so sure," challenged the certainty that Mr. Smith alone was the problem or had the problem—a certainty which had been shared by Mr. Smith, his family, and the many mental health professionals he had encountered.

The therapist's framework was structural family therapy, a body of theory and techniques that approaches the individual in his social context. Therapy based on this framework is directed toward changing the organization of the family. When the structure of the family group is transformed, the positions of members in that group are altered accordingly. As a result, each individual's experiences change.

The theory of family therapy is predicated on the fact that man is not an isolate. He is an acting and reacting member of social groups. What he experiences as real depends on both internal and external components. The paradoxical duality of the human perception of reality is explained by Ortega y Gasset in a parable: "Peary relates that on his polar trip he traveled one whole day toward the north, making his sleigh dogs run briskly. At night he checked his bearings to determine his latitude and noticed with great surprise that he was much further south than in the morning. He had been toiling all day toward the north on an immense iceberg drawn southwards by an ocean current." Human beings are in the same situation as Commander Peary on the iceberg. Man's experience is determined by his interaction with his environment.

To say that man is influenced by his social context, which he also influences, may seem obvious. Certainly the concept is not new; it was familiar to Homer. But it is a new approach to base mental health techniques on this concept.

The traditional techniques of mental health grew out of a fascination with individual dynamics. This preoccupation dominated the field and led therapists to concentrate on exploring the intrapsychic. Of necessity, the resulting treatment techniques focused exclusively on the individual, apart from his surroundings. An artificial "boundary" was drawn between the individual and his social context. In theory, this boundary was recognized as artificial, but in practice it was maintained by the process of therapy. As the patient was treated in isolation, the data encountered were inevitably restricted to the way he alone felt and thought about what was happening to him; such individualized material in turn reinforced the approach to the individual apart from his context and provided little possibility for corrective feedback. The very richness of the data available discouraged other approaches. As a result, the individual came to be viewed as the site of pathology.

A therapist oriented to individual therapy still tends to see the individual as the site of pathology and to gather only the data that can be obtained from or about the individual. For instance, an adolescent boy might be referred to therapy because he is shy and daydreams in class. He is a loner, with difficulty relating to his peers. A therapist who operates in individual sessions would explore the boy's thoughts and feelings about his present life and the people in it, the historical development of his conflict with parents and siblings, and the compulsive intrusion of this conflict into extrafamilial, seemingly unrelated situations. He would establish contact with the family and the school, but to understand the boy and the boy's relationship with his family, he would rely mainly on the content of the boy's communication and on transferential phenomena. An internal cognitive-affective rearrangement is regarded as the necessary step to facilitate improvement of the presenting problem.

A therapist working within this framework can be compared to a technician using a magnifying glass. The details of the field are clear, but the field is severely circumscribed. A therapist working within the framework of structural family therapy, however, can be compared to a technician with a zoom lens. He can zoom in for a closeup whenever he wishes to study the intrapsychic field, but he can also observe with a broader focus.

If the same boy were referred to a family therapist, the therapist would explore his interactions within significant life contexts. In family interviews, the therapist would observe the relationship of the boy and his mother, with its mingled closeness and hostility. He might see that when the boy talks in the presence of his parents, he rarely addresses his father, or that when he does talk to his father, he tends to do so through his mother, who translates and explains her son to her husband. He might notice that other siblings seem more spontaneous, interrupt the parents, and talk to the father and mother alike. Thus, the therapist does not have to depend on the boy's descriptions of his father, mother, and siblings to postulate the introjection of the familial figures. The family members are present, demonstrating behavior in relation to the boy that can be operationally described. The broader focus and the greater flexibility opened to the therapist enhance the possibilities for therapeutic intervention. The therapist is not restricted to the family interaction as internalized by the boy, but can himself experience the way in which the family members support and qualify each other. He then develops a transactional theory to explain the phenomena he is observing. He can also be in touch with the boy's school, since the presenting problem is related to school performance, and the theories and techniques of family therapy lend themselves readily to work with the individual in contexts other than the family.

Thus, the family therapist does not conceive of an "essential" personality, remaining unchanged throughout the vicissitudes of different contexts and circumstances. He sees the boy as a member of different social contexts, acting and reacting within them. His concept of the site of pathology is much broader, and so are the possibilities for intervention.

Excerpted from *Families and Family Therapy* by S. Minuchin, 1974. Cambridge, MA: Harvard University Press. Reprinted with permission.

Leaving Wiltwyck, Minuchin assumed the position of director at the Philadelphia Child Guidance Clinic. He hired Jay Haley as director of research, and along with Haley and Braulio Montalvo, developed what is now known as the structural approach. Probably his greatest claim to fame is his work with very difficult clients, and in particular, his work with the families of anorexic girls. These "psychosomatic families" helped Minuchin refine his theory considerably (Minuchin, Rosman, & Baker, 1978). Minuchin retired in 1986. He still conducts training, but functions more as a commentator on the profession than as a theorist or practitioner (Simon, 1992) and a writer: two recent books are *Assessing Families and Couples: From Symptom to System* (Minuchin, Nichols, & Lee, 2007) and a second edition of *Working with Families of the Poor* (P. Minuchin, Colapinto, & Minuchin, 2007), originally published in 1998 with wife Patricia as one of the authors. The Minuchin Center for the Family (http://www.minuchincenter.org/index.php) is in New York City, training professionals and consulting with families and organizations.[1]

CENTRAL CONSTRUCTS

FAMILY STRUCTURE

"Family structure is the invisible set of functional demands that organizes the ways in which the family members interact" (Minuchin, 1974, p. 51). In essence, family structure is a set of rules that tells who talks to whom, who plays with whom (and in what ways), and so forth. Family members can join together in *coalitions* (two or more members become close buddies, so to speak). Who sides with whom in arguments is particularly important. Interaction patterns are critical because they tend to be repeated and institutionalized, become part of the family's and individual members' identities, and determine how everyone is to behave. Patterns of interaction also tell you about hierarchy, or

[1] For ease of reading, references to Salvadore Minuchin's work are cited without an initial.

power, in families (P. Minuchin et al., 2007). In essence, these repeated patterns of interaction *are* the family structure. Certain forms of family structure are conducive to individual and family dysfunction, as will be described in the section on health and dysfunction.

John, the structural therapist working with Jean and Derril, first notes that there are several structures in their immediate household. Mother and son clearly have formed a coalition. Father is distant from the family. He decides to look at these in terms of subsystems.

Subsystems

Families naturally differentiate into subsystems, or smaller groupings within the family (Minuchin, 1974). Subsystems help to get the work of the family done, such as when the adult partners form a parental subsystem to raise children. An individual can even be a subsystem, and larger subsystems can be formed according to sex, generation, interest, or function (Minuchin, 1974, p. 52). An individual can be a member of more than one subsystem, and further, a member of subsystems in multiple families. For example, a woman can be a youngest daughter, a spouse, a mother, an aunt, and so forth. If she and her brother-in-law like to ride horses, they can form a subsystem around this interest.

John sees the subsystems of kid (Derril), woman (Jean), and parental (Jean and in some ways, Jean and Al). Jean's daughter is yet another relevant subsystem, and her family has spousal, parental, and kid subsystems, too. John thinks that Derril and Jean also are a subsystem of sorts. Although the interaction seems limited, Jean is a member of subsystems of her family of origin—the sibling subsystem.

Boundaries

Critical to structural therapy is the idea of boundaries, or the rules that specify who participates in a subsystem (Minuchin, 1974). Boundaries protect the integrity of a subsystem and should be flexible but clear. A too-rigid boundary around a subsystem creates isolation of those individuals, depriving them of the protection of the family and opportunities to learn about life from other members. Very blurred boundaries between subsystems create a situation in which everyone's business is everyone else's. Such a system can become overwhelmed and stressed beyond its capacities. When boundaries are too rigid, the system is said to be *disengaged*, and when boundaries are very unclear, it is said to be *enmeshed* (Minuchin, 1974). For example, a teenage girl is acting out, yet when her mother tries to correct her, her father interferes. Minuchin would say that this pattern is indicative of a weak boundary between the parental subsystem and the daughter—the father and daughter are in coalition or enmeshed.

Boundaries in a system can be observed in a number of ways (Minuchin & Fishman, 1981). Where family members sit in a counseling session can provide hypotheses about subsystem functioning. Do the children sit next to each other, or does one sit between the parents? How the family talks is also indicative of boundaries—who speaks for whom, who interrupts whom, and who is quiet.

John sees that there are boundary issues in Jean and Derril's situation. The boundaries are weak between the parental and child subsystems (i.e., Jean and Derril have more of a sibling relationship than a parent–child one). This family seems to be enmeshed. Also, it appears that this new subsystem has rigid boundaries around it: Dad does not join it, and it seems to be impervious to any input from the surrounding environment.

Earlier in the family's history, the parental subsystem seems to have involved Derril at times, particularly when Al and Jean were fighting. Now the spousal subsystem is nonexistent, and the parental subsystem is disengaged in that Al is not taking a parental role with Derril.

THEORY OF THE PERSON AND DEVELOPMENT OF THE INDIVIDUAL

Structural family theorists are more interested in the development of the family than that of the individual. Minuchin and Fishman (1981) proposed four main stages of family development: couple formation, families with young children, families with school-age or adolescent children, and families with grown children (p. 23). Each of these transition points involves either the addition of a subsystem or a challenge to already established ones.

When becoming a couple, partners must shift loyalties from their families of origin to the new entity, the partnership (Minuchin, 1974). A natural feature of human development is that at some point, an adolescent will begin to differentiate more from the family of origin. Ultimately, he will separate from them by going to college or moving out of the family home for other reasons. This change will seriously affect the family subsystems. If he was a member of the kid subsystem, his role and function will be missing. If he was a caretaker for younger children, his parents will need to adjust to his absence. If he was in coalition with either parent, his loss will be traumatic. These are just a few examples of the stresses brought on by these transitions.

Minuchin (1974) maintained that the individual's personal identity is composed of a balance between individuality and belonging. Families are a critical source of the individual's sense of separateness and togetherness, primarily through subsystem membership (remember, an individual can be considered a subsystem, too).

One thing that structural theorists are sure about is that systems change. If you watch families, social service agencies, hospitals, or any other kind of system, you will observe periods of stability, but because human systems are open-ended, times of transition (P. Minuchin, et al., 2007).

Derril is entering adolescence. John notes that this transition seems difficult for Jean and Derril. They are both struggling with the change from small child who is always near mother (belonging) and an adolescent developing his own personhood (individuality). Part of this process is Derril's struggle to strengthen his subsystem boundaries.

HEALTH AND DYSFUNCTION

At the most general level, structural family therapists discuss dysfunction in terms of the ways in which the family relates (Aponte & Dicesare, 2002; Minuchin et al., 2007). Families tend to experience difficulties when old patterns of relating don't work. These dynamics are particularly evident in times of transition whether the transitions are "normal" parts of the cycle of life (e.g., the birth of a new child) or not (such as natural disaster; P. Minuchin et al., 2007).

More specifically, Minuchin tended to speak in terms of too-rigid or too-blurred boundaries among subsystems, or in other words, enmeshment or disengagement (Minuchin, 1974). Aponte and VanDeusen (1981) provided a more elegant definition: "Functional and dysfunctional levels are determined by the adequacy of the fit of a system's structural organization to the requirements of an operation in a set of circumstances" (p. 313). Something about the structure is not adaptive to the events of life, and often, enmeshment or disengagement is not helping the family (although sometimes these patterns are fine).

When the disengaged family is stressed and needs to adapt, it does not respond because the rigid boundaries in the system keep the stress from being transmitted to all members of the system. In enmeshed families, the blurred boundaries between subsystems enable the immediate and intense transmission of stress and potentially excessive reactions (Minuchin, 1974). In essence, the enmeshed family responds instantly to threat by freaking out. In contrast, the disengaged family seems not to care about its members. Disengaged families tend to allow a lot of individuality, whereas enmeshed families expect conformity and loyalty (Minuchin, 1974).

Minuchin and his colleagues learned valuable things about family structure and function from observing psychosomatic families. Psychosomatic families are those in which children present with symptoms that are more severe than would be expected based on the biological aspects of the disorder, such as asthma or anorexia nervosa. These observations led Minuchin, Rosman, and Baker (1978) to theorize that these families had five important similarities. Although originally intended to describe the psychosomatic families, these qualities have acquired a more general usage in describing family structure.

Minuchin and colleagues maintained that psychosomatic families are enmeshed, overprotective of members, rigid in the face of change, and have difficulties resolving conflict. However, the key characteristic in these families is the child's involvement in the parental relationship. In essence, the child's symptom serves as the regulator in the system, assisting in the avoidance of conflict between the parents. Three such situations generally characterize the types of alignments found in families (Aponte & VanDeusen, 1981). Although these alignments may temporarily relieve stress, they have long-term consequences because they negatively affect the functioning of the children (Kerig, 1995).

In one common pattern, parents who are in conflict and can't deal with it bind together to focus on the afflicted child, a pattern called *detouring* or *scapegoating* (Minuchin, 1974). The couple system looks calm and united, but they are channeling their stress to the child. The child is defined as the family's problems, becomes a victim, and develops symptoms. The process is perpetuated when the parents in some way reinforce the symptom.

Two other patterns are evident when the parental dyad is openly split, *parent–child coalition* and *triangulation*. Parent–child coalition refers to the situation in which the child is recruited into a stable partnership with one parent in opposition to the other. In triangulation, the child finds himself caught in the middle—he can't risk expressing his feelings or opinions because to do so would be to side with one parent over the other. Essentially, the parents are competing for the validation of the child, and a parent may attack the child if he or she perceives the child as joining with the other parent (Minuchin, 1974). It is important to note that although these patterns are often described in terms of parent–child relations, triangulation and detouring occur among other family member configurations, such as when two sisters triangulate their little brother.

Healthy families are those in which structures are clearly defined and flexible. Thus, these systems can change as needed, such as when a new stage of development is imminent (Aponte & VanDeusen, 1981). Minimal levels of triangling, detouring, and parent–child coalition are present in healthy families because the parental dyad is appropriately boundaried. Within the spouse system, togetherness and distance are balanced (Becvar & Becvar, 2006). The spouses are supportive and accommodating of each other.

In a healthy family, the kid subsystem benefits from the support of the parental and spousal systems (Becvar & Becvar, 2006). Children feel free to explore and grow. In structural theory, the healthy individual can maintain a good balance between individuation and belonging to the family.

John knows that somehow the system of this family is not adaptive. He has an idea that Derril is involved in a coalition with his mother, but he is also a factor in the parental subsystem. Jean and Al argue quite a bit about what is to be done with Derril, a sign that Derril is incorporated in that subsystem. The weak boundaries around the child and adult woman subsystem are allowing stress to be transmitted freely from Jean to Derril and vice versa. Further, the system is stressed by Derril's attempts to establish a clearer identity. His angry acting-out behavior appears to be a facet of this struggle to become a person separate from his mother and father. Al, who is disengaged from the family, seems relatively unaffected by the processes in the family; he is the outsider in the Derril-Jean-Al triangle.

NATURE OF THERAPY

ASSESSMENT

The first thing the structural therapist does is assess family structure. No formal assessment methods are used; the therapist simply asks himself a series of questions (Minuchin, 1974), such as: Who is the spokesperson of the family? Who selected or designated the spokesperson and why? Who is the true executive of the family? What are the other members doing while the spokesperson talks? Are they attentive or dismissive? Aponte and Dicesare (2002) note that contemporary structural therapists have been known to use genograms to assess what Minuchin et al. (2007) call the structurally oriented historical explanation (see the section on Bowen theory for a more detailed description of genograms).

John watches Jean and Derril interact and wishes that he had Al in the room as well. However, Jean contends that she and Al would fight too much to make sessions productive.

Jean and Derril's interaction mostly consists of Jean telling Derril how disrespectful he is. She does most of the talking, explaining that she doesn't understand why he does what he does. Derril responds minimally unless he gets angry. Then he tells his mother not to get in his face. Jean and Derril report that they sometimes "play" with each other, but that when

Jean asks Derril to stop and he doesn't, Jean gets angry. John also infers that Jean and Derril are in an enmeshed system, based on the report that they spend most of their free time together, Derril's role in the home, and his freedom to comment on his mother's appearance. A mother–child cross generational coalition has been formed, probably having its roots in the conflict between Jean and Al.

OVERVIEW OF THE THERAPEUTIC ATMOSPHERE AND ROLES OF CLIENT AND COUNSELOR

Structural therapy is active and present focused. Minuchin (1974) wrote, "The tool of this therapy is to modify the present, not to explore and interpret the past" (p. 14). Although I risk being obvious here, it is important to keep in mind that the target of the structural family therapist's intervention is the family, not the individual member.

The role of the counselor in structural family therapy is that of expert. The therapist joins the family (more on joining later), but maintains a stance as a leader in the counseling process. Minuchin et al. (2007) contend that it is easier to say what a structural therapist is NOT than what he is, writing

> A therapist isn't fair or just, or a politically correct practitioner; not an ethicist, not a logistician, not all knowing. The therapist is a practitioner of change. But change is always resisted: by the familiarity of well-traveled pathways, by a family's conviction about the way things are, by the competitive tension between the "selves in relation" that make up a family, and by the demands for change that family members make on each other. (p. 13; quotes in original)

The personality of Minuchin is often confused with the qualities and roles of the structural therapist. Minuchin is a very charismatic guy who is not afraid to be pushy. Obviously, it is not a requirement that one be pushy to be a structural family therapist, but one must be willing to be very active, and as you can see from the foregoing quote, at time willing to violate social norms (at least according to Minuchin).

John takes an active role with Jean and Derril, asking questions and generally directing their conversation. He joins with both of them in small ways, identifying with Jean's frustration and with Derril's attempts to be an individual.

GOALS

The structural therapist is intent on changing the structure of the family system, and thereby the experiences of its members (Minuchin, 1974). The problem presented is to be solved, but structural therapists does so by joining the family in "ways that impede old patterns of thinking and relating and build on their strengths to generate new patterns leading to immediate, palpable results" (Aponte & Dicesare, 2002, p. 1).

John's goal is to help Jean and Derril become individuals but still remain connected as mother and son. In essence, he wants to rearrange the boundaries in this system, tightening those around the individual subsystems (Jean's and Derril's personal spaces) and creating a stronger boundary between the parental and child subsystems.

PROCESS OF THERAPY

The structural family therapist is the leader of the system but also must become a member of it, a process that Minuchin called *joining* (Minuchin & Fishman, 1981). As Minuchin and Fishman put it, the "therapist is in the same boat with the family but he [*sic*] must be the helmsman" (p. 29). Joining is not a technique, but a mental set on the part of the therapist that conveys to the family that he is on their side and will work with and for them. Structural family therapists join the family by disclosing similarities with them, by supporting family members, or by conveying understanding of their perspectives. However, Minuchin is careful to point out that family therapists must be able to move in and out of family interaction—sometimes acting as a pseudomember of the family, other times as an observer (Minuchin, Lee, & Simon, 1996).

Minuchin et al. (2007) outline a four-step model of family assessment (pp. 9–12). In step 1, Opening Up the Presenting Complaint, the therapist's job is to help the family reframe the problem as systemic. Step 2, Highlighting Problem-Maintaining Interactions, involves clarifying and emphasizing the thing that the family does to maintain the problem, with particular attention to interactions that support the problem. A structurally-oriented historical exploration is in order in step 3, Structurally Focused Exploration of the Past. The adults in the family are asked to look at how their experiences have shaped their present (restricted) views of themselves and others. The structural counselor is most interested in keeping this conversation focused on history that bears directly on the presenting problem. Finally, in step 4, An Exploration of Alternative Ways of Relating, clients and therapist the explore alternatives to the present problem-maintaining interactions.

P. Minuchin and colleagues point out that it is important, particularly working with really stressed families, to recognize and acknowledge family strengths. It is also critical that counselors realize that it is inevitable that the counselor, as he joins the system, will be tempted to also join the family's view of the problem and their version of how problems should be solved (P. Minuchin et al., 2007). If you are working from a structural perspective, it is your job to keep in mind that the task is to help the client(s) see the world differently and act accordingly.

John carefully joins Jean and Derril in their plight. He understands Jean's worries about Derril's future. He talks with Derril about their mutual interest in sports, particularly basketball. Because John is African American, his personal qualities are a joining point with this family.

THERAPEUTIC TECHNIQUES

According to Minuchin and Fishman (1981), three general strategies are used in structural therapy: challenges are made to the (a) view of the symptom, (b) family structure, and (c) family reality (p. 67). Because Minuchin and Fishman's presentation is so clear and organized, this summary in this section relies mainly on their comments, unless otherwise noted.

A number of techniques can be used in the service of the three general strategies. *Reframing* is used to influence how the symptom is viewed. Three techniques are identified to change the family's view of the symptom: enactment, focusing, and achieving intensity. To *challenge the family structure*, the therapist engages in boundary making, unbalancing, and teaching the family about the complementarity of roles and functions (p. 69). The *family reality is challenged* through paradoxical techniques, using cognitive interventions, and emphasizing the strengths the family already possesses.

ENACTMENT

Minuchin is famous for having families perform interactions in the therapy session. This strategy is based on the notion that families won't often tell the counselor about their problems in relating to one another, so watching their interaction in session is instructive. The therapist can simply observe or intervene in the sequences the family demonstrates (Minuchin & Fishman, 1981). For example, if the children in a session are acting out, Minuchin will ask the parents to solve the problem. Observing how the parents interact with their children provides valuable information about how the parental and kid subsystems operate. If one parent is abdicating her role, the counselor can step in and ask the parent to engage, thereby encouraging the reestablishment of the two-person parental subsystem.

John thinks that mini-enactments are going to help Jean and Derril. He accomplishes this by talking to each alone after sending the other out of the room. Sometimes he simply tells the other that the topic is not his or her business. He also has them talk about problem areas and everyday things, directing the conversation so that Jean is parental in her approach to Derril, keeping her cool and making reasonable decisions and rules. Speaking calmly rather than in her accusing sibling mode helps to establish the parent–child boundary.

FOCUSING

In any counseling session, the therapist must choose a focus for his attention because the family presents a wide array of data about how they function. Basically, the therapist chooses the most important element in the family's presentation, and that choice is dictated by structural theory. A potential pitfall, warned Minuchin, is theoretical tunnel vision (Minuchin & Fishman, 1981). The counselor must be aware of his choice of focus and sensitive to the effects of narrowing his focus. Focusing can be used to take the spotlight off the identified patient by examining other dynamics in the family, such as the relationship between the parents or the caretaking efforts of a sibling.

John focuses on parenting with Jean, asking her to discuss what she thinks good parenting is. He asks if she can talk these things over with Al, wondering if she wants to get Al more involved with the parenting process. John also asks a lot about Derril's social life, implying that he needs to develop a network of supports outside of the family.

ACHIEVING INTENSITY

Because families have a shared way of looking at the world, they often have difficulty hearing the therapist's message. Hearing the message really means that the family experiences the therapist's reality in a way that will help the family structure shift. Achieving intensity is not a separate operation; several interventions can be used to achieve this goal, and they vary depending on the level of involvement with the family (Minuchin & Fishman, 1981). The counselor may simply repeat her message many times during a session. For example, the therapist may decide that 6-year-old James is acting incompetent to help others in the family feel better about themselves. The counselor will make this statement many times, and will also ask all of the participants how they experience this sequence.

Intensity can also be enhanced when the counselor asks families to go beyond the point at which they tend to interrupt stressful interactions. Most dyads or families have a point at which things get too hot and the interaction is discontinued. Asking the participants to "hang in there" at that point will continue the heat, and this journey into new territory has the potential to create new perceptions and patterns. Changing the distance between the therapist and family members (e.g., getting down on one's knees to talk to a small child or getting very close to an adult) can also increase intensity. Although primarily used as a boundary-creating maneuver, changing the seating arrangements among family members can also be used to intensify the counseling process (Minuchin & Fishman, 1981).

John repeats his contention that Derril is still trying to take care of Mom—protecting her from the world as he has protected her from his father at times. He asks Derril to talk about how he does this, and he asks Jean how that makes her feel.

When Jean and Derril are talking about a recent fight he had at school, Derril becomes sulky and quiet. John jumps in and helps Derril continue the conversation with his mother, encouraging him to talk more like a grown-up.

BOUNDARY MAKING

Another well-known structural technique involves tactics that create better boundaries within a family system. Boundary interventions can be very simple, such as when the counselor insists that the person to whom he asked a question answer the question (rather than someone else in the family). Members of the family can also be asked to change places. The classic example is when a child who is psychologically between the parents is moved from a chair between them to one next to the therapist, who sits facing the couple.

Many of John's interventions could be described as boundary making. When John helps Jean and Derril speak to each other differently, it is a boundary intervention. John stops Jean from interrupting Derril and vice versa. This allows each to speak his or her own piece and become more of an individual. When John talks with Jean or Derril individually, this is a boundary intervention. He asks Jean or Derril to complete some task or attend a social event separately over the period between sessions. If John succeeds in bringing Al into therapy, he will try to establish a boundary around the parental subsystem. This intervention might be more effective if John sends Derril out of the room for some period of time or if he asks Derril to sit off to the side and observe. However, just having Al and Jean talk about parenting Derril would be helpful.

UNBALANCING

This technique is intended to change the hierarchy within the family. The structural family counselor sides with a less powerful person in the system, or with a subsystem, and thereby steals the power of the more powerful. Alternately, a family member or system can be ignored. Needless to say, these are tricky interventions, and they raise ethical issues about the potential effects on the family and individual members. Minuchin and Fishman (1981) cautioned that the counselor must always be aware of the stress level of family members, particularly when siding with one member against more powerful others.

John considers siding with Derril in an attempt to gain him more autonomy. He could do this by telling Jean that he and Derril are going to have a heart-to-heart about what Derril should do to grow up. John thinks that this intervention would be stressful for both Derril and Jean. Derril would feel not only the stress of abandoning his mom, but also the pressure of growing up. It is possible that Jean could become anxious and then angry in reaction to this intervention.

TEACHING COMPLEMENTARITY

Simply put, the structural family therapist wants to give family members a sense that they are part of something bigger than themselves (Minuchin & Fishman, 1981). The therapist intervenes to teach the members how their behaviors fit together to create the system and define their collective worldview. Increasing members' senses of belonging and contributing can be accomplished in many ways. A challenge to the family's way of viewing the problem (that it is inside the identified patient, or IP) can establish a new, but shared, experience for the family. For example, the IP can be described as the family healer (Minuchin & Fishman, 1981, p. 195). The family can rethink its conviction that the IP is controlling them. The problem can be expanded to include more than one person—for instance, that dad and daughter are having "problems in their relationship."

John helps Derril and Jean see that they must work as a mother–son team, but in ways appropriate to Derril's age. He observes that Jean sometimes treats Derril as much younger than he is and at others times, as her partner. Derril sometimes reacts to his mother as if he were addressing an age mate. John makes interventions that redefine "the problem" (i.e., Derril) as one that involves Jean, too. Also, John talks to Derril and Jean about the kind of relationship they have, intending to reorient them into one that is more complementary.

Strategic Therapy

OVERVIEW

Strategic Therapy evolved from the work of the early systems theorists, primarily the "Palo Alto group" at the Mental Research Institute (MRI), a collection of researchers studying communication processes, most notably in the families of schizophrenics (Guerin & Chabot,1995; Watzlawick, Beavin, & Jackson, 1967). The MRI researchers included Gregory Bateson, Jay Haley, Don Jackson, and John Weakland, and they are perhaps most famous for their description of double-bind communication. Observed to happen repeatedly in families of schizophrenics, double-bind communication occurs when one family member gives a message to another that is really two contradictory messages, one conveyed on the verbal channel, the other on the nonverbal channel of communication. The target of this communication is unable to escape the situation, and as a result, over time develops psychological symptoms as a way of dealing with an impossible predicament (Nichols, 2006). A simple example of double-bind communication might be the following. Imagine your partner or parent saying "Of course you should go to the quilting party." However, the way she says it conveys "Going to the quilting party is the last thing I want you to do; as a matter of fact, I will fall apart if you do go and it will be your fault." Two messages are expressed, but they conflict. What do you do?

Jay Haley extended the MRI group's work and went on to become the foremost proponent of Strategic Therapy (Carlson, 2002). Haley, to say the least, was a bit of a maverick. Rather than the traditional degree in psychology or medicine, Haley's degree is a master's in arts and communication (Becvar & Becvar, 2006). Haley has consistently delighted in skewering the traditional psychotherapy club. One of his books, *The Power Tactics of Jesus Christ and Other Stories* (1969) does quite a bit of this skewering of entrenched institutions (as you could guess by its title), including an analysis of the power dynamics of psychoanalysis and of the mental hospitals of the 1950s and 1960s. Haley died in 2007, but his website can still be found at www.jay-haley-on-therapy.com.

Haley was much influenced by master therapist Milton Erickson (see Chapter 14 for more information). It is also helpful to know that he spent 10 years working with Minuchin developing Structural Family Therapy. The definitive statement of Strategic Therapy is probably Haley's book *Problem-Solving Therapy* (1987), which actually has first and second editions. Another leading proponent of Strategic Family Therapy is Cloe Madanes, who was at one time married to Haley. Madanes' book *Strategic Family Therapy* (1981) is considered an excellent resource on this approach. Another relatively recent source on this approach is Haley and Richeport-Haley's 2003 book *The Art of Strategic Therapy*.

Strategic therapists, like structural therapists, are interested in family hierarchy; power within the family is an essential way of understanding symptomatic presentations. The difference between strategic and structural therapists, according to Haley and Madanes (1981), is that strategic therapists pay more attention to the repetitive patterns of communication and behavior within the family than do the structuralists.

This theory is shorter on concepts and techniques than others, possibly because the strategic therapists believe that the way to change is to design specific tasks for each individual problem. There is no theory of personality associated with this approach.

CENTRAL CONSTRUCTS

COMMUNICATION

Strategic therapists are interested in the repetitive sequences of interaction that are seen in families and dyads (O'Connor, 1986). Communication happens on two levels: the digital and the analogic, or metaphoric (Haley, 1987). Digital communication occurs when statements have only one meaning—a sort of yes/no or on/off situation. Everyone mostly understands the meaning intended, and things are rational and precise. For example, I can count the number of times Jenny has temper tantrums in a day.

Analogic communication is the kind that happens between people, and the hallmark is that statements can have meanings on multiple levels. For example, when Sara and John fight over who is to clean the bathroom, the fight is overtly about the cleaning, but it is probably also a statement about how they relate. According to the strategic therapist, relationships between people happen on the level of analogic communication. For example, Haley (1987) maintained that the symptom or problem bringing the client to therapy is really a metaphor for his current relationship situation.

Haley (1987) also recognized another way to cut the communication pie: into report (or content) and command (or relationship) aspects. The report level is concerned with the actual content of a verbal message. The command level is largely nonverbal, and it conveys the relationship between the interactants. Using the example of Sara and John above, if the tense and angry Sara says to John "I am so tired of having to remind you to clean the bathroom" the content level is exactly what you read (she is tired of reminding), but the relationship message is that Sara gets to tell John that he has to clean, a clear statement that she is in charge.

Morgan, the strategic therapist, wonders how Derril's behavior is a metaphor for the family's distress. One possibility is that the metaphor resides in the "in your face" routine. This family has a history, it seems, of getting in each other's faces. When one tries to coerce the other, or blame or label, the other retaliates in kind, somewhat like Derril's behavior at school. Morgan looks closely at Derril and Jean's communication patterns to see what the command level is suggesting about their struggles.

HIERARCHIES

Any organization has hierarchies, and families are no exception. Hierarchies involve power, and thus, this concept is often seen as problematic. The traditional hierarchy in a family defines the parental dyad as in charge of the kids (Madanes, 1981). Even more traditionally, this structure often implies that the man is in charge and all must obey him. Haley (1987) protested that although we must accept the existence of hierarchies, this admittance does not dictate that a particular structure *must* exist. He cautioned that simply seeing an unjust hierarchy in a family is not justification for changing it. Hierarchies are to be changed when necessary to change symptoms, and only then.

Morgan sees that the hierarchy in this family is not entirely clear. Jean is the mom, yes, but often she seems to act like a teenager with Derril. Derril sometimes acts much younger and sometimes much older than he is in relationship to his mother. Dad's role is that of outsider.

THEORY OF THE PERSON
AND DEVELOPMENT OF THE INDIVIDUAL

Strategic therapists don't have a formal theory of personality. They have some ideas about development, but generally they attend to points of transition in the life span. According to Haley (1973), the important life stages in Strategic Therapy are (a) the courting period,

(b) early marriage, (c) childbirth and dealing with the young, (d) middle marriage, (e) weaning parents from children, and (e) retirement and old age. In his book on Erickson's methods, *Uncommon Therapy* (Haley, 1973), Haley devoted a chapter to each of these stages, illustrating them with examples from Erickson's work.

Morgan notes that Derril is on the verge of adolescence. Although Derril is only 12, he is showing signs of growing up.

HEALTH AND DYSFUNCTION

Strategic therapists see dysfunction is defined as rigid, repetitive interactive behavior (Becvar & Becvar, 2006; Haley, 1987). They evolve over time as people try to manage their relationships with others (Carlson, 2002).

For Madanes (1981) and Haley (1987; Haley & Richeport-Haley, 2003), problems in families result from problematic hierarchies, or what Madanes calls "incongruous hierarchical organization in the family" (1981, p. 67). These hierarchies, it is implied, are inextricably linked to the rigid interactive behavior of family members. For example, when George has a symptom and thereby distracts the parents from difficulties in the couple's relationship, he is assuming inappropriate power within the family system. The parents focus on George and do "more of the same" with him, trying the same responses to his behavior time and time again (and typically, escalating each time).

If there is a problem child in a family, according to Haley, then someone has crossed a generational boundary and become too involved with a child (not necessarily the symptomatic one, although that is common; 1987). The situation is at its worst when the dysfunctional coalition is denied or concealed. Also, the ganging up process is repeated—that is, cross-generational coalitions are not necessarily problematic unless they become routine (Haley, 1987). Haley and Richeport-Haley (2003) also point to two other common problems seen in family hierarchy: parents forming coalitions in opposition to one another, and in-laws violating boundaries.

Ironically, the symptom is seen as a metaphor for the problem but also as an attempt to solve the problem (O'Connor, 1986). Kids cooperate with feuding parents by appearing with symptoms that distract them from the conflict (Cheung, 2005). So George's temper tantrums express the rage between the two parents, but are also attempts to distract his parents from this painful situation.

You might have guessed by now that strategic therapists spend little time discussing healthy people and families. Haley (1987) noted that even confused or distorted hierarchies can reside in healthy families. Stanton (1981) gave one strategic version of health: "Healthy families are less preoccupied with themselves and their own motivations or problems, showing less interest in any kind of 'search for insight'" (p. 363).

By deduction, we would assume that healthy families, from a strategic perspective, would have clear hierarchies that are consistent with the family's context (i.e., the culture in which it lives; Stanton, 1981). Few entrenched cross-generational coalitions would be observed in these families. These families would somehow figure out how to navigate the transitions in the family life cycle without confusion or collusion. Communication patterns are clear and flexible.

Morgan observes that Jean and Derril seem to have a cross-generational coalition. However, this teamwork is not denied, and in some instances, it is adaptive, such as in completing household chores. However, Derril's behavior suggests that something is not working, and Morgan guesses that his acting-out behavior is both symbolic of the conflict between his parents (in your face!) and also a way of distracting Jean from her loneliness and pain.

NATURE OF THERAPY

ASSESSMENT

No formal assessment or diagnosis is used in Strategic Therapy. In fact, strategic therapists in the past were seen as radicals because they were critical of diagnostic labels, suggesting that "to label someone as 'schizophrenic,' 'delinquent,' or 'manic-depressive' is to participate in the creation of the problem that the therapy must solve. Sometimes the label creates a problem, so that the solution is made more difficult to cure" (Madanes, 1981, p. 20). Even more outrageous to some was the strategic camp's insistence that psychoactive medication should be immediately discontinued because it defines the client as "mentally ill" instead of simply misbehaving (Madanes, 1981). Nowadays, strategic therapists seem much less adamant about these issues, advocating that the therapist should work to establish good relationships with other professionals, including psychiatrists who are prescribing medication (Haley & Richeport-Haley, 2003).

The strategic therapist assesses the family through observation of interactions, which will provide information about hierarchies and where they might be dysfunctional. The strategic therapist can also gain information by deliberately intervening in the family and observing how it responds (Stanton, 1981).

Morgan watches carefully as Jean and Derril discuss what brings them to counseling. She looks at who presents the problem (Jean), how Derril responds to this presentation (by presenting his own version), and how Jean reacts to Derril's presentation. The actual content of these presentations is not as important as the quality of their interaction; the two seem to be operating from approximately the same level of power.

OVERVIEW OF THE THERAPEUTIC ATMOSPHERE AND ROLES OF CLIENT AND COUNSELOR

Strategic family therapy is generally brief, and the therapist is very active and directive (O'Connor, 1986). The focus of counseling is generally on the present, and the therapist assumes responsibility for the structure of the counseling process (Carlson, 2002).

Unlike most other approaches, Strategic Therapy considers the social context of the presenting problem to include professionals who have influence and control over the clients, such as medical professionals who prescribe drugs and administer inpatient treatment (Haley, 1987; Madanes, 1981). These institutions and individuals can be problematic because they "not only focus on an individual, but are also antifamily" (Haley, 1980, p. 53). Strategic therapists are flexible in their use of locations and time frames for therapy (Haley, 1987). Sessions can be held in homes, in schools, or in the traditional office space. Sessions are known to range from the sacred 50 minutes to multiple hours (Haley, 1987).

The therapist in Strategic Therapy shoulders the total responsibility for the outcome of therapy (Carlson, 2002). Relatively few expectations are expressed about the role of the clients in Strategic Therapy.

Morgan takes charge of the therapy situation. She is active and begins her task of helping Jean and Derril define a solvable problem. Although she is aware of the role of Derril's school in this situation (defining Derril as a problem kid), she decides that she will not intervene there unless at some point it seems necessary.

GOALS

The goal of the strategic therapist is very simple and straightforward: to resolve the presenting problem (Madanes, 1981). The problem "should be something one can count, observe, measure, or in some way know one is influencing" (Haley, 1987, p. 39). Ultimately, the strategic counselor wants people to *behave differently;* she doesn't care much about insight (Haley, 1987). In fact, Haley and Richeport-Haley (2003) point out that pushing for insight can be a problem, because many clients are not comfortable with interpretations. Another way to look at the goal of therapy from this perspective is that counseling helps individuals navigate the transition between the life stages. That is, clients become clients because they have experienced a crisis in one stage of development and are unable therefore to move to the next stage. For example, Haley (1980) maintained that adolescents become schizophrenic because they are having difficulty leaving home.

The strategic therapist's interest in patterns of communication that support distorted hierarchies also leads to interest in changing the routine patterns presented by the clients. Thus, the strategic therapist strives to help the clients learn more complex ways of communicating and interacting with their systems (Madanes, 1981). As Stanton (1981) put it, "Strategic therapists more commonly use the family's overtly expressed goals or target complaints as rallying points for actually altering dysfunctional sequences" (p. 366). In other words, the therapist appears to be digital in his focus on the presented problem, but is analogic in conceptualization and intervention.

Strategic therapists deal with client resistance in a unique way—they "go with" the family and thereby avoid power struggles (Stanton, 1981). They also use indirect or paradoxical directives as a way of inducing change by using resistance. These interventions are discussed in more detail later.

The agreed-upon goal is to help Derril stay out of trouble. The number of times he gets in trouble at school can be counted. Morgan thinks that to do this, she will help Derril grow up and help Jean develop a life outside of her relationship with Derril. Achieving these goals requires changing how this pair relates to each other and to the outside world.

PROCESS OF THERAPY

One of the first tasks of the strategic therapist is to work with the family to formulate a problem that is solvable (Haley, 1987). Therapy can then proceed, but beware, because Haley and Richeport-Haley (2003) warn us that "what makes therapy difficult for trainees is that life is so complex that you have to design therapy for each case and you have to be innovative" (p. xv).

Haley had quite a bit to say about the conduct of the first session of counseling. He thought that it was important to have everyone in the household present for at least the first session (1987), saying, "It is possible to change a person by seeing him alone, but the skill required is often too much to ask of the average therapist" (p. 11). Carlson (2002) had a different view—he opined that effective therapy could happen without everyone there.

Haley (1987) divided the first counseling session into five stages: social, problem, interaction, goal setting, and task setting. In the *social* stage, the therapist chitchats with the family, getting to know the members. It is important to get everyone to talk in this stage so that all family members know they are important to the counseling process. The counselor also uses the behavior of the family in the social stage to observe important family processes, such as parenting, general family mood, and the roles and power structures in the family. The strategic therapist formulates *tentative* hypotheses based on these observations, but does *not* divulge these to the family (Haley, 1987).

The *problem* stage begins when the therapist asks what brought the family to counseling. Family members' responses to this question are informative. Everyone must have a chance to give his or her views on the problem, but Haley recommends that the adult who is least involved with the identified problem be queried first. However, the counselor must be very careful to be respectful and courteous to the individual who has the most power to bring the family back to therapy. These individuals are typically not the same people! Haley also cautions that it is inadvisable to start with the problem child because he might conclude that the counselor blames him.

In the problem stage, the therapist should have an attitude of "helpful interest" (Haley, 1987, p. 27). He should not offer advice, even if someone requests it. Family members should be asked for their opinions, not their feelings, about the situation. All the time, the counselor is making observations about the family, but again, she is not to convey these or any interpretations about what she sees. The discussion of the problem should move from general statements to a more specific construction, and the latter should ideally involve more than one person.

The next stage of the first session is the *interaction* stage (Haley, 1987). Family members are directed to talk to each other about the problem. The intent of the strategic therapist is, ideally, to actually see the problem in its full glory. If someone in the family is anxious, she can be asked to get anxious in the session so that the counselor can observe what happens. The therapist can also get a good view of the family's hierarchy through this process.

Once the family has interacted, they move to the *goal-setting* stage, in which the problem is clearly defined in a solvable way (Haley, 1987). The problem must be observable so the family and therapist know when things are getting better. Rather than setting the goal to reduce John's anxiety, the therapist wants more specific goals, such as stopping John's stuttering, increasing John's excursions outside of his home to three per week, and so on.

Sometimes, but sometimes not, a final stage of the first session is entered, called *task setting* (Haley, 1987). If the counselor is clever enough, she will prescribe some homework for the family to complete before the next session. Directives of this sort are essential to Strategic Therapy and will be discussed in more detail in the section on techniques.

When Morgan asked Jean to bring Al to the first therapy session, Jean reacted very emphatically, saying that it would be of no use because he was not part of the family. Although Morgan thought that this arrangement was not quite ideal, she accepted it.

Morgan greets Jean and Derril and chats with them a little about everyday stuff. She asks if they had any difficulty finding her office, where they live, and so forth. Fairly quickly, though, Morgan proceeds to asking Jean and Derril what brings them in. Jean mostly describes the problem, with Derril remaining silent. At one point, Derril gets angry and breaks into his mother's monologue. Morgan observes these events and begins to form hypotheses. She moves Jean and Derril into the interaction phase by asking them to talk to each other about the problem. Observing this discussion, Morgan notes that the two relate as equals rather than as mother and son. Mother blames a lot, and Derril blames others for his behavior—they get in his face.

Morgan struggles to help Jean and Derril define the problem as solvable. She defines the problem as a joint effort of Jean and Derril to keep him out of trouble at school. Jean needs to take charge in this process of helping Derril to grow up and take responsibility for his own behavior. Perhaps if he grows up, he will find some new ways to deal with conflict.

Privately, Morgan decides that Derril is taking care of his mother at the expense of taking care of his own life. Jean needs to help Derril see that she doesn't need to be taken care of. If Morgan can create a more functional hierarchy for Jean and Derril, this problem should take care of itself.

THERAPEUTIC TECHNIQUES

DIRECTIVES

The strategic therapist almost always issues directives to the family, often as tasks to be performed at home over the intervals between sessions. Directives are used to accomplish the therapeutic goal of getting people to behave differently. They also change the relationship with the therapist—it is intensified because the clients live with the therapist in the form of her directives for a whole week (Haley, 1987). The use of directives also helps the counselor gather information. Whether the clients obey or disobey, they are still communicating.

Two kinds of directives are used in Strategic Therapy: direct, or straightforward, and indirect, or paradoxical (Haley, 1987; Haley & Richeport-Haley, 2003). Direct interventions are those in which the counselor simply tells the client what to do. They are used when the therapist expects that the family will comply (O'Connor, 1986). Directives are not the same as giving advice. Haley (1987) noted that "giving good advice means the therapist assumes that people have rational control of what they are doing. To be successful in the therapy business, it may be better to drop that idea" (p. 61). Good advice is what everyone gives the family, so that, for example, "telling people that they should treat each other better is not useful to them" (Haley, 1987, p. 61). More useful are directives that alter the patterns of communication, and hence the hierarchy, in the family.

One example of a straightforward directive is penance (Haley & Richeport-Haley, 2003). This form is used when clients feel sorry and awful; the therapist gives them something to do that is helpful to others (p. 9).

Paradoxical directives are used when the therapist thinks the family will probably resist a direct intervention. Two general forms of paradox are described by Haley and Richeport-Haley (2003): restraining orders (which instruct the client *not* to change) and symptom prescription. These interventions are designed to place the client in a no-win situation. To illustrate this dilemma, O'Connor (1986) described the directive given to a child obsessing about vomiting. The 10-year-old was told to sit for an hour each day in the family kitchen and think about vomiting (and only then). If Charlie obeys, then he demonstrates control over his symptom. If Charlie disobeys, the symptom is gone!

Any directive given must be clear, precise, and understood by all members of the family (Haley, 1987). All members of the family should have a part in the task. Directives should clarify, not confuse, hierarchies. Of course, Haley noted that sometimes (but not very often) it is helpful to give confusing directives, involve less than the complete family, or confuse the family hierarchy. Finally, someone in the family should be made responsible for reporting on the family's performance at the next counseling session. If the family has followed the directive, fine. If they have not, they should not be let off easily (Haley, 1987).

A special form of paradoxical directive is the *ordeal*. The goal of the ordeal is to make the symptom more trouble than it is worth in terms of controlling relationships with others. The client will then voluntarily give up the symptom. The assumption behind this approach is that the individual who gives up her symptom will then have to find new ways of relating to others that are more adaptive.

Haley (1984) described three characteristics of ordeals. First, as noted earlier, the ordeal must be worse than the symptom. Second, the ordeal must be something the person is able to do and not object to on moral or ethical grounds. Third, the ordeal must not harm the client or anyone else (1984, p. 7). As with directives, there are two kinds of ordeals. A *straightforward ordeal* requires the performance of an unpleasant but "good for you" task upon occurrence of the symptom. Clients are asked about things that they should do more of (e.g., exercising, cleaning house, and so forth). Once the symptom is clearly specified, the client is told to perform the ordeal if the symptom occurs. Haley (1984) noted that it is best if the ordeal is performed in the middle of the night! I once gave a client an ordeal to help him with insomnia. He decided that he needed to clean out his garage. I instructed him that if he could not sleep 20 minutes after getting in bed, he should get up and clean his garage. This client found that he had very little trouble getting to sleep in the next few weeks and that his garage remained dirty.

Paradoxical ordeals are directives that demand the performance of the symptom. From one perspective, simply having to perform the symptom could be considered an ordeal. Another tactic is to require the performance under aversive conditions. One interesting aspect of paradoxical ordeals is that if the client complies, the symptom becomes voluntary, under the client's control (Haley, 1984). The alternative, noncompliance with the directive, is to give up the symptom.

In addition to straightforward and paradoxical directives, which can be, at times, ordeals, therapy itself can be viewed as an ordeal. There are numerous ways to *make the therapist the ordeal*. On a very basic level, the fact that the client has to pay to discuss her inadequacies in front of what seems to be a problem-free person makes the therapist troublesome. Haley described several instances of using payments to the therapist as ordeals, with the agreement that the therapist can do whatever he wants to with the money. In one case, each time a client binged and vomited, she had to pay the therapist, beginning with a penny. Every time she repeated this behavior, the amount doubled (Haley, 1984). The first time she vomited, she owed a penny, the second time 2 cents. The third time the client threw up, she owed 4 cents, then 8, then 16 cents, and so on. For the client who throws up 10 times a day, this can be a very expensive contract. She went from vomiting from 4 to 25 times a day to vomiting only 6 times in the first week after the assignment. In the second week, she vomited only once and then stopped completely.

Confrontation and interpretation of the client's behavior by the therapist often result in clients having to acknowledge things they'd rather not. Reframing or redefining the client's behaviors in ways the client does not like constitutes an unpleasant experience. Anger can be redefined as a way of caring about someone. If the client is resisting a certain task, the counselor can characterize this behavior as the client being protective of herself or others. This reconceptualization puts the client in charge of her behavior.

Ordeals involving two or more persons are typically used when families are available to participate. The ordeal of the binging and vomiting client described earlier is a good example of this type of ordeal (because the therapist was involved). Another example is having the mother of a bed-wetting child get him up at dawn to practice his handwriting (Haley, 1984).

Morgan considers the directives she could give Jean and Derril. Some straightforward options are telling Jean to get a life (i.e., directing her to do something on her own over the next week) and devising a way for Derril to help her out in this. She considers having Jean give Derril more autonomy when it comes to school, not calling his teachers weekly as she has been. Derril must comply by giving his mother a daily summary of events when she gets home from work.

Paradoxical alternatives might involve moving Jean and Derril closer together, hoping for noncompliance. Morgan considers asking Jean and Derril to devise more ways to spend time with each other and could intensify this directive into an ordeal by having them play cards for 2 hours every night. She also thinks about having Jean go to school with Derril every day. She could get detailed daily reports on his behavior.

Reframing

Sometimes, changing the way the clients perceive the problem is helpful. In fact, reframing can be one way to transform a problem from intractable to solvable. Obsessions can be transformed into worrying or even thinking about, which seems much less threatening.

Morgan can reframe Derril's acting out as a way of taking care of his mother—he keeps her busy with his problems, distracting her from her struggles to be a single mom who has few friends.

Exaggerating the Hierarchical Problem

Directives can be used to exaggerate the hierarchy identified as distorted. Haley (1987) noted that two such approaches can be used. In the first, the more distant parent is put in charge of a child who is in coalition with the involved parent. However, interventions of this first type can be problematic because they can induce conflict in the couple's relationship. An alternative is to exaggerate the involvement of the family members in coalition to disrupt it. Haley (1973) described a case in which Erickson intervened with a mother concerned about her 12-year-old son's bed-wetting. Erickson prescribed an ordeal, insisting that the mother get up at 4:00 A.M. every night and check her son's bed. If it was wet, she was to wake him, and he was to then improve his handwriting by copying passages out of a book until 7:00 A.M. The bed-wetting disappeared very quickly.

PRETEND DIRECTIVES

Madanes (1981) contributed the idea of pretend directives to the strategic arsenal. She suggested that it was useful to use these directives in two ways: (a) have the symptomatic person pretend to have the symptom in the counseling session or (b) have the parents of a symptomatic child pretend to need the child's help. When an adult is directed to pretend to have a symptom, the partner or spouse is directed to give a critical analysis of the presentation. In the second instance, in which the parents pretend to need help, the child is to pretend to help. In this approach, the symptom becomes less real, and pretending to have it serves the same function as having it. Thus, the client can give up the "real" symptom (Nichols, 2002). Also, the individual might be more likely to experiment with different kinds of behaviors if the situation is framed as play (Becvar & Becvar, 2006).

Morgan considers using a pretend directive in session, telling Jean to ask for Derril's help on developing a social life.

Bowen's Family Systems Theory

OVERVIEW

This version of FS theory is the brainchild of Murray Bowen (1913–1990). To distinguish it from other systems approaches, I will refer to it as Bowen's Family Systems Theory (BFST). This approach is widely acknowledged as the most elegant theoretical construction among the family system theories (Gurman & Kniskern, 1981).

Bowen, a psychiatrist, began his theoretical work working with schizophrenics at the Menninger Clinic from 1946 to 1954. He later moved to the National Institute of Mental Health (NIMH) and then to Georgetown University. A detailed history of the development of Bowen's thought is found in Kerr (1981).

Bowen is best known for two pioneering advances in the family therapy area. First, while at NIMH, he experimented with hospitalizing the entire families of schizophrenics, practicing what Kerr (1981) called family group therapy (p. 230). In these studies, he began to note the intense emotional processes in these families, but his concurrent outpatient work suggested that the differences between these families and those with less severe dysfunction was a matter of quantity, not quality.

A second contribution of Bowen was his analysis of his own journey to differentiate from his family of origin (a version of this paper can be found in Bowen, 1978 and you can read a little bit of it in Box 13.3). Bowen presented this analysis to a group of family therapy theorists and researchers and then soon began teaching this approach to his students.

If you read a lot of BFST literature, you will find that some authors distinguish between traditional and nontraditional BFST, or Bowen and Bowenian variants, according to Guerin and Guerin (2002). The traditional form is that practiced by Bowen himself, was long-term, and focused on getting the client to work on family of origin issues. Bowenian therapy is a broadened version of the therapy, and seems as likely to intervene in the present (e.g., with the current family system, or focus on the presenting symptom) as it is to focus on multigenerational issues (Murdock, 2007). In this chapter, I will attempt to offer points from both perspectives.

Box 13.3

An Excerpt from Bowen's *On the Differentiation of Self*

An important triangle at work at this time was the one between my mother, my second brother, and me. I had worked very hard on the triangle with my parents and me, assuming that my problem would be solved. Now a new version of the problem had been displaced onto the new triangle. When conflict arose in the business, my mother would communicate by some means, if not directly, that I was on her side, and my brother would react as if this was reality. I began to perceive some of this development on trips. The process would emerge in the form of gossip-type stories which in an emotional system communicate, "We two are together on this issue. We are in agreement about that other third person." One of the better ways to disengage from such a triangling "secret" communication is to go to the third person and report the message in a neutral way. I was out of effective contact with my second brother then and the only move I could make was to tell my mother that I was neutral. She would say that she respected my position and I would assume she was acting neutral about me with others. I would leave town and the family would react as if I was on her side.

Action is required when words fail to detriangle in emotional systems. My mother has always used "secret" communications to facilitate her position in the emotional system. One of my early responses to her communication was to listen, and I thought I could listen without taking sides. In retrospect, this maneuver was one of the key triggers for my early fusions into the emotional system. Listening to such communications without response, pretending that one is not involved, does not fool an emotional system. When I was aware that "no response" was not effective, I began using comments such as, "That's one of the better stories." This method was a little more effective. In retrospect, I undoubtedly was responding while I kidded myself that I was neutral. I had worked much more actively on the triangle with my father, mother, and myself and I had been more effective in detriangling from that. There had been several exchanges about "secrets" that turned the tide in that area. The first one was a letter in which mother communicated some negative story about my father. In the next mail I wrote to my father to say that his wife had just told me this story about him, and I wondered why she told me instead of telling him. He showed the letter to her, and she fussed about not being able to trust me. Several letters such as this, plus similar exchanges when I was with both parents, had been reasonably effective at detriangling me from them. During that period, mother made comments about my reading too much between the lines, and I made comments about her writing too much between the lines.

The triangling pattern in my family of origin, which is the usual one in all emotional systems, was most intense during stress periods. Various family members were grouped on the corners of the primary triangle, except that the grouping would be somewhat different, depending on the emotional issues. The two on the togetherness side of a triangle would talk about the outsider. With various versions of different issues being discussed in four separate households, and with me in reasonably good contact with them all, it was possible to keep a good reading of the family emotional tension. My first brother has hardly been mentioned in this report. His lifelong position in the family has been one of moderate involvement and acting uninvolved, with statements that he would be willing to help anytime if he was needed but that he did not want to "just talk."

Excerpted from *Family Therapy in Clinical Practice* by M. Bowen, 1978. New York: Jason Aronson. Reprinted with permission.

CENTRAL CONSTRUCTS

DIFFERENTIATION OF SELF

The most basic construct in BFST is differentiation of self from the family of origin. According to Bowen, it is an inherent feature of all living organisms that they must balance pulls of togetherness and separateness (Wetchler & Piercy, 1996). Differentiation of self is a lifelong process of balancing these forces (Kerr & Bowen, 1988).

Differentiation is both an individual and a family construct. Individuals have characteristic levels of differentiation, but the overall levels of differentiation of their families of origin mostly determine the individual's level. Differentiation should be thought of as a continuum; people and families fall along a range from very low differentiation to relatively high differentiation. For purposes of explanation, though, we tend to compare the characteristics of individuals with low and high levels of this construct.

Individuals who are relatively well differentiated have a solid sense of self. They are clear about where they end and others begin. They are able to distinguish thought from feeling, and their behavior is guided by their own principles and cognitions rather than emotional factors (Guerin & Guerin, 2002). Individuals who display low levels of differentiation are said to be *reactive;* they respond based on emotions as compared to individuals with higher levels of differentiation, who respond on the basis of objective thought, or what some term "clearheadedness" (Friedman, 1991).

In relationships, individuals with higher levels of differentiation are able to stay in intimate contact with others while maintaining a solid sense of self (Kerr, 1984). This quality, termed emotional autonomy, should not be confused with denying one's needs for other people. Distancing on the basis of such denial is termed a "pseudo independent posture" (Kerr, 1984, p. 9) and is evidence of a lack of emotional autonomy.

The term *fusion* is almost synonymous with low differentiation of self, and it seems to have at least two meanings in BFST. In Bowen's early writing, he spoke of fusion as meaning that the individual's emotional and intellectual systems are inseparable (Bowen, 1978). The emotional system tends to dominate behavior, and usually the emotionality is activated by anxiety in an important other or in a critical relationship (Guerin & Guerin, 2002).

A second definition refers to the low-differentiated individual's tendency to fuse the self into a "common self with others" (Bowen, 1978, p. 472). This process is seen most clearly in intimate relationships such as marriages. Such fusion creates "emotional bliss" (p. 473), but it is difficult to maintain. One individual in the dyad tends to absorb higher levels of self and becomes dominant, or stronger, whereas the other adapts and looks weaker. The weaker-appearing individual is then likely to develop symptoms. The emphasis here is on terms such as *looks* and *appears* stronger or weaker because Bowen maintained that we tend to involve ourselves with significant others who are at about the same level of differentiation as we are (Bowen, 1978). The borrowing of self in the fusion process makes one individual look more together than the other looks.

Jacob, Jean and Derril's BFST therapist, starts his work with the premise that both Jean and Derril are relatively low on the range of differentiation of self. They appear to be fused in their relationship—neither has a strong sense of self separate from the other. Both seem to be emotionally reactive as evidenced by what happens when conflict erupts.

CHRONIC ANXIETY

Closely related to differentiation is what Bowen called chronic anxiety. Both constructs are considered to be natural biological phenomena (Friedman, 1991). Chronic anxiety is a nonthinking phenomenon that is basic to survival. It is basically the organism's response to *imagined* threat, as compared to acute anxiety, which is a response to real threat (Kerr & Bowen, 1988). Although Bowen maintained that chronic anxiety is not caused by any specific factors, it is seen as generated mainly by relationship disturbance (Kerr & Bowen, 1988, p. 113). Chronic anxiety is integral to understanding psychological dysfunction. Symptoms are a method of controlling, or in Bowenian terms, binding, anxiety. Friedman (1991) wrote, "*Chronic anxiety is understood to be the primary promoter of all symptoms, from schizophrenia to cancer, from anorexia to birth defects. The antidote, and the preventive medicine, always is differentiation*" (p. 140; italics in original). Here, I will pause to comment that the definitions of differentiation, chronic anxiety, and stress seem to overlap in Bowen's system, causing some fuzziness in at least my understanding of the relations among these concepts. Sometimes, stress, differentiation, and anxiety appear to be separate, independent constructs. However, at other points, Bowen seems to use these terms interchangeably, or at least implies that the three qualities covary perfectly.

Jacob guesses that there is a great deal of chronic anxiety in Jean and Derril's system and is a significant factor in the struggles they face. In fact, Jacob is fairly certain that Jean responds to this undercurrent by focusing intently on Derril. Derril responds to the pressure by acting out.

TRIANGLES

Bowen thought that the most basic unit of human interaction was the triangle (Kerr & Bowen, 1988). To state the obvious, a triangle involves three people. At any time, two of the people are the "in" group, and the third is on the outside. Triangles can form when the level of tension rises in a relationship or family (Kerr, 1981). If the anxiety present in the system is not bound by one person (see the discussion of the development of health and dysfunction), then the tension can be absorbed by one member of a dyad fusing with a third person. The "out" person may feel relieved or very uncomfortable with his position. Triangling is connected to differentiation in that individuals who have lower levels of differentiation (or families low in differentiation) are more likely to triangle because of the higher levels of emotionality present (Kerr, 1981).

Guerin, Fogarty, Fay, and Kautto (1996) note that triangles keep people stuck. They maintain that "in active triangles, people are never free. Their responses to events are constrained and predictable. They are unable to consider alternatives" (p. 35). So, when you see your client acting in repetitive ways in relation to others (particularly to a specific other), you should suspect that a triangle is activated. However, Guerin et al. also note that not every three-person structure is a triangle. Three people can interact with each other in two-person relations without pulling the third one in.

Jacob sees a triangle with Jean and Derril on the inside and Al on the outside. The original conflict arose between Jean and Al, and apparently, she fused with Derril to bind the anxiety in the system.

EMOTIONAL DISTANCE

Emotional proximity can be chosen, or it can be the result of reactivity. Everyone uses distancing sometimes, which is also called *emotional cutoff* (Papero, 1990). People with relatively high levels of differentiation can choose to distance from one another because they are busy with other things. However, folks with lower levels of differentiation often reactively distance from important others (family) because the level of anxiety in relationships is intolerable. Cutoff can be good, because it decreases anxiety, or bad, because it deprives the individual of the support of the family (Kerr & Bowen, 1988).

Derril's dad, Al, has dealt with the conflicted relationship with Jean by cutting himself off from her and Derril. In this process, he has probably fused into his relationship with his new girlfriend, because Jacob guesses that Al probably has a similar level of differentiation as Jean.

SIBLING POSITION

Borrowing from Toman's (1961) work, Bowen wrote about the influence of birth order on individuals' relationship tendencies (see Chapter 4 for more information on birth order). Declaring that "I believe that no single piece of data is more important than knowing the sibling position of people in the present and past generations" (1978, p. 385), Bowen (1978) thought that deviation from what was expected based on a particular birth position provided information on levels of differentiation and family functioning. For example, if an oldest child acts like we expect an "only" to act, triangulation is probably occurring. The gender composition among a set of siblings is also important: it is one thing to be a youngest daughter with two older sisters and quite different to be the same in a male sibling group. Sibling position also influences couple functioning: two eldests are likely to fight about who gets to be in charge whereas a youngest and oldest might have fewer disagreements in this area (Papero, 1990).

Jacob notes that Derril is an only child in the current system. His 20-year-old sister is considered to be of another family from a conceptual standpoint. Derril does not share the limelight with anyone and this undoubtedly has influenced who he is. He notes that Jean is an eldest (with younger brothers and sisters) and Al a youngest with an older sister. At first glance, this pairing should be relatively complementary, so Jacob wonders why this was not the case for Jean and Al.

THEORY OF THE PERSON
AND DEVELOPMENT OF THE INDIVIDUAL

For Bowen, the essential feature of human life (and further, in nature) is differentiation, the balancing of the two natural forces of individuality and togetherness (Kerr, 1981). Both processes are considered to be biologically rooted, but the relative level of differentiation is transmitted by the family.

Bowen thought that families projected their levels of differentiation onto their members through the nuclear family emotional system (Wetchler & Piercy, 1996). Kerr and Bowen asserted that "people who marry have the same level of differentiation of self. When they marry, the two spouses become the primary 'architects' of the nuclear family emotional atmosphere . . . and each child born . . . is incorporated into that atmosphere" (p. 225; quotes in original). Further, this process operates across generations, and it is called the *multigenerational transmission process.*

As a result of the qualities of its members (their levels of differentiation) and factors external to the family, each family has an average level of chronic anxiety over time. The total amount of chronic anxiety experienced and the ways in which it is bound (triangles, couple conflict, symptoms, etc.) determines the average level of differentiation of family members. Some kids may be a little more differentiated than others, but these differences are not likely to be extreme (Kerr & Bowen, 1988). If one child becomes the object of the family projection process, then she will develop lower differentiation than the family average while other kids may achieve higher levels. When Frank, the kid with the lowest level of differentiation, takes a partner, the partner, according to BFST, will be at Frank's level of differentiation, creating a system with a lower level of differentiation than Frank's family displayed. The same pattern would be true for Nicole, who has a level of differentiation higher than that of her family of origin. These divergences, according to the theory, account for the range of differentiation observed over generations of a family and also across people in general.

Jean and Al have transmitted their levels of differentiation to Derril, who is now struggling to individuate as an adolescent. The multigenerational process of transmission of differentiation predicts that Jean and Al's families of origin probably showed a lot of anxiety, triangulation, and cutoff.

HEALTH AND DYSFUNCTION

From a BFST perspective, symptoms appear as a result of the characteristic style of emotional functioning of the family (Kerr & Bowen, 1988). Symptoms appear most often in families with lower levels of differentiation. Given a group of individuals who are low in differentiation, symptoms could potentially pop up in any member when stress levels rise, according to Bowen. Three general patterns of dysfunction are seen: conflict in the couple's relationship, dysfunction in a member of the parental couple, and dysfunction in a child. For example, if the family's style is to put the anxiety into the couple relationship, high-stress periods result in the partners fighting. If the tendency is to create dysfunction in one person, a child or one of the parents will become "sick," either physically or psychologically (Kerr & Bowen, 1988). Families with higher levels of differentiation are not immune to symptoms. Kerr and Bowen noted that if stressed enough for a long enough period of time, even well-differentiated families can develop dysfunction.

Dysfunction can also be conceptualized from a more individualistic perspective, using the construct of differentiation of self. An important construct in BFST is anxiety, defined as the "response to an individual or organism to threat, real or imagined" (Kerr & Bowen, 1988; p. 112). Differentiation of self and anxiety combine to determine the level of an individual's functioning, and specifically, the level of *chronic anxiety* in an individual's relationship system is key. "Symptom development, therefore, depends on the amount of stress *and* on the adaptiveness of the individual or family to stress" (p. 112; italics in original). One important source of stress is the level of chronic anxiety in relationship systems (Kerr & Bowen, 1988). Because individuals low in differentiation are less adaptive to stress, they tend to get into trouble more often and more easily than do individuals with higher levels of differentiation.

Jacob thinks that this family's style shows two of the three patterns of dealing with anxiety. Formerly the anxiety erupted as fights between Jean and Al. However, when Al cut off and fused with his current girlfriend, the anxiety resulted in symptoms in Derril—his acting-out behavior. Periodically, the stress in the environment combined with Jean's focus on Derril results in his disruptive, emotionally reactive behavior.

NATURE OF THERAPY

Assessment

Assessment in a family systems approach is accomplished through two basic techniques, one informal and one formal. Informal assessment is accomplished through questioning; the BFST counselor uses a directed set of questions to assess the characteristics of the individual, his family of origin, and his current nuclear family, if applicable.

BFST counselors are very interested in the level of emotionality present in clients, because "emotional intensity is not to be feared, but it is to be respected" (Kerr & Bowen, 1988, p. 328). If a client is under a lot of stress and is fairly low in adaptability (differentiation), the therapist must take care not to disturb this precarious position.

Assessment in this model can also involve looking at the primary method of anxiety binding used by the client. Remember, anxiety can be bound into relationship conflict, symptoms in one of the partners, or symptoms in a child. The BFST therapist wants to see which of these is prominent in a client's presentation because he believes that treatment may need to proceed differently depending on the mode (Kerr & Bowen, 1988). For example, if the major method is the continual adaptation of one relationship partner to the other (resulting in loss of self and the appearance of symptoms), the BFST counselor may decide to see the partners separately. Counseling them together may even make the de-selfed partner worse!

Kerr and Bowen (1988) recommended that if the major mechanism for anxiety is over-involvement with a child (triangling), the therapist probably wants to have the parents work on their own differentiation from their families of origin first, excluding the child from therapy. The rationale for this approach is that the emotional bond with the child is just too intense for much progress to be made. Getting the parents to differentiate is thought to help them be more observant and objective in their relationships with the kid.

The *genogram* is the primary method of formal assessment in BFST. Basically, a genogram looks like a family tree that shows the members of an individual's family, usually over three generations. Some BFST counselors developed fancy notation that symbolizes the nature of the various relationships depicted on the genogram. For example, if you absolutely hate your cousin Fred, a zigzaggy line would be drawn between you and him on your genogram.

Jacob's genogram for Jean and Derril's family is shown in Figure 13.1. He notes that Al is un-employed. This underfunctioning in respect to his current partner (who is a nuclear scientist), replicates the situation in his family of origin. Also, Al is a youngest child, a boy, and therefore likely to be the object of much parental attention. Jean is an eldest, probably used to taking care of her siblings, and in particular, Jerome, who may be the focus of Jean's family's tension.

Jacob observes the high level of emotionality present in Jean's communication and Derril's tendency to alternate between being sulky (cutting off) or reacting angrily to Jean.

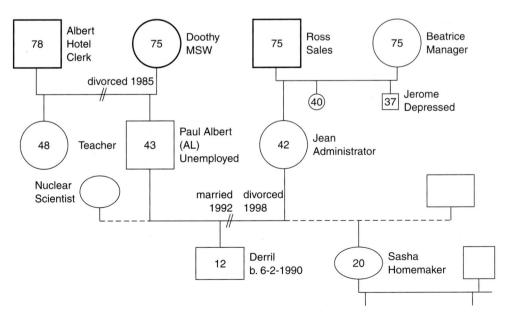

FIGURE 13.1. Genogram of Jean and Derril's Family.

He asks questions about how Jean's family communicates (anger followed by emotional cutoff) and about her siblings and their relationships, both current and historically. Jacob decides that because the issue seems to be overinvolvement of Jean and Derril, his first task should be to help Jean differentiate from her family of origin.

OVERVIEW OF THE THERAPEUTIC ATMOSPHERE AND ROLES OF CLIENT AND COUNSELOR

Because the basic goal of BFST is differentiation, and differentiation is such a difficult task, traditional BFST can be much longer in duration than other types of family therapy. The therapist is very active in this approach, but in a way that could be seen as very different from that observed in other approaches to counseling. The BFST therapist, above all, seeks to "*stay detriangled* from the emotional process" (Kerr, 1981, p. 255; italics in original). The therapist presents objectively and unemotionally. BFST therapists maintain that to stay detriangled, one needs to deal with facts, not feelings, and practice a calm vocal tone (Nichols & Schwartz, 2001). If a therapist finds himself reacting emotionally to the work with clients, Guerin et al. would say that the therapist has become triangled and the work of therapy will be compromised. For example, if I find myself getting mad at one member of a couple, I need to recognize this as triangulation and find a way to free myself.

BFST therapy is often described as *coaching* (Carter & McGoldrick, 2005). The therapist is the coach, and the client is the athlete; the analogy is apt because BFST counselors believe that most of what happens in therapy is the result of the client's work. The therapist just helps him get started and cheers him on through the process of differentiating from the family of origin (Bowen, 1978). Carter and Orfanidis (1976) described coaching as a process in which the coach supports the client without becoming triangled into the client's system. For example, siding with the client against other family members would be bad coaching. In essence, the BFST counselor will "expect and resist attempts to get him to provide direct emotional support, approval or reassurance. The coach will not want to become emotionally more important to a client than his family members are, nor to be more concerned or responsible for the client's life decisions and actions than the client is himself" (Carter & Orfanidis, 1976, p. 216).

Jacob is fairly neutral in his approach to Jean and Derril. He asks a lot of questions and works to stay detriangled. He is respectful to both as individuals, asking for their opinions on the situation. As he begins to move into helping Jean differentiate from her family, he will act as a coach to her in this process.

GOALS

The goal of BFST is to help the individual (or individuals) differentiate from the family of origin (Wetchler & Piercy, 1996). Kerr and Bowen (1988) noted that the reduction of anxiety in the individual and/or system is critical, too, because it will relieve symptoms. It is important to note that differentiation does *not* mean cutting off from one's family, emotionally or otherwise. The differentiated person is in contact with the family system, but her behavior is not dictated by family patterns. Altering one's level of differentiation will help the client to become more adaptive to stress and less reactive in relationships, all of which will contribute to the demise of symptoms.

Because of the typical pattern of this family, Jacob decides that the best way to intervene is to encourage Jean to differentiate from her family of origin so that Derril will be more free to do the same. This should decrease the fusion between them. Most likely, he will begin to see Jean alone as she negotiates this process. However, for the first part of therapy, Jacob will work with the dyad, decreasing the level of anxiety so that both Jean and Derril can function a little more effectively in their lives.

PROCESS OF THERAPY

The BFST therapist emphasizes insight, but action in the form of interacting differently with family of origin members is critical. As you will see in this section, one of the most common assignments to clients in BFST is to journey home and observe family interactions. The therapist teaches the client about the operation of family systems, but the client must go and watch for herself how her family puts the principles into effect. Then, the client is expected to change how she interacts with her family.

Bowen thought that counselors wanting to do BFST should work on their own levels of differentiation. Kerr and Bowen (1988) noted that "the more a therapist has worked on differentiation of self in his own family, the more he will be able to get closely involved with a clinical family and still be 'outside' the system" (p. 285; quotes in original). Essentially, the therapist needs to undergo BFST therapy himself so that he can competently provide help to others.

Jacob is sure that he will need to work with Jean to schedule visits with her family of origin. He teaches her about triangles, reactivity, and emotional cutoff.

THERAPEUTIC TECHNIQUES

There are really no set techniques associated with BFST (Kerr, 1981). In fact, Bowen was evidently dismissive of technique, preferring to emphasize understanding of the family system (Nichols, 2006). The BFST therapist then coaches the individual in his struggle for differentiation from the family of origin.

Commonly, clients go on "journeys" to work on differentiating, and it is best that they go alone rather than with a spouse, children, or sibling. Other approaches are to use telephone conversations or letters. The goal of these journeys, which should be taken when emotions are running high in the family, is to have the client observe the process of the family and attempt, if she is ready, to act differently. Detriangling (see the following paragraphs) is particularly important in these journeys.

One of the major tactics used by BFST counselors is *process* questioning (Nichols, 2006). The therapist uses these questions about how clients participate in their lives and relationships to avoid the emotionality often associated with content questions. An example of a process question might be when Terry, the therapist, asks Amy, "What happens in your family when your little brother Dayton has a temper tantrum?"

In the 1978 book *Family Therapy in Clinical Practice*, a compilation of Bowen's papers, Bowen described three methods by which the client works toward better differentiation of self. First, he endeavors to establish and maintain *person-to-person relationships* with members of his family (p. 540). Difficult to achieve, these relationships involve talking directly to another without talking about third parties or topics that are impersonal. Bowen recommended that the client establish a person-to-person relationship with every (living) person in the family of origin (Bowen, 1978).

A second objective for individuals wishing to increase their levels of differentiation is to *learn to be a better observer of family interactions, and better at controlling emotional reactions.* These two tasks are linked, according to Bowen, because observing and learning about our families leads to less emotional reactivity, which then frees us to be better observers. However, Bowen warned that no one is perfect. It is impossible to be a completely objective observer of one's own family, but one can make progress with hard work.

Detriangling is the third route to differentiation; in fact, Bowen called it "an absolute necessity" (1978, p. 542). To detriangle, one needs to be in continual contact with two other family members around an emotional issue. You can't take sides with either of the other members, nor can you defend yourself—you must be objective and neutral. You can't even be silent on the issue because that will be perceived by the others as an emotional response. Detriangling is best practiced when there is some form of emotional upswing in the family because under calm situations families will try to bury emotional issues. Clients are thus encouraged to "go home" to visit during holidays (always stressful!) or when there are illnesses or deaths in the family. In the broader, Bowenian approach to BFST, the therapist can also bring the members of the triangle into therapy and intervene directly to reorganize the interactions (Guerin et al., 1996).

I would be remiss to neglect to mention the role of taking an I-position in BFST counseling. Both the therapist and the client are expected to use the I-position, which is "a clear statement, neither offensive or defensive, of one's thoughts and feelings on a subject" (Carter & Orfanidis, 1976). Taking an I-position is a sign of differentiation.

Now that Jean understands the basic ideas of BFST, Jean and Jacob devise journeys home for her. She is to visit with her mother, sister, and brother, observing how she is pulled into triangulation, even though these family members live separately from one another. Mother wants to talk about father with Jean. Sister wants to talk about their brother's problems with depression. Jean, the eldest child, is expected to intervene in her parent's relationship and help her little brother. She feels pulled to take Mother's side against Father.

Jean struggles to maintain a person-to-person relationship with each family member and to not talk about other family members in the context of another relationship. As Jacob coaches Jean, he asks her to describe the family's ways of interacting with her. He explores the triangle between the parents and little brother and also the sibling triangle of Jean, her sister, and her little brother. Together, they devise ways for Jean to stay out of these triangles and to function more autonomously.

EVALUATION OF THE FAMILY SYSTEMS APPROACHES

Family Systems Theory, as is the case with other theories, has its critics. Strategic Therapy draws a good deal of the fire for its use of strategies such as paradoxical interventions.

These strategies are questioned on ethical grounds because they are seen as manipulating the client without the client's consent (Hampton, 1991). Haley (1987), of course, retorted that it is impossible to do counseling without manipulating clients because you are trying to get them to change. However, Minuchin has his share of critics, too (Golann, 1988). Feminists have been quite clear in their criticisms of systems approaches (see the later discussion of cultural and gender issues). Still others accuse FS theory of being simplistic and mechanical.

The roles of therapist as powerful expert and client as passive object have also been questioned. The postmodern, constructivist theorists maintain that since we construct all reality, there is no absolute truth for the therapist to know. This position implies that the client is as much of an expert as the counselor (Becvar & Becvar, 2006).

QUALITIES OF THE THEORY

It is difficult to evaluate FS approaches on my usual dimensions because the four theories presented here are very different from one another. For instance, some aspects of BFST seem to be relatively *operationalizable* and *testable*, but others are less so (binding anxiety, for example). Satir's theory is, at times, pretty vague. On the other hand, we have certainly learned how to measure self-esteem. Strategic and structural propositions about structure and hierarchy have been tested (see the discussion of this under "Research Support"), and the results are somewhat supportive of structural concepts.

FST is considered *empirically valid* in some forms. Family therapy in general has been found to be effective (Sexton & Alexander, 2002; Shadish & Baldwin, 2003), although you will see from the following reviews that at least one study found that the effects of systems interventions appear not to be as strong as those resulting from behavioral approaches.

RESEARCH SUPPORT

Outcome research. Reviews of family and relationship (i.e., "marital") therapy generally find that, overall, these approaches are effective (Diamond & Josephson, 2005; Rowe, Gozez, & Liddle, 2006; Sexton & Alexander, 2002; Shadish et al., 1993). Assessments of the efficacy of family interventions, particularly when they are using meta-analysis, tend to lump all of the approaches discussed in this chapter under the label "systems interventions" rather than separating them out. Although systems approaches are found to be effective, it is often difficult to determine what this exactly means. For example, Shadish and Baldwin (2003) reviewed 30 meta-analyses of couples and family interventions and declared the approach effective. Shadish and colleagues (1993) meta-analyzed 163 studies (all using random assignment of participants to groups) and found that although systems approaches as a group produced an effect size significantly different from zero, this effect (0.28) appeared to be much smaller than that found for behavioral or psychoeducational approaches (0.56), for instance. A more specific analysis of these data (testing only studies that compared two or more approaches in the same project) found that for family therapy, behavioral approaches did better than all other orientations *except* systems approaches.

Shadish and colleagues' meta-analysis included very few studies of FS theory (14), and those tested only two of the approaches described in this chapter—structural (one study), strategic (three studies), and structural–strategic integration (one study). No tests of Satir's or Bowen's approaches were found. Unfortunately, there does not seem to be a lot of research around using the controlled clinical trial method (randomization, manualization, and control group) to test classic FS approaches.

Using traditional review method, Diamond and Josephson (2005) pronounced that family-based approaches to treatment were effective across a large range of presenting problems. They note, however, that very little research is available that addresses the underlying theoretical structures of the treatments that have been tested.

Friedlander (2001) reviewed the outcome research on family approaches, also noting that most studies did not test FS theory. She concluded that theoretical approaches generally produce similar outcomes, and that systems approaches have generally been supported for marital problems, adolescent delinquency, and substance abuse (p. 501). Some evidence exists for the effectiveness of FS therapy with drug abuse and children's psychosomatic disorders.

The point that is easily overlooked in considering reviews of outcome research is that looking at effectiveness according to diagnostic category (e.g., depression, anxiety, substance abuse) is contrary to systems thinking (Friedlander, 2001). Think about it: once you've conferred a diagnosis, you have branded the problem as within the individual.

Several research programs that test hybrid systems approaches have succeeded in clearly specifying treatment packages and have proceeded to produce good results. Multisystemic Therapy (MST) is one of these, and true to its name involves intervening in wide range contexts involved when kids get in trouble (e.g., school, home, family). Family interventions focus on family affect and parenting practices. Research findings for this approach, including the results of randomized controlled trials, are very supportive (Rowe et al., 2006). Another systemic approach with good research support is Strategic Structural Systems Engagement, an intervention based in structural theory that is aimed at getting clients into therapy (Szapocznik & Kurtines, 1989). This intervention seems helpful with a client group that is known for underutilizing mental health services, Hispanic families, and has been successful with Hispanic families in which the IP was a drug user (Santisteban et al., 1996; Szapocznik et al., 1988).

In what might be seen as evidence bearing on structural and strategic theory, Mann, Bourduin, Henggeler, and Blaske (1990) compared Multisystemic Family Therapy and individual therapy with a group of adolescent offenders. They found that MST produced more improvement across time than individual therapy. Further, Mann et al.'s results indicated that cross-generational coalitions in these families were related to family relationships (e.g., family conflict and supportiveness) and symptoms, and that improvement in symptoms was related to changes in parental relationships.

Theory-Testing Research. It seems that more theory-testing research has been conducted on FS approaches than outcome research, although the coherence and quality of these investigations varies. Many studies have tested the predictions of structural family systems therapy and, indirectly, Strategic Therapy because the majority of these studies look at family hierarchy. Some of these studies are explicitly tests of one of the theories (mostly structural), whereas others are presented as tests of more general statements that would be endorsed by many orientations. For example, much research has supported the prediction that parental conflict is related to dysfunction in both kids and parents (Davis, Hops,

Alpert, & Sheeber, 1998; Kerig, 1995). Because of the sheer volume of research available, I will review only a select group of studies.

Many studies have examined family alignment patterns, which would seem to be fairly direct tests of structural or strategic ideas. For example, Kerig (1995) studied families characterized (by the members) as triangulated, detouring, cohesive, or disengaged. She found much support for structural theory. Parents in families that were characterized as relying on triangulation reported more conflict and more negative affect in comparison to cohesive and detouring families. Kids in detouring families reported feeling more responsible for their parent's problems and were found to have more internalizing problems (i.e., depression and anxiety in comparison to acting out) than kids in other kinds of families. Contrary to predictions, children in triangulated families did not show more dysfunction than children in other families, but Kerig maintained that the lack of difference was because most of these kids were involved in a coalition with a parent. She reasoned that the coalition was a source of support for these children. Unfortunately, this study did not distinguish between triangulation and stable cross-generational coalitions.

Northey, Griffin, and Krainz (1998) looked at structural theory's hypothesis that psychosomatic families display marital distress and have difficulty resolving disagreements. Their results only partially supported structural theory in that families with asthmatic children appeared to avoid disagreement and engage children in parental discourse. However, Northey and colleagues found no support for the contention that the primary motivation for detouring was to decrease marital conflict (asthmatic couples detoured regardless of level of couple distress). These researchers suggested that instead of seeing these dynamics as problematic, we should consider that families with a chronically ill child may avoid stress by avoiding parental conflict and involving children in parental discourse.

Other research has demonstrated that family coalitions are related to psychological distress (Jacobvitz & Bush, 1996) and that clearly boundaried families with few cross-generational alliances are related to adolescent achievement and good coping skills (Perosa & Perosa, 1993). Adaptive family structure and effective parental subsystems are associated with less acting-out behavior among young children (Schoppe, Mangelsdorf, & Frosch, 2001).

Empirical tests of Bowen's theory have produced promising results. Miller, Anderson, and Keala (2004) reviewed the literature and found support for the theory in terms of relationships between differentiation, anxiety, relationship satisfaction, and psychological dysfunction. For example, Murdock and Gore (2004) documented that differentiation and stress levels interact to predict psychological symptoms—individuals lower in differentiation showed more symptoms than under high levels of stress than those higher in differentiation. Under low levels of stress, these differences were less pronounced. Skowron and colleagues (Knauth, Skowron, & Escobar, 2006; Skawron, 2000) have linked differentiation and various outcome measures (e.g., social problem solving among adolescents). One theoretical issue still in contention is the role of stress or chronic anxiety in the differentiation-dysfunction relationship. Some research has found stress to be a moderator (Murdock & Gore, 2004) and other studies that stress mediates the relationship between differentiation and distress (Knauth et al., 2006).

Differentiation has also been related to psychological reactance, a finding that would confirm BFST predictions (Johnson & Buboltz, 2000). Tuason and Friedlander (2000) established that the construct of differentiation seemed to be applicable cross-culturally, at least for a sample of Filipino individuals. In this study, differentiation was inversely related to psychological distress, supporting Bowen's theory. However, they found no support for the family systems prediction that levels of differentiation are the result of multigenerational transmission. In contrast, Harvey, Curry, and Bray (1991) demonstrated that parents' levels of individuation and intimacy were directly related to those of their children, supporting the multigenerational transmission hypothesis.

Bowen predicted that individuals would choose partners who had similar levels of differentiation to their own. This hypothesis has received very mixed support in the literature, with some studies confirming and others disconfirming (Day, St. Clair, & Marshall, 1997; Greene & Mabee, 1992; Kosek, 1998; Miller et al., 2004). In summary, it appears that Bowen's ideas about differentiation of self are supported when it comes to psychological functioning, but perhaps are less supported with family or couples processes (Miller et al., 2004).

In what at first glance looks like an outcome study, Bartle-Haring, Glad, and Vira (2005) assessed the relations between differentiation of self (using a measure that primarily taps emotional reactivity) and psychological symptoms across nine sessions of therapy. Although they found that differentiation predicted initial levels of symptoms, it did not predict the rate of change across sessions. All of the clients improved over time in therapy. Although this study may seem somewhat disappointing to fans of BFST, a number of questions can be raised about it. This was not a randomly controlled trial, nor was the therapy specifically BFST, so it can not be construed as an outcome assessment of the model. Bowen would predict that differentiation should relate to outcome in therapy; however, given that we know little about the therapy provided in this study (at a university-based training clinic) conclusions from this study are tentative at best.

ISSUES OF INDIVIDUAL AND CULTURAL DIVERSITY

Feminist therapists have great difficulty with traditional FS theory (Braverman, 1988; Nichols, 2006). Feminists believe that the neutral stance of systems theory and concepts such as circular causality can result in excusing the perpetrators of battering and child abuse. The very common "dysfunctional triangle" of the overinvolved mother, distant father, and smothered child is based on the patriarchal system because women have few options outside of the home. Lerner (1988) observed that

> as long as men are the makers and shapers of culture in the world outside the home, as long as women are not free to define the terms of their own lives, as long as society continues to convey the message that mother *is* the child's environment, then the basic dysfunctional triad of distant, overfunctioning father, emotionally intense, overinvolved mother with a child with little room to grow up, is a natural outgrowth and microcosm of the culture. (p. 51, italics in original)

Feminist therapists also argue that FS theory reinforces traditional family structure, which is based on the patriarchal model of male in power. Structural Family Therapy is, in particular, a target of these criticisms (Simon, 1992). The idea that "enmeshment" of the mother and child as pathological is seen as problematic; similar criticisms have been offered about Bowen's construct of differentiation (discussed later). The argument is that even if this structure is pathological (and that is questionable), it is the result of cultural factors that deprive women of other outlets and pressure them to conform, and should be recognized as such (Bograd, 1990). Feminists also point out that very often, if someone in the family is absent in therapy, it is the father, which can reinforce the stereotypical perception of the mother as caregiver and father as breadwinner.

Similar observations have been made about Bowen's construct of differentiation. Lerner (1988) pointed out that the description of highly differentiated individuals is synonymous with the stereotypical view of men, whereas low differentiation appears identical to stereotypes about women.

FS approaches are also susceptible to the charge of cultural bias. Most models of ideal family functioning were developed based on the Caucasian middle-class nuclear family (Falicov & Brudner-White, 1983; Imber-Black, 1990). However, Structural Family Therapy is an exception to this characterization; Minuchin developed his theory during his work with poor inner-city youth and their families.

Falicov and Brudner-White (1983) argued that the bias toward structures, norms, and practices of middle-class European American families could lead therapists to ignore the adaptiveness of other family structures and processes. For example, "intrusion" by grandparents might be adaptive in cultures in which close extended family ties are common. Further, theories that encourage the exploration of extended family relationships, such as Bowen's, have the potential to be culturally insensitive because they tend to support separating (differentiating) from the extended family, an individualistic value that is contrary to the norms of many cultures. Encouraging a close-knit Latino family to differentiate would be counter to the tradition of *familismo* found in Hispanic/Latino cultures (Sue & Sue, 2003). African American families also involve the extended family in a wide range of family issues and functions, so FS approaches could be problematic with these clients as well. Similarly, triangling is often adaptive among working-class families because spouses in these systems rely on networks of personal friends for support and help (Falicov & Brudner-White, 1983).

On the other hand, too much attention to cultural features can be hazardous, according to the family theorists. Montalvo and Gutierrez (1983) warned that the family systems therapist can become "merely delighted and empathic toward the exotic aspects of the family's culture rather than focused on how these are employed to facilitate or block problem solving" (p. 18).

FS theorists have extensively addressed issues of cultural diversity in their work (cf., Carter & McGoldrick, 2005). Minuchin, you recall, began his work with disadvantaged inner-city youths, and he often comments on the cultural differences among families and family structures (Minuchin, Lee, & Simon, 1996). Chang and Yeh (1999) reviewed several of the approaches to FS theory described in this chapter, noting that each has strengths for working with families of Asian origin. For example, the emphasis on multigenerational issues in Bowen's theory is consistent with the values of Asian cultures, and Chang and Yeh suggested that coaching can help these families balance the powers of the family and the individual. Bowen's approach and structural theory can also help these families in the struggle to acculturate to other cultures that are more individualistic than traditional Asian ones, according to these authors. Also, the role of the therapist as active, expert coach or leader in the FS approach is consistent with the expectations of individuals who are of Asian origin.

Haley and Richeport-Haley (2004) noted that Strategic Therapy is consistent with the expectations of many clients from cultures other than Western European because

(1) The family and or social network is included in the therapy. (2) Therapy does not stress exploration nor insight. (3) It is action oriented, not discussion oriented. (4) The therapist maintains a position of expertise and authority. (5) The client receives concrete advice. (6) The therapist maintains a posture of courteous concern. (p. 28)

They go on to describe four different ways to approach clients who have belief systems that diverge from those typically seen in Western European cultures. First, and perhaps most controversial, would be to ignore cultural differences and treat the problem as usual. Although acknowledging that this approach can be counter to the values of some clients' cultures, Haley and Richeport-Haley contended that this mode would help clients to challenge cultural behaviors that are giving them trouble in "mainstream" American reality. They describe a case in which this method was used with a violent Hispanic family, noting that they violated the traditional values of respect for authority (respeto) in encouraging the wife to be less submissive and obedient to the husband. Dragging the husband into therapy and requiring him to bare his personal life also was counter to this value. A second approach is to use aspects of the client's belief system to solve the problem. For example, good spirits can be enlisted to fight against evil ones. The third and fourth ways to deal with alternative belief systems are to refer the client to an indigenous healer or to collaborate with one in therapy.

Less attention is paid to other-than-heterosexual couples in traditional family systems theory. Only fairly recently have the experiences of gay, lesbian, and bisexual (GLB) couples and families become a topic of interest, but this interest is clearly increasing (Johnson & Colucci, 2005; Greenan, 1996; Johnson & Colucci, 1999).

THE CASE STUDY

The case of Jean and Derril lends itself well to the classic FST conceptualization of overinvolved mother and distant father. I chose it because it allows an opportunity to evaluate the tendency in FS theory to pathologize this structure. That the clients are of different cultural groups is an interesting addition to the complexity of this presentation.

Feminists would question the characterization of Jean and Derril as enmeshed or undifferentiated—or at least the assumption that this situation is the problem. They would point out that Jean's behavior is simply fierce protection of her son in the face of a racist world (Bograd, 1990). Jean is likely struggling economically as a single parent, and this dynamic finds itself into her relationship with Derril in her hope that he will succeed according to the prevailing cultural norms.

Should Derril's father be brought back into the system? Some would question this assumption. He has been physically abusive to Jean in the past and shows few signs of wanting to be involved with Derril. Many would question the validity of the idea that two parents are better than one.

What are the cultural implications of encouraging Derril and Jean to differentiate? Is this construct or process adaptive in doing counseling with members of the African American culture?

Summary

Family systems theorists see human behavior as stemming from the power of the system, which is composed of the members of a family structure and their various relationships, roles, and interactions. Family systems theorists assume that influencing one part of the system will influence all of the other parts. Thus, they do not locate psychological dysfunction in an individual (the IP); rather, they see dysfunction as a product of the circular, repetitive interactions observed in a family.

The four theories reviewed in this chapter share the basic systems assumption but vary in how they think about systems and how to intervene in them. Satir focuses mostly on communication patterns and members' senses of self-esteem. She strives to bring love and caring to a situation often fraught with faulty communication and dysfunctional rules, which are exacerbated by the members' low self-worth.

Structural Family Therapy focuses on the interplay of the family's subsystem in terms of how the arrangements in the family help it achieve life tasks. These theorists emphasize a balance between togetherness and individuality, like Bowen, but they tend to intervene by changing the structure of the family or the permeability of its system boundaries.

Strategic systems therapists focus on interaction patterns and hierarchies. They are attentive to issues of control and power in relationships and find that when families are in distress a hierarchy is out of whack. Interventions in Strategic Therapy are intended to change interactional patterns and thus the hierarchical arrangement of the family.

Bowen's Family Systems Theory emphasizes differentiation in the context of the family emotional system. Triangles are considered key in the functioning of individuals within systems, and clients are taught to recognize these and escape functioning within them. Many times, BFST counselors will urge adult clients to differentiate from their own families of origin before attempting to deal with current relationship or family issues.

Outcome research seems to support family interventions, but the largest portion of these efforts has been directed at interventions other than systems ones. Still, a significant number of studies support the utility of a family systems approach. Theory-testing research, which largely assesses concepts taken from Structural, Strategic, and BFST, is generally supportive. Contradictory or nonconfirming findings have been reported in all areas, however.

Family systems theorists have been criticized for upholding a model of white, middle-class families that is not applicable to individuals from other cultural or ethnic origins. The model originated with a distinct heterosexual bias, and feminists argue that cultural norms about the roles of men and women are embedded in these systems.

Visit Chapter 13 on the Companion Website at **www.prenhall.com/murdock** for chapter-specific resources and self-assessments.

CHAPTER 14

Solution-Focused Therapy

Steve de Shazer

Kelly is a 22-year-old Caucasian male who comes to counseling to deal with problems of anger control. Currently working as a technical writer, Kelly earned his bachelor's degree in journalism 3 years ago.

Kelly is single (never married) and lives with his parents in their home in a large city. He has a steady girlfriend, Janet, and they plan to be married, but are not formally engaged.

Kelly reports that he wants to work on "problems with my temper." He sees himself as an "angry person" and reports being easily offended, tending to "blow up" when really frustrated. In the past, Kelly has occasionally thrown things when extremely angry, but never directly at anyone. Most often, these incidents happen when he is in conflict with his parents and less often with his girlfriend, Janet.

Kelly is perfectionistic about his appearance, environment, and work, and says that this perfectionism sometimes leads to an overconcern about details and frustration with others who do not share his standards. Although Kelly admits that he resents authority figures, he says that he does not have problems with his anger in work settings. Occasionally his "perfectionism" causes Kelly to be frustrated with the performances of his coworkers, but he is generally able to deal with this feeling in a constructive way. In fact, Kelly reports that he is more likely to be passive at work, accepting "mistreatment" from employers and remaining in an unfulfilling job despite feeling that he is not challenged by his work.

Kelly's nonverbal presentation is somewhat stiff and tense. He alternates between seeming angry and sad when he talks about his troubles.

BACKGROUND

What I am going to call Solution-Focused Therapy (SF Therapy for short) draws from two separate approaches, both of which are rooted in early communications/systems theory and draw from the work of Milton Erikson (more on this to follow). The first variant of SF Therapy is associated with Steve de Shazer and Insoo Kim Berg of the Center for Brief Family therapy. A second version of SF Therapy is attributable to Bill O'Hanlon and colleagues. O'Hanlon has used the terms *solution centered, possibility therapy*, and *collaborative, competency-based counseling* to refer to his approach, but most recently seems to refer to it as Possibility therapy. Because *Solution-Focused Therapy* seems to be the most widely recognized term, I will use it in this chapter. A review of the history of this theoretical approach can be found in Cade and O'Hanlon (1993) and Nunnally, de Shazer, Lipchick, and Berg (1986).

de Shazer, Berg, and several other colleagues (principally Elam Nunnally and Marvin Wiener) established the Brief Family Therapy Center (BFTC) in 1978 in Milwaukee, Wisconsin (Nunnally et al., 1986). This group reports that their earliest sessions were conducted in the de Shazer-Berg living room, with one member of the team handling the video camera. From these small beginnings, the BFTC has grown to international recognition. The BFTC has a website at www.brief-therapy.org.

Most of the writers in the solution-focused tradition share an admiration of the work of Milton Erickson (see Haley, 1973, for a description of Erickson's work). In fact, Bill O'Hanlon served as Erickson's gardener for a year because he desperately wanted to train with Erickson and could not afford to pay for it (O'Hanlon, 1986). The solution-focused theorists were intrigued by Erickson's use of language, metaphor, and hypnosis to draw out clients' strengths so that they can be applied to current problems (de Shazer, 1982). In this process, Erickson could be seen to accept the worldview and life patterns of the client, helping the client to use them in new ways. de Shazer and colleague Joseph Berger spent a significant amount of time trying to develop a theory around Erickson's work, which, although it obviously involved interactional (communication) elements, seemed almost magical. de Shazer (1998) reported that these efforts were not successful; indeed "Erickson, it turned out, was correct in saying that he did not have a Theory. He perhaps had many theories, but not quite one per case" (p. 3).

Steve de Shazer and Insoo Kim Berg met at the Mental Research Center in Palo Alto (see Chapter 13 for more information on the MRI). Thus, Solution-Focused Therapy incorporates some of the ideas of the communications orientation to psychotherapy that originated at MRI (Watzlawick, Weakland, & Fisch, 1974). These researchers initially began their work by studying communication in families of people diagnosed as schizophrenic, finding that certain patterns of interaction were particularly common in such families. They later broadened their ideas to conceptualize most psychological dysfunction as rooted in interactional patterns. One of the most significant aspects of the MRI group's work as far as ST therapists are concerned is the conceptualization of client problems as resulting from "more of the same" syndrome, a cycle wherein clients' failed efforts to solve problems result in their trying even harder but using the same strategies.

de Shazer and Berg were married for 28 years, and died within a year and a half of each other fairly recently. Steve de Shazer passed away in 2005. His last book, *More Than Miracles: The State of the Art of Solution-Focused Therapy* (with Yvonne Dolan), was published posthumously in 2007. You can read a bit from this book in Box 14.1. A year and a half later, Insoo Kim Berg died unexpectedly on January 10, 2007. Berg had recently completed a book on coaching from an SF perspective (Berg & Szabo, 2005).

Box 14.1

The Therapist's Mind-Set Using the Miracle Question

We think it makes a difference whether or not the therapist assumes that clients have the capacity to create meaningful descriptions of what they want their lives to look like and how they want to be in the world. Asking the miracle question both implies and demands faith in the client's capacity to do this and the question needs to be asked in a manner that communicates this faith.

When asking the miracle question, or teaching the concept in training seminars, we have learned that the way you ask the question is very important, i.e., you have to ask the question as if you really want to hear the answer *and* you believe the client has the ability to give a good answer.

Some therapists are afraid to ask the miracle question because, they do not have faith that their clients have the capacity to answer it productively. This results in a sort of catch-22: Faith that clients experiencing serious problems will be able to answer the miracle question can only develop as a result of hearing clients respond beneficially; however, the therapist won't ask questions to invite these responses if he or she doesn't have faith in the clients' capacity to create them. If we believe that a client has the capacity to describe a problem then we must also believe that he or she is capable of describing what "better" than that problem would be.

Over the years in our training programs and workshops, we have heard people ask, "Aren't you afraid that this sort of question might lead people into false hopes or denial? What do you do if a client with AIDS says he won't have AIDS, or a man whose wife left him answers with "She'd be there in the bed with me when I woke up"?

We believe that in most cases people who come to therapy are all too aware of the realities of the conditions they are experiencing, and have the ability to recognize wishful thinking for exactly what it is. On the other hand, starting out by acknowledging what one hopes for that is not going to happen can be a first step toward identifying some useful things that *are* possible to make happen. Steve de Shazer tells a story of a client who lost his left arm in an industrial accident. When asked the miracle question the client answered that he'd wake up with his left arm in place. Steve answered "Sure," and since he didn't know how to go on he waited. A long silence ensued and then the man added: "I guess you mean something that could happen," and Steve nodded. The man then went on to describe how he would get up and make breakfast with only one arm. There was never any talk again about getting the arm back.

It is obvious that many people with serious illnesses and handicaps wish they were well ("he'd wake up with his left arm in place") and there is no danger in them expressing this. When we acknowledge and validate ("Sure"), most people move to a realistic view (". . . I guess you mean something that could happen").

Clients know what's possible and what isn't. They know that talking with us won't give them back their arms, bring back the dead, or cure them or their loved ones of AIDS. Furthermore, it is important to recognize that ultimately the miracle question is not so much about figuring out what would be a "dream come true" miracle for this person or family as it is about discovering, identifying, and replicating the tangible, observable effects of it.

Excerpted from *More Than Miracles* by S. de Shazer and Y. Dolan (2007). New York: Haworth Press.

Bill O'Hanlon's website can be found at http://www.brieftherapy.com/ and the title of a recent book is *Change 101: A Practical Guide to Creating Change in Life or Therapy* (2006). The two major professional organizations in SF Therapy are the European Brief Therapy Association (http://www.ebta.nu/index.html) created in 1994 and the Solution Focused Brief Therapy Association founded in the United States in 2002 (http://www.sfbta.org).

BASIC PHILOSOPHY

Solution-focused (SF) therapists are serious optimists. They believe in the power of language to create and define reality, and therefore, that there are no absolute truths (de Shazer, 1994).

The dual influences of the MRI approach and Milton Erickson's work fused to produce a constructivist theory that proposes that humans create their realities, and if trouble develops, they can recreate them in ways that are more helpful to them. SF therapists emphasize the joint psychological construction of the therapy situation that allows therapists and clients to create new ways of viewing their lives and through these constructions formulate solutions to the problems clients bring to counseling. Approaching clients with the attitude that they have strengths and resources to solve their complaints, solution-focused counselors create an interaction designed to maximize client potential.

The SF therapist calls the client the "customer" and the problem the "complaint." In this way, the SF approach emphasizes that the client knows where he wants to go and is motivated to get there. The counselor is merely "hired" because she has some expertise in constructing solutions.

SF counseling's propositions are presented as countering the assumptions found in so-called traditional approaches to psychotherapy. For instance, whereas other approaches maintain that change is difficult, the SF theorists argue that change is constant. Other "myths" of traditional therapeutic approaches according to the SF theorists are presented in Box 14.2.

In beginning her work with Kelly, Mary, a Solution-Focused Therapist, starts with the expectation that therapy will not take long and that Kelly can easily resolve his complaint. She is on the alert for Kelly's strengths and resources, and will surely note that he had the intelligence and persistence to complete a college degree. Mary approaches Kelly with the attitude that change is easy to achieve and that she would be surprised if Kelly did not change.

<u>Box 14.2</u>

Myths of "Traditional" Therapy

1. There are always deep, underlying causes for symptoms—client problems are symptoms of these causal factors.
2. Awareness or insight is necessary for change or symptom reduction—we must understand the cause of the symptom for people to get better.
3. Amelioration or removal of symptoms is useless or shallow at best and harmful or dangerous at worst.
4. Symptoms serve functions.
5. Clients are ambivalent about change and resistant to therapy.
6. Real change takes time; brief interventions are shallow and do not last.
7. Focus on identifying and correcting pathology and deficits. Traditional therapies look for pathology, the Solution-Focused therapist says "If you look, you will find it."

From O'Hanlon & Weiner-Davis (1989), pp. 26–30.

In countering the ideology of traditional approaches to psychotherapy, O'Hanlon and Weiner-Davis (1989) identified some important assumptions of Solution-Focused Therapy. These principles are as follows:

1. Clients have resources and strengths to resolve complaints.

The therapist's job is to help the client access these abilities and put them to work in the interest of solving the problem. Clients are often so focused on their difficulties that they forget about their strengths. It is essential that the Solution-Focused therapist remind them.

Kelly worries that his explosions of anger prove that he is out of control, that he is indeed an "angry person," and that his relationships will be destroyed if he does not change. His counselor Mary acknowledges Kelly's concerns, but she is also alert for Kelly's personal strengths and brings them to Kelly's attention. For instance, Mary commends Kelly for his sensitivity to and caring for others, which resulted in his coming to counseling. She asks Kelly about his work and comments on his ability to concentrate and focus on a task until it is completed to his satisfaction (rather than construing this process as "perfectionism"). Mary recognizes Kelly's desire to get tasks done well, including his motivation to improve his personal relationships.

2. Change is constant.

According to the SF philosophy, if one assumes that change is constant, one will behave as though change is inevitable. Basically, the solution-focused therapist conveys to the client verbally and nonverbally that she would be surprised if the problem persisted. O'Hanlon might add that clients must work hard not to change—see his 11 ways to stay stuck in Box 14.3 on page 470.

Mary presents with the attitude that she expects change and expects it soon. She asks Kelly about what his life will be like when he changes, not if he changes.

3. The SF therapist's job is to identify and amplify change.

In any approach to counseling, therapists create a reality with the client through the questions they ask and the things they choose to focus on or ignore. SF therapists identify what seems to be working, label it, and work on making it happen more often.

Kelly says that he argues with his parents about many things, from what football game to watch on Saturday afternoon to what his responsibilities and rights are within the household. However, there are times when he does not "blow up." Mary is quite interested in these exceptions to his patterns. Mary tries to find out how Kelly manages to avoid blowing up and asks him to do the same things in other situations.

4. It is usually unnecessary to know a great deal about the complaint to resolve it.

According to O'Hanlon and Weiner-Davis (1989), therapists can get stuck because they have "too much information about the complaint and too little information about the solution" (p. 38). Instead, SF therapists find out what clients are already doing that is working. Once the therapist and client have identified the characteristics of trouble-free times, the client can work toward doing these things all of the time.

Mary discovers that Kelly can often tell his girlfriend Janet when he is upset with her, which usually results in the two of them talking about a difficult issue and resolving it. Mary is not very interested in the particular issue involved, but more in how Kelly was able to approach the situation calmly rather than exploding. Kelly reveals that the solution to the situation is that he distracts himself for a few minutes before he approaches Janet. Mary immediately asks Kelly how he can do this in other situations, for instance, when conflict is impending with one of his parents.

5. It is not necessary to know the cause or function of a complaint to resolve it.

Going to the therapist is typically the last resort. Before they get to counseling, most clients have spent a lot of time trying to figure out what caused their problems because mainstream culture teaches that if we can find the cause, the solution will follow (O'Hanlon & Weiner-Davis, 1989). It is obvious to SF counselors that this rumination has not helped their customers. However, because we are brainwashed by society, the media, and therapists, our customers sometimes still ask the "expert" *why* they have the problem. A SF therapist might simply counter with "would it be enough if the problem were to disappear and you never understood why you had it?" (O'Hanlon & Weiner-Davis, 1989, p. 41).

Mary is not very interested in Kelly's personal history, nor would she spend much time delving into the history of the anger problems. In contrast, Kelly, who has been brainwashed by society, probably thinks that his anger problem is the result of some very complicated events way back in his childhood. No doubt his troublesome parents had something to do with it!

6. A small change is all that is necessary; a change in one part of the system can effect change in another part of the system.

A small, positive change raises our clients' confidence, and buoyed by the counselor's support, they begin to believe that they can create more changes. O'Hanlon and Weiner-Davis (1989) offered Milton Erickson's snowball metaphor of change as an illustration: once a snowball gets rolling down a hill, "the therapist merely needs to stay out of the way" (1989, p. 42).

A major goal for Mary is to find, in the first session, some small change Kelly could make that he would perceive as positive. For example, Kelly typically fights with his father over what football game to watch on Saturdays. Mary discovers that Janet likes football and usually agrees with Kelly about which games to watch. Mary asks if Kelly could ask Janet to bring over her portable television and join him and his father for the coming Saturday games. That way, Kelly could alternate between games. Not only might this change his relationship with Dad, but it might also enhance his partnership with Janet.

7. Clients define the goal.

Solution-focused counselors dispute the idea that there is any one "correct" way to live (O'Hanlon & Weiner-Davis, 1985). Refusing to believe that there is some "real problem" that underlies the symptom leads solution-focused therapists to insist that clients determine the goals for treatment. The only exceptions to this rule are illegal or patently unrealistic goals.

Some therapists' first response to Kelly's situation might be to opine that he should move out of his parents' home. After all, he is 24 and employed. Shouldn't he be "mature enough" to live on his own? As an SF counselor, Mary joins with Kelly in his desire to find a solution for his problems with anger, implicitly acknowledging that it is his valid choice to remain in his parents' home.

8. Rapid change or resolution of problems is possible.

The first session is considered particularly powerful in the SF approach. Through reconstructing their views of their situations along with the counselor, clients typically see that they already know how to resolve the complaint. If the client still sees a need for change at the conclusion of the initial session, the counselor expects the client to go off and do whatever else is needed to create solutions before the next session.

During his first session with Mary, Kelly realizes that he has the negotiation skills necessary to avoid his outbursts of anger. After all, he is able to get along with his coworkers, and his relationship with Janet is not all that stormy. He need only apply these skills to his interactions with his parents.

9. There is no one "right" way to view things; different views may be just as valid and may fit the facts just as well.

Although many different views of a situation are valid, some are more helpful than others, according to the SF approach. When clients come to counseling, they are problem focused. Adopting a solution-oriented view is seen as more likely to produce change.

Our clients' views of problems often promote the "more of the same" syndrome (Watzlawick et al., 1974). Typically, if attempts to solve the problem don't work, the old adage "if at first you don't succeed . . ." seems to apply, and clients tend to "try try again" with the same strategies. SF theorists maintain that different views of the problem might lead to different strategies or even to defining the problem as not a problem! My client Jean's 9-year-old son developed a distressing tendency to tell his mother "I hate you" when she corrected his behavior. Jean's typical response was to lecture him about how this was an inappropriate thing to say. What she was doing had little effect on the young man's behavior, so we decided to have Jean stop doing more of the same and instead do something different—ignore these statements because he probably didn't mean them anyway. This strategy was apparently successful; the frequency of the "I hate yous" decreased. Further, when the boy did say this, the mother was not bothered by it any longer so she was much more relaxed in her interactions with him.

Kelly reports that he experiences his most troublesome outbursts when his parents "pick at him" and "treat him like a child." He views this behavior as controlling and evidence that his parents do not view him as an adult. When he gets angry, he is attempting to convince them of the "wrongness" of their actions, and when they have these talks, Kelly progressively raises the volume of his voice, trying to really get their attention. When the volume approach does not work, he will occasionally throw something. However, Kelly's angry outbursts are not working to change his parents' behaviors, and Kelly begins to realize that his own behavior is, in fact, rather childlike. Mary sees Kelly's escalation as "more of the same" and attempts to get him to do something, anything, different the next time conflict looms with his parents. She might also try to portray Kelly as "sensitive" rather than "easily offended" or "defensive."

10. Focus on what is possible and changeable rather than on what is impossible and intractable.

The complaints that SF therapists and their clients address are those that are amenable to change.

Mary would never attempt "personality reconstruction," but she might attempt to help Kelly have fewer angry outbursts.

HUMAN MOTIVATION

Hard-core SF therapists really don't care what motivates people in general. They simply observe what clients want to achieve and use clients' identified strengths and resources to help them reach solutions.

Even so, O'Hanlon (2006) distinguishes between positive and negative motivation, and further, past, present, and future motivation. Positive and negative motivation refer to our tendencies to move toward things we want and away from those we wish to avoid. In O'Hanlon's view, our behavior can be informed by each of these in the moment, or by experiences/expectations of them in past or future. He provides an example of a young man who was negative past motivated (in O'Hanlon's terminology) by the assertion of his high school counselor that he was not "college material" (2006, p. 3). The young man ended up with a Ph.D.!

CENTRAL CONSTRUCTS

EXCEPTIONS

An SF therapist starts with the basic assumption that regardless of the severity of a client's presenting problem, there are always times when the problem does not happen. The SF counselor takes the stance that she would be very surprised if there were not exceptions to the complaint. The motivation behind this belief is to help clients to see that the complaint is not always present and that they already are successful and happy at times. The therapist works with the client to find ways to increase those activities that have produced the exceptions.

Invariably, clients have not paid attention to exceptions. Clients are often quite surprised when the therapist focuses on the times that are trouble-free rather than on the presenting complaint. They are used to thinking about the complaint, and they typically have been exposed to (some would say indoctrinated by) the traditional models of psychotherapy that spend a lot of time on how and why the problem occurs.

Kelly's therapist, Mary, will be hard at work from the beginning of the first session to find exceptions to his "angry personality," which they have since redefined as troubles in expressing anger and negotiating conflict. She will be likely to ask him about when he has disagreed with his parents but not had an angry explosion, and what he did to manage to avoid it. Kelly has invested a lot of effort in trying to figure out why he is so "angry" with little result. When Mary encourages him to think of times when he isn't angry or can negotiate agreement with someone, he is pleasantly surprised and even smiles in response to her questions.

CHANGE TALK

The goal of an SF interview is to talk about the client's problem in ways that bring about change (de Shazer, 1989). Complaints are discussed in terms of specific behaviors amenable to change rather than using negatively valenced labels. Use of the presumptive terms in place of probabilistic language (such as *when* rather than *if*) in talking about change emphasizes that the counselor firmly expects change to occur (Corcoran, 2005). For example, the therapist can ask the client "when you (perform the exception) what do things look like?"

Discussions with Mary about times when he is not angry (i.e., when he is happy and content) help Kelly construct a situation in which it is acknowledged that anger is transient, not a personality trait fixed at birth. Relabeling the "angry personality" as difficulties in communicating (or perhaps temper tantrums) suggests that the troubles will be easy to banish. Mary asks Kelly "When you communicate well, how would you describe your relationship with your mother?"

SOLUTIONS

Solution-focused counselors believe that if we "accept the client's complaint as the reason for starting therapy, therapists should, by the same logic, accept the client's statement of satisfactory improvement as the reason for terminating therapy" (de Shazer, 1991, p. 57). Rather than focusing on the client's complaints, SF counseling concentrates on what would be perceived by the client as an acceptable solution to the problem—a difference that would make a difference.

Kelly, by his report, wants to deal with his problems with anger. Mary, accepting Kelly's goals, helps him to identify times when he negotiates conflict satisfactorily and works with him to decide how to do this more often.

STRENGTHS AND RESOURCES

The aspiring SF counselor needs to adopt a special view of people. Rather than looking for their weaknesses (because if you look under every rock for pathology, you'll certainly find it), the SF therapist emphasizes the strengths of clients and the resources they already can access. These qualities are put to work finding the solutions to complaints.

Cade and O'Hanlon (1993, p. 138) related the story of a client who was known for her work training difficult horses. After asking her to elaborate how she did so well with these beasts, the therapist asked if these principles could be applied to dealing with her troubles with her husband!

Mary works hard to identify and emphasize Kelly's strengths and the skills he can use in the service of reaching his preferred solution. She discovers that he is bright and likes to solve puzzles. He clearly is good at attending to detail and has the ability to concentrate intensely.

THEORY OF THE PERSON AND DEVELOPMENT OF THE INDIVIDUAL

SF advocates do not postulate a theory of the individual or of dysfunction. This theory is more a theory of counseling than a theory of human nature. A solution-focused therapist does not care where the problem comes from and is not very interested in the history of the individual or of the problem except in special, very rare, circumstances. For example, in discussing one of the most difficult problems therapists confront, severe psychological dysfunction such as schizophrenia, O'Hanlon and Rowen (2003) note that "when some medications were found to be helpful in managing the symptoms of such disorders, it was hailed as proof that the disorders had a biological basis. This is akin to arguing that if you take cocaine and it helps lift your depression, you have a biological disorder involving cocaine deficiency" (p. 19). Acknowledging that the jury is still out about the origins of these dysfunctions, O'Hanlon and Rowen advocate that SF techniques can be helpful if the therapist maintains an awareness of neurological and biochemical influences that wax and wane in these presentations.

Mary spends no time wondering about any personality theory or factors in Kelly's childhood. Such factors are just not relevant to the kind of counseling she offers.

HEALTH AND DYSFUNCTION

The diagnosis in Solution-Focused Therapy is as follows: a customer has come with a complaint. SF therapists are not concerned with notions of health or dysfunction—they simply listen to the client's construction of the problem, look for exceptions, and construct solutions. The client determines what is healthy; that is, the customer determines the goals of therapy. Therapists who think that their personal version of the problem (e.g., its causes and meaning) is the only correct one are suffering from "delusions of certainty or theory countertransference" (Hudson & O'Hanlon, 1991).

Despite the emphasis on listening to each client as an individual, the SF therapist could also say that "all complaints are alike. In almost all cases, the client's complaint includes wanting the absence of something without having any idea about what a reasonable replacement might be" (de Shazer, 1988, p. 52). Often, the therapist helps the client redefine the complaint in solution-oriented terms, a process called reframing (de Shazer, 1991).

Another way of looking at dysfunction is that clients are stuck. O'Hanlon (2006) has some ideas about this, which you can read about in Box 14.3.

In Kelly's case, he wants to lose the temper tantrums, but has not decided how to behave instead of having fits. Kelly comes to Mary thinking that he needs to get rid of his angry and compulsive personality. Alternatively, he could think that Mary needs to help him figure out ways to change those around him, particularly his parents. Mary acknowledges these ideas, but will then proceed to help Kelly redefine the complaint in a way that leads to solutions.

Box 14.3

How NOT to Change

Eleven Strategies for Staying Stuck

1. Don't listen to anybody.
2. Listen to everybody.
3. Endlessly analyze and don't make any changes.
4. Blame others for your actions or problems.
5. Blame yourself or put yourself down regularly.
6. Keep doing the same thing that doesn't work.
7. Keep focusing on the same things when that focus doesn't help.
8. Keep thinking the same thoughts when those thoughts don't help.
9. Keep putting yourself in the same unhelpful environment.
10. Keep relating to the same unhelpful people.
11. Put more importance on being right than on changing.

From *Change 101* by B. O'Hanlon (2006), p. 162. Used with permission.

NATURE OF THERAPY

ASSESSMENT

SF advocates do not believe in traditional assessment; they would say that assessing the client belongs in the medical, problem-focused approach to counseling. Instead, SF counselors *interview for solutions* from the very start of counseling (DeJong & Berg, 2002).

Mary asks lots of questions of Kelly, but they are focused on the exceptions to his complaints of angry outbursts ("disagreements with his parents") and his strengths and resources.

OVERVIEW OF THE THERAPEUTIC ATMOSPHERE

Therapists at the Milwaukee BFTC use a team-assisted approach to counseling similar to that used by family systems therapists, although Nunnally and colleagues (1986) reported that the groups developed the procedures independently. Counselors typically work with a team of consultant therapists, who are usually behind a one-way mirror. Often, sessions are videotaped as well. Sometime during the session (normally toward the end), the therapist takes a break to consult with the team and normally returns with some compliments for the client and a homework task to be completed between sessions. The team, along with the therapist, is seen as an integral part of the psychotherapy system (de Shazer, 1991).

Typically, clients in Solution-Focused Therapy complete four to five sessions, and most find their solutions in fewer than 10 sessions. Sometimes, clients attend only a single session of counseling and emerge as satisfied customers.

SF Therapy is seen as a collaborative venture (Guterman, 2006). The therapist's task in the first session is to establish a working, cooperating relationship with the client, a process de Shazer calls "developing fit" (1988, p. 90). In establishing the relationship, the therapist invites client cooperation by initiating cooperating behaviors. Clients will then reciprocate by demonstrating their versions of cooperating behaviors.

The relationship in SF counseling is described as having a special kind of intimacy and harmony. Counselor and client pay attention to what the other says and respect each other's worldviews as valid and meaningful (de Shazer, 1988). De Shazer and Dolan (2007) write that SF therapists "almost never pass judgments about their clients, and avoid making any interpretations about the meanings behind their wants, needs, or behaviors. The therapist's role is viewed as trying to expand rather than limit options" (p. 4).

O'Hanlon and Weiner-Davis (1989) pointed out that language can be used to help establish the therapeutic relationship. Initially, SF therapists are likely to adopt some of the client's language as a way to join the client. The SF therapist then gently helps the client channel the language used about the complaint into more solution-oriented forms (i.e., change and exception talk).

Berg and Shafer (2004), in writing about working with clients mandated to treatment, summarized the SF approach to cooperating in the following way:

> Cooperating with clients means learning how to stand side by side with them, not facing against them, as in a competition . . . we see things from clients' perspectives and eliminate the "professional posture" of judging them. Clients do not need one more failure or one more label as "incompetent" or "difficult." The most important contribution a

practitioner can make during the initial contact is to shape clients' experience in a way that is different from any other negative professional experiences they may have encountered in the past. Clients need the opportunity and the latitude to make choices instead of feeling coerced to comply; to feel understood instead of being labeled" (p. 90, quotes in original).

Mary adopts Kelly's language of "angry person" to begin with, so that he feels at ease in the first session. Kelly, of course, is a little tentative at first because he is afraid that Mary will see him as childish and reject his version of the problem. Mary joins Kelly in his frustration and comments on how he is very sensitive to others, which is demonstrated by his sadness after he has a fight with his parents or Janet.

ROLES OF CLIENT AND COUNSELOR

The SF counselor is expected to take responsibility for what happens in sessions. SF therapists have special knowledge about how problems are maintained and changed. In this sense, the therapist is an expert in change, but not about the client's particular problem. Clients have all the necessary knowledge about their particular complaints along with the ability to change things. The therapist focuses on the text (what the client says needs to be different) without making any further assumptions (de Shazer, 1994).

SF counseling is an energetic process, with the therapist taking the lead and using a series of questions designed to elicit information relevant to exceptions and solutions. The client is seen as an active collaborator in this process and as responsible for doing whatever is necessary to solve the problem.

de Shazer (1988) identified three types of clients: visitors, complainants, and customers. *Visitors* are clients who don't have any complaints. They are often in the counselor's office because someone else has told them to be there. In fact, in the case of visitors, de Shazer pointed out that the real client is probably not in the office. Thinking about the client as "visiting" rather than "involuntary" avoids creating an "involuntary" therapist. An involuntary client paired with an involuntary therapist is a recipe for trouble. According to de Shazer, the way to deal with a "visitor" is to be nice, be on his side, focus on what works, and give compliments.

Complainants are signaling that therapy can begin. No matter how diffuse, vague, or confusing the problem, at least there is a problem! The complainant has come with some expectation that change will happen as a result of therapy. I once had a client, Sue, who came to therapy because she was depressed. How did she know she was depressed? She found herself tearing up at Kodak commercials. No other symptoms of "depression" were reported. I never really did decide whether she was a visitor or complainant, and I am sad to say that our work together was not successful, at least by my standards.

Clients who bring a complaint and the desire to do something about it are called *customers*. Ideal clients for any therapist, these individuals can be given tasks to complete with the expectation that they will oblige.

De Jong and Berg (2007) note that the distinction between visitors, complainants, and customers, although helpful to understand, is not currently used all that often. They contend that it is simply more respectful and helpful to assess the extent to which clients have clarified their goals as a way of assessing, rather than placing them in formal categories.

Mary is quite active in her sessions with Kelly and confidently accepts her job as an expert in change. Kelly appears to be a customer in his presentation to Mary because he indicates a problem and a desire to change. Mary expects Kelly to be a collaborator in the change process and to work hard to make solutions happen. If Kelly had been coerced into therapy by his parents or Janet, his girlfriend, the situation might be very different. He might then be a visitor. If Kelly were a visitor, Mary would empathize with his difficult situation, but not be inclined to go further.

GOALS

Berg and Shafer note that "SFT begins with finding out what the *client* wants" (2004, p. 85; italics in the original). The counselor works with the client to develop the specific, attainable, and concrete goals that are essential in SF Therapy. These goals should be observable. As noted earlier, even very small changes lead to more change, so no reasonable objective should be dismissed as trivial. Often the counselor will ask the client, "What will be the first sign of change?" This question searches for the smallest increment of change that is meaningful to the client.

Regardless of the complaint, the goals of the good SF therapist are as follows:

1. Change the *doing* of the situation that is perceived as problematic
2. Change the *viewing* of the situation
3. Evoke *resources, strengths, and solutions* to bring to the situation perceived as problematic (O'Hanlon & Weiner-Davis, 1989, p. 126)

The SF counselor is wary of "absence" goals (Cade & O'Hanlon, 1993; de Shazer, 1988)—that is, goals that specify that something will go away but do not specify what fills the vacuum. The best goals are those that specify what replaces the unwanted behaviors.

When asked what he wants to get out of therapy, Kelly says that he wants to stop being an angry person. He also wants to be less perfectionistic. He mentions "not yelling" or "not flying out of the house in a fury" or "not throwing any object within reach." Mary notes that these are "absence goals" and begins to look for the behaviors that sometimes replace the yelling ones.

Mary asks Kelly if it would make sense to focus on how he will have discussions at normal volume with his parents. He could learn some negotiation skills. Kelly says that he'd like to be more easygoing overall, which might lead to being able to relax at work, too. Mary asks Kelly how he will know he is more easygoing. What will be the first sign?

PROCESS OF THERAPY

Solution-focused counselors want action, and right away! The very first and most critical task of counseling is defining (actually redefining) the problem. Client and counselor negotiate the nature and meaning of the client's complaint (Guterman, 2006). For example, a client would be asked, "What do you mean by 'depressed'?" or more likely, "What is it like when you are not depressed?" Adopting the client's lingo, so to speak, is a way the SF therapist enters the client's world and joins with him in constructing the therapeutic relationship.

Once the therapeutic relationship is established, the counselor will gradually begin to use change talk, suggesting words that have less negative connotations than those typically used by the client, and that also imply change rather than a static state of affairs. A "speech phobic" client might be termed "nervous," or a depressed client "sad." Most important, the SF counselor is trying to change labels to specific descriptions of behavior that are more amenable to change.

SF counselors focus on the present, not the past. Even though clients often think that a detailed exploration of the past is necessary to progress, SF counselors think that there is a risk of becoming bogged down in problem talk if there is too much focus on the past. They tend to treat historical information only as a source of possible solutions (Rossiter, 2000).

Solution-focused therapists have proclaimed the death of client resistance (actually, they admit to murdering it in cold blood; de Shazer, 1998, p. 5) and have reportedly had a funeral for it (Cade & O'Hanlon, 1993). de Shazer noted, "when the therapist focuses on what it is exactly that the client wants and lets that be the guide, there is no need for a concept of 'resistance'" (1994, p. 61, quotes in original).

SF counselors don't recognize transference and countertransference in the way that many other theoretical approaches do. However, they do identify "theory countertransference," which is the therapist's tendency to get carried away and see everything through the lens of her pet theory (O'Hanlon & Rowan, 2003).

Solution-focused counselors place great emphasis on the first session of therapy (Guterman, 2006). At the start of the session, the SF therapist will take some time to join with the client, chitchatting about things that have nothing to do with the problem. However, very quickly the counselor moves into working with the client to reconstruct the problem or what Guterman (2006) calls "coconstructing a problem and goal" (p. 46). First, the counselor will ask for a brief description of the problem but immediately follow with series of questions designed to extract information about exceptions to the problem—times when things are progressing smoothly, past solutions to the current problem, and the person's strengths and resources. Box 14.4 shows a list of questions offered by O'Hanlon and Weiner-Davis (1989). The SF therapist is aware of, and asks about, pretreatment change (i.e., change between the time the client called for an appointment and the appointment).

The initial goal of the first session is to create a solvable complaint, at the very least, and at best, to solve the problem. In difficult cases, the SF therapist seeks to introduce uncertainty about the problem; that is, to somehow raise questions about the client's construction of the complaint (de Shazer, 1988). "Therapeutic misunderstanding" of the client's story is often used by the counselor to loosen the certainty with which the client holds his view of the problem. For example, a client might report that he is "compulsive." The SF counselor might wonder if this is really a time management problem because the client finds himself working too many hours.

The remainder of the first session is devoted to finding exceptions to the complaint and exploring these; the counselor and client construct concrete, solvable goals and then look at ways to reach these goals. At the end of the session, the counselor typically gives the client a solution-relevant task to complete over the interval between sessions, which can range from a week to months.

In the remaining sessions of counseling, the counselor wants to use the "more of the same" principle to her advantage—continuing to do what works and abandoning what doesn't. Sessions begin with checking the results of homework assignments. Counselors ask clients about what happened over the interval that they'd like to continue.

Box 14.4

A Series of Solution-Focused Questions

1. What is different about the times when _____ (the exception happens)?
2. How did you get that to happen?
3. How does it make your day go differently when _____ (the exception happens)?
4. Who else noticed that _____ (exception)? In what way could you tell that she/he noticed? What did he/she do or say?
5. How did you get her/him to stop _____ ?
6. How is that different from the way you might have handled it _____ (one week, one month, etc.) ago?
7. What do you do for fun? What are your hobbies or interests?
8. Have you ever had this difficulty in the past? How did you resolve it then? What would you need to do to get that to happen again?

From *In Search of Solutions: A New Direction in Psychotherapy* (pp. 85–92) by William Hudson O'Hanlon and Michele Weiner-Davis. Copyright © 1989 by William Hudson O'Hanlon and Michele Weiner-Davis. Used by permission of W. W. Norton & Company, Inc.

Once clients tell what was good in the interval between sessions, the counselor responds with past-tense questions about these positives. Examples of these questions might be: How did you get that to happen? How did it (the positive change) make your day go differently? The SF counselor wants to talk about the good things that happened for the entire session, if possible (and sometimes it is). Although the SF theorists would argue that many clients accomplish what they need very quickly (i.e., in one session), O'Hanlon and Weiner-Davis (1989) identified three groups of clients:

1. The miracle group (one-session cure)
2. The so-so group (report having a better week but are not convinced that the problem is completely solved)
3. The same or worse group (pp. 147–151)

Working with the *miracle* client is easy—the counselor simply focuses on the change and maintaining it. Clients are asked to think about factors that could lead to setbacks. Plans can then be made to defeat these. Sometimes clients are skeptical that change will last; they have seen improvement in the problem before that did not last long. The SF therapist respects this healthy caution rather than seeing it as resistance and helps the client explore previous patterns. The counselor then asks the client to specify a short period of time of change in the problem that would really make a difference. SF therapists do not generally prescribe relapses, but if setback seems likely, then ups and downs are conceptualized as part of the normal process of solving the complaint. At the end of the session, the counselor asks the client if he would like to schedule another session. A "check-up" session is scheduled with most clients.

Dealing with the *so-so* group is a little trickier. These clients respond to questions about what good things happened with a description of the difficulties they encountered.

According to O'Hanlon and Weiner-Davis, the counselor should immediately interrupt the client to refocus on positives. The client should always be assured that the difficulties will be discussed later in the session.

After the positives are exhausted, solution-oriented procedures are then used to work on the difficulties the client reports. Exceptions are sought, and sometimes scaling questions are used (see the section on techniques).

The *same or worse* clients, of course, are the toughest customers. The wise SF therapist never accepts these negative reports automatically. Closer examination often reveals the small change needed to alter the client's perception of his first session outcome. My clients Susan and George came to their first session struggling so mightily with their relationship that they described themselves as "not a couple." At the start of the second session, they characterized their week as no better than previous ones, but I soon discovered that they had spent more time together during the week and had even gone out for a special dinner over the weekend. These behaviors certainly seemed more like a couple to me.

Same or worse clients sometimes truly see the problem as persisting. SF theorists advise that when that happens, the therapist should ask two sets of basic questions:

1. Who is our customer? Who is complaining? Who wants to see change?
2. What is the goal? How will we know when we've gotten there? (O'Hanlon & Weiner-Davis, 1989, p. 152)

Sometimes these questions will reveal that the real customer is not in the session.

A final caution. Searching for strengths and solutions can sometimes be "more of the same." As with any therapeutic approach, rigid or dogmatic behavior on the part of the therapist can be detrimental to client progress. Sometimes it's possible to get carried away with searching for strengths and solutions—clients may just have a hard time seeing it that way. Particularly with same or worse clients, it may also be helpful to consider that the therapist and therapy may be part of the problem rather than part of the solution. Solution-focused counselors who persist in the strengths/solutions approach in these circumstances are simply doing more of the same. O'Hanlon and Weiner-Davis suggested that in this situation, it might be wiser to resort to exploring the complaint pattern, or occasionally, to get pessimistic, such as when a warring couple is asked how in the heck they manage to stay together. Taking a pessimistic stance is considered a last-ditch tactic (Corcoran, 2005).

Mary is aware that redefining the problem is her first task. She asks Kelly to relate situations in which his "attention to detail" is not a problem or even when it is helpful. They explore situations in which he is able to contain his anger, or more simply, when he does not yell or throw things. When Kelly talks about his parents "pissing him off" or treating him like a child, Mary asks, "What is happening when you aren't pissed off? What is happening when they treat you like an adult? When you are able to negotiate differences with your parents without yelling, what is different?"

THERAPEUTIC TECHNIQUES

SF Therapy has numerous techniques, many of which are designed so that they can be adapted to a wide range of complaints. However, the therapist has to really pay attention to what she is doing because "technique" in SF Therapy can be as subtle as how you word a question to a client. A very general strategy in SF counseling is to identify exceptions and then encourage the client to do more of the same (Guterman, 2006).

QUESTIONS

Solution-focused counselors rely heavily on questioning the client. A special SF tactic is the *presuppositional question*, which gives the respondent few options. A classic presuppositional question is when the attorney asks the client, "Have you stopped beating your wife?" (O'Hanlon & Weiner-Davis, 1989, p. 80). In SF Therapy, presuppositional questions are used to emphasize change possibilities and the strengths of the client. For example, the classic SF question is, "When the problem is not present, how are things different?" Notice that the phrasing is not "*if* the problem were not present." The good presuppositional question already assumes that success happens. Presuppositional questions are open ended, but do not leave room for negative answers.

Pichot and Dolan (2003) identified several types of questions used by SF therapists. Some of these are discussed next (the Miracle and Scaling questions). Others are *difference* (e.g., what difference did it make for you to say good morning to your daughter every day this week?), and *relationship* (e.g., how will your husband know when you are no longer depressed?) questions. In general, when questions are used, they are usually followed with more questions intended to elaborate on details, thus making the solution more vivid for client and counselor.

Mary has used a number of presuppositional questions with Kelly, such as, What is going on when your parents treat you like an adult? What happens? What difference does that make in your relationship to your mother? Your father?

NORMALIZING THE PROBLEM

This technique helps clients feel as though they are not "crazy" or extreme in their situations. One way to normalize is to ask clients, "How can you tell the difference between [the stated problem] and [a normalized explanation of it]? (O'Hanlon & Weiner-Davis, 1989, p. 97). Normalizing compliments are a special case of normalizing the problem and usually take the form of commending the client for his or her strength in handling a very difficult situation.

Mary asks Kelly how he knows the difference between his parents treating him like a child and their expressing their caring for him. She also tells Kelly, "Given the circumstances, I am very impressed with how often you do keep your cool. It's kind of tough to grow out of being the kid, huh?"

COMPLIMENTS

People love compliments! Counselors should keep this in mind and comment on the great things clients are doing at any opportunity (De Jong & Berg, 2007). Reframing, or positive connotation, is a particularly helpful way of complimenting clients. For instance, when one member of a couple is very vigilant, the therapist can choose to see this behavior as "paying attention to what is going on in the relationship." One other good way of complimenting clients is to point to things that they have already done toward a solution. De Jong and Berg (2007) note that clients often self-compliment; the therapist should notice and reinforce these. However, it is important in all of these cases that the compliments be real (not used just to cheerlead) and based squarely in information provided by the client.

Mary congratulates Kelly on his success in dealing with situations in which he gets into conflict with his girlfriend, Janet. He is also sensitive to relationships and cares a lot for other people. In fact, he cares so much that he came to counseling!

MIRACLE QUESTION

A trademark technique in SF Therapy is the miracle question (Berg, 2005). Designed to help clients figure out what they want from therapy without having to spend a lot of time contemplating problems and their causes, the miracle question goes something like this: "Suppose that one night, while you were asleep, there was a miracle and this problem was solved. How would you know? What would be different?" (de Shazer, 1988, p. 5). de Shazer and Dolan (2007) note that the miracle question can have several functions in SF counseling: to help clients figure out their goals for Therapy, for one. They also contend that asking the miracle question helps clients get a sense that parts of the solution are already happening—the detailed questions that are used to follow up invariably get to things that have happened in the client's life that are related to the miracle. Typically, the miracle question is followed with a scaling question (see the following section) that asks the client where they are now on a 1–10 scale ranging from 0 (just decided to go to the counselor) to 10 (the miracle is accomplished; de Shazer & Dolan (2007).

Mary asks Kelly this question in the hope that he can generate some concrete indicators of how he will know when the problem is solved. Mary would also like to know how Kelly's parents (or Janet) will know when Kelly is different.

SCALING QUESTIONS

Scaling questions can be used in several ways. The most common is, "On a scale from 0 to 10, with 0 being the worst the problem has ever been and 10 being the problem is completely solved, where are you today?" (Cade & O'Hanlon, 1993; de Shazer, 1988, 1994). Note that the question stacks the deck in the counselor's favor because it is fairly unlikely that the problem is at its absolute worst when the client is in the session.

Once clients give a number on the scale, they are often asked, "What one or two things could you do this week to bring you up two points?" Alternately, they can be given homework, such as keeping track of all the seven or eight things that happen between sessions. Scaling questions can also be used as confidence builders by setting the anchors as 0 representing absolutely no confidence that the complaint will be solved and 10 absolute certainty that it will be (Cade & O'Hanlon, 1993).

Mary asks Kelly to rate his anger on a 1 to 10 scale. He says that it is a 6. When asked what one thing he could do this week to bring himself up to a 7, Kelly thinks for a while.

Finally, he says that he could count to 10 before he answers any questions that his mother or father asks.

PREDICTION TASKS

Prediction tasks are often used when exceptions to the problem seem random (de Shazer, 1988). Clients are asked to stop sometime during their day—for example, before they go to sleep at night—and predict whether the problem or exception will occur the next day.

If Kelly could not identify circumstances in which he felt like a laid-back guy (i.e., was more patient with others), he might be asked to predict each night whether he would have that feeling the next day. He would be asked to track the accuracy of his predictions.

FAST-FORWARD QUESTIONS

Fast-forward questions can be used when clients absolutely cannot think of exceptions (O'Hanlon & Weiner-Davis, 1989). The counselor then asks them to mentally project themselves into a future in which the problem does not exist. Because of the speculative nature of this question, a great deal of time must be devoted to getting the client to be specific (asking such things as, "How will your life be different?" "Who will be the first to notice?" "What will he or she do or say?" and "How will you respond?").

Mary sends Kelly to 2 years from now and asks him to describe his laid-back self. Kelly says that he is able to negotiate with his parents. He reports that he helps folks at work with things that are important to him and is able to relax about the rest of the stuff. Mary is quite pleased with this view of Kelly's future.

ASKING ABOUT THE PROBLEM

Exploring the problem is a last-ditch effort used when the client can't think of exceptions (O'Hanlon & Weiner-Davis, 1989). This tactic is typically used to find a pattern in the complaint that can be altered (remember, a small change is a great place to start).

The therapist asks detailed, specific questions in attempting to elicit the exact sequence of events in the problem chain. This inquiry is *not* intended, of course, to elicit causes or any such nonsense, but to document the exact problem sequence so that a small change can be suggested that will hopefully lead to larger change. Also, because the "more of the same" principle suggests that problems are maintained by people's faulty change attempts, information is needed about these to reverse them.

Because Kelly is responding so positively to solution talk and readily finding exceptions, Mary feels no great need to ask a lot about the problem.

EXTERNALIZING

Drawing from White and Epston's work (1990), O'Hanlon and Rowan (2003) suggest that giving the problem a name and placing it outside of the client can be helpful. You can read much more about this technique in Chapter 15 on Narrative Therapy.

Mary and Kelly decide that Temper has gotten the best of Kelly in the past. It is now time for Kelly to look at ways in which he has defeated Temper and put it in its place.

First Session Formula Task

"Between now and the next time we meet, I would like you to observe, so that you can describe to me what happens in your (pick one: family, life, marriage, relationship) that you want to continue to have happen" (de Shazer, 1985, p. 137). Although not a presuppositional question, this task makes use of the assumption that something good is already happening in the client's life. Clients, who are often very obsessed with what's wrong, are startled when the therapist asks them what's right. According to O'Hanlon and Weiner-Davis (1989), clients often do something new, different, and good in response to this task, even though it requests no change.

Mary assigns Kelly the first session formula task, and he comes back with a list of things he likes about his life. He is happy with his relationship with Janet and mostly likes his work. Mary asks what he likes about his relationship with Janet; she is setting him up for a generic task.

Generic Task

Once goals have been established, the client can be asked to keep track of what he is doing this week that _____ [makes him feel more in control, makes him less stressed, and so forth] (O'Hanlon & Weiner-Davis, 1989). The idea is to fill in the blank with the exception situation. A variant of this task that works particularly well with addictive or compulsive processes is the "pay attention to what you do when you overcome the urge to _____" assignment.

Kelly reports feeling tense much of the time, which seems to make it easier for him to lose his temper. As part of reframing Kelly's problem, Mary and he decide that he needs to be more relaxed. Mary therefore gives Kelly the assignment of keeping track of what he does during the week that makes him more relaxed.

Breaking Patterns

Almost anything that changes the pattern of the complaint can be helpful. O'Hanlon (O'Hanlon, 2006, pp. 57–90; O'Hanlon & Weiner-Davis, 1989, pp. 130–132) suggests some ways of interrupting the sequence. Examples of these tactics include the following:

Changing any body behavior associated with the pattern. O'Hanlon (2006) reports directing overeaters to eat with the wrong hand (i.e., the nondominant one). I am sure this would raise my awareness as I clumsily spilled food on my lap.

Changing timing or duration of the pattern. For example, couples can be asked to fight from 6:00 to 6:17 A.M. every day (see the discussion of structured fights). A person who is anxious about giving a speech could be asked to be anxious 2 hours before the speech and get it over with. Client Denise compulsively checks doors 10 times before she goes to bed (to see if she has locked them). She could be asked to check the doors 25 times instead of 10.

Changing the location of the pattern's performance. O'Hanlon (2006) offered a particularly amusing example of changing the location. A couple reported having nasty fights. They were instructed to go immediately into their bathroom the moment they begin to argue. The husband was told to undress and lie in the bathtub while the wife sits fully clothed on the toilet. The couple was instructed to continue the fight. When they tried to follow the therapist's orders, of course they couldn't and broke into laughter. After that incident the couple found themselves looking toward their bathroom and laughing whenever a discussion started to get tense.

Adding at least one new element to the complaint pattern. A client trying to quit smoking would be instructed to place his cigarettes in some difficult-to-reach place (a neighbor's mailbox, for instance). O'Hanlon (2006) describes having a client put on her most favorite shoes before she allowed herself to binge.

Linking the complaint performance to the performance of some burdensome activity. This technique resembles Haley's (1963) benevolent ordeal. One of my clients was having trouble falling asleep at night because he was ruminating on angry thoughts. Because he had occasionally lamented that his garage needed cleaning and he hated that task, I told him that if he did not sleep within 20 minutes of hitting the bed, he was to get up and clean the garage. After all, he might as well use his nonsleeping time productively. At his next session he reported absolutely no problems falling asleep over the preceding week!

Changing the context of the complaint. A client having trouble eating sufficiently (notice that she was not characterized as anorexic!) who normally eats alone could be instructed to always eat in the presence of others.

Change the clothing worn during the pattern. Watch out if I am wearing purple! It means that I am in a bad mood. I should probably wear green instead.

Mary decides on an ordeal task for Kelly to alter the performance of his temper outbursts. Kelly, who does not like to write about his personal experiences, is asked to write down everything he wants to say to his parents before he tells them about it. The minute he begins to be annoyed with something they've said, he is to go directly to his room, sit at his desk, and write out his complaints. He can then give this written summary to his parents.

SURPRISE TASK

This assignment is often used with couples or families and directs clients to do one or two things that will surprise family members or partners. Clients are instructed as follows: "Do at least one or two things that will surprise your parents (partner). Don't tell them what it is. Parents (partner), your job is to see if you can tell what it is that she/he is doing. Don't compare notes; we will do that next session" (O'Hanlon & Weiner-Davis, 1989, p. 137). If the target person is a young child, the rest of the family can be asked to leave the room while the counselor coaches the child on strategies that he can use to stump the family (Reiter, 2004).

No one says that therapy can't be fun sometimes! Clients who really engage in this task generally enjoy it. They become solution-focused detectives (i.e., searching for good things, not bad). At the least, this task can introduce change into patterns of interaction in a positive way. Sometimes the surprises even turn into solutions.

Mary wonders what might happen if she could get Kelly's folks into counseling and give them the surprise task. When Kelly and his parents return for the next session, she would not ask them what they did for the other. Instead, she would ask Kelly what he detected that his father did and vice versa. Mom would be asked the same question about Kelly and Dad. Sometimes this process results in giving credit to the other for things they didn't do intentionally, such as when Kelly praises Mom for cooking his favorite vegetable—boiled carrots. Mom secretly thinks, "I thought he hated boiled carrots," but is gracious in accepting Kelly's appreciation.

WRITE, READ, AND BURN

This task is useful for obsessive or depressive thinking (de Shazer, 1985). The client is instructed to write about the problem on even-numbered days for a specified period of time, even if he only has a few sentences to write. On odd days, the client is to read the notes and then burn them. Between writing, reading, and burning, the client is to put off thinking about the problem until the regularly scheduled time.

As de Shazer noted, this task literally makes the client's troubles go up in smoke (p. 121)! Also, write, read, and burn helps clients achieve distance from their concerns and become more objective. Most clients find that after a few days they have better things to do than to dwell on the problem.

On even days, Mary tells Kelly to make a long list of things his parents do that make him mad. On odd days he is to burn his lists after reading them over.

STRUCTURED FIGHT

This technique is a version of changing the pattern of the complaint often used with couples. The SF counselor instructs the clients to fight in the following way: (a) Toss a coin to decide who goes first. (b) The winner gets to bitch for 10 uninterrupted minutes. (c) The other gets 10 minutes. (d) There must be 10 minutes of silence before tossing the coin again (de Shazer, 1985).

Kelly could invite his parents to argue with him three times in the next week. They follow the 10-minute sequence, each of them complaining and listening. If they are not finished after one round, they wait 10 minutes and repeat the process.

DO SOMETHING DIFFERENT

Designed to disrupt the "more of the same" syndrome that maintains problems, this task is often used when one person is complaining about the behavior of another person and has tried "everything" to get the other to change, to no avail (de Shazer, 1985).

Mary tells Kelly to do something different the next time he is headed for an argument with his parents. He takes her advice, and the next time he senses that his parents are going to criticize him, he breaks into a dance, skipping around the living room. His parents collapse in laughter.

SOLUTION-ORIENTED HYPNOSIS

In contrast to traditional uses of hypnosis, the SF therapist uses it to summon skills that support solutions. This unique approach to hypnosis apparently originated with therapists of the "Ericksonian" school who used it to "access unconscious resources" (O'Hanlon & Weiner-Davis, 1989, p. 139). The implication is that the resources evoked are those that are thought to be beyond the client's conscious control.

Mary hypnotizes Kelly and asks him to see himself responding to his parents calmly. He sees himself doing so and even cracking jokes about how they care so much about him that he can't stand it.

EVALUATION OF THE THEORY

Solution-Focused Therapy is a relative newcomer to the psychotherapy scene. These authors are prolific, fun to read, and, for the most part, very good at arguing their cases. Because they are mostly practicing counselors, their writings are filled with case studies that illustrate the practical applications of their theory. Further, they attempt to collect data on their approach, and the results of these efforts are promising. The SF approach is appealing to many because of its brevity.

On the other hand, Miller (1994), in a very entertaining critique of SF counseling, pointed out that SF's claims of being different (quicker and better) are not supported by a review of the psychotherapy research. He pointed out that the average number of sessions for clients in any type of counseling is around five sessions. Further, you already know from reading Chapter 1 that very little evidence exists that demonstrates that any one theoretical approach produces better outcomes than others. The wise sage in Miller's article, Brief Throat, concludes, "The main impact of the solution-focused model—and any model of therapy, for that matter—is on the therapists that adhere to and practice the model's theoretical tenets and techniques and *not* on their clients!" (p. 29; italics in original). By saying this, Miller was pointing primarily to two issues: that the therapist's belief in her system boosts her effectiveness, and that across approaches, common factors produce client change. Claims that something special is happening in SF counseling, therefore, are simply ways to keep folks interested and invested in the approach.

Solution-Focused Therapy can be criticized on the charge that it is superficial; it lacks a theoretical structure through which client complaints can be understood. Piercy, Lipchik, and Kiser (2000) have suggested that SF theory should attend more to emotion and that its practitioners should be more flexible in their approaches to their clients. de Shazer and Dolan (2007) contend that an emphasis on emotions stems from traditional views of therapy in which such inner states are privileged over external or social and made into mystical, problematic things. They reply that SF Therapy

> does not view emotions as problems to be solved but rather views them as some of the many resources that clients have for constructing something "better." In other words, helping clients construct situations where they "feel better" and where they can remember that they feel better is one part of successfully constructing and "reinforcing" solutions by paying attention to the context in which emotions happen, SFBT keep them in

their proper home, which is the client's everyday life, rather than making them an esoteric, mysterious phenomenon inside of the individual. (p. 149)

Those who choose other theoretical orientations that are concerned with underlying
causal structures (e.g., psychoanalytic, existential) are likely to see SF Therapy as shallow.
Proponents of the view that symptoms serve functions (i.e., almost all of the other counseling theories) would suggest that simple symptom relief would not last unless the function were replaced by some other means.

QUALITIES OF THE THEORY

Precision and Testability. Because there is so little actual theory in SF Therapy, it would be
difficult to operationalize the approach. Off the top of my head, a few possibilities suggest
themselves, however. One might be able to track the exceptions identified by clients and
relate them to outcomes. Certainly, solution statements could be counted.

Empirical Validity. Despite the efforts of SF Therapy's proponents to empirically validate
their approach, most of the presentations of the theory rely on traditional (nonempirical)
case study materials. Because relatively few empirical studies have been conducted on SF
Therapy, the efficacy of this approach is not considered established.

RESEARCH SUPPORT

SFT has some empirical support, but because of the relative recency of the approach, the
corpus of data is relatively small compared to other approaches. Therefore, I will bypass
my usual division of this section into outcome and theory-testing research.

Macdonald (2007) compiled a list of studies relevant to SFT, finding 6 randomly controlled trials that supported the efficacy of the approach. Of particular interest was an
unpublished meta-analysis of 22 studies that found significant, but small-effect sizes that
favored SFT (Kim, 2006, cited by Macdonald, 2007). Although De Jong and Berg (2007)
cite a number of reviews in support of the approach, several are not published in refereed
journals and the quality of research is uneven.

Bertolino and O'Hanlon (2002) build a case for SF Therapy based on the common
factors approach to psychotherapy outcome (see Chapter 1). They maintained that
client factors are the single most powerful factors in therapy outcome and that these factors are reflective of client strengths, resources, and social support. Taking a collaborative, strength-based approach to counseling thus is based on empirical data. The
therapist's assumption that change will happen bolsters "placebo" effects and builds
client expectations.

Much to their credit, de Shazer and the therapists at the Brief Family Therapy Center
(BFTC) have collected outcome data on some of their clients (De Jong & Berg, 2007; de
Shazer, 1985, 1991). A study of 275 clients who presented for therapy at the BFTC in
1992 and 1993 found that 7 to 9 months after therapy, 45% of the 136 clients who could
be contacted reported that their goals had been met in therapy; 32% reported some
progress; 23% reported that they had made no progress in meeting their goals. Keep in
mind that these are informal survey data, helpful, but subject to many potential pitfalls in
terms of experimental design.

In a study of the first session formula task, de Shazer and Molnar (1984) had therapy team members (who were behind the one-way mirror) rate client responses to the first session task. They found that 57% of the 56 clients studied reported improvement between the first and second sessions. The average client in this study attended five sessions. In follow-up interviews conducted between 6 and 12 months after therapy, 23 of the 28 clients responding reported that their main complaint was "better." Interestingly, 25 of the 28 clients had mentioned a secondary complaint, and 11 of them (all from the successful cases) reported that improvement was seen in the secondary area as well, a finding that supports the "ripple effect." It is important to note, as did de Shazer, that these studies were exploratory in nature. No control or comparison groups were included, and random assignment of clients to therapists was not used, thus leaving the studies open to strong criticism on grounds of internal validity. Nonetheless, these therapists are commended on their attempts to validate their approach.

Studies conducted by researchers other than those at the Brief Family Therapy Center appear to have found similar results. Gingerich and Eisengart (2000) reviewed a selection of outcome studies of SF Therapy. Generally, they found that clients in SF counseling showed improvement relative to untreated clients (or standard treatment, such as in rehabilitation care). However, the methodological quality of the studies varies widely. To illustrate the state of the research on SF counseling, I will briefly review a few studies.

Wettersten, Lichtenberg, and Mallinckrodt (2005) explored the relationship between the working alliance and outcome in SF Therapy and Brief Interpersonal Therapy (BIT). Reasoning that the alliance should be more important in BIT than SF Therapy, Wettersten et al. compared a sample of 26 clients who received SF Therapy with an archival sample who had completed BIT. Interestingly, the results showed that the alliance scores of the two groups were similar when measured early in treatment and at termination. However, levels of symptom change, which overall, were similar in the two groups, were only correlated with the alliance for the BIT group. Wettersten et al. suggest that these findings indicate that although an alliance is necessary in SF Therapy, it is not a mechanism of change. This conclusion would be acceptable to proponents of SF Therapy, who would be pleased with the results for symptom change and also for client satisfaction, which was similar for the two groups.

Jakes and Rhodes (2003) reported on an interesting study of SF and cognitive-behavioral (CB) strategies with clients who had delusions. Five clients were intensively studied at baseline (no treatment) and as they were then treated with a SF and 2 CB interventions (schema-focused cognitive therapy and cognitive therapy focused on challenging the delusion) in that order. They observed that 2 of these clients (who were diagnosed with chronic psychosis as well as delusion for at least one year) responded positively (in terms of decreasing belief in their delusions) when they were treated with SF. All clients decreased their negative views about the self, and Jakes and Rhodes indicate that this effect was seen mostly in the SF phase of treatment. However, because this was a multiple case study design, we must be cautious in drawing causal inferences from its results.

Lee (1997) found that 65% of a sample of families participating in SF Therapy reported that their goals were either partly or completely met. This study was based on client self-report and did not include comparison groups. Clients engaged in an average of 5.5 sessions over 3.9 months. Beyebach, Morejon, Palenzuela, and Rodriguez-Arias (1996) reported that a study of 39 outpatients found an 80% goal achievement rate. De Jong and Hopwood

(1996) studied 275 clients who completed an average of 2.9 sessions. Forty-five percent of these clients reported achieving their goals, and 32% reported making "some progress."

Zimmerman, Prest, and Wetzel (1997) studied 36 couples treated in groups, comparing them to a control group of untreated couples. Couples receiving SF Therapy showed more improvement on the Dyadic Adjustment Scale compared to control couples. However, these results must be interpreted cautiously because of other methodological concerns with this research (e.g., the treatment group couples were distressed and seeking therapy; the control group couples did not identify themselves as dissatisfied with their relationships).

Individuals diagnosed as schizophrenic and their families were the participants in another study (Eakes, Walsh, Markowski, Cain, & Swanson, 1997). An interesting addition to the therapy in this study was that near the end of each session, the therapeutic team came from behind the one-way mirror and changed places with the family! This procedure then allowed the family to observe the team discussing the family's strengths and resources.

No standard outcome measures were used in Eakes and colleagues' study; instead, the researchers chose to examine perceptions of the family environment among control and treated participants. Clients who received Solution-Focused Therapy reported increases in family expressiveness and participation in social and recreational activities. In contrast, an untreated control group did not show these changes and instead increased in the degree to which they perceived disagreement among family members about the nature of the family environment.

Two studies have focused on the patterns of change among clients in SF Therapy. Interestingly, these studies were based on a research definition of SF Therapy developed by the European Brief Therapy Association (EBTA). The EBTA definition is as follows:

First session

The therapist . . .
1. . . . asks and follows up on the Miracle Question.
2. . . . asks and follows up on the Progress Scale Question (On a scale, where 10 stands for the day after the miracle and 0 stands for when the problems that brought you in were at their worst, where would you put yourself right now?).
3. . . . compliments the client(s) at the end of the session.

Second and following sessions

The therapist . . .
4. . . . asks "What is better?" at the beginning of the session and follows up on it.
5. . . . asks and follows up on the Progress Scale Question.
6. . . . compliments the client(s) at the end of the session.

Therapists will have to adjust to the exact wording and (where applicable) timing of these elements, as described in the following sections of this treatment protocol. Therapies where one or more of these elements are missing in one or more of the sessions can not be included in the sample.

Adapted from EBTA, 2007, European Brief Therapy Association Outcome Study: Research Definition Description of the Treatment.

Reuterlov, Lofgren, Nordstrom, Ternstrom, and Miller (2000) asked a sample of clients "what is better?" and examined their responses relative to scaling responses from the end of that same session. To ascertain whether clients had changed, they compared the scaling responses obtained to those from the immediately preceding session. Some clients reply in the negative, and the approved SF procedure would be for the therapist to deconstruct this outcome and by the end of the session, the client should report improvement. Contrary to this supposition, Reuterlov et al. found that 87% of their clients stayed the same or declined by the end of the session (based on comparisons of ratings to those in a previous session). Thus, it seems that deconstructing client's negative reports might be a mistake—the therapist in this situation might need to "do something different."

De Vega and Beyebach (2004) set out to replicate Reuterlov et al.'s work with a sample of clients in Spain. Although De Vega and Beyebach found a similar pattern (about 63% of clients starting off negatively did not report improvement at the end of the session), the percentage of clients reporting improvement at the end of the session approximately tripled that found by Reuterlov et al. (37.5% vs. 13%). De Vega and Beyebach conclude that they are not quite as certain about the problematic nature of deconstruction—perhaps further research will reveal in what circumstances it is helpful and under which conditions it is not. However, it is worth noting that the samples in these two studies were different (Sweden vs. Spain) and the therapists differed, too.

Based on the foregoing review and other studies that report success rates from 64 to 75% (Macdonald, 1994, 1997; Reimer & Chatwin, 2006), it appears that SF Therapy is associated with desirable client change. Although these data may seem very convincing at first glance, it is important to remember that most of these studies were seriously flawed when evaluated according to standards generally accepted by psychotherapy outcome researchers (e.g., Chambless & Hollon, 1998; Lambert & Ogles, 2004). Thus, it is probably safe to conclude that the efficacy of Solution-Focused Therapy has not yet been established.

ISSUES OF INDIVIDUAL AND CULTURAL DIVERSITY

Because de Shazer and his colleagues maintain that they construct the view of the problem along with the client, they argue that they enter the client's world, avoiding any imposition of the counselor's perspective on the client (de Shazer, 1994). Great care is taken to take the client's presentation at face value and initially to work within the client's perceptual framework. Thus, these theorists would probably argue that their approach is, in fact, culturally bound, but to that of the client rather than to the culture of the theory or counselor. SF proponents have explored the use of this approach with a wide range of clients and presentations, including male cross-dressing (Dzelme & Jones, 2001), and religious/spiritual concerns (Guterman & Leite, 2006).

Corcoran (2000) evaluated the appropriateness of SF Therapy in working with African American and Mexican American clients. She contended that the SF emphasis on a brief approach, future orientation, and solutions rather than problems fit well for these clients. Further, Corcoran maintained that the SF approach "conveys respect for the unique world views of clients and how they solve problems" (2000, p. 11).

Berg and Miller (1992) and Chang and Yeh (1999) specifically evaluated the utility of SF Therapy for clients who are of Asian origin. Although these authors warned that to act on stereotypes of Asians or Asian Americans alone is risky, they maintained that certain aspects of SF counseling are very consistent with these clients' ideologies. They pointed out that because Asian Americans tend to seek counseling as a last resort, they are often in crisis, which leads to a desire to focus on problems. Indeed, in general, individuals of Asian heritage are thought to be more comfortable problem solving than addressing emotional content (Berg & Miller, 1992). This problem focus helps the Asian client cope with the feelings of shame that are so powerful in the Asian culture. SF counseling would seem to be a good match for these clients because of its emphasis on rapid change as a result of an intense problem (solution) focus. Berg and Miller also noted that when therapists focus on exceptions, they are helping the Asian client "save face," an important cultural process. An even more specific application of SF Therapy with Asian clients was presented by Lee and Mjelde-Mossey (2006), who discussed using the approach to help East Asian elders and their families to address the problem of cultural dissonance.

Nonetheless, some of the same criticisms can be directed at this approach that are commonly directed at other theories of counseling. From a broad perspective, the notion of solutions may be culturally linked. For example, the search for exceptions is often behaviorally oriented and typically results in prescriptions for behavioral change. This individualistic focus may neglect the needs of individuals from more relationship-oriented cultures such as Latino/Latina or American Indian. However, Berg and Miller (1992) pointed out that SF counselors often help clients to explore exceptions by asking about how important others view the situation, thereby acknowledging the critical nature of these relationships. Individuals who have experienced oppression and discrimination (e.g., the physically challenged; African Americans; gays, lesbians, and bisexuals, or Latinos/Latinas) may find it difficult to focus narrowly on problems when so many social and cultural factors influence their daily lives.

SF Therapy is very focused and directive, which may clash with the values of clients from cultures that are less problem-oriented in their approaches to living. Women may find that the focus on problems and solutions neglects relationship themes that are important to them and de-emphasizes cultural factors that restrict their ability to directly problem solve. At the extreme, solution-focused counselors tend to follow almost a formula in dealing with clients, leading to very specific prescribed questions or tasks. For example, techniques such as scaling that reflect the pragmatic Western ideology may be foreign to clients from cultures other than traditional western cultures.

Dermer, Hemesath, and Russell (1998) pointed out that SF Therapy's emphasis on a collaborative relationship between client and counselor is consistent with feminist perspectives on counseling. However, they also asserted that SF theorists overlook the power of stereotypic roles and that the neutral stances of SF therapists may reinforce the (patriarchal) status quo. This neutral stance may also lead to the failure to assign responsibility for problems such as domestic violence even though the violence itself is condemned.

Rossiter (2000) noted that the SF therapist's eschewal of the past can potentially be problematic, particularly when working with clients from groups who have historically been oppressed or have experienced physical or sexual abuse. Encouraging the client to testify about injustices they have experienced is an important political event, according to Rossiter. Discouraging talk about the past is a serious mistake that potentially aligns the therapist with the historically privileged and powerful:

> it is chilling to contemplatetherapy being used widely to conspire with silence by rendering history invisible and trivializing the symptoms (forms of telling) of injustice by managing them as "complaints." In such circumstances, the culture that therapy helps to create is invested in denial, repression, and abuse of power (p. 158; quotes in original).

THE CASE STUDY

Understanding Kelly's presentation from the SF perspective is at first a little daunting. He speaks in problem language and labels himself as "an angry person" and "a perfectionist." It is somewhat difficult to find exceptions in his initial description although they are not difficult to imagine. He is clearly a customer (not a visitor or complainant) and is open to change, which makes it easier to use the SF approach. He identifies clear goals and has a number of strengths upon which the SF counselor, Mary, can draw. Because Kelly is a Caucasian male, potential issues of cultural bias are reduced. In summary, SF theory seems to fit well with Kelly's presentation.

Summary

SF counselors approach counseling with a model that focuses on client strengths and resources. It is a constructivist approach and is presented as a radical alternative to traditional models of counseling. Instead of spending a lot of time dissecting the client's (customer's) problem, attention is directed toward times when the complaint does not happen, or exceptions. Solutions are emphasized in this approach, and great care is taken to use language and techniques that emphasize exceptions rather than problem occurrences.

SF therapists do not use formal assessment, and they see the therapy relationship as collaborative. The SF counselor is an expert on change, but the client is the expert on how and what to change. The goals of therapy are set by the client, and the SF counselor's job is to redefine the problem so that it is solvable. The SF counselor helps the client to avoid doing more of the same and to increase the performance of exceptions to the problem.

Very little outcome research exists in support of SF therapy. What does appear is methodologically suspect. The constructivist approach of SF counseling may be beneficial for clients of diverse backgrounds, but the individualistic, solve-your-problem focus of SF counseling may neglect environmental factors that influence client presentations.

Visit Chapter 14 on the Companion Website at **www.prenhall.com/murdock** for chapter-specific resources and self-assessments.

CHAPTER 15

Narrative Therapy

Michael White

The Kennedy family comes to counseling in hopes of helping the eldest daughter, Rachael (17 years old), in her struggle with anorexia. David and Melanie, the parents, have been divorced for 4 years. Rachael's problems developed when she was 13 years old, around the time her parents separated. There are two other children in the family, Jeff (age 12) and Jessica (age 15).

David and Melanie report that their marriage ended because David "came out." Another factor in the couple's history was Melanie's drinking—she was apparently physically abusive to the children when she was drinking, resulting in frequent conflict with David as well. Melanie reports that she has been sober for 4 years.

Rachael, according to her mother, just could not handle her parents' break-up, the news that her father was gay, and her mother's entry into alcohol rehabilitation. In addition, Rachael reports that she was almost raped by an uncle when she was 15 years old. Rachael says that when the family lived together, her father was perfectionistic and demanding, insisting that she perform at the highest levels in schoolwork and athletics. When she did not meet these standards, he would tell her that she was going nowhere with her life. Rachael readily admits that her anorexia is a form of "passive suicide."

Rachael has been hospitalized three times for her problems and the family is referred to counseling by the psychiatrist with whom she has most recently been working. Multiple forms of treatment have been attempted, including hypnosis, antidepressant medication, individual psychotherapy, music therapy, and Eating Disorders Anonymous. Rachael reported that until about a year ago she used laxatives, diuretics, and diet pills to maintain a low body weight. She currently weighs about 105 pounds and is considered severely underweight for her height. She restricts her food intake and exercises several times a day.

For the most part, the family is coming to therapy to see if they can help Rachael. However, David does not see how family therapy can help—he sees the problem as Rachael's and states that she just needs to get her act together and start eating.

BACKGROUND

Essentially, narrative therapists see life as a process of storytelling. Narrative Therapy (NT) is a relatively recent development and it is firmly situated in the social constructivist approach to psychotherapy. For some, what is disconcerting about this approach is that there is no one True Story. I will have more to say on this issue later.

The names most commonly associated with the NT approach are Michael White and David Epston. The "bible" of the theory is White and Epston's (1990) book *Narrative Means to Therapeutic Ends*. One hotbed of NT is the Dulwich Centre in Adelaide, Australia, co-directed by Michael and Cheryl White. You can find their website at www.dulwichcentre.com.au/index.htm. Check out www.narrativeapproaches.com/ for David Epston's website. In Box 15.1, you'll find a selection of Michael White's writing about a client, Robert, that will give you a sense of how he thinks about his work.

Box 15.1

A Case from Michael White

Robert was referred to therapy over abusive behavior in relation to his partner and one of his children. This abuse had only been recently disclosed. He had agreed to leave the family home, and the appropriate police and court measures were in the process of being instituted.

During our early contact, discussion centered on Robert's responsibility for perpetrating the abuse,* on the identification of the survivors' experiences of abuse, on the real short-term and possible long-term traumatic effects of this on the life of the survivors, and on determining what he might do to take responsibility to mend what might be mended.

Following this work, I asked Robert whether he would be prepared to join me in some speculation about the conditions and the character of men's abusive behavior. This he agreed to do, so I asked him a series of questions within the category of those represented below:

- If a man wanted to control and to dominate another person, what sort of structures and conditions could he arrange that would make this possible?
- If a man desired to dominate another person, particularly a woman or a child, what sort of attitudes would be necessary in order to justify this?
- If a man decided to make someone his captive, particularly a woman or a child, what sort of strategies and techniques of power would make this feasible?

During this speculation, particular knowledges about men's ways of being that are subjugating of others were articulated, techniques and strategies that men could rely upon to institute this subjugation were identified, and various structures and conditions that support abusive behavior were reviewed. I then asked Robert to determine which of these attitudes he had given his life to, which of these strategies had been dominant in shaping his relationships with others, and which of these conditions and structures had provided the framework for his life. This was followed by further discussion centered on a review of the historical processes through which Robert had been recruited into the life space that was fabricated of these attitudes, techniques, and structures.

Robert was invited to take a position on these attitudes, strategies, and structures. Would he continue to subject his life to this particular knowledge of men's way of being? To what extent did he think it was reasonable to live life as "power's instrument," as an instrument of terror? To what extent did he wish to cooperate with these strategies and tactics that so devastated the lives of others? In view of his developing understanding of the real effects of his actions, did he think it acceptable to depend upon these structures and conditions as a framework for his life?

As this work progressed, Robert began to experience a separation from these attitudes and an alienation from these structures and techniques of power and control. His previously familiar and taken-for-granted ways of being in relation to women and children—and for that matter, his previously familiar and taken-for-granted ways of being with other men—no longer spoke to him of the truth of who he was as a man. For Robert to challenge his abusive behavior no longer meant taking action against his own "nature," and he was now able to take entire responsibility for the abuse that he had perpetrated on others.

In the space that Robert stepped into as a result of this separation, we were able to find various unique outcomes, that is, occasions upon which his behavior had not been compelled by those previously familiar and taken-for-granted ways of being as a man. I asked Robert to evaluate these unique outcomes. Did he see these outcomes as desirable? Did he feel positively about them? Or were they of no consequence to him? As Robert concluded that these outcomes were desirable, I asked him to share with me how he had reached this conclusion.

As our work progressed, the identification of these unique outcomes provided a point of entry for an "archeology" of alternative and preferred knowledges of men's ways of being, knowledges that Robert began to enter. For example, in response to my encouragement to give meaning to these unique outcomes, to determine what ways of "being" as a man were reflected in them, Robert recalled an uncle who was quite unlike other men in his family; this was a man who was certainly compassionate and non-abusive. Robert subsequently did some homework on this uncle, and this contributed significantly to his knowledge of some of the more intimate particularities of this alternative way of being.

Robert's family had signaled a strong desire to explore the possibilities of reuniting. As Robert had begun to separate from those attitudes and practices that had justified and supported his abusive behavior, and as he had entered into an exploration of alternative and preferred knowledges of men's ways of being, the time seemed right to convene a meeting with the family.** Understanding his responsibility to provide safeguards to family members, he agreed to participate in certain structures that would contribute significantly to the security of family members. These included (a) a meeting with representatives† of his partner and his child to disclose his responsibility for and the nature of the abuse, (b) a willingness to participate in weekly escape from secrecy meetings‡ with his family and the nominated representatives, and (c) a preparedness to cooperate with other family members in the development of a contingency plan should any family member again feel threatened by abuse.

Over time, Robert traded a neglectful and strategic life for one that he, and others, considered to be caring, open, and direct.

Excerpted from "Deconstruction and Therapy" by M. White. In S. Gilligan and R. Rice (eds.) *Therapeutic Conversation* (pp. 22–80) 1993. New York: W. W. Norton.

'I would refer readers to Alan Jenkin's book *Invitations to Responsibility* (1990), for an excellent discussion of this and other aspects of work with men who abuse others.

'The counseling of family members in relation to the abuse and other issues was undertaken concurrently in a different context.

'I do not believe it is ever sufficient for men to take entire responsibility for perpetrating abuse, to identify the experience of those abused, to get in touch with the short-term and possible long-term effects of the abuse, to develop a sincere apology, to work on ways of repairing what might be repaired, and to challenge the attitudes that justify such behavior and the conditions and techniques of power that make abuse possible.

If that is where it ends, although the man may experience genuine remorse, he is likely to re-offend because he has no other knowledges of men's ways of being to live by. For there to be any semblance of security that this will not occur, I believe that it is essential that these men be engaged in the identification and the performance of alternative knowledges of men's ways of being.

†These representatives must be nominated by the child and the non-offending spouse. They can be relatives who do not have a history of abusive behavior or persons known to them in the community.

‡Escape from secrecy meetings are held weekly in the first place, and gradually move to a monthly basis over a period of two years. At each of these meetings, events of the past week or so are reviewed. Events which reflect a reappearance of any of those attitudes, strategies, conditions, and structures that provided the context for past abuse can be identified and challenged.

Different family members take turns at minute-taking for these meetings and in the posting of these minutes to the therapist (frequently with the assistance of the representatives). The family member whose turn it is to take this responsibility is encouraged to append his or her confidential comments to these minutes. If the therapist does not receive the minutes of a meeting on schedule, s/he immediately follows this up. From time to time the therapist joins these meetings to review progress.

It is not possible to overemphasize the importance of local accountability in this work. State intervention can be highly effective in bringing about the immediate cessation of abuse, but local accountability structures are essential to the establishment of secure contexts.

For an excellent discussion of the significance of secrecy in structuring a context for abuse, I would refer readers to Amanda Kamsler and Lesley Laing's "Putting an end to secrecy" (1990).

Beels (2001) provides a history of White and Epston's collaboration in creating NT and the following section draws significantly from his work. White and Epston are both social workers by training and are more likely to be found doing family therapy than individual therapy. As an undergraduate, Epston majored in anthropology and also worked for Australia's Northern Territory Department of Aboriginal Welfare. According to Beels, he held many diverse jobs and then "dropped out into the hippie world of Vancouver, Canada" (p. 166), in the late '60s or early '70s. Epston eventually returned to New Zealand in the late '70s and began to work with children and families.

A native of Adelaide, White worked for the Department of Welfare while working on his degree in social work and then in a children's hospital. An interesting tidbit about his training: the first therapy approach he learned was Person-Centered Theory.

White and Epston reportedly met at the First Australian Family Therapy conference in 1980 and found a mutual interest in anthropology as a basis for family therapy. The influence of this foundation can be clearly seen in the NT commitment to grounding individuals' stories in cultural and historical contexts. This emphasis, along with the physical genesis of NT in Australia and New Zealand, probably led to the interest among these therapists in community-level interventions such as the Dulwich Centre's consultations with Aboriginal people's councils. Beels (2001) maintains that other major influences on the evolution of NT were White and Epston's '60s-era life experiences, and the fact that neither had been intensively trained in the psychoanalytic tradition.

Currently, NT has a sizable international following and social constructivism is considered a cutting edge of family therapy (Carr, 1998). You can see a really good example of Narrative Therapy on the *Theories in Action* DVD, featuring therapist Jim Kreider with the client Helen. The major websites for this approach are probably Epston's and White's (listed earlier) but you can easily find others through a quick search. The *Australia and New Zealand Journal of Family Therapy* can be found at http://www.anzjft.com/resources.htm and *Gecko*, a practice-based journal about Narrative Therapy is described at http://narrativebooks.com/journals.php?journal=16.

BASIC PHILOSOPHY

NT, as noted earlier, is rooted in social constructivist philosophy. Pure social constructivists believe that there is no objective social reality; instead, the way we view ourselves, others, and the entire social world in which we live is created (constructed) by social processes, and most significantly, through our interactions with others.

An important aspect of the NT philosophy is the analysis of social power, which is rooted in the ideas of the French philosopher Foucault (White & Epston, 1990). In this view, power is seen as determining the truths by which society operates, which in turn, strongly influence the stories individuals create about their lives. You may see similarities with a feminist ideology in this NT perspective and these are not accidental. Both approaches are considered political stances as much as they are ways of helping. An NT therapist would be very comfortable with the phrase "the personal is political."

Power and knowledge (that accepted by the dominant culture) are inseparable. In fact, it is difficult to see the relationship, for the workings of power are disguised under the notion of "truth." For example, western European culture generally accepts the notion of an objective reality (outside of us) that can be known by scientific method. One who departs from this version of reality is usually known by those around her as "crazy" and is rendered powerless (think of how folks talk about psychic advisors, for example).

Further, White and Epston (1990) tell us:

> If we accept that power and knowledge are inseparable—that a domain of knowledge is a domain of power and a domain of power is a domain of knowledge—and if we accept that we are simultaneously undergoing the effects of power and exercising power over others, then we are unable to take a benign view of our own practices. Nor are we able simply to assume that our practices are primarily determined by our motives, or that we can avoid all participation in the field of power/knowledge through an examination of such motives. (p. 29)

Because therapy is part of the domains of knowledge/power it is possible for it to become a form of social control. If one accepts this stance, then, a critical evaluation of our actions as counselors in terms of power is in order. Further, because NT often supports and encourages clients to question the dominant stories of their cultures, the NT counselor is aware that therapy is a form of social/political action (White & Epston, 1990). There is a distinct sense of social activism in this approach, nicely captured by Doan (1998): "narrative therapy concerns itself with the deliverance of clients from the weight of oppressive and totalizing stories via liberating the client's voice and preferences" (p. 219).

NT counselors approach clients from a perspective that emphasizes health and strengths (Semmler & Williams, 2000). This stance, combined with NT's insistence that reality is socially created, leads to a questioning of traditional psychological perspectives. In the words of the Dulwich Centre website: "narrative therapy questions pathologising practices" (Commonly asked questions about narrative therapy: Is narrative therapy anti-medication?). NT therapists don't particularly like the term *client*, and the term *patient* is even worse. Michael White has been known to reject the terms *counseling, therapy,* and *treatment* because they convey power messages, instead referring to himself as a conversational host. Other important values in NT are accountability of the therapist to clients and, like feminism, the commitment to make therapy as transparent to clients as is possible (recall the feminist value of demystifying therapy).

Here is a bit of Michael White's writing to give you a flavor of his position on therapy and politics:

> In therapy, I have participated with persons in challenging various practices of power, including those that relate to: (a) the technologies of the self—the subjugation of the self through the discipline of bodies, soul, thoughts, and conduct according to specified ways of being (including the various operations that are shaping of bodies according to the gender-specific knowledges); (b) the technologies of power—the subjugation of others through techniques such as isolation and surveillance, and through perceptual evaluation and comparison. (1993, p. 54)

Deepa is the NT therapist who has agreed to work with the Kennedy family. She is 30 years old, of Asian Indian descent, an important influence on her choice of NT; her ethnicity is a constant point of reference in her work. Approaching Rachael's family with the knowledge of her own background and the awareness that historical and cultural influences affect their lives, Deepa is particularly attentive to the power differential that is inherent in the therapeutic relationship, traditional views of anorexia, and cultural discourses that suggest that women maintain a slim figure to be considered attractive.

HUMAN MOTIVATION

NT theorists don't spend a lot of time talking about what motivates people, probably because they are so intently focused on an individual client's story. Further, taking a stance in this area might be seen as limiting the possibilities of persons to create their own versions of a meaningful life. Given the emphasis on personally constructed meaning in this approach, however, it would probably be safe to say that NTs would view the tendency to create meaning as a central feature of human existence (Morgan, 2000).

Deepa considers that Rachael and her family are struggling to create meaning out of the various life events in their experiences. Rachel is likely to be struggling with the meaning of sexuality and womanhood. Deepa guesses that in listening to their accounts of how the present came to be, she will understand this family's perspectives and how they make sense of the current situation.

CENTRAL CONSTRUCTS

STORIES

Human life, according to the NT tradition, is a series of stories. These stories are created over time through our attempts to connect events in our experiences and in this way, derive meaning from them (Morgan, 2000). Morgan (2000) writes that "for narrative therapists, stories consist of events linked in sequence across time according to plot" (p. 5). The process begins when we start connecting a number of events into a plot or the beginnings of a story. Once these first connections are made, it begins to be easy to gather more events that are consistent with the story line; in the words of the NT theorists—events become "privileged" over other events and are included in what becomes the *dominant* story for the individual (Morgan, 2000). For example, I learn the tango, and then salsa. I begin to create a story about myself that I like to dance. I begin to live this story, and it creates meaning for me in my life. I then take up tap dancing. I now have a story of myself as Nancy the dancer.

In contrast to dominant stories are *alternate stories* (White & Epston, 1990). We all live such complex lives that invariably there are aspects of our experience that do not get included in or are hidden by dominant stories. These aspects are known as alternate stories, and are often important in helping our clients (more on this follows).

Stories, however, are not created in isolation; they are created through the interactions we have with others. Stories are also heavily influenced by the culture in which the person participates. In fact, NT theorists use the terms *cultural discourse* or *dominant discourse* to refer to culturally based "truths" that influence our lives (Zimmerman & Dickerson, 2001). Those who comply or accept these discourses are in the "in" group and those who don't are marginalized. An example of a Western European cultural discourse is individualism—the idea that a person should develop a strong sense of self separate from others. Other examples of cultural discourses are sexism, classism, racism, heterosexism, adultism, developmentalism, and capitalism (Zimmerman & Dickerson, 2001).

One special type of story is a *problem-saturated story*, which is what people bring to counseling (Payne, 2000). For most clients, the problem saturated story is the dominant story of their lives at that time—it is what prompts them to come to counseling.

Rachael's family brings the problem-saturated story about Rachael's anorexia to counseling, seeking Deepa's help. Currently, it is the dominant story for this family and is heavily situated in cultural discourses about acceptable roles and appearances for women. The family also tells the story of Melanie's journey from alcoholism to sobriety and David's coming out process.

THINNESS AND THICKNESS

These adjectives refer to the qualities of the stories people tell. Thin stories contain few events and are relatively sparse in detail. Thick stories, on the other hand, are very elaborate and rich in nature. Stories get thick because they are told again and again, and they are usually embellished upon with each telling. More detail and description is added to the original, sparse story, making the retold story more vivid and complete. Dominant stories are rich and thick; alternative stories tend to be sparse and thin.

How one views the problem-saturated stories that persons bring to counseling is a matter of perspective. From the perspective of the dominant culture, forms of "psychopathology" carry rich, detailed stories that serve to reinforce the existing power structure. However, when thinking about the individual who is burdened by the dominant story, one can also see the problem-saturated story as relatively thin and unitary, because it contains a label and cultural discourse and tends to obscure the uniqueness of the individual and the power politics inherent in the label. That is, the social power and oppression embedded in the label are unrecognized and simply go unquestioned. Problem-saturated stories are also very restricted views of the person that don't include details about her strengths and competence.

The Kennedy family has a rich, thick story about Rachael's problems that is highly connected to the dominant discourses of society about "anorexia." They describe her refusal to eat, her hospitalizations, therapy—it is clear to Deepa that they see her troubles as a sickness that resides in her. Her father thinks that Rachael needs to get her act together—this may be her last chance. Deepa thinks that this description of Rachel is very influenced by power and politics and represents a very thin view of who Rachel really is as a person.

UNIQUE OUTCOMES

Unique outcomes are events that are not part of the dominant, problem-saturated story (White & Epston, 1990). They are the exceptions to the problem's rule and are very important in helping clients escape the tyranny of the problem. Often found in alternate stories, unique outcomes usually become part of the *preferred story* (here read "therapy goals") for the client. The NT therapist is very interested in unique outcomes and spends a lot of time asking detailed questions about them, getting the client to expand upon her description.

Deepa sees a glimmer of hope in the family reports that Rachael no longer uses laxatives or diuretics. She has also managed to stop purging and Deepa sees these as potential examples of unique outcomes. Deepa will remember these things as she begins to talk with Rachael and her family, and will search for further instances that are counter to the family's dominant story.

THEORY OF THE PERSON AND DEVELOPMENT OF THE INDIVIDUAL

NT counselors don't have much use for a general theory of development of individuals. Smith (1997), in discussing using NT with children and adolescents, maintains that traditional theories of development (containing developmental "milestones" and normative patterns) are sometimes helpful. However, NT therapists are usually more interested in the client's unique trajectory through life, cultural context, and her personal understanding of the current situation.

Zimmerman and Dickerson (2001) suggest that we are all multiversioned or multistoried. How we behave in a given situation depends upon which story has the most influence at that point in time. For example, they suggest that "under the influence of patriarchy a man might be inclined to dominance and over entitlement. However, the same person, under the influence of compassion (as a way of being) might respond quite differently" (Zimmerman & Dickerson, 2001, p. 419).

Thus, the NT counselor sees humans as having multiple selves; the expressions of these are situationally determined. However, because mainstream Western society is so individualistic, we cling to the idea that we have one self and experience others in the same way (Zimmerman & Beaudoin, 2002). These understandings of self are heavily influenced by dominant cultural discourses operating around individuals, as just noted. The notion of a single self is deeply ingrained in Western European culture—so much that it rarely occurs to us to think differently. So, Sarah who would rather climb trees than play with the Barbies is labeled a tomboy because she violates the cultural discourse about girls. The quiet boy who would rather help his mother cook than play soccer likewise violates the cultural discourse about boys and is seen as odd or unusual.

Deepa recognizes that Rachael is in the general developmental period termed adolescence but makes no assumptions about what this experience means to Rachael. Deepa does see Rachael as struggling to define herself and after listening to Rachael, understands that currently, for Rachael, self is anorexia.

HEALTH AND DYSFUNCTION

NT counselors believe that individuals come to therapy because the stories by which they are living do not sufficiently represent their life experiences (White & Epston, 1990). Something about the story doesn't fit with the client's view of how things are or should be. They become very focused on this particular story and the client's presentation is said to be problem saturated. As White and Epston note: "persons organize their lives around specific meanings and . . . in so doing, they inadvertently contribute to the "survival" of, or what is often called the "career" of, the problem" (1990, p. 3 qutoes in original).

Several authors have attempted to identify commonalities across clients in terms of problem stories. For example, West and Bubenzer (2002) described three problematic narratives: Ongoing Conflict, Not Being Appreciated, and A Continual Lack of Trust (p. 266). Doan (1998) suggested that it is possible that two central narratives are common to all people: Fear and Love. He maintains that it is inherent in the human condition that we can choose life stories that are saturated by one of these two themes, the consequences of which I am sure you can imagine. An amusing and informative reference is Doan's interviews with these two entities. Investigative reporters were hired to conduct the interviews in unbiased manners because although it was possible for therapists to interview Love, when they tried to interview Fear, they tended to try somehow to change it. These influence attempts invariably resulted in Fear prematurely terminating the interview and being labeled "suspicious" and "resistant" by the therapists (p. 220).

The term "preferred narrative" is probably the closest thing to "healthy person" in this approach. The client presents with a problem-saturated story that she experiences as not fitting her life experience. The therapist then helps the client find the preferred story.

Deepa thinks that Rachael is somehow not happy with the current story of her life and her family generally agrees. They are contributing to the story of anorexia by focusing heavily on it and defining Rachael almost solely on the basis of this story. Although it is not entirely clear yet to Deepa, she thinks that perhaps another way to see this story is that it is partially one of

Rachael feeling Not Appreciated or Unloved. Deepa hopes to understand this story more deeply, and to help Rachael and her family find a preferred story that better suits them.

NATURE OF THERAPY

Most simply put, NT is a place where the client tells the therapist a story, the therapist listens, and the two make what they can out of it. Beels (2001) offered the following metaphor: "the telling and hearing of the story are a collaboration on one of many versions, one of many ways that consultant and client can travel across the landscape of experience together, perhaps retracing their path again and again, ultimately looking for a preferred path to a preferred place" (p. 163).

Deepa begins with the Kennedy family by simply asking them to describe their experiences. The members of the family eagerly comply, and Deepa tries to listen to each family member intently.

ASSESSMENT

NT practitioners are not very likely to use formal assessment; the assumptions behind such systems are generally inconsistent with NT philosophy. First, traditional models of assessment assume a single reality to which the therapist has access. Second, these processes tend to be pathology-oriented and may ignore cultural or other contextual factors.

Assessment in an NT model is seen as a continuous process that is focused on understanding clients' perspectives on their lives (Smith, 1997). Particular attention is paid to the cultural and other contexts of the client's experiences. Multiple perspectives are honored such that "the initial focus of therapy is on trying to grasp the local meanings and understandings of everyone involved" (Smith, 1997, p. 29).

A thorough exploration of the problem is critical in the NT approach. Morgan (2000) recommends examining the problem's tricks, intentions, plans, motives, and deceits and lies, among other things (p. 25). Discussing the problem in these ways helps to externalize it.

As members of the Kennedy family tell their stories, Deepa listens to each one closely, acknowledging their perspectives. As she listens, Deepa affirms the various views of the problem, but she generally refers to Rachael's situation as "her problems with eating" or her "problems with anorexia" rather than as Anorexia (as a formal diagnosis). She asks about Anorexia's ways of operating, how it "tricks" Rachael into not eating and exercising a lot. What does Anorexia tell Rachael about herself and who she should be?

OVERVIEW OF THE THERAPEUTIC ATMOSPHERE

The collaborative nature of the therapeutic relationship leads to a therapeutic process that proceeds at the pace of the client (Carr, 1998). The client's language is used, or privileged, rather than the therapist's. It is common for the NT counselor to overtly check with the client to see if it is OK to proceed and also to see if the therapist understands her story accurately and is on the right track (White, 2004).

Deepa begins with the Kennedy family by asking if it is OK for her to ask them some questions so that she can understand them and the influence of Anorexia in their lives. She suggests that they will work together to find out what the family thinks might be better ways to live.

ROLES OF CLIENT AND COUNSELOR

In NT, the therapist is a collaborator or consultant; clients are the true experts on their lives (Carr, 1998). Semmler and Williams (2000) provide a delightful characterization of the roles of client and counselor in NT: the therapist is a "curious learner" and the client is a "senior partner whose own wisdom and experience, rather than the counselors', are resources for change" (p. 53). Enron and Lund (1996) describe the therapist in NT as akin to the television show detective Columbo. Columbo was a humble guy in a rumpled old trench coat who presented a very distinct interview style. Often complimenting his interviewees on their willingness to help and perceptive observations, he assumed an attitude of curiosity and respect. His approach, simply put, was one of "not knowing" about the current crime but as knowledgeable about putting pieces together to solve problems.

Deepa's orientation to Rachael and her family is one of not knowing—she makes no assumptions about how the problem gained its life and energy and how things will proceed in this consultation. She recognizes the Kennedy family members as the experts in this discussion and works hard to understand their points of view.

GOALS

What NT counselors want is new, more satisfying, stories for their clients. More formally stated, the goal of NT is to deconstruct problem-saturated stories and to re-author narratives that support preferred outcomes (West & Bubenzer, 2002, p. 366).

Deepa hopes that she can work collaboratively with the Kennedy family to help them define new stories, or preferred outcomes, in their experiences. It is likely that the preferred outcome of this family is to get out from under the tyranny of Anorexia and begin to tell stories about themselves as a loving, caring family. This process will require deconstruction of the story of Rachael the Anorexic.

PROCESS OF THERAPY

Beels (2001, pp. 177–178) identifies three stages of NT. First, through listening to the story of the problem, it is recast as an affliction of the client. To do this, the therapist and client concentrate on the effects rather than the causes of the problem. These efforts help in the process of externalizing the problem (see the following).

Next, alternatives to the problem are explored, and an alternate story is created through focusing on *unique outcomes*, or times when the problem was not manifest. The client is asked to decide if this story is the *preferred story*, if her actions or situation are more consistent with her experiences and more acceptable to her than was the problem-saturated story. As it begins to develop, this story will include plans and strategies to strengthen the story line, and details opportunities for the new story to take place. The preferred story characterizes the client as capable, rather than downtrodden, as able to stand up to the problem. This process is sometimes called *re-authoring, re-storying* or *re-membering* (Monk, 1997; Morgan, 2000; White & Epston, 1990) and is described as "relocating a person/family's experience in new narratives, such that the previously dominant story becomes obsolete. In the course of these activities, people's own lives, relationships, and relationships to their problems are redescribed" (White & Epston, 1990, p. 127).

Finally, and in Beels' view, most importantly, the therapist and client build a support group to help the client continue the new story. The support group is chosen by the client and can be family, friends, or entire communities (such as the AntiAnorexia League; see the description under "Taking It Back Practices"). Supporters can be imaginary, too . . . think of the cartoon characters Calvin and Hobbes. Hobbes is recruited to deal with all kinds of problems that Calvin externalizes. The support group believes in the preferred story and helps to create this "new" reality for the client.

An important process in NT is *externalizing*. In externalizing, the NT therapist helps the client to recast the problem as something outside of her by carefully listening to the client's story and asking a lot of questions about it, particularly about the effects of the problem on the client and people around her. This kind of questioning is called *relative influence questioning* (more on this follows). In effect, the "problem becomes the problem, and then the person's relationship with the problem becomes the problem (White & Epston, 1990, p. 40). Usually, but not always, the problem is given a name to emphasize its separateness from the person (Beels, 2001). Some examples include Trouble, Misery, Tantrums, Guilt, and Bad Habits.

Externalizing the problem is thought to help clients take a stand against it (Zimmerman & Dickerson, 2001). It is often considered as a political activity in which client and therapist expose the problem as the oppressive agent of the power structure of the dominant culture. An NT counselor, might, for example, see a depressed client as under the influence of Sadness. She asks: What are the effects of Sadness? How does Sadness influence your relationships with others? What does Sadness tell you about yourself? Sadness tells the client she is not meeting someone's (society's) standards; it is oppressive and dictatorial. Together, therapist and client can find ways it can be resisted and overthrown. You can read about a good example of problem naming in Box 15.2, "The Story of Sneaky Poo."

Box 15.2

The Story of Sneaky Poo

An interesting and engaging case described by White and Epston is that of "sneaky poo," the story of a 6-year-old encopretic boy. Nick, the boy, had "accidents" nearly daily, and even more traumatizing for the family was his tendency to play with the poo, smearing walls, creating balls with it, secreting it in clothes, corners of the house, and bathroom drains. Relative influence questioning of Nick and his family revealed that "the poo was making a mess of Nick's life by isolating him from other children and by interfering with his school work. By coating his life, the poo was taking the shine off his future and was making it impossible for him and others to see what he was really like as a person"

(p. 44). His mother was at her wits' end, ready to give up, and seeing herself as a failure as a parent. His father was very embarrassed about the poo, and this shame was driving him to isolate himself from relatives and friends. All of the relationships in the family were affected by the poo; "it was wedged between Nick and his parents, Sue and Ron. The relationship between him and Sue had become somewhat stressed, and much of the fun had been driven out of it. And the relationship between Nick and Ron (the father) had suffered considerably under the reign of tyranny perpetrated by the poo. Also, since their frustrations with Nick's problems always took center stage in their discussions, the poo had been highly influential in the relationship between Sue (the mother) and Ron, making it difficult for them to focus their attention on each other" (p. 44).

White and Epston helped Nick and his parents identify instances where Nick was able to outwit Sneaky Poo—when he resisted smearing or playing with it in other ways. Sue identified situations where she did not feel overwhelmed and miserable. Ron could not recall *not* being embarrassed by the poo, but was open to revealing his terrible secret to a work colleague. How could they reauthor their story?

The narrative therapist helped this family identify their resources that could be used to quit being ruled by Sneaky Poo. Nick decided that he would no longer be "tricked" into being Sneaky Poo's playmate. Ron decided that he could reveal his problem to others, and Sue had some notions about how to refuse Sneaky Poo's invitations to misery.

After three sessions, this family had conquered Sneaky Poo. Nick was making more friends, and Sue and Ron talked to other parents, finding that they were not alone in their worry about parenting skills. By taking Sneaky Poo out of Nick and renaming it as the enemy, this family was able to unite and defeat it. They did this by revising their relationships with the problem. Nick was awarded the Breaking the Grip of Sneaky Poo certificate for his efforts.

From White, M. & Epston, D. (1990). *Narrative Means to Therapeutic Ends.* NY: W. W. Norton & Company.

Externalizing conversations have a special character. By giving the problem a name, it is given a life of its own, and is often cast as "recruiting" the client to its cause (White & Epston, 1990). Often, problems are situated in dominant discourses, which calls for a special kind of *deconstruction:* the examination of the influences of cultural truths in the genesis of the problem (Zimmerman & Dickerson, 2001).

NT therapists are quick to point out, however, that in cases of violence of or other abuse of others, perpetrators are not let off. Externalizing the problem does not mean that the person escapes responsibility for his or her contribution to its existence. An important part of externalizing is to understand the ideas or practices that underlie the behavior (Russell & Carey, 2004). "Violence" is not simply externalized in these cases—the individual is instead seen as under the influence of "stinking thinking" or cultural discourses of superiority or power (Russell & Carey, 2004).

There is some concern about externalizing conversations becoming overemphasized in NT. White (2004), while acknowledging the value of these conversations, maintains that they are not always present in his work with clients. Externalizing is only the beginning of the journey—the focus must next turn to the exploration of unique outcomes.

Dominant stories are often supported by lots of plot and don't go away easily. They are therefore sometimes difficult to deconstruct. This perspective is one way in which NT counselors would view "resistance" on the part of the client. In social constructivist approaches, client resistance is also seen as the client's attempt to protect the view of self and world if these are threatened by the prospect of change (Richert, 2003).

Deepa engages Rachael and her family in detailed discussions of Anorexia. How does Anorexia manage to get the upper hand with Rachael? What does Anorexia tell Rachael about herself? Is Perfection a friend of Anorexia or its child? Anorexia is seen as taking charge of this family, and in particular, running Rachael's life. It is a tyrant that interferes with the family's mission. Deepa asks how it does this. Who is most affected other than Rachael? Are there times when Anorexia does not get the upper hand?

Deepa finds that the story of Anorexia is very detailed and complex. It is intertwined with the stories of Divorce and Alcohol or Drinking. There is also the issue of the sexual abuse of Rachael by her uncle and it is not clear to Deepa how this story plays out in relation to the others. It is clear to Deepa that Anorexia is a sneaky and powerful entity that tells Rachael that she is fat and unworthy. She is not perfect and also weak, for Anorexia manages to outwit her; it carries with it the force of society's judgments about women and their appearances.

THERAPEUTIC TECHNIQUES

QUESTIONING

The major technique in NT is asking questions. They are critical in helping the client deconstruct the dominant story and a major vehicle in the process of externalizing the problem (Zimmerman & Dickerson, 2001). NT counselors believe that the questions asked of clients generate experience; that is, questions can bring about new ways of seeing things (Freedman & Combs, 1996).

One very important kind of questioning is *relative influence questioning* (Carr, 1998). These questions help the client explore two critical sets of information: (a) the influence of the problem in her life, most importantly, in her relationships with others, and (b) her influence on the problem (White & Epston, 1990).

The first set of questions includes some like these:

Who was in charge at that moment, you or the problem?
Who sides with the problem?
What has Trouble tried to get you to do lately that you didn't want to do?
How does Guilt get between you and your husband?

The second kind of questions are intended to help the individual see what influence she has on the problem and usually involve a focus on times when she is able to resist the influence of the problem.

Examples of this second sort include:

This is a pretty powerful problem. How have you managed to keep it from getting even more difficult?
How did you avoid Trouble when it wanted you to come out and play?
How did you act to make Anger take a break from bothering you?

Questions are also important in reinforcing alternative stories, containing unique outcomes. Here are some examples of these:

How did you manage to do this? Can you give me some idea of what it took?
Did you almost chicken out? How did you keep going?
Were there things going on in other areas of your life that helped you take these steps?

Another way of categorizing questioning is in terms of *Landscape of Action* and *Landscape of Consciousness.* These are used in both examining the dominant and alternate (preferred) stories. Landscape of action questions require the client to situate outcomes in a sequence across time. Landscape of Consciousness questions are used to help the client reflect on the material gleaned from action questions and to give it meaning (White, 1992).

Deepa asks many questions of Rachael and her family, listening closely, and checking frequently to make sure she understands what they are telling her. How does Anorexia influence relationships in the family? What has been the pattern of Anorexia's influence over time? How does Anorexia trick Rachael into thinking she is incompetent, weak, fat, ugly, and so forth? She thinks about a similar series of questions on Divorce, Drinking, and Abuse, but because the family is so focused on Anorexia, she decides to stay with their dominant story for now.

Deepa is very interested in times when Rachael has been able to escape the influence of Anorexia. How did Rachael manage to defy Anorexia and stop binging, purging, and taking laxatives? Who is on Rachael's side against Anorexia? Have there been any times recently when Rachael has been able to resist Anorexia's commands? How did she do this?

VISUALIZATION

One way to help clients externalize is to use mental imagery. A compelling example was offered by Semmler and Williams (2002) who described the case of an African American woman who was struggling with issues of racism. The client eventually constructed a series of mental images in which racist messages became bricks tossed in her path. She would visualize herself picking up the bricks and giving them back to the individuals who tossed them.

Deepa asks Rachael to relax and visualize what Anorexia looks like, and how its voice sounds. Rachael constructs the image of Anorexia as a fat, strong, bully. It is hard to tell what sex Anorexia is and although it speaks to her in an authoritative, critical voice, Rachael is again unsure whether this voice is masculine or feminine. Can Rachael trick the bully somehow so that it can no longer push her around? Should she try to make friends with it?

Other family members provide their images of Anorexia and they range from a slimy octopus-like creature (Jeff's) to a jailer (Melanie's). Deepa helps each member look at ways that they could defeat Anorexia. How to help Rachael take away the keys or cloud the octopus' water?

OUTSIDER WITNESS PRACTICES

As the name implies, the outsider witness practice involves inviting a special person or group of persons to participate in therapy conversations (Russell & Carey, 2004). This practice is also sometimes called a *definitional ceremony.* White (2004) describes this technique as rooted in the tradition of acknowledgement. Its primary purpose is to develop a rich, thick story line for the client, often about the preferred story. In this process, values become clearly identified and negative perceptions can be diminished or defeated.

This technique involves the client(s) and an outsider-witness group. The witness(es) can be the other partner in a couple, family members, friends—anyone who is deemed relevant by the client(s). The ceremony begins with the client telling a story of her choosing and the witnesses listening carefully. At some point (determined by the therapist) the witnesses are invited to recount what was most salient for them in the client's story. They are encouraged to explain why they were drawn to aspects of the client's story, what they mean to them, and what images they evoked.

Following the witnesses' retelling, the therapist then interviews the client, asking some of the same questions: what stood out in the witnesses' retelling, what images emerged for the client about her life in this process, and what meanings were salient for the client.

Outsider witness procedures can take many forms depending on the needs of the client. Sometimes, the witnesses are members of the client's family or immediate friends. In other instances, the witnesses are former clients who have dealt with similar problems. For example, Russell and Carey (2004) describe a situation in which women who were formerly in abusive relationships attended a client's therapy session. These women listened and then respectfully responded to the client's description of her relationship with her brother, who helped her survive the abuse.

Sometimes outsider witness practices are used to help further establish the preferred story. People who are identified by the client as the most likely to believe in the client's ability to change can be invited to hear the client tell the preferred story and react to it. They might also become allies of the client in establishing the preferred story.

Deepa thinks that outsider witness practices may be very useful to Rachael and her family. One form that Deepa considers is having Rachael describe how she managed to stop binging, purging, and using laxatives. The family members could listen and then comment on what was most important to them in what they heard. Rachael could also describe her dreams for her future as someone who has escaped the clutches of Anorexia.

ACCOUNTABILITY PRACTICES

Sometimes NT counselors turn the tables on clients, and ask them to interview the therapists on how they are conducting the counseling (Zimmerman & Dickerson, 2001). Interviewing members of the clients' salient groups (e.g., persons of the same gender, ethic identity, sexual orientation) can also increase accountability.

Deepa checks with the Kennedy family about how they think the therapy is going, and on her work with them. Because he was initially pessimistic, she interviews David about how he thinks therapy is progressing and respectfully asks him to evaluate her performance. However, Deepa makes sure that everyone in the family has a voice in this evaluation process.

REFLECTION PRACTICES

Originally, systemic therapists employed teams of other therapists, often behind one-way mirrors, to help the therapists (usually a co-therapy team) by providing a different, "external" perspective on what was going on in the counseling session. NT therapists have adopted this practice, but use it in a unique way. In the traditional approach, the team behind the mirror would either call the therapists out during the session to give them advice, or debrief with them after the session. In the NT approach, the clients and therapist talk, observed by the team, but then sometime during the session, the two groups switch places (Freedman & Combs, 1996). The team then discusses, while the clients observe, what they witnessed in the therapy session, offering questions, impressions, and ideas. Following this interaction, the two groups change places again and the clients are encouraged to reflect on and comment upon what they heard from the reflecting team. In essence, the use of a reflecting team is another form of the outsider witness practice. The underlying rationale when tapping the expertise of other therapists is that increasing the visibility of the reflecting team emphasizes the collaborative, transparent, relationships critical to the NT approach (Freedman & Combs, 1996).

Deepa considers that she has several colleagues who are accustomed to serving on reflecting teams, and at least one who is familiar with struggles with Anorexia. She decides to invite these colleagues to serve as a reflecting team, after ascertaining that this procedure is acceptable to the Kennedy family. Three NT colleagues observe the family as Deepa interviews them about recent developments in their lives and Rachael's progress in outwitting Anorexia. The team then emerges from behind the one-way mirror and conveys their impressions to the family. One comments on the obvious caring and concern among the family members, despite the hardships they have suffered. Another remarks that she was touched by Melanie's description of how she defeated Alcohol and wonders what this means to Rachael.

TAKING IT BACK PRACTICES

This term applies to both therapists and clients in NT. For therapists, the philosophy of NT counselors suggests that the therapist (or a reflecting team) tell the client how she/they have been influenced by the client (Zimmerman & Dickerson, 2001). What is in other approaches deemed a negative event, that is, influence of the therapist by the client, is seen in NT as a positive. NT counselors acknowledge that therapy changes both client and counselor (Carr, 1998).

Taking it back is also seen when clients are given the opportunity to share their experiences with others, such as when they help other clients by revealing their struggles and triumphs with similar problems (Carr, 1998). This sharing often happens in the context of outsider witness practice but can also be seen in larger-scale efforts. A great example of the latter form of this practice, the Anti-Anorexia League, is documented at David Epston's website, which houses the League's archives. The Anti-Anorexia League is a group of individuals who have been influenced by anorexia and have worked to combat this influence. Many have survived anorexia and they offer their stories in the interest of helping others. According to Epston and Maisel (2006), 200–300 people have contributed to the archive, motivated to express their protest of, and disobedience to, anorexia.

Deepa will certainly alert Rachael to the existence of the Anti-Anorexia League and ask if she wishes to contribute or participate in any way. Deepa conveys her respect for Rachael's struggles and remarks that others may be able to learn from her. Rachael thinks that she might learn a great deal from studying the archives of the league and seems encouraged to learn that others have struggled in ways similar to hers and found satisfactory new stories.

WRITTEN ARTIFACTS

NT counselors often use written documents as ways of reinforcing or celebrating the accomplishments of their clients. Because the written word is considered more powerful than the spoken, these artifacts are important evidence for the client and others of the client's new story. These artifacts can be letters, certificates, memos, lists; virtually anything that is dreamed up by the therapist and client (Payne, 2000). For example, White and Epston (1990) describe the "Certificate of Concentration" and the "Escape from Tantrums Certificate" (pp. 196–197) given to commemorate therapeutic success stories. They refer to these items as counter documents because they oppose the oppressive dominant discourse that has been influencing the client's life. You can read about another example in Box 15.3, "All It Takes Is A Party," which combines a written artifact (an invitation) with a ceremonial intervention.

Box 15.3

All It Takes Is a Party

David Epston (1992) shows us how to eliminate temper tantrums, the Narrative Therapy way.

In 1979, David Epston was called to work with a family in which the daughter was having uncontrollable temper tantrums. In attempting to discuss the matter with the young woman, Nolene, her family, and her boyfriend, Epston discovered two important things: that Nolene was embarrassed for her boyfriend to learn about the tantrums (he reported that it was beyond belief that she would behave in such a way around him) and that talking to embarrassed adolescents sometimes requires a little calculated misunderstanding. Because he was having difficulty understanding her, he deliberately "heard" Nolene say that she wanted to buy a pumpkin. With this off-beat approach, he lured Nolene into a conversation, peppered with random references to pumpkin pie, "a wonderful treat," "the national dessert of Canada," "pumpkin pie with whipped cream," and so forth.

What began as a desperate measure to communicate with Nolene evolved into a symbol used in the Temper Tantrum Control Programme, which can be tailored to fit most individuals experiencing seemingly out-of-control behaviors, especially anger. First the therapist gets a thorough description of the temper tantruming, including its influence on the identified tantrummer and her family members. In most cases, the therapist finds out that temper tantrums most affect the tantrummer, making her look immature and silly. Proceeding, the therapist then gets the family to agree on carrying out the Programme; the commitment of the tantrummer is particularly critical.

A key person in the family, usually the mother, is given the task of monitoring the tantrummer and to signal her when there is a tantrum coming on. The parent is warning the tantrummer that a recording session is in the offing—that is, if warnings are ignored, her temper tantrum will be recorded via audiotape. Three warnings are given, at 1 minute intervals, meaning that the tantrummer can tantrum for 3 minutes. If she does not stop after the third warning, a tape recorder is turned on.

The tantrummer then is given the responsibility of writing a letter to individuals who don't know about the tantrum behavior (i.e., the "problem free context," p. 57). The recipients of the letter are usually the tantrummer's 3 best friends. Nolene's letter read as follows:

Dear (guest)—

I would like to invite you to my house on (date, time) to have a piece of pumpkin pie and whipped cream and listen to a recording. I will be disappointed if you don't come.

Clearly, Nolene does not want to really have to play the tape, although having a party and eating pie would be fun.

The family is invited to come back in a given period of time and if successful (which according to Epston, most are) describe what they did to overcome temper. This session is audiotaped as well, and the clients are asked if the therapist could share it with future individuals experiencing temper tantrums.

NT therapists sometimes send clients letters in between sessions. Used to reinforce events in therapy, letters sometime summarize session content, and are often used to comment on unique outcomes or offer new perspectives on the problem-saturated stories of clients. "Readiness letters" can be composed for clients who are reluctant about therapy to acknowledge the client's choice and control in her life. An interesting example was provided by White and Epston (1990) in which Jay, a young man who was incapacitated by headaches, was sent a letter, part of which read as follows:

To prove your readiness, Jay, the Team suggests the following:
That between now and when we meet again, if you are ready (we, once again, want you to know we have no doubts about your ability), you will initiate several approaches to a more self-embracing (instead of a self-erasing) lifestyle without your Mum or Dad providing you with either an initiative or instruction. For example, washing the boat without being asked. Jay, you are to keep a list of each and every one of your initiatives and not divulge them to your parents. Janis and Blair, you are to keep a secret list noting any initiatives that you have observed Jay taking. (p. 168)

Deepa decides to send a summary letter to the Kennedy family after the first counseling session. In this letter, she describes her perceptions of the family and compliments them on their persistence in the face of great challenges from the two As—Alcohol and Anorexia. She wonders what Rachael has observed over the years in Melanie that allowed her to defeat Alcohol and if Rachael sees any of these strengths in herself. Rachel replies that her mother's determination and never-give-up attitude has been inspirational. . . . She is determined to get in touch with these qualities within her.

EVALUATION

Perhaps the most common criticism of NT (and of social constructivist approaches more generally) is that it is difficult to read and understand. Partly, this difficultly is due to the language used—terms such as discourse, languaging, and privileging are not typically found in your average theory of counseling. Hayward (2003), a proponent of NT, argues that in order to really convey the new ideas of NT the unfamiliar is necessary to convey the uniqueness of the approach. He says, "If we accept that language creates our perspectives as well as reflects them, then different language practices will be required to access different perspectives and to think outside of what is routinely taught" (p. 186).

Minuchin (1998) has criticized the NT approach for "losing the family." He points out that although NT theorists emphasize the socially-embedded nature of reality, they in practice ignore the relationships between people because they do not attend to the relationship patterns and structures in their clients' families. Essentially, he is disappointed that NT does not include a more defined theoretical structure when he writes "I began to ask myself whether this metatheory concerning the construction of reality had a theory about families at all. How would this theory explain bonding? Or the affiliations between family members that create subgroups, and sometimes scapegoating? How does it explain the way conflict between parents affects their children's views of themselves? How does it frame the complexities of divorce and remarriage, or the way individual family members select certain family functions and certain styles of interpersonal transactions?"(p. 398). He contends that NT practitioners, who are not adverse to working with individual family members, unduly privilege the individual voice, and then skip the family context in their practice of relating individual stories to cultural discourses.

Efran and Clarfield (1992) ride to the defense of social constructivist therapies (in the general sense), pointing out that to assume the label does not automatically mean that "anything goes." Essentially, they argue that constructivism is simply another metaphor or descriptive device and that too often, advocates of this position obscure matters by weaving "a virtually impenetrable fog of abstraction" (p. 202). Further, they urge constructivist therapists to accept their expertise and to take positions, opining that "we regret that some constructivists feel inclined to deny that they are in this sort of 'influence' business" (p. 202).

QUALITIES OF THEORY

Oerationalizable/Testable. You will generally not find hard-core NT advocates out doing empirical research. The postmodern approach adopted by the NT camp recognizes two types of knowledge: the "expert" knowledge of traditional science and the "local" knowledge of individuals and communities. They are very suspicious of generalizations, and thus tend to see the products of traditional science (i.e., expert knowledge) as merely hypotheses that can be subjected to local tests (Payne, 2000).

Despite the reservations of NT proponents, there are probably ways to operationalize NT's constructs, relying on self-report or observational methods. It would be much easier to do outcome research on this approach than theory-testing, because there are few theoretical constructs in this approach and no elaborate theory linking them, as Minuchin (1997) has pointed out.

Empirically Valid. Because of the scarcity of the research on this approach and the difficulty in testing it, the question of empirical validity is not easy to answer. However, supporters of this approach would argue that the issue of empirical validity is rooted in the traditional, expert-knowledge-based view of science and is therefore not very relevant to the verification of NT. Local knowledge (i.e., client and therapist stories of therapy) would be more legitimate and useful. Further, Lock, Epston, Maisel, and de Faria (2005) point out that accessing expert knowledge (via the traditional system of scientific verification) can legitimize dominant cultural stories that emphasize the location of health and dysfunction as properties of individuals, not problems to be re-storied.

Research Support

Outcome Research. Etchison and Kleist (2000) presented a review of research on NT, although they indicated that the literature on this perspective was indeed sparse. Speculating about the reasons for the scarcity of research, they suggested that the newness of the approach and the philosophical stance of NT proponents (as just described) were significant factors. Lack of training in qualitative methods, seen as particularly appropriate to the NT approach, was also seen as an impediment to research in this area. Although they found that NT was useful in working with families, they cautioned that the limited research base precluded general statements about the efficacy of this approach with any specific family issue. With these reservations in mind, I will briefly review several examples of research on NT.

Besa (1994) examined NT in a sample of 6 families experiencing parent-child conflict. Using quantitative methods (parents' count of frequencies of child behaviors), they found that 5 out of the 6 families reported improvement.

St. James-O'Connor, Meakes, Pickering, and Schuman, (1997) used ethnographic methods to study clients' experiences in NT. Eight families participated in semistructured interviews, clients of the researchers, who were situated in a university hospital outpatient clinic. They reported that six overall themes appeared in their qualitative analysis of the data: externalizing conversation, unique outcomes and alternate story, developing personal agency, consulting and reflecting teams, building the audience, and helpful/unhelpful aspects of therapy. All of the families reported a reduction in the severity of the problem over therapy, although those who had been in therapy longer reported greater gains than those who had been in for only a short time. St. James-O'Connor et al. also noted two themes that clients most often recognized in therapy: increasing feelings of personal agency, and issues around reflecting teams (both positive and negative impressions of these). It is interesting that they further described clients' desires to talk with the reflecting teams; evidently, in their version of NT, this was not a routine practice as it is described elsewhere. Finally, to their surprise, discussions of externalizing conversations were much rarer than the other themes.

A different perspective was taken by Smith, Winton, and Yoshioka (1992), who examined therapists' perceptions of reflecting teams. Using participant-observation methods, they observed and interviewed the members of a training team using NT. Overall, the therapists reported that they found reflecting teams to be useful, provided a good working relationship had been established with clients and that the input of the teams did not confuse clients with too many perspectives and opinions. This technique was seen as particularly useful in resolving therapeutic impasses.

Theory-Testing Research. Piran and Cormier (2005) offered a study that could be construed as testing the theoretical propositions underlying NT. In a study of 394 women, they examined the relationships between eating-disordered behaviors and attitudes and three internalized social expectations: (a) silencing the self in relationships in favor of the wants and needs of others, (b) anger suppression (hypothesized to be in response to cultural norms), and objectification of their bodies. Consistent with their predictions (and those that could be derived form NT theory), they found that all three of these qualities were significantly related to eating-disordered characteristics. On the basis of these results, Piran and Cormier argued that deconstruction of these social discourses would be particularly important in helping young women fight anorexia and bulimia.

An important aspect of NT is transforming the story of the problem as one located within the person/client to one external to the client, or one that is interpersonal or systemic. Coulehan, Friedlander, and Heatherington (1998) looked at this phenomenon in a sample of 8 families in NT. They found that in successful families (4 of the 8), 3 out of 4 were observed to have made this shift. In another study, Friedlander, Heatherington, and Marrs (2000) used conversation analysis (a qualitative technique) to study constructivist therapists' responses to client blaming statements. They reasoned that blaming statements were particularly problematic for therapists in this camp because although blaming is thought to be counterproductive in family therapy, confronting or challenging such client behavior could be construed as contrary to a constructivist approach (i.e., it negates the client's view of reality). Judges reviewed six tapes of well-known constructivist therapists and found three overall categories of response to client blaming: ignoring/diverting, acknowledging/challenging, and reframing. Within these categories, the most frequent response was focusing on the positive, which fell in the ignoring/diverting category. Friedlander and her colleagues maintained that these findings were consistent with a constructivist stance, and particularly an NT approach, for blaming is generally the problem-saturated story, whereas a focus on positive events would likely fit within the realm of unique outcomes.

ISSUES OF INDIVIDUAL AND CULTURAL DIVERSITY

Proponents of NT argue that this approach is perfect for use with individuals from diverse backgrounds. Payne (2000) opines that even though he assumes that most current psychotherapy approaches are anti-isms (e.g., racism, sexism, classism, heterosexism, and so forth), "the emphasis in narrative therapy on the need for continual vigilance against the more subtle manifestations of these elements is particularly consistent and emphatic" (p. 31). Semmler and Williams (2002) suggest that NT's emphasis on the socially constructed nature of problems allows for the externalization of problems such as racism, which might otherwise be internalized by clients. They also point out that dominant cultural stories often diverge from those of individuals who are of minority groups, and worse, can have negative effects on them. Deconstructing these dominant narratives can help clients identify with the prized aspects of their own cultures.

NT counselors, however, warn that as with any approach to therapy, NT can't just be blindly applied in cultures other than the ones in which it originated (Dulwich Centre website). Differences in traditions across cultures (such as reliance on written or oral traditions, acceptability of asking direct questions) may influence the applicability of the approach. Ideally, according to the Dulwich Centre website, the therapist should be of the same culture as the client.

The values of NT are consistent with those of feminist therapy, proponents of which would heartily support the ideas about collaboration with clients and the demystification of the therapy process. NT's stance against oppressive practice would also seem to promote the growth of female clients and indeed, clients from any group that has been the target of such practices in past or present. Indeed, Nylund and Nylund (2003) argue that NT is useful in helping men question the traditional structures that have supported male dominance and power in relation to women.

The NT perspective on sexual orientation is to recognize the influence of the dominant cultural discourse about sexuality that privileges heterosexuality over homosexuality. Thus, NT is also considered to be a good approach for working with those whose sexual orientations are other than heterosexual. Logan (2002) described such work, and maintained that "coming out is a process in which a person 'rewrites' the story they have about themself [*sic*]" (p. 140).

THE CASE STUDY

Conceptualizing the case of Rachael was relatively easy from the NT perspective. NT proponents are very interested in anorexia/bulimia and write extensively on this topic (e.g., Maisel, Epston, & Borden, 2004). However, my opinion is that although it is easy to discuss the conceptualization of anorexia from an NT approach, actualizing this in practice might be more difficult. It might be quite difficult for clients to perceive anorexia as something external to the identified client. The same might be true for conceptualizing Drinking/Alcohol.

Summary

Narrative Therapy is a constructivist approach in which counselor and clients collaborate to create new life stories. NT therapists recognize that we create our realities through our language, and further, that cultures have dominant discourses that determine who gets power and control and who doesn't. Thus, NT therapists are very attuned to issues of social justice and power. People and problems are always viewed with an awareness of the cultural context in which they are embedded.

Clients come to NT counseling because the stories that are dominant in their lives do not fit some aspects of their experiences. The NT counselor listens closely to the client's story, attempting to understand the dominant themes but also looking for alternative stories or unique outcomes, cases in which the problem-staturated story does not hold. The goal of NT counseling is to help the client deconstruct the problem-saturated dominant story and to thereby create opportunities to choose among other, more preferred outcomes. Questioning is a major technique in this approach, and it is often aimed at externalizing the problem, which means that the person is separated from the problem and the problem becomes the person's relationship with it rather than part of the person. It is important that therapist and client examine all the influences in the life of the problem and their sources, but most importantly, the client and the therapist examine times when the client is able to resist the problem and focus on how this happened. A new story can then be created based upon the deconstructed version of the client's story. In the words of our

NT therapist on the DVD *Theories in Action,* the client and counselor engage in a process of "collaborative co-construction of a unique re-description" of the client's life (Jim Krieder, personal communication, March 30, 2007).

Other techniques of NT involve engaging important individuals or groups of individuals in the client's struggle with the problem. Outsider witness practices, in which carefully selected others listen to the client's story and then reveal their reactions to it are often employed. Written artifacts such as letters and certificates of achievement are also used to reinforce clients' process and progress in therapy.

NT, because it originates in the constructivist camp, does not lend well to traditional scientific approaches. Proponents of NT are critical of dominant discourses that emphasize the existence of one true reality that can be explained only through a culturally approved set of scientific methods. Therefore, little traditional theory testing or outcome research can be found that is specific to NT counseling.

Issues of cultural and individual diversity seem to be handled well in an NT perspective. Advocates of NT emphasize local and cultural influences in the stories lived by clients and also the deconstruction of dominant (culturally based) narratives that seem to negatively affect clients.

Visit Chapter 15 on the Companion Website at **www.prenhall.com/murdock** for chapter-specific resources and self-assessments.

CHAPTER 16

Conclusion

Consider the following scenarios:

1. *Scarlett's therapist believes that the current disarray in her relationship with Rhett is the result of unconscious forces that stem from her childhood. Rhett is simultaneously the father that Scarlett desires and a forbidden object. Scarlett is transferring her anger at her father's rejection to Rhett, and will eventually interact with her therapist in similar ways.*

2. *Irrational beliefs are the problem behind Scarlett's current distress. She believes that everyone must love her and the world must treat her kindly or life is unacceptable. Scarlett's counselor resolves to teach her the ABCs so that she will adopt rational beliefs such as, "It's too bad that Rhett left; I'd rather he hadn't, but that doesn't make me a worthless worm."*

3. *Scarlett is coming to counseling because she is hurting in the area of belonging needs. She experiences a problematic relationship and has placed both Rhett and Bonnie in her quality world. However, she has persisted in attempting to control their behaviors and abdicated responsibility for her own. She is anxietying, angering, and depressing because she is attempting to meet her need for love in the best way that she can.*

4. *Scarlett is clearly in need of interventions to change her behavior. Her therapist will focus on the anxiety attacks that seem to lead to her fainting. Cognitive and behavioral techniques will be used to intervene when Scarlett begins to feel anxious. Exposure therapy will be most helpful for her.*

5. *Unfinished business is clearly getting in the way of Scarlett's creative adaptation to the world. She has an unmet need for love that has become figure; as a result, she can't freely experience her feelings.*

6. *Scarlett is not successful in the life tasks of love, work, and society. She is discouraged and pursuing a socially useless lifestyle. Clearly, she needs to find ways to achieve power that don't involve selfish motives such as winning the battle with Rhett. Her selfish ways of getting attention need to be seen for what they are.*

7. *Rhett and Scarlett's relationship had been stabilized by the triangulation with their daughter, Bonnie. Rhett and Bonnie appear to have formed a cross-generational coalition. Now that Bonnie is gone, these parents are confronted with mourning the death of their child along with the conflict in their relationship. Rhett responds by emotionally distancing from Scarlett, and she is tempted to pursue him.*

8. *Scarlett has been oppressed by society in that the rules say that she can't experience her personal power because she is a woman. She has met with a good deal of rejection over the course of her life because she displayed qualities that are not ladylike, such as starting her own business and freely speaking her mind. Rhett left partly because her anger over being oppressed by white men became directed at him.*

9. *It is not important why Scarlett behaves as she does. She and her counselor need to decide exactly what the problem is and reconsider it. Scarlett is lonely and afraid. Examining times when she is* not *lonely and afraid, she and her counselor work to make these events happen more frequently.*

10. *Activation of the loss and threat modes are behind Scarlett's current distress. She shows depressive schematic functioning ("things will* never *get better") and anxiety-generating thoughts ("I am inadequate to handle the world by myself"). These constellations of thoughts are bringing on Scarlett's dysfunctional emotions and behavior.*

11. *Scarlett is clearly experiencing an existential crisis. The loss of Bonnie has brought her face-to-face with her own mortality, causing her to question her life meaning. She is using the hope of Rhett as the ultimate rescuer to ward off existential anxiety and terror, but this defense has failed because Rhett, confronted with his own mortality, ran away (probably exercising the defense of specialness).*

12. *Scarlett is experiencing incongruence between her self and experience. Her need for positive regard from self and others has led her to avoid experiences that are inconsistent with her vision of herself, which is as a sweet, feminine, Southern lady. Her anger at her circumstances is not consistent with this self-image so she attempts to deny it. She becomes depressed, but the anger erupts at times because her defenses are weak.*

13. *Scarlett seems to have a fragmented sense of herself. Her recent losses are stressing her, making it difficult for her to relate to others on an even keel. This is why she's been distant all these years with Rhett; something about him activates feelings that she can't understand or control. Early dysfunction in relationship with her parents (her father's drinking is likely to be a sign of this) is likely to be the source of these dynamics.*

14. *Something about Scarlett's current version of her life is terribly at odds with how she'd like to be. She is trapped and oppressed by the power structure embedded in her current life story and is desperately seeking a different outcome. She is an independent woman yet feels caught between social pressure to return to stereotypic ways (settle down with Rhett) and the desire to be herself and live her own story.*

Key to Scarlett's therapists: 1. Psychoanalysis; 2. Rational Emotive Behavior Therapy; 3. Reality Therapy; 4. Behavior Therapy; 5. Gestalt Therapy; 6. Individual Psychology; 7. Family Systems Therapy; 8. Feminist Therapy; 9. Solution-Focused Therapy; 10. Cognitive Therapy; 11. Existential Theory; 12. Person-Centered Therapy; 13; Neoanalytic Theory; 14. Narrative Therapy

What do you think about the various descriptions of Scarlett? You undoubtedly have recognized that each paragraph is a very brief conceptualization derived from each of the theories reviewed in this book (if you are puzzled about any of them, check the key at the end of the descriptions). Which one do you think makes the most sense? Will one vision help Scarlett more than the others? The answers to these questions should help guide you in your search for the right theoretical orientation for you at this stage of your career.

Now that you've worked your way through 14 theories of counseling and psychotherapy, you may be a little overwhelmed. It may seem to you that there are just too many interesting approaches—too many roads on the map or too many kinds of cars in which to travel. The 14 approaches covered in this book all have some form of empirical support, they make sense, and most of them have been around for a while. You probably like parts of all of them. You may hate parts of some of them. You may be somewhere between the extremes. However, I've rarely seen anyone emerge from a basic theory course absolutely certain that one of the major approaches is the perfect fit. More commonly, students are a little bewildered and still wondering how to choose among all of the theories.

In Chapter 1, I outlined some considerations that I believe are important in considering theories. As you now know, theories vary widely on these dimensions, and you are probably wondering which of these dimensions is the most important. If I were pressed to answer, I'd probably say empirical support. That answer may not seem helpful to you, though, because all of the theoretical systems I presented have empirical support to some degree or another. One way out of this dilemma might be to choose the theory with the "best" empirical support—probably Behavior or Cognitive Therapy.

However, there is another way of looking at the situation. Given that the research evidence demonstrates that the major approaches to counseling produce client change relative to no treatment, empirical support does not have to be the sole criterion in selecting your orientation. The other factors I discussed in Chapter 1 are helpful too. In essence, you need to find an approach that fits with who you are, your philosophical assumptions, and how you understand human existence. It is not my intent in this last chapter to exhaustively compare the theories along these dimensions. However, I will attempt to provide some examples of how the approaches differ on what I believe to be some key dimensions. I invite you to answer the following questions as I present them:

IS THIS A GOOD THEORY?

What do you think of the research evidence presented in support of this theory?
Is the theory testable? Are the predictions derived from the theory precise?
Is the approach practical?

One way to progress in the dilemma of theory choice is to evaluate the approaches we have studied along the dimensions of "good theory." In the chapters, I evaluated each theoretical perspective on the dimensions of precision/testability and empirical support. The various approaches fell out along a continuum on these two dimensions. In the sections that follow, I will briefly compare the theories on these qualities.

EMPIRICALLY VALID

To some extent or another, all of the theoretical systems reviewed have outcome data to support their efficacy. The quality of these data vary, however, with the behavior and cognitive approaches having status as empirically supported treatments. Other perspectives have less rigorous outcome support (Rational Emotive Behavior Therapy, Individual Psychology, Person-Centered Therapy, and Gestalt Therapy). Empirical verification can be found for aspects of Family Systems Therapy, Feminist Therapy, and Individual Psychology. Probably the least evidence for empirical verifiability is found for Reality Therapy, Narrative Therapy, and Solution-Focused Therapy. Gestalt Therapy receives indirect support from the work of Greenberg and colleagues in Process-Experiential Psychotherapy. The status of Person-Centered Theory is also mixed, with good support for Rogers' ideas about the importance of the therapeutic relationship in support of the theory. The data are less convincing regarding the specific predictions of PC theory. Psychoanalytic theory in the broadest sense is supported by research that seems to confirm the existence and influence of unconscious processes, and several short-term psychoanalytic approaches have received empirical support, and one (Interpersonal Psychotherapy as described in Chapter 1) is considered empirically supported.

STIMULATING

As I noted in Chapter 1, all of the approaches that I chose to present are stimulating in one way or another. Judging by the surveys of counselors' theoretical orientations, some are more popular than others. Cognitive and behavioral approaches, for example, seem to have the most adherents. In terms of stimulating thought, Psychoanalysis seems to have cornered the market. Newer approaches such as Narrative Therapy and Solution-Focused Therapy have been receiving a lot of attention in the practice community. Many counselors adopt a Feminist Therapy philosophical approach or consider existential questions within the structure of one or more other theories.

PRACTICAL

Many theories have a large number of specific techniques that are applied to problems presented by the client (behavior, cognitive, family systems). Person-Centered, Existential, and Feminist Therapy tend to be a little more vague or global in their techniques. Narrative therapists seem a little mystifying at times, at least in the way they write and talk about their approach.

Some would argue that psychoanalysis is not very practical anymore because it just takes too long to do a real analysis. Solution-Focused Therapy is at the opposite end of the spectrum; its proponents claim very quick "cures," sometimes in a single session. However, there really are therapists out there doing classic analysis, complete with couch (as you have observed on your DVD), so for a certain group of clients this approach is viable. Students are often impatient with the unfolding process of Person-Centered Therapy because they want to help the client right away. To these students, it seems impractical to sit back and wait for the client to grow.

A focus on the problem as defined by the client might be seen as the most practical route to helping. In other words, take the client's word for it—the problem is not the result of early childhood experiences or irrational beliefs. If you take this position, then Behavior, Cognitive, Family Systems, or Solution-Focused Therapy might be for you. However, I think it would be naive to assume that these approaches do absolutely no translation of the client problem presentation. For example, the cognitive therapist must turn the problem the client brings into one in which thinking is central and then persuade the client to buy the Cognitive Therapy model.

YOUR PHILOSOPHICAL ASSUMPTIONS

Considering your assumptions about people is critical to choosing your theory because, for the most part, these broad statements about human nature are not testable. Take a minute and think about the following questions:

> Do you think humans are mostly inherently good, neutral, or evil?
> Do you think that there is one concrete reality out there that we can access? Or do you believe that multiple views of reality exist?
> Is human behavior the result of biology, learning, or the influence of others (i.e., social relationships)?
> Is it important to look at the person as a whole, or should specific behavior be the target of observation?

In the basic philosophy section of the chapters, I attempted to describe theories along these dimensions. To begin with the obvious, Psychoanalysis seems to have a rather gloomy picture of humanity, whereas Person-Centered folks have been accused of wearing rose-colored glasses. Other theories are not as explicit about the basic character of human nature, so they could fit with a position of neutrality on this dimension.

What do you think about the idea that anatomy is destiny? Some theorists insist that behavior is socially determined (the behaviorists and the feminists, for example), whereas others place much more weight on inherent or biological factors. Even Albert Ellis thinks that irrationality is an innate human characteristic (as is rationality).

If you believe in an objective reality, (i.e., one real, true reality), you might find Behavior Therapy most compatible with your leanings, or oddly enough, Psychoanalysis, with its certainty about the origins of behavior. Reality therapists would seem to be the ultimate in objectivity. The constructivist approaches, such as Narrative Therapy, Solution-Focused Therapy, Gestalt Therapy, or Person-Centered Therapy, are much more concerned with how the individual interprets the world.

Think about your goals for counseling. Are they focused on specific behavior change or overall global well-being? Is your client to be happy or symptomless? Do you think human functioning is connected to family, work, and environmental cues, or is it the result of specific thoughts or needs?

YOUR BELIEFS ABOUT HUMAN BEHAVIOR

Some experts would say that we shouldn't even be talking about *beliefs* here; we should stick to the scientific evidence in understanding human behavior. If you are close to this position, recognize that and choose an approach with a lot of empirical support or an empirically supported treatment. You may want to take a more moderate position. In that case, choosing an approach that is consistent with your ideas about human functioning (provided it has some empirical support) is probably the best route to becoming a good therapist. Consider the following questions, which are loosely derived from my system for case conceptualization presented in the first chapter.

- *What do you believe motivates human behavior?*

  Table 16.1 contrasts the 14 views of human motivation presented in this book. Do you buy the notion of the unconscious as the prime mover of human activity? Psychoanalysts do, and cognitive therapists seem to be proposing unconscious influence in the forms of protoschemas or modes. Behavior therapists are less vocal on this issue. We can infer that they see behavior as stemming from a motivation to survive and adapt to the environment. More narrowly, for behaviorists, humans move toward positive stimuli and away from aversive ones. They would attend little to unconscious processes, even if they believed in them. Systems theorists would probably acknowledge influences outside of our awareness (i.e., the family system), but those things are very different from

TABLE 16.1
VIEWS OF HUMAN MOTIVATION

Psychoanalysis	Pessimistic; humans motivated by instinctual drives of sex, aggression
Neoanalytic Approaches	Pessimistic but maybe less so that psychoanalysis; instinctual drives recognized but so is the power of the ego
Individual Psychology	Optimistic; humans motivated by striving for superiority and feelings of community
Person-Centered Therapy	Optimistic; humans motivated to actualize their potential
Existential Therapy	Depends on which approach; some optimistic, some pessimistic (the only certainty is death). Humans search for meaning.
Gestalt Therapy	Optimistic; humans motivated to grow (meet needs) but also to attain harmony with the environment (homeostasis)
Behavior Therapy	Neutral; humans motivated to adapt to the environment and obtain resources to survive; immediate behavior controlled by environmental sources—the consequences of behavior
Rational Emotive Behavior Therapy	Neutral; humans are human, rational and irrational
Cognitive Therapy	Neutral; humans motivated to adapt to the environment and obtain resources to survive; cognition primary in behavior; recent versions recognize unconscious structures/processes in generating behavior
Reality Therapy	Optimistic; humans motivated by basic needs, but most important, the need for love and belonging
Feminist Therapy	No clear statement, but power and intimacy are important
Family Systems Therapy	Varies with approach: Bowen is neutral; the tension between individuality and togetherness drives behavior; Satir is optimistic; humans motivated to grow and love; strategic and structural approaches do not closely consider motivation.
Solution-Focused Therapy	Neutral; no real statements on motivation
Narrative Therapy	Optimistic; humans motivated to seek meaning

TABLE 16.2
MAJOR THEORETICAL CONSTRUCTS

Psychoanalysis	Id, ego, superego; psychosexual stages of development
Neoanalytic Approaches	Internalized representations of others, defenses, relational matrix
Individual Psychology	Striving for superiority; basic tasks; lifestyle; social interest; family constellation
Person-Centered Therapy	Actualizing tendencies; self and experience; congruence and incongruence
Existential Therapy	Modes of being; ultimate concerns (death, freedom, meaning, aloneness); anxiety, defenses
Gestalt Therapy	Contact; needs; cycle of awareness; polarities
Behavior Therapy	Classical conditioning; operant conditioning; social learning
Rational Emotive Behavior Therapy	Beliefs, rational and irrational
Cognitive Therapy	Beliefs; schemas; modes
Reality Therapy	Basic needs; quality world; total behavior; choice theory
Feminist Therapy	Gender; personal is political
Family Systems Therapy	Family as a system; communication; subsystems and boundaries; triangles; family hierarchy; differentiation of self; chronic anxiety
Solution-Focused Therapy	Exceptions; solutions; client strengths and resources
Narrative Therapy	Stories, unique outcomes

the influences proposed by Psychoanalysis or Person-Centered Theory, which would also acknowledge unconscious activity.

- *What are the principal constructs that help to explain experience?*

Table 16.2 reviews some of the major theoretical constructs of the 14 theories covered in this book. Are "deep" psychological constructs such as modes, lifestyle, and needs essential to understanding our clients? Do we need to critically examine the effects of patriarchy? Can we help a client by simply focusing on what she would like to have happen, the times when things are going well? Do we really carry around a mental picture of our ideal self or mental representations of those who satisfy our needs? Is the content of the client's belief influential in determining her behavior? Is our fear of being alone a major consideration?

- *How do you see the process of human development? Is it important in determining current behavior, or can we bypass this theoretical step?*

Developmental aspects of the 14 approaches are shown in Table 16.3. Although they may not address it specifically, all of these theories would acknowledge the biological/physiological processes of growth associated with human development. How the physiological processes interact with psychological processes of development is described differently across the various theories. To help your client, do you need some structure that describes psychological development? Does the past live in the present, or is the past irrelevant?

- *List the characteristics of a healthy person. Which approach fits best with your ideas?*

What factors are the most important in psychological health? Do you focus on thoughts? Do you focus on creative, growth-oriented behavior or whether the individual

TABLE 16.3
VIEWS OF HUMAN DEVELOPMENT

Psychoanalysis	Psychosexual stages are innate; early experience paramount
Neoanalytic Approaches	Early experience critical; instinctual drives
Individual Psychology	Family environment influences development along with innate creative processes and the drive for superiority
Person-Centered Therapy	Development is toward maximization of potential; influenced by family, other significant individuals
Existential Therapy	No specific model
Gestalt Therapy	Humans progress from environmental to self-support; need satisfaction affected by the surrounding environment and individuals in it
Behavior Therapy	Development is the process of learning
Rational Emotive Behavior Therapy	Innate biological and psychological tendencies interact with social influences
Cognitive Therapy	Early life experience influences development of schemas; modal functioning largely innate
Reality Therapy	Strength of basic needs is innate; development influenced by individuals around the person
Feminist Therapy	Emphasizes the influences of gender and power
Family Systems Therapy	Varies across approaches but all emphasize family influences
Solution-Focused Therapy	No formal statements
Narrative Therapy	No specific statement

is making good choices that do not violate the rights of others and the rules of social groups? What about our thoughts about our finiteness? Do these play a role? Does the individual require a healthy family or rational society to be healthy? Table 16.4 sketches the versions of healthy persons presented by the theories covered in this book.

- *What is the relative importance of family, intimate others, friends, and so on, in a person's functioning?*

Can you help a client by working with that person as an individual? With the exception of some Family Systems Approaches, the answer is yes. However, the relative influence of family members and events varies among approaches. Individual Psychology would see family as a critical influence, whereas many other theories would see family as a source of learning only in a very general way. Of course, family influences are pivotal in psychoanalytic theory.

Feminist Therapy sees relationships as critical, particularly those between men and women, and a woman's relationships with other women are a key source of support. Existential therapists see authentic relationships with others as very important.

- *Relatively speaking, how important are behavior, cognition, and affect in the ways we function?*

Do you think that attention to emotion is the most important thing that happens in counseling? If so, you may want to consider Psychoanalysis, Gestalt Therapy, or

TABLE 16.4
VIEWS OF PSYCHOLOGICAL HEALTH

Psychoanalysis	Low levels of repressed urges; healthy defenses; mature ego
Neoanalytic Approaches	Coherent sense of self; adapted ego
Individual Psychology	Socially useful strivings for superiority; successful at basic tasks; acceptance of self as human and therefore fallible
Person-Centered Therapy	Congruence between self and experience; self-acceptance; authentic expression of experience
Existential Therapy	Authenticity; awareness of ultimate concerns
Gestalt Therapy	Satisfaction of needs; awareness of experience; authenticity
Behavior Therapy	Adaptive behavior
Rational Emotive Behavior Therapy	Mostly rational beliefs; rational life philosophy
Cognitive Therapy	Adaptive beliefs leading to adaptive behavior
Reality Therapy	Basic needs relatively satisfied; healthy relationships
Feminist Therapy	Aware of social influences on experience; able to set and reach life goals unencumbered by social constraints
Family Systems Therapy	Healthy family structures and communication patterns
Solution-Focused Therapy	Complaints do not exist
Narrative Therapy	Preferred outcomes; new fulfilling story

Person-Centered Theory. If you see thoughts as relatively more important than feeling or behavior in terms of functioning, your choice might fall in the Cognitive Therapy camp (CT or REBT). If behavior is of most interest, then Behavior or Reality Therapy seems right, but so might Solution-Focused or Family Systems Therapy. If you think social influences are critical, try Narrative Therapy or Feminist Therapy.

YOUR PERSONAL STYLE: APPROACH AND TECHNIQUE

- *Are you an active type, or are you more able to sit back and wait?*
- *Do you think the client or the therapist should lead in determining what happens in sessions?*
- *Do you think the therapist or client should take responsibility for what happens in counseling?*
- *Are you a problem solver?*

Different theories naturally lead to different ways of doing counseling. Some approaches rely heavily on formal assessment, for example. Recall that formal assessment refers to ritualized kinds of procedures, such as giving tests (such as the Rorschach or the Beck Depression Inventory) or administering structured techniques (such as Adlerian early recollections). Informal assessment means talking with the client or simply observing the client's behavior during the counseling session.

Table 16.5 presents the ways in which each of the 14 theories approach assessment. Qualities of the therapeutic approach and the relationship between client and therapist are summarized in Table 16.6. Table 16.7 on page 524 compares the goals of the various counseling theories, and Table 16.8 on page 525 lists common techniques associated with each approach.

In Box 1.3 of Chapter 1, I presented some research evidence that suggested that philosophical assumptions and interpersonal tendencies may be factors in the choice of theoretical

TABLE 16.5
Orientations to Assessment

Psychoanalysis	Both formal and informal used; therapist's observations initially determine the appropriateness of therapy; projective techniques considered useful; target is unconscious processes
Neoanalytic Approaches	Observation of the client's ways of relating to the therapist
Individual Psychology	Formal and informal are considered useful; counselor's observations important; target is means of achieving power/superiority; family constellation and early recollections significant
Person-Centered Therapy	Not appropriate; creates distance between counselor and client
Existential Therapy	Not appropriate; could interfere with the authenticity of the therapeutic relationship
Gestalt Therapy	Formal assessment generally not used; informal assessment focused on client experiencing, particularly emotional functioning
Behavior Therapy	Formal assessment critical; normally behavioral observation by the therapist, significant other, or self-observation; paper-and-pencil objective measures sometimes used
Rational Emotive Behavior Therapy	Formal and informal are acceptable; primary target is belief(s)
Cognitive Therapy	Formal, objective, symptom-focused measures frequently used; critical to assess thoughts, often using paper-and-pencil surveys; targets are thoughts, beliefs
Reality Therapy	Informal assessment; target is needs, particularly belonging/love
Feminist Therapy	No assessment advocated; therapist observation of social/environmental influences important
Family Systems Therapy	Formal assessment not used; therapist observation of family patterns critical
Solution-Focused Therapy	No assessment used; client determines the problem; focus is on exceptions to the problem
Narrative Therapy	Not appropriate; limits the story of the client and therapist

TABLE 16.6
General Qualities of the Approach to Therapy

Psychoanalysis	Formal; doctor-patient relationship; long-term process
Neoanalytic Approaches	Formal; depending on variant can be doctor-patient; long term
Individual Psychology	Collaborative; therapist is educator and model; therapist as human, fallible; relatively long term
Person-Centered Therapy	Authentic therapist in equal, genuine relationship with client; can be long term
Existential Therapy	Authentic unknowing therapist, client as fellow-traveler; long term
Gestalt Therapy	Counseling an authentic encounter between therapist and client; length of therapy varies
Behavior Therapy	Therapist is teacher/consultant, client is learner; generally a short-term approach
Rational Emotive Behavior Therapy	Therapist is teacher/consultant, client is student; generally short term
Cognitive Therapy	Therapist is teacher/consultant, client is student; elements of doctor-patient relationship; generally short term
Reality Therapy	Therapist is genuine and direct; short-term approach
Feminist Therapy	Egalitarian relationship essential; client is empowered; length of therapy varies
Family Systems Therapy	Therapist is expert who joins the family as an honorary member; generally short term
Solution-Focused Therapy	Therapist is consultant to client who determines the goals; considered a brief therapy approach
Narrative Therapy	Collaborative, equal relationship essential; length varies

TABLE 16.7
Goals of Counseling/Therapy

Psychoanalysis	Resolve unconscious conflict; insight; healthy defenses
Neoanalytic Approaches	Integrated self; adapted ego; insight
Individual Psychology	Convert selfish life style into socially useful one; correct basic mistakes; insight
Person-Centered Therapy	Resolve incongruence between self and experience
Existential Therapy	Understanding of life; authenticity, freedom
Gestalt Therapy	Awareness; self-support; harmony with the environment leading to growth
Behavior Therapy	Adaptive behavior
Rational Emotive Behavior Therapy	Rational thoughts; rational life philosophy, including knowledge of ABCs
Cognitive Therapy	Modify distorted thought patterns; knowledge of the cognitive model
Reality Therapy	Healthy choices that satisfy basic needs, especially belonging/love needs
Feminist Therapy	Empower client to reach life goals; understand, resist, and subvert oppressive influences
Family Systems Therapy	Satir: increase self-esteem of family members; release blocked potential of family members; clear communication. Structural: change the family structure thereby resolving the presenting problem. Strategic: resolve the presenting problem; modify dysfunctional hierarchies. Bowen: increase the level of differentiation of self from family of origin
Solution-Focused Therapy	Resolve the complaint; increase exceptions to the complaint
Narrative Therapy	Reauthor preferred narratives

orientations. Those philosophical assumptions are included in the previous section, "Your Philosophical Assumptions" (e.g., objective vs. subjective, emphasis on physical vs. psychological causation, holism vs. elementarism).

Interpersonal dominance was the interpersonal dimension that emerged from our data. Those who endorsed a psychoanalytic orientation appeared to see themselves as more interpersonally dominant compared to those who endorsed the other orientations. Do not be put off by the use of the term *dominant;* yes, it has some negative connotations in our culture, but the way it is used technically is a little different. First, the degree of dominance observed in behavior spans a continuum, and in fact, extreme dominance is problematic. A therapist displaying rigid and extreme levels of dominant behavior would not be a very good therapist. In considering dominance in the context of theoretical orientation, we could see it as the willingness to take charge of the counseling enterprise or the general activity level of the therapist. However, these two forms of dominant behavior are not exactly the same thing in therapy. The degree to which the therapist takes charge of the session is related to the level of activity observed to some degree, but not totally. For instance, in Psychoanalysis, the therapist is clearly in charge (setting the rules for free association, making interpretations of behavior—the doctor role), yet relatively passive behaviorally, letting the client free associate. In Person-Centered Therapy, the therapist is active, but the directiveness of this approach is less obvious.

TABLE 16.8
TECHNIQUES

Psychoanalysis	Free association; interpretation of transference; dream analysis
Neoanalytic Approaches	Free association, interpretation of transference, dream analysis
Individual Psychology	Interpretation; encouragement; natural and logical consequences; acting as if; pushing the button; catching oneself; creating images; pleasing someone; paradoxical intention
Person-Centered Therapy	No techniques; therapist provides conditions of empathy, unconditional positive regard, and genuineness (congruence)
Existential Therapy	Self-disclosure, dream analysis; paradox; bracketing; guided fantasy
Gestalt Therapy	Therapist self-disclosure; dialogues; playing the projection; working with polarities; making the rounds; taking responsibility; exaggeration; reversals; dream work; bodywork
Behavior Therapy	Relaxation; flooding; exposure and response prevention; systematic desensitization; aversive techniques; paradoxical intention; shaping; reinforcement; extinction; punishment; assertiveness training; stimulus control; covert conditioning; modeling; behavioral self-control
Rational Emotive Behavior Therapy	Disputing; bibliotherapy; proselytizing; recording therapy sessions; reframing; stop and monitor; rational coping strategies and rational emotive imagery; flamboyant therapist actions; humor; forceful coping statements; role-playing; dialogues; reinforcement; skills training; in vivo desensitization; shame attacking
Cognitive Therapy	Questioning; downward arrow; thought recording; behavioral experiments; activity scheduling; graded tasks; assertiveness training; problem solving; imagery and role-playing
Reality Therapy	Questioning; bibliotherapy; doing the unexpected; humor; therapist self-disclosure; metaphor; physical activity/meditation; allowing or imposing consequences
Feminist Therapy	Gender role analysis; self-disclosure; assertiveness training
Family Systems Therapy	Satir: family sculpting; family stress ballet; communication analysis; therapist communications; family thermometer; parts party. Structural: enactment; focusing; achieving intensity; boundary making; unbalancing; teaching complementarity. Strategic: directives; reframing; exaggerating the hierarchical problem; pretend directives. Bowen: process questioning; detriangling; coaching; I-position.
Solution-Focused Therapy	Questions; asking about the problem; normalizing the problem; compliments; miracle question; scaling questions; prediction tasks; fast-forward questions; first session formula task; generic task; altering the performance of the complaint; surprise task; write, read, and burn; structured fight; doing something different; solution-oriented hypnosis
Narrative Therapy	Externalizing; questioning, visualization, accountability practices; refection practices; written artifacts

Your preference for activity is fairly important in choosing an approach. If you are very active and like to solve puzzles, a theory such as Solution-Focused Therapy, Family Systems Therapy, Reality Therapy, or one of the cognitive or behavioral approaches may be for you. If you are more laid-back, think Psychoanalysis or Person-Centered Theory. Of course, Psychoanalysis has its share of puzzles to solve, too.

THE ROLE OF YOUR CLIENTS: DIVERSITY
IS HERE TO STAY

The type of clients with whom you expect to work is yet another factor in the theory choice equation. If you are going to work primarily with children, some approaches would seem to fit better than others, but then again, all of the approaches could be modified to work with kids. Because of the need to narrow the focus of this book, at least one approach very popular in working with children, play therapy, is not covered here. You might want to check it out.

Data and experience verify that the world is changing. It is becoming a much more diverse place than it was even 5 years ago. Cultural and ethnic groupings that used to be considered minority are quickly approaching majority status. For both pragmatic and ethical reasons, you have a responsibility to decide if the approach you choose can be used without bias with clients from varying backgrounds.

I have provided evaluations of each of the major theories in terms of their strengths and weaknesses in working with clients who are from other than Caucasian, Western European, Protestant backgrounds. I have considered issues of sex and sexual orientation. You will need to personally evaluate these assertions. Most approaches have a decided bias toward individualism or the notion that independence and separateness are the hallmarks of psychological health. Will Person-Centered Theory really help a client from a disadvantaged background who is struggling with very basic life support tasks? Does the notion of differentiation embedded in Family Systems approaches limit your ability to help clients from collectivistic cultures?

I hope that these questions have helped you to more clearly settle on the route that you choose to follow in your journeys with your clients. Yet I find myself still returning to the question, Why choose one approach? Can't we use the best of all or a set of theories as seems appropriate? This question brings us to a consideration of what are known as eclectic or integrative approaches.

ECLECTIC AND INTEGRATIVE APPROACHES
TO PSYCHOTHERAPY

As early as 1930, attempts were made to integrate approaches to psychotherapy, namely the two dominant theories of the time, Behaviorism (classical conditioning) and Psychoanalysis (Goldfried & Norcross, 1995). In 1936 Rosenzweig wrote his famous paper on the common factors operating in the different approaches to counseling (Rosenzweig, 1936/2002). These early efforts are recognized as pioneering, but the nature of eclecticism and integrationism is a little different in the 2000s.

Generally, we now recognize four general approaches to the thorny problem of eclecticism in psychotherapy: technical eclecticism, common factors, theoretical integration and assimilative integration (Gold & Stricker, 2006; Norcross, 2005). However, Norcross (2005) warns that in practice, these approaches are not so easily distinguishable. For purposes of clarity, however, it is useful to discuss them separately, so I will do so in the following sections.

The eclectic approach is perhaps most clearly articulated by those who assume a stance of *technical eclecticism.* These therapists adopt techniques from various approaches without endorsing the theoretical assumptions behind them. However, there does seem to be an assumption that many technical eclectics have a unifying theoretical system that guides their selection of techniques.

Lazarus, who developed Multimodal Therapy (MMT), is probably the best-known proponent of this approach. A Behavior Therapy orientation informs this approach, specifically, Social-Cognitive Learning Theory (Lazarus, 2006). According to Lazarus, MMT is "predicted on the assumption that most psychological problems are multifaceted, multidetermined, and multilayered, and that comprehensive therapy calls for a careful assessment of seven parameters or "modalities"—behavior, affect, sensation, imagery, cognition, interpersonal relationships and biological processes" (2000, p. 107). Substituting drugs for biological processes (Lazarus contends that this substitution is appropriate because biological processes are most often treated with drugs), we get the memorable acronym BASIC ID. Once a BASIC ID assessment is completed with a client, techniques appropriate to the modalities most salient in the client's presentation are selected. MMT has been criticized, as have eclectic approaches in general, for a lack of research support (Beutler, Consoli, & Williams, 1995). Also, MMT neglects social and environmental factors and provides no specific guidelines for the selection of interventions (Beutler et al., 1995).

Theoretical integrationist approaches are a second alternative to traditional theory. In this paradigm, two or more theoretical systems are merged. In essence, these approaches attempt to take the best of all worlds and "smush" them together (London, 1986). Early attempts to merge psychoanalysis with behaviorism represented this camp; however, these systems never really caught on.

One well-elaborated approach that exemplifies the current status of theoretical integrationism is exemplified by the theory presented in Box 16.1, the Transtheoretical approach (Prochaska, DiClemente, & Norcross, 1992; Prochaska, & Norcross 2007). Initially based on studies of individuals who actually changed addictive behaviors (e.g., cigarette smoking), this approach combines all theories of counseling by postulating generic *processes* of change (initially generated by a conceptual analysis of the major theories of psychotherapy) and identifying common *stages* of change across clients. The stages and processes fit together as shown in Table 16.9. The Transtheoretical approach has the strength of being based on empirical observations of the change process, and its proponents have steadily built the research base for the system. However, this approach could also be criticized on the grounds of cultural bias, mainly because of its emphasis on individualism. Also, because this approach was developed on very specific behaviors, it is more difficult to apply to more diffuse client presentations.

Box 16.1

Transtheoretical Therapy

Prochaska and Norcross (2007) argued that the major approaches to counseling are more similar in how change happens than in the actual material to be changed. They proposed a model that integrates elements from many theoretical perspectives, called Transtheoretical Therapy (TT). TT identifies three basic dimensions of change: *processes, stages,* and *levels.*

TABLE 16.9
STAGES OF CHANGE IN WHICH CHANGE PROCESSES ARE MOST EMPHASIZED

Stages of Change				
Precontemplation	Contemplation	Preparation	Action	Maintenance
Consciousness raising				
Dramatic relief				
	Environmental reevaluation			
	Self-reevaluation			
		Self-liberation		
			Contingency management	
			Counterconditioning	
			Stimulus control	

Note: Processes of change are centered between columns to show the overlap between stages.

Source: Prochaska, J. O. & Norcross, J. C. (2007). *Systems of Psychotherapy: A Transtheoretical Analysis (6th Ed.).* Belmont, CA: Thomson Brooks/Cole.

PROCESSES OF CHANGE

Understanding how people change is partially achieved through understanding what they do when they attempt to change their own behaviors. TT presents ten basic processes associated with change:

1. Consciousness raising
2. Catharsis/Dramatic relief (emotional expression)
3. Self-reevaluation
4. Environmental reevaluation
5. Self-liberation
6. Social liberation
7. Contingency management
8. Counterconditioning
9. Stimulus control
10. Helping relationship

STAGES OF CHANGE

Not every client who walks in your door is going to be ready to leap into action. Prochaska and Norcross (2007) identified seven possible stages of change: precontemplation, contemplation, preparation, action, maintenance, recycling, and termination. Understanding these stages is fairly straightforward and helps to shed light on what processes of change might be most useful to clients as they progress through them (see Table 16.9). The following material is summarized from Prochaska, DiClemente, and Norcross (1992) and Prochaska and Norcross (2002 and 2007).

In *precontemplation,* the client is not even thinking about change. Precontemplators who show up for counseling are not likely to be happy because they are likely to be there because someone else has forced them there (e.g., family, courts). The best a TT counselor can do in this circumstance is to try to create some awareness through consciousness-raising techniques or help the client gain emotional release through dramatic relief.

Clients who are in the *contemplation* stage are beginning to think about change; they perceive a problem and are thinking about what to do about it in a serious way. According to TT theorists, clients can stay in the contemplation stage for a very long time. Like those in the precontemplation stage, these individuals will not respond well to traditional, action-based therapeutic approaches.

The first attempts to change behaviors are seen in the *preparation* phase. For instance, a client who wishes to quit smoking will cut down on the amount of cigarettes she smokes in a day, or institute some ritual that must be preformed before smoking. However, the person has not reached the full commitment to change that is seen in subsequent stages.

Significant, committed behavior change occurs in the *action* stage. One day of serious change is recognized as action stage status.

After 6 months of change, the individual is considered to be in the *maintenance* stage. During this stage the individual is working to maintain and consolidate her gains. It is well known that change is very difficult, and for particularly stubborn problems such as smoking or substance abuse, relapse is common. Thus, for some problems, maintenance may be a lifelong experience.

Recycling refers to the observation that most people don't maintain change on the first attempt—they must recycle to the beginning and try again. Thus, the process of change is seen as a spiral rather than as a ramp. Counselors can help by providing some relapse prevention training, which is directed at avoiding relapse and also at recycling after one occurs (which it typically does with additive behavior within the 3 months of termination of treatment; Prochaska & Norcross, 2007).

Termination is said to occur when the individual no longer has to fight relapse. Termination of counseling and the termination of the problem do not always coincide.

TT advocates realize that individuals do not progress through the stages in a simple stage-by-stage fashion. Relapses occur, and the individual cycles back to a preceding stage from either the action or maintenance stage.

LEVELS OF CHANGE

Levels of change are interrelated areas of functioning in which intervention for change can be made. TT theorists identify five levels of change:

1. Symptom/situational problems
2. Maladaptive cognitions
3. Current interpersonal conflicts
4. Family/systems conflicts
5. Intrapersonal conflicts (Prochaska & Norcross, 2007, pp. 524–525)

The levels are ordered according to how "deep" the problem is seen to be in terms of historical influences and relevance to the individual's sense of self. Different approaches to psychotherapy focus on different levels of change. For example, psychoanalysis is concerned with intrapersonal (within the individual) conflicts. Family systems counselors zero in on family/systems conflicts. According to Prochaska and Norcross (2003), the critical factor is that client and counselor agree on the level or levels to which they attribute the problem.

THERAPY

Most important to the TT therapist is to assess the three constructs identified as essential to the change process. TT therapists assess the *stage* of change of the client, the kind of *processes* the client is using or has used, and which of the *problem levels* are relevant (Prochaska & Norcross, 2002).

In intervening with clients, TT advocates attempt to put together in one approach their knowledge about stages, levels, and processes of change. As Goldfried and Norcross (1995) put it, "Efficient behavior change depends on doing the right things (processes) at the right time (stages)" (p. 263). Thus, recommended interventions are different for clients in different stages of change. For example, using consciousness-raising techniques with clients in the action stage is a mistake. Clients in this stage benefit from approaches emphasizing behavioral processes such as contingency management (Prochaska & Norcross, 2007). Likewise, using action-oriented techniques with a client in the contemplation or preparation stages is not likely to work (Goldfried & Norcross, 1995). As far as level of intervention is concerned, the first preference of a TT counselor is to intervene at the symptom/situational level because the symptom or situation is usually what has brought the client to therapy. Attempting change at the deeper levels is more complicated because some of the problem causes may be out of awareness or intimately tied to the client's sense of self. Change of this kind takes longer (Prochaska & Norcross, 2007).

TT counselors realize that the levels are interconnected, however, so that change at one level can introduce change at other levels, too. Interpersonal conflicts often involve dysfunctional cognition, for example, and changing one may affect the other (Prochaska & Norcross, 2002a).

TECHNIQUES

The TT approach does not specify techniques per se; instead, these theorists outline strategies for intervention. The aim of the strategies is to help the client progress through the stages of change using the processes of change. These processes can be embedded within an existing theory of personality/psychotherapy or independent of a traditional counseling theory.

Shifting levels is one of these strategies; it is used when problems can't be eliminated by working at a given level (Prochaska & Norcross, 2002a). For example, consider the client dealing with depression resulting from the loss of a significant relationship. He starts work focusing on his symptoms. However, progress is slow to nonexistent. In response, the therapist might need to shift from the symptom level to the maladaptive cognitive level because cognitions seem to be supporting and exacerbating the symptoms. If the depression involves the loss of a significant relationship, the cognitive focus might not work, either. The therapist can then go to any one of the other levels as seems appropriate.

A second strategy is intervening at a *key level* (Prochaska & Norcross, 2003). In the case of some client presentations, the level applicable is fairly obvious, such as with simple phobia. The counselor focuses on the symptom level. In other client presentations, the key level is not all that obvious.

The *maximum impact* strategy is invoked when the problem seems to have elements at multiple levels (Prochaska & Norcross, 2007). Interventions are devised to affect several levels of the client's problem.

SUMMARY AND EVALUATION

Transtheoretical therapy theorists identify three important elements of the counseling process: processes of change, stages of change, and levels of change. Counselors must first assess where the client is in terms of the stages of change before deciding on useful processes and levels. Interventions are directed at a key level of change, and sometimes shifting levels is seen as a useful strategy. Techniques are not specified; all interventions that create the processes of change are acceptable.

The TT approach is relatively new, yet the response to this conceptualization among helping professionals has been positive. The proponents of TT, Prochaska, Norcross, and colleagues, have worked hard to establish empirical support for their approach and have amassed an impressive amount of data in this process. From a diversity viewpoint, this approach seems to adopt the traditional individualistic stance, although the recognition that clients sometimes are not ready to change may allow room for family and social factors that have significant implications in client presentations. Further, the proponents of TT would argue that the approach is broad and flexible enough to be used in ways that are sensitive to individual and cultural diversity.

Another important integrative approach is *assimilative integration*. In this model, the therapist is firmly committed to the theoretical assumptions and structures of one model, but adds techniques and assumptions from other theoretical systems in a deliberate way. For example, Stricker and Gold (2005) describe Assimilative Psychodynamic Psychotherapy, which has a theoretical basis in Relational Psychoanalysis (Chapter 3) but employs techniques from Behavioral, Experiential, and Family Systems approaches. In this approach, three tiers of functioning are identified: interpersonal relatedness (Tier 1), cognition, perception, and emotion (Tier 2), and psychodynamic conflict, self-representations, and object representation (Tier 3). Clients are assessed on all three levels and then interventions are designed that enhance client strengths and address dysfunction on each level. An overall goal is to target issues on levels 1 and 2 that might impede successful work on level 3. To give you a better sense of this approach, here is an example from Stricker and Gold (2005, p. 224):

> . . . consider the patient who suffers from a Tier 2 problem of self-critical thinking. In addition to thinking about ways to help this person to test these thoughts and to modify them, we explore the possible role of Tier 3 (psychodynamic) factors in motivating such thinking, and we consider such thoughts to be a potential defense against unconscious issues such as hostility toward a loved one with whom the patient is identified. Then, and perhaps most importantly, we ask ourselves, and attempt to explore clinically, the question of whether these thoughts can and need be changed through exploration of their unwitting symbolic and defensive role or whether their modification via the use of active, cognitive techniques would be a more effective step that would lead us to the same exploratory goal. Another component of this piece of the assessment would be to think about the interpersonal or transferential impact of the active intervention. . . .

Other assimilative approaches include Cognitive-Behavioral Assimilative Integration (Castonguay, Newman, Borkovec, Holtforth, & Maramba, 2005) and the Interpersonal-Cognitive approach proposed by Safran and colleagues (Marcotte & Safran, 2002; Safran, 1998; Safran & Segal, 1990). These approaches would have the drawbacks traditionally associated with the major theories they access and varying degrees of empirical support.

A final approach is the Common Factors perspective, which was briefly reviewed in Chapter 1. In closing I present a common factors model that emphasizes the value of a theoretical structure, or belief system, in the counseling process but also recognizes the common factors inherent in the healing relationship.

THE CONTEXTUAL MODEL

A few years ago, Bruce Wampold (2001) undertook a comprehensive review of the research on psychotherapy outcome in an attempt to promote a better understanding of the counseling process. In conceptualizing the research, Wampold identified two models of helping, the medical model and the contextual model.

The *medical* model is based on the premise that different treatments produce treatment-related specific effects that cure the client or patient. It is so named because in medical research, the emphasis is on specific biological effects of treatments; "psychological" effects are seen as simply confusing the matter. In classic medical research, using a placebo pill filters out psychological effects. The situation in psychotherapy, however, is a little different: both the specific and placebo effects are psychological.

Nonetheless, in psychotherapy research, medical model advocates try to identify the specific effects of therapy and relegate nonspecific effects, such as those associated with the counseling relationship, to a lesser status. So, for instance, the latest advocates of the medical model, the proponents of the Empirically Supported Treatment (EST) approach, say things like: "We define ESTs as clearly specified psychological treatments shown to be efficacious in controlled research with a delineated population. . . . we suggest that practitioners and research will profit from knowing which treatments are effective for which clients or patients" (Chambless & Hollon, 1998, p. 7).

Yet you recall from Chapter 1 that there were very few differences between the various theoretical approaches in terms of client outcomes. Even the elaborate client–treatment matching studies such as the NIMH study of depression and Project MATCH fail to uncover specific effects of treatment and client characteristics. Wampold used this information to support a different conception of psychotherapy. After reviewing an amazing amount of psychotherapy outcome research from a common factors perspective, Wampold argued that the most powerful influences in counseling outcome are the therapeutic relationship and therapist allegiance. Therapist allegiance, in this context, is interpreted as the extent to which the therapist believes her approach is beneficial.

Wampold proposed that the operation of psychotherapy is better captured by what he called the *contextual* model. Derived from Frank and Frank's (1991) work, this model is based on the assumption that "the aim of psychotherapy is to help people feel and function better by encouraging appropriate modifications in their assumptive worlds, thereby transforming the meanings of experiences to more favorable ones" (p. 30). People come to therapy because they are demoralized, not because of their symptoms. For these reasons, all successful therapy has the following ingredients:

1. A therapeutic relationship in which the client can confide in the therapist and in which there is a level of emotionality.
2. The relationship is conducted in a setting connected to a healing mission.
3. There is rationale or conceptual formulation about the client's symptoms and ideas about how to resolve them.
4. The rationale, which need not be "true," must be accepted by client and therapist.
5. The rationale must be consistent with the worldview and values of the client or the counselor must help the client understand and accept it.
6. The conceptual system leads to a ritual or procedure that requires the active involvement of client and therapist.

Adapted from Wampold [2001], p. 25.

Can you see the implications of this model for what you intend to do as a therapist? First, you must establish the right kind of relationship with your client. Further, you and your client must believe in what you are doing, and this belief must lead to active engagement in a process expected to lead to healing.

CONCLUSION

Clients do not come to therapy with a theoretical explanation of what's wrong in their lives. If they do have an explanation, most of the time it is not helping them. Your task as a counselor is to think critically about the helping process. That evaluation can now be based on the large amount of information that I have conveyed to you in this book. The approaches I chose to present are generally recognized as the major theoretical approaches to counseling (give or take a few, depending on whom you ask) and would seem to be a good starting point for your exploration of the counseling process. You could do worse than adopting one of these theories as you begin to work with clients.

If you consider Wampold's perspective, in some ways it really doesn't matter whether you are an advocate of the medical or contextual model. In essence, what you need is a theory in which you can believe. Again, I suggest that your belief is best placed in one of the major approaches to counseling rather than in more obscure, relatively untested models. Further, trying to create your own eclectic approach at this stage of your career would likely result in a less than coherent system that would be hard to communicate to your client.

For now, I think I have said what I can. I leave to you the ultimate decision about your commitment to a theoretical stance. I wish you the best in your journey and would welcome feedback on my thoughts.

REFERENCES

Abela, J. R. Z., & D'Alessandro, D. U. (2002). Beck's cognitive theory of depression: A test of the diathesis-stress and causal mediation components. *British Journal of Clinical Psychology, 1,* 111–128.

Abramowitz, J. S. (1997). Effectiveness of psychological and pharmacological treatments for obsessive-compulsive disorder. *Journal of Consulting and Clinical Psychology, 65,* 44–52.

Adams, B. N. (1972). Birth order: A critical review. *Sociometry, 35,* 411–439.

Adler, A. (1927). Individual psychology. *Journal of Abnormal and Social Psychology, 22,* 116–122.

Adler, A. (1969). *The science of living.* (H. L. Ansbacher, Ed. and Trans.). New York: Doubleday. (Original work published 1929)

Adler, A. (1982). *Co-operation between the sexes.* (H. L. Ansbacher & R. R. Ansbacher, Eds. & Trans.). New York: Norton.

Adler, A. (1998a). *Understanding human nature.* (C. Brett, Trans.). Center City, MN: Hazelden. (Original work published 1927)

Adler, A. (1998b). *What life could mean to you.* (C. Brett, Trans.). Center City, MN: Hazelden. (Original work published 1931)

Adler, K. (1994). Socialist influences on Adlerian psychology. *Journal of Individual Psychology, 50,* 131–141.

Alford, B. A., & Beck, A. T. (1997a). *The integrative power of cognitive therapy.* New York: Guilford Press.

Alford, B. A., & Beck, A. T. (1997b). The relation of psychotherapy integration to the established systems of psychotherapy. *Journal of Psychotherapy Integration, 7,* 275–289.

Alford, B. A., & Beck, A. T. (1997c). Therapeutic interpersonal support in cognitive therapy. *Journal of Psychotherapy Integration, 7,* 105–117.

Alleyne, A. (1998). Which women? What feminism? In I. B. Seu & M. C. Heenan (Eds.), *Feminism and psychotherapy* (pp. 43–56). London: Sage.

Almeida, R. (2003). Creating collectives of liberation. In L. B. Silverstein & T. J. Goodrich (Eds.), Feminist family therapy: Empowerment in social context (pp. 293-306). Washington, D.C.: American Psychological Association.

American Psychiatric Association. (2000). *Diagnostic and statistical manual of mental disorders* (DSM-IV-TR) (4th ed.). Washington, DC: Author.

American Psychological Association. (1992). Ethical principles of psychologists and code of conduct. *American Psychologist, 47,* 1597–1611.

American Psychological Association. (2006). *Guidelines for psychological practice with girls and women.* Washington, DC: Author.

American Psychological Association, Division 17, Counseling Psychology. (1979). Principles concerning the counseling and therapy of women. *The Counseling Psychologist, 8,* 21.

Amerikaner, M., Elliot, D., & Swank, P. (1988). Social interest as a predictor of vocational satisfaction. *Journal of Individual Psychology, 44,* 316–323.

Anderson, W. T. (2004). The upstart spring: *Esalen and the human potential movement: The first 20 years.* Lincoln, NE: iUniverse, Inc. (also referenced in Gestalt chapter).

Ansbacher, H. L. (1962). Was Adler a disciple of Freud? A reply. *Journal of Individual Psychology, 18,* 126–135.

Ansbacher, H. L. (1969). Introduction. In A. Adler, *The science of living* (pp. vii–xxii). New York: Doubleday. (Original work published 1929)

Ansbacher, H. L. (1970). Alfred Adler: A historical perspective. *American Journal of Psychiatry, 127,* 777–782.

Ansbacher, H., & Ansbacher, R. (Eds.). (1956). *The individual psychology of Alfred Adler.* New York: Basic Books.

Antony, M. M., & Roemer, L. (2003). Behavior therapy. In A. S. Gurman & S. B. Messer (Eds.), *Essential psychotherapies: Theory and practice* (2nd ed., pp. 182–223). New York: Guilford Press.

Aponte, H. J., & Dicesare, E. J. (2002). Structural family therapy. In J. Carlson & D. Kjos (Eds.), *Theories and strategies of family therapy* (pp. 1–18). Boston: Allyn & Bacon.

Aponte, H. J., & VanDeusen, J. M. (1981). Structural family therapy. In A. S. Gurman & D. P. Kniskern (Eds.), *Handbook of family therapy* (pp. 310–360). New York: Brunner/Mazel.

Arlow, J. A. (2005). Psychoanalysis. In R. J. Corsini & D. Wedding (Eds.), *Current Psychotherapies* (pp. 15–51). Belmont, CA: Brooks/Cole-Thompson Learning.

Arnkoff, D. B., & Glass, C. R. (1995). Cognitive therapy and psychotherapy integration. In D. K. Freedheim (Ed.), *History of psychotherapy: A century of change* (pp. 657–694). Washington, DC: American Psychological Association.

Aron, A., & Corne, S. (Eds.) (1994). Writings for a liberation psychology: Ignacio Martin-Baro. Cambridge, MA: Harvard University Press.

Arrendondo, P., Toporek, R., Brown, S. P., Jones, J., Locke, D., Sanchez, J., et al. (1996). *Operationalization of the multicultural counseling competencies.* Alexandria, VA: Association for Multicultural Counseling and Development.

Asay, T. P., & Lambert, M. J. (1999). The empirical case for the common factors in therapy: Quantitative findings. In M. A. Hubble, B. L. Duncan, & S. D. Miller (Eds.), *The heart and soul of change* (pp. 23–55). Washington, DC: American Psychological Association.

Association for Behavior Analysis International. (2006). Understanding behavior analysis. Retrieved December 20, 2006, from http://www.abainternational.org/BA/FAQ3.asp

Bach, P., & Hayes, S. C. (2002). The use of acceptance and commitment therapy to prevent the rehospitalization of psychotic patients: A randomized controlled trial. *Journal of Consulting and Clinical Psychology, 70,* 1129–1139.

Bachelor, A. (1988). How clients perceive therapist empathy: A content analysis of "received" empathy. *Psychotherapy, 25,* 227–240.

Baer, B. E., & Murdock, N. L. (1995). Nonerotic dual relationships between therapists and clients: The effects of sex, theoretical orientation, and interpersonal boundaries. *Ethics and Behavior, 5,* 131–145.

Baker, H. S. (1989). Definition of splitting in object relations theory. *American Journal of Psychiatry, 147* (9), 1252.

Ballou, M. (2005). Threats and challenges to feminist therapy. *Women and therapy, 28,* 201–210.

Ballou, M. (2006). Critical self-reflection necessary but not sufficient. *International Journal of Reality Therapy, 26,* 27–28.

Ballou, M., & Brown, L. S. (Eds.) (2002). *Rethinking mental health and disorder: Feminist perspectives.* New York: Guilford Press.

Bandura, A. (1969). *Principles of behavior modification.* New York: Holt, Rinehart & Winston.

Bandura, A. (1974). Behavior theory and the models of man. *American Psychologist, 29,* 859–869.

Bargad, A., & Hyde, J. S. (1991). A study of feminist identity development in women. *Psychology of Women Quarterly, 15,* 181–201.

Barrett-Lennard, G. T. (1959). *Dimensions of perceived therapist response related to therapeutic change.* Unpublished doctoral dissertation, University of Chicago.

Barrett-Lennard, G. T. (1986). The Relationship Inventory now: Issues and advances in theory, method, and use. In L. Greenberg & W. Pinsof (Eds.), *The psychotherapeutic process* (pp. 439–476). New York: Guilford Press.

Bartle-Haring, S., Glade, A. C., & Vira, R. (2005). Initial levels of differentiation and reduction in psychological symptoms for clients in marriage and family therapy. *Journal of Marital and Family Therapy, 31,* 121–131.

Bass, M. L., Curlette, W. L., Kern, R. M., & McWilliams, A. E. (2002). Social interest: A meta-analysis of a multidimensional construct. *Journal of Individual Psychology, 58,* 4–34.

Bauman, S., & Waldo, M. Existential theory and mental health counseling: If it were a snake, it would have bitten! *Journal of Mental Health Counseling, 20,* 13–28.

Beach, D. A. (2005). The behavioral interview. In R. J. Craig (Ed.), *Clinical and diagnostic interviewing* (pp. 91–105). Lanham, MD: Jason Aronson.

Beal, D., Kopec, A. M., & DeGuiseppe, R. (1996). Disputing clients' irrational beliefs. *Journal of Rational-Emotive and Cognitive-Behavior Therapy, 14,* 215–229.

Beck, A. T. (1964). Thinking and depression: II. Theory and therapy. *Archives of General Psychiatry, 10,* 561–571.

Beck, A. T. (1976). *Cognitive therapy and the emotional disorders.* Madison, WI: International Universities Press.

Beck, A. T. (1991). Cognitive therapy as *the* integrative therapy. *Journal of Psychotherapy Integration, 1* (3), 191–198.

Beck, A. T. (1993). Cognitive therapy: Past, present and future. *Journal of Consulting and Clinical Psychology, 61,* 194–198.

Beck, A. T. (1996). Beyond belief: A theory of modes, personality, and psychopathology. In P. M. Salkovskis (Ed.), *Frontiers of cognitive therapy* (pp. 1–25). New York: Guilford Press.

Beck, A. T. (1997a). Cognitive therapy: Reflections. In J. Zeig (Ed.), *The evolution of psychotherapy: The third conference* (pp. 55–64). New York: Brunner/Mazel.

Beck, A. T. (1997b). The past and future of cognitive therapy. *Journal of Psychotherapy Practice and Research, 6,* 276–284.

Beck, A. T. (1999). Cognitive aspects of personality disorders and their relation to syndromal disorders: A psychoevolutionary approach. In C. R. Cloninger (Ed.), *Personality and psychopathology* (pp. 411–430). Washington, DC: American Psychiatric Press.

Beck, A. T. (2005). The current state of cognitive therapy. *Archive of General Psychiatry, 62,* 953–959.

Beck, A. T., Baruch, E., Balter, J. M., Steer, R. A., & Warman, D. M. (2004). A new instrument for measuring insight: The Beck Cognitive Insight Scale. *Schizophrenia Research, 68,* 319–329.

Beck, A. T., & Clark, D. A. (1997). An information processing model of anxiety: Automatic and strategic processes. *Behavior Research and Therapy, 35,* 49–58.

Beck, A. T., & Emery, G. (1985). *Anxiety disorders and phobias: A cognitive perspective.* New York: Basic Books.

Beck, A. T., & Emery, G. (2005). *Anxiety disorders and phobias: A cognitive perspective.* New York: Basic Books.

Beck, A. T., Epstein, N., Brown, G., & Steer, R. A. (1988). An inventory for measuring clinical anxiety: Psychometric properties. *Journal of Consulting and Clinical Psychology, 56,* 893–897.

Beck, A. T., Freeman, A., et al. (1990). *Cognitive therapy of personality disorders.* New York: Guilford.

Beck, A. T., Freeman, A., Davis, D. D., and Associates (2004). *Cognitive therapy of personality disorders* (2nd ed.). New York: Guilford Press.

Beck, A. T., & Rector, N. A. (2000). Cognitive therapy of schizophrenia: A new therapy for the new millennium. *American Journal of Psychotherapy, 54,* 291–300.

Beck, A. T., & Rector, N. A. (2005). Cognitive approaches to schizophrenia: Theory and therapy. *Annual Review of Clinical Psychology, 1,* 577–606.

Beck, A. T., Rush, A. J., Shaw, B. F., & Emery, G. (1979). *Cognitive therapy of depression.* New York: Wiley.

Beck, A. T., Ward, C., Mendelson, M., & Erbaugh, J. (1961). An inventory for measuring depression. *Archives of General Psychiatry, 6,* 561–571.

Beck, A. T., & Weishaar, M. E. (2005). Cognitive therapy. In R. J. Corsini & D. Wedding (Eds.), *Current psychotherapies,* (7th ed., pp. 238–268). Belmont, CA: Brooks/Cole.

Beck, A. T., Wright, F. D., Newman, C. F., & Liese, B. (1993). *Cognitive therapy of substance abuse.* New York: Guilford Press.

Beck, J. S. (1995). *Cognitive therapy: Basics and beyond.* New York: Guilford Press.

Beck, J. S. (2004). Cognitive therapy, behavior therapy, psychoanalysis and pharmacotherapy: A cognitive continuum. In A. Freeman, M. J. Mahoney, P. Devito, & D. Martin (Eds.), *Cognition and psychotherapy* (pp. 197–220). NY: Springer.

Beck, J. S. (2005). *Cognitive therapy for challenging problems: What to do when the basics don't work.* NY: Guilford Press.

Beckvar, D. S., & Beckvar, R. J. (2006). *Family therapy* (6th ed.). Boston: Allyn & Bacon.

Beels, C. C. (2001). *A different story . . . the rise of narrative in psychotherapy.* Phoenix, AZ: Zeig, Tucker & Theisen.

Beevers, C. G., & Miller, I. W. (2005). Unlinking negative cognition and symptoms of depression: Evidence of a specific treatment effect for cognitive therapy. *Journal of Consulting and Clinical Psychology, 73*, 68–77.

Benton, M. K., & Schroeder, H. E. (1990). Social skills training with schizophrenics: A meta–analytic evaluation. *Journal of Consulting and Clinical Psychology, 58*, 741–747.

Berg, I. K., (2005). The state of miracles in relationships. *Journal of Family Psychotherapy, 16*, 115–118.

Berg, I. K., & DeJong, P. (2005). Engagement through complimenting. *Journal of Family Psychotherapy, 16*, 51–56.

Berg, I., & Miller, S. D. (1992). Working with Asian American clients: One person at a time. *Journal of Contemporary Human Services, 73*, 356–363.

Berg, I. K., & Shafter, K. C. (2004). Working with mandated substance abusers: The language of solutions. In S. L. A. Straussner (Ed.), *Clinical work with substance abusing clients*, 2nd ed. (pp. 82–102). New York: Guilford Press.

Berg, I. K., & Szabo, P. (2005). *Brief coaching for lasting solutions.* NY: W. W. Norton.

Bergman, D. (1951). Counseling method and client responses. *Journal of Consulting Psychology, 15*, 216–224.

Berk, L. E. (2007). *Development across the lifespan*, (4th ed.). Boston: Allyn & Bacon.

Berman, J. S., Miller, R. C., & Massman, P. J. (1985). Cognitive therapy versus systematic desensitization: Is our treatment superior? *Psychological Bulletin, 97*, 451–461.

Bernard, M. E. (1998). Validation of the general attitude and belief scale. *Journal of Rational-Emotive and Cognitive-Behavioral Therapy, 16*, 183–196.

Bernard, M. E., & DiGiuseppe, R. (1989). Rational-emotive therapy today. In M. E. Bernard & R. DiGiuseppe (Eds.), *Inside rational-emotive therapy: A critical appraisal of the theory and therapy of Albert Ellis* (pp. 1–7). New York: Academic Press.

Bernard, M. E., Ellis, A., & Terjesen, M. (2006). Rational-emotive behavioral approaches to childhood disorders: History, theory, practice, and research. In A. Ellis & M. E. Bernard (Eds.), *Rational emotive behavioral approaches to childhood disorders* (pp. 3–84). New York: Springer.

Bertolino, B., & O'Hanlon, B. (2002). *Collaborative, competency–based counseling and therapy.* Boston: Allyn & Bacon.

Besa, D. (1994). Evaluating narrative family therapy using single system research designs. *Research on Social Work Practice, 4*, 309–326.

Beutler, L. E. (1998). Identifying empirically supported treatments: What if we didn't? *Journal of Consulting and Clinical Psychology, 66*, 113–120.

Beutler, L. E., Consoli, A. J., & Williams, R. E. (1995). Integrative and eclectic therapies in practice. In B. Bongar & L. E. Beutler (Eds.), *Comprehensive textbook of psychotherapy* (pp. 274–292). New York: Oxford University Press.

Beutler, L. E., Machado, P. P. P., & Neufeldt, S. A. (1994). Therapist variables. In A. E. Bergin & S. L. Garfield (Eds.), *Handbook of psychotherapy and behavior change* (4th ed., pp. 229–269). New York: Wiley.

Beyebach, M., Morejon, A. R., Palenzuela, D. L., & Rodriguez-Arias, J. L. (1996). Research on the process of solution-focused brief therapy. In S. D. Miller, M. A. Hubble, & B. L. Duncan (Eds.), *Handbook of solution focused brief therapy.* San Francisco: Jossey–Bass.

Bieling, P. J., & Kuyken, W. (2003). Is cognitive case formulation science or science fiction? *Clinical Psychology: Science and Practice, 10*, 52–69.

Binder, J. L., Strupp, H. H., & Henry, W. P. (1995). Psychodynamic theories in practice: Time-limited dynamic psychotherapy. In B. Bonger & L. E. Beutler (Eds.), *Comprehensive textbook of psychotherapy* (pp. 48–63). New York: Oxford University Press.

Bird, B. E. I. (2005). Understanding dreams and dreamers: An Adlerian perspective. *Journal of Individual Psychology, 61*, 200–216.

Bishop, D. R. (1993). Applying psychometric principles to the clinical use of early recollections. *Journal of Individual Psychology, 49*, 153–165.

Blankstein, K. R., & Segal, Z. V. (2001). Cognitive assessment: Issues and methods. In K. S. Dobson (Ed.), *Handbook of cognitive-behavioral therapies* (pp. 40–85). New York: Guilford Press.

Blau, S. (1998). Introduction. In A. Ellis & S. Blau (Eds.), *The Albert Ellis reader.* Secaucus, NJ: Carol.

Bograd, M. (1990). Scapegoating mothers: Conceptual errors in systems formulations. In M. P. Mirkin (Ed.), *The social and political contexts of family therapy* (pp. 69–88). Boston: Allyn & Bacon.

Bohart, A. (1991). The missing 249 words: In search of objectivity. *Psychotherapy, 28*, 497–503.

Bohart, A. C., Elliott, R., Greenberg, L. S., & Watson, J. C. (1992). Empathy. In J. C. Norcross (Ed.), *Psychotherapy relationships that work: Therapist contributions and responsiveness to patients* (pp. 89–108). New York: Oxford University Press.

Bond, F. W., & Dryden, W. (1996). Why two central REBT hypotheses appear untestable. *Journal of Rational-Emotive and Cognitive-Behavior Therapy, 14*, 29–40.

Bornstein, R. F. (2005). Reconnecting psychoanalysis to mainstream psychology: Challenges and opportunities. *Psychoanalytic Psychology, 22*, 323–340.

Bowen, M. (1978). *Family therapy in clinical practice*. New York: Jason Aronson.

Bowman, C. E. (1998). Definitions of Gestalt therapy: Finding common ground. *Gestalt Review, 2* (2), 97–107.

Bozarth, J. D., Zimring, F. M., & Taush, R. (2001). Client-centered therapy: The evolution of a revolution. In D. J. Cain & J. Seeman (Eds.), *Humanistic psychotherapies: Handbook of research and practice* (pp. 147–188). Washington, DC: American Psychological Association.

Brabeck, M., & Brown, L. (1997). Feminist theory and psychological practice. In J. Worell & N. G. Johnson (Eds.), *Shaping the future of feminist psychology: Education, research and practice* (pp. 15–36). Washington, DC: American Psychological Association.

Braverman, L. (Ed.). (1988). *A guide to feminist family therapy*. New York: Harrington Park Press.

Breger, L., & McGaugh, J. L. (1973). Critique and reformulation of "learning-theory" approaches to psychotherapy and neuroses. In T. Millon (Ed.), *Theories of personality and psychopathology* (2nd ed., pp. 407–426). New York: Holt, Rinehart, & Winston. (Reprinted from *Psychological Bulletin*, 1965, *33*, 338–358)

Brenner, C. (1982). *The mind in conflict*. New York: International Universities Press.

Bretz, H. J., Heekerens, H., & Schmitz, B. (1994). A meta-analysis of the effectiveness of gestalt therapy. *Zeitschrift Fuer Klinische Psychologie, Psychiatrie und Psychotherapie, 42* (3), 241–260.

Breuer, J., & Freud, S. (1937). *Studies in hysteria* (A. A. Brill, Trans). Boston: Beacon Press. (Original work published 1895)

Briere, J. (1995). Science versus politics in the delayed memory debate. *The Counseling Psychologist, 23*, 290–293.

Brothers, B. J. (2000). Virginia Satir. In M. Suhd, L. Dodson, & M. Gormori (Eds.), *Virginia Satir: Her life and circle of influence* (pp. 1–102). Palo Alto, CA: Science and Behavior Books.

Brown, G. K., Have, T. T., Henriques, G. R., Xie, S. X., Hollander, J. E., & Beck, A. T. (2005). Cognitive therapy for the prevention of suicide attempts. *Journal of the American Medical Association, 294*, 563–570.

Brown, G. K., Newman, C. F., Charlesworth, S. E., Crits–Christoph, & Beck, A. T. (2004). An open clinical trial of cognitive therapy for Borderline Personality Disorder. *Journal of Personality Disorders, 81*, 257–271.

Broverman, I. K., Broverman, D. M., Clarkson, F., Rosenkrantz, P., & Vogel, S. (1970). Sex-role stereotyping and clinical judgments of mental health. *Journal of Consulting and Clinical Psychology, 45*, 250–256.

Brown, L. S. (1994). *Subversive dialogs*. New York: Basic Books.

Brown, L. S. (1995). Toward not forgetting: The science and politics of memory. *The Counseling Psychologist, 23*, 310–314.

Brown, L. S. (2000). Feminist therapy. In C. R. Snyder & R. E. Ingram (Eds.), *Handbook of psychological change: Psychotherapy processes and practices for the 21st century* (pp. 358–380). New York: Wiley.

Brown, L. S. (2006). Still subversive after all these years: The relevance of feminist therapy in the age of evidence-based practice. *Psychology of Women Quarterly, 30*, 15–24.

Brown, L. S., & Liss-Levinson, N. (1981). Feminist therapy I. In R. J. Corsini (Ed.), *Handbook of innovative psychotherapies* (pp. 299–314). New York: Wiley.

Brown, L. S., Riepe, L. E., & Coffey, R. L. (2005). Beyond color and culture: Feminist contributions to paradigms of human difference. *Women and Therapy, 28*, 63–92.

Buckley, P. (2003). Revolution and evolution: A brief intellectual history of American psychoanalysis during the past two decades. *American Journal of Psychotherapy, 57*, 1–17.

Bugental, J. T., & Bracke, P. E. (1992). The future of existential-humanistic psychotherapy. *Psychotherapy: Theory, Research, Practice, and Training, 29*, 28–33.

Bugental, J. F. T., & Kleiner, R. I. (1993). Existential psychotherapies. In G. Stricker & J. R. Gold (Eds.), *Comprehensive handbook of psychotherapy integration* (pp. 101–112). New York: Plenum Press.

Burlin, F. D., & Guzzetta, R. A. (1977). Existentialism: Toward a theory of psychotherapy for women. *Psychotherapy: Theory, Research and Practice, 14*, 262–266.

Burnett, P. C. (1988). Evaluation of Adlerian parenting programs. *Journal of Individual Psychology, 44*, 63–76.

Burns, D. D. (1980). *Feeling good: The new mood therapy*. New York: Signet.

Butler, A. C., Chapman, J. E., Forman, E. M., & Beck, A. T. (2006). The empirical status of cognitive-behavioral therapy: A review of meta-analyses. *Clinical Psychology Review, 26*, 17–31.

Cade, B., & O'Hanlon, W. H. (1993). *A brief guide to brief therapy*. New York: Norton.

Caffaro, J. (1991). A factor analytic study of deflection. *The Gestalt Journal, 14* (1), 73–94.

Campbell, B., Schellenberg, E. G., & Senn, C. Y. (1997). Evaluating measures of contemporary sexism. *Psychology of Women Quarterly, 21*, 89–102.

Cambell, L., White, J., & Stewart, A. (1991). The relationship of psychological birth order to actual birth order. *Individual Psychology, 47*, 380–391.

Carlson, J. (2002). Strategic family therapy. In J. Carlson & D. Kjos (Eds.), *Theories and strategies of family therapy* (pp. 80–97). Boston: Allyn & Bacon.

Carlson, J., Watts, R. E., & Maniacci, M. (2006). *Adlerian therapy*. Washington, DC: American Psychological Association.

Carr, A. (1998). Michael White's narrative therapy. *Contemporary Family therapy, 20*, 485–503.

Carter, B., & McGoldrick, M. (Eds.). (1999). *The expanded family life cycle: Individual family and social perspectives*. Boston: Allyn & Bacon.

Carter, B., & McGoldrick, M. (2005). Coaching at various stages of the life cycle. In B. Carter & M. McGoldrick (Eds.), *The expanded family life cycle* (3rd ed., pp. 436–254). New York: Allyn & Bacon.

Carter, E. A., & Orfanidis, M. M. (1976). Family therapy with one person and the family therapist's own family. In P. J. Guerin, Jr. (Ed.), *Family therapy: Theory and practice* (pp. 193–219). New York: Gardner Press/Wiley.

Casement, A. (2002). Psychodynamic therapy: The Jungian Approach. In W. Dryden (Ed.), *Handbook of individual therapy* (pp. 77–102). London: Sage.

Cashdan, S. (1988). *Object relations therapy: Using the relationship.* New York: Norton.

Cassidy, J., & Shaver, P. R. (Eds.). (1999). *Handbook of attachment: Theory, research, and application.* New York: Guilford Press.

Castonguay, L. G., Newman, M. G., Borkovec, T. D., Holtforth, M. G., & Maramba, G. G. (2005). Cognitive-behavioral assimilative integration. In J. C. Norcross & M. R. Goldfried (Eds.), *Handbook of psychotherapy integration* (pp. 214–262). New York: Oxford University Press.

Cautela, J. R. (1994). Covert conditioning: Assumptions and procedures. In J. R. Cautela & A. J. Kearney (Eds.), *Covert conditioning casebook* (pp. 3–10). Pacific Grove, CA: Brooks/Cole.

Cautela, J. R., & Kastenbaum, R. (1967). A reinforcement survey schedule for use in therapy, training, and research. *Psychological Reports, 20,* 1115–1130.

Chamberlain, J. M., & Haaga, D. A. F. (2001). Unconditional self-acceptance and responses to negative feedback. *Journal of Rational-Emotive and Cognitive-Behavior Therapy, 19,* 177–189.

Chambless, D. L. (1986). [Contributing topic editor's introduction]. *The Behavior Therapist, 1,* 7–10.

Chambless, D. L., & Gillis, M. M. (1993). Cognitive therapy of anxiety disorders. *Journal of Consulting and Clinical Psychology, 61,* 248–260.

Chambless, D. L., & Hollon, S. D. (1998). Defining empirically supported therapies. *Journal of Consulting and Clinical Psychology, 66,* 7–18.

Chang, T. H., & Yeh, R. L. (1999). Theoretical framework for therapy with Asian families. In K. S. Ng (Ed.), *Counseling Asian families from a systems perspective* (pp. 3–13). Alexandria, VA: American Counseling Association.

Chantler, K. (2005). From disconnection to connection: 'Race', gender and the politics of therapy. *British Journal of Guidance and Counselling, 33,* 239–256.

Chen, C. P. (1995). Counseling applications of RET in a Chinese cultural context. *Journal of Rational–Emotive and Cognitive-Behavior Therapy, 13,* 117–128.

Chernin, J., & Holden, J. M. (1995). Toward an understanding of homosexuality: Origins, status and relationship to individual psychology. *Journal of Individual Psychology, 51,* 90–101.

Chesler, P. (1972). *Women and madness.* Garden City, NY: Doubleday.

Chester, A., & Bretherton, D. (2001). What makes feminist counselling feminist? *Feminism & Psychology, 11,* 527–545.

Cheung, S. (2005). Strategic and solution-focused couples therapy. In M. Harway (Ed.), *Handbook of couples therapy* (pp. 194–210). New York: Wiley.

Chodorow, N. J. (1978). *The reproduction of mothering.* Berkeley, CA: University of California Press.

Chodorow, N. J. (1989). *Feminism and psychoanalytic theory.* New Haven, CT: Yale University Press.

Chodorow, N J. (2002). Prejudice exposed: On Stephen Mitchell's pioneering investigations of the psychoanalytic treatment and mistreatment of homosexuality. *Studies in Gender and Sexuality, 3,* 61–72.

Clark, D. A. (2004). Cognitive-behavioral theory and treatment of obsessive-compulsive disorder. In R. L. Leahy (Ed.), *Contemporary cognitive therapy: Theory, research, and practice* (pp. 161–183). New York: Guilford Press.

Clark, D. A., & Beck, A. T. (1999). *Scientific foundations of cognitive theory and therapy of depression.* New York: Wiley.

Clark, D. M., & Ehlers, A. (1993). An overview of the cognitive theory and treatment of panic disorder. *Applied and Preventive Psychology, 2,* 131–139.

Clarkson, P. (1989). *Gestalt counselling in action.* London: Sage.

Clarkson, P., & Mackewn, J. (1993). *Fritz Perls.* Thousand Oaks, CA: Sage.

Coan, R. W. (1979). *Psychologists: Personal and theoretical pathways.* New York: Irvington.

Cole, P. H. (1998). Affective process in psychotherapy: A gestalt therapist's view. *The Gestalt Journal, 21* (1), 49–72.

Coleman, E. Z. (1988). Room to grow: How divergent approaches to counseling can enrich one another. *British Journal of Guidance and Counseling, 16,* 21–32.

Colledge, R. (2002). *Mastering counseling theory.* New York: Palgrave Macmillan.

Collins, R. L., & McNair, L. D. (1986). Black women and behavior therapy: Exploring the biases. *The Behavior Therapist, 1,* 7–10.

Comas-Diaz, L., & Greene, B. (Eds.). (1994). *Women of color: Integrating ethnic and gender identities in psychotherapy.* New York: Guilford Press.

Combs, A. W. (1988). Some current issues for person-centered therapy. *Person-Centered Review, 3,* 263–276.

Contratto, S. (2002). A feminist critique of attachment theory and evolutionary psychology. In M. Ballou & L. S. Brown (Eds), *Rethinking mental health and disorder* (pp. 29–47). New York: Guilford Press.

Contratto, S., & Rossier, R. (2005). Early trends in feminist theory and practice. *Women and Therapy, 28,* 7–26.

Cooper, M. (2003). *Existential therapies.* London: Sage.

Corcoran, J. (2000). Solution-focused family therapy with ethnic minority clients. *Crisis Intervention, 6,* 5–12.

Corcoran, J. (2005). Building strengths and skills: A collaborative approach to working with clients. NY, US: Oxford University Press.

Corey, D. W. (1951). *The homosexual in America.* New York: Greenberg.

Corey, G. (2001). *Theory and practice of counseling and psychotherapy* (6th ed.). Belmont, CA: Brooks/Cole.

Corey, G. (2004). *Theory and practice of counseling and psychotherapy.* NY: Wadsworth.

Cornelius-White, J. H. D., & Cornelius-White, C. F. (2005). Reminiscing and predicting: Rogers's beyond words speech and commentary. *Journal of Humanistic Psychology, 45,* 383–396.

Cornett, C. W., & Hudson, R. A. (1986). Psychoanalytic theory and affirmation of the gay lifestyle: Are they necessarily antithetical? *Journal of Homosexuality, 12*(1), 97–108.

Corsini, R. J., & Wedding, D. (Eds.). (2000). *Current psychotherapies* (6th ed.). Itasca, IL: Peacock.

Corsini, R. J., & Wedding, D. (2005). *Current psychotherapies* (7th Ed). Belmont, CA: Thompson/Brooks-Cole.

Coulehan, R., Friedlander, M., & Heatherington, L. (1998). Transforming narratives: A change event in constructivist family therapy. *Family Process, 37,* 17–33.

Coyne, J. C., & Gotlib, I. H. (1983). The role of cognition in depression: A critical appraisal. *Psychological Bulletin, 94,* 472–505.

Coyne, J. C., & Gotlib, I. (1986). Studying the role of cognition in depression: Well-trodden paths and cul-de-sacs. *Cognitive Therapy and Research, 10,* 695–705.

Craighead, W. E. (1990). There's a place for us: All of us. *Behavior Therapy, 21,* 3–23.

Cramer, D. (1988). Self-esteem and facilitative close relationships: A cross-lagged panel correlation analysis. *British Journal of Social Psychology, 27,* 115–126.

Cramer, D. (1994). Self-esteem and Rogers' core conditions in close friends: A latent variable path analysis of panel data. *Counselling Psychology Quarterly, 7,* 327–337.

Cramer, D., & Buckland, N. (1995). Effect of rational and irrational statements and demand characteristics on task anxiety. *The Journal of Psychology, 129,* 269–275.

Crandall, J. E. (1981). *Theory and measurement of social interest: Empirical tests of Alfred Adler's concept.* New York: Columbia University Press.

Crits-Christoph, P. (1992). The efficacy of brief dynamic psychotherapy: A meta-analysis. *The American Journal of Psychiatry, 149,* 151–158.

Crits-Christoph, P. (1997). Limitations of the Dodo Bird verdict and the role of clinical trials in psychotherapy research: Comment on Wampold et al. (1997). *Psychological Bulletin, 122,* 216–220.

Crits-Christoph, P., & Connolly, M. B. (1998). Empirical basis of supportive-expressive psychodynamic psychotherapy. In R. F. Bornstein & J. M. Masling (Eds.), *Empirical studies of the therapeutic hour* (pp. 109–151). Washington, DC: American Psychological Association.

Crits-Cristoph, P., Siqueland, L., Blaine, J., Frank, A., Luborsky, L., Onken, L. S., Muenz, L. R., Thase, M. E., Weiss, R. D., Gastfriend, D. R., Woody, G.E., Barber, J. P., Butler, S. F., Dayley, D., Salloum, I., Bishop, S., Najavits, L. M., Lis, J.,

Mercer, D., Griffin, M. L., Moras, K., & Beck, A. T. (1999). Psychosocial treatments for cocaine dependence: National Institute on Drug Abuse Collaborative Cocaine Treatment Study. *Archives of General Psychiatry, 56,* 493–502.

Crocker, S. F. (1999). *A well-lived life.* Cambridge, MA: GIC Press.

Crumbaugh, J., & Maholick, L. (1964). *Purpose in life test.* Murfreesboro, TN: Psychometric Affiliates.

Curtis, F. (1994). Gestalt couples therapy with lesbian couples: Applying theory and practice to the lesbian experience. In G. Wheeler & S. Backman (Eds.), *On intimate ground: A gestalt approach to working with couples* (pp. 188–209). San Francisco: Jossey-Bass.

Curtis, R. C., & Hirsch, I. (2003). Relational approaches to psychoanalytic psychotherapy. In A. S. Gurman & S. B. Messer (Eds.), *Essential psychotherapies: Theory and practice* (pp. 69–106). NY: Guilford Press.

Daniels, V. (2003). The working corner: "Making the rounds" or the "go-around." *Gestalt! 7,* no pagination specified (according to psychinfo).

David, D., Montgomery, G. H., Macavei, B., & Bovbjerg, D. H. (2005). An empirical investigation of Albert Ellis' binary model of distress. *Journal of Clinical Psychology, 61,* 499–516.

David, D., Szentagotai, A., Eva, K., & Macavei, B. (2005). A synopsis of rational-emotive behavior therapy (REBT) fundamental and applied research. *Journal of Rational-Emotive and Cognitive Behavior Therapy, 23,* 175–221.

Davidson, G. C. (1976). Homosexuality: The ethical challenge. *Journal of Consulting and Clinical Psychology, 44,* 157–162.

Davies, M. F. (2006). Irrational beliefs and unconditional self-acceptance. I. Correlational evidence linking two key features of REBT. *Journal of Rational-Emotive & Cognitive Behavior Therapy, 24,* 113–124.

Davis, B. T., Hops, H., Alpert, A., & Sheeber, L. (1998). Child responses to parental conflict and their effect on adjustment: A study of triadic relations. *Journal of Family Psychology, 12,* 163–177.

Davis, D., & Padesky, C. (1989). Enhancing cognitive therapy with women. In A. Freeman, K. M. Simon, L. E. Beutler, & H. Arkowitz (Eds.), *Comprehensive handbook of cognitive therapy* (pp. 535–557). New York: Plenum Press.

Davis, S. N. (2003). Sex stereotypes in commercials targeted toward children: A content analysis. *Sociological Spectrum, 23,* 407–424.

Day, H. D., St. Clair, S., & Marshall, D. D. (1997). Do people who marry really have the same level of differentiation of self? *Journal of Family Psychology, 11,* 131–135.

Deci, E. (1995). *Why we do what we do.* New York: Penguin.

Deffenbacher, J. L., Oetting, E. R., & DiGiuseppe, R. A. (2002). Principles of empirically supported interventions applied to anger management. *The Counseling Psychologist, 30,* 262–280.

De Jong, P., & Berg, I. K. (2007). Interviewing for solutions. Belmont, CA: Brooks/Cole.

De Jong, P., & Hopwood, L. E. (1996). Outcome research on treatment conducted at the brief family therapy center 1992–1993. In S. D. Miller, M. A. Hubble, & B. L. Duncan (Eds.), *Handbook of solution focused brief therapy* (pp. 272–298). San Francisco: Jossey-Bass.

Demer, S. B., Hemesath, C. W., & Russell, C. S. (1998). A feminist critique of solution-focused therapy. *The American Journal of Family Therapy, 26,* 239–250.

Derogatis, L. R. (1994). SCL-90-R: Symptom checklist-90-R : Administration, scoring & procedures manual. Minneapolis, Minnesota: National Computer Systems.

DeRubeis, R. J., & Crits-Christoph, P. (1998). Empirically supported individual and group psychological treatments for adult mental disorders. *Journal of Consulting and Clinical Psychology, 66,* 37–52.

de Shazer, S. (1982). *Patterns of brief therapy.* New York: Guilford Press.

de Shazer, S. (1985). *Keys to solution in brief therapy.* New York: Norton.

de Shazer, S. (1988). *Clues: Investigating solutions in brief therapy.* New York: Norton.

de Shazer, S. (1991). *Putting difference to work.* New York: Norton.

de Shazer, S. (1994). *Words were originally magic.* New York: Norton.

de Shazer, S. (1998). *Beginnings.* Unpublished manuscript.

de Shazer, S., & Dolan, Y. (2007). *More than miracles: The state of the art of solution focused therapy.* New York: Haworth Press.

de Shazer, S., & Molnar, A. (1984). Four useful interventions in brief family therapy. *Journal of Marriage and Family Therapy, 10,* 297–304.

De Vega, M. H., & Beyebach, M. (2004). Between-session change in solution-focused therapy: A replication. *Journal of Systemic Therapies, 23,* 18–26.

Diamond, G., & Josephson, A. J. (2005). Family-based treatment research: A 10-year update. *Journal of the Academy of Child and Adolescent Psychiatry, 44,* 872–887.

DiGiuseppe, R. (1991a). A rational-emotive model of assessment. In M. E. Bernard (Ed.), *Using rational-emotive therapy effectively* (pp. 151–172). New York: Plenum Press.

DiGiuseppe, R. (1991b). Comprehensive cognitive disputing in RET. In M. E. Bernard (Ed.), *Using rational-emotive therapy effectively* (pp. 173–195). New York: Plenum Press.

DiGiuseppe, R. (1995a). A rational-emotive model of assessment. In W. Dryden (Ed.), *Rational emotive behavior therapy: A reader* (pp. 73–93). London: Sage.

DiGiuseppe, R. (1995b). Comprehensive cognitive disputing. In W. Dryden (Ed.), *Rational emotive behavior therapy: A reader* (pp. 108–129). London: Sage.

DiGiuseppe, R., Leaf, R., Exner, T., & Robin, M. W. (1988). The development of a measure of irrational/rational thinking. Paper presented at the World Congress of Behavior Therapy, Edinburgh, Scotland. (Cited in David, D., Szentagotai, A., Eva, K., & Macavei, B. 2005)

DiLorento, A. O. (1971). *Comparative psychotherapy: An experimental analysis.* Chicago: Aldine-Atherton.

DiNardo, P. A., Brown, T. A., & Barlow, D. H. (1994). Anxiety disorders interview schedule of DSM-IV. Albany, NY: Graywind.

Dinkmeyer, D. C., Dinkmeyer, D. C., Jr., & Sperry, L. (1987). *Adlerian counseling and psychotherapy.* Upper Saddle River, NJ: Merrill/Prentice Hall.

Dinkmeyer, D., & Dreikurs, R. (1963). *Encouraging children to learn: The encouragement process.* Upper Saddle River, NJ: Prentice Hall.

Dinkmeyer, D. C., Jr., & Sperry, L. (2000). *Counseling and psychotherapy: An integrated individual psychology approach* (3rd ed). Upper Saddle River, NJ: Merrill/Prentice Hall.

Division of Counseling Psychology, Committee on Definition. (1956). Counseling psychology as a specialty. *American Psychologist, 11,* 282–285.

Doan, R. E. (1998). Interviewing fear and love: Implications for narrative therapy. In M. F. Hoyt, (Ed.), *The handbook of constructive therapies: Innovative approaches from leading practitioners.* (pp. 219–240). San Francisco, CA: Jossey-Bass.

Dobson, K. S. (1989). A meta-analysis of the efficacy of cognitive therapy for depression. *Journal of Consulting and Clinical Psychology, 57,* 414–419. doi: 10.1049/e11:20071405

Dobson, K. S., & Shaw, B. F. (1988). The use of treatment manuals in cognitive therapy: Experience and issues. *Journal of Consulting and Clinical Psychology, 56,* 673–680.

Donaldson, G. (1996). Between practice and theory: Melanie Klein, Anna Freud and the development of child analysis. *Journal of the History of the Behavioral Sciences, 32,* 160–176.

Douglas, C. (2005). Analytical Psychotherapy. In R. J. Corsini & D. Wedding (Eds.), *Current Psychotherapies* (7th ed., pp. 96–129). Belmont, CA: Brooks/Cole.

Downing, N. E., & Roush, K. L. (1985). From passive acceptance to active commitment: A model of feminist identity development for women. *The Counseling Psychologist, 21,* 3–87.

Dozois, D. J. A., & Backs-Dermott, B. J. (2000). Sociotropic personality and information processing following imaginal priming: A test of the congruency hypothesis. *Canadian Journal of Behavioral Science, 32,* 117–126.

Dreikurs, R. (1952–1953). The psychological interview in medicine. *American Journal of Individual Psychology, 10,* 99–122.

Dreikurs, R. (1953). *Fundamentals of Adlerian psychology.* Chicago: Alfred Adler Institute.

Dryden, W. (1994). *Progress in rational emotive behavior therapy.* London: Whurr.

Dryden, W. (1995a). The use of chaining in rational emotive therapy. In W. Dryden (Ed.), *Rational emotive behavior therapy: A reader* (pp. 94–99). London: Sage.

Dryden, W. (1995b). Vivid methods in rational-emotive therapy. In W. Dryden (Ed.), *Rational emotive behavior therapy: A reader* (pp. 151–174). London: Sage.

Dryden, W. (1995c). *Brief rational emotive behavior therapy.* New York: Wiley.

Dryden, W. (1996). Rational emotive behavior therapy. In W. Dryden (Ed.), *Handbook of individual therapy* (pp. 304–327). London, England, and Thousand Oaks, CA: Sage.

Dryden, W., & Mytton, J. (1999). *Four approaches to counselling and psychotherapy.* New York: Routledge.

Dryden, W., & Neenan, M. (2006). *Rational emotive behavior therapy: 100 Key points and techniques.* New York: Routledge.

Dryden, W., & Yankura, J. (1993). *Counselling individuals: A rational-emotive handbook* (2nd ed.). London: Whurr.

Duan, C., & Hill, C. E. (1996). The current state of empathy research. *Journal of Counseling Psychology, 43,* 261–274.

Dzelme, K., & Jones, R. A. (2001). Male cross-dressers in therapy: A solution-focused perspectives for marriage and family therapists. *The American Journal of Family Therapy, 29,* 293–305.

Eagly, A. H. (1995). The science and politics of comparing women and men. *American Psychologist, 50,* 145–158.

Eakes, G., Walsh, S., Markowski, M., Cain, H., & Swanson, M. (1997). Family-centered brief solution-focused therapy with chronic schizophrenia: A pilot study. *Journal of Family Therapy, 19,* 145–158.

Eckstein, D., Milliren, A., Rasmussen, P. R., & Willhite, R. (2006). An Adlerian approach to the treatment of anger disorders. In E. L. Feindler (Ed.), *Anger-related disorders: A practitioner's guide to comparative treatments* (pp. 257–276). New York: Springer.

Edgette, J. S., & Prout, M. (1989). Cognitive and behavioral approaches to the treatment of anorexia nervosa. In A. Freeman, K. M. Simon, L. E. Beutler, & H. Arkowitz (Eds.), *Comprehensive handbook of cognitive therapy* (pp. 367–384). New York: Plenum.

Efran, J. S., & Clarfield, L. E. (1992). Contructionist therapy: Sense and nonsense. In S. McNamee & K. J. Gergen (Eds.), Therapy as social construction (pp. 200–217). London: Sage.

Egan, G. (2006). *Essentials of skilled helping.* Belmont, CA: Thompson Wadsworth.

Elkin, I. (1994). The NIMH Treatment of Depression Collaborative Research Program: Where we began and where we are. In A. Bergin and S. Garfield (Eds.), *Handbook of psychotherapy and behavior change* (4th ed., pp. 114–139). New York: Wiley.

Elkin, L., Shea, M. T., Watkins, J. T., Imber, S. D., Sotsky, S. M., Collins, J. F., et al. (1989). NIMH Treatment of Depression Collaborative Research Program: General effectiveness of treatments. *Archives of General Psychiatry, 46,* 971–983.

Elliot, R. (2001). The effective of humanistic therapies: A meta-analysis. In D. J. Cain & J. Seeman, (Eds.) , *Humanistic psychotherapies: Handbook of research and practice* (pp. 57–81). Washington, DC: American Psychological Association.

Elliot, R. (2002). The effectiveness of humanistic therapies: A meta-analysis. In D. J. Cain & J. Seeman (Eds.), *Humanistic psychotherapies: Handbook of research and practice* (pp. 57–82). Washington, DC: American Psychological Association.

Elliot, R., Watson, J. C., Goldman, R. N., & Greenberg, L. S. (2004). *Learning emotion-focused therapy: The process experiential approach to change.* Washington, DC: American Psychological Association.

Elliott, D., Amerikaner, M., & Swank, P. (1987). Early recollections and the vocational preference inventory as predictors of vocational choice. *Journal of Individual Psychology, 43,* 353–359.

Ellis, A. (1979a). Toward a new theory of personality. In A. Ellis & J. M. Whitley (Eds.), *Theoretical and empirical foundations of rational-emotive therapy* (pp. 7–32). Monterey, CA: Brooks/Cole.

Ellis, A. (1979b). Rejoinder: Elegant and inelegant RET. In A. Ellis & J. M. Whitley (Eds.), *Theoretical and empirical foundations of rational-emotive therapy* (pp. 240–267). Monterey, CA: Brooks/Cole.

Ellis, A. (1979c). The practice of rational-emotive therapy. In A. Ellis & J. M. Whitley (Eds.), *Theoretical and empirical foundations of rational-emotive therapy* (pp. 61–100). Monterey, CA: Brooks/Cole.

Ellis, A. (1985). The evolution of rational-emotive therapy (RET) and cognitive-behavior therapy (CBT). In J. K. Zeig (Ed.), *The evolution of psychotherapy.* New York: Brunner/Mazel.

Ellis, A. (1987). The impossibility of achieving consistently good mental health. *American Psychologist, 42,* 364–375.

Ellis, A. (1989). Comments on my critics. In M. E. Bernard & R. DiGiuseppe (Eds.), *Inside rational-emotive therapy: A critical appraisal of the theory and therapy of Albert Ellis* (pp. 199–233). San Diego, CA: Academic Press.

Ellis, A. (1990). Rational-emotive therapy. In J. K. Zeig & W. M. Munion (Eds.), *What is psychotherapy? Contemporary perspectives.* San Francisco: Jossey-Bass.

Ellis, A. (1991). Using RET effectively: Reflections and interview. In M. Bernard (Ed.), *Using rational-emotive therapy effectively: A practitioner's guide.* New York: Plenum Press.

Ellis, A. (1992a). My early experiences in developing the practice of psychology. *Professional Psychology: Research and Practice, 23,* 7–10.

Ellis, A. (1992b). The revised ABCs of rational-emotive therapy (RET). In J. K. Zeig (Ed.), *The evolution of psychotherapy: The second conference* (pp. 79–91). New York: Brunner/Mazel.

Ellis, A. (1994a). *Reason and emotion in psychotherapy* (rev. ed.). New York: Birch Lane Press.

Ellis, A. (1994b). Rational emotive behavior therapy approaches to obsessive-compulsive disorder (OCD). *Journal of Rational-Emotive and Cognitive-Behavior Therapy, 12,* 121–141.

Ellis, A. (1995a). Fundamentals of REBT for the 1990s. In W. Dryden (Ed.), *Rational emotive behavior therapy: A reader* (pp. 1–30). London: Sage.

Ellis, A. (1995b). Reflections on rational emotive therapy. In M. J. Mahoney et al. (Eds.), *Cognitive and constructive psychotherapies: Theory, research, and practice* (pp. 69–73). New York: Springer/ Washington, DC: American Psychological Association.

Ellis, A. (1995c). Rational-emotive therapy approaches to overcoming resistance. In W. Dryden (Ed.), *Rational emotive behavior therapy* (pp. 184–211). London: Sage.

Ellis, A. (1996a). *Better, deeper, and more enduring brief therapy: The rational emotive behavior therapy approach.* New York: Brunner/Mazel.

Ellis, A. (1996b). Responses to criticism of rational emotive behavior therapy (REBT) by Ray DiGiuseppe, Frank Bond, Windy Dryden, Steve Weinrach, and Richard Wessler. *Journal of Rational-Emotive and Cognitive-Behavior Therapy, 14,* 97–120.

Ellis, A. (1997a). The evolution of Albert Ellis and rational emotive behavior therapy. In J. K. Zeig (Ed.), *The evolution of psychotherapy: The third conference* (pp. 69–78). New York: Brunner/Mazel.

Ellis, A. (1997b). REBT with obsessive-compulsive disorder. In J. Yankura & W. Dryden (Eds.), *Using REBT with common psychological problems.* New York: Springer.

Ellis, A. (1998a). How rational emotive behavior therapy belongs in the constructivist camp. In M. F. Hoyt (Ed.), *Handbook of constructive therapies: Innovative approaches for leading practitioners* (pp. 83–99). San Francisco: Jossey-Bass.

Ellis, A. (1998b). The biological basis of human irrationality. In A. Ellis & S. Blau (Eds.), *The Albert Ellis reader* (pp. 271–291). Secaucus, NJ: Carol.

Ellis, A. (1999a). Treatment of borderline personality disorder with rational emotive behavior therapy. In C. R. Cloninger (Ed.), *Personality and psychopathology.* Washington, DC: American Psychiatric Press.

Ellis, A. (1999b). Early theories and practices of rational emotive behavior therapy and how they have been augmented and revised during the last three decades. *Journal of Rational-Emotive and Cognitive-Behavior Therapy, 17,* 69–93.

Ellis, A. (1999c). Why rational-emotive therapy to rational emotive behavior therapy? *Psychotherapy, 36,* 154–159.

Ellis, A. (1999d). Rational emotive behavior therapy as an internal control psychology. *International Journal of Reality Therapy, 19,* 4–11.

Ellis, A. (1999e). *How to make yourself happy and remarkably less disturbable.* Atascadero, CA: Impact.

Ellis, A. (2001). Rational and irrational aspects of countertransference. *Journal of Clinical Psychology, 57,* 991–1004.

Ellis, A. (2002). *Overcoming resistance: A rational emotive behavior therapy integrated approach* (2nd ed.). New York: Springer.

Ellis, A. (2003). How to deal with your most difficult client—you. *Journal of Rational Emotive & Cognitive Behavior Therapy, 21,* 203–213.

Ellis, A. (2004a). Why I (really) became a therapist. *Journal of Rational-Emotive & Cognitive-Behavior Therapy, 22,* 73–77.

Ellis, A. (2004b). Post-September 11 perspectives on religion, spirituality, and philosophy in the personal and professional lives of selected REBT cognoscenti: A response to my colleagues. *Journal of Counseling and Development, 82,* 439–442.

Ellis, A. (2004c). Why rational emotive behavior therapy is the most comprehensive and effective form of behavior therapy.

Journal of Rational-Emotive and Cognitive-Behavior Therapy, 22, 85–92.

Ellis, A. (2005a). *The myth of self-esteem: How Rational Emotive Behavior Therapy can change your life forever.* Amherst, NY: Prometheus Books.

Ellis, A. (2005b). Rational-emotive behavior therapy. In R. J. Corsini & D. Wedding (Eds.), *Current psychotherapies* (pp. 166–201). Belmont, CA: Brooks/Cole.

Ellis, A., & Dryden, W. (1997). *The practice of rational emotive behavior therapy* (2nd ed.). New York: Springer.

Ellis, A., & Joffe, D. (2002). A study of volunteer clients who experienced live sessions of rational emotive behavior therapy in front of a public audience. *Journal of Rational-Emotive & Cognitive-Behavior Therapy, 20,* 151–158.

Ellis, A., & MacLaren, C. (1998). *Rational emotive behavior therapy: A therapist's guide.* Atascadero, CA: Impact.

Ellis, A., & MacLaren, C. (2005). *Rational emotive behavior therapy: A therapist's guide* (2nd ed.). Atascadero, CA: Impact.

Emmelkamp, P. M. G. (1990). Anxiety and fear. In A. S. Bellack, M. Hersen, & A. E. Kazdin (Eds.), *International handbook of behavior modification and therapy* (2nd ed., pp. 283–305). New York: Plenum Press.

Emmelkamp, P. M. (2004). Behavior therapy with adults. In M. J. Lambert (Ed.), *Bergin and Garfield's handbook of psychotherapy and behavior change* (5th ed., pp. 393–446). New York: Wiley.

Engles, G. I., Garnefski, N., & Diekstra, R. F. (1993). Efficacy of rational-emotive therapy: A quantitative analysis. *Journal of Consulting and Clinical Psychology, 61,* 1083–1090.

Enns, C. Z. (1987). Gestalt therapy and feminist therapy: A proposed integration. *Journal of Counseling and Development, 66,* 93–95.

Enns, C. Z. (1993). Twenty years of feminist counseling and therapy: From naming biases to implementing multifaceted practice. *The Counseling Psychologist, 21,* 3–87.

Enns, C. Z. (1995). Toward integrating feminist psychotherapy and feminist philosophy. *Professional Psychology: Research and Practice, 23,* 453–466.

Enns, C. Z. (2004). *Feminist theories and feminist psychotherapies: Origins, themes, and variations* (2nd ed.). New York: Haworth Press.

Enns, C. Z. (2000). Gender issues in counseling. In S. D. Brown & R. W. Lent (Eds.), *Handbook of counseling psychology* (3rd ed., pp. 601–669). New York: Wiley.

Enns, C. Z., & Hackett, G. (1990). Comparison of feminist and nonfeminist women's reactions to variants of nonsexist and feminist counseling. *Journal of Counseling Psychology, 37,* 33–40.

Enns, C. Z., McNeilly, C. L., Corkery, J. M., & Gilbert, M. S. (1995). The debate about delayed memories of child sexual abuse: A feminist perspective. *The Counseling Psychologist, 23,* 181–279.

Enright, J. B., (1970). An introduction to gestalt techniques. In J. Fagan & I. L. Shepherd (Eds.), *Gestalt therapy now* (pp. 107–124). New York: Harper & Row.

Enron, J. B., & Lund, T. W. (1996). *Narrative solutions in brief therapy.* New York: Guilford Press.

Epston, D. (1992). Temper tantrum parties: Saving face, losing face, or going off your face! In D. Epston, & M. White. *Experience, contradiction, narrative & imagination: Selected papers of David Epston and Michael White.* South Australia: Dulwich Centre Publications.

Epston, D., & Maisel, R. (2006). The history of the archives of resistance: Anti-anorexia/anti-bulemia. Retrieved from http://www.narrativeapproaches.com/antianorexia%20folder/anti_anorexia_index.htm

Erikson, E. (1959). *Identity and the life cycle.* NY: International Universities Press.

Ernst, C., & Angst, J. (1983). *Birth order.* New York: Springer.

Espin, O. M. (1993). Feminist therapy: Not for or by white women only. *The Counseling Psychologist, 21,* 103–108.

Espin, O. M. (1994). Feminist approaches. In L. Comas-Diaz & B. Greene (Eds.), *Women of color: Integrating ethnic and gender identities in psychotherapy* (pp. 265–286). New York: Guilford Press.

Etchison, M., & Kleist, D. M. (2000). Review of narrative therapy: Research and utility. *The Family Journal: Counseling and Therapy for Couples and Families, 8,* 61–66.

European Brief Therapy Association. (2007). European Brief Therapy Association outcome study: Research definition description of the treatment. Retrieved January 5, 2007, from http://www.ebta.nu/page2/page30/page30.html

Evans, J., Hernon, J. Lewis, G., Araya, R., & Wolke, D.(2005). Negative self-schemas and the onset of depression in women: longitudinal study. *British Journal of Psychiatry, 186,* 302–307.

Evans, K. M., Kincade, E. A., Marbley, A. F., & Seem, S. R. (2005). Feminism and feminist therapy: Lessons from the past and hopes for the future. *Journal of Counseling and Development, 81,* 269–277.

Eysenck, H. J. (1952). The effects of psychotherapy: An evaluation. *Journal of Consulting Psychology, 16,* 319–321.

Eysenck, H. J. (1960). Learning theory and behavior therapy. In H. J. Eysenck (Ed.), *Behaviour therapy and the neuroses* (pp. 4–21). New York: Macmillan.

Eysenck, H. J., & Wilson, G. D. (1973). *The experimental study of Freudian theories.* London: Methuen.

Falicov, C. J., & Brudner-White, L. (1983). The shifting family triangle: The issue of cultural and contextual relativity. In J. C. Hansen & C. J. Falicov (Eds.), *Cultural perspectives in family therapy* (pp. 51–67). Rockville, MD: Aspen Systems.

Fernbacher, S. (2005). Cultural influences and considerations in gestalt therapy. In A. L. Woldt & S. M. Toman (Eds.), *Gestalt therapy: History, theory and practice* (pp. 117–132). Thousand Oaks, CA: Sage.

Ferster, C. B. (1983). Behavioral approaches to depression. In T. Millon (Ed.), *Theories of personality and psychopathology* (3rd ed., pp. 372–383). New York: Holt, Rinehart & Winston.

Fiebert, M. S. (1997). In and out of Freud's shadow: A chronology of Adler's relationship with Freud. *Journal of Individual Psychology, 53,* 241–269.

Field, N. P., & Horowitz, M. (1998). Applying an empty-chair monologue paradigm to examine unresolved grief. *Psychiatry, 61,* 279–287.

Fine, R. (1979). *A history of psychoanalysis.* New York: Columbia University Press.

Fisch, R. (1990). To thine own self be true. . . . Ethical issues in strategic therapy. In J. K. Zeig, S. G. Gilligan, et al. (Eds.), *Brief therapy: Myths, methods and metaphors* (pp. 429–436). New York: Brunner/Mazel.

Fischer, A. R., & Good, G. E. (2004). Women's feminist consciousness, anger, and psychological distress. *Journal of Counseling Psychology, 51,* 437–446.

Fischer, A. R., Jome, L. M., & Atkinson, D. R. (1998). Reconceptualizing multicultural counseling: Universal healing conditions in a culturally specific context. *The Counseling Psychologist, 26,* 525–588.

Fischer, C. T. (1991). Phenomenological-existential psychotherapy. In M. Hersen, A. E. Kazdin, & A. S. Bellack (Eds.), *The clinical psychology handbook,* (2nd ed., pp. 534–550). New York: Pergamon Press.

Fischer, C. T., McElwain, B., & DuBoise, J. T. (2000). Existential approaches to psychotherapy. In C. R. Snyder & R. E. Ingram (Eds.), *Handbook of psychological change* (pp. 243–257). New York: Wiley.

Fischer, S. K. (1993). A proposed Adlerian theoretical framework and intervention techniques for gay and lesbian couples. *Journal of Individual Psychology, 49,* 438–449.

Fishman, D. B., & Franks, C. M. (1997). The conceptual evolution of behavior therapy. In P. L. Wachtel & S. B. Messer (Eds.), *Theories of psychotherapy: Origins and evolution* (pp. 131–180). Washington, DC: American Psychological Association.

Fitzgerald, L., & Nutt, R. (1986). The Division 17 principles concerning the counseling/psychotherapy of women: Rationale and implementation. *The Counseling Psychologist, 14,* 180–216.

Flores, L. Y., Carrubba, M. D., Good, G. E. (2006). Feminism and Mexican American adolescent women: Examining the psychometric properties of two measures. *Hispanic Journal of Behavioral Sciences, 28,* 48–64.

Foa, E. B., & Franklin, M. E. (1999). Cognitive behavior therapy. In M. Hersen & A. S. Bellack (Eds.), *Handbook of comparative interventions for adult disorders* (pp. 359–377). New York: Wiley.

Fodor, I. G. (1985). Assertiveness training for the eighties: Moving beyond the personal. In L. B. Rosewater & L. E. A. Walker (Eds.), *Handbook of feminist therapy: Women's issues in psychotherapy* (pp. 257–265). New York: Springer.

Fonagy, P., & Target, M. (1996). Prediction of outcome of child psychoanalysis: A retrospective study of 763 cases at the Anna Freud Center. *Journal of the American Psychoanalytic Association, 44,* 27–77.

Forisha, B. L. (1981). Feminist psychotherapy II. In R. J. Corsini (Ed.), *Handbook of innovative psychotherapies* (pp. 315–332). New York: Wiley.

Fosshage, J. L. (2003). Contextualizing self psychology and relational psychoanalysis: Bi-directional influence and proposed synthesis. *Contemporary Psychoanalysis, 39,* 411–448.

Fowers, B. J., Applegate, B., Tredinnick, M., & Slusher, J. (1996). His and her individualisms? Sex bias and individualism in psychologists' responses to case vignettes. *Journal of Psychology, 130,* 159–174.

Frank, J. D., & Frank, J. B. (1991). Persuasion and healing: A comparative study of psychotherapy (3rd ed.). Baltimore: Johns Hopkins University Press.

Frankel, J. B. (1998). Are interpersonal and relational psychoanalysis the same? *Contemporary Psychoanalysis, 34,* 485–500.

Frankl, V. (1963). *Man's search for meaning: An introduction to logotherapy.* New York: Pocket Books.

Frankl, V. E. (1984). *Man's search for meaning.* New York: Pocket Books.

Franks, C. M., & Barbrack, C. R. (1990). Behavior therapy with adults: An integrative perspective for the nineties. In M. Hersen, A. E. Kazdin, & A. S. Bellack (Eds.), *The clinical psychology handbook* (2nd ed., pp. 551–566). New York: Pergamon Press.

Freedman, J., & Combs, G. (1996). Narrative therapy: The social construction of preferred realities. New York: Norton.

Freeman, A., Schrodt, G. R., Gilson, M., & Ludgate, J. W. (1993). Group cognitive therapy with inpatients. In J. H. Wright, M. E. Thase, A. T. Beck, & J. W. Ludgate (Eds.), *Cognitive therapy with inpatients: Developing a cognitive milieu* (pp. 121–153), New York: Guilford Press.

Freire, E. S., Koller, S. H., Piason, A., & da Silva, R. B. (2005). Person-centered therapy with impoverished, maltreated, and neglected children and adolescents in Brazil. *Journal of Mental Health Counseling, 27,* 225–237.

Freud, A. (1936). *The ego and the mechanisms of defense.* Madison, CT: International Universities Press.

Freud, A. (1974). Introduction to psychoanalysis: Lectures for child analysts and teachers. *In the Writings of Anna Freud* (p. 200). Oxford, England: International Universities Press.

Freud, S. (1909). Analysis of a phobia in a five-year-old boy. In *Collected papers of Sigmund Freud* (Vol. 3, pp. 49–295). New York: Basic Books.

Freud, S. (1910). The Origin and Development of Psychoanalysis. *American Journal of Psychology, 21,* 181–218. Retrieved from http://psychclassics.yorku.ca/Freud/Origin/ index.htm

Freud, S. (1949). *An outline of psycho-analysis.* New York: Norton. (Originally published 1940)

Freud, S. (1952). *A general introduction to psycho-analysis.* (J. Riviere, Trans.). New York: Washington Square. (Original work published 1920)

Freud, S. (1953). The interpretation of dreams. In J. Strachey (Ed. and Trans.), *The standard edition of the complete psychological works of Sigmund Freud, Vol. 4* (pp. 1–626). London: Hogarth. (Original work published 1900)

Freud, S. (1955a). Beyond the pleasure principle. In J. Strachey (Ed. and Trans.), *The standard edition of the complete psychological works of Sigmund Freud, Vol. 18* (pp. 1–66). London: Hogarth. (Original work published 1920)

Freud, S. (1955b). From the history of an infantile neurosis. In J. Strachey (Ed. and Trans.), *The standard edition of the complete psychological works of Sigmund Freud, Vol. 17* (pp. 7–122). London: Hogarth. (Original work published 1918)

Freud, S. (1957a). "Wild" psycho-analysis. In J. Strachey (Ed. and Trans.), *The standard edition of the complete psychological works of Sigmund Freud, Vol. 11* (pp. 219–227). London: Hogarth. (Original work published 1910)

Freud, S. (1957). Repression. In J. Strachey (Ed. and Trans.), *The standard edition of the complete psychological works of Sigmund Freud, Vol. 14* (pp. 146–158). London: Hogarth. (Original work published 1915)

Freud, S. (1958). Observations on transference love. In J. Strachey (Ed. and Trans.), *The standard edition of the complete psychological works of Sigmund Freud, Vol. 12* (pp. 157–171). London: Hogarth. (Original work published 1915)

Freud, S. (1958). On beginning the treatment. In J. Strachey (Ed. and Trans.), *The standard edition of the complete psychological works of Sigmund Freud, Vol. 12* (pp. 121–144). London: Hogarth. (Original work published 1913)

Freud, S. (1958). Recommendations to physicians practicing psycho-analysis. In J. Strachey (Ed. and Trans.), *The standard edition of the complete psychological works of Sigmund Freud, Vol. 12* (pp. 109–120). London: Hogarth. (Original work published 1912)

Freud, S. (1961). The ego and the id. In J. Strachey (Ed. and Trans.), *The standard edition of the complete psychological works of Sigmund Freud, Vol. 19* (pp. 13–59). London: Hogarth Press. (Original work published 1923)

Freud, S. (1961). Some psychological consequences of the anatomical distinction between the sexes. In J. Strachey (Ed. and Trans.), *The standard edition of the complete psychological works of Sigmund Freud, Vol. 19* (pp. 243–258). London: Hogarth. (Original work published 1925)

Freud, S. (1963). Introductory lectures on psycho-analysis, Part III. General theory of the neuroses. In J. Strachey (Ed. and Trans.), *The standard edition of the complete psychological works of Sigmund Freud, Vol. 16* (pp. 243–463). London: Hogarth. (Original work published 1917)

Freud, S. (1964a). New introductory lectures on psychoanalysis. In J. Strachey (Ed. and Trans.), *The standard edition of the complete psychological works of Sigmund Freud, Vol. 22* (pp. 3–182). London: Hogarth. (Original work published 1933)

Freud, S. (1964b). An outline of psychoanalysis. In J. Strachey (Ed. and Trans.), *The standard edition of the complete psychological works of Sigmund Freud, Vol. 23* (pp. 141–207). London: Hogarth. (Original work published 1940)

Freud, S. (1989a). An autobiographical study. In P. Gay (Ed. and Trans.), *The Freud reader*. New York: Norton. (Original work published 1925)

Freud, S. (1989b). Three essays on the theory of sexuality. In P. Gay (Ed. and Trans.), *The Freud reader*. New York: Norton. (Original work published 1924)

Friedan, B. (1963). *The feminine mystique*. New York: Norton.

Friedlander, M. L. (2001). Family therapy research: Science into practice, practice into science. In M. P. Nichols & R. C. Schwartz (Eds.), *Family therapy: Concepts and methods* (pp. 485–521). Boston: Allyn & Bacon.

Friedlander, M. L., Heatherington, L., & Marrs, A. (2000). Responding to blame in family therapy: A narrative/constructionist perspective. *American Journal of Family Therapy, 28*, 133–146.

Friedman, E. H. (1991). Bowen theory and therapy. In A. S. Gurman & D. P. Kniskern (Eds.), *Handbook of Family therapy* (Vol. 2, pp. 134–170). New York: Brunner/Mazel.

Friedman, N. (2003). Bringing together some early and later gestalt therapy theory concepts. *International Gestalt Journal, 26*, 59–78.

Fuller, G. B., & Fuller, D. L. (1999). Reality therapy approaches. In H. T. Prout & D. T. Brown (Eds.), *Counseling and psychotherapy with children and adolescents* (pp. 302–350). New York: Wiley.

Gaffan, E. A., Tsaousis, I., Kemp-Wheeler, S. M. (1995). Researcher allegiance and meta-analysis: The case of cognitive therapy for depression. *Journal of Consulting and Clinical Psychology, 63*, 966–980.

Galatzer-Levy, R. M., Bachrach, H., Skolnikoff, A., & Waldron, S. (2000). *Does psychoanalysis work?* New Haven, CT: Yale University Press.

Garfield, S. L. (1989). The client-therapist relationship in rational-emotive therapy. In M. E. Bernard & R. DiGiuseppe (Eds.), *Inside rational-emotive therapy*. New York: Academic Press.

Garfield, S. L. (1995). The client-therapist relationship in rational emotive therapy. *Journal of Rational-Emotive and Cognitive-Behavior Therapy, 13*, 101–116.

Gay, P. (1988). *Freud: A life for our time*. New York: Norton.

Gay, P. (Ed. and Trans.). (1989). *The Freud reader*. New York: Norton.

Geller, J. D., Norcross, J. C., & Orlinsky, D. E. (2005). The question of personal therapy. In J. D. Geller, J. C. Norcross, & D. E. Orlinsky (Eds.), *The psychotherapist's own psychotherapy* (pp. 3–11). New York: Oxford University Press.

Gendlin, E. T. (1990). The small steps of the therapy process: How they come and how to help them come. In G. Lietaer, J. Rombauts, & R. Van Balen (Eds.), *Client-centered and experiential psychotherapy in the nineties*. Louvain, Belgium: Leuven University Press.

Gendlin, E. T. (1996). *Focusing-oriented psychotherapy: A manual of the experiential method*. New York: Guilford Press.

Gentry, J. M., Winer, J. L., Sigelman, C. K., & Phillips, F. L. (1980). Adlerian lifestyle and vocational preference. *Journal of Individual Psychology, 36*, 80–86.

Ghent, E. (2001). Relations: Introduction to the first IARPP Conference. *IARPP E-News, 1(2)*. Retrieved from http://www.iarpp.org/html/resources/newsletter_1_1.cfm#article4.

Ghent, E. (2002). Relations: Introduction to the first IARPP Conference. *IARPP E-News, 1(2)*. Retrieved April 26, 2007, from http://www.iarpp.org/html/resources/newsletter_1_1.cfm# article4.

Gilbert, L. A. (1980). Feminist therapy. In A. M. Brodsky & R. T. Hare-Mustin (Eds.), *Women and psychotherapy* (pp. 245–265). New York: Guilford Press.

Gilbert, L. A., & Rader, J. (2007). Feminist counseling. In A. Rochlen (Ed.), *Applying counseling theories: An on-line, case based approach* (pp. 225–238). Upper Saddle River, NJ: Prentice Hall.

Gilbert, L. A., & Scher, M. (1999). *Gender and sex in counseling and psychotherapy*. Needham Heights, MA: Allyn & Bacon.

Gingerich, W. J., & Eisengart, S. (2000). Solution-focused brief therapy: A review of the outcome research. *Family Process, 39*, 477–577.

Glass, C. R., & Arnkoff, D. B. (1992). Behavior therapy. In D. K. Freedheim (Ed.), *History of psychotherapy: A century of change* (pp. 587–628). Washington, DC: American Psychological Association.

Glasser, W. (1965). *Reality therapy: A new approach to psychiatry*. New York: Harper & Row.

Glasser, W. (1968). *Schools without failure*. New York: HarperCollins.

Glasser, W. (1976). *Positive addiction*. New York: Harper & Row.

Glasser, W. (1990). *The quality school*. New York: HarperCollins.

Glasser, W. (1992a). Reality therapy. In J. K. Zeig (Ed.), *The evolution of psychotherapy: The second conference* (pp. 270–278). New York: Brunner/Mazel.

Glasser, W. (1992b). Response by Dr. Glasser. In J. K. Zeig (Ed.), *The evolution of psychotherapy: The second conference* (pp. 282–283). New York: Brunner/Mazel.

Glasser, W. (1998). *Choice theory: A new psychology of personal freedom*. New York: HarperCollins.

Glasser, W. (2000a). *Counseling with choice theory: The new reality therapy*. New York: HarperCollins.

Glasser, W. (2000b). *Reality therapy in the year 2000*. Paper presented at the Evolution of Psychotherapy Conference, Anaheim, CA. Retrieved from http://www.wglasserinst.com/rt2000.htm

Glasser, W. (2002). *Unhappy teenagers: A way for parents and teachers to reach them*. New York: HarperCollins.

Glasser, W. (2003). *Warning: Psychiatry can be hazardous to your mental health*. New York: HarperCollins.

Glasser, W. (2004). A new vision for counseling. *The Family Journal: Counseling for Couples and Families, 12*, 339–341.

Glasser, W. (n.d.). Focusing on chemistry instead of compassion: Psychiatry takes another step in the wrong direction. Retrieved November 23, 2001, from http://www.wglasser-inst.com/chemistry.htm

Glasser, W., & Glasser, C. (2000). *Getting together and staying together: Solving the mystery of marriage.* New York: HarperCollins.

Glasser, W., & Wubbolding, R. (1995). Reality therapy. In R. Corsini & D. Wedding (Eds.), *Current psychotherapies* (5th ed., pp. 293–321). Itasca, IL: Peacock.

Gloaguen, V., Cottraux, J., Cucherat, M., & Blackburn, I. M. (1998). A meta-analysis of the effects of cognitive therapy in depressed patients. *Journal of Affective Disorders, 49*, 59–72.

Gloaguen, V., Cottraux, J., Cucherat, M., & Blackburn, I. (1998). A meta-analysis of the effects of cognitive therapy in depressed patients. *Journal of Affective Disorders, 49*, 59–72.

Gochman, S. I., Allgood, B. A., & Geer, C. R. (1982). A look at today's behavior therapists. *Professional Psychology, 13*, 605–609.

Golann, S. (1988). On second-order family therapy. *Family Process, 27*, 51–65.

Gold, J., & Stricker, G. (2006). Introduction: An overview of psychotherapy integration. In G. Stricker & J. Gold (Eds.), *A Casebook of Psychotherapy Integration* (pp. 3–16). Washington, DC: American Psychological Association.

Goldfried, M. R., & Davison, G. C. (1994). *Clinical behavior therapy.* New York: Wiley.

Goldfried, M. R., & Norcross, J. C. (1995). Integrative and eclectic therapies in historical perspective. In B. Bongar & L. E. Beutler (Eds.), *Comprehensive textbook of psychotherapy* (pp. 254–273). New York: Oxford University Press.

Gonzales, J. E., Nelson, J. R., Gutkin, T. B., Saunders, A., Galloway, A., & Shwery, C. S. (2004). Rational Emotive Therapy with children and adolescents: A meta-analysis. *Journal of Emotional and Behavioral Disorders, 12*, 222–235.

Good, G. E., Gilbert, L., & Scher, M. (1990). Gender aware therapy: A synthesis of feminist therapy and knowledge about gender. *Journal of Counseling and Development, 68*, 376–380.

Good, G., Thoreson, R., & Shaughnessy, P. (1995). Substance use, confrontation of impaired colleagues, and psychological functioning among counseling psychologists: A national survey. *The Counseling Psychologist, 23*, 703–720.

Goodman, R. F., Morgan, A. V., Juriga, S., & Brown, E. J. (2004). Letting the story unfold: A case of client-centered therapy for childhood traumatic grief. *Harvard Review of Psychiatry, 12*, 199–212.

Goodyear, R. K., Murdock, N. L., Lichtenberg, J. W., McPherson, R. S., Koetting, K. K., & Petren, S. (in press). Stability and change in counseling psychologists' identities, roles, functions, and career satisfaction across fifteen years. *The Counseling Psychologist.*

Gossette, R. L., & O'Brien, R. M. (1992). The efficacy of rational emotive therapy in adults: Clinical fact or psychometric artifact? *Journal of Behavior Therapy and Experimental Psychiatry, 23*, 9–24.

Gould, R. A., Buckminster, S., Pollack, M. H., Otto, M. W., & Yap, L. (1997). Cognitive-behavioral and pharmacological treatment for social phobia: A meta-analysis. *Clinical Psychology, 4*, 291–306.

Grawe, K., Caspar, F., & Ambuhl, H. (1990). Differentielle psychotherapieforschung: Vier therapieformen. *Vergleich. Zeitschrift fur Klinische Psychologie, 19*, 287–376.

Gray, J. (1992). *Men are from Mars, women are from Venus.* New York: HarperCollins.

Grazioli, R., & Terry, D. J. (2000). The role of cognitive vulnerability and stress in the prediction of postpartum depressive symptomatology. *British Journal of Clinical Psychology, 39*, 329–347.

Greenan, D. E. (1996). Men and dependency: The treatment of a same-sex couple. In S. Minuchin, W. Lee, & G. M. Simon (Eds.), *Mastering family therapy: Journeys of growth and transformation* (pp. 175–192). New York: Wiley.

Greenberg, J., Pyszczynski, T., Soloman, S., Rosenblatt, A., Veeder, M., Kirkland, S., & Lyon, D. (1990). Evidence for terror management theory II: The effects of mortality salience on reactions to those who threaten or bolster the cultural worldview. *Journal of Personality and Social Psychology, 59*, 308–318.

Greenberg, J. R. (1999). Theoretical models and the analyst's neutrality. In S. A. Mitchell & L. Aron (Eds.), *Relational psychoanalysis: The emergence of a tradition* (pp. 133–152). Hillsdale, NJ: Analytic Press.

Greenberg, J. R., & Mitchell, S. A. (1983). *Object relations in psychoanalytic theory.* Cambridge, MA: Harvard University Press.

Greenberg, L. S., & Dompierre, L. M. (1981). Specific effects of gestalt two-chair dialogue on intrapsychic conflict in counseling. *Journal of Counseling Psychology, 28*, 288–294.

Greenberg, L., Elliott, R., & Lietaer, G. (1994). Research on experiential psychotherapies. In A. E. Bergin & S. L. Garfield (Eds.), *Handbook of psychotherapy and behavior change* (4th ed., pp. 509–539). New York: Wiley.

Greenberg, L. S., Elliott, R., Watson, J. C., & Bohart, A. C. (2001). Empathy. *Psychotherapy, 38*, 380–384.

Greenberg, L. S., & Foerster, F. S. (1996). Task analysis exemplified: The process of resolving unfinished business. *Journal of Consulting and Clinical Psychology, 64*, 439–446. Retrieved from http://spider.apa.org/ftdocs/ccp/1996/june/ccp6434390.html

Greenberg, L. S., Goldman, R., & Angus, L. (2001). The York II psychotherapy study on experiential therapy of depression. Unpublished manuscript, York University. Cited in Elliot et al., 2004.

Greenberg, L. S., & Rice, L. N. (1997). Humanistic approaches to psychotherapy. In P. L. Wachtel & S. B. Messer (Eds.), *Theories of psychotherapy: Origins and evolution* (pp. 97–130). Washington, DC: American Psychological Association.

Greenberg, L. S., Rice, L. N., Rennie, D. L., & Toukmanian, S. G. (1991). York University psychotherapy research program. In L. E. Beutler & M. Crago (Eds.), *Psychotherapy research: An international review of programmatic studies* (pp. 175–182). Washington, DC: American Psychological Association.

Greenberg, L. S., & Watson, J. C. (1998). Experiential therapy of depression: Differential effects of client-centered relationship conditions and active experiential interventions. *Psychotherapy Research, 8,* 210–224.

Greenberg, L. S., Watson, J. C., & Lietaer, G. (1998). *Handbook of experiential psychotherapy.* New York: Guilford Press.

Greene, G. J., Hamilton, N., & Rolling, M. (1986). Differentiation of self and psychiatric diagnosis: An empirical study. *Family Therapy, 13* (2), 187–194.

Greene, G. J., & Mabee, T. F. (1992). Differentiation of self and marital adjustment of clinical and nonclinical spouses. In B. J. Brothers (Ed.), *Couples therapy, multiple perspectives: In search of universal threads* (pp. 133–151). New York: Haworth Press.

Greever, K. B., Tseng, M. S., & Friedland, B. U. (1973). Development of the Social Interest Index. *Journal of Consulting and Clinical Psychology, 41,* 454–458.

Grieger, R. (1989). A client's guide to rational-emotive therapy (RET). In W. Dryden & P. Trower (Eds.), *Cognitive psychotherapy: Stasis and change.* London: Cassel.

Grosskurth, P. (1986). *Melanie Klein: Her world and her work.* Cambridge, MA: Harvard University Press.

Guerin, K., & Guerin, P. (2002). Bowenian family therapy. In J. Carlson & D. Kjos (Eds.), *Theories and strategies of family therapy* (pp. 126–157). Boston: Allyn & Bacon.

Guerin, P. J., & Chabot, D. R. (1995). Development of family systems theory. In D. K. Freedheim (Ed.), *History of psychotherapy: A century of change* (pp. 225–260). Washington, DC: American Psychological Association.

Guerin, P. J., Fogarty, T. F., Fay, L. F. & Kautto. J. G. (1996). *Working with relationship triangles: The one-two-three of psychotherapy.* New York: Guilford Press.

Gurlin, F., & Guzzetta, R. A. (1977). Existentialism: Toward a theory of psychotherapy for women. *Psychotherapy: Theory, Research, and Practice, 14,* 262–266.

Gurman, A. S., & Fraenkel, P. (2002). The history of couple therapy: A millennial review. *Family Process, 41,* 199–260.

Gurman, A. S., & Kniskern, D. P. (1981). *Handbook of family therapy.* New York: Brunner/Mazel.

Guterman, J. T. (2006). *Mastering the art of Solution-focused counseling.* Alexandria, VA: American Counseling Association.

Guterman, J. T., & Leite, N. (2006). Solution-focused counseling for clients with religious and spiritual concerns. *Counseling and Values, 51,* 39–52.

Haaga, D. A., Dyck, M. J., & Ernst, D. (1991). Empirical status of cognitive theory of depression. *Psychological Bulletin, 110,* 215–236.

Haaga, D. A. F., & Davison, G. C. (1989). Slow progress in rational-emotive therapy outcome research: Etiology and treatment. *Cognitive Therapy and Research, 13,* 493–508.

Haaga, D. A. F., & Davison, G. C. (1993). An appraisal of rational-emotive therapy. *Journal of Consulting and Clinical Psychology, 61,* 215–220.

Haber, R. (2002). Virginia Satir: An integrated, humanistic approach. *Contemporary Family Therapy, 24* (1), 23–34.

Hackett, G., Enns, C. Z., & Zetzer, H. A. (1992). Reactions of women to nonsexist and feminist counseling: Effects of counselor orientation and mode of information delivery. *Journal of Counseling Psychology, 39,* 321–330.

Hagan, K. L. (1993). *Fugitive information: Essays from a feminist hothead.* New York: HarperCollins.

Hajzler, D. J., & Bernard, M. E. (1991). A review of rational-emotive education outcome studies. *School Psychology Quarterly, 6* (1), 27–49.

Haldeman, D. C. (1994). The practice and ethics of sexual orientation conversion therapy. *Journal of Consulting and Clinical Psychology, 62,* 221–227.

Haley, J. (1963). *Strategies of psychotherapy.* New York: Grune & Stratton.

Haley, J. (1969). *The power tactics of Jesus Christ and other stories.* New York: Grossman.

Haley, J. (1973). *Uncommon therapy: The psychiatric techniques of Milton H. Erickson, M. D.* New York: Norton.

Haley, J. (1980). *Leaving home: The therapy of disturbed young people.* New York: McGraw-Hill.

Haley, J. (1984). *Ordeal therapy.* San Francisco: Jossey-Bass.

Haley, J. (1987). *Problem-solving therapy* (2nd ed.). San Francisco: Jossey-Bass.

Haley, J., & Madanes, C. (1981). Dimensions of family therapy. In C. Madanes, *Strategic family therapy* (pp. 1–18). San Francisco: Jossey-Bass.

Haley, J., & Richeport-Haley, M. (2003). *The art of strategic therapy.* New York: Brunner-Routledge.

Hall, C. S. (1954). *A primer of Freudian psychology.* New York: Mentor.

Hamilton, N. G. (1988). *Self and others: Object relations.* Northvale, NJ: Jason Aronson.

Hamilton, N. G. (1989). A critical review of object relations. *American Journal of Psychiatry, 146* (12), 1552–1560.

Hampton, B. R. (1991). Ethical issues in the practice of strategic therapy. *Psychotherapy in Private Practice, 9* (2), 47–59.

Hare-Mustin, R. T. (1994). Discourses in the mirrored room: A postmodern analysis of therapy. *Family Process, 33,* 19–35.

Harman, R. L. (Ed.). (1990). *Gestalt therapy discussions with the masters.* Springfield, IL: Charles C. Thomas.

Harrington, N. (2006). Frustration intolerance beliefs: Their relationship with depression, anxiety, and anger, in a clinical population. *Cognitive Therapy and Research, 30,* 699–709.

Harris, S., Davies, M. F., & Dryden, W. (2006). An experimental test of a core REBT hypothesis: Evidence that irrational beliefs lead to physiological as well as psychological arousal. *Journal of Rational Emotive and Cognitive-Behavior Therapy, 24,* 101–111.

Hartmann, H. (1939). Ego psychology and the problem of adaptation. NY: International Universities Press

Harvey, D. M., Curry, C. J., & Bray, J. H. (1991). Individuation and intimacy in intergenerational relationships and health patterns across two generations. *Journal of Family Psychology, 5,* 204–236.

Harvey, V. S., & Retter, K. (1995). The development of the basic needs survey. *Journal of Reality Therapy, 15* (1), 76–80.

Hayes, S. C. (2002). Acceptance, mindfulness and science. *Clinical Psychology, 9*, 101–106.

Hayes, S. C., Luoma, J. B., Bond, F. W., Masuda, A., & Lillis, J. (2006). Acceptance and commitment therapy: Model, processes and outcomes. *Behavior Research and Therapy, 44*, 1–25.

Hayes, S. C., Strosahl, K. D., & Wilson, K. G. (1999). *Acceptance and commitment therapy. An experiential approach to behavior change.* New York: Guilford Press.

Hays, P. A., & Iwamasa, G. Y. (2006). *Culturally responsive cognitive-behavioral therapy.* Washington, DC: American Psychological Association.

Hayward, M. (2003). Critiques of narrative therapy: A personal response. *ANZIFT, 24*, 183–189.

Henry, W. P., Strupp, H. H., Schacht, T. E., & Gaston, L. (1994). Psychodynamic approaches. In A. E. Bergin & S. L. Garfield (Eds.), *Handbook of psychotherapy and behavior change* (pp. 467–508). New York: Wiley.

Hensley, P. L., Nadiga, D., & Uhlenhuth, E. H. (2004). Long-term effectiveness of cognitive therapy in major depressive disorder. *Depression and Anxiety, 20*, 1–7.

Heppner, P. P., Kivlighan, D. M., Jr., & Wampold, B. E. (2007). *Research design in counseling* (3rd ed.) Pacific Grove, CA: Thompson-Brooks/Cole.

Herrington, A. N., Matheny, K. B., Curlette, W. L., McCarthy, C. J., & Penick, J. (2005). Lifestyles, coping resources, and negative life events as predictors of emotional distress in university women. *Journal of Individual Psychology, 61*, 343–364.

Hettema, J., Steele, J., & Miller, W. R. (2005). Motivational interviewing. *Annual Review of Clinical psychology, 1*, 91–111.

Hill, C. E. (2004). *Helping skills: Facilitating exploration, insight, and action.* Washington, DC: American Psychological Association.

Hill, C. E., & Corbett, M. M. (1993). A perspective on the history of process and outcome research in counseling psychology. *Journal of Counseling Psychology, 30*, 3–24.

Hoffman, E. (1994). *The drive for self.* Reading, MA: Addison-Wesley.

Hoffman, S. G. (2006). The importance of culture in cognitive and behavioral practice. *Cognitive and Behavioral Practice, 13*, 243–245.

Holdstock, L. (1990). Can client-centered therapy transcend its monocultural roots? In G. Lietaer, J. Rombauts, & R. Van Balen (Eds.), *Client-centered and experiential psychotherapy in the nineties.* Louvain, Belgium: Leuven University Press.

Hollon, S. D., & Kendall, P. C. (1980). Cognitive self-statements in depression. Clinical validation of an automatic thoughts questionnaire. *Cognitive Therapy and Research, 4*, 383–395.

Hollon, S. D., Shelton, R. D., & Davis, D. D. (1993). Cognitive therapy for depression: Conceptual issues and clinical efficacy. *Journal of Consulting and Clinical Psychology, 61*, 270–275.

Horney, K. (1932). The dread of women. *International Journal of Psychoanalysis, 13*, 348–360.

Horney, K. (1967). The distrust between the sexes. In H. Kelman (Ed.), *Feminine psychology.* New York: Norton. (Originally published 1930).

Howatt, W. A. (2001). The evolution of reality therapy to choice theory. *International Journal of Reality Therapy, 21*, 7–11.

Hoyt, M. F. (Ed.) *The handbook of constructive therapies: Innovative approaches from leading practitioners.* San Francisco Jossey-Bass.

Hudson, P. O., & O'Hanlon, W. H. (1991). *Rewriting love stories.* New York: Norton.

Hunter, P., & Kelso, E. N. (1985). Feminist behavior therapy. *The Behavior Therapist, 10*, 201–204.

Hycner, R. H. (1987). An interview with Erving and Miriam Polster: The dialogical dimension in gestalt therapy. *The Gestalt Journal, 10* (2), 27–66.

Hyde, J. S. (2005). The gender similarities hypothesis. *American Psychologist, 60*, 581–592.

Imber-Black, E. (1990). Multiple embedded systems. In M. P. Mirkin (Ed.), *The social and political contexts of family therapy* (pp. 3–18). Boston: Allyn & Bacon.

Ivey, A. E., D'Andrea, M., Ivey, M. B., & Simek-Morgan, L. (2002). *Counseling and psychotherapy: A multicultural perspective.* Boston: Allyn and Bacon.

Ivey, A., & Ivey, M. B. (2007). *Intentional interviewing and counseling: Facilitating client development in a multicultural society.* Belmont CA: Wadsworth.

Iwata, B A., Kahng, S. W., Wallace, M. D., & Lindberg, J. S. (2000). The functional analysis model of behavioral assessment. In J. Austin & J. E. Carr (Eds.), *Handbook of applied behavior analysis* (pp. 61–90). Reno, NV: Context.

Jacobson, E. (1929). *Progressive relaxation.* Chicago: University of Chicago Press.

Jacobson, N. S. (1997). Advancing behavior therapy means advancing behaviorism. *Behavior Therapy, 28*, 629–632.

Jacobvitz, D. B., & Bush, N. F. (1996). Reconstructions of family relationships: Parent-child alliances, personal distress, and self-esteem. *Developmental Psychology, 32*, 732–743.

Jakes, S. C., & Rhodes, J. E. (2003). The effect of different components of psychological therapy on people with delusions: Five experimental single cases. *Clinical Psychology and Psychotherapy, 10*, 302–315.

Jakubowski, P. A. (1977a). Assertive behavior and clinical problems of women. In E. I. Rawlings & D. K. Carter (Eds.), *Psychotherapy for women: Treatment toward equality* (pp. 147–167). Springfield, IL: Charles C. Thomas.

Jakubowski, P. A. (1977b). Self-assertion training procedures for women. In E. I. Rawlings & D. K. Carter (Eds.), *Psychotherapy for women: Treatment toward equality* (pp. 168–190). Springfield, IL: Charles C. Thomas.

Jamison, C., & Scogin, F. (1995). The outcome of cognitive bibliotherapy with depressed adults. *Journal of Consulting and Clinical Psychology, 63,* 644–650.

Jensen, J. P., Bergin, A. E., & Greaves, D. W. (1990). The meaning of eclecticism: New survey and analysis of components. *Professional Psychology: Research and Practice, 21,* 124–130.

Johansen, T. M. (2005). Applying individual psychology to work with clients of the Islamic faith. *Journal of Individual Psychology, 61,* 174–184.

Johnson, G. B. (1966). Penis envy? Or pencil needing? *Psychological Reports, 19,* 758.

Johnson, P., & Buboltz, W. C. (2000). Differentiation of self and psychological reactance. *Contemporary Family Therapy, 22* (1), 91–102.

Johnson, P., Smith, A. J., & Nelson, M. D. (2003). Predictors of social interest in young adults. *Journal of Individual Psychology, 59,* 281–292.

Johnson, T. W., & Colucci, P. (1999). Lesbians, gay men, and the family life cycle. In B. Carter & M. McGoldrick (Eds.), *The expanded family life cycle* (3rd ed., pp. 346–361). Boston: Allyn & Bacon.

Johnson, T. W., & Colucci, P. (2005). Lesbians, gay men, and the family life cycle. In B. Carter & M. McGoldrick (Eds.), *The expanded family life cycle* (3rd ed. pp. 346–361). New York: Allyn & Bacon.

Johnson, W. R., & Smith, E. W. L. (1997). Gestalt empty-chair dialogue versus systematic desensitization in the treatment of phobia. *Gestalt Review, 1* (2), 150–162.

Jones, E. (1927). Symposium on child-analysis. *International Journal of Psychoanalysis, 8,* 387–391.

Jones, J., & Trower, P. (2004). Irrational and evaluative beliefs in individuals with anger disorders. *Journal of Rational Emotive and Cognitive-Behavior Therapy, 22,* 153–169.

Jones, M. C. (1960a). The elimination of children's fears. In H. J. Eysenck (Ed.), *Behaviour therapy and the neuroses* (pp. 38–44). New York: Macmillan. (Reprinted from *Journal of Experimental Psychology, 1924, 7,* 383–390)

Jones, M. C. (1960b). A laboratory study of fear: The case of Peter. In H. Eysenck (Ed.), *Behaviour therapy and the neuroses* (pp. 45–51). New York: Macmillan. (Reprinted from *Pedagogical Seminary, 1924, 31,* 308–315).

Jordan, E. W., Whiteside, M. M., & Manaster, G. J. (1982). A practical and effective research measure of birth order. *Journal of Individual Psychology, 38,* 253–260.

Jordan, J. V., & Hartling, L. M. (2002). New developments in relational-cultural theory. In M. Ballou & L. S. Brown (Eds.), *Rethinking mental health and disorder: Feminist perspectives* (pp. 48–70). New York: Guilford Press.

Josefowitz, N., & Myran, D. (2005). Towards a person-centred cognitive behavior therapy. *Counselling Psychology Quarterly, 18,* 329–336.

Juntunen, C. L., Atkinson, D. R., Reyes, C., & Gutierrez, M. (1994). Feminist identity and feminist therapy behaviors of women psychotherapists. *Psychotherapy, 31,* 327–333.

Kal, E. F. (1994). Reaction to "Applying psychometric principles to the clinical use of early recollections" by D. Russell Bishop. *Journal of Individual Psychology, 50,* 256–261.

Kanfer, F. H., & Karoly, P. (1972). Self-control: A behavioristic excursion into the lion's den. *Behavior Therapy, 3,* 398–416.

Kantrowitz, R. E., & Ballou, M. (1992). A feminist critique of cognitive-behavioral therapy. In L. S. Brown & M. Ballou (Eds.), *Personality and psychopathology: Feminist reappraisals* (pp. 70–87). New York: Guilford Press.

Kanus, W., & Wessler, R. L. (1976). Rational-emotive problem simulation. *Rational Living, 11* (2), 8–11.

Kaplan, A. G., & Yasinski, L. (1980). Psychodynamic perspectives. In A. M. Brodsky & R. T. Hare-Mustin (Eds.), *Women and psychotherapy* (pp.191–216). New York: Guilford Press.

Kaplan, M. (1983). A woman's view of the DSM-III. *American Psychologist, 20,* 786–792.

Kareem, J., & Littlewood, R. (1992). *Intercultural therapy: Themes, interpretations and practice.* London: Blackwell Science.

Karon, B. P., & Widener, A. J. (1995). Psychodynamic therapies in historical perspective: "Nothing human do I consider alien to me." In B. Bongar & L. E. Beutler (Eds.), *Comprehensive textbook of psychotherapy* (pp. 2–47).

Karon, B. P., & Widener, A. J. (1996). Psychodynamic therapies in historical perspective. In B. Bonger & L. E. Beutler (Eds.), *Comprehensive textbook of psychotherapy* (pp. 24–47). New York: Oxford University Press.

Kasler, J., & Nevo, O. (2005). Early recollections as predictors of study area choice. *Journal of Individual Psychology, 61,* 217–232.

Kassoff, B. (2004). The queering of relational psychoanalysis: Who's topping whom? *Journal of Lesbian Studies, 8,* 159–176.

Kazdin, A. E. (1978). *History of behavior modification.* Baltimore: University Park Press.

Kazdin, A. E. (2001). *Behavior modification in applied settings* (6th ed.). Belmont, CA: Wadsworth.

Kearney, A. B. (1994). The use of covert conditioning in the treatment of obsessive compulsive disorder. In J. R. Cautela & A. J. Kearney (Eds.), *Covert conditioning casebook* (pp. 22–37). Pacific Grove, CA: Brooks/Cole.

Keene, K. K., & Wheeler, M. S. (1994). Substance use in college freshmen and Adlerian life-style themes. *Journal of Individual Psychology, 50,* 97–109.

Keijsers, G. P. J., Schaap, C. P. D. R., & Hoogduin, C. A. L. (2000). The impact of interpersonal patient and therapist behavior on outcome in cognitive-behavior therapy: A review of empirical studies. *Behavior Modification, 24,* 264–297.

Keller, J. (2002). Blatant stereotype threat and women's math performance: Self-handicapping as a strategic means to cope with obtrusive negative performance expectations. *Sex Roles, 47,* 193–198.

Kellogg, S. (2004). Dialogical encounters: Contemporary perspectives on "chairwork" in psychotherapy. *Psychotherapy: Theory, Research, Practice, Training, 41,* 310–320.

Kerig, P. K. (1995). Triangles in the family circle: Effects of family structure on marriage, parenting, and child adjustment. *Journal of Family Psychology, 9,* 28–43.

Kern, R. M. (1976). Life Style Inventory Questionnaire. Atlanta: Georgia State University.

Kern, R., Gfroerer, K., Summers, Y., Curlette, W., & Matheny, K. (1996). Life-style, personality and stress coping. *Journal of Individual Psychology, 52,* 42–53.

Kernberg, O. F. (1984). *Severe personality disorders: Psychotherapeutic strategies.* New Haven, CT: Yale University Press.

Kernberg, O. F. (1996). The analyst's authority in the psychoanalytic situation. *Psychoanalytic Quarterly, 65,* 137–157.

Kernberg, O. F. (2001). Recent developments in the technical approaches of the English-langage psychoanalytic schools. *Psychoanlaytic Quarterly, LXX,* 519–547.

Kernberg, O. F. (2005). The influence of Joseph Sandler's work on contemporary psychoanalysis. *Psychoanalytic Inquiry, 25,* 173–183.

Kerr, M. E. (1981). Family systems theory and therapy. In A. S. Gurman & D. P. Kniskern (Eds.), *Handbook of family therapy* (pp. 226–264.). New York: Brunner/Mazel.

Kerr, M. E. (1984). Theoretical base for differentiation of self in one's family of origin. *The Clinical Supervisor, 2*(2), 3–36.

Kerr, M. E., & Bowen, M. (1988). *Family evaluation: An approach based on Bowen theory.* New York: Norton.

Kim, J. S. (2006). Examining the effectiveness of solution-focused brief therapy: A meta-analysis using random effects modeling. Cited by Macdonald, A. J. (2007). Solution-focused therapy evaluation list. Retrieved March 23, 2007, from http://www.psychsft.freeserve.co.uk/sfb.html

Kim, K. (2002). The effect of a reality therapy program on the responsibility for elementary school children in Korea. *International Journal of Reality Therapy, 22,* 30–33.

Kim, J. (2006). The effect of a bullying prevention program on responsibility and victimization of bullied children in Korea. *International Journal of Reality Therapy, 26,* 4–8.

Kindler, A. (2007). Self psychology. In A. B. Rochlen (Ed.), *Applying counseling theories: An on-line, case-based approach* (pp. 53–74). Upple Saddle River, NJ: Prentice-Hall.

Kirsch, I., & Lynn, S. J. (1999). Automaticity in clinical psychology. *American Psychologist, 54,* 504–515.

Kirschenbaum, H. (2004). Carl Rogers's life and work: An assessment on the 100th anniversary of his birth. *Journal of Counseling and Development, 82,* 116–124.

Kirschenbaum, H., & Henderson, V. L. (Eds.). (1989). *The Carl Rogers reader.* Boston: Houghton Mifflin.

Kirschenbaum, H., & Jourdan, A. (2005). The current status of Carl Rogers and the person-centered approach. *Psychotherapy: Theory, Research, Practice, Training, 42,* 37–51.

Klein, M. (1926). The psychological principles of early analysis. In *The Writings of Melanie Klein,* London: Hogarth Press, 1981, Vol. 1, 128–138.

Klein, M. (1927). Symposium on Child-Analysis. *International Journal of Psychoanalysis, 8,* 339–370.

Klein, M. (1952). The origins of transference. *International Journal of Psycho-analysis, 33,* 433–438.

Klein, M. H., Michels, J. L., Kolden, G. G., & Chisholm-Stockard, S. (2001). Congruence or genuineness. *Psychotherapy, 38,* 396–400.

Klein, M., Riviere, J., Searl, N., Sharpe, E., Glover, E., & Jones, E. (1927). Symposium of Child Analysis, *International Journal of Psychoanalysis, 8,* 339–391.

Kleiner, F. B. (1979). Commentary on Albert Ellis' article. In A. Ellis & J. M. Whitley (Eds.), *Theoretical and empirical foundations of rational-emotive therapy* (pp. 188–192). Monterey, CA: Brooks/Cole.

Klerman, G. L., & Weissman, M. M. (1993). Interpersonal psychotherapy for depression: Background and concepts. In G. L. Klerman & M. M. Weissman (Eds.), *New applications of interpersonal psychotherapy.* Washington, DC: American Psychiatric Association Press.

Klerman, G. L., Weissman, M. M., Rounsaville, B. J., & Chevron, E. S. (1984). *Interpersonal theory of depression.* New York: Basic Books.

Kline, P. (1972). *Fact and fantasy in Freudian theory.* London: Methuen. (American edition published by Harper & Row)

Kluft, R. P., Loftus, & E. F. (2007). Issue 8: Are Repressed Memories Real? In Nier, Jason A. (2007). *Taking sides: Clashing views in social psychology* (2nd ed., pp. 152–171). New York: McGraw-Hill.

Knauth, D. G., Skowron, E. A., & Escobar, M. (2006). Effect of differentiation of self on adolescent risk behavior. *Nursing Research, 55,* 336–345.

Koenig, A. M., & Eagly, A. H. (2005). Stereotype threat in men on a test of social sensitivity. *Sex Roles, 52,* 489–496.

Kohut, H. (1977). *The restoration of the self.* New York: International Universities Press.

Kohut, H. (1984). In A. Goldberg & P. Stepansky (Eds.), *How does analysis cure?* Chicago: The University of Chicago Press.

Kolenberg, R. J., & Tsai, M. (1995). Functional analytic psychotherapy: A behavior approach to intensive treatment. In W. O'Donohue & L. Krasner (Eds.), *Theories of behavior therapy: Exploring behavioral change.* Washington, DC: American Psychological Association.

Kosek, R. B. (1998). Self-differentiation within couples. *Psychological Reports, 83,* 275–279.

Kovacs, M., & Beck, A. T. (1978). Maladaptive cognitive structures in depression. *The American Journal of Psychiatry, 135,* 525–533.

Krebs, L. L. (1986). Current research on theoretically based parenting programs. *Journal of Individual Psychology, 42,* 375–387.

Kuehnel, J. M., & Liberman, R. P. (1986). Behavior modification. In I. L. Kutash & A. Wolf (Eds.), *Psychotherapist's casebook* (pp. 240–262). San Francisco: Jossey-Bass.

Kuhn, T. S. (1970). *The structure of scientific revolutions* (2nd ed.). Chicago: University of Chicago Press.

Kupers, T. A. (1997). The politics of psychiatry: Gender and sexual preference in DSM-IV. In M. R. Walsh (Ed.), *Women, men, and gender: Ongoing debates* (pp. 340–347). New Haven, CT: Yale University Press.

LaFond, B. A. G. (2000). Glasser's reality therapy approach to relationships: Validation of a choice theory basic needs scale. *Dissertation Abstracts International, 60* (7–B), 3615B.

Laird, T. G., & Shelton, A. J. (2006). From an Adlerian perspective: Birth order, dependency, and binge drinking on a historically Black university campus. *Journal of Individual Psychology, 62,* 3–17.

Lambert, M. J., & Bergin, A. E. (1994). The effectiveness of psychotherapy. In A. E. Bergin & S. L. Garfield (Eds.), *Handbook of psychotherapy and behavior change* (pp. 143–189). New York: Wiley.

Lambert, M. J., & Ogles, B. M. (2004). The efficacy and effectiveness of psychotherapy. In M. J. Lambert (Ed.), *Bergin and Garfield's Handbook of Psychotherapy and Behavior Change* (5th Ed. pp. 139–193) New York: Wiley.

Lantz, J., & Gregoire, T. (2000a). Existential psychotherapy with couples facing breast cancer: A twenty year report. *Contemporary Family Therapy, 22,* 315–327.

Lantz, J., & Gregoire, T. (2000b). Existential psychotherapy with Vietnam veteran couples: A twenty-five year report. *Contemporary Family Therapy, 22,* 19–37.

Lantz, J., & Raiz, L. (2004). Existential psychotherapy with older adult couples: A five-year treatment report. *Clinical Gerontologist, 27* (3), 39–54.

Last, C. G., & Hersen, M. (1994). Clinical considerations. In C. G. Last & M. Hersen (Eds.), *Adult behavior therapy casebook* (pp. 3–12). New York: Plenum Press.

Lawrence, D. H. (2004). The effects of reality therapy group counseling on the self-determination of persons with developmental disabilities. *International Journal of Reality Therapy, 23,* 9–15.

Lawson, D. M., & Brossart, D. F. (2004). The association between current intergenerational family relationships and sibling structure. *Journal of Counseling and Development, 82,* 472–482.

Lazarus, A. A. (1989). The practice of rational-emotive therapy. In M. E. Bernard & R. DiGiuseppe (Eds.), *Inside rational-emotive therapy: A critical appraisal of the theory and therapy of Albert Ellis* (pp. 95–112). San Diego, CA: Academic Press.

Lazarus, A. A. (1996). *Behavior therapy and beyond.* Northvale, NJ: Jason Aronson.

Lazarus, A. A. (2000). Multimodal strategies with adults. In S. Carlson & L. Sperry (Eds.), *Brief therapy with individuals and couples* (pp. 106–124). Phoenix, AZ: Zeig, Tucker & Theisen.

Lazarus, A. (2006). Multimodal therapy: A seven-point integration. In G. Stricker & J. Gold (Eds.), *A Casebook of Psychotherapy Integration* (pp. 17–28). Washington, DC: American Psychological Association.

Leahy, R. L. (2004) (Ed.). *Contemporary cognitive therapy: Theory, research, and practice.* New York: Guilford Press.

Leahy, R. L., Beck, J., & Beck, A. T. (2005). Cognitive therapy for the personality disorders. In S. Strack (Ed.) *Handbook of personology and psychopathology* (pp. 442–461). New York: Wiley.

Leak, G. K. (2006). An empirical assessment of the relationship between social interest and spirituality. *Journal of Individual Psychology, 62,* 59–69.

Leary, T. F. (1957). *Interpersonal diagnosis of personality.* New York: Ronald.

Lee, M. Y. (1997). A study of solution-focused brief family therapy: Outcomes and issues. *The American Journal of Family Therapy, 5,* 3–17.

Lee, M. Y., & Mjelde-Mossey, L. (2004). Cultural dissonance among generations: A solution-focused approach with east Asian elders and their families. *Journal of Marital and Family Therapy, 30,* 497–513.

Leiberman, M. A., Yalom, I. D., & Miles, M. B. (1973). *Encounter groups: First facts.* New York: Basic Books.

Lejuez, C. W., Hopko, D. R., Levine, S., Gholkar, R., & Collins, L. M. (2006). The therapeutic alliance in behavior therapy. *Psychotherapy: Theory, Research, Practice, Training, 42,* 456–468.

Lemoire, S. J., & Chen, C. P. (2005). Applying person-centered counseling to sexual minority adolescents. *Journal of Counseling and Development, 83,* 146–154.

Leonsky, E. M., Kaplan, N. R., & Kaplan, M. L. (1986). Operationalizing gestalt therapy's processes of experiential organization. *Psychotherapy, 23,* 41–49.

Lerner, H. G. (1988). Is family systems theory really systemic? A feminist communication. In L. Braverman (Ed.), *A guide to feminist family therapy* (pp. 47–63). New York: Harrington Park Press.

Leuzinger-Bohleber, M., & Target, M. (2002) (Eds.), *Outcomes of psychoanalytic treatment: Perspectives for therapists and researchers.* New York: Brunner-Routledge.

Levin, R. B. (1966). An empirical test of the female castration complex. *Journal of Abnormal Psychology, 71,* 181–188.

Levitsky, A., & Perls, F. S. (1970). The rules and games of gestalt therapy. In J. Fagan & I. L. Shepherd (Eds.), *Gestalt therapy now* (pp. 140–149). New York: Harper & Row.

Levy, K. N., Clarkin, J. F., Yeomans, F. E., Scott, L. N., Wasserman, R. H., & Kernberg, O. F. (2006). The mechanism of change in the treatment of borderline personality disorder with transference focused psychotherapy. *Journal of Clinical Psychology, 62,* 481–501.

Lewis, T. F., & Osborn, C. J. (2004). An exploration of Adlerian lifestyle themes and alcohol-related behaviors among college students. *Journal of Addictions & Offender Counseling, 25,* 2–17.

Lieberman, M. A., Yalom, I. D., Miles, M. B. (1973). *Encounter Groups: First Facts*. New York: Basic Books.

Lietaer, G. (1990). The client-centered approach after the Wisconsin Project: A personal view on its evolution. In G. Lietaer, J. Rombauts, & R. Van Balen (Eds.), *Client–centered and experiential psychotherapy in the nineties*. Louvain, Belgium: Leuven University Press.

Lijtmaer, R. M. (1998). Psychotherapy with Latina women. *Feminism & Psychology, 8*, 537–543.

Linehan, M. M. (1993). *Cognitive-behavioral treatment of borderline personality disorder*. New York: Guilford Press.

Linnenberg, D. M. (2006). Thoughts on reality therapy from a pro-feminist perspective. *International Journal of Reality Therapy, 26*, 23–26.

Loeschen, S. (1998). *Systematic training in the skills of Virginia Satir*. Pacific Grove, CA: Brooks/Cole.

Loewald, H. W. (1989). On the therapeutic action of psychoanalysis. In *Papers on psychoanalysis*. New Haven, CT: Yale University Press.

Lock, A., Epston, D., Maisael, R., deFaria, N. (2005). Resisting anorexia/bulimia: Foucauldian perspectives in narrative therapy. *British Journal of Guidance and Counseling, 33*, 315–322.

Loftus, E. F. (1993). The reality of repressed memories. *American Psychologist, 48*, 518–537.

Loftus, E. F., & Ketcham, K. (1994). *The myth of repressed memory*. New York: St. Martin's Press.

Logan, B. (2002). Weaving new stories over the phone: A narrative approach to a gay switchboard. In D. Dengborough (Ed.), *Queer counseling and narrative practice* (pp. 138–159). Adelaide, South Australia: Dulwich Centre Publications.

Logan, E., Kern, R., Curlette, W., & Trad, A. (1993). Couples adjustment, life-style similarity and social interest. *Journal of Individual Psychology, 49*, 456–467.

London, P. (1986). *The modes and morals of psychotherapy* (2nd ed.). New York: Holt, Rinehart & Winston.

LoPiccolo, J. (1990). Sexual dysfunction. In A. S. Bellack, M. Hersen, & A. E. Kazdin (Eds.), *International handbook of behavior modification and therapy* (2nd ed., pp. 547–580). New York: Plenum Press.

Loyd, B. D. (2005). The effects of reality therapy/choice theory principles on high school students' perception of needs satisfaction and behavioral change. *International Journal of Reality Therapy, 25*, 5–9.

Lyons, L. C., & Woods, P. J. (1991). The efficacy of rational-emotive therapy: A quantitative review of the outcome research. *Clinical Psychology Review, 11*, 357–369.

Macaskill, N. D., & Macaskill, A. (1996). Rational-emotive therapy plus pharmacotherapy versus pharmacotherapy alone in the treatment of high cognitive dysfunction depression. *Cognitive Therapy and Research, 20*, 575–592.

Macavei, B. (2005). The role of irrational beliefs in the rational emotive behavior therapy theory of depression. *Journal of Cognitive and Behavioral Psychotherapies, 5*, 73–81.

Macdonald, A. J. (2007). Solution-focused therapy evaluation list. Retrieved March 23, 2007 from http://www.psychsft.freeserve.co.uk/sfb.html

MacDougall, C. (2002). Rogers's person-centered approach: Consideration for use in multicultural counseling. *Journal of Humanistic Psychology, 42*, 48–65.

Mackewn, J. (1997). *Developing gestalt counseling*. London: Sage.

Madanes, C. (1981). *Strategic family therapy*. San Francisco: Jossey-Bass.

Maddi, S. R. (1996). *Personality theories: A comparative analysis* (6th ed.). Pacific Grove, CA: Brooks/Cole.

Maddi, S. R. (2005). The existential/humanistic interview. In R. J. Craig (Ed.), *Clinical and diagnostic interviewing* (2nd ed., pp. 106–130). Lanham, MD: Jason Aronson.

Mahler, M. S. (1972). On the first three subphases of the separation-individuation process. *International Journal of Psychoanalysis, 53*, 333–338.

Mahler, M. S., Pine, F., & Bergman, A. (1975). *The psychological birth of the human infant*. New York: Basic Books.

Mahoney, M. J. (1997). Psychotherapists' personal problems and self-care patterns. *Professional Psychology: Research and Practice, 28*, 14–16.

Mahoney, M. J., Lyddon, W. J., & Alford, D. J. (1989). An evaluation of the rational-emotive theory of psychotherapy. In M. E. Bernard & R. DiGiuseppe (Eds.), *Inside rational-emotive therapy: A critical appraisal of the theory and therapy of Albert Ellis* (pp. 69–94). San Diego, CA: Academic Press.

Maina, G., Forner, F., & Bogetto, F. (2005). Randomized controlled trial comparing brief dynamic and supportive therapy with waiting list condition in minor depressive disorders. *Psychotherapy and Psychotherapy and Psychosomatics, 74*, 43–50.

Maisel, R., Epston, D., & Borden, A. (2004). *Biting the hand that starves you: Inspring resistance to anorexia/bulimia*. New York: Norton.

Malouff, J. M., & Schutte, N. S. (1986). Development and validation of a measure of irrational belief. *Journal of Consulting and Clinical Psychology, 54*, 860–862.

Manaster, G. J. (1990). Adlerian psychotherapy. In R. D. Chessick, M. A. Mattoon, G. J. Manaster, & R. J. Corsini (Eds.), *Classical approaches*. Section in J. K. Zeig & W. M. Munion (Eds.), *What is psychotherapy? Contemporary perspectives* (pp. 34–53). San Francisco: Jossey-Bass.

Manaster, G., Painter, D., Deutch, J., & Overholt, B. (Eds.). (1977). *Alfred Adler: As we remember him*. Chicago: North American Society of Adlerian Psychology.

Manaster, G. J., & Perryman, T. B. (1974). Early recollections and occupational choice. *Journal of Individual Psychology, 30*, 302–311.

Manaster, J. (1977). Alfred Adler: A short biography. In G. Manaster, D. Painter, J. Deutch, & B. Overholt (Eds.), *Alfred Adler: As we remember him*. Chicago: North American Society of Adlerian Psychology.

Mancoske, R. J., Standifer, D., & Cauley, C. (1994). The effectiveness of brief counseling services for battered women. *Research on Social Work Practice, 4*, 53–63.

Mann, B. J., Bourduin, C. M., Henggeler, S. W., & Blaske, D. M. (1990). An investigation of systemic conceptualizations of parent-child coalitions and symptom change. *Journal of Consulting and Clinical Psychology, 58*, 336–344.

Marcotte, D., & Safran, J. D. (2002). Cognitive-interpersonal psychotherapy. In F. W. Kaslow, (Ed.), *Comprehensive Handbook of Psychotherapy: Integrative/eclectic, Vol. 4.* (pp. 273–293). Hoboken, NJ: Wiley.

Marecek, J., & Kravetz, D. (1998). Power and agency in feminist therapy. In I. B. Seu & M. C. Heenan (Eds.), *Feminism and psychotherapy* (pp. 13–29). London: Sage.

Markowitz, J. C., & Swartz, H. A. (1997). Case formulation in interpersonal psychotherapy of depression. In T. D. Eells (Ed.), *Handbook of psychotherapy case formulation* (pp. 192–222). New York: Guilford Press.

Marsh, E. J. (1985). Some comments on target selection in behavior therapy. *Behavioral Assessment, 7*, 63–78.

Marshall, W. L., & Gauthier, J. (1983). Failures in flooding. In E. B. Foa & P. M. G. Emmelkamp (Eds.), *Failures in behavior therapy* (pp. 82–103). New York: Wiley.

Martell, C. R. (2007). Behavioral therapy. In A. Rochlen (Ed.). *Applying counseling theory: An on-line, casebased approach* (pp. 143–156). Upper Saddle River, NJ: Prentice Hall.

Masling, J. M., Bornstein, R. F., Fishman, I., & Davila, J. (2002). Can Freud explain women as well as men? A meta-analytic review of gender differences in psychoanalytic research. *Psychoanalytic Psychology, 19*, 328–347.

Maslow, A. H. (1962). Was Adler a disciple of Freud? A note. *Journal of Individual Psychology, 18*, 125.

Massad, P. M., & Hulsey, T. L. (2006). Exposure therapy renewed. *Journal of Psychotherapy Integration, 16*, 417–428.

Masson, J. M. (1984). *The assault on truth: Freud's suppression of the seduction theory.* New York: Farrar, Straus, & Giroux.

Matsuyuki, M. (1998). Japanese feminist counseling as a political act. *Women & Therapy, 21* (2), 65–77.

Maultsby, M. C., Jr., & Ellis, A. (1974). *Techniques for using rational-emotive imagery.* New York: Institute for Rational-Emotive Therapy.

May, R. (1982). The problem of evil: An open letter to Carl Rogers. *Journal of Humanistic Psychology, 22*, 10–21.

May, R., & Yalom, I. (2005). Existential Psychotherapy. In R. J. Corsini & D. Wedding (Eds.), *Current Psychotherapies* (7th ed., pp. 269–298). Belmont, CA: Brooks/Cole.

McGovern, T. E., & Silverman, M. (1986). A review of outcome studies of rational-emotive therapy from 1997 to 1982. In A. Ellis & R. M. Grieger (Eds.), *Handbook of rational-emotive therapy* (pp. 81–102). New York: Springer.

McLellan, B. (1999). The prostitution of psychotherapy: A feminist critique. *British Journal of Guidance and Counselling, 27*, 325–337.

McLendon, J. A., & Davis, B. (2002). The Satir system. In J. Carlson & D. Kjos (Eds.), *Theories and strategies of family therapy* (pp. 170–189). Boston: Allyn & Bacon.

McNally, R. J., Perlman, C. A., Ristuccia, C. S., & Clancy, S. A. (2006). Clinical characteristics of adults reporting repressed, recovered, or continuous memories of childhood sexual abuse. *Journal of Consulting and Clinical Psychology, 74*, 237–242.

Mead, G. H. (1934). *Mind, self and society.* Chicago: University of Illinois Press.

Meichenbaum, D. (1977). *Cognitive-behavior modification.* New York: Plenum Press.

Meichenbaum, D. (1993). Changing conceptions of cognitive behavior modification: Retrospect and prospect. *Journal of Consulting and Clinical Psychology, 61*, 202–204.

Melnick, J., & Nevis, S. M. (1998). Diagnosing in the here and now: A Gestalt therapy approach. In L. S. Greenberg, J. C. Watson, & G. Lietauer (Eds.), *Handbook of experiential psychotherapy* (pp. 428–447). New York: Guilford Press.

Melnick, J., & Nevis, S. M. (2005). Gestalt therapy methodology. In A. L. Woldt & S. M. Toman (Eds.), *Gesalt therapy: History, theory and practice* (pp. 101–115). Thousand Oaks, CA: Sage.

Merry, T., & Tudor, K. (2006). Person-centred counseling and psychotherapy. In C. Feltham & I. E. Horton (Eds.), *The Sage handbook of counseling and psychotherapy* (2nd ed., pp. 292–297). London: Sage.

Mickel, E., & Boone, C. (2001). African centered family mediation: Building on family strengths. *International Journal of Reality Therapy, 21*, 38–41.

Milan, M. A. (1990). Applied behavior analysis. In A. S. Bellack, M. Hersen, & A. E. Kazdin (Eds.), *International handbook of behavior modification and therapy* (2nd ed., pp. 67–84). New York: Plenum Press.

Miller, J. B. (1991). The development of women's sense of self. In J. V. Jordan, A. G. Kaplan, J. B. Miller, I. P. Stiver, & J. L. Surrey (Eds.), *Women's growth in connection: Writings from the Stone Center* (pp. 11–26). New York: Guilford Press.

Miller, M. V. (1989). Introduction to gestalt therapy verbatim. *The Gestalt Journal, 12* (1), 5–24.

Miller, R., & Berman, J. S. (1983). The efficacy of cognitive behavior therapies: A quantitative review of the research evidence. *Psychological Bulletin, 94*, 39–53.

Miller, R. B., Anderson, S., & Keala, D. K. (2004). Is Bowen theory valid?: A review of basic research. *Journal of Marital & Family Therapy, 30*, 453–466.

Miller, S. D. (1994). The solution conspiracy: A mystery in three installments. *Journal of Systemic Therapies, 13*, 18–37.

Miller, W. R. (1983). Motivational interviewing with problem drinkers. *Behavioral Psychotherapy, 11*, 147–172.

Mills, B. (1997). A psychometric examination of gestalt contact boundary disturbances. *Gestalt Review, 1*, 278–284.

Minuchin, P., Colapinto, J., & Minuchin, S. (2007). *Working with families of the poor* (2nd ed.). New York: Guilford Press.

Minuchin, S. (1974). *Families and family therapy.* Cambridge, MA: Harvard University Press.

Minuchin, S. (1998). Where is the family in narrative family therapy? *Journal of Marital and Family Therapy, 24,* 397–403.

Minuchin, S., & Fishman, H. C. (1981). *Family therapy techniques.* Cambridge, MA: Harvard University Press.

Minuchin, S., Lee, W., & Simon, G. M. (1996). *Mastering family therapy: Journeys of growth and transformation.* New York: Wiley.

Minuchin, S., Montalvo, B., Gurney, B., Rosman, B., & Schumer, F. (1967). *Families of the slums.* New York: Basic Books.

Minuchin, S., Nichols, M. P., & Lee, W. (2007). *Assessing families and couples: From symptom to system.* Boston, MA: Allyn & Bacon.

Minuchin, S., Rosman, B. L., & Baker, L. (1978). *Psychosomatic families: Anorexia nervosa in context.* Cambridge, MA: Harvard University Press.

Mishne, J. M. (1993). *The evolution and application of clinical theory: Perspectives from four psychologies.* New York: Free Press.

Mitchell, S. A. (1978). Psychodynamics, homosexuality, and the question of pathology. *Psychiatry, 41,* 254–263.

Mitchell, S. A. (1992). True selves, false selves, and the ambiguity of authenticity. In N. J. Skolnick & S. C. Warshaw (Eds.), *Relational perspectives in psychoanalysis* (pp. 1–20). Hillsdale, NJ: Analytic Press.

Mitchell, S. A. (1988). *Relational concepts in psychoanalysis: An integration.* Cambridge, MA: Harvard University Press.

Mitchell, S. A. (1997). *Influence and autonomy in psychoanalysis.* Hillsdale, NJ: Analytic Press.

Mitchell, S. A. (1998). The analyst's knowledge and authority. *Psychoanalytic Quarterly, 67,* 1–31.

Mitchell, S. A. (2004). My psychoanalytic journey. *Psychoanalytic Inquiry, 24*(4) 531–541.

Mitchell, S. A., & Black, M. J. (1995). *Freud and beyond: A history of modern psychoanalytic thought.* New York: Basic Books.

Modell, A. (1990). Common ground or divided ground? *Psychoanalytic Inquiry, 14,* 201–211.

Mollon, P. (2007). Self psychology psychoanalysis: Releasing the unknown self. Retrieved on March 21, 2007, from http://www.selfpsychologypsychoanalysis.org/mollon.shtml

Monk, G. (1997). How narrative therapy works. In G. Monk, J. Winslade, K. Crocket, & D. Epston (Eds.), *Narrative therapy in practice: The archaeology of hope* (pp. 3–31). San Francisco, CA: Jossey-Bass.

Montalvo, B., & Gutierrez, M. (1983). A perspective for the use of the cultural dimension in family therapy. In J. C. Hansen & C. J. Falicov (Eds.), *Cultural perspectives in family therapy* (pp. 15–32). Rockville, MD: Aspen Systems.

Monte, C. F. (1999). *Beneath the mask: An introduction to theories of personality* (6th ed.). Fort Worth, TX: Harcourt Brace.

Monte, C. F., & Sollod, R. N. (2003). *Beneath the mask: An introduction to theories of personality* (7th ed.). New York: Wiley.

Moradi, B., & Subich, L. M. (2002a). Feminist identity development measures: Comparing the psychometrics of three instruments. *The Counseling Psychologist, 30,* 66–86.

Moradi, B., & Subich, L. M. (2002b). Perceived sexist events and feminist identity development attitudes: Links to women's psychological distress. *The Counseling Psychologist, 30,* 44–65.

Moradi, B., Subich, L. M., & Phillips, J. C. (2002). Revisiting feminist identity development theory, research and practice. *The Counseling Psychologist, 30,* 6–43.

Morgan, A. (2000). *What is narrative therapy? An easy to read introduction.* Adelaide, South Australia.

Mosak, H. H. (1985). Interrupting a depression: The pushbutton technique. *Journal of Individual Psychology, 41,* 210–214.

Mosak, H. H. (2005). Adlerian psychotherapy. In R. J. Corsini & D. Wedding (Eds.), *Current psychotherapies* (6th ed.). Itasca, IL: Peacock.

Mosak, H. H., & DiPietro, R. (2006). *Early recollections: Interpretive method and application.* New York: Routledge.

Mosak, H. H., & Dreikurs, R. (1977a). The tasks of life II: The fourth life task. In H. H. Mosak (Ed.), *On purpose.* Chicago: Alfred Adler Institute.

Mosak, H. H., & Dreikurs, R. (1977b). The tasks of life II: The fifth life task. In H. H. Mosak (Ed.), *On purpose.* Chicago: Alfred Adler Institute.

Mosak, H. H., & Maniacci, M. P. (1998). *Tactics in counseling and psychotherapy.* Itasca, IL: Peacock.

Mosak, H. H., & Maniacci, M. P. (1999). *A primer of Adlerian psychology: The analytic-behavioral-cognitive psychology of Alfred Adler.* London: Taylor & Francis.

Mosak, H. H., & Schneider, S. (1977). Masculine protest, penis envy, women's liberation and sexual equality. *Journal of Individual Psychology, 32,* 193–202.

Mosher L. (2001). Treating madness without hospitals: Soteria and its successors. In K. J. Schneider, J. F. T. Bugetntal, & J. F. Pierson (Eds.), *The handbook of humanistic psychology: Leading edges in theory, practice and research* (pp. 389–402). Thousand Oaks, CA: Sage.

Mozdzierz, G. J., & Mozdzierz, A. B. (1997). A brief history of the Journals of Individual Psychology. *Journal of Individual Psychology, 53,* 275–285.

Murdock, N. L. (1991). Case conceptualization: Applying theory to individuals. *Counselor Education and Supervision, 30,* 355–365.

Murdock, N. L. (2001, August). Theoretical orientation: Personal orientation and that of the counselor's counselor. In

R. H. McPherson (Chair), *National Counseling Psychology Survey: Culture, personal orientation and life satisfaction.* Symposium presented at the annual meetings of the American Psychological Association, San Francisco.

Murdock, N. L. (2007). Family systems theory. In A. B. Rochlen (Ed.) *Applying counseling theories: An online case–based approach* (pp. 209–224). Upper Saddle River, NJ: Prentice Hall.

Murdock, N. L., Banta, J., Stromseth, J., Viene, D., & Brown, T. M. (1998). Joining the club: Factors related to counselors' theoretical orientations. *Counselling Psychology Quarterly, 11*, 63–78.

Murdock, N. L., & Brooks, R. P. (1993). Some scientist-practitioners do. *American Psychologist, 48*, 1293.

Murdock, N. L., & Gore, P. A. (2004). Differentiation, stress, and coping: A test of Bowen theory. *Contemporary Family Therapy, 26*, 319–335.

Murdock, N. L., & Wang, D. C. (in press). Humanistic Approaches. In H. E. A. Tinsley & S. Lease (Eds.), *Encyclopedia of Counseling*, Thousand Oaks, CA: Sage.

Murphy, T. F. (1984). Freud reconsidered: Bisexuality, homosexuality, and moral judgment. *Journal of Homosexuality, 9* (2–3), 56–77.

Murray, K. (2006). A call for feminist research: A limited client perspective. *The Family Journal: Counseling and Therapy for Couples and Families, 14*, 169–173.

Myers, I. B., & McCaulley, M. H. (1985). *MBTI Manual: A guide to the development and use of the Myers–Briggs Type Indicator.* Palo Alto, CA: Consulting Psychologists Press.

Nathan, P. E. (2000). The Boulder Model: A dream deferred—or lost? *American Psychologist, 55*, 250–252.

Neenan, M., & Dryden, W. (1996). Trends in rational emotive behavior therapy: 1955–95. In W. Dryden (Ed.), *Developments in psychotherapy: Historical perspectives* (pp. 213–237). London, England/Thousand Oaks, CA: Sage.

Neenan, M., & Dryden, W. (2000). *Essential rational emotive behavior therapy.* London: Whurr.

Nelson, M. O. (1991). Another look at masculine protest. *Journal of Individual Psychology, 47*, 490–497.

Nelson-Jones, R. (2000). *Six key approaches to counselling and therapy.* London: Continuum.

Nemeroll, C. J., & Karoly, P. (1991). Operant methods. In F. H. Kanfer & A. P. Goldstein (Eds.), *Helping people change* (4th ed., pp. 122–160). New York: Pergamon.

Newman, C. F., & Beck, A. T. (1990). Cognitive therapy of affective disorders. In B. B. Wolman & G. Stricker (Eds.), *Depressive disorders: Facts, theories, and treatment methods* (pp. 343–367). New York: Wiley.

Newton, B. J., & Mansager, E. (1986). Adlerian life-styles among Catholic priests. *Journal of Individual Psychology, 42*, 367–374.

Nichols, M. P. (2002). *The essentials of family therapy.* Boston: Allyn & Bacon.

Nichols, M. P. (2006). *Family therapy: Concepts and methods,* (7th ed.). Boston: Allyn & Bacon.

Nichols, M. P., & Schwartz, R. C. (2001). *Family therapy: Concepts and methods.* Boston: Allyn & Bacon.

Nishimura, N. (2004). Counseling biracial women: An intersection of multiculturalism and feminism. *Women and Therapy, 27*, 133–145.

Norcross, J. C. (1987). A rational and empirical analysis of existential psychotherapy. *Journal of Humanistic Psychology, 27*, 41–68.

Norcross, J. C. (2005). A primer on psychotherapy integration. In J. C. Norcross & M. R. Goldfried (Eds.), *Handbook of psychotherapy integration* (pp. 3–23). New York: Oxford University Press.

Norcross, J. C., Beutler, L. E., & Levant, R. F. (Eds.). (2006). *Evidence-based practices in mental health: Debate and dialogue on the fundamental questions.* Washington, DC: American Psychological Association.

Norcross, J. C., & Guy, J. D. (2005). The prevalence and parameters of personal therapy in the United States. In J. D. Geller, J. C. Norcross, & D. E. Orlinsky (Eds.), *The psychotherapist's own psychotherapy* (pp. 165–176). New York: Oxford University Press.

Norcross, J. C., Hedges, M., & Castle, P. H. (2001). Psychologists conducting psychotherapy in 2001: A study of the Division 29 membership. *Psychotherapy: Theory, Research, Practice, Training, 39*, 97–102.

Norcross, J. C., Karpiak, C. P., & Santoro, S. O. (2005). Clinical psychologists across the years: The division of clinical psychology from 1960 to 2003. *Journal of Clinical Psychology, 61*, 1467–1483.

Norcross, J. C., Koocher, G. P., & Garofalo, A. (2006) Discredited Psychological Treatments and Tests: A Delphi Poll. *Professional Psychology: Research and Practice, 37*, 515–522.

Norcross, J. C., Strausser-Kirtland, D., & Missar, C. D. (1988). The processes and outcomes of psychotherapists' personal treatment experiences. *Psychotherapy, 25*, 36–43.

Nord, G., Wieseler, N. A., & Hanson, R. H. (1991). Aversive procedures: The Minnesota experience. *Behavioral Residential Treatment, 6* (3), 197–205.

Northey, S., Griffin, W. A., & Krainz, S. (1998). A partial test of the psychosomatic family model: Marital interaction patterns in asthma and nonasthma families. *Journal of Family Psychology, 12*, 220–235.

Nunnally, E., de Shazer, S., Lipchick, E., & Berg, I. (1986). A study of change: Therapeutic theory in process. In D. E. Efron (Ed.), *Journeys: Expansion of the strategic-systemic therapies* (pp. 77–96). New York: Brunner/Mazel.

Nutt, R. L. (1979). Review and preview of attitudes and values of counselors of women. *The Counseling Psychologist, 8*, 18–20.

Nye, R. D. (1986). *Three psychologies.* Belmont, CA: Brooks/Cole.

Nylund, D., & Nylund, D. A. (2003). Narrative therapy as a counterhegemonic practice. *Men and Masculinities, 5*, 386–394.

O'Connor, J. J. (1986). Strategic psychotherapy. In I. L. Kutash & A. Wolf (Eds.), *Psychotherapist's casebook* (pp. 489–520). San Francisco: Jossey-Bass.

Oei, T. P. S., & Free, M. L. (1995). Do cognitive behavior therapies validate cognitive models of mood disorders? A review of the empirical evidence. *International Journal of Psychology, 30*, 145–179.

Oei, T. P. S., Hansen, J., & Miller, S. (1993). The empirical status of irrational beliefs in rational emotive therapy. *Australian Psychologist, 28*, 195–200.

O'Hanlon, B. (2006). *Change 101: A practical guide to creating change in life or therapy.* New York: Norton.

O'Hanlon, B., & Rowan, T. (2003). *Solution oriented therapy for chronic and severe mental illness.* New York: Norton.

O'Hanlon, W. H. (1986). Fragments for a therapeutic autobiography. In D. E. Efron (Ed.), *Journeys: Expansion of the strategic-systemic therapies* (pp. 30–39). New York: Brunner/Mazel.

O'Hanlon, W. H., & Weiner-Davis, M. (1989). *In search of solutions.* New York: Norton.

Okonji, J. M. A., Ososkie, J. N., & Pulos, S. (1996). Preferred style and ethnicity of counselors by African American males. *Journal of Black Psychology, 22*, 329–339.

O'Leary, E. (1992). *Gestalt therapy: Theory, practice and research.* London: Chapman & Hall.

O'Leary, E. (1997). Confluence versus empathy. *The Gestalt Journal, 20* (1), 137–154.

O'Leary, E., Sheedy, G., O'Sullivan, K., & Thoresen, C. (2003). Cork older adult intervention project: Outcomes of a gestalt therapy group with older adults. *Counselling Psychology Quarterly, 16*, 131–143.

Ollendick, T. H., & King, N. J. (2006). Empirically supported treatments typically produce outcomes superior to non-empirically supported treatment therapies. In J. C. Norcross, L. E. Beutler, & R. F. Levant (Eds.), *Evidence-based practices in mental health: Debate and dialogue on the fundamental questions* (pp. 308–317). Washington, DC: American Psychological Association.

Orford, J. (1986). The rules of interpersonal complementarity: Does hostility beget hostility and dominance, submission? *Psychological Review, 93*, 365–377.

Padesky, C. A. (2004). Aaron T. Beck: Mind, man, and mentor. In R. L. Leahy (Ed.), *Contemporary cognitive therapy: Theory, research, and practice* (pp. 3–26). New York: Guilford Press.

Paivio, S. C., & Greenberg, L. S. (1995). Resolving "unfinished business": Efficacy of experiential therapy using empty-chair dialogue. Journal of Consulting and Clinical Psychology, 63, 419–425. Retrieved from http://spider.apa.org/ftdocs/ccp/1995/june/ccp633419.html

Paludi, M. A. (2002). *The psychology of women* (2nd ed.). Upper Saddle River, NJ: Prentice Hall.

Papero, D. V. (1990). *Bowen family systems theory.* Boston: Allyn & Bacon.

Parlett, M., (2005). Contemporary gestalt therapy: Field theory. In A. L. Woldt & S. M. Toman (Eds.), *Gestalt therapy: History, theory and practice* (pp. 41–63). Thousand Oaks, CA: Sage.

Parlett, M., & Hemming, J. (1996a). Developments in gestalt therapy. In W. Dryden (Ed.), *Developments in psychotherapy: Historical perspectives* (pp. 91–110). Thousand Oaks, CA: Sage.

Parlett, M., & Hemming, J. (1996b). Gestalt therapy. In W. Dryden (Ed.), *Handbook of individual therapy* (pp. 194–218). Thousand Oaks, CA: Sage.

Paskauskas, A. (1988). *The complete correspondence of Sigmund Freud and Ernest Jones 1908–1939.* Cambridge, MA: Harvard University Press.

Patterson, C. H. (1984). Empathy, warmth, and genuineness in psychotherapy: A review of reviews. *Psychotherapy, 21*, 431–438.

Patterson, C. H. (2000). *Understanding psychotherapy: Fifty years of client-centred theory and practice.* Ross-on-Wye, UK: PCCS Books.

Payne, M. (2000). *Narrative therapy: An introduction for counselors.* London: Sage.

Perkins–Dock, R. E. (2005). The application of Adlerian family therapy with African American families. *Journal of Individual Psychology, 61*, 233–249.

Perls, F. S. (1947). *Ego, hunger, and aggression.* London: Allen & Unwin.

Perls, F. S. (1969a). *Gestalt therapy verbatim.* Lafayette, CA: Real People Press.

Perls, F. S. (1969b). *In and out the garbage pail.* Lafayette, CA: Real People Press.

Perls, F. S. (1970a). Four lectures. In J. Fagan & I. L. Shepherd (Eds.), *Gestalt therapy now* (pp. 14–38). New York: Harper & Row.

Perls, F. S. (1970b). Dream seminars. In J. Fagan & I. L. Shepherd (Eds.), *Gestalt therapy now* (pp. 204–233). New York: Harper & Row.

Perls, F. S., Hefferline, R. F., & Goodman, P. (1951) *Gestalt therapy: Excitement and growth in the human personality.* New York: Dell.

Perls, L. (1992). Concepts and misconceptions of gestalt therapy. *Journal of Humanistic Psychology, 32* (3), 50–56.

Perosa, S. L., & Perosa, L. M. (1993). Relationships among Minuchin's structural family model, identity achievement, and coping style. *Journal of Counseling Psychology, 40*, 479–489.

Persons, J. B., & Tompkins, M. A. (1997). Cognitive-behavioral case formulation. In T. D. Eells (Ed.), *Handbook of psychotherapy case formulation* (pp. 314–339). New York: Guilford Press.

Peterson, A. V. (2000). Choice theory and reality therapy. *TCA Journal, 28* (1), 41–49.

Peterson, A. V., Chang, C., & Collins, P. L. (1998). The effects of reality therapy and choice theory training on self-concept among Taiwanese university students. *International Journal for the Advancement of Counseling, 20*, 79–83.

Peterson, R. D., Tantleff-Dunns, S. & Bedwell, J. S. (2006). The effects of exposure to feminist ideology on women's body image. *Body Image, 3*, 237–246.

Peven, D. E., & Shulman, B. H. (1986). Adlerian psychotherapy. In I. L. Kutash & A. Wolf (Eds.), *Psychotherapist's casebook.* San Francisco: Jossey-Bass.

Phillips, R. D., & Gilroy, F. D. (1985). Sex role stereotypes and clinical judgments of mental health: The Broverman findings re-examined. *Sex Roles, 12*, 179–193.

Philpot, C. L., Brooks, G. R., Lusterman, D. D., & Nutt, R. L. (1997). *Bridging separate gender worlds: Why men and women clash and how therapists can bring them together.* Washington, DC: American Psychological Association.

Pichot, T., & Dolan, Y. M. (2003). *Solution-focused brief therapy: Its effective use in agency settings.* New York: Haworth Clinical Practice Press.

Piercy, F. P., Lipchik, E., & Kiser D. (2000). Miller and deShazer's article on "emotions in solution-focused therapy." *Family Process, 39*, 25–28.

Piran, N., & Cormier, H. C. (2005). The social construction of women and disordered eating patterns. *Journal of Counseling Psychology, 52*, 549–558.

Polster, E., & Polster, M. (1973). *Gestalt therapy integrated.* New York: Random House.

Polster, M., & Polster, E. (1990). Gestalt therapy. In J. K. Zeig & W. M. Munion (Eds.), *What is psychotherapy?* (pp. 103–107). San Francisco: Jossey-Bass.

Pope, K. S., & Tabachnick, B. G. (1994). Therapists as patients: A national survey of psychologists' experiences, problems, and beliefs. *Professional Psychology: Research and Practice, 25*, 247–258.

Poyrazli, S. (2003). Validity of Rogerian therapy in Turkish culture: A cross cultural perspective. *Journal of Humanistic Counseling, Education, and Development, 42*, 107–115.

Prendergast, M., Podus, D., Finney, J., Greenwell, L., & Roll, J. (2006). Contingency management for treatment of substance use disorders: A meta-analysis. *Addiction, 101*, 1546–1560.

Pretzer, J., & Beck, J. T. (2004). Cognitive therapy of personality disorders. In R. L. Leahy (Ed.), *Contemporary cognitive therapy: Theory, research, and practice* (pp. 299–318). New York: Guilford Press.

Prochaska, J. O. (1999). How do people change, and how can we change to help many more people? In M. A. Hubble, B. L. Duncan, & S. D. Miller (Eds.), *The heart & soul of change: What works in therapy* (pp. 227–255). Washington, DC: American Psychological Association.

Prochaska, J. O., DiClemente, C. C., & Norcross, J. C. (1992). In search of how people change: Applications to addictive behaviors. *American Psychologist, 47*, 1102–1114.

Prochaska, J. O., & Norcross, J. C. (1983). Contemporary psychotherapists: A national survey of characteristics, practices, orientations and attitudes. *Psychotherapy: Theory, Research and Practice, 20*,161–173.

Prochaska, J. O., & Norcross, J. C. (2002). Stages of change. In J. C. Norcross (Ed.), *Psychotherapy relationships that work* (pp. 303–313). New York: Oxford University Press.

Prochaska, J. O., & Norcross, J. C. (2003). *Systems of psychotherapy: A transtheoretical approach.* Pacific Grove, CA: Brooks/Cole.

Prochaska, J. O., & Norcross, J. C. (2007). *Systems of psychotherapy: A transtheoretical approach* (6th ed.). Belmont, CA: Brooks/Cole.

Project MATCH Research Group. (1997). Matching alcoholism treatments to client heterogeneity: Project MATCH posttreatment drinking outcomes. *Journal of Studies on Alcohol, 58*, 7–29.

Prouty, G. (1998). Pre-therapy and pre-symbolic experiencing: Evolutions in person-centered/experiential approaches to psychotic experience. In L. S. Greenberg, J. C. Watson, & G. Lietaer (Eds.), *Handbook of experiential psychotherapy* (pp. 388–409). New York: Guilford Press.

Quintar, B., Lane, R. C., & Goeltz, W. B. (1998). Psychoanalytic theories of personality. In D. F. Barone, M. Hersen, & V. B. Van Hasselt (Eds.), *Advanced personality* (pp. 27–55). New York: Plenum Press.

Rader, J., & Gilbert, L. A. (2005). The egalitarian relationship in feminist therapy. *Psychology of Women Quarterly, 29*, 427–435.

Radtke, L., Sapp, M., & Farrell, W. C. (1997). Reality therapy: A meta analysis. *Journal of Reality Therapy, 17*, 4–9.

Raff, J. (2007). Analytical (Jungian) Psychology. In A. B. Rochlen (Ed.), *Applying counseling theory: An on-line, case-based approach* (pp. 21–36). Upper Saddle River, NJ: Prentice Hall.

Raimey, V. C. (Ed.). (1950). *Training in clinical psychology.* Upper Saddle River, NJ: Prentice Hall.

Randall, E. (2001). Existential therapy of panic disorder: A single system study. *Clinical Social Work Journal, 29*, 259–267.

Raskin, N. J. (1952). An objective study of the locus-of-evaluation factor in psychotherapy. In W. Wolff & J. A. Precker (Eds.), *Success in psychotherapy.* New York: Grune & Stratton.

Rector, N. A. (2004). Cognitive theory and therapy of schizophrenia. In R. L. Leahy (Ed.), *Contemporary cognitive therapy: Theory, research, and practice* (pp. 244–265). New York: Guilford Press.

Reimer, W. L., & Chatwin, A. (2006). Effectiveness of solution focused therapy for affective and relationship problems in a private practice context. *Journal of Systemic Therapies, 25*, 52–67.

Reinecke, M. A., & Freeman, A. (2003). Cognitive therapy. In A. S. Gurman & S. B. Messer (Eds.), *Essential psychotherapies: Theory and practice,* (2nd ed., pp. 224–271). New York: The Guilford Press.

Reinecke, M. A., Ryan, N. E., & DuBois, D. (1998). Cognitive-behavior therapy of depression and depressive symptoms during adolescence: A review and meta-analysis. *Journal of the American Academy of Child and Adolescent Psychiatry, 37*, 26–34.

Reiter, M. D. (2004). The surprise task: A solution-focused formula task for families. *Journal of Family Psychotherapy, 15,* 37–45.

Reitman, D. (1997). The relation between cognitive and behavioral therapies: Commentary on "Extending the goals of behavior therapy and of cognitive behavior therapy." *Behavior Therapy, 28,* 341–345.

Reuterlov, H., Lofgren, T., Nordstrom, K., Ternstrom A., & Miller, S. D. (2000). What is better? A preliminary investigation of between-session change. *Journal of Systemic Therapies, 19,* 111–115.

Reynolds, G. S. (1968). *A primer of operant conditioning.* Glenview, IL: Scott Foresman.

Rice, L. N., & Greenberg, L. S. (1992). Humanistic approaches to psychotherapy. In D. K. Freedheim (Ed.), *History of psychotherapy: A century of change* (pp. 197–224). Washington, DC: American Psychological Association.

Richert, A. J. (2003). Living stories, telling stories, changing stories: Experiental use of the relationship in narrative therapy. *Journal of Psychotherapy Integration, 13,* 188–210.

Rickman, J. (Ed.). (1957). *A general selection from the works of Sigmund Freud.* New York: Doubleday.

Rilling, M. (2000). John Watson's paradoxical struggle to explain Freud. *American Psychologist, 55,* 301–312.

Roazen, P. (2002). *The trauma of Freud: Controversies in psychoanalysis.* New Brunswick, NY: Transaction.

Robin, M. W., & DiGiuseppe, R. (1997). "Shoya Moya Ik Baraba": Using REBT with culturally diverse clients. In J. Yankura & W. Dryden (Eds.), *Special applications of REBT* (pp. 39–68). New York: Springer.

Robins, C. J., & Chapman, A. L. (2004). Dialectical behavior therapy: Current status, recent developments, and future directions. *Journal of Personality Disorders, 18,* 73–89.

Robinson, L. A., Berman, J. S., & Neimeyer, R. A. (1990). Psychotherapy for the treatment of depression: A comprehensive review of controlled outcome research. *Psychological Bulletin, 108,* 30–49.

Rogers, C. R. (1942). *Counseling and psychotherapy.* Boston: Houghton Mifflin.

Rogers, C. R. (1951). *Client-centered therapy: Its current practice, implications, and theory.* Boston: Houghton Mifflin.

Rogers, C. R. (1957). The necessary and sufficient conditions of therapeutic personality change. *Journal of Consulting Psychology, 21,* 95–103.

Rogers, C. R. (1958). A process conception of psychotherapy. *American Psychologist, 13,* 142–149.

Rogers, C. R. (1959). A theory of therapy, personality, and interpersonal relationships, as developed in the client-centered framework. In S. Koch (Ed.), *Psychology: A study of a science* (pp. 184–256). New York: McGraw-Hill.

Rogers, C. R. (1961). *On becoming a person.* Boston: Houghton Mifflin.

Rogers, C. R. (1966). Client-centered therapy. In S. Arieti (Ed.), *American handbook of psychiatry* (pp. 183–200). New York: Basic Books.

Rogers, C. R. (1967). Carl. R. Rogers. In E. Boring & G. Lindzey (Eds.), *A history of psychology in autobiography.* New York: Appleton-Century-Crofts.

Rogers, C. R. (1972). *Becoming partners.* New York: Delacorte.

Rogers, C. R. (1977). *On personal power.* London: Constable.

Rogers, C. R. (1980). *A way of being.* Boston: Houghton Mifflin.

Rogers, C. (1982). Notes on Rollo May. *Journal of Humanistic Psychology, 22,* 8–9.

Rogers, C. R. (1986a). Client-centered therapy. In I. L. Kutash & A. Wolf (Eds.), *Psychotherapist's casebook* (pp. 197–208). San Francisco: Jossey-Bass.

Rogers, C. R. (1986b). Reflection of feelings. *Person-Centered Review, 1,* 375–377.

Rogers, C. R. (1987). Comment on Shlien's article "A countertheory of transference." *Person-Centered Review, 2,* 182–188.

Rogers, C. R., & Freiberg, H. J. (1994). *Freedom to learn* (3rd ed.). Upper Saddle River, NJ: Merrill/Prentice Hall.

Rogers, C. R., Gendlin, E. T., Kiesler, D. V., & Truax, C. (Eds.). (1967). *The therapeutic relationship and its impact: A study of psychotherapy with schizophrenics.* Madison: The University of Wisconsin Press.

Rogers, N. (1993). *Beyond Carl Rogers.* London: Constable.

Rorschach, H. (1942). *Psychodiagnostics: A diagnostic test based on perception* (P. Lemkau & B. Kronenburg, Trans). Berne, Switzerland: Huber.

Rosenthal, T. L., & Steffek, B. D. (1991). Modeling methods. In F. H. Kanfer & A. P. Goldstein (Eds.), *Helping people change* (4th ed., pp. 70–121). New York: Pergamon Press.

Rosenzweig, S. (2002). Some implicit common factors in diverse methods of psychotherapy: "At last the Dodo said, 'Everybody has won and all must have prizes.'" *Journal of Psychotherapy Integration, 12,* 5–9. (Reprinted from *American Journal of Orthopsychiatry, 6,* 412–415)

Ross, R., Frances, A., & Widiger, T. A. (1997). Gender issues in DSM-IV. In M. R. Walsh (Ed.), *Women, men, and gender: Ongoing debates* (pp. 348–357). New Haven, CT: Yale University Press.

Rossiter, A. (2000). The professional is political: An interpretation of the problem of the past in solution-focused therapy. *American Journal of Orthopsychiatry, 70,* 150–161.

Rothbaum, B. O., Anderson, P., Zimrand, E., Hodges, L., Lang, D., & Wilson, J. (2006). Virtual reality exposure therapy and standard (in vivo) exposure therapy in the treatment of fear of flying. *Behavior Therapy, 37,* 80–90.

Rowe, C. L., Gozez, L., & Liddle, H. A. (2006). Family therapy research: Empirical foundations and practice implications. In M. P. Nichols (Ed.), *Family therapy: Concepts and methods,* (7th ed., pp. 399–440). Boston: Allyn & Bacon.

Rule, W. R. (2006). Lifestyle self-awareness and the practitioner: Understanding and reframing resistance using angels and devils as metaphor. In W. R. Rule & M. Bishop (Eds.), *Adlerian lifestyle counseling* (pp. 45–53). New York: Routledge.

Rule, W. R., & Bishop, M., (Eds.). (2006). *Adlerian lifestyle counseling*. New York: Routledge.

Russell, S., & Carey, M. (2004). *Narrative therapy: Responding to your questions*. Adeaide, South Australia: Dulwich Centre Publications.

Ruthven, A. J. (1992). A person-centered/humanistic approach to intervention. In R. C. D'Amato & B. A. Rothlisberg (Eds.), *Psychological perspectives on intervention: A case study approach to prescriptions for change* (pp. 95–111). New York: Longman.

Sabik, N. J., & Tylka, T. L. (2006). Do feminist identity styles moderate the relation between perceived sexist events and disordered eating? *Psychology of Women Quarterly, 30*, 77–84.

Sachese, R. (1990). Concrete interventions are crucial: The influence of the therapist's processing proposals on the client's intrapersonal exploration in client-centered therapy. In G. Lietaer, J. Rombauts, & R. Van Balen (Eds.), *Client-centered and experiential psychotherapy in the nineties*. Louvain, Belgium: Leuven University Press.

Safran, J. D., & Segal, Z. V. (1990) *Interpersonal process in cognitive therapy*. Lanham, MD: Jason Aronson.

Safran, J. D. (1998). *Widening the scope of cognitive therapy*. New York: Jason Aronson.

Sanchez, W. (1998). Quality world and culture. *International Journal of Reality Therapy, 17* (2), 12–16.

Sanchez, W., Perez-Prado, E. M., & Cadavid, M. (1998). A Puerto Rican quality world. *International Journal of Reality Therapy, 17* (2), 17–23.

Saner, R. (1989). Culture bias of gestalt therapy: Made-in-U.S.A. *The Gestalt Journal, 12* (2), 57–71.

Sansone, D. (1998). Research, internal control and choice theory: Where's the beef? *International Journal of Reality Therapy, 17* (2), 4–6.

Santisteban, D. A., Szapocznik, J., Perez-Vidal, A., Kurtines, W. M., Murray, E. J., & LaPerriere, A. (1996). Efficacy of intervention for engaging youth and families into treatment and some variables that may contribute to differential effectiveness. *Journal of Family Psychology, 10*, 35–44.

Sapp, M. (1997). *Counseling and psychotherapy*. Lanham, MD: University Press of America.

Sartre, J. P. (1956). *Being and nothingness*. New York: Philosophical Library.

Satir, V. (1967). *Conjoint family therapy*. Palo Alto, CA: Science and Behavior Books.

Satir, V. (1972). *Peoplemaking*. Palo Alto, CA: Science and Behavior Books.

Satir, V. (1975). *You as a change agent*. In V. Satir, J. Stachovwiak, & H. A. Taschman (Eds.), *Helping families to change* (pp. 37–63). New York: Jason Aronson.

Satir, V. (1978). *Your many faces*. Berkeley, CA: Celestial Arts.

Satir, V. (1988). *The new peoplemaking*. Mountain View, CA: Science and Behavior Books.

Satir, V. (2000). The therapist story. In M. Baldwin (Ed.), *The use of self in therapy* (2nd ed., pp. 17–27). New York: Haworth.

Satir, V., & Baldwin, M. (1983). *Satir step by step*. Palo Alto, CA: Science and Behavior Books.

Satir, V., Banmen, J., Gerber, J., & Gomori, M. (1991). *The Satir model: Family therapy and beyond*. Palo Alto, CA: Science and Behavior Books.

Saunders, K. J., Kashubeck-West, S. (2006). The relations among feminist identity development, gender-role orientation, and psychological well-being in women. *Psychology of Women Quarterly, 30*, 199–211.

Scharff, J. S., & Scharff, D. E. (1995). *The primer of object relations therapy*. Northvale, NJ: Jason Aronson.

Schigl, B. (1998). *Evaluationssudie zur Integrativen Gestalttherapie: Wirkungen und Wirkfaktoren-aus katamnestischer Sicht ehemaliger KlientInnen* [Evaluative study on integrative Gestalt psychotherapy]. Vienna, Austria: Endbericht zum Forschungsprojekt der Fachsektion fur Integrative Gestalttherapie in OAGG. (cited in Strumpfel & Goldman, 2001).

Schneider, K. J. (2003). Existential-humanistic psychotherapies. In A. S. Gurman & S. B. Messer (Eds.), *Essential psychotherapies* (2nd ed., pp. 149–181). New York: Guilford Press.

Schneider, M. F. (2007). Adlerian psychology. In A. B. Rochlen (Ed.), *Applying counseling theories: An online, case-based approach* (pp. 37–52). Upper Saddle River, NJ: Prentice Hall.

Schoenewolf, G. (1990). *Turning points in analytic therapy: The classic cases*. Northvale, NJ: Jason Aronson.

Schoppe, S. J., Mangelsdorf, S. C., & Frosch, C. A. (2001). Coparenting, family process, and family structure: Implications for preschoolers' externalizing behavior problems. *Journal of Family Psychology, 15*, 526–545.

Schulenberg, S. E. (2003). Approaching Terra Incognita with James F. T. Bugental: An interview and overview of existential-humanistic psychotherapy. *Journal of Contemporary Psychotherapy, 33*, 273–285.

Scorzelli, J. F., & Reinke-Scorzelli, M. (1994). Cultural sensitivity and cognitive therapy in India. *The Counseling Psychologist, 22*, 603–610.

Seager, M. (2003). Problems with client-centred therapy. *The Psychologist, 16*, 400–415.

Sears, R. R. (1943). *Survey of objective studies of psychoanalytic concepts*. New York: Social Science Research Council.

Seeman, J. (1990). Theory as autobiography: The development of Carl Rogers. *Person-Centered Review, 5*, 373–386.

Seligman, M. E. P. (1975). *Helplessness: On depression, development, and death*. San Francisco: Freeman.

Seligman, M. E. P. (1995). The effectiveness of psychotherapy: The *Consumer Reports* study. *American Psychologist, 50*, 965–974.

Semmler, P. L., & Williams, C. B. (2000). Narrative therapy: A storied context for multicultural counseling. *Journal of Multicultural Counseling and Development, 28*, 51–60.

Serok, S., & Zemet, R. M. (1983). An experiment of gestalt group therapy with hospitalized schizophrenics. *Psychotherapy: Theory, Research and Practice, 20*, 417–424.

Sexton, T. L., & Alexander, J. F. (2002). Family-based empirically supported interventions. *The Counseling Psychologist, 30*, 238–261.

Shadish, W. R., & Baldwin, S. A. (2003). Meta-analysis of MFT interventions. *Journal of Martial and Family Therapy, 29*, 547–570.

Shadish, W. R., Montgomery, L. M., Wilson, P., Wilson, M. R., Bright, I., & Okwumabua, T. (1993). Effects of family and marital psychotherapies: A meta-analysis. *Journal of Consulting and Clinical Psychology, 61*, 992–1002.

Shapiro, D. A., Barkham, M., Rees, A., Hardy, G., Reynolds, S., & Startup, M. (1994). Effects of treatment duration and severity of depression on the effectiveness of cognitive behavioral and psychodynamic-interpersonal psychotherapy. *Journal of Consulting and Clinical Psychology, 62*, 522–534.

Shapiro, D. A., & Shapiro, D. (1982). Meta-analysis of comparative therapy outcome studies: A replication and refinement. *Psychological Bulletin, 92*, 581–604.

Sherman, A. R. (1973). *Behavior modification: Theory and practice.* Monterey, CA: Brooks/Cole.

Sherry, A. (2005). The constructivist approach to counseling. In A. Rochlen (Ed.), Applying counseling theories: An online, case-based approach (pp. 239–254). Upper Saddle River, NJ: Prentice Hall.

Shlien, J. M., Mosak, H. M., & Dreikurs, R. (1962). Effect of time limits: A comparison of two psychotherapies. *Journal of Counseling Psychology, 9*, 31–34.

Shorkey, C., & Whiteman, V. (1977). Development of the Rational Behavior Inventory: Initial validity and reliability. *Educational and Psychological Measurements, 37*, 527–534.

Shostrom, E. L. (Producer). (1965). *Three approaches to psychotherapy* [Film]. Orange, CA: Psychological Films.

Shulman, B. H. (1973). *Contributions to individual psychology.* Chicago: Alfred Adler Institute.

Shulman, B., & Mosak, H. (1977). Birth order and ordinal position: Two Adlerian views. *Journal of Individual Psychology, 33*, 114–121.

Silverman, M. S., McCarthy, M., & McGovern. T. (1992). A review of outcome studies of rational emotive therapy from 1982–1989. *Journal of Rational-Emotive and Cognitive-Behavior Therapy, 10*, 111–186.

Simon, R. M. (1972). Sculpting the family. *Family Process, 11*, 49–51.

Simon, R. (1992). *One on one: Conversations with the shapers of family therapy.* Washington, DC: The Family Therapy Network and New York: Guilford Press.

Singer, A. (1994). Gestalt couples therapy with gay male couples: Enlarging the therapeutic ground of awareness. In G. Wheeler & S. Backman (Eds.), *On intimate ground: A gestalt approach to working with couples* (pp. 166–187). San Francisco: Jossey-Bass.

Skinner, B. F. (1953). *Science and human behavior.* New York: Free Press.

Skinner, B. F. (1971). *Beyond freedom and dignity.* New York: Bantam/Vintage.

Skinner, B. F. (1976). *Walden Two.* New York: Macmillan.

Skinner, N. F. (1977). Failure to support a test for penis envy. *Psychological Reports, 80*, 754.

Skowron, E. A. (2000). The role of differentiation of self in marital adjustment. *Journal of Counseling Psychology, 47*, 229–237.

Skowron, E. A., & Friedlander, M. L. (1998). The Differentiation of Self Inventory: Development and initial validation. *Journal of Counseling Psychology, 45*, 235–246.

Sloane, R. B., Staples, F. R., Cristol, A. H., Yorkston, N. J., & Whipple, K. (1975a). *Psychotherapy vs. behavior therapy.* Cambridge, MA: Harvard University Press.

Smith, C. (1997). Introduction: Comparing traditional theories with narrative approaches. In C. Smith & D. Nylund (Eds.), *Narrative therapies with children and adolescents* (pp. 1–52). New York: Guilford Press.

Smith, D. L. (1982). Trends in counseling and psychotherapy. *American Psychologist, 37*, 802–809.

Smith, E. W. L. (1991). Gestalt, a Dionysian path. *The Gestalt Journal, 14* (2), 61–69.

Smith, M. L., & Glass, G. V. (1977). Meta-analysis of psychotherapy outcome studies. *American Psychologist, 32*, 752–760.

Smith, M. L., Glass, G. V., & Miller, T. I. (1980). *The benefits of psychotherapy.* Baltimore: Johns Hopkins University Press.

Smith, T. E., Winton, M., Yashioka, M. (1992). A qualitative understanding of reflective-teams II: Therapists' perspectives. *Contemporary Family Therapy, 14*, 419–432.

Smith, T. W. (1989). Assessment in rational-emotive therapy: Empirical access to the ABCD model. In M. E. Bernard & R. DiGiuseppe (Eds.), *Inside rational-emotive therapy: A critical appraisal of the theory and therapy of Albert Ellis* (pp. 199–233). San Diego, CA: Academic Press.

Smith, T. W., & Allred, K. D. (1986). Rationality revisited: A reassessment of the empirical support for the rational-emotive model. In P. C. Kendall (Ed.), *Advances in cognitive-behavioral research and therapy, Vol. 5* (pp. 63–87). New York: Academic Press.

Smith, T. W., Houston, B. K., & Zurawski, R. M. (1984). Irrational beliefs and the arousal of emotional distress. *Journal of Counseling Psychology, 31*, 190–201.

Soloman, A., & Haaga, D. F. (1995). Rational emotive behavior therapy research: What we know and what we need to know. *Journal of Rational-Emotive and Cognitive-Behavior Therapy, 13*, 179–191.

Solomon, S., Greenberg, J., & Pyszczynski, T. (2004). The cultural animal: Twenty years of terror management theory and research. In J. Greenberg, S. L. Koole, & T. Pyszczynski (Eds.), *Handbook of experimental existential psychology* (pp. 13–34). New York: Guilford Press.

Spangenberg, J. J. (2003). The cross-cultural relevance of Person-Centered counseling in postapartheid South Africa. *Journal of Counseling and Development, 81,* 48–54.

Spiegel, S. B. (1979). Separate principles for counselors of women: A new form of sexism. *The Counseling Psychologist, 8,* 49–50.

Spiegler, M. D., & Guevremont, D. C. (2003). *Contemporary behavior therapy* (4th ed.). Pacific Grove, CA: Brooks/Cole.

Spinelli, E. (1997). *Tales of un-knowing.* Washington Square, NY: New York University Press.

Spinelli, E. (2001). Psychosis: New existential, systemic, and cognitive-behavioral developments. *Journal of Contemporary Psychotherapy, 31,* 61–67.

Spinelli, E. (2002). The therapeutic relationship as viewed by existential psychotherapy: Re-embracing the world. *Journal of Contemporary Psychotherapy, 32,* 111–118.

St. Clair, M. (2000). *Object relations and self psychology: An introduction* (3rd ed.). Pacific Grove, CA: Brooks/Cole.

St. Clair, M. (2004). *Object relations and self psychology* (4th ed.). Belmont, CA: Brooks/Cole.

St. James-O'Connor, T., Meakes, E., Pickering, M., & Schuman, M. (1997). On the right track: Client experience of narrative therapy. *Contemporary Family therapy, 19,* 479–495.

Staemmler, F. M. (2004). Dialogue and interpretation in gestalt therapy. *International Gestalt Journal, 27,* 33–57.

Stanton, M. D. (1981). Strategic approaches to family therapy. In A. S. Gurman & D. P. Kniskern (Eds.), *Handbook of family therapy* (pp. 361–402). New York: Brunner/Mazel.

Steele, C. M., Aronson, J. (1995). Stereotype Threat and the Intellectual Test Performance of African Americans. *Journal of Personality and Social Psychology, 69,* 797–811.

Stein, H. T. (2000). Adlerian overview of birth order characteristics. Retrieved November, 7, 2000, from http://ourworld.compuserve.com/homepages/hstein/borthord.htm

Stein, H. T., & Edwards, M. E. (1998). Classical Adlerian theory and practice. In P. Marcus & A. Rosenberg (Eds.), *Psychoanalytic versions of the human condition: Philosophies of life and their impact on practice.* New York: New York University Press.

Steinbrueck, S. M., Maxwell, S. E., & Howard, G. S. (1983). A meta-analysis of psychotherapy and drug therapy in the treatment of unipolar depression with adults. *Journal of Consulting and Clinical Psychology, 51,* 856–863.

Steketee, G., & Cleere, L. (1990). Obessional-compulsive disorders. In A. S. Bellack, M. Hersen, & A. E. Kazdin (Eds.), *International handbook of behavior modification and therapy* (2nd ed., pp. 307–332). New York: Plenum Press.

Stiles, W. B., Barkham, M., Twigg, E., Mellor-Clark, J., & Cooper, M. (2006). Effectiveness of cognitive-behavioural, person-centred and psychodynamic therapies as practised in UK National Health Service settings. *Psychological Medicine, 36,* 555–566.

Strasser, F., & Strasser, A. (1997). *Existential time-limited therapy.* New York: Wiley.

Stricker, J., & Gold, J. (2005). Assimilative psychodynamic psychotherapy. In J. C. Norcross & M. R. Goldfried (Eds.), *Handbook of psychotherapy integration* (pp. 221–240). New York: Oxford University Press.

Strozier, C. B. (2006). Heinz Kohut. Retrieved from http://www.psychologyoftheself.com/kohut/strozier1.htm

Strumpfel, U. (2004). Research on gestalt therapy. *International Gestalt Journal, 27,* 9–59.

Strumpfel, U., & Goldman, R. (2001). Contacting gestalt therapy. In D. J. Cain & J. Seeman (Eds.), *Humanistic psychotherapies: Handbook of research and practice* (pp. 189–219). Washington, DC: American Psychological Association.

Stuart, S. (2006). Interpersonal psychotherapy: A guide to the basics. *Psychiatric Annals. 36,* 542–550.

Stuhr, U., & Meyer, A. E. (1991). Hamburg Short Psychotherapy Comparison experiment. In M. Crago & L. Beutler (Eds.), *Psychotherapy research: An international review of programmatic studies.* Washington, DC: American Psychological Association.

Sue, D. W., Ivey, A. E., & Pedersen, P. B. (1996). *A theory of multicultural counseling and therapy.* Pacific Grove, CA: Brooks/Cole.

Sue, D. W., & Sue, D. (2003). *Counseling the culturally diverse: Theory and practice* (4th ed.). New York: Wiley.

Suinn, R. M. (1969). The STABS, a measure of test anxiety for behavior therapy: Normative data. *Behavior Research and Therapy, 7,* 335–339.

Sulliman, J. R. (1973). *The development of a scale for the measurement of social interests.* Unpublished doctoral dissertation, Florida State University, Tallahassee.

Svartberg, M., & Stiles, T. C. (1991). Comparative effects of short-term psychodynamic psychotherapy: A meta-analysis. *Journal of Consulting and Clinical Psychology, 59,* 704–714.

Sweeney, T. J. (1989). *Adlerian counseling.* Bristol, PA: Accelerated Development.

Sweet, A. A. (1984). The therapeutic relationship in behavior therapy. *Clinical Psychology Review, 4,* 253–272.

Sweitzer, E. M. (2005). The relationship between social interest and self-concept in conduct disordered adolescents. *Journal of Individual Psychology, 61,* 55–79.

Syzmanski, D. M., Baird, M. K., & Kornman, C. L. (2002). The feminist male therapist: Attitudes and practices for the 21st century. *Psychology of Men and Masculinity, 3,* 22–27.

Szapocznik, J., & Kurtines, W. (1989). *Breakthroughs in family therapy with drug abusing problem youth.* New York: Springer.

Szapocznik, J., Perez-Vidal, A., Brickman, A. L., Foote, F. H., Santisteban, D., Hervis, O., et al. (1988). Engaging adolescent drug abusers and their families in treatment: A strategic structural systems approach. *Journal of Consulting and Clinical Psychology, 56*, 552–557.

Szapocznik, J., Rio, A., Murray, E., Cohen, R., Scopetta, M., Rivas-Vazquez, A., et al. (1989). Structural family versus psychodynamic child therapy for problematic Hispanic boys. *Journal of Consulting and Clinical Psychology, 57*, 571–578.

Szentagotai, A., & Kallay, E. (2006). The faster you move the longer you live—A test of rational emotive behavior therapy? *Journal of Cognitive and Behavioral Psychotherapies, 6*, 69–80.

Task Force on Promotion and Dissemination of Psychological Procedures, Division of Clinical Psychology of the American Psychological Association (1995). Training and dissemination of empirically validated psychological treatment: Report and recommendations. *The Clinical Psychologist, 48*, 3–23.

Taub, R. R. (1995). An Adlerian approach to the treatment of a contemporary Little Hans. *Journal of Individual Psychology, 51*, 332–344.

Tavris, C. (1993). The mismeasure of woman. *Feminism and Psychology, 3*, 149–168.

Taylor, S. E., & Brown, J. D. (1988). Illusion and well-being: A social psychological perspective on mental health. *Psychological Bulletin, 103*, 193–210.

Tham, E. (2001). The meaning of choice theory for the women of Albania. *International Journal of Reality Therapy, 21*, 4–6.

Thompson, C. L., & Rudolph, L. B. (2000). *Counseling children* (5th ed.). Belmont, CA: Brooks/Cole.

Thompson, J. K., & Williams, D. E. (1985). Behavior therapy in the 80's: Evolution, exploitation, and the existential issue. *The Behavior Therapist, 8*, 47–50.

Tillet, R. (1994). The clinical usefulness of gestalt therapy. *British Journal of Psychotherapy, 112*, 290–297.

Toman, W. (1961). *Family constellation.* New York: Springer.

Tremblay, J. M., Herron, W. G., & Schultz, C. L. (1986). Relation between therapeutic orientation and personality in psychotherapists. *Professional Psychology: Research and Practice, 17*, 106–110.

Truax, C., & Carkhuff, R. (1965). Experimental manipulation of therapeutic conditions. *Journal of Counseling Psychology, 29*, 119–124.

Tuason, M. T., & Friedlander, M. L. (2000). Do parents' differentiation levels predict those of their adult children? And other tests of Bowen theory in a Philippine sample. *Journal of Counseling Psychology, 47*, 27–35.

Tudor, K., & Worrall, M. (2006). *Person-centered therapy: A clinical philosophy.* London: Routledge.

Turner, B. F., & Turner, C. B. (1991). Bem Sex-Role Inventory stereotypes for men and women varying in age and race among National Register psychologists. *Psychological Reports, 69*, 931–944.

Tyson, G. M., & Range, L. M. (1987). Gestalt dialogs as a treatment for mild depression: Time works just as well. *Journal of Clinical Psychology, 43*, 227–231.

Ullmann, L. P., & Krasner, L. (1965). *Case studies in behavior modification.* New York: Holt, Rinehart & Winston.

Usher, C. H. (1989). Recognizing cultural bias in counseling theory and practice: The case of Rogers. *Journal of Multicultural Counseling and Development, 17*, 62–71.

Van der Veen, F. (1967). Basic elements in the process of psychotherapy: A research study. *Journal of Consulting Psychology, 31*, 295–303.

Van der Veen, F. (1998). Core principles of the person-centered approach. Retrieved from http://www.centerfortheperson.org/page28.html

Van Deurzen-Smith, E. (1988). *Existential counseling in practice.* London: Sage.

Van Deurzen-Smith, E. (1997). *Everyday mysteries: Existential dimensions of psychotherapy.* London: Routledge.

Van Deurzen, E. (2006). Existential counseling and therapy. In C. Feltham & I. E. Horton (Eds.), *The SAGE handbook of counseling and psychotherapy* (2nd ed., pp. 281–285). London: Sage.

van Oppen, P., van Balkom, A. J. L. M., de Haan, E, & Van Dyck, R. (2005). Cognitive therapy and exposure in vivo alone and in combination with Fluvoxamine in Obsessive-Compulsive Disorder: A 5-year follow-up. *Journal of Clinical Psychiatry, 66*, 1415–1422.

Vontress, C. E. (1985). Existentialism as a cross-cultural counseling modality. In P. Pedersen (Ed.), *Handbook of cross-cultural counseling and therapy* (pp. 207–212). Westport, CT: Greenwood Press.

Wadden, T. A., & Bell, S. T. (1990). Obesity. In A. S. Bellack, M. Hersen, & A. E. Kazdin (Eds.), *International handbook of behavior modification and therapy* (2nd ed., pp. 449–473). New York: Plenum Press.

Wagner-Moore, L. (2004). Gestalt therapy: Past, present, theory, and research. *Psychotherapy: Theory, Research, Practice, Training, 41*, 180–189.

Walker, N. (1957). *A short history of psychotherapy in theory and practice.* New York: Noonday Press.

Wallen, R. (1970). Gestalt therapy and gestalt psychology. In J. Fagan & I. L. Shepherd (Eds.), *Gestalt therapy now* (pp. 8–13). New York: Harper & Row.

Wallerstein, R. S. (1986). *Forty-two lives in treatment: A study of psychoanalysis and psychotherapy.* New York: Guilford Press.

Wallerstein, R. S. (1989). The Psychotherapy Research Project of the Menninger Foundation: An overview. *Journal of Consulting and Clinical Psychology, 57*, 195–205.

Wallerstein, R. S. (2002). The growth and transformation of American ego psychology. *Journal of the American Psychoanalytic Association, 50*, (1), 135–169.

Walsh, M. R. (Ed.). (1997). *Women, men, and gender: Ongoing debates.* New Haven, CT: Yale University Press.

Walsh, R. A., & McElwain, B. (2001). Existnential psychotherapies. In D. J. Cain & J. Seeman (Eds.), *Humanistic psychotherapies: Handbook of research and practice* (pp. 253–278). Washington, DC: American Psychological Association.

Walton, D. E. (1978). An exploratory study: Personality factors and the theoretical orientations of therapists. *Psychotherapy: Theory, Research, and Practice, 14,* 390–395.

Walts, R. E., & Engels, D. W. (1995). Thedife task of vocation: A review of Adlerian researxxh literature. TCA *Journal, 23,* 9–20.

Wampold, B. E. (2001). *The great psychotherapy debate.* Mahwah, NJ: Erlbaum.

Wampold, B. E., Lichtenberg, J. W., & Waehler, C. A. (2002). Principles of empirically supported intervention in counseling psychology. *The Counseling Psychologist, 30,* 197–217.

Wampold, B. E., Mondin, G. W., Moody, M., Stich, F., Benson, K., & Ahn, H. (1997). A meta-analysis of outcome studies comparing bona fide psychotherapies: Empirically, "All must have prizes." *Psychological Bulletin, 122,* 203–215.

Waterhouse, R. L. (1993). "Wild women don't have the blues": A feminist critique of "person-centred" counseling and therapy. *Feminism and Psychology, 3,* 55–61.

Watkins, C. E., Jr. (1982). A decade of research in support of Adlerian psychological theory. *Journal of Individual Psychology, 38,* 90–99.

Watkins, C. E., Jr. (1992a). Adlerian-oriented early memory research: What does it tell us? *Journal of Personality Assessment, 59,* 248–263.

Watkins, C. E., Jr. (1992b). Birth order research and Adler's theory: A critical review. *Journal of Individual Psychology, 48,* 357–366.

Watkins, C. E., Jr. (1994). Measuring social interest. *Journal of Individual Psychology, 50,* 69–96.

Watkins, C. E., Jr., & Guarnaccia, C. A. (1999). The scientific study of Adlerian theory. In R. E. Watts & J. Carlson (Eds.), *Interventions and strategies in counseling and psychotherapy.* Philadelphia: Accelerated Development.

Watkins, C. E., Jr., Lopez, F. G., Campbell, V. L., & Himmell, C. D. (1986). Contemporary counseling psychology: Results of a national survey. *Journal of Counseling Psychology, 33,* 301–309.

Watson, G. S., & Gross, A. M. (1999). Behavior therapy. In M. Hersen & A. S. Bellack (Eds.), *Handbook of comparative interventions for adult disorders* (pp. 25–47). New York: Wiley.

Watson, J. B., & Morgan, J. J. (1917). Emotional reactions and psychological experimentation. *American Journal of Psychology, 28,* 163–174.

Watson, J. B., & Rayner, R. (2000). Conditioned emotional reactions. *American Psychologist, 55,* 313–317. (Reprinted from *Journal of Experimental Psychology,* 1920, *3,* 1–14)

Watson, J. C., Gordon, L. B., Stermac, L., Steckley, P., & Kalogerakos, F. (2003). Comparing the effectiveness of process-experiential with cognitive behavioral psychotherapy in the treatment of depression. *Journal of Consulting and Clinical Psychology, 71,* 773–781.

Watts, R. E., Peluso, P. R., & Lewis, T. F. (2005). Expanding the acting as if technique: An Adlerian/constructive integration. *Journal of Individual Psychology, 61,* 380–387.

Watzlawick, P., Beavin, A. B., & Jackson, D. D. (1967). *Pragmatics of human communication.* New York: Norton.

Watzlawick, P., Weakland, J. H., & Fisch, R. (1974). *Change: Principles of problem formation and resolution.* New York: Norton.

Weinrach, S. (1990). Rogers and Gloria: The controversial film and the enduring relationship. *Psychotherapy, 27,* 282–290.

Weinrach, S. (1991). Rogers' encounter with Gloria: What did Rogers know and when? *Psychotherapy, 28,* 505–506.

Weinrach, S. G. (1996). Reducing REBT's "wince factor": An insider's perspective. *Journal of Rational-Emotive and Cognitive-Behavior. Therapy, 14,* 63–78.

Weishaar, M. E. (1993). Aaron T. Beck. London, England/Thousand Oaks, CA: Sage.

Weissman, A. N., & Beck, A. T. (1978). *Development and validation of the Dysfunctional Attitude Scale: A preliminary investigation.* Paper presented at the annual meeting of the American Educational Research Association, Toronto, Canada.

Weissman, M. M., & Markowitz, J. C. (1994). Interpersonal psychotherapy: Current status. *Archives of General Psychiatry, 51,* 599–606.

Weissman, M. M., & Markowitz, J. C. (1998). An overview of interpersonal psychotherapy. In J. C. Markowitz (Ed.), *Interpersonal psychotherapy* (pp. 1–27). Arlington, VA: American Psychiatric Association Press.

Wenzel, A., Sharp, I. R., Brown, G. K., Greenberg, R. L., & Beck, A. T. (2006). Dysfunctional beliefs in panic disorder: The Panic Belief Inventory. *Behaviour Research and Therapy, 44,* 819–833.

Wenzel, A., Sharp, I. R., Sokol, L., & Beck, A. T. (2006). Attentional fixation in panic disorder. *Cognitive Behaviour Therapy, 35,* 65–73.

Wessler, R. L. (1996). Idiosyncratic definitions and unsupported hypotheses: Rational emotive behavior therapy as pseudoscience. *Journal of Rational-Emotive and Cognitive-Behavior Therapy, 14,* 41–61.

West, J. D., & Bubenzer, D. L. (2002). Narrative family therapy. In J. Carlson & D. Kjos (Eds.), *Theories and strategies of family therapy,* (pp. 353–381). Boston, MA: Allyn and Bacon.

Weston, D. (1998). The scientific legacy of Sigmund Freud: Toward a pschodynamically informed science. *Psychological Bulletin, 124,* 333–371.

Wetchler, J. L., & Piercy, F. P. (1996). Transgenerational family therapies. In F. P. Piercy, D. H. Sprenkle, J. L. Wetchle, et al. (Eds.), *Family therapy sourcebook* (2nd ed., pp. 25–49). New York: Guilford Press.

Wettersten, K. B., Lichtenberg, J. W., & Mallinckrodt, B. (2005). Associations between working alliance and outcome in Solution-Focused Brief Therapy and brief interpersonal therapy. *Psychotherapy Research: 15*, 35–43.

Wexler, D. A., & Rice, L. N. (Eds.). (1974). *Innovations in client-centered therapy.* New York: Wiley.

Wheeler, G. (1991). *Gestalt reconsidered.* New York: Gardner Press/Gestalt Institute of Cleveland Press.

Wheeler, G., & Backman, S. (Eds.). (1994) *On intimate ground: A gestalt approach to working with couples.* San Francisco: Jossey-Bass.

Wheeler, M. S., Kern, R. K., & Curlette, W. L. (1991). Life-style can be measured. *Journal of Individual Psychology, 47*, 229–240.

Wheeler, M. S., Kern, R., & Curlette, W. (1993). BASIS-A Inventory. Highlands, NC: TRT.

Whiston, S. C. (2002). Career counseling and interventions. *The Counseling Psychologist, 30*, 218–237.

White, M. (1985). Fear busting and monster taming: An approach to the fears of young children. *Dulwich Centre Review*, 29–34.

White, M. (1992). Deconstruction and therapy. In D. Epston & M. White (Eds.), *Experience, contradiction, narrative and imagination: Selected papers of David Epston & Michael White 1989–1991* (pp. 109–151). South Austraila: Dulwich Centre Publications.

White, M. (1993). Deconstruction and therapy. In S. Gilligan & R. Price (Eds.), *Therapeutic conversations* (pp. 22–80). New York: Norton.

White, M., & Epston, D. (1990). *Narrative Means to Therapeutic Ends.* New York: Norton.

Widiger, T. A., & Settle, S. A. (1987). Broverman et al. revisited: An artifactual sex bias. *Journal of Personality and Social Psychology, 53*, 463–469.

Williams, C. B. (2005). Counseling African American women: Multiple identities—multiple constraints. *Journal of Counseling and Development, 83*, 278–283.

Wilson, G. T. (1987). Chemical aversion conditioning as a treatment for alcoholism. *Behavior Research and Therapy, 25*, 503–516.

Wilson, G. T. (2005). Behavior therapy. In R. J. Corsini & D. Wedding (Eds.), *Current psychotherapies* (7th ed., pp. 202–237). Belmont, CA: Brooks/Cole.

Winnicott, D. W. (1965). *The maturational processes and the facilitating environment.* New York: International Universities Press.

Wolfe, J. (1986). RET and women's issues. In A. Ellis & R. M. Grieger (Eds.), *Handbook of rational-emotive therapy* (pp. 397–421). London, England/Thousand Oaks, CA: Sage.

Wolfe, J. L. (2007). Rational emotive behavior therapy (REBT). In A. Rochlen (Ed.), *Applying counseling theories: An online, case-based approach* (pp. 177–191). Upper Saddle River, NJ: Prentice Hall.

Wolitzky, D. L. (2005). The theory and practice of traditional psychoanalytic treatment. In A. S. Gurman & S. B. Messer (Eds.), *Essential psychotherapies* (2nd ed.). New York: Guilford Press.

Wolitzky, D. L., & Eagle, M. N. (1997). Psychoanalytic theories of psychotherapy. In P. L. Wachtel & S. B. Messer (Eds.), *Theories of psychotherapy: Origins and evolution* (pp. 39–96). Washington, DC: American Psychological Association.

Wolpe, J. (1960). Reciprocal inhibition as the main basis of psychotherapeutic effects. In H. J. Eysenck (Ed.), *Behaviour therapy and the neuroses* (pp. 88–113). New York: Macmillan.

Wolpe, J. (1985). Existential problems and behavior therapy. *The Behavior Therapist, 8*, 126–127.

Wolpe, J. (1990). *The practice of behavior therapy* (4th ed.). New York: Pergamon Press.

Wolpe, J. (1992). Toward better results in the treatment of depression: The analysis of individual dynamics. In J. K. Zeig (Ed.), *The evolution of psychotherapy: The second conference* (pp. 129–138). New York: Brunner/Mazel.

Wolpe, J. (1997). Thirty years of behavior therapy. *Behavior Therapy, 28*, 633–635.

Wong, E. C., Kim, B. S., Zane, N. W. S., Kim, I. J., & Huang, J. S. (2003). Examining culturally based variables associated with ethnicity: Influences on credibility perceptions of empirically supported interventions. *Cultural Diversity and Ethnic Minority Psychology, 9*, 88–96.

Woods, M. D., & Martin, D. (1984). The work of Virginia Satir: Understanding her theory and technique. *The American Journal of Family Therapy, 12* (4), 3–11.

Woolfolk, R. L., & Sass, L. A. (1989). Philosophical foundations of rational-emotive therapy. In M. E. Bernard & R. DiGiuseppe (Eds.), *Inside rational-emotive therapy: A critical appraisal of the theory and therapy of Albert Ellis* (pp. 9–26). San Diego, CA: Academic Press.

Worell, J., & Johnson, D. (2001). Therapy with women: Feminist frameworks. In R. K. Unger (Ed.), *Handbook of the psychology of women and gender* (pp. 317–329). New York: Wiley.

Worell, J., & Johnson, N. G. (1997). *Shaping the future of feminist psychology: Education, research and practice.* Washington, DC: American Psychological Association.

Worell, J., & Remer, P. (2003). *Feminist perspectives in therapy,* (2nd ed.). New York: Wiley.

Wright, J. H., & Beck, A. T. (1996). Cognitive therapy. In R. E. Hales & S. C. Yudofsky (Eds.), *The American Psychiatric Press synopsis of psychiatry* (pp. 1011–1038). Washington, DC: American Psychiatric Press.

Wubbolding, R. E. (2000). *Reality therapy for the 21st century.* Philadelphia: Brunner-Routledge.

Wubbolding, R. E. (2007). Reality therapy. In A. Rochlen (Ed.), *Applying counseling theories: An online, case-based approach* (pp. 193–207). Upper Saddle River, NJ: Prentice Hall.

Wubbolding, R. E., Al-Rashidi, B., Brickell, J., Kakitani, M., Kim, R. I., Lennon, B., et al. (1998). Multicultural awareness: Implications for reality therapy and choice theory. *International Journal of Reality Therapy, 17* (2), 4–6.

Wubbolding, R. E., & Brickell, J. (1998). Qualities of the reality therapist. *International Journal of Reality Therapy, 17* (2), 47–49.

Wubbolding, R. E., & Brickell, J. (2000). Misconceptions about reality therapy. *International Journal of Reality Therapy, 19* (2), 264–265.

Wubbolding, R. E., Brickell, J., Imhof, L., Rose, I. K., Lojk, L., Al-Rashidi, B. (2004). Reality therapy: A global perspective. *International Journal for the Advancement of Counseling, 26*, 219–228.

Wyche, K. F., & Rice, J. K. (1997). Feminist therapy: From dialogue to tenets. In J. Worell & N. G. Johnson (Eds.), *Shaping the future of feminist psychology: Education, research and practice* (pp. 57–71). Washington, DC: American Psychological Association.

Yalof, J. (2005). Psychoanalytic interviewing. In R. J. Craig (Ed.), *Clinical and diagnostic interviewing* (2nd ed., pp. 57–90). New York: Jason Aronson.

Yalom, I. D. (1980). *Existential psychotherapy.* New York: Basic Books.

Yalom, I. D. (2002). *The gift of therapy.* New York: Harper Perennial.

Yalom, I., & Leszcz, M. (2005). *The theory and practice of group psychotherapy,* (5th ed.). New York: Basic Books.

Yalom, V., & Bugental, J. F. T. (1997). Support in existential-humanistic psychotherapy. *Journal of Psycho-therapy Integration, 7*, 119–129.

Yankura, J., & Dryden, W. (1994). *Albert Ellis.* London: Sage.

Yankura, J., & Dryden, W. (1994). *Doing RET: Albert Ellis in action.* New York: Springer.

Yates, A. J. (1960). Symptoms and symptom substitution. In H. J. Eysenck (Ed.), *Behaviour therapy and the neuroses* (pp. 22–27). New York: Macmillan.

Yoder, J. (2003). *Women and gender: Transforming psychology,* (2nd ed.). Upper Saddle River, NJ: Prentice Hall.

Yoder, J. D. (1981). The existential mode and client anxiety: Or she chose to hold a porcupine. *Personnel and Guidance Journal, 59*, 279–283.

Yontef, G. M. (1995). Gestalt therapy. In A. S. Gurman & S. B. Messer (Eds.), *Essential psychotherapies: Theory and practice* (pp. 261–303). New York: Guilford Press.

Yontef, G. M. (2005). Gestalt theory of change. In A. L. Woldt & S. M. Toman (Eds.), *Gestalt therapy: History, theory and practice* (pp. 81–100). Thousand Oaks, CA: Sage

Yontef, G. M., & Fuhr, R. (2005). Gestalt therapy theory of change. In A. L. Woldt, & S. M. Toman, (Eds.), *Gestalt therapy: History, theory, and practice* (pp. 81–100). Thousand Oaks, CA, US: Sage Publications, Inc.

Yontef, G. M., & Jacobs, L. (2000). Gestalt therapy. In R. J. Corsini & D. Wedding (Eds.), *Current psychotherapies* (6th ed., pp. 303–339). Itasca, IL: Peacock.

Yontef, G., & Jacobs, L. (2005). Gestalt therapy. In R. J. Corsini & D. Wedding (Eds.), *Current psychotherapies* (6th ed. pp. 299–336). Belmont, CA: Brooks/Cole.

Young, J. E., Beck, A. T., & Weinberger, A. (1993). Depression. In D. H. Barlow (Ed.), *Clinical handbook of psychological disorders: A step-by-step treatment manual* (2nd ed., pp. 240–177). New York: Guilford Press.

Zanardi, C. (Ed.). (1990). *Essential papers on the psychology of women.* New York: New York University Press.

Zarski, J., Sweeney, T. J., & Barcikowski, R. S. (1977). Counseling effectiveness as a function of counselor social interest. *Journal of Counseling Psychology, 24*, 1–5.

Zeig, J. K. (1992). Discussion. In J. K. Zeig (Ed.), *The evolution of psychotherapy: The second conference* (pp. 278–282). New York: Brunner/Mazel.

Ziegler, D. J. (1999). The construct of personality in rational emotive behavior therapy (REBT) theory. *Journal of Rational-Emotive and Cognitive-Behavior Therapy, 17*, 19–32.

Ziegler, D. J. (2000). Basic assumptions concerning human nature underlying rational emotive behavior therapy (REBT) personality theory. *Journal of Rational-Emotive and Cognitive-Behavior Therapy, 18*, 67–85.

Zimmerman, G., Favrod, J., Trieu, V. H., & Pomini, V. (2004). The effect of cognitive-behavioral treatment on the positive symptoms of schizophrenia spectrum disorders: A meta-analysis. *Schizophrenia Research, 77*, 1–9.

Zimmerman, J. L., & Dickerson, V. C. (2001). Narrative therapy. In R. J. Corsini (Ed.), *Handbook of innovative therapy* (pp. 415–426). New York: Wiley.

Zimmerman, T. S., Prest, L. A., & Wetzel, B. E. (1997). Solution-focused couples therapy groups: An empirical study. *Journal of Family Therapy, 19*, 125–144.

Zimring, F. (1990). Cognitive processes as a cause of psychotherapeutic change: Self-initiated processes. In G. Lietaer, J. Rombauts, & R. Van Balen (Eds.), *Client centered and experiential psychotherapy in the nineties.* Louvain, Belgium: Leuven University Press.

Zimring, F. M., & Raskin, N. J. (1992). Carl Rogers and client/person-centered therapy. In D. K. Freedheim (Ed.), *History of psychotherapy: A century of change.* Washington, DC: American Psychological Association.

Zinker, J. (1977). *Creative process in gestalt therapy.* New York: Random House.

Zurawski, R. M., & Smith, T. W. (1987). Assessing irrational beliefs and emotional distress: Evidence and implications of limited discriminant validity. *Journal of Counseling Psychology, 34*, 224–227.

Zuroff, D. C., Mongrain, M., & Santor, D. A. (2004). Conceptualizing and measuring personality vulnerability to depression: Comment on Coyne and Whiffen (1995). *Psychological Bulletin, 130*, 489–511.

Name Index

SUBJECT INDEX